D1376407

HITLER'S FATAL MISCALCULATION

Hitler's decision to declare war on the United States has baffled generations of historians. In this revisionist new history of those fateful months, Klaus Schmider seeks to uncover the chain of events which would incite the German leader to declare war on the United States in December 1941. He provides new insights not just on the problems afflicting German strategy, foreign policy and war production but, crucially, how they were perceived at the time at the top levels of the Third Reich. Schmider sees the declaration of war on the United States not as an admission of defeat or a gesture of solidarity with Japan, but as an opportunistic gamble by the German leader. This move may have appeared an excellent bet at the time, but would ultimately doom the Third Reich.

KLAUS H. SCHMIDER has been with the Royal Military Academy Sandhurst since May 1999. He is the co-author of Volume 8 of the official German history of World War II, *Das Deutsche Reich und der Zweite Weltkrieg* (2007).

Cambridge Military Histories

Edited by

HEW STRACHAN, Professor of International Relations, University of St Andrews, and Emeritus Fellow of All Souls College, Oxford

GEOFFREY WAWRO, Professor of Military History and Director of the Military History Center, University of North Texas

The aim of this series is to publish outstanding works of research on warfare throughout the ages and throughout the world. Books in the series take a broad approach to military history, examining war in all its military, strategic, political and economic aspects. The series complements *Studies in the Social and Cultural History of Modern Warfare* by focusing on the 'hard' military history of armies, tactics, strategy and warfare. Books in the series consist mainly of single author works – academically rigorous and ground-breaking – which are accessible to both academics and the interested general reader.

A full list of titles in the series can be found at:
www.cambridge.org/militaryhistories

HITLER'S FATAL MISCALCULATION

Why Germany Declared War on the United States

KLAUS H. SCHMIDER

Royal Military Academy Sandhurst

CAMBRIDGE
UNIVERSITY PRESS

CAMBRIDGE
UNIVERSITY PRESS

University Printing House, Cambridge CB2 8BS, United Kingdom

One Liberty Plaza, 20th Floor, New York, NY 10006, USA

477 Williamstown Road, Port Melbourne, VIC 3207, Australia

314–321, 3rd Floor, Plot 3, Splendor Forum, Jasola District Centre,
New Delhi – 110025, India

79 Anson Road, #06–04/06, Singapore 079906

Cambridge University Press is part of the University of Cambridge.

It furthers the University's mission by disseminating knowledge in the pursuit of
education, learning and research at the highest international levels of excellence.

www.cambridge.org
Information on this title: www.cambridge.org/9781108834919
DOI: 10.1017/9781108870405

First published 2021

Printed in the United Kingdom by TJ Books Ltd., Padstow, Cornwall

A catalogue record for this publication is available from the British Library

Library of Congress Cataloging-in-Publication data
Names: Schmider, Klaus, author.
Title: Hitler's fatal miscalculation : why Germany declared war on the United States / Klaus
H. Schmider, Royal Military Academy, Sandhurst.
Other titles: Why Germany declared war on the United States
Description: Cambridge, United Kingdom ; New York, NY : Cambridge University Press,
2021. | Series: Cambridge military histories | Includes bibliographical references and index.
Identifiers: LCCN 2020021818 | ISBN 9781108834919 (hardback) | ISBN 9781108870405
(ebook)
Subjects: LCSH: Germany – Foreign relations – United States. | United States – Foreign
relations – Germany. | Hitler, Adolf, 1889–1945. | World War, 1939–1945 – Causes. | World
War, 1939–1945 – Germany. | World War, 1939–1945 – United States.
Classification: LCC D751 .S37 2021 | DDC 940.53/43–dc23
LC record available at https://lccn.loc.gov/2020021818

ISBN 978-1-108-83491-9 Hardback

Days before he was due to leave Berlin for the United States, CBS correspondent William Shirer reflected on the odds of a US–German war breaking out in the near future:

'The clash is as inevitable as that of two planets hurtling inexorably through the heavens towards each other. As a matter of fact, it may come sooner than almost all Americans at home imagine. An officer of the High Command somewhat shocked me the other day while we were discussing the matter. He said: "You think Roosevelt can pick the moment most advantageous to America and Britain for coming into the war. Did you ever stop to think that Hitler, a master at timing, may choose the moment for war with America – a moment which he thinks will give him the advantage?"

'I must admit I never did.'

—William L. Shirer, *Berlin Diary: The Journal of a Foreign Correspondent, 1934–1941*, entry for 1 December 1940[1]

---

[1] London: Hamish Hamilton 1941, pp 463–4. Excerpt reprinted by permission of Don Congdon Associates, Inc. © 1941, renewed 1968 by William L. Shirer. My thanks to my colleague Ed Yorke for bringing this source to my attention.

CONTENTS

FIGURES

MAPS

PREFACE

The seed for this book was arguably planted on a weekend about forty years ago. My father and I were out walking the family dog, when conversation turned to the circumstances surrounding the recent fall of South Vietnam. At the time, though only a precocious ten- or eleven-year-old, I had already started to take a serious interest in the general subject area that would eventually become my profession. When I made a rather critical comment about the supposedly meddling nature of US foreign policy, my father challenged me to come up with an example. I found myself struggling at first, then hit on one that seemed to be the perfect fit: 'The American declaration of war on Germany in 1941,' I volunteered.

To this day I can still remember the expression on my father's face. Confusion, bafflement, irritation and horror were visibly vying for control over his features – in light of the fact that he was wearing shades, no small feat. After regaining his composure he told me calmly and deliberately: 'Son – we declared war on them.' Even though I did not realise it at the time, I had just had my first lesson as a baby historian: always make sure you check your sources before you go on to deliver a lecture. Over the years, I came to realise that my gaffe that day was rendered more understandable by what appeared to be the unique nature of the episode in question: to a far greater extent than any other event that has decisively shaped history in recent times, this one appeared to defy any attempts at rationalisation. Over the years, quite a few of my students have expressed astonishment when they learnt in seminar that it was Germany who declared war on the USA in December 1941, rather than the other way around. Even film directors and novelists have occasionally introduced this event into the narrative when they needed to confront their protagonists with a development which was sure to leave them utterly bemused, baffled or even horrified.[2]

As for my father, he went on to teach me many things besides who initiated the German–American war in 1941. Together with my mother, he continued

---

[2] For example, see *Des Teufels General*, directed by Helmut Käutner (Real-Film, 1954), and Robert Harris, *The Ghost* (London: Hutchinson 2007), p 41.

to encourage my interest in the past in all sorts of ways and encouraged me to take up this career at a critical juncture in my life. When the time came to write this book, his constant enquiries about its progress were one of the key factors in convincing me that I had hooked something big. For this, and many other things besides, this book is dedicated to both my parents.

ACKNOWLEDGEMENTS

First of all, a vote of thanks to Tim Bean, Peter Lieb, Evan Mawdsley, Sönke Neitzel, Felix Römer, Ben Shepherd, Brendan Simms and Karl-Günther Zelle for taking time from their busy schedules to read the manuscript in its entirety or in part and share their feedback with me. It goes without saying that the responsibility for any remaining errors is mine alone.

Truman Anderson, Pier Paolo Battistelli, Joseph Blandino, Lutz Budrass, Christopher Duffy, Marcus Faulkner, Ed Flint, Paul Fröhlich, Christian Hartmann, Jörg Hillmann, Johannes Hürter, Gerhard Krebs, Takuma Melber, Axel Niestle, Berthold Sander-Nagashima, Nobuo Tajima, Simon Trew and Ed Yorke selflessly shared the fruits of their research with me or drew my attention to sources I would otherwise have overlooked. Matthias Strohn and Peter Lieb provided priceless assistance in decrypting handwritten sources, as did Tim Bean in the search for the ever-elusive MOMP. Particular thanks to Professor Ellen Gibbels, Dr Tamer Farghal and Dr Irina Tavlaridou for assisting a clueless humanities graduate in understanding the pathology of Parkinson's disease and the effects of assorted prescription drugs from the 1940s.

At the Royal Military Academy Sandhurst, the library staff repeatedly went above and beyond the call of duty to make sure this ship finally reached a safe port. Thanks to Andrew and John for signing off on those exotic-sounding inter-library loans, time and again breathing life into that steam-driven reader-printer and shoring up my will power at critical moments with generous helpings of the library's sherry (cream). I am equally grateful to Mel for keeping me up to date on incoming journals and to Ken for rescuing from a pile of cardboard a collection of microfiches to which they had been consigned by Dr Schmider in a moment of true academic absent-mindedness. Thanks also to Margaret and her team at Graphics for putting up with those countless last-minute requests for scans and binding. The author is also indebted to the staff of the library of the German Historical Institute for their selfless assistance rendered over the years.

At the War Studies department, Sarina, Alisa, Duncan, Peter, Simon, Tim, Chris, Claus, Alex, Stewart, James, Ed, Greg, as well as the two Pauls and two Steves, not only supported this endeavour with valuable suggestions and ideas;

even more importantly, the tolerance and good humour with which they regarded the process, which saw the author, while physically present at the department, increasingly removed from more and more aspects of its day-to-day running because he was away commuting between the Berghof and the Neue Reichskanzlei, is proof of the uniqueness of the central corridor of the Faraday Hall's first floor as a work place in academe.

The Schmider family provided a truly unique setting in researching and writing this monograph. My brother in true selfless fashion found ways to relieve me of tasks which, while not rooted in the history of the Third Reich, were nevertheless important and even urgent. My wife actually kept tabs on my working hours and on more than a few occasions would actually scold me when she felt I had not spent enough time on the PC. I am reliably informed by my colleagues that such behavioural patterns are not standard issue among historian's spouses. Our son again and again provided a helping hand (or rather, hand, arm and leg) in IT-related matters and thus played a key role in preparing this manuscript for publication in the world of the twenty-first century.

ABBREVIATIONS AND GERMAN
AND RUSSIAN TERMS

AA	Auswärtiges Amt (German foreign ministry)
ADAP	*Akten zur deutschen auswärtigen Politik* (post-war edition of German diplomatic communications)
AEF	American Expeditionary Force (the US Army command deployed in France in 1917–18)
AHA	*Allgemeines Heeresamt* (General Army Office of the OKH)
AK	*Armeekorps* (higher command formation of the German field army encompassing between two and five divisions)
BA/MA	Bundesarchiv/Militärarchiv, Freiburg (central archive for Prussian/German military records since 1867)
BA-Kobl.	Bundesarchiv/Koblenz
BA-Lichterf.	Bundesarchiv/Lichterfelde, Berlin (central archive for NSDAP records)
Bd.	Band (volume)
BdE	*Befehlshaber des Ersatzheeres* (commanding officer of the Replacement Army)
BdU	*Befehlshaber der Unterseeboote* (commanding officer of the U-boat arm)
Buna	name of the synthetic rubber produced between 1936 and 1945 by IG Farben. Made up of the first two letters of butadiene and natrium (German for sodium)
CHJ	*The Cambridge History of Japan* (history of Japan, published in seven volumes between 1989 and 2001)
CPSU	Communist Party of the Soviet Union
CUP	Cambridge University Press
DDI	*I Documenti Diplomatici Italiani* (post-war edition of Italian diplomatic communications)
DRZW	*Das Deutsche Reich und der Zweite Weltkrieg* (semi-official history of Germany in World War II published in thirteen volumes between 1979 and 2008)
FHO	*Fremde Heere Ost* (OKH department tasked with collecting intelligence on the Red Army)
Geschwader	Luftwaffe unit made up of three Gruppen and comprising 120 aircraft

GRT	Gross Register Tonnage (measure of the internal volume of a merchant ship)
GRU	Glavnoje Rzvedyvatel'noje Upravlenije (Fourth [Intelligence] Directorate of the Red Army Staff), foreign intelligence service of the Red Army
Gruppe	Luftwaffe unit with a paper strength of forty aircraft
HGr	*Heeresgruppe* (army group)
IfZ	Institut für Zeitgeschichte, München (Institute for Contemporary History)
IJA	Imperial Japanese Army
IJN	Imperial Japanese Navy
IWM	Imperial War Museum
JG	*Jagdgeschwader* (single-engine fighter wing)
KG	*Kampfgeschwader* (bomber wing)
KTB Halder	*Kriegstagebuch* (personal office diary) of German Army chief of staff *Generaloberst* Franz Halder
KTB OKW	*Kriegstagebuch* (official war diary) of the German armed forces' high command
KTB Seekriegsleitung	*Kriegstagebuch* (official war diary) of the German admiralty
MBPH	*'Magic' background of Pearl Harbor* (edition of decrypted Japanese diplomatic traffic)
MOMP	Mid-Ocean Meeting Point
n.d.	no date
NSDAP	Nationalsozialistische Deutsche Arbeiterpartei
OKH	Oberkommando des Heeres (German Army high command)
OKW	Oberkommando der Wehrmacht (German armed forces' high command)
Ostheer	German term for the Army in the East (term used for the totality of ground units fighting under army command in Russia)
OUP	Oxford University Press
PA/AA	Politisches Archiv des Auswärtigen Amtes (archive of the German foreign ministry)
pb	paperback edition
RAM	*Reichsaußenminister* (the German foreign minister)
RLM	Reichluftfahrtministerium (German air ministry)
RSA	*Hitler. Reden. Schriften. Anordnungen* (edition of Adolf Hitler's speeches, letters and articles from 1925 to 1933, published in twelve volumes between 1991 and 2000)
SD	Sicherheitsdienst der SS (foreign intelligence service of the SS)
Skl	Seekriegsleitung (German admiralty)
Stavka	Stavka Verkhovonogo Glavnokomandovaniya (wartime Supreme Headquarters of the Soviet armed forces)

StS	*Staatssekretär* (German equivalent of permanent secretary in the civil service structure)
TB Bock	*Tagebuch* (personal diary) of *Generalfeldmarschall* Fedor von Bock (Army Group Centre)
TB Goebbels	*Tagebuch* (personal diary) of *Reichspropagandaminister* Joseph Goebbels
TB Leeb	*Tagebuch* (personal diary) of *Generalfeldmarschall* Ritter von Leeb (Army Group North)
TMWC	Trial of the Major War Criminals (multi-volume transcript of the record of the 1945–6 Nürnberg trial)
UP	University Press
USNIP	United States Naval Institute Press
WFSt	*Wehrmachtführungsstab* (OKW's headquarter staff for the operational direction of the war)
WiRüAmt	*Wehrwirtschaft- und Rüstungsamt* (OKW office for economic coordination)
ZG	*Zerstörergeschwader* (heavy fighter wing)

~

Introduction

In the last days of November 1941, Nazi Germany's strategic situation was ambiguous: its armies were in possession of most of continental Europe and fighting deep inside the USSR, but the momentum of the Wehrmacht's war machine appeared to be spending itself. At sea, in relation to the numbers of U-boats available, sinkings had been dropping since June; the German surface fleet was unlikely to pick up the slack, since it had just had fuel restrictions imposed on it that all but ruled out a resumption of Atlantic operations. In the air, night-time RAF bombing raids were becoming a feature of everyday life, reaching deeper and deeper into hitherto untouched areas of German geography. On the Russian Front, which consumed most of the assets of the army and air force, operations were still in progress, aimed at rendering untenable the situation of the defenders of Leningrad and Moscow and forcing the surrender of Sevastopol. On the downside, Army Group South had just been forced to abandon its most recent prize – the city of Rostov – to the counter-attacking Red Army, an event that definitely had to be rated as a 'first' in the annals of the Russo–German war. Crucially, the war economy, which needed to deliver maximum output if the armed forces of the Third Reich were to have even a remote chance of meeting the conflicting priorities set by their warlord, had entered a period of crisis. Neither enough labour nor raw materials were available to meet the demands for the coming year, 1942.

This was the backdrop to the conversation that Adolf Hitler had with his armaments minister, Fritz Todt, and the industrialist, Walter Rohland, in the Neue Reichskanzlei on 29 November. Rohland had just returned from an inspection tour of the Eastern Front, where both the quantity and quality of Soviet armour facing Army Group Centre had left him deeply impressed. Todt, as an NSDAP veteran of some standing, was able to talk to the dictator with unprecedented candour, and on this occasion he did. The enemy coalition, he said (including growing Lend-Lease deliveries from the USA in his calculation), was already capable of producing armoured vehicles at such a prodigious rate that the concluding of a negotiated compromise peace was absolutely unavoidable.

Hitler did point out to Todt that the possibilities of such an endeavour were next to non-existent, which was no doubt accurate; merely preparing the ground for a peace initiative would undoubtedly have required toppling the government of one of the three main belligerent nations at that time – Germany, Great Britain and the USSR. Even so, the fact remains that Todt's warning had been preceded by a virtually identical assessment by *Generaloberst* Friedrich Fromm of the *Allgemeines Heeresamt* a month earlier. Surely, for any statesman caught in such a quandary the logical conclusion had to be that the mere continuation of hostilities would from now on be heavily dependent on avoiding moves that were likely to lead to a further escalation of them.

At the time of Todt's warning, no commitment had yet been made to Tokyo, so reasons of prestige are unlikely to have played a role in deciding the dictator's mind for him, when on 11 December he went on to declare war on the United States. It was without a doubt the one decision which, while being completely avoidable, also irreversibly doomed the Third Reich. Three generations of historians have been thoroughly baffled by it and expressed this sentiment in colourful language. In 1973, Norman Rich termed it 'the greatest single mistake of [Hitler's] career'.[1] Five years later, Sebastian Haffner described it as the most 'incomprehensible' of a series of blunders that turned 'a complete victory into an unavoidable defeat'.[2] To Hitler's future biographer Ian Kershaw, it was nothing so much as 'a futile gesture';[3] a few years later Kershaw added that it was 'more irrational than any decision taken to date'.[4] According to Mark Lowenthal, it was 'one of his most irrational policy decisions'.[5] Williamson Murray and Alan Millett agreed in sprit, terming it 'one of the worst mistakes Hitler made',[6] while to Andrew Roberts it was both an 'unimaginably stupid thing' and a 'suicidally hubristic act'.[7] P. M. H. Bell described it as simply 'freakish and irrational'.[8] Antony Beevor with commendable English understatement refrained from such hyperbole, but still described it as 'rash to say the least'.[9] One of the historians interviewed for

[1] Norman Rich, *Hitler's War Aims: Ideology, the Nazi State and the Course of Expansion* (London: André Deutsch 1973), p 245.

[2] Sebastian Haffner, *Anmerkungen zu Hitler* (München: Kindler 1978; Fischer pb 2003), pp 135–41.

[3] Ian Kershaw, *The Nazi Dictatorship: Problems and Perspectives of Interpretation* (London and New York: Bloomsbury 1985; 2015 rp), p 184.

[4] Ian Kershaw, *Hitler: Profiles in Power* (London: Longman 1991), p 159.

[5] Mark Lowenthal, 'Roosevelt and the Coming of War: The Search for United States Policy, 1937–1942'; in: *Journal of Contemporary History*, Vol. 16 (1981), pp 413–40, esp. p 430.

[6] Williamson Murray and Alan Millett, *A War to Be Won: Fighting the Second World War* (New Haven: Yale UP 2000), pp 135–6.

[7] Andrew Roberts, *The Storm of War: A New History of the Second World War* (London: Allen Lane 2009), pp 193–6.

[8] P. M. H. Bell, *Twelve Turning Points of the Second World War* (New Haven: Yale UP 2011), pp 77–8.

[9] Antony Beevor, *The Second World War* (London: Weidenfeld & Nicholson 2012), pp 278–9.

Ken Burns' recent documentary on Theodore and Franklin Roosevelt speculated that it must have been made in 'a fit of absent-mindedness and contempt without thinking it through'.[10] Both Klaus Fischer and Rainer Schmidt concluded that it was the equivalent of a historical riddle too far. According to the former, 'the definitive answer will probably never be known, buried forever in irrational motivation',[11] while to the latter it simply defied rational analysis: he described it as the 'the most mysterious decision of the entire war'.[12] So mysterious in fact that quite a few historians have studiously avoided engaging with it in any shape or form, even in the context of publications whose subject would appear to make the inclusion of a sub-chapter or at least a sidebar unavoidable.[13]

Widespread mystification notwithstanding, a couple of schools of thought on the issue have gradually emerged since the 1960s, and it is to these we must now turn. In 1965, German historian Andreas Hillgruber published a massive tome about 'Hitler's strategy, 1940/41'. Although it mostly dealt with the decision-making process that led ultimately to the German dictator unleashing the invasion of the USSR in June 1941, it also briefly touched on his decision to declare war on the USA five and a half months later.[14] To Hillgruber, this event did not lend itself to the kind of analysis one might ordinarily use to make sense of a strategic decision. The only way to explain such a move was by assuming that, as early as mid-November, Hitler had resigned himself to the fact that his way of vanquishing enemies Blitzkrieg-style had come to grief on the resistance of the Red Army. Hence, declaring war on Washington was not a path freely chosen, but 'a gesture meant to cover up the fact that he was no longer in a position to determine the momentum of the war, since the initiative for all subsequent strategic decisions had passed to the enemy coalition'. It came with the added bonus of placing another major obstacle in the path of

---

[10] 'Ken Burns: The Roosevelts: An Intimate History', 2014 PBS documentary (episode 6).

[11] Klaus P. Fischer, *Nazi Germany: A New History* (London: Constable 1995), p 475.

[12] Rainer F. Schmidt, *Der Zweite Weltkrieg. Die Zerstörung Europas* (Berlin: be.bra 2008), pp 116–19.

[13] B. H. Liddell Hart, *History of the Second World War* (New York: G. P. Putnam's Sons 1970); James L. Stokesbury, *A Short History of World War II* (London: Robert Hale 1982); Patrick Hearden, *Roosevelt Confronts Hitler: America's Entry into World War Two* (Dekalb: Northern Illinois UP 1987); Robert E. Herzstein, *Roosevelt and Hitler: Prelude to War* (New York: Paragon House 1989); Alan F. Wilt, *War from the Top: German and British Military Decision Making during World War II* (London and New York: I. B. Tauris & Co 1990); Williamson Murray and Allan Millett (eds.), *Calculations. Net assessment and the coming of World War II* (New York: The Free Press 1992); Steven Casey, *Cautious Crusade: Franklin D. Roosevelt, American Public Opinion and the War against Nazi Germany* (New York: OUP 2001); Norman Stone, *A Short History of World War Two* (London: Penguin 2014 pb); Henrik Eberle, *Hitlers Weltkriege. Wie der Gefreite zum Feldherrn wurde* (Hamburg: Hoffmann & Campe 2014).

[14] Andreas Hillgruber, *Hitlers Strategie. Politik und Kriegführung 1940–1941* (Frankfurt a.M.: Bernard & Graefe 1965), pp 540–54.

'oppositional forces in the military leadership seeking to find a way out of the hopeless conflict that was now developing'.[15]

Hillgruber effectively divested of any rationality what could be seen as one the most momentous strategic decisions of the twentieth century. This was especially so in later publications where Hillgruber even dropped the idea that Hitler's aim, at least in part, was to force his military elite to discard thoughts of a separate peace.[16] Thus, Hillgruber reduced any thought process that may have taken place to the kind of reaction more commonly associated with sulking teenagers. Such an interpretation had the welcome side effect of further reducing the standing of an already thoroughly loathsome personality, which may go a long way towards explaining its remarkable longevity. For the next half century, many authors of general histories of World War II and biographies of Adolf Hitler adopted this line or slight variations thereof;[17] a few even spelled out what Hillgruber had only implied, namely that by giving up on the idea of seeking an orthodox military victory in the midst of an ongoing total war, the dictator had chosen a path that could lead only to self-immolation. The obvious conclusion to draw from this was that such an option would be acceptable to him only if by taking it he would be guaranteed the extinction of his domestic enemies. Hence, out of sheer spite, he now began implementing a policy of genocide aimed at his main domestic enemy (the Jews).[18] Rather remarkably, Hillgruber's influence can even be traced in his phraseology, which some historians adopted wholly or in part. This author knows of only one instance where the plausibility of this interpretation of events was openly called into question.[19]

The early 1980s saw the emergence of two novel interpretations, which in contrast to Hillgruber's both attempted to look for a genuine strategic rationale. In a 1980 article, Gerhard Weinberg made the case that German decision-

---

[15] Ibid., pp 553–4.

[16] Andreas Hillgruber, *Deutsche Großmacht- und Weltpolitik im 19. und 20. Jahrhundert* (Düsseldorf: Droste 1978), pp 197–222.

[17] Joachim Fest, *Hitler. Eine Biographie* (Frankfurt: Proplyäen 1973), p 892; Haffner, *Anmerkungen*, pp 135–41; Jürgen Förster, 'Das Unternehmen Barbarossa – eine historische Ortsbestimmung'; in: Horst Boog et al, *Der Angriff auf die Sowjetunion* (Stuttgart: DVA 1983) [= Das Deutsche Reich und der Zweite Weltkrieg, Bd. 4], pp 1086–8; Harald Steffahn, 'Hitler als Soldat und militärischer Führer'; in: Christian Zentner and Friedemann Bedürftig (eds.), *Das große Lexikon des Zweiten Weltkriegs* (München: Südwest Verlag 1993), pp 254–7; Joachim Fest, *Speer. Eine Biographie* (Berlin: Alexander Fest Verlag 1999), p 178; Rafael Seligmann, *Hitler. Die Deutschen und ihr Führer* (München: Ullstein 2004), pp 258–66; Klaus P. Fischer, *Hitler and America* (Philadelphia: Pennsylvania UP 2011), pp 152–67.

[18] Haffner, *Anmerkungen*, pp 162–7; Gregor Schölgen, *Jenseits von Hitler. Die Deutschen in der Weltpolitik von Bismarck bis heute* (Berlin: Propyläen 2005), pp 196–8; Fischer, *Hitler and America*, pp 152–67.

[19] Guntram Schulze-Wegner, *Die deutsche Kriegsmarine-Rüstung 1942–1945* (Hamburg: E.S. Mittler 1997), p 225.

making in November and December 1941 was determined by both a chronic underestimation of American military potential and the wish to seize a rare opportunity to finally get Japan to initiate hostilities against the British Empire.[20] An agenda by Berlin to actively seek war with the USA was assumed as a given. In addition, a state of war would allow the Kriegsmarine's submarine arm to reap a rich harvest in the waters off the Americas – as indeed turned out to be the case from January to June 1942. Weinberg also addressed the question of Berlin neglecting to demand a quid pro quo from Tokyo, like a declaration of war on the USSR. In his view, Hitler refrained from such a move because of a concern about Japanese strategic overreach that might result from this and because he was reluctant to raise questions that might give the pro-peace faction in Tokyo one last chance to challenge the consensus for going to war.[21]

In 1981, Eberhard Jäckel offered a different explanation: without criticising Hillgruber by name, he questioned the plausibility of a 'suicidal impulse' as the main driver for a major strategic decision. Instead, he developed an idea first put forward by Klaus Reinhardt in 1972, who had made a case for Hitler being resigned in November 1941 to the Americans joining the British in the very near future.[22] Only through a Japanese declaration of war would it be possible to force the Americans to split their armed forces between two oceanic theatres. Hence the need to bring Japan into the war at any diplomatic price.[23] While both Weinberg and Jäckel did a more creditable job than Hillgruber, insofar as they managed to move the debate away from musings about self-immolation and back into the realm of strategy, their essays raised as many questions as they answered. They did not explain which US move was probably key in making Hitler accept the inevitability of war with the USA or what estimate made him conclude that Washington would deploy a large part of its assets to the Far East, rather than prioritising Europe straightaway. Nor did they address a number of areas (especially the air

---

[20] Gerhard Weinberg, 'Germany's Declaration of War on the United States: A New Look'; in: Hans L. Trefousse (ed.), *Germany and America: Essays on Problems of International Relations and Immigration* (New York: Columbia UP 1980) [= Brooklyn College Studies on society in change, Vol. 21], pp 54–70.

[21] Ibid., p 67.

[22] Klaus Reinhardt, *Die Wende vor Moskau. Das Scheitern der Strategie Hitlers im Winter 1941/42* (Stuttgart: DVA 1972), pp 181–4. At the same time, Reinhardt failed to completely divest himself from Hillgruber's idea that Hitler was resigned to losing the war as early as mid-November.

[23] Eberhard Jäckel, 'Die deutsche Kriegserklärung an die Vereinigten Staaten von 1941'; in: Friedrich J. Kroneck and Thomas Oppermann (eds.), *Im Dienste Deutschlands und des Rechts. Festschrift für Wilhelm G. Grewe zum 70 Geburtstag am 16. Oktober 1981* (Baden-Baden: Nomos Verlagsgesellschaft 1981), pp 117–37. An English translation – albeit missing a third of the source notes of the original – can be found in Eberhard Jäckel, *Hitler in History* (London: UP of New England 1984), pp 66–87.

war, the critical situation in Russia and the production crisis of the German war economy), which appeared to make a compelling case for strategic retrenchment. Crucially, they failed to explain why the Japanese announcement of impending hostilities in the Pacific and the news of the Pearl Harbor attack were not simply met with a vague promise of indirect support and in due course possibly an opportunistic expansion of submarine activity in the Atlantic. Contrary to what some authors allege to this day,[24] the Tripartite Pact was defensive in nature and the strategic distraction desired by the German government had just been delivered free of charge. Even so, the Jäckel theory in particular went on to achieve considerable currency in academic circles.[25] It was adopted by the official German history,[26] and in 1987 it received the ultimate accolade when Hillgruber himself championed it in one of the last articles he ever wrote.[27] Two years later, Enrico Syring built on it to present a variant, which pointed to the need to include the military situation in Russia in any detailed analysis of the events of those days – a point so far omitted by all historians.[28] Due to its briefness, the Syring article inevitably shared many of the limitations of the essays by Weinberg and Jäckel, but it still constitutes the best attempt to analyse Hitler's decision in the context of contemporary events.

Over the following years, most historians touching on this subject tended to restrict discussion of it to a paragraph or two at the most; there was usually a clear dividing line between those favouring either Hillgruber or Jäckel, but even that could get blurred at times.[29] Only one historian attempted to

---

[24] John Lukacs, *The Hitler of History* (New York: Alfred Knopf 1997), pp 153–9.

[25] Marlis Steinert, *Hitler* (München: C. H. Beck 1994), p 521; Herbert Sirois, *Zwischen Illusion und Krieg. Deutschland und die USA 1933-1941* (Paderborn: Ferdinand Schöningh 2000), pp 255–61; Richard J. Evans, *The Third Reich at War* (London: Allen Lane 2008), pp 243–4; Roberts, *Storm of War*, p 194; Lars Lüdicke, *Griff nach der Weltherrschaft. Die Aussenpolitik des Dritten Reiches 1933-1945* (Berlin: be.bra 2009), pp 149–50; Peter Longerich, *Hitler. Biographie* (München: Siedler 2015), p 827; Stephen G. Fritz, *The First Soldier: Hitler as Military Leader* (New Haven: Yale UP 2018), pp 218–19; Ralf-Georg Reuth, *Kurze Geschichte des Zweiten Weltkriegs* (Berlin: Rowohlt 2018), pp 187–8.

[26] Bernd Wegner, 'Hitlers Strategie zwischen Pearl Harbor und Stalingrad'; in: DRZW 6, pp 97–127, esp. pp 99–100.

[27] Andreas Hillgruber, 'Hitler und die USA 1933–1945'; in: Otmar Franz (ed.), *Europas Mitte* (Göttingen: Musterschmidt 1987), pp 125–44.

[28] Enrico Syring, 'Hitlers Kriegserklärung an Amerika vom 11. Dezember 1941'; in: Wolfgang Michalka (ed.), *Der Zweite Weltkrieg. Analyse. Grundzüge. Forschungsbilanz* (München: Piper 1989), pp 683–96.

[29] Udo Schmidt, *Hitlers Englandbild und seine strategischen Entscheidungen im Zweiten Weltkrieg* (München: GRIN Verlag 1998), pp 107–20; Ralf-Georg Reuth, *Hitler. Eine politische Biographie* (München: Piper 2003), pp 546–51; Schölgen, *Jenseits von Hitler*, p 198; Lars Lüdicke, *Hitlers Weltanschauung. Von 'Mein Kampf' bis zum 'Nero-Befehl'* (Paderborn: Schöningh 2016), pp 169–71.

combine key elements of the theories of Hillgruber, Jäckel and Weinberg.[30] In 1995, Gerhard Weinberg attempted an original approach that involved reprising many of the points he had made in 1980, especially the existence of a long-term agenda on the German side, stretching back as far as June 1939, to initiate hostilities against the USA. At the same time, he took a closer look at the hardware of war that was on display in both sides' arsenals in 1941. He reached the conclusion that for the German dictator the main Japanese contribution to the Tripartite Pact lay in its surface fleet – at the time the third largest in the world.[31] In early 1939, the Kriegsmarine had had plans to give Germany a sizeable blue-water navy, but the start of the war later that year, along with the United Kingdom's continuing the fight after Dunkirk, had forced these to be put on hold. Since German capital ships had thus far taken at least four years to build, a German high seas presence that might do more than occasionally inconvenience the Anglo–Americans appeared an increasingly remote prospect. Tokyo joining the European Axis would go a long way towards filling this gap. This explanation was not only plausible but also supported by the Führer's idiosyncratic fondness for the Japanese Navy, which is borne out by existing sources.[32]

Ian Kershaw in 2007 likewise saw a particular theatre of war as the key to understanding the decision to declare war on the USA. In the longest piece yet written on the topic, he rejected the notion that the dictator had simply acted out a 'grandiose moment of megalomaniac madness'.[33] Instead, he pointed to the problems that had arisen out of the US Navy's increasingly assertive presence in the eastern half of the North Atlantic and the growing likelihood of war arising therefrom. Hitler's foreign minister, Joachim von Ribbentrop, was the first to raise this issue in the dock at Nürnberg. He claimed that in private conversation Hitler had justified declaring war on the USA by pointing to the momentum towards conflict created by the shooting war between the Kriegsmarine and the US Navy's Atlantic Fleet.[34] Other historians before Kershaw had touched on this, but none had attempted to analyse it in such detail. American interference in the naval sphere had taken different forms.

---

[30] Volker Ullrich, *Adolf Hitler. Die Jahre des Untergangs* (Berlin: Fischer 2018), pp 254–5.

[31] Gerhard L. Weinberg, *A World at Arms: A Global History of World War II* (Cambridge: CUP 1995), pp 249–52, 262–3.

[32] Ibid. This particular aspect of Weinberg's explanation is certainly far more believable than any variant of the Hillgruber theory and deserved to receive a greater echo than it did. At the time of writing only Max Hastings, *All Hell Let Loose: The World at War, 1939–1945* (London: Harper Press 2011), p 197, has taken his cue from it.

[33] Ian Kershaw, *Fateful Choices: Ten Decisions that Changed the World 1940–1941* (London: Allen Lane 2007), pp 382–430.

[34] *Trial of the Major War Criminals before the Military Court in Nuremberg (TMWC)*, Vol. X, (Nürnberg 1947), pp 297–8. Also: 'Document 8. Ribbentrop, Hitler and War. Memorandum for Justice Jackson (June 1945)'; in: Richard Overy (ed.), *Interrogations: The Nazi Elite in Allied Hands* (London: Allen Lane 2001), pp 318–22.

A Neutrality Patrol that had acted in a thoroughly unneutral fashion since September 1939 was followed by the granting of repair facilities for Royal Navy vessels in US ports, the basing of troops and ships in Iceland in July 1941 and the start of convoying from mid-September 1941. In the grand scheme of things, Kershaw was inclined to follow Jäckel. Standing back and allowing the Americans to concentrate on Japan was not really an option for Berlin, since this might mean the obliteration of the Far Eastern partner. US resources had to be split while American rearmament was still in a preliminary stage. Hence, a mere escalation of the undeclared war between the US Navy and the Kriegsmarine could not suffice.

It is my contention that none of the explanations put forward can explain the decision by the German leadership to push the USA into hostilities. The Hillgruber theory borders on the ahistorical, since it clearly views the decision through the lens of the events of 1945, when attempts by Hitler to render Germany's defeat as comprehensive and destructive as possible are undeniable. Identifying a similar pattern of behaviour in late November and early December of 1941, when Germany occupied most of the European continent and had an army group bearing down on Moscow, requires a truly major leap of faith.

The Jäckel theory and its offshoots, while clearly superior, come with their own set of limitations. For one thing, some of those proposing it give us a Hitler a little too anxious about doing the right thing by his Japanese allies, whether out of a sense of moral commitment,[35] or because he feared they might be obliterated by the USA unless he were to force Washington to direct part of its forces against Germany first.[36] Such selflessness definitely clashes with his known track record in treating any of his other allies or satellites. Furthermore, none of its proponents has integrated into their analysis an examination of the German military situation in Russia, in the air and on the factory floor. Nor can they explain the curious haste shown by Hitler and his diplomats during the last days of peace with the USA. The Japanese had not made their entry into the war conditional upon a German declaration of war on the USA; the Germans in turn did not even attempt to get something tangible in return, a blockade of Vladivostok being the most obvious thing they could have been expected to insist upon. Instead, a suggestion along these lines by the German ambassador in Tokyo was curtly dismissed. It is thus obvious that a major reassessment of these events is long overdue, especially in a day and age where even such aspects of Hitler's life as his interest in art,[37]

[35] For examples, see Peter Brett, *The USA and the World, 1917–1945* (London: Hodder & Stoughton 1997), p 122, Lukacs, *Hitler of History*, pp 153–9, as well as Warren F. Kimball, *Forged in War: Roosevelt, Churchill and the Second World War* (New York: William Morrow 1997), pp 123–4.

[36] Schölgen, *Jenseits von Hitler*, pp 197–8.

[37] Birgit Schwarz, *Geniewahn: Hitler und die Kunst* (Wien: Böhlau Verlag 2009).

architecture[38] and Wagnerian opera,[39] as well as his strengths and limitations as a wordsmith of the German language,[40] are coming in for serious revisionist treatment.

It is only fair to stress that the author was encouraged in his task by the work of two colleagues who have re-examined areas that have a direct bearing on this issue: ideally, these two titles should be read together with this work. Evan Mawdsley has produced what is in effect a new global history of the events during the fortnight that saw the final moves in the escalation to global conflict.[41] Brendan Simms has made a compelling argument that Hitler's ideology incorporated a major anti-American slant from its earliest days, thus considerably easing any decision-making process leading to a declaration of war.[42] This work, by contrast, will endeavour to answer the question of whether it could also have been driven by a rational weighing of pros and cons not subject to ideology. This book will examine the information that reached the dictator over the course of 1941 in all fields of military strategy as well as foreign and economic policy with a direct or indirect bearing on relations with Japan and the USA. It will endeavour to establish what kind of 'frame of reference' Hitler would have been working from in the months before 11 December 1941.[43] No assumptions will be made about news of a particular event – no matter how well publicised – actually reaching the dictator or one of his closest collaborators unless the means by which it was conveyed to them survives. Hence, a Tokyo power struggle, a speech by the British prime minister or a vote in the US Senate will only enter the narrative of this book if an intelligence agency, senior military command or foreign ministry department of the Third Reich kept a contemporary record of it in the form of a memo, diary entry or set of briefing minutes. Instances where the older scholarship made mistaken assumptions about the information available to the Führer prior to 11 December will be highlighted. Speculation about the extent to which the dictator's temperament or mood swings could have affected

---

[38] Wolfram Pyta, *Hitler. Der Künstler als Politiker und Feldherr* (München: Siedler 2015), pp 47–177.

[39] Sebastian Werr, *Heroische Weltsicht. Hitler und die Musik* (Köln: Böhlau Verlag 2014); Hermann Grampp, 'Großonkel Leitwolf'; in: *Frankfurter Allgemeine Zeitung* (25.7.2018) – 'Geisteswissenschaften' supplement.

[40] Helmuth Kiesel, 'War Adolf Hitler ein guter Schriftsteller ?'; in: *Frankfurter Allgemeine Zeitung* (4.8.2014) – 'Feuilleton' supplement.

[41] Evan Mawdsley, *December 1941: Twelve Days that Began a World War* (New Haven: Yale UP 2011).

[42] Brendan Simms, *Hitler: Only the World Was Enough* (London: Allen Lane 2019).

[43] The recent work by Neitzel and Welzer constitutes a powerful reminder that the decisions of past generations can only be fully understood if any kind of information that reached them after the fact is deliberately ignored. See Sönke Neitzel and Harald Welzer, *Soldaten. Protokolle vom Kämpfen, Töten und Sterben* (Frankfurt a.M.: S. Fischer 2011), esp. pp 16–82.

a particular decision will be avoided; instead, an attempt will be made to square what is still widely regarded as a 'freakish and irrational decision' with a recent characterisation of the dictator by an eminent scholar, who concedes that 'Hitler, irrespective of his politically fixated aims, was a man possessed of a remarkable strategic instinct'.[44]

[44] Bernd Wegner, *Von Stalingrad nach Kursk*; in: DRZW Bd. 8, p 37 (fn 156).

Hitler's Pre-War Assessment of the United States and Japan

1.1 United States[1]

The deterioration in US–German relations from the mid-1930s onwards forced Hitler to indulge in considerable spin whenever the subject of the USA had to be addressed in a public forum.[2] Long before that, however, he had given a great deal of thought to the future role of the United States (or, as he preferred to call it, the *Amerikanische Union*) in world affairs. Most of these musings are to be found in public speeches and the records of private conversations as well as in the draft of his unpublished *Second Book*, a follow-up volume to *Mein Kampf* with a clear emphasis on foreign affairs. Unlike *Mein Kampf*, no part of the *Second Book* was ever redacted for publication.

It is important to realise that Hitler completed the *Second Book* at a time (June–July 1928) when the USA barely featured in German politics in general or those of the NSDAP in particular. The election of the Republican Warren Harding to the presidency (November 1920) and the death of Woodrow Wilson (February 1924) had removed the latter as a figure of hatred for the German Right; the Young Plan still lay a year in the future. Moreover, Enrico Syring has made a convincing case that no source from that period offers so much as a hint that Hitler expected to find himself as German chancellor in the foreseeable future; instead, he was resigned to doing little more than prepare the ground for a successor by political agitation.[3] Thus, these reflections offer a unique insight into what a Hitler unaffected by the pressures of real political

---

[1] For a more comprehensive analysis of the evolution of Hitler's view of the United States than is possible here, the reader is referred to the important new work by Brendan Simms: *Hitler: Only the World Was Enough* (London: Allen Lane 2019).

[2] The speeches he gave on 28 April 1939 and 30 January 1941 are cases in point. Max Domarus (ed.), *Hitler. Reden und Proklamationen, 1932–1945*, Bd. II (Wiesbaden: R. Löwit 1973), pp 1148–78; 1657–64.

[3] Enrico Syring, *Hitler. Seine politische Utopie* (Berlin: Propyläen Verlag 1994), pp 241–76. An assessment supported by a number of statements Hitler himself made during the period in question. See, for instance, 'Handschriftlicher Brief Rudolf Heß an Gret Georg, Schweinfurt (27.11.1924)'; in: Wolf-Rüdiger Heß and Dirk Bavendamm (eds.), *Rudolf Heß. Briefe 1908–1933* (München: Langen Müller 1987), pp 355–6. According to Ian Kershaw, Hitler likely as not made the mental transition from agitator to future leader

power thought of the USA. How exactly he arrived at this assessment is to some extent subject to conjecture. It is, however, possible to single out a few influencing factors.

1.1.1   First Impressions (1918–1923)

Thanks to recent research by Brendan Simms we are in a position to put a date on the first contact between *Gefreiter* Hitler and representatives of the American nation: after his regiment's first brush with a US Army unit near Rheims on 17 July 1918, he was detailed to drop off two POWs at the field headquarters of the Twelfth Royal Bavarian Infantry Brigade.[4] We do not know what (if anything) transpired between them along the way, but a reference made in a public speech nine years later as likely as not refers to this encounter.[5] Hitler alleged that those captured Americans – most probably because one or both of them still spoke German – served as a powerful reminder to him of the net loss which foreign migration to America had meant for pre-war Germany. Whether coincidentally or not, one of the very first public speeches he had given while still employed as a political agitator by the Reichswehr in post-revolutionary Munich also appears to have addressed this issue[6] – the net loss which pre-war Germany had sustained through migration.[7] By December 1919, he was quoting the United States in one breath with Britain whenever he lashed out at the enemy alliance that kept defeated Germany pinned to the ground. This is not altogether surprising since these

during his imprisonment in Landsberg. Ian Kershaw, *Hitler 1889–1936: Hubris* (London: Allen Lane 1998), pp 218–19.

[4] Bayerisches Hauptstaatsarchiv, Abt. IV, Kriegsarchiv, 16. RIR, Nr. 10 ('Stab Juli 1918') as quoted by Brendan Simms, '"Against a World of Enemies": the Impact of the First World War on the Development of Hitler's Ideology'; in: *International Affairs* 90:2 (2014), pp 317–36, esp. p 324.

[5] '20 Millionen Deutsche zuviel Rede auf NSDAP-Versammlung in Ansbach (26.3.1927)'; in: Bärbel Dusik (ed.), *Hitler. Reden, Schriften, Anordnungen. Band II: Juli 1926–Juli 1927* (München et al: K. G. Saur 1992), pp 193–219, esp. p 202. This multi-volume edition of Hitler's early speeches and proclamations will henceforth be quoted as RSA.

[6] On this phase of Hitler's life, see Othmar Plöckinger, *Unter Soldaten und Agitatoren. Hitlers prägende Jahre im deutschen Militär 1918–1920* (Paderborn et al: Ferdinand Schöningh 2013).

[7] Simms, 'World of Enemies', p 329. The speech took place on 24 August 1919 and carried the title '*Auswanderung*' (emigration). The text does not survive. See also 'Rede auf einer NSDAP-Versammlung (München, 6. Juli 1920)' as well as 'Der deutsche Arbeiter und die Friedensverträge. Rede auf einer NSDAP-Versammlung (München, 31. Mai 1921)'; in: Eberhard Jäckel and Axel Kuhn (eds.), *Hitler. Sämtliche Aufzeichnungen 1905–1924* (Stuttgart: DVA 1980). A small number of documents included in this edition were later found to be forgeries. They are listed in Jäckel/Kuhn, 'Neue Erkenntnisse zur Fälschung von Hitler-Dokumenten'; in: *Vierteljahrhefte für Zeitgeschichte* Bd. 32 (1984), Nr. 1, pp 163–9.

early speeches – not all of which survive – still often fit the mould of orthodox right-wing German opinion in 1919–21 on the USA and President Wilson in particular. According to this discourse, the US President had entered the war in 1917 to save the Allies from an increasingly likely defeat and, by extension, American banks from financial ruin.[8] Wilson then mischievously 'tricked' the Germans into opening armistice talks by the apparent generosity of the Fourteen Points peace offer he put forward in January 1918, thus leaving Germany prostrate before the victors at Versailles.[9]

While it is true that these broadsides against the victors of 1918 were sometimes accompanied by harsh personal expletive, Hitler saved most of his venom for the German politicians who, according to him, had done the Allies' dirty work for them.[10] The US President, on the other hand, he sometimes granted a degree of grudging respect, for pulling off such a feat.[11] The fact that the US Senate had refused to approve the country's membership of the League of Nations was also something Hitler felt stood in contrast to the undignified behaviour of the German political class in trying to be accepted into that august body.[12] American legislation aimed at keeping Native Americans and African Americans in a state of segregation and at stemming the influx of non-white immigrants into the country was another thing Hitler could approve of.[13]

---

[8] For good examples of this, see 'Deutschland vor seiner tiefsten Erniedrigung (München, 10. Dezember 1919)'; 'Friede der Versöhnung oder der Gewalt. Rede auf einer NSDAP-Versammlung (München, 22. September 1920)'; 'Der Weltkrieg und seine Macher. Rede auf einer NSDAP-Versammlung (Landshut, 28. Februar 1921)' all in: Jäckel/Kuhn (eds.), *Aufzeichnungen*, pp 96–9, 233–7, 327–9.

[9] For a good example of this, 'Der Daitsche Staatsmann. Aufsatz (München, 28. April 1921)'; in: Jäckel/Kuhn (eds.), *Aufzeichnungen*, pp 371–3. It goes without saying that this train of thought conveniently overlooked the fact that Germany had chosen to avail herself of this offer only in October 1918 and after having brought the Allies to the brink of defeat in March–April 1918.

[10] In the case of President Wilson, a sarcastic *Friedensapostel* (peace prophet) was the one most commonly used. 'Moral and physical syphilitic American' ('*moralischen und physischen amerikanischen Syphilitikers*') constituted an – admittedly unique – all-time low. See 'Der Daitsche Staatsmann. Aufsatz (München, 28. April 1921)'; in: Jäckel/Kuhn (eds.), *Aufzeichnungen*, pp 371–3.

[11] In: 'Gegen den Völkerbund. Rede auf einer NSDAP-Versammlung' (München 5. November 1920)'. Also 'Versailles, Deutschlands Vernichtung (München, 24. November 1920)'. Both in: Jäckel/Kuhn (eds.), *Aufzeichnungen*, pp 257–8, 265–9.

[12] 'Gegen den Völkerbund. Rede auf einer NSDAP-Versammlung (5. November 1920)'; in: Jäckel/Kuhn (eds.), *Aufzeichnungen*, pp 257–8.

[13] 'Politik und Rasse. Warum sind wir Antisemiten? Rede auf einer NSDAP-Versammlung (München, 20. April 1923)'; in: Jäckel/Kuhn (eds.), *Aufzeichnungen*, pp 906–10. A manifestation of approval that is of more than academic interest. New scholarship has revealed that the debate among Nazi jurists which would precede the proclamation of the Nürnberg laws of 1935 was informed to a considerable degree by American racist

It needs to be stressed, however, that these judgements, while noteworthy, did not stand at the heart of Hitler's image of the USA in the early 1920s. Even at this early stage of his career, the one thing he was most consistent about was his anti-Semitism. Even though to him the United States was a country run on material greed, he appeared willing to discriminate between ordinary Americans and the Jewish money-lending class which supposedly was in the process of usurping that country's government.[14] The America of the late nineteenth and early twentieth centuries he described as 'an evolving civilisation', which was now being progressively corrupted by the 'Jews of Wall Street'.[15] Even the country's entry into World War I was something he was willing to put down to the influences of British propaganda and 'the Jewish media of America', which had, after all, pulled off 'a real masterpiece: to goad a people both numerous and peaceful which cared as much about the struggle in Europe as it did about the North Pole, to join the most cruel war ever for the sake of "culture".'[16]

It is difficult to ascertain whether this set of prejudices already amounted to a sort of programme that included the blueprint for a future American–German confrontation. Some recent research points to the possibility that Hitler's anti-Semitism may in fact have originated from the perceived need to remove an imagined Jewish barrier standing between a resurgent German Right and a no-holds-barred struggle against Anglo–American capitalism.[17] There is some support for this, especially a 1919 speech where the United States is described as an 'absolute adversary' and thus placed ahead even of the hereditary enemy, France;[18] in a similar address from May 1920 the future dictator makes a point of discriminating between those foreign powers whose enmity is incidental and arguably a consequence of foolish pre-1914 policies (Russia is mentioned in this context) and those which have to be seen as sworn enemies of the German Reich (France, Great Britain and the USA).[19] Over and above this, both a draft and a manuscript from 1923, point to a reason for this

---

legislation. See James Q. Whitman, *Hitler's American Model: The United States and the Making of Nazi Racial Law* (Princeton and Oxford: Princeton UP 2017).

[14] 'Deutschland vor seiner tiefsten Erniedrigung. Rede auf einer DAP-Versammlung (München, 10. Dezember 1919)'; in: Jäckel/Kuhn (eds*.), Aufzeichnungen*, pp 96–9.

[15] 'Positiver Antisemitismus der Bayerischen Volkspartei. Rede auf einer NSDAP-Versammlung (München, 2. November 1922)'; in: Jäckel/Kuhn (eds.), *Aufzeichnungen*, pp 717–21.

[16] 'Weltjude und Weltbörse, die Urschuldigen am Weltkriege. Rede auf einer NSDAP-Versammlung (München, 13. April 1923)'; in: Jäckel/Kuhn (eds.), *Aufzeichnungen*, p 891.

[17] Simms, 'World of Enemies', pp 330–1.

[18] 'Deutschland vor seiner tiefsten Erniedrigung. Rede auf einer DAP-Versammlung (München, 10. Dezember 1919)'; in: Jäckel/Kuhn (eds.), *Aufzeichnungen*, pp 96–9.

[19] 'Die Macher am Weltkrieg. Rede auf einer Versammlung des Deutschvölkischen Schutz- und Trutzbundes (Stuttgart, 26. Mai 1920)'; in: Jäckel/Kuhn (eds.), *Aufzeichnungen*, pp 135–6.

ranking that might go beyond raving anti-Semitism. According to these, Hitler had taken careful note of the failure – unique among the great powers of the time – of any kind of socialist party to establish a major foothold within the body politic of the United States.[20] To him, this was a crucial issue, because this was arguably the only political force that had had the power to stop war in 1914 and, in the German case, actually did so in 1918, with consequences that led directly to Versailles. The Americans' apparent immunity to this kind of threat was something that left him deeply impressed.[21]

1.1.2   Reading Matter

Hitler read voraciously, albeit in an unsystematic fashion that tended to favour biographies and military history. Unlike Stalin, he would only occasionally jot down marginal notes in the pages of books, making it difficult for the latter-day researcher to discriminate among the books which he read, just skimmed over or merely owned.[22] The ranks of the third category were swollen by numerous gifts from admirers, which in many cases went straight onto the shelves of his main libraries in Berlin, Munich and Berchtesgaden, never to be touched again by the recipient's hand.[23] As a rule of thumb, the likelihood of Hitler devoting serious time to a book must have decreased considerably with every year he spent in power. The 1920s, on the other hand, have to be seen as a key period in two senses. First, his mind was still open to some new ideas and his view of the world had not yet hardened into a set of prejudices.[24] Second, the leisure enforced on him by his prison sentence (November 1923–December 1924) and

---

[20] A fact he highlighted in a brief article written for the Hearst papers more than eight years later. While on this occasion he may have been playing to American expectations, it's still obvious that the point had rankled with him, if nothing else. 'Rundfunkrede-New York American vom 13.12.1931 (11. Dezember 1931)'; in: RSA, Bd. IV.2, pp 256–9.

[21] 'Börsendiktatur, Ursachen des Weltkrieges, das Los der Beamten, Bolschewismus. Stichworte zu Reden (o.O., post- April 1923)'; 'Weltjude und Weltbörse, die Urschuldigen am Weltkriege. Rede auf einer NSDAP-Versammlung (München, 13. April 1923)'; both in: Jäckel/Kuhn (eds.), *Aufzeichnungen*, pp 856–62.

[22] Stalin consumed both books and files at a prodigious rate never matched by his arch-enemy. On his reading habits, see Zhores Medvedev and Roy Medvedev, 'Stalin's Personal Archive: Hidden or Destroyed? Facts and Theories'; in: Zhores A. Medvedev and Roy A. Medvedev, *The Unknown Stalin* (London: I.B. Tauris 2003), pp 57–94, esp. pp 88–91.

[23] In a recent examination of Hitler's reading habits, Timothy Ryback estimated that approximately two-thirds of Hitler's 16,000 volumes fell into this category. Timothy Ryback, *Hitler's Bücher. Seine Bibliothek. Sein Denken* (Köln: Fackelträger 2010), p 22.

[24] Albert Speer, in an early statement to Allied interrogators, claimed that Hitler had repeatedly admitted to him that everything he was trying to achieve was an outflow of ideas he had formed between his thirtieth and fortieth birthdays (1919–1929). Ulrich Schlie (ed.), *Albert Speer. Die Kransberg-Protokolle 1945. Seine ersten Aussagen und Aufzeichnungen* (München: Herbig 2003), p 98 (1.8.1945).

the following period of languishing political fortunes meant that, by force of circumstance, he had plenty of time on his hands.[25]

Erwin Rosen's *Amerikaner* is a ninety-page booklet issued by a popular German publisher in 1920;[26] its author – a well-travelled German who had lived in the USA in the 1890s – sought to explain to his readers the mentality of the average American citizen and how this had contributed to making the USA both a land of plenty and an economic superpower. We are lucky in having a source which confirms that Hitler read this book while serving his sentence in Landsberg prison. In a letter by Rudolf Heß to his family dated 19 May 1924, he refers to Hitler 'devouring' Rosen's book.[27] Since our image of Hitler is that of a man notorious for taking on board other views only if they tended to reinforce his own prejudices, the obvious expectation is for *Amerikaner* to be a rabidly anti-American diatribe peppered with racist and anti-Semitic slurs. Closer examination reveals it to be an account that is not just completely devoid of the obligatory rants against President Wilson so prevalent among German political publications of the time, but also characterised by a surprisingly friendly attitude towards American society. The average American is described as having a healthy zest for life and hard work. Americans' constant proclamations of their country's greatness, while grating to European ears, are increasingly being borne out by reality, the author asserts. Their almost childlike naivete coexists side by side with a 'zeal for action' passed down from one generation to the next, which manifests itself in snappy decision-making and a 'violent passion for competition'.[28] Where politics are concerned, two points stand out, which Hitler undoubtedly would have agreed with. Rosen stresses that irrespective of flowery rhetoric, American politicians will never hesitate to put the interests of their country before those of the League of Nations. Second – especially in the context of worldwide events at the time that Hitler was reading the book[29] – working-

---

[25] Of this period in particular Hitler admitted to Heß in 1928 that the failure of the 1923 coup had been a blessing in disguise. Among other things, the time he was forced to spend in gaol 'had given him the time to reassess his situation and acquire fundamentally new insights'. See 'Handschriftlicher Brief Rüdolf Heß an Ilse Heß (8.3.1928)'; in: Heß/ Bavendamm (eds.), *Briefe*, pp 390–1. The timing of this statement is crucial: at the time, nothing indicated an imminent upswing in the NSDAP's fortunes, which would have allowed Hitler to put a positive gloss on past misfortunes.

[26] Erwin Rosen, *Amerikaner* (Leipzig: Dürr & Weber 1920). Rosen, who also served in the French Foreign Legion in 1905–6, is better known as the author of the memoir *In the Foreign Legion* (1910).

[27] 'Handschriftlicher Brief Rudolf Heß an Ilse Pröhl (18.5.1924)'; in: Heß/Bavendamm (eds.), *Briefe*, pp 326–39, esp. p 328.

[28] Rosen, *Amerikaner*, p 37.

[29] 1919–20 saw a rash of revolutionary uprisings in central and eastern Europe as well as civil war in Russia and the Soviet invasion of Poland. In the USA, a number of terrorist acts and widespread industrial action led to the Great Red Scare. There is a whole library of scholarly

class Americans, who are constantly seeking to improve their lot by making the most of the opportunities available to them, have proven completely immune to the temptations of communist ideology.[30]

A year or two after reading Rosen, Hitler settled down to a book of a completely different ilk. Madison Grant (1865–1937) was a well-connected eugenicist from an old New York family, who agitated throughout the early 1900s against mixed marriages and for a limitation of immigration quotas. This effort peaked with his role in collecting the data that underpinned the 1924 Federal Immigration Act. This law fixed quotas that all but ruled out East Asian immigration, sharply reduced the numbers allowed to East European Jews and Italians, while favouring others (like Germans) seen as more desirable. A prolific writer, Grant's most influential work by far was *The Passing of the Great Race* (1916), which was translated into a number of languages, with the German edition coming out in early 1925. Grant essentially stood Darwinist theory on its head by insisting that throughout history the 'Nordic' race, while consistently victorious in its march of conquest through most of Europe and the Middle East, had invariably succumbed to its inferior, but more numerous subject peoples. In recent centuries, conflagrations like the Thirty Years War and the Great War had meant that the Nordic countries involved had suffered demographic setbacks they could ill afford. As a result, Germany could no longer be counted in the front ranks of the purely Nordic nations: only between 9 and 19 million of its people were, according to Grant, still worthy of the label 'Nordic'. The United States, he insisted, was still reasonably safe by virtue of the fact that the state rested on solid racial foundations put down in the late eighteenth and early nineteenth centuries, when the first substantial waves of migrants to cross the Atlantic were composed of individuals from northern European countries. Even so, the aforementioned historical pattern would assert itself, without protection from new legislation that saw to both the limitation of immigration and the sterilisation of the unfit.

The extent of Grant's influence on Hitler's thinking is difficult to assess because broadly similar ideas were being put forward at the time by other commentators.[31] However, we do know that Hitler referred to Grant and his

---

works on these events; for a succinct summary, see Anthony Read, *The World on Fire: 1919 and the Battle with Bolshevism* (New York and London: W. W. Norton 2008).

[30] Rosen, *Amerikaner*, pp 41–57, esp. p 53.

[31] A paragraph in the first volume of *Mein Kampf* appears to indicate considerable familiarity with Grant's theories; this is rendered problematic, however, by the fact that the first volume of *Mein Kampf* was published in July 1925 and so a few weeks before the publication of the German language translation of Grant's book. Hence, an article espousing similar theories in the *Zeitschrift für Geopolitik* of January 1924 by the academic Franz Termerit appears to be the more likely source, especially since we know that Hitler had access to back issues of this journal through Professor Haushofer.

thinking on at least one occasion in a major speech and even bowed to the harsh judgement Grant had made about Germany's deteriorating Nordic status.[32] In a key paragraph in the unpublished *Second Book* Hitler fully integrated into his ideology the notion of the constantly victorious, yet equally constantly threatened Nordic race on its march through history.[33] In further speeches he fully echoed Grant's thinking about the wasteful losses endured by both countries on the battlefields of World War I and even adopted an unflattering (and to a German public of the time, probably strangely unintelligible) comparison between the USA and Mexico that Grant had used to illustrate the baleful consequences of racial intermarriage. Finally, he wrote Grant a letter in which he thanked him effusively and described *The Passing of the Great Race* as his bible.[34] While Grant's influence on Hitler is key in the sense that his theory probably encouraged Hitler to transfer his racial ideology to a continental scale, he also nurtured in him a view of the United States which broadly speaking took into account the fact that it was a country of considerable demographic and economic potential. That Hitler should have arrived at this conclusion at least in part by the roundabout route of his racial pseudo-science did not make this assessment any less accurate.

1.1.3 Public and Private Statements, Mein Kampf and the Second Book, 1924–1933

Of all the value judgements that Hitler ever made about the USA, those that have endured the longest have been the anti-Semitic and racist diatribes of the wartime years. They are confirmed by the impressions of a few of his fellow travellers, such as Fritz Wiedemann and Ernst Hanfstaengl. The latter wrote in 1970 that 'to Hitler the US apparently was nothing more than a country ruled by gangsters, corrupt politicians and Jews and where public order – such as it was – was determined by the rate of kidnappings, stock exchange crashes and millions of unemployed'.[35] This chapter will attempt to explore why these statements stand in such contrast to other, much less well-publicised ones.

See Christian Hartmann, Thomas Vordermayer, Othmar Plöckinger and Roman Töppel (eds.), *Hitler, Mein Kampf. Eine kritische Edition* (München: Institut für Zeitgeschichte 2016), p 745.

[32] 'Warum sind wir Nationalisten? Rede auf NSDAP-Versammlung in München (6.4.1927)'; in: RSA, Bd. II.1, pp 235–41, esp. p 236. Grant had calculated that Germany's purely 'Nordic' population currently stood at a mere '9 or 10 million inhabitants', figures Hitler repeated in his address.

[33] Gerhard L. Weinberg, Christian Hartmann, Klaus Lankheit (eds.), *Hitler. Reden. Schriften. Anordnungen (Februar 1925 bis Januar 1933). Band II A. Aussenpolitische Standortbestimmung nach der Reichstagswahl* (München: K. G. Saur 1995), p 87.

[34] Grant kept the letter carefully filed away and developed the habit of sharing its contents with fellow travellers sympathetic to his cause. Ryback, *Bücher*, p 149.

[35] Ernst Hanfstaengl, *Zwischen Weißem und Braunem Haus* (München: Piper 1970), p 280.

At no other time since joining the Bavarian Army in 1914 was Hitler better able to make the most of (admittedly enforced) leisure than during the incarceration after the failed coup attempt of November 1923. He greatly benefitted from the fact that existing legislation allowed him to serve his time under a privileged regime of *Festungshaft* reserved to political detainees.[36] Especially after he and a number of accomplices were moved to the fortress of Landsberg, treatment can only be described as a pale reflection of what awaited ordinary inmates of the German prison system of the time. This was compounded by the obvious sympathy with which the warden of the institution and the guards treated their famous charges; they were allowed regular visits from the outside, unlimited access to books and newspapers and showered with culinary gifts from admirers all over Germany. Cells were not locked in daytime and the inmates were allowed to wander around their wing and even the prison gardens at will. Hitler put on weight and began work on the manuscript that would become *Mein Kampf*.[37] Of the seven co-conspirators who had been sent to Landsberg at the same time as Hitler, the one closest to him was probably Rudolf Heß. Destined to become world-famous by his flight to Scotland in May 1941 and forty-year-long post-war imprisonment in Spandau, he had joined the newly founded NSDAP in July 1920 and soon turned into one of its most zealous agitators. By 1922–3, he had become one of the individuals closest to Hitler. After spending a few months on the run from the authorities, he turned himself in and joined his beloved *Tribun* in Landsberg, where he was delighted to find him in excellent shape.[38] The extent to which the much better educated Heß played a marginal or major role in the writing of *Mein Kampf* is irrelevant in this context;[39] what is important is that the two grew even closer than they had been before the coup, thus laying the foundation for Heß's being made Deputy Führer after he left Landsberg. Together with the hotel-like, but still somewhat cramped living conditions at Landsberg, this would give Heß a unique glimpse into Hitler's reflections on the world around him. In a draft letter dated 9 April 1924, Heß

---

[36] For an excellent analysis of the historical and legal context of *Festungshaft*, see Peter Fleischmann, *Hitler als Häftling in Landsberg am Lech* (Neustadt an der Aisch: PH.C.W. Schmidt 2015), pp 20–33.

[37] On living conditions in Landsberg, see Holger Herwig, *The Demon of Geopolitics. How Karl Haushofer 'Educated' Hitler and Hess* (New York and London: Rowman & Littlefield 2016), pp 90–4, and David King, *The Trial of Adolf Hitler* (London: Macmillan 2017), pp 303–23.

[38] 'Handschriftlicher Brief Rudolf Heß an Ilse Pröhl (18.5.1924)'; in: Heß/Bavendamm (eds.), *Briefe*, pp 326–9, esp. p 326. As Heß put it to his fiancée: 'the period of enforced leisure is beneficial to him.'

[39] The extent to which early drafts of *Mein Kampf* benefitted from Heß's input is still contentious. For more detailed views on this see Kershaw, *Hitler I*, pp 241–50, as well as Othmar Plöckinger, *Geschichte eines Buches: Adolf Hitler's Mein Kampf 1922–1945* (München: Oldenbourg Verlag 2006), pp 146–9.

reflected on Hitler's broad range of interests, including technical processes aimed at facilitating human progress. In a recent conversation, the future Führer had dwelt at length on the successes which the Ford Motor Company had achieved in the mass production of cars.[40] In view of Henry Ford's by then well-known anti-Semitism, the historian would be justified in assuming that it was the US magnate's prejudices, rather than his latest industrial achievements, that had attracted Hitler's attention. In the following weeks and months, however, Hitler would return to the subject of the American way of life time and again. On 16 May, Heβ again summarised many of Hitler's musings, this time for the benefit of his mother. Among the subjects singled out for special attention was the future of the motor car as the main means of transport for the working class 'as in America', Germany still being many years away from such a state of affairs.[41] On 27 May, Heβ reported a conversation where Hitler had dwelt in considerable detail on the latest rage from America as far as architecture was concerned – skyscrapers. Hitler even expressed a desire to have the NSDAP's new party headquarters installed in such a building, as a deliberate snub to the *Theutschvölkischen* within the movement, as he put it.[42] On 16 June 1924, Heβ – apparently for the first time – appended to one of the letters he sent his fiancée a virtual word-by-word record of a monologue by Hitler. Again, the subject was the need to make wider use of available technology to ease the travails of day-to-day life, a task Hitler saw as the defining challenge for his generation. He went so far as to state that it was necessary to treat the United States as an example to be followed (*'Man soll sich ein Beispiel an Amerika nehmen'*).[43] German car manufacturers demanding a rise in tariffs in order to gain some protection from US competitors should be told to work harder and achieve similar results. In a different context, even the American Yellowstone Park was praised as a model institution which Germany would do well to emulate.[44]

Otto Wagener was a relative newcomer to Hitler's court.[45] A veteran of World War I and the post-war Freikorps, he came from a well-off background and supported various far-right causes in the 1920s. Starting in 1927, some of

---

[40] 'Maschinenschriftliche Ausarbeitung von Rudolf Heβ (9.4.1924)'; in: Heβ/Bavendamm (eds.), *Briefe*, pp 317–21, esp. p 319.

[41] 'Handschriftlicher Brief Rudolf Heβ an Klara Heβ, Reichsoldsgrün (16.5.1924)'; in: Heβ/ Bavendamm (eds.), *Briefe*, pp 322–5, esp. p 324.

[42] A reference to representatives of the far Right both within and outside the NSDAP who sought a return to old 'Germanic' values of pre-modern times. 'Handschriftlicher Brief Rudolf Heβ an Ilse Pröhl (27.5.1924)'; in: Heβ/Bavendamm (eds.), *Briefe*, pp 329–31.

[43] 'Anlage zu Dokument 342: Handschriftliche Aufzeichnung Rudolf Heβ von einem Gespräch mit Adolf Hitler (16.6.1924)'; in: Heβ/Bavendamm (eds.), *Briefe*, pp 339–40.

[44] Ibid.

[45] The following is mostly a summary of Henry Ashby Turner, 'Otto Wagener, Der vergessene Vertraute Hitlers'; in: Ronald Smelser et al (eds.), *Die braune Elite II. 21 weitere biographische Skizzen* (Darmstadt: WBG 1993), pp 243–53.

his wartime comrades who had joined the Nazi cause encouraged him to attend speeches and rallies. Finally, during the August 1929 rally of the NSDAP in Nürnberg, the head of the SA, Oskar Pfeffer von Salomon, a good friend from his Freikorps days, introduced him to Hitler. It appears that he was made the offer to join the party and become Pfeffer von Salomon's chief of staff more or less on the spot. When a year later Hitler and Pfeffer had a massive falling out, which led to the latter tendering his resignation, Wagener decided to stay. In early 1931 he made room for a new appointee as SA chief of staff: Ernst Röhm, a member of the NSDAP's old guard, who had just returned from a stint in Bolivia as a soldier of fortune. A move that appeared to relegate Wagener to the sidelines actually brought him closer to Hitler. He volunteered to set up a cell within the NSDAP's leadership that would have as its sole remit the study of the problems afflicting the German economy. His experience as a manager of several companies before 1929 gave him a modicum of expert knowledge in the subject. As luck would have it, the NSDAP's central offices were just in the process of moving house to the newly built Braunes Haus in Munich and, whether by chance or by design, Wagener ended up in an office next door to Hitler's. The latter took a liking to his fellow southerner, included him in his retinue and repeatedly asked him to accompany him on the numerous trips he made all over Germany.

By the spring of 1932, Wagener had developed a political theory based on the progressive evolution of private companies into entities collectively owned by their most productive workers. Sketchy at best (and in all likelihood, completely impractical), this theory soon lost ground to voices within the NSDAP leadership who advocated a close cooperation with private industry, with a view to attaining political power. In September 1932, Wagener resigned his position and for a few months acted as a political lobbyist for the party in Berlin. From April to June 1933, after the NSDAP's seizure of power, he briefly held the ill-defined position of Reich commissioner for the economy until he fell foul of his rival Göring. He lost all power and never returned to politics. His relevance to this account lies in the fact that while a POW in British hands, he spent much of 1945–6 rewriting from memory diaries he had kept throughout much of the 1929–33 period. They consist of a chronologically arranged series of sixty-two anecdotal snapshots, usually revolving around a particular incident or conversation, often (though by no means always) with Hitler at its centre.[46] Where he describes events subject to verification half a century later, his account is remarkably accurate. The fact that we know for certain that he was part of Hitler's close retinue for most of the January 1931–September 1932 period gives this source additional credibility. Some of the differences of opinion on economics he records between himself and the future

---

[46] Henry Ashby Turner Jr, (ed.), *Hitler aus nächster Nähe. Aufzeichnungen eines Vertrauten 1929–1933* (Frankfurt a.M.: Ullstein 1978).

Führer ring true; they tally with what we know about the controversies within the party at the time about what economic policy to espouse – a subject area on which Nazi dogma had so far been vague. As already stated, Wagener had a stake in these discussions, which might make him a less than absolutely faithful chronicler of the exchanges.[47] However, even though he claims to have made several unsuccessful attempts to steer Hitler away from confrontation with the USSR, he appears to have been non-committal on the subject of the USA. What his record does reflect is that throughout the summer of 1931 and possibly as late as 1933 he and Hitler had several exchanges during which the latter dwelt at some length on the future role of the United States in world politics.[48] In Hitler's view, the USA was preordained to pursue a policy of expansion in order to meet the problem of industrial overproduction. This issue had if anything been exacerbated and not alleviated by the Great Depression then enveloping the world.[49] The only way to check this in the long term would be for Europe to form a union under German leadership, after having brought the Ukraine into the fold with a view to acquiring self-sufficiency in raw materials. Should Europe fail to do this, the USA could not fail eventually to establish a global hegemony.[50] Hitler was willing to concede that President Roosevelt might sincerely be pursuing economic recovery as a means to restore prosperity to the masses hit by the Depression. But he prophesied that the President would fail in this endeavour and would ultimately turn to war in order to vanquish permanently any economic competitors.[51] Nor did the world of racial politics provide any solace for this bleak outlook. Hitler freely acknowledged that the Nordic element predominated in the United States and that there was little doubt that in due course the Americans too would become one people.[52]

---

[47] On the reliability of Wagener's writings in general see Turner (ed.), *Aufzeichnungen*, pp VI–XVI. It is noteworthy that even after 1945, Wagener refused to adopt the posture of a 'prophet without honour'. Instead, he freely conceded that his course might have not have brought victory either.

[48] Turner (ed.), *Aufzeichnungen*, pp 280–97 (fragments 33, 34 and 35). The chronology at this point is slightly blurry, since there is at least one reference to Franklin Delano Roosevelt, who was after all only elected in November 1932 and inaugurated in March 1933. It is likely that Wagener incorporated a later conversation between him and Hitler into the account.

[49] Turner (ed.), *Aufzeichnungen*, p 280 (fragment 33), p 281 (fragment 34), p 296 (fragment 35).

[50] Turner (ed.), *Aufzeichnungen*, p 293 (fragment 35).

[51] Turner (ed.), *Aufzeichnungen*, p 296 (fragment 35).

[52] Turner (ed.), *Aufzeichnungen*, p 288–9 (fragment 35): '*So wird auch Amerika mit der Zeit ein Volk werden.*' Statements which he made to Albert Speer in the second half of the war appear to contradict this assessment. It should be borne in mind, however, that by then Germany's deteriorating situation put him in a situation where statements made to his closest collaborators were increasingly marked by wishful thinking, his joyful reaction at

References to the United States and its people are far from infrequent in *Mein Kampf*, the two-volume programmatic diatribe Hitler wrote in Landsberg and in the months after his release.[53] However, they are not assembled in a coherent way that might point the reader towards the future shape of US–German relations; instead, they stand on their own. What is important is the fact that nearly all of them express admiration or even awe at American achievements. A case in point is a paragraph in the second volume discussing the proliferation of technical innovations coming out of the USA. According to the future dictator's interpretation, this had to be seen as the direct result of a culture of social mobility that allowed people of modest means to reap the reward of their labours, thus creating a powerful incentive for individuals from all walks of life to put their minds to work in a manner that would benefit both them and the state.[54] Other features of the inter-war United States also meet with his approval – its sheer size for one thing. In contrast to the British and French empires, whose size was mostly underpinned by vulnerable overseas territories, the USA boasted an enormous and unmatched continental 'base' with just a few overseas possessions.[55] To Hitler this alone was enough to rule out a future European war against the enemies of 1914, aimed at re-establishing Germany's borders of 1914. The way he saw it, even a successful conclusion of such a war would leave Germany still struggling to outflank Britain or 'match the size of the [American] Union'.[56] It was with some glee, however, that he looked forward to the intensification of US–British rivalries over commerce and naval supremacy, since such a conflict was likely to 'doom England' unless backed by a major ally.[57] Finally, Hitler paid Washington the highest imaginable accolade. The Americans' long tradition of shunning marriages with 'lesser races',[58] along with the new legislation that all but barred migration by Asians and considerably lowered the quotas for Eastern Europeans,[59] showed that they were engaged in a serious attempt at preventing 'the lowering of the quality of their race'.[60]

Hitler continued to observe American affairs carefully from afar. In the original edition of *Mein Kampf* the wording hinted at the likelihood that the Americans' endeavour to maintain the numerical supremacy of the Nordic

Roosevelt's death on 16 April 1945 being a case in point. Schlie (ed.), *Kransberg-Protokolle* (7.9.1945), p 231.

[53] Volume I appeared in July 1925, Volume II in December 1926. Hartmann et al (eds.), *Mein Kampf*, p 69.

[54] Ibid., p 1093 f.

[55] Ibid., p 401.

[56] Ibid., p 1651.

[57] Ibid., p 1617.

[58] Ibid., p 743. Hitler contrasted this tradition with the high levels of racial inter-marriage in many Latin American countries.

[59] Ibid., p 1117.

[60] Ibid., p 743.

races in their country would be doomed in the long run. In the 1930 edition, however, a minor but important amendment indicated that the author had reached the conclusion that the struggle for Nordic supremacy in the USA was still open-ended.[61]

Hitler developed these ideas over the years, and by the time he sat down to write the *Second Book*,[62] they formed the groundwork for an entire chapter exclusively dedicated to the USA.[63] In it, and in contrast to most other spokesmen for the far Right in Germany at the time, Hitler did not merely bemoan the cultural encroachment symbolised by US feature films and jazz bands, but reflected on the reasons behind this budding hegemony. To him neither mere numbers nor the size of the country could explain this success. Echoing Grant, he stressed that the key factor was the racial homogeneity and hence compatibility of the bulk of the migrants, who in any case constituted the pick of their generation.[64] This fact was reflected both in the daring they exhibited by the mere decision to migrate and in their emergence at the top of the ensuing Darwinist scramble for resources that the expansion of the white settlers across the continent had entailed. The combination of this quality of *Menschenmaterial* (human resources) with the sheer extent of land capable of development accounted for the country's unique potential. However, Hitler was not carried away by the romantic image of settlers engaged in a perpetual struggle against Native Americans and the untameable wilderness – an image that had in any case belonged to the past for two generations. Instead, and harking back to his reflections on the subject in Landsberg, he singled out the future of the car industry as an image to impress upon his readers the pointlessness of engaging the USA in peaceful competition for markets. To him, the motorisation of modern society was 'an issue of immeasurable importance for the future'.[65] The 1920s had seen US car production multiply many times over, with European producers struggling to stay in the race. In Hitler's view, this was an exercise in futility, since the size of the US domestic market enabled American car producers to implement economies of scale that would always allow them to out-produce and outbid competitors. The same logic was

---

[61] Ibid. The first edition spoke of the existing racial supremacy by the Germanic races in the United States which would, however, come to an end when they fell prey to race defilement. This sentence was given a new meaning in 1930 with the omission of 'when' and its substitution by 'if'.

[62] Weinberg et al, *Aussenpolitische Standortbestimmung*, pp 81–92.

[63] It is rather misleadingly titled '*Weder Grenzpolitik noch Wirtschaftspolitik noch Paneuropa*', which may account for the fact why some historians have overlooked it. See Barbara Zehnpfennig, *Adolf Hitler: Mein Kampf. Studienkommentar* (München: Wilhelm Fink 2011), p 216.

[64] Weinberg el al, *Aussenpolitische Standortbestimmung*, pp 91–2.

[65] Weinberg et al, *Aussenpolitische Standortbestimmung*, p 84.

applicable to any other industry. Hitler made light of the idea that a long-term European union would be enough to meet the USA on anything like equal terms. This would be possible only under the leadership of a powerful hegemon and after legislation similar to that of the 1924 US Immigration Law had been implemented across the European continent. Failure to bring about such a state of affairs, he stressed in the conclusion of the manuscript, would lead to 'the overpowering of the world by the American Union'.[66]

The true importance of these private and semi-private musings can only be realised by comparing and contrasting them with the public statements Hitler made around the same time.[67] The first time he reflected on American affairs after the publication of *Mein Kampf* appears to have been in an article sold as a brochure in February 1926. There he noted that Britain was impaled on the horns of a dilemma: it found itself having to choose between a Japanese and an American alliance; ties of history and kinship suggested the latter, he noted, but it was equally obvious that this would only hurry along the inevitable process whereby the United States would dethrone Britain as the power that still currently ruled the waves – just.[68] On 4 July 1926, he dwelt at length on the tragedy which the immigration – and hence, loss – of millions of Germans to the Americas constituted for the German nation.[69] On 26 March 1927 he returned to the same theme, making it more evocative by mentioning the encounter between himself and American POWs being marched to the rear in 1918.[70] On 6 April 1927 he publicly quoted Grant's estimate of Germany's 'racial deterioration' and heaped praises upon the new restrictive American Immigration Law, which he compared favourably with the alleged incompetence of the German government in this area.[71] On 26 June 1927, he went much further, describing the USA as 'a pillar of the white race'.[72] On 6 August 1927, he returned to the theme of the net loss which generations of

---

[66] Ibid., p 88, 181.

[67] The first attempt to match the two was undertaken by Jürgen-Peter Schmied. See 'Hitlers Amerikabild vor der "Machtergreifung"'; in: *Geschichte in Wissenschaft und Unterricht* 2002, Nr. 12, pp 714–26. According to Schmied, Hitler simply used the USA as an instrument with which to highlight alleged wrongs in German society in his public speeches. Such an assessment seems questionable in light of both the sheer abundance of such references, but also the way in which they are mirrored by statements he made in private conversation.

[68] 'Die Südtiroler Frage und das deutsche Bündnisproblem (12.2.1926)'; in: RSA, Bd. I, pp 291–2.

[69] 'Politik, Idee und Organisation. Rede auf NSDAP-Parteitag in Weimar (4. Juli 1926)'; in: RSA, Bd. II.1, pp 17–25.

[70] '20 Millionen Deutsche zuviel ! Rede auf NSDAP-Versammlung in Ansbach (26. März 1927)'; in: ibid., pp 193–219, esp. pp 201–2.

[71] 'Warum sind wir Nationalisten? Rede auf NSDAP-Versammlung in München (6. April 1927)'; in: ibid., pp 235–41, esp. pp 236–7.

[72] 'Freiheit und Brot. Rede auf NSDAP-Versammlung in Dörflas (26. Juni 1927)'; in: ibid., pp 386–403, esp. p 392.

mass migration to the Americas had meant for Germany and again asked his audience to cast their minds back only a few years, to when the German Imperial Army found itself facing more and more former Germans in the ranks of the 1918 American Expeditionary Force (AEF). He also reminded any German toying with the idea of migrating across the Atlantic to escape the spectre of European conflict that the United States was a nation very much born and bred in violence, so much so that he described it as a country conquered according to 'our' principles.[73] On 10 October 1928, while making a general point about Europe's alleged dearth of arable land, he dwelt at length on the subject of the standard of living Americans were enjoying at the time, irrespective of their almost complete disregard for the social needs of the working class. What is noteworthy is that he freely conceded that individual for individual, Americans were every bit as hardworking and inventive as Germans – a compliment he almost never paid to the people of other nations.[74]

In November 1928 American affairs featured in both an article and a speech: the former was a review of current affairs written for the *Illustrierter Beobachter*, in which he also analysed the recent outcome of the US presidential elections. He ridiculed those German observers who had seen the race exclusively in terms of the implications it was going to have for the future of Prohibition. In his judgement, the only thing that really mattered was that President-elect Hoover had made it unambiguously clear he was willing to protect US industry with high tariffs. Accordingly, neither American 'economic-imperialist plans' nor 'the attempts by US capital to take over and monopolise foreign industries' was likely to cease.[75] On 30 November 1928 he returned to his old core theme with regards to the USA: generations spent attracting immigrants from Nordic countries and recent legislation which ruthlessly barred from entry the sick, the weak and the criminally disposed put the USA in a position where 100 million Americans would, according to Hitler, always outweigh 1,000 million Russians. It was this simple fact of life that made the USA such a 'global threat'.[76] On 17 April 1929 he returned to a favourite theme: the preponderance of the ever-growing US car industry and the well-nigh futility of trying to match its output.[77] A speech in Nürnberg

---

[73] 'Was ist Nationalsozialismus? Rede auf NSDAP-Versammlung in Heidelberg (6. August 1927)'; in: RSA, Bd. II.2, pp 439–52, esp. p 443 (quote). It is difficult to ascertain with certainty whether 'our principles' alluded to the ways of European history or the Social Darwinist principles of the NSDAP.

[74] 'Die Panzerkreuzer- Narretei der Kommunisten. Rede auf NSDAP-Versammlung in München (10. Oktober 1928)'; in: RSA, Bd. III.1, pp 121–49, esp. pp 130–1.

[75] 'Politik der Woche – Artikel (17.11.1928)'; in: RSA, Bd. III.1, pp 240–1.

[76] 'Freiheit und Brot. Rede auf NSDAP-Versammlung in Hersbruck (30. November 1928)'; in: RSA, Bd. III.1, pp 261–87, esp. p 269.

[77] 'Rede auf NSDAP-Veranstaltung in Annaberg (17. April 1929)'; in: RSA, Bd. III.2, pp 202–12, esp. 209–10.

delivered on 4 August 1929 stressed the issue of past German migratory waves, which according to him had been nothing but a disastrous drain on the country, and the US legislation to keep out the weak, feeble-minded or racially suspect. It was the combination of the two, Hitler said, that made Washington a 'never-ending threat' to Europe.[78]

The Great Crash of October 1929, as well as the implementation of the Young Plan so loathed by the German Right, should have put a major dent in Hitler's admiration for American society. Quite undaunted by this, he continued to dwell on the general topic of US potential. An article dated 29 January 1930 which he wrote for the *Völkischer Beobachter* had as its topic the Conference on Naval Disarmament, which had started in London a few days previously. However, when he discussed the economic potential behind the naval policy of the great powers, it was the USA that occupied centre stage. That country was blessed with unfathomable resources and populated by 'a racial selection of Europe's best which had grown there over centuries'. That ultimate accolade, however, did not stop him from predicting that 'a dire fate awaited all of Europe if no way could be found to somehow put a stop to the expansionism of America's economy'.[79] On 1 December 1930, while giving a brief address to Hamburg businessmen, he returned to the theme of US competition. America, he maintained, was both overly rich and engaged in the process of cornering the global market in most, though not (yet) all products.[80] On 25 June 1931, irrespective of the ravages the Depression had made in America, he continued to reflect on the country's virtually unlimited potential. Demography and geography had created a state that was in the process of elbowing aside European manufacturers in areas of industry they had seen as their own only years before. If some of these industries had been spared so far, it was only because the American competition had not yet found the time to move into them. As a threat to Europe, he went on, the United States rivalled even that bête noire of the Right, the USSR and international communism.[81] A speech delivered on 26 January 1932 before a group of Ruhr industrialists appears to have been the last occasion prior to the forming of his government on which he discussed the threat posed by American capitalism.[82] The speech was weighted to favour themes where National Socialists and

---

[78] 'Appell an die deutsche Kraft. Rede auf NSDAP-Reichsparteitag in Nürnberg (4. August 1929)'; in: RSA, Bd. III.2, pp 345–52, esp. p 347–8.

[79] 'Die Hintergründe der Londoner Flottenkonferenz – Artikel (29.1.1930)'; in: RSA, Bd. IV.1, pp 43–4.

[80] 'Rede vor dem National-Klub von 1919 in Hamburg (1. Dezember 1930)'; in: RSA, Bd. IV.1, pp 141–4, esp. p 142.

[81] 'Rede auf DSNStB-Versammlung in Erlangen (25. Juni 1931)'; in: ibid., pp 413–31, esp. pp 416–17.

[82] 'Rede vor dem Industrie-Club in Düsseldorf (26. Januar 1932)'; in: RSA, Bd. IV.3, pp 74–97.

captains of industry would struggle the least to find common ground, and hence dwelt at length on the internal and external threats posed by Soviet-style communism. Even here, however, he managed to slip in a paragraph on the unique nature of the challenge posed by the *Amerikanische Union*. As he saw it, the unique nature of this phenomenon was defined by two characteristics: first, the economies of scale enjoyed by the USA, which were permanently beyond the reach of any European nation; second, the fact that the sheer size of the American domestic market should really obviate the need for any kind of export-oriented economy, thus strongly suggesting the latter was somehow tied up with a higher aggressive design.[83]

Hitler's thoughts on the USA during this period are noteworthy for two reasons. First, there is a remarkable coincidence between statements made in private conversation, semi-private musings in his *Second Book* and statements which he made for the record in public speeches. Second, this was before the murderous anti-Semitism of his government (1933–41) and the success of his policy of aggression (1938–41) brought him into increasing conflict with the United States and forced him first to seek to assuage and then to confront an increasingly hostile reaction from the USA.[84] During this earlier period of the 1920s and early 1930s, he was able to speak with much greater freedom.

1.1.4   Input from Individuals with Access to Hitler

Ernst Hanfstaengl was very much the odd man out in the ranks of the *alte Kämpfer* (literally, 'old fighters'), NSDAP militants who had joined the party or the SA well before 1933.[85] He came from an affluent background, was American on his mother's side and had studied at Harvard from 1905 to 1909, where he made the acquaintance of the young Franklin Delano Roosevelt, among others. Even more strikingly – in view of the premium placed by the National Socialists on the *Fronterlebnis* ('fraternity of the

---

[83] Ibid., pp 86–7.

[84] Especially in the early years of his regime (1933–6) Hitler was still capable of marshalling considerable charm and wit when meeting American visitors. For a typical example, see the conversation with William Randolph Hearst in 1934: David Nasaw, *The Chief: The Life of William Randolph Hearst* (Boston and New York: Houghton & Mifflin Company 2001), pp 496–7.

[85] In view of the rather minor and transient role which Hanfstaengl played on the stage of the Third Reich, he has been remarkably well served by the scholarly attention invested in him. See David G. Marwell, *Unwanted Exile: a Biography of Dr. Ernst 'Putzi' Hanfstaengl* (State University of New York PhD 1988); David G. Marwell, 'Ernst Hanfstaengl – des "Führers" Klavierspieler'; in: Ronald Smelser et al (eds.): *Die braune Elite II. 21 weitere biographische Skizzen* (Darmstadt: WBG 1993) pp 137–49; Peter Conradi, *Hitler's Piano Player: The Rise and Fall of Ernst Hanfstaengl, Confidant of Hitler, Ally of FDR* (London: Duckworth 2005). Marwell's PhD is mainly concerned with Hanfstaengl's time in exile in the USA.

trenches') – he then sat out World War I in New York, where he managed the family's art gallery from 1911 to 1920. On his return to Munich he attended a speech by Hitler for the first time in November 1922 and emerged mesmerised. Over the following year he found himself increasingly drawn into the orbit of Hitler's social circle. Though a gifted piano player whose renditions of Wagner appeared to touch a chord in Hitler, other reasons seem to have played a part too. At the time, the fledgling NSDAP had barely any other members who could boast the affluence or cosmopolitan background of Hanfstaengl. The former, his affluence, would pay for a new printing press for the *Völkischer Beobachter*; his cosmopolitan background turned him into a sort of unofficial spokesman capable of handling occasional interview requests by foreign media representatives. At the same time, he introduced Hitler to a small but growing number of individuals from Munich's high society, who would be the beginning of a network of sympathisers in high places. By the spring and summer of 1923, irrespective of the fact that Hanfstanegl was not even a party member, the two men were meeting almost daily.[86]

The collapse of the November 1923 coup against the Weimar Republic revealed his commitment to the Nazi cause as somewhat lukewarm, however. After returning from a brief exile in Austria, he devoted himself to academic studies, gaining a history PhD in the process. Even though his villa continued to be a popular meeting point for Hitler and a select few of the NSDAP's leadership in the late 1920s, it took the NSDAP's landslide victory in the September 1930 elections to revive Hanfstaengl's interest in politics. The party's change in fortunes brought a sudden surge in interest from foreign journalists. Since most party VIPs lacked the language skills – or for that matter, charm or manners – to be trusted with an interview situation, Hitler himself decided that somebody of Hanfstaengl's background was needed as a go-between and coach.[87] This position he fulfilled in an informal fashion from September 1930. By the end of 1931, the decision was made to turn it into an official full-time position; he was given a salary, an office staff and the mission to 'sell' the idea of a National Socialist Germany to the outside world. From then onwards he became the point of contact for eminent foreign journalists like Louis P. Lochner, Sefton Delmer, John Gunther, Karl von Wiegand, Djuna Barnes and Dorothy Thompson, who were trying to secure an interview with Hitler or some other party bigwig.[88] By far his greatest coup

---

[86] On the relationship between Hitler and Hanfstaengl during that period see Marvell, *Klavierspieler*, pp 140–3, as well as Conradi, *Piano Player*, pp 43–64.

[87] For this decision see ibid., pp 79–80.

[88] Ibid., pp 83–131. On the experience of US journalists in the Germany of the 1930s, see Carmen Müller, *Weimar im Blick der USA: Amerikanische Auslandskorrespondenten und öffentliche Meinung zwischen Perzeption und Realität* (Münster: LIT 1997) as well as Michaela Hoenicke Moore, *'Know your Enemy': The American Debate on Nazism, 1933–1945* (Cambridge: CUP 2010), esp. pp 41–60.

involved a reversal of roles: he secured an interview with William Randolph Hearst, who was taking a cure at a southern German spa in August 1934. This was followed by a much-publicised audience for the American newspaper baron at Hitler's Reichskanzlei.[89] The triumph proved to be short-lived, however: in trying to ensure tolerable working conditions for foreign journalists – if nothing else – he emerged as a voice of moderation and this made him increasingly vulnerable at Hitler's court. In October 1934, Hanfstaengl fell from grace after losing out to a rival in an intrigue.[90] He was banished from Hitler's circle and fled Germany in February 1937.

While there is no doubt that Hanfstaengl threw himself heart and soul into the task of presenting an acceptable face of the NSDAP and its Führer to foreign journalists, we know much less about the extent to which he managed to influence Hitler with his particular views on the USA. According to his post-war memoirs, he did try to impress upon him the need for a 'rational' relationship with the United States, which would preclude a repeat of the gratuitous clash of 1917–18. But he freely concedes that he only stirred Hitler's interest when talk turned to subjects of a very specific, rather than fundamental nature.[91] In the absence of other sources, it is thus impossible to assert that Hanfstaengl was a major influence on Hitler's views on the USA.[92] The extent and success of his attempts in that direction must remain speculative.

From February 1933 to January 1938 Hitler's most senior and influential military advisor was his war minister (*Reichswehrminister*), *General der Infanterie* Werner von Blomberg.[93] He has gone down in history as the man instrumental in 'handing the Wehrmacht to Hitler' as well as for his ignominious fall after marrying a young lady of ill repute in January 1938.[94] Military historians know him as an open-minded individual who was keen to integrate civilian agencies and ideas into the war of the future. Until the eve of Blomberg's dismissal, Hitler showed an unprecedented degree of trust in

---

[89] Conradi, *Piano Player*, pp 172–5. See Nasaw, *The Chief*, pp 488–99, for a depiction of these events based on sources close to Hearst.

[90] For slightly different interpretations of what may have transpired prior to Hanfstaengl's fall from grace see Marvell, *Klavierspieler*, pp 145–6 and Conradi, *Piano Player*, pp 176–82.

[91] Hanfstaengl, *Weißem und Braunem Haus*, pp 45–7. According to Hanfstaengl, Hitler kept probing him on disparate subjects like the quality of American-built cars, on what it felt like to live in a high-rise building and how the American public was disposed towards the Jewish minority.

[92] Conradi comes closest to making a strong case for this, but provides no supporting source note. Conradi, *Piano Player*, pp 48–9.

[93] He was promoted to the rank of *Generaloberst* on 30 August 1933 and elevated to *Generalfeldmarschall* (the first of the newly minted Wehrmacht) on 20 April 1936.

[94] For an extensive discussion of these issues the reader is referred to the biography by Schäfer. Kirstin A. Schäfer, *Werner von Blomberg – Hitlers erster Feldmarschall. Eine Biographie* (Paderborn: Ferdinand Schöningh 2006).

him, which at times seems to have bordered on genuine friendship; even after the general's retirement, he continued to speak highly of him.[95] This ensured that Blomberg enjoyed a truly privileged position among the most senior Wehrmacht officers of the early Third Reich. An often overlooked fact is his role in acquainting Hitler with the military past of the United States. Blomberg spoke excellent English,[96] and he took a keen interest in the history of the American Civil War, which he felt was a subject unduly neglected at German military academies.[97] While a *Generalleutnant*, he had carried out an extensive tour of various bases and training establishments of the US Army between 24 September and 3 December 1930.[98] He was unimpressed by what he saw at West Point, where so far as he was able to tell the syllabus placed greater stress on spit and polish than on modern tactics.[99] While he levelled similar criticism at the National Guard units organised at state level, he nonetheless judged them to be valuable as an institution, because of the pro-military attitude they fostered.[100] He singled out for particular praise the work done at the War College and within the reserve units attached to learning institutions, like the

[95] It appears that this relationship stemmed in part from the gratitude Hitler felt towards Blomberg for having checked (vastly exaggerated) army opposition to the NSDAP's seizure of power in 1933. For an example of this, see Hildegard von Kotze (ed.), *Heeresadjutant bei Hitler* (Stuttgart: DVA 1974), pp 20–1 (entry for 20 April 1938) and p 61 (entry for 10 September 1939). Once safely ensconced in power, Hitler went on record as contrasting Blomberg's smooth running of his ministry with affairs at the Auswärtiges Amt, where relatively minor functionaries where allowed to obstruct the new government's policies at every turn. See Jürgen Matthäus and Frank Bajohr (eds.), *Alfred Rosenberg. Die Tagebücher von 1934 bis 1944* (Frankfurt a. Main: S. Fischer Verlag 2015), pp 120–1 (entry for 14 May 1934). See also IfZ, ZS 285/1–4 'Protokoll zur im Auftrag des Deutschen Insituts f. Zeitgeschichte durchgeführten Befragung Herrn K.J. v. Puttkamers am 12.3.1952' and Nicolaus von Below, *Als Hitlers Adjutant 1937–1945* (Selent: Pour le Merite 1999 rp), p 51.

[96] We have it on the authority of *Hauptmann* Karl Boehm-Tettelbach, Blomberg's Luftwaffe adjutant and himself a native speaker, that the general's English was 'first rate' (*ausgezeichnet*). Karl Boehm-Tettelbach, *Als Flieger in der Hexenküche* (Mainz: Hase & Koehler 1981), p 29.

[97] Schäfer, *Blomberg*, p 237 (Fn 453).

[98] BA/MA, RH 2/1825 'Generalleutnant von Blomberg. Bericht über mein Kommando zu der Armee der Vereinigten Staaten (1.1.1931)'. For an analysis of his trip and the agendas driving it, see Paul Fröhlich, *"Meine Reise ergab in dieser Beziehung sehr gute Aufklärung für unsere Belange." Die militärische Zusammenarbeit der Reichswehr mit der U.S. Army 1918–1933* (unpublished MA thesis, Universität Potsdam 2009), pp 85–90. My thanks to Paul Fröhlich for providing me with a copy of his thesis.

[99] BA/MA, RH 2/1825 'Generalleutnant von Blomberg. Bericht über mein Kommando zu der Armee der Vereinigten Staaten (1.1.1931)', pp 79–80. Blomberg's companion on this trip, *Oberst* Kühlental, judged West Point to be 'horrifyingly antediluvian' (*erschreckend vorsintflutlich*). See RH 2/1825 'Bericht des Oberst Kühlenthal über seinen Aufenthalt in den Vereinigten Staaten von Amerika (n.d.)', p 31.

[100] BA/MA, RH 2/1825 'Generalleutnant von Blomberg. Bericht über mein Kommando zu der Armee der Vereinigten Staaten (1.1.1931)', pp 95–9. Blomberg and Kühlental visited a unit of the New York National Guard.

Reserve Officer Training Corps embedded in 325 colleges all over the country.[101] If there was one factor still limiting US military effectiveness in Blomberg's view, it was the fact that too many of its officers had to hone their skills in theoretical exercises rather than by being in command of men, an inevitable consequence of the ratio between officers and enlisted men then prevailing. Of course, only a standing army could change that, but as matters stood around the turn of the years 1930–1, such a sea change – advantageous though it would be to the country's role in world affairs – appeared unlikely.[102] In more general terms, Blomberg admired the unique way in which American society had coalesced around the idea of technical progress and economic prosperity. Irrespective of differences in ethnic background and economic income, Americans were remarkably homogenous in their outlook on life and their concerns. More importantly, as Blomberg put it, 'it is possible to conclude that such a people will lend itself to be led'.[103]

Figure 1.1 Werner von Blomberg (far left) and the service chiefs reporting to Hitler (right). Blomberg's assessment of American military potential tended to complement the opinion Adolf Hitler had already formed in his mind.
(ullstein bild/ullstein bild via Getty Images)

[101] Ibid., pp 99–102.
[102] Ibid., pp 112–13.
[103] Ibid., pp 121–5.

The general was prone to exaggerate the extent of his influence on Hitler. Even so, it is fair to assume that throughout his time as minister for the armed forces, he must on average have met Hitler on a near-weekly basis. The extent to which he used this opportunity to widen the Führer's horizons with regard to US military affairs would probably be a matter for speculation were it not for a casual aside made by a US journalist in a 1942 publication. Frederick Oechsner was head of the United Press International's Berlin office from 1932 to 1941 and in this capacity managed to interview Hitler on four occasions. On one of these he gained access (whether because he was left unsupervised or through the good offices of a sympathetic adjutant remains open to speculation) to the library of the new German chancellor. In the 1942 book *This Is the Enemy* he gives one of the better descriptions of its holdings, even allowing for a couple of polemical asides calculated to cast America's enemy no. 1 in a poor light.[104] He estimated the number of books on military history as nearing 7,000.[105] Though the majority of these dealt with the lives and campaigns of one of 'the German and Prussian potentates', other subjects were covered too. Of particular noteworthiness was the fact that 'there is Theodore Roosevelt's work on the Spanish–American War, also a book by General von Steuben, who drilled our troops during the American Revolution. Blomberg, when he was war minister, presented Hitler with 400 books, pamphlets and monographs on the United States armed forces and he has read many of these'.[106] He also added that Hitler had no hesitations in having books in a foreign language translated if they caught his interest.

Another potential influence was Fritz Wiedemann, who had served together with Hitler on the staff of the regimental HQ of 16. Bavarian *Reserve-Infanterieregiment* throughout much of World War I. Back then, Wiedemann had been the regimental adjutant and as such one of Hitler's superiors.[107] By all accounts, they got on well, though a bit of mischief may also have played a part when Hitler offered Wiedemann a position as his adjutant in 1921. At the time, Wiedemann was fully engaged running a successful dairy factory and he politely declined. When his business ran into trouble in the early 1930s, however, he remembered the offer and asked his old runner for a job. After spending most of 1934 as the adjutant of Rudolf Heß, he moved on to become Hitler's *Persönlicher Adjutant* in January 1935. His role is of some relevance to this account because in November and December 1937 together

---

[104] 'Some 800 to 1,000 books are simple, popular fiction, many of them pure trash in anybody's language.' Frederick Oechsner, *This Is the Enemy* (London: William Heinemann 1942), p 81.

[105] A fairly accurate estimate, if one allows for the fact that Oechsner would only have been able to take in the holdings of one of the two main libraries (either at the Reichskanzlei or the one in the Berghof at Berchtesgaden).

[106] Oechsner, *Enemy*, pp 79–80.

[107] For an account of Hitler's and Wiedemann's time on the Western Front, see Thomas Weber, *Hitler's First War* (Oxford: OUP 2010), esp. pp 96–234.

with his wife he undertook a four-week long trip through the United States which saw him visit (among other places) New York, Washington, Chicago, San Francisco and Los Angeles.[108] In his 1964 memoirs, he alleged that on the subject of the United States, Hitler 'was inclined to believe any nonsense which was put to him'; accordingly he was determined to collect evidence on his travels to enlighten the dictator on his return.[109] Seeing that this statement comes from a member of Hitler's close entourage writing after the war, it would normally have to be taken with a fistful of salt. However, Wiedemann's growing estrangement from the regime in general and his concern over the underestimation of US power in particular can be corroborated from independent sources of the time.[110]

Knowing that Hitler took a serious interest in architecture, he gifted him thirty richly illustrated books on recent feats of the US building industry, like the Empire State Building and the Hoover Dam. The recipient of this generous gift appears to have taken an interest, but only to the extent that he instructed Speer to plan his next projects with the specific aim of topping these structures. Wiedemann was also able to report at length about his impressions, when Hitler gave him an afternoon to do so in early 1938.[111] A few weeks later, however, the Führer refused to sign up to the 1939 World Exhibition in New York over a perceived slight, at which point Wiedemann seems to have given up on further attempts to get Hitler acquainted with the USA. A year later he was sacked over his increasingly obvious lack of enthusiasm for Hitler's war course and posted as consul general to San Francisco.[112]

Hans-Heinrich Dieckhoff was Germany's ambassador in Washington from mid-May 1937 to late November 1938,[113] and as such oversaw bilateral relations between the two countries during the crucial period when they first reached crisis point. He was ideally suited to the task since he had already served with the embassy in Washington as a *Botschaftsrat* (counsellor) from November 1922 to December 1926. Back then, Dieckhoff had acquired a reputation for familiarising himself with the politics of the country and the forces underpinning it to a remarkable degree – a trait that would stand him in good stead on his return to

---

[108] Wiedemann, *Feldherr*, pp 215–18.

[109] Wiedemann, *Feldherr*, p 215.

[110] 'Botschafter Dieckhoff an Ministerialdirektor Weizsäcker (20.12.1937)'; in: ADAP, Serie D, Bd. I, pp 537–9. Also Weber, *Hitler's First War*, pp 322–5 and Heike B. Görtemaker, *Hitlers Hofstaat. Der innere Kreis im Dritten Reich und danach* (München: C.H. Beck 2019), pp 259–65.

[111] Wiedemann, *Feldherr*, pp 220–2.

[112] Wiedemann, *Feldherr*, pp 234–5.

[113] For much of what follows, the author is indebted to the author of the excellent biography on Dieckhoff: Sylvia Taschka, *Hans-Heinrich Dieckhoff, Diplomat ohne Eigenschaften? Die Karriere des Hans-Heinrich Dieckhoff, 1884–1952* (Stuttgart: Franz Steiner 2006) [= Transatlantische Historische Studien, Vol. 25].

the USA in 1937.[114] Even more remarkably, his cables from the 1920s had reflected a pro-Weimar attitude not commonly found among the elite reared under the old empire.[115] This manifested itself in scathing criticism of the political Right at home in Germany, in particular its agitation against the endeavour of the Auswärtiges Amt to get the USA to intervene as an 'honest broker' in its attempts to restructure Germany's reparations payments. Dieckhoff saw the agitation as counterproductive, on one noteworthy occasion referring to the activities of the NSDAP as 'that Hitler-rubbish', which he deemed to be 'more dangerous than commonly assumed'.[116]

It is impossible to say whether Hitler at any point learned of this unflattering assessment. In any case, Dieckhoff was informed in March 1937 that he was to take over from his predecessor Hans Luther to retrieve a deteriorating situation. Taking up his post on 15 May, he was able to draw on the good will he and his wife had accumulated in the previous decade. Even journalists known to be highly critical of the new Germany were at first inclined to give the new envoy the benefit of the doubt.[117] For his part, Dieckhoff appears to have seen his main task as carrying out some provisional damage control in order to stop relations from worsening even further. In his eighteen months as German ambassador he bombarded his superiors with dire warnings about the USA's potential and that the outbreak of a new European war would see America siding with Britain either straightaway or after a brief period of transition. Initiatives virtually guaranteed to enrage the Americans were those that appeared to indicate a spread of National Socialism by way of alliance (with Italy or Japan) or by spreading political sedition. As history showed, Dieckhoff was powerless to prevent the alliances, but scored a success of sorts when he managed to convince his government to cut most ties with the *Amerikadeutscher Volksbund*, a party of Nazi sympathisers made up of German-Americans attempting to square their American nationality with the ideology and trappings of National Socialism.[118]

Beyond this, it is difficult to assess to what extent Dieckhoff was able to form Hitler's view of the United States. We have anecdotal evidence that by May 1938 Hitler was getting sorely exasperated by the tone and content of Dieckhoff's cables. In Hitler's view, they did not reflect the manifest reluctance in US government circles to get involved in any kind of European conflict and were much too 'pessimistic' in tone.[119] This appears to be confirmed by an

---

[114] Taschka, *Diplomat*, pp 72–3.

[115] Dieckhoff had joined the Auswärtiges Amt in 1912.

[116] Taschka, *Diplomat*, p 85. The fact that he offered this assessment nine months before Hitler's coup attempt of November 1923 makes it even more prescient.

[117] On Dieckhoff's arrival in Washington, Taschka, *Diplomat*, pp 166–9.

[118] Taschka, *Diplomat*, pp 174–91.

[119] Theo Sommer, *Deutschland und Japan zwischen den Mächten* (Tübingen: J. C. B. Mohr 1962) p 122, fn 29. The exchange in question took place in May 1938 between Hitler and

event that occurred a few months later. While spending his summer holidays in Germany, Dieckhoff repeatedly tried – and failed – to get an audience with Hitler; when an interview finally came about through the intercession of Wiedemann, he found himself dismissed after a conversation of five minutes.[120] What little influence he may have had around that time dwindled fast after his recall to Germany following the events of the *Reichskristallnacht* of November 1938. Technically, he remained ambassador to the USA until December 1941. He seems to have been copied into most or even all of the communications between the embassy and Berlin.[121] He also intervened on occasions when he felt that the caretaker envoy, Hans Thomsen, and the military attaché, Friedrich von Boetticher, were diverging ever so slightly from the line he had set, especially as regards America's political will to intervene in the war.[122] His opinion was still sought whenever German–American relations had reached yet another impasse or when a propaganda ploy had to be found to counter yet another pro-British move by the Roosevelt administration. Even so, it was inevitable that his influence would wane with every passing month.

It may have been with a view to counter this development that on 9 January 1941 he composed a memo for Ribbentrop that is remarkable for the insight it gives into the workings of the mind of a German 'appeaser' in early 1941.[123] He stressed that he was setting out to disprove the theory that in view of the current US help for beleaguered Britain, a 'proper' state of war between Berlin and Washington was unlikely to constitute much of a change. He went into considerable detail to explain that this would give heart to the other enemies of the Axis, virtually rule out a separate peace with Britain and grant the US President sweeping war powers, which would allow him to multiply many times over his country's already considerable military potential. In the face of such a menace, Germany, he went on, could not but 'keep cool' and refuse all challenges and provocations that might come its way. However, in the last paragraph he conceded that there was one conceivable American transgression that would make a German–American clash 'inevitable'. Should the US government dismantle its neutrality legislation prohibiting the sailing of US merchantmen into British waters and cap this by escorting American

---

Eugen Ott, ambassador in Tokyo, and concerned the influence US power in the Pacific region might have on Japanese decision making. It has to be stressed that this account was not recorded on the day, but passed on to Sommer by Ott in a 1955 interview.

[120] Taschka, *Diplomat*, pp 178–9.

[121] Even most of the reports that the SD intelligence service compiled on US affairs in 1940–1 found their way into his in tray, as the distribution lists appended to these documents prove. They can be found under PA/AA, Inland II g, 337–341.

[122] For examples of this, see Taschka, *Diplomat*, pp 194–5, 201–2.

[123] 'Aufzeichnung des Botschafters Dieckhoff (9.1.1941)'; in: ADAP, Serie D, Bd. XI.2, pp 883–5.

convoys straight into British ports, 'a completely new situation would be created'.[124] It is quite possible that he decided to end his paper on this bellicose note because such a development seemed a very long way off and because a wholly uncompromising peace stance would have consigned his memo to Ribbentrop's waste basket. On the other hand, it may also have reflected his innermost thinking. Either way, it gives us an interesting insight into what level of US involvement in the Anglo–German war was regarded unacceptable both by Kriegsmarine admirals and diplomats.

On 19 April 1933 *Generalleutnant* Friedrich von Boetticher took over as the first German military attaché in Washington since 1917.[125] He proved to be an excellent choice, who established cordial working relations with the relatively small circle of senior US army officers who in those days worked for the US Army chief of staff in Washington DC's Munitions Building. He was conscious of the fact that fourteen years after Versailles, he was likely to be regarded as a 'Hun' and worked hard to overcome prejudices among his hosts. He was aided in this by two strengths. For one thing, he had already established cordial relations with a small number of US army officers who travelled to Germany in the 1920s to research German assessments of the AEF's war in 1917–18. In his capacity as head of the Reichswehr's *Heerestatistische Abteilung* (Department for Army Statistics), it fell to Boetticher to assist them in this task and smooth over any frictions.[126] In addition, he had a keen interest in and remarkable knowledge of the military history of the US Civil War which never ceased to impress American friends with whom he toured the sites of battlefields in nearby Virginia, Maryland and Pennsylvania. We do not know when Hitler got into the habit of having Boetticher's reports presented to him in raw form; a statement recorded by his army adjutant in June 1939 strongly implies that by then he had been reading them for at least a few months.[127]

By that stage a bizarre decision Ribbentrop had taken in early January to boycott invitations to official occasions hosted by Americans put the attaché in a unique position. German army officers posted abroad as attachés continued to be subordinate to Oberkommando des Heeres (OKH),[128] and not the Auswärtiges Amt. This allowed Boetticher unfettered access to his old sources

---

[124] Ibid., p 885.

[125] Recently Boetticher has been the subject of an excellent biography. See Alfred M. Beck, *Hitler's Ambivalent Attaché: Lt. Gen. Friedrich von Boetticher in America, 1933–1941* (Washington DC: Potomac Books 2005).

[126] Beck, *Ambivalent Attaché*, pp 23–33.

[127] Kotze (ed.), *Heeresadjutant*, pp 46–7, n.d. (June 1939): 'Of all political reports, those by Boetticher pleased him the most; he was capable of looking behind the scenes, knew how to judge the Americans and their views and was also capable of assessing what to weigh and how to judge the latter.'

[128] As of 8 April 1940 the *Attachegruppe* was turned into a department of the *Oberquartiermeister IV* section of the general staff of the Army. In November 1939, Ribbentrop relaxed the original prohibition, but it proved difficult to recover the ground

and circle of acquaintances, which virtually turned him into a substitute ambassador. Dieckhoff's successor Thomsen more or less resigned himself to this state of affairs and even willingly co-signed cables that covered both political and military affairs but were clearly authored only by Boetticher, since he kept referring to himself in the singular.

This quirk alone would have made it impossible to disguise from Hitler or any of his senior military advisers who was actually running things in Washington. Accordingly, it greatly exasperated both Ribbentrop and Ernst von Weizsäcker, the permanent secretary (*Staatssekretär*) at the Auswärtiges Amt, in Berlin. Finally, when in late May 1941 the coverage of an important Roosevelt speech was yet again hijacked by the general, Ribbentrop succeeded in enforcing a division of labour which ensured that Thomsen reported on key political events by himself.[129] If this new arrangement caused any friction between Thomsen and Boetticher, it has not been recorded; it is perfectly possible that a change in the general's personal circumstances in the months before Pearl Harbor encouraged his silent acquiescence in losing his de facto ambassadorship.[130]

Together with his assistant air attaché, Hauptmann Peter Riedel, who from July 1938 kept an eye on the growth of American air power, Boetticher filed reports which were by and large accurate within a certain time frame. What set the general apart from Dieckhoff was the tone of his cables. To the ambassador a clash with the USA was something to be avoided at almost any price; Boetticher, while not denying the human and industrial potential of the country, began to shift his focus to the myriad of problems that confronted the Americans after Roosevelt announced a massive mobilisation in May 1940. This was justified insofar as most historians would agree that throughout 1940–1 US strategy was crippled by a major mismatch between ends and means. This manifested itself most clearly in the struggle to turn funds – which were available – into an adequate number of shipyards, factories, barracks, tanks, planes and, most importantly, trained men – which were not available. Boetticher also stressed time and again that these problems would be multiplied many times over by the need to support Great Britain and the increasing likelihood of conflict not just with Germany, but Japan too. As

---

lost in the meantime. See 'Thomsen an Unterstaatssekretär Woermann (21.10.1939)', esp. fn 4; in: ADAP, Serie D, Bd. VIII, p 260.

[129] PA/AA, StS USA, Bd. 6, 'Thomsen an den Herrn Staatssekretär. Geheime Reichssache (23.5.1941)'. Finding himself upbraided yet again by his superiors for the manner in which he had allowed Boetticher to routinely report on non-military matters, Thomsen pointed out that the general was being encouraged in this by the 'repeated praise' which he kept receiving from the 'highest quarters' (*von höchster Stelle*). In the bureaucratic language of the Third Reich, this term generally referred to Adolf Hitler.

[130] At the time, Boetticher's twenty-three-year old son was hospitalised with depression in a Maryland hospital. See Beck, *Ambivalent Attaché*, pp 192.

a result of this, too many of his cables placed rather too much stress on problems that were likely to be remedied in the mid-term, with only a handful giving the US Army its full due as a potential enemy endowed with considerable human and material resources.[131] As for the big picture, it can safely be described as the general's blind spot. Only once did he dwell at length on the stage when the US armed forces were likely to be able seize a limited strategic initiative and the possible consequences this might have for the Axis.[132] The simple fact that the United States by dint of its size and location on the globe was practically invulnerable to any strategic threat Germany might be capable of marshalling in the early 1940s was not once brought up. Taken together, these sins of omission and commission undoubtedly produced a rather skewed intelligence picture of a potential enemy caught in a phase of uniquely transient vulnerability.

On Dieckhoff's departure from Washington in November 1938, forty-seven-year-old career diplomat Hans Thomsen took over as caretaker envoy. Any attempt to determine the actual impact he had in shaping Hitler's view of the United States should really be impossible, in view of the way in which he allowed himself to be elbowed aside by the attaché in 1939–41. Although he was still co-signing the cables from Washington, their diction and the persistent use of the first person singular made it clear they had been authored by Boetticher. While this exasperated Ribbentrop, it did not apparently do so with Hitler, who was full of praise for Boetticher's work in the American capital. It is thus a stroke of luck for the historian that by early June 1941 Ribbentrop temporarily enforced the new routine on the Washington embassy that finally forced Thomsen to write and sign his own cables.[133] For the first time Hitler would be given the opportunity of passing comment on two different reporting styles. Failure to do so might imply that he no longer took the time to read a fair number of the reports himself, an understandable assumption in view of the time that running the Russian campaign would demand of him in the summer and autumn of 1941. Proof to the contrary is provided by an August entry in the Seekriegsleitung's war diary: 'The Führer has noted with approval that reports of the envoy in Washington have proved to be unerring in their assessment of US political affairs and the political

---

[131] PA/AA, StS USA, Bd. 9, 'Boetticher und Thomsen an Auswärtiges Amt. Betreffend amerikanisches Heer (5.11.1941)'.

[132] PA/AA, StS USA, Bd. 7, 'Boetticher & Thomsen an Auswärtiges Amt (30.7.1941)'.

[133] 'Ribbentrop an die Botschaft in Washington. Für Geschaftsträger persönlich (26.5.1941)' as well as 'Ribbentrop an die Botschaft in Washington. Für Geschaftsträger persönlich (27.5.1941)' and 'Ribbentrop an die Botschaft in Washington. Für Geschaftsträger persönlich. (1.6.1941)' all in: PA/AA, StS USA, Bd. 6. By September, cables written in the old 'Boetticher style' were beginning to reappear, though not to the same extent as had been the case before.

intentions of the President.'[134] The entry also recorded the intention to copy the Japanese foreign ministry into some of these reports to help it reach a realistic appraisal of America's strengths and weaknesses. When compared to Boetticher's communications, Thomsen's, though almost never substantially different in content, tend to be briefer and less burdened by the liberal use of invectives ('Jews', 'warmongers', 'busybodies'). Post-war allegations that Thomsen allowed himself to be turned by the Americans into an agent of influence who in early December 1941 spoonfed Hitler tainted intelligence to encourage a declaration of war have yet to be corroborated by contemporary US sources. Since these telegrams covered the same ground as the reports that he, Boetticher and Dieckhoff had repeatedly submitted over the last year, this allegation cannot be taken at face value.[135]

In the spring of 1942, Hitler reminisced over lunch on the work done by the two men who had been his eyes and ears in Washington in 1939–41. He praised them both as observers who had never allowed themselves to be 'bluffed' and who had been unerring in their judgements. It is noteworthy that Thomsen's contribution did not vanish behind the larger role played by Boetticher. Hitler stated that he intended to single Thomsen out for a particularly challenging position after the war.[136]

All the individuals listed so far had regular access to Hitler either from a distance (Dieckhoff, Boetticher, Thomsen), through frequent personal contact (Hanfstaengl, Blomberg) or both (Wiedemann) over a prolonged period of time. Other personalities with an informed opinion on the USA only had fleeting opportunities to catch a moment or two of the Führer's time, with many such visits undoubtedly going by unrecorded.

---

[134] Werner Rahn and Gerhard Schreiber (eds.), *Kriegstagebuch der Seekriegsleitung 1939–1945. Teil A, Bd. 24* (Herford: Mittler & Sohn 1991), p 165 (entry for 20 August 1941) The term used in the entry is *Geschäftsträger*, i.e. the correct term to describe Thomsen's position, thus clearly setting him apart from Boetticher.

[135] Thomas Toughill, *A World to Gain: The Battle for Global Dominance and Why America Entered WW II* (Forest Row: Clairview 2003), pp 118–22.

[136] '18.5.1942 mittags (Wolfsschanze)'; in Henry Picker (ed.), *Hitlers Tischgespräche im Führerhauptquartier* (München: Propyläen 2003), pp 442–3. It is important to stress that the editions of Hitler's musings published in the English-speaking world as 'table talk' or 'monologues' are not word-by-word recordings of his spoken words, but a summary of key points of a conversation which struck one of the NSDAP functionaries (Henry Picker or Heinrich Heim) detailed for the task of recording them as particularly important. While the content is usually accurate, comparisons with other sources have revealed discrepancies in wording, nuance and context. For a thorough analysis of this source, see the excellent Mikael Nilsson, 'Hitler redivivus.' Hitlers Tischgespräche' und 'Monologe im Führerhauptquartier' – eine kritische Untersuchung; in: *Vierteljahrshefte für Zeitgeschichte* Bd. 67 (2019), Nr. 1, pp 105–45.

One of the more famous journalists and travel writers of the Germany of the inter-war years was the Austrian-born Colin Ross (1885–1945). Even though he studied engineering and economics between 1905 and 1910, he took to journalism, becoming a war correspondent before World War I, a profession he stuck to once the war broke out. In the inter-war years he travelled widely to most continents of the world and wrote a number of bestselling books about his exploits, three of which had the United States as their subject.[137] A witness statement from the main Nürnberg War Crimes Trial suggests that in October 1939 the Hitler Youth leader, Baldur von Schirach, came up with the idea of introducing him to Hitler in the hope that he would impress upon the Führer the hopelessness of ever challenging the USA. If this really was the idea behind the scheme, it produced ambivalent results.[138] Hitler met Ross in the Reichskanzlei for one hour around noon on 12 March, 1940. The chemistry between the two appears to have been quite good, because Ross was asked to return in two days' time to have lunch with Hitler. The contents of their talk were recorded by Walther Hewel, Ribbentrop's liaison at Führer's Headquarters.[139] Some of what Ross said reflected the common wisdom of most contemporary observers, such as the predominant role played in US political affairs by a relatively small, near-aristocratic clique centred on the East Coast and mostly descended from seventeenth-century English and Dutch settlers. They tended to be willing to cooperate with Britain but were distrustful of Germany. Americans of German descent were highly regarded by their countrymen and well integrated, but also rather anxious to be seen as such.[140]

---

[137] Bodo-Michael Baumunk, *Colin Ross: Ein deutscher Revolutionär und Reisender 1885–1945* (unpublished MA thesis, Tübingen University 1991). *Unser Amerika* had as its subject the story of the German-Americans and their contribution to the rise of America as a great power. Two further titles discussed extensive trips through Canada and Mexico, respectively.

[138] 'The Nizkor Project'. The Trial of the German Major War Criminals. Sitting at Nuremberg, Germany 27 May to 6 June 1946: www.nizkor.org/trials-of-german-major-war-criminals (accessed 26 April 2014). The statement was made by Hartmann Lauterbacher, a witness for the defence of Schirach. The chronology (the witness specifically refers to Ross still being away on travels outside Germany in October 1939 and not returning for a number of months which would account for his not meeting Hitler until mid-March) supports the story, but it needs to be kept in mind that the account was no doubt somewhat embellished for effect.

[139] 'Aufzeichnung des Vortragenden Legationsrats Hewel, Persönlicher Stab RAM. Unterredung des Führers mit Herrn Colin Ross am 12. März 1940 von 12–13 Uhr (12.3.1940)'; in: ADAP, Serie D, Bd. VIII.1, pp 714–17.

[140] A direct consequence of the social marginalisation and occasional mob violence many of them had found themselves subjected to in 1917–18. For an analysis of the precarious position of German-Americans during World War I, the reader is referred to Katja Wüstenbecker, *Deutsch-Amerikaner im Ersten Weltkrieg. US-Politik und nationale Identitäten im Mittleren Westen* (Stuttgart: Franz Steiner 2007), esp. pp 214–44.

This accounted for the futility of trying to instrumentalise them in any capacity on behalf of the new Germany.

In other areas, the views Ross put forward bordered on the bizarre and beg the question whether he had been coached to present them in this fashion with a view to pleasing the Führer. He seriously suggested bringing about an entente with the USA by illustrating to the Americans – with the help of a map drawn by himself – the fact that existing British 'spheres of influence' constituted a greater threat to the US position in the Western Hemisphere than anything Germany might have in store. As far as the fate of European Jews was concerned, he proposed to increase the rate of forced Jewish migration to the USA, with a view to deliberately increasing anti-Semitism there. Once this had occurred, the Americans would gladly agree to a 'constructive' solution put forward by the German government, preferably in the form of an overseas territory set aside for the purpose of creating a Jewish state. The possibility of a US–German clash in the near future does not appear to have been the prevailing theme of the discussion. Only when the conversation turned to the sitting US President and his re-election prospects was this subject touched on in an almost offhand manner. According to Ross, Roosevelt had come to power in the same year as Hitler and with a similar agenda, but had so far met with only a modicum of success due to the level of domestic opposition to some of his New Deal–connected schemes. His hostility towards Hitler was thus mainly motivated 'by jealousy'. Ross apparently would not be drawn on Roosevelt's prospects in November but unhesitatingly predicted that in the case of his re-election, he would be in a position to take the country to war should he choose to do so ('*dass er dann das amerikanische Volk in den Krieg führen könne, wenn er es wolle*').[141]

1.2 Japan

In contrast to the embarrassment of riches facing the historian researching Hitler's views on the United States, references to Japan are much thinner on the ground. Insofar as the Far Eastern country features at all in his early

---

[141] 'Aufzeichnung des Vortragenden Legationsrats Hewel, Persönlicher Stab RAM. Unterredung des Führers mit Herrn Colin Ross am 12. März von 12–13 Uhr (12.3.1940)'; in: ADAP, Serie D, Bd. VIII.1, p 717. According to a visitor who was present at the lunch of 14 March, Ross also shared his thoughts on the Sino-Japanese War with Hitler. The way he saw it, Japan was hopelessly stuck, while Chiang-Kai-Check, whom he held in high regard, could afford to fight a long war of attrition. There was no question of the Japanese having the means of intervening in another conflict. The fact that Hitler chose to quiz his well-travelled guest first on the United States and then on the crisis in the Far East seems unlikely to have been a coincidence. Elke Fröhlich (ed.), *Die Tagebücher von Joseph Goebbels. Bd. I.7: Juli 1939-März 1940* (München: K.G. Saur 1998), pp 349–50 (entry for 15 March 1940).

utterances, the remarkable thing is a complete absence of resentment or bitterness. After all, Japan had unexpectedly sided with the Entente in 1914 and had joined British Empire forces in rolling up Germany's colonial possessions in the South Pacific and on the Chinese mainland. The fact that the German state had expended copious amounts of 'soft power' in previous decades by sending numerous academic delegations and military missions to assist with the modernisation of the Nipponese empire should have made this particularly irksome.

Factors aiding reconciliation may have been the brevity of the only campaign involving a sizeable body of troops on each side (the siege of Tsingtao, 28 September–7 November 1914),[142] as well as the regal treatment afforded German and Austrian POWs held in Japan between 1914 and 1919.[143] To a German politician looking to split the alliance of the victors of 1918, however, another event would have carried greater weight. In 1915, Japan had run into firm opposition from its allies when it tried to impose the so-called Twenty-One Demands on a militarily impotent China. Had Japan managed to enforce this agenda, it would have gone a long way towards turning the newborn Chinese Republic into a Japanese satellite state in all but name. British and particularly American pressure forced Japan to withdraw the demands in their original form, but any discerning observer would have been able to register the beginnings of a rift between Japan and the other 1918 victors.

1.2.1   First Impressions (1904–1920)

The outcome of the Russo–Japanese War (1904–5) had a major impact on Western perceptions of the Nipponese empire, and it appears that young Adolf Hitler was no exception to the rule. In Mein Kampf,[144] as well as in numerous private conversations during the war,[145] he claimed that he had rooted for the Asian power right from the start. This reflected a divide between Austrian-German and Czech students in his class, the latter being left disconsolate when the news of the Russian defeat was confirmed. He had a certain penchant for the Imperial Japanese Navy, and some comments from the 1940s suggest that this

---

[142] The German and Austrian defenders numbered around 5,000 men; 60,000 Japanese besiegers were supported by 15,000 British soldiers.

[143] Gerhard Krebs, "Die etwas andere Kriegsgefangenschaft"; in: Rüdiger Overmanns (ed.): In der Hand des Feindes. Kriegsgefangenschaft von der Antike bis zum Zweiten Weltkrieg (Köln: Böhlau 1999), pp 323–37.

[144] Hartmann et al (eds.), Mein Kampf, p 445.

[145] 'Führerhauptquartier 21.9.1941, mittags. H/Fu.'; in: Werner Jochmann (ed.), Adolf Hitler. Monologe im Führerhauptquartier 1941-1944 (München: Bertelsmann 2000 rp), p 64. His press spokesman Otto Dietrich wrote after the war that Hitler spoke repeatedly of the key role that the Russo-Japanese War had played in forming his early image of Japan. Otto Dietrich, 12 Jahre mit Hitler (Köln: Atlas 1955), p 84.

was tied to the latter's 'birthday' at the battle of Tsushima in 1905.[146] In *Mein Kampf* he would even lambast Imperial Germany's supposedly half-hearted shipbuilding polices by contrasting them with the Japanese approach, which had made the difference between victory and defeat in 1905.[147] Japan joining the Entente powers does not seem to have affected his feelings towards the country one way or another. In a speech he delivered on 26 May 1920 he implied that he was happy to let bygones be bygones by asserting that Japan had been forced into arraying itself on the enemy side by its agenda of checking European expansion in the Far East.[148] Thereafter, he did not return to the topic.

1.2.2   Reading Matter

The fact that Hitler ever bothered to read a more or less scholarly book on Japan would probably be lost to history were it not for Rudolf Heß's assiduous work as a court chronicler in Landsberg gaol. In a letter written in May 1924 to his fiancée, he mentioned in passing that Hitler was reading Professor Karl Haushofer's 'book on Japan' (*'Er liest zur Zeit des Generals Japan-Buch'*).[149] Since by then the highly prolific Haushofer already had five monographs dealing with Japanese subjects to his name,[150] identifying the title would pose a problem were it not for two clues. It stands to reason that a matter-of-fact, almost offhand reference to *'das Japan-Buch'* implies a degree of familiarity, which the recipient of the letter would be able to pick up on. Only a few months before, Heß had received a gift copy of *Japan und die Japaner* from his friend Haushofer and began reading it more or less immediately.[151] Heß also

---

[146] 'Wolfsschanze 4./5.1.1942, nachts. Gast: Sepp Dietrich H/Fu' as well as 'Führerhauptquartier 19.6.1943 Mü/Ad'; both in: Jochmann (ed.), *Monologe*, pp 177, 402.

[147] Hartmann et al (eds.), *Mein Kampf*, p 290. According to Hitler's interpretation, the defensive mindset of the German admiralty had led it to favour ship designs mounting smaller gun calibres, despite alternatives being available.

[148] 'Die Macher am Weltkrieg. Rede auf einer Versammlung des Deutschvölkischen Schutz- und Trutzbundes (Stuttgart, 26.5.1920)'; in: Jäckel/Kuhn (eds.), *Aufzeichnungen*, pp 135–6.

[149] 'Heß an Ilse Pröhl (18./19.5.1924)'; in: Heß/Bavendamm (eds.), *Briefe*, p 328.

[150] *Dai Nihon. Betrachtungen über Groß-Japans Wehrkraft, Weltstellung und Zukunft* (Berlin 1913); *Der deutsche Anteil an der geographischen Erschließung Japans und des japanischen Erdraums, und deren Förderung durch den Einfluß von Krieg und Wehrpolitik* (Erlangen PhD 1914); *Grundrichtungen in der geographischen Entwicklung des japanischen Reiches* (University of Munich Habilitation 1919); *Das japanische Reich in seiner geographischen Entwicklung* (Wien 1921); *Japan und die Japaner. Eine Landeskunde* (Leipzig 1923).

[151] 'Rudolf Heß an Karl Haushofer (13.9.1923)' and 'Rudolf Heß an Karl Haushofer (6.10.1923)'; both in: Hans-Adolf Jacobsen (ed.), *Karl Haushofer. Leben und Werk, Bd. II. Ausgewählter Schriftwechsel 1917–1946* (Boppard a. Rhein: Haraldt Boldt 1979) [= Schriften des Bundesarchivs, Bd. 24/II], pp 20–1, 22–6. Though Heß does not allude to the title, the first letter describes the cover art of the original edition in such detail that an error can be safely ruled out.

refers to the special interest Hitler had shown in chapters discussing Japanese architecture. None of the monographs about Japan Haushofer had so far published included dedicated chapters to architecture, but *Japan und die Japaner* does discuss the subject over a total of five pages.[152]

Japan und die Japaner is a relatively short (160-page) introduction to Japanese affairs divided into chapters on geography, topography, climate, economy, society and history. Haushofer wrote it with the stated intent of giving German readers an insight unburdened by 'the selfish agendas of foreign powers'.[153] Haushofer's love for tortuous and overlong sentences makes it a tiresome read. At the same time, an uninitiated reader would have been left more confused than enlightened by the extreme brevity with which he narrates some phases of Japanese history – hardly a topic many Germans of the time would have had an even passing acquaintance with. Assessing the impact this book may have had on Hitler is speculative at best, but a few salient points that would have been of greater interest to him than others can be suggested. The most important would have been the book's mantra that Japan is a country without 'living space'. This forced the government to permit the migration of up to 600,000 of its people per year, either to colonies or protectorates like Korea or farther afield to California and Hawaii.[154] According to Haushofer, this migratory wave was unique insofar as the government made it its priority that expatriate subjects, irrespective of where they settled, retain a high degree of loyalty towards the Land of the Rising Sun.[155] Haushofer describes the Japanese people as a hardy race remarkably inured to suffering, whether their own or other people's.[156] He is full of praise throughout the book for the manner in which they have mastered the unprecedented challenge of engineering in two generations the transition from an early modern society to being an industrial power. According to him, the main reason this has been achieved with so little friction is that a country untouched by invasion or mass immigration for more than 2,000 years can boast supreme 'racial homogeneity', a theme he returns to time and again in the text.[157] He describes the country as currently finding itself at a crossroads, with further expansion to the north (China and/or the USSR) or the south (Southeast Asia) by peaceful or other means as the two major options. The author is candid in stating his belief that Japan's future lies to the north, but stops well short of making a prediction.[158]

---

[152] Haushofer, *Japan*, pp 47–50, 56.
[153] Ibid., p 3.
[154] Ibid., pp 13.
[155] Ibid., pp 157–8.
[156] Ibid., pp 44, 50, 72.
[157] Ibid., pp 10, 41–2, 103, 127, 137–8.
[158] Ibid., pp 157–60.

1.2.3 Public and Private Statements, Mein Kampf *and the* Second Book

Hitler's references to Japan before his chancellorship are not only few in number but also brief in nature, more often than not serving as a foil or contrast. Moreover, they offer little clue as to whether he saw in Japan a future rival or ally. On 2 December 1921 he referred to the country as the 'one remaining independent state' which 'international Jewdom' was attempting to strangulate.[159] In the late summer of 1923, he impressed upon a visiting US journalist that the NSDAP's attitude to Jews bore a resemblance to that shown by the Federal government to Japanese migrants reaching American shores. The Japanese, according to Hitler, 'have ruined no state. They are not carriers of Bolshevism.' Nonetheless, he continues, 'We look upon the Jews as you look upon the Japanese.'[160]

There is some evidence that on Hitler's release from Landsberg prison, Haushofer's influence had left a mark on his thinking. In a conversation with Hanfstaengl which took place in December 1924, Hitler waxed lyrical about the 'racial purity' and 'soldierly virtues' of the Japanese people engaged in a struggle for living space, making them natural partners for Germany in a future alliance against Russia.[161] With the exception of a couple of very brief comments, however, there are few references of substance to Japan in *Mein Kampf,* first published the following year. The theme from the 1921 speech surfaced again in the second volume of *Mein Kampf.* There, he spoke of Japan as an obstacle to the spread of international Jewry across the globe. He took up this theme again in the preface he wrote to a programmatic pamphlet published by the party two months later; he basically rationalised Britain's recent refusal to extend the alliance treaty with Japan by referring to the inevitable Jewish plotting. This was virtually a foregone conclusion, he said, because for racial reasons Jews were incapable of infiltrating Japanese society as they were allegedly doing with any number of European countries. Hence, ways had to be found to isolate Japan and leave her surrounded by a coalition of hostile powers.[162] By Hitler's standards, this was an accolade, and together with some of the other statements discussed, it appears to suggest that the idea of Imperial Japan as his favourite coalition partner had formed in his mind by 1925–6 at the latest.

---

[159] 'Der Jude als Menschenfreund. Rede auf einer NSDAP-Versammlung' (2 December 1921); in: Jäckel/Kuhn (eds.), *Aufzeichnungen,* p 528.

[160] 'Interview mit George Sylvester Viereck'; in: ibid., 1023–6. The exact date on which the interview took place is lost to history, but it appears to have been before October 1923.

[161] Hanfstaengl, *Weissem und Braunem Haus,* p 168.

[162] Hartmann et al (eds.), *Mein Kampf,* p 1621. 'Die Südtiroler Frage und das Deutsche Bündnisproblem'. Aufsatz (12 February 1926); in: RSA, Bd. I, pp 269–93, esp. pp 292–3.

However, such a judgement needs to be qualified. Both in *Mein Kampf* and a public speech delivered in April 1928, Hitler stressed that the Japanese were not a people capable of 'creating' culture (his use of the term implied that he meant scientific progress rather than the arts), but only of adapting or using it.[163] The fact that the Japan of the 1920s was still to a large extent dependent on imports of Western high-end technology would have made such a comment doubly hurtful to any Japanese observer of German politics. Around the same time, Hitler had started to bracket Japan with China and India as a group of nations that the West was well advised to exclude from access to technological secrets. While incapable of unassisted innovative thinking, these countries boasted unlimited reserves of cheap labour that could put them in a position to produce the same goods as the West, but at much cheaper retail prices.[164]

Following this rather contradictory pattern of praise and condescension, in a public speech in May 1928 he elevated the previously patronised Asian nation to the lofty status of 'troublemaker' being hounded by the Western (read: Jewish) media. Here, he was in all likelihood referring to criticism aroused by a recent deployment of Japanese troops to the Shandong peninsula which resulted in a serious clash with Chinese Kuomintang forces near the city of Jinan (3–10 May 1928).[165] It needs to be kept in mind, however, that this was little more than a casual aside in a long-winded speech dealing with the alleged power of Jewish-controlled media rather than Far Eastern affairs.[166] The fact that two references to Japan in two months did not mark a sea change in his perception of the Far Eastern empire can be gleaned from his *Second Book*, which he produced that summer. In a manuscript running to more than 200 pages and boasting an extensive chapter dealing with the long-term threat posed by the USA, Japan barely featured. Passing reference had been made in *Mein Kampf* to the re-emerging of US–Japanese irritations after the end of World War I,[167] and given the *Second Book*'s clear focus on foreign policy,

---

[163] Hartmann et al (eds.), *Mein Kampf*, p 757. See also 'Freiheit und Brot. Rede auf NSDAP-Versammlung in Bayreuth (14 April 1928)'; in: RSA, Bd. II.2, pp 773–8, esp. p 776. The Japanese were not the only people alluded to in this context, but seeing that Hitler placed them in the same bracket as 'kaffirs', 'negroes' and 'hottentots' this would not have afforded them much comfort.

[164] 'Die deutsche Not und unser Weg. Rede auf NSDAP-Versammlung in Neustadt a.d. Aisch (15.1.1928)'; in: RSA, Bd. II.2, p 616; 'Rede auf NSDAP-Veranstaltung in Annaberg (17.4.1929)'; in: RSA, Bd. III.2., p 210; 'Rede auf NSDAP-Versammlung in Weimar (8.2.1931)'; in: RSA, Bd. IV.1, p 193; 'Interview mit Universal Service (18.8.1932)'; in: RSA, Bd. V.1, p 313 f.

[165] On the second Shandong expedition, see Edward J. Drea, *Japan's Imperial Army: Its Rise and Fall, 1853–1945* (Lawrence: Kansas UP 2009), pp 163–5.

[166] 'Adolf Hitler entlarvt. Rede auf NSDAP-Versammlung in München (23 May 1928)'; in: RSA, Bd. II.2, p 851.

[167] Hartmann et al (eds.), *Mein Kampf*, p 1617.

expanding on this theme would have seemed like a natural choice. The point has been made that any discussion of Japan was dropped from *Mein Kampf* in order to avoid irritating the British, whom Hitler was still trying to woo at the time.[168] However, in light of the fact that the *Second Book* never even got as far as the pre-publishing stage, the omission of even a sidebar on Japan is striking, all the more so since US–Japanese relations had just suffered a major blow with the passing of openly anti-Asian immigration legislation in the USA in 1924.

Following the attention he briefly gave Japan in 1924, Hitler's next reference to the empire was rather long in coming and highlights what can be described as plain lack of interest. In a November 1930 speech, he denigrated a proposal for a multilateral treaty of disarmament by pointing out the need to keep the USSR in check. The way he saw it, nothing short of a defence treaty encompassing all non-communist nations on the planet 'including the USA and even Japan' – an utterly fanciful notion clearly beyond the means of 1930s diplomacy – would be needed to make this viable. It turned the entire matter under discussion into a moot point.[169] Again, Hitler was using a reference to the Japanese Empire as a means to make a point barely connected to Far Eastern affairs.

The first step towards a fundamental reassessment of Japan's potential as an ally appears to have come about as a result of the Japanese Army's occupation of Manchuria (September 1931). This brought a diplomatic crisis in its train, culminating in Japan's decision to quit the League of Nations in March 1933. Both Gregor Straβer in a December 1931 speech and Hitler himself in an interview with a Japanese daily the following month expressed their pleasure that somebody was finally challenging the existing balance of power as represented by the League of Nations.[170] By themselves, these public statements may not have meant much, especially since Hitler's statement to the Japanese journalists ('the NSDAP's posture towards Japan is exclusively defined by the degree of support which it can receive from Japan in its struggle for revision of the Versailles treaty'[171]) fell somewhat short of a passionate endorsement of German–Japanese amity. However, a contemporary observer in the guise of German diplomat Erich Kordt would later – in 1950 – point to the immediate aftermath of the Manchurian Crisis as the point when Hitler first began to take notice of Japan in a serious way. The invasion and annexation of Manchuria attracted his attention, but what really sold him on Japan was the fact that the country's government decided to cut the Gordian knot by walking out on

---

[168] Spang, *Haushofer und Japan*, p 390.

[169] 'Deutschland und Frankreichs Abrüstung. Erklärung (7 November 1930)'; in: RSA, Bd. IV.1, pp 65–73, esp. p 73.

[170] For both documents, see 'Interview mit Tokio Asahi Shimbun (3 January 1932)'; in: RSA, Bd. IV.3, p 12–13.

[171] Ibid.

the League. Only from that point on did Hitler, according to Kordt, begin to think of Japan as a 'potential ally, especially against the Soviet Union'.[172]

1.2.4 Input from Individuals with Access to Hitler[173]

Professor Albrecht Haushofer has been a person of interest to historians of the Third Reich for some time. A career officer of the Bavarian Army, he had spent a year in Japan in 1909–10 and returned to Germany having formed a highly positive impression of Japanese society.[174] He served in World War I, retiring as a *Generalmajor* in 1919, and went on to become an unsalaried lecturer at Munich University in the same year. In the 1920s, he managed to reach a considerable audience through his highly prolific output and a monthly radio feature – a first in the young history of German broadcasting.[175] His chosen subject was *Geopolitik*, a field of research seeking to establish the extent to which geography and climate determined a country's historical evolution and future policy options.[176] This included thoughts on the concept of *Lebensraum* (living space) and the possible need to expand borders deemed to be detrimental to a nation's natural evolution, though he remained vague about whether wars of conquest were a legitimate

---

[172] Erich Kordt, *Nicht aus den Akten* (Stuttgart: Union Deutsche Verlagsgesellschaft 1950), p 122. German political and military elites continued to be rather tepid on the idea of an alliance with Japan until at least 1935–6. See Spang, *Haushofer und Japan*, p 385.

[173] A former officer of the Austro-Hungarian Army, who according to one of Hitler's adjutants played a major role in forming the Führer's exalted image of the warrior spirit of Japan's armed forces could not be identified before going to print. See Wiedemann, *Feldherr*, p 225. Of Friedrich Wilhelm Hack and Hermann vom Raumer, who for a few years advised the Auswärtiges Amt on Far Eastern affairs, no proof exists that they were ever in a position to directly submit reports to Hitler, much less brief him in person. Accordingly, their names have not been included in this line-up. On Hack and Raumer, see Christian W. Spang, 'Wer waren Hitlers Ostasienexperten? Teil I & II'; in: OAG Notizen 4/2003, pp 10–16, and OAG-Notizen 5/2003, pp 12–24.

[174] Haushofer's life has been the subject of many books and articles. As far as the Japanese dimension of his work is concerned, the best is Christian W. Spang, *Karl Haushofer und Japan. Die Rezeption seiner geopolitischen Theorien in der deutschen und japanischen Politik* (München: IUDICUM 2013) [= Monographien aus dem Deutschen Insititut für Japanstudien, Bd. 52].

[175] On Haushofer's career as a writer and commentator in those years, see Spang, *Haushofer und Japan*, pp 146–208 and Herwig, *Demon*, pp 111–68.

[176] A pithy definition of *Geopolitik* as understood by Haushofer is extremely difficult to arrive at on account of its multi-faceted nature and numerous built-in ambiguities and contradictions. The definition proposed by Holger Herwig ('a study of the influence of such factors as geography, economics and demography on the politics and esp. the foreign policy of a state') is as good as any other and a lot more intelligible than anything put forward by Haushofer himself. See Holger Herwig, 'Geopolitik: Haushofer, Hitler and Lebensraum'; in: *Journal of Strategic Studies*, Vol. 22, Nos. 2/3 (June–September 1999), pp 218–41.

tool to achieve this.[177] As far as the options open to German foreign policy were concerned, he advocated alliances or at least close cooperation with Japan and the USSR; the one country against which he consistently harboured feelings of hostility was the United States.[178] Haushofer was introduced to Hitler by his student Rudolf Heβ in July 1921. When Heβ found himself imprisoned in Landsberg gaol after the failed coup of 1923, Haushofer paid him at least eight extensive visits. On most (possibly all) of these visits he also met Hitler.[179] He developed a habit of bringing the two men books and journals and discussing their contents during his next visit. Visits by a minor celebrity such as he was did not go unnoticed, attracting the attention both of the Allied leadership in the 1940s and of many historians afterwards. The latter felt justified in making the assumption that Haushofer's thoughts on 'living space' must to some degree have influenced Hitler's thinking on the subject;[180] from there to inferring that Haushofer had a major role in the writing of *Mein Kampf* hardly required a leap of faith.[181]

For the purposes of this study, the extent to which Haushofer moulded Hitler's views on Japan is far more important. Again it is thanks to Hanfstaengl that we have a record of Hitler's frame of mind on the subject post-Landsberg. On two separate occasions in his memoirs, Hanfstaengl bemoaned how Heβ and Haushofer were filling Hitler's mind with all kinds of 'nonsense' regarding the alleged military potential of Japan; to the cosmopolitan Hanfstaengl such infatuation could not but lead to a gratuitous confrontation with the USA.[182] Hitler and Haushofer continued to meet at irregular intervals throughout the 1920s and 1930s, even though in the majority of cases the backdrop would be

---

[177] On Haushofer's notion of *Lebensraum*, see Hans-Adolf Jacobsen, *Karl Haushofer. Leben und Werk. Band I. Lebensweg 1869–1946 und ausgewählte Texte zur Geopolitik* (Boppard am Rhein: Haraldt Boldt 1979) [= Schriften des Bundesarchivs, Bd. 24/I], pp 245–58.

[178] Spang, *Haushofer und Japan*, pp 291, 360–1, 398. Also Herwig, *Demon*, p 156.

[179] Post-war, Haushofer and some of his supporters alleged that he had actually tried to keep a certain distance between himself and Hitler during this period. On this see Spang, *Haushofer und Japan*, pp 366–9, 386 and Herwig, *Demon*, pp 92–3. The circumstantial evidence still indicates that he is almost certain to have met Hitler as well as Heβ during most of his prison visits, especially since their respective cells were just feet apart and kept open throughout the day. In addition, the inmates also shared a furnished common room. That the prisoners routinely received visitors in their quarters is proven by a letter written by Rudolf Heβ. See 'Machinenschriftlicher Brief Rudolf Heβ an Ilse Pröhl, München (11.6.1924)'; in: Heβ/Bavendamm (eds.), *Briefe*, pp 332–3. Fleischmann, *Landsberg* only engages with the subject of visitors entered in the Landsberg log as having come to see Hitler, rather than Heβ.

[180] For an overview of these early interpretations of Haushofer's work see the excellent summary provided by Spang, *Haushofer und Japan*, pp 33–52, 463–79.

[181] Recent research has tended to discredit this notion. See Plöckinger, *Adolf Hitler's 'Mein Kampf'*, pp 143–6.

[182] Hanfstaengl, *Weissem und Braunem Haus*, p 93, 168, 211.

an event involving a number of other people, such as a dinner party or a wedding. Hitler and Ribbentrop put Haushofer's reputation in Japan to good use when they employed him as a go-between during the process of gradual rapprochement with Tokyo in 1934–6.[183] Whether Haushofer was able to reverse the process by influencing the regime is more difficult to assess, especially if one considers that his last meeting with Hitler took place in November 1938 and appears to have ended acrimoniously.[184] His idea of a 'continental bloc' involving a German–Soviet–Japanese alliance appeared to take shape when Hitler and Stalin signed a non-aggression pact in August 1939; the Tripartite Pact of September 1940 seemed like the next logical step on this road. However, there is no record of the Führer having sought the professor's advice in the months before, and by December 1940 he had become thoroughly disenchanted with the idea of continuing to cooperate with the USSR. Even if – against all the evidence – Haushofer at that stage still had the means of reaching out to Hitler and imparting advice, it does not seem like the latter was bothering to listen. Thus, the invasion of the Soviet empire by the Wehrmacht in June 1941 would appear like a natural parting of ways between Haushofer and the regime.

As it happened, this had already been presaged by a wholly unconnected event. On 10 May, the professor's protégé Heß departed for Scotland in the hope that he might be able to broker a peace deal; on learning of this, Hitler was beside himself with rage and blamed Haushofer and his son Albrecht for putting the Deputy Führer up to such a nonsensical scheme.[185] Although Haushofer retained all his honours and his position, he lost much of the ready access he had previously enjoyed to the high and mighty of the Third Reich.[186] The idea that either Hitler or anybody close to him would have sought or heeded his advice on the subject of joining Japan in a war with the USA at some point over the next seven months can thus be safely discounted.

---

[183] Spang, *Haushofer und Japan*, pp 409–38.

[184] Herwig, *Demon*, pp 162–3. According to Herwig, 'Geopolitik', p 233, a further meeting took place in February 1939, though he neglects to give a source for this.

[185] Kotze (ed.), *Aufzeichnungen Engel*, pp 104–5 (entries for 12 and 13 May 1941); TB Goebbels, Bd. I.9, pp 310–18 (entries for 13–16 May 1941); Matthäus/Bajohr (eds.), *Rosenberg Tagebücher*, p 386 (entry for 14 May 1941). The idea that Hitler was play-acting because he had originally supported the idea of the flight continues to enjoy some currency to this day among a minority of historians. The little-noticed John Harris and Richard Wilbourn, *Rudolf Hess: A New Technical Analysis of the Hess Flight, May 1941* (Stroud: Spellmount 2014), actually puts forward genuinely new evidence that appears to support this possibility.

[186] This may have been as a consequence of Hitler issuing instructions to shut him out or due to the actions of medium-level party officials adept at anticipating their masters' presumed wishes. According to Spang, *Haushofer*, pp 373–81, the latter seems the more likely of the two. A diary entry by Joseph Goebbels could suggest either. TB Goebbels, Bd. I.9, p 416 (entry for 1 July 1941).

Generalmajor Eugen Ott was a Swabian army officer who, after a transition from the artillery arm to the prestigious general staff in 1917, was invited to join the Reichswehr of the Weimar Republic after the war – a privilege he shared with only 4,000 officers.[187] After spending most of 1933 as an exchange officer with Japanese artillery units in Nagoya and Manchuria, he was sent back to the Far East as military attaché in Tokyo, a position he held from April 1934 to April 1938. Rather than leave Japan on completion of his tour of duty, he was promoted on the spot to fill the vacancy left by the ailing ambassador Herbert von Dirksen and went on to serve four and a half years as the senior representative of the Auswärtiges Amt in the Japanese capital.

Ott was burdened with some political baggage, since he had been a close collaborator of the then *Oberst* Kurt von Schleicher from 1923 to 1929. During his time as the Weimar Republic's last head of government (December 1932–January 1933), Schleicher found himself at the centre of an initiative by various establishment players that could potentially have grown into a major check on Hitler's rise to power.[188] As a result, he and a number of his associates were on the death list that formed the script of the Night of the Long Knives on 30 June 1934. The existing documentary record does not indicate whether or not Ott's name ever featured in this document, and he would in any case have been safely out of the henchmen's reach by then. Nor is there any conclusive evidence that his name was tainted by association afterwards. Hitler spoke favourably of him once or twice before the war, while Göring for unknown reasons appears to have held a grudge of sorts against him.[189]

The extent to which Ott's reports from Tokyo during the critical phase of 1941 shaped Hitler's assessment of Japan's potential as a military ally is difficult to answer. As the year progressed, the tone of the ambassador's cables grew increasingly weary whenever the subject of Japan's willingness to align with the Axis came up – a clear reflection of the futility of trying to discern the direction of Japanese government politics. While the German leader's satisfaction with the tone and content of the reports emanating from the Washington embassy

---

[187] There is at present no biography of Ott. A lot of useful information can be found in Jürgen W. Schmidt, 'Eugen Ott – Freund und Quelle von Richard Sorge'; in: Heiner Timmermann et al (eds.), *Spionage, Ideologie, Mythos – der Fall Richard Sorge* (Münster: LIT 2005) [= Dokumente und Schriften der Europäischen Akademie Otzenhausen, Bd. 113], pp 88–104.

[188] This scheme involved inciting the NSDAP's *Reichsorganisationsleiter*, Gregor Straßer, and his followers of the left wing of the party to cooperate with the Schleicher government. Together with other issues plaguing the party at the time (especially a scarcity of funds) this plan might have brought about a challenge to Hitler's leadership or even a split within the NSDAP. See Udo Kissenkoetter, *Gregor Straßer und die NSDAP* (Stuttgart: DVA 1978), pp 162–77, 181–90, and Benjamin Carter Hett, *The Death of Democracy: The Rise of Hitler* (London: Heinemann 2018), pp 164–70.

[189] Schmidt, 'Eugen Ott', pp 92, 94.

Figure 1.2 Ambassador Eugen Ott (centre): the constant shifts and turns of Tokyo politics left the ambassador as exasperated and confused as any other Western envoy. (ullstein bild/ullstein bild via Getty Images)

is a matter of record, no such echoes have survived of Ott's reporting. What is a fact is that when the Japanese in early November first approached the Tokyo embassy, with a view to convincing the Germans to join them in their imminent war against the USA, Ott's credibility had just taken a serious blow with the arrest in Tokyo of the German journalist and GRU spy Richard Sorge.[190] Sorge was a gregarious and charismatic personality who had befriended Ott

[190] The story of the Sorge spy ring has enjoyed abundant historiographical attention. Chalmers Johnson, *An Instance of Treason: Ozaki Hotsumi and the Sorge Spy Ring* (Stanford: Stanford UP 1964); Frederick William Deakin and G. R. Storry, *The Case of Richard Sorge* (New York: Harper & Row 1966); Gordon W. Prange, *Target Tokyo: The Story of the Sorge Spy Ring* (New York: McGraw-Hill 1984); Robert Whymant, *Stalin's Spy: Richard Sorge and the Tokyo Espionage Ring* (London and New York: Tauris 1997) and Owen Matthews, *An Impeccable Spy: Richard Sorge, Stalin's Master Agent* (London: Bloomsbury 2019) are the most important monographs on the subject. The allegation that Stalin routinely disregarded Sorge's warnings has recently been challenged. See David Glantz, 'The Impact of Intelligence Provided to the Soviet Union by Richard Sorge on Soviet Force Deployments from the Far East to the West in 1941 and 1942'; in: *Journal of Slavic Military Studies*, Vol. 30 (2017), No. 3, pp 453–81.

and some of the attachés from 1934 onwards.[191] On a number of occasions when surprises sprung by the erratic and unfathomable nature of Japanese politics had left the embassy staff dumbfounded Sorge, assisted by a Japanese asset close to government circles, had made predictions that turned out to be remarkably accurate.[192] In this manner, he managed to become a permanent fixture at the embassy and personal counsellor to Ott and his attachés in all but name. At the peak of his influence, he was repeatedly given access to sensitive documents and invited to join regular evaluation meetings looking into Japanese military affairs with Ott in the presiding chair;[193] by 1940 he and the ambassador had adopted the habit of ushering in the day with a working breakfast.[194] The revelation that a man who had had the run of the embassy for years had been a Soviet asset all along sent shockwaves through the German foreign ministry, Japanese attempts at keeping the matter under wraps not-withstanding. However, it does not seem that the combined weight of these events, along with Ott's association with Schleicher, cowed him into following the party line to a greater degree than he would otherwise have done. The reports he sent in the last weeks of peace if anything indicate a certain willingness to remind Berlin that entering the US–Japanese conflict consti-tuted a move that warranted substantial concessions from the Japanese, which had not been forthcoming.[195]

1.3   Conclusion

Over the years, historians attempting to make sense of Hitler's assessment of the USA have divided into two schools: one tends to see him as a leader, who while cunning, was limited in his capability to assess a country like the United States by his ignorance of the world beyond Germany's borders and by his

---

[191] For a vivid description of Sorge's outgoing nature, see Kordt, *Akten*, pp 425–9. The extent to which some of the diplomats allowed feelings of friendship to violate security protocol is difficult to gauge in individual cases. According to Prange, *Target Tokyo*, p 198, Sorge established a particularly good rapport with Ott, *Oberstleutnant* Friedrich von Scholl (assistant military attaché) and *Oberstleutnant* Wolfgang Nehmitz (assistant air attaché); Whymant, *Stalin's Spy*, p 305, broadly agrees with this assessment, but sees naval attaché Wenneker playing a more important role than Nehmitz.

[192] Especially with regards to the insurrection by Imperial Japanese Army officers (February 1936) and the likely course of events after the Marco Polo Bridge Incident (July 1937). Prange, *Target Tokyo*, pp 120–6, 177–9.

[193] Whymant, *Stalin's Spy*, pp 104–5, 111–14.

[194] Prange, *Target Tokyo*, p 261; Matthews, *Impeccable Spy*, pp 189, 202–3, 229–31. After the war, Ott waged a minor campaign to refute allegations by the West German media that he had routinely allowed Sorge access to confidential information. Some of the corres-pondence from that period can be found in IfZ, Nachlass Ott, ZS/A 32, Bd. 8.

[195] For a more detailed discussion of Ott's reporting in those weeks, see the chapter on German-Japanese relations.

deeply ingrained racial prejudices.[196] The other sees him unduly influenced by Washington's gradual shift from neutrality in 1933 to open hostility by 1938–9. Hitler's 'positive' or at least non-committal view of America thus gave way to a 'negative' one as relations between the two countries gradually deteriorated.[197] Based on the evidence presented here, a third model seems to be more likely: of a Hitler who by virtue of his Social Darwinist view of world affairs became convinced that the further rise of the USA, given its sheer size, ethnic make-up and economic potential, was probably unstoppable. At some point between the early to mid-1920s, he concluded that a major clash (its exact nature and timing as yet undetermined) would almost certainly be inevitable between the United States and a Europe under German leadership. Some of the features of this view of the future, such as the expectation that the process would result in the Anglo-Saxon powers falling out with each other and London ultimately taking Germany's side, were clearly delusional. In other ways, it could be said to have been a remarkably prescient foretelling of the United States' rise to superpower status and what the post-war world would look like. The notion that a long-held racist conceit led him to chronically underestimate American power and that this in turn coloured his strategic estimates is untenable.[198] If anything, the exact opposite was the case.

The fact that some of the people who attempted to educate him on American potential were rebuffed, while he appeared to be more receptive to the opinions of others, is not inconsistent with this interpretation. On the evidence available, it can be safely stated that Hanfstaengl, Wiedemann and Dieckhoff did their best to impress on him that confrontation with the USA was something to be avoided at almost any cost. This clashed with a view he had formed at some point in the 1920s, from which he would not budge and which Colin Ross may have unwittingly encouraged. Accordingly, he disregarded their opinions on the matter. Blomberg and Boetticher, on the other hand, were different. For one thing, it is possible to make a compelling case that Blomberg returned from the USA in late 1930 with a view of that country's potential that was eerily similar to the assessment Hitler himself had arrived at by the late 1920s. Even more importantly, as professional officers, neither Blomberg nor Boetticher

---

[196] An interpretation most recently espoused by Wolfram Pyta, *Hitler. Der Künstler als Politiker und Feldherr. Eine Herrschaftsanalyse* (München: Siedler 2015), p 494.

[197] A theory most recently proposed in Klaus P. Fischer, *Hitler and America* (Philadelphia: Pennsylvania UP 2011), p 37.

[198] A view held among others by Gerhard Weinberg, 'Germany's Declaration of War on the United States: A New Look'; in: Hans L. Trefousse (ed.), *Germany and America: Essays and Problems of International Relations and Immigration* (NY: Columbia UP 1980) [= Brooklyn College Studies on Societies in change, Vol. 21], pp 54–70. Also Williamson Murray and Alan Millett, *A War to Be Won: Fighting the Second World War* (Cambridge, Mass.: Harvard UP 2000), pp 135–6 and David Reynolds, *America: Empire of Liberty* (London: Allen Lane 2009), p 362.

presumed to engage their commander-in-chief in a debate over matters of state policy. Instead, they just provided him with data on the military strengths and weaknesses of a power that appeared more and more likely with every passing day to confront the new Germany in the near future. This was the sort of advice Hitler found practical and helpful.

With regards to Japan, there is little evidence available that indicates that Hitler had given serious and consistent thought to the Far Eastern country's potential as a possible ally before 1933. Hanfstaengl may have been exasperated by Haushofer's apparent success in filling Hitler's head with ideas about Japanese martial prowess, but the dearth of substantial references to Japan in the speeches and writings of the 1920s is nothing short of striking and stands in contrast to the consistence and substance of references to the USA. Almost without fail, whenever Japan is introduced into the narrative, it is to serve as a foil to help Hitler make a point barely connected to Asian affairs. Most telling is the absence of Japan in the *Second Book*. In a manuscript which goes to great lengths to describe the threat hanging over Europe's future on account of the economic preponderance of the *Amerikanische Union*, the seemingly obvious idea of bringing Japan into play as a possible counterweight is not even mooted. Thus, the conclusion to be drawn is that at least until 1932, and in contrast to the United States, Japan barely featured in Hitler's thoughts. His interest grew in an opportunistic fashion and in synchronicity with every step Japan took that appeared to guarantee a lasting antagonism between it and its former allies. By early 1941, with all hopes of peace with Britain dashed and Italy a major disappointment as an ally, Japan finally became the focus of German alliance politics. Even then, Hitler would occasionally be over-whelmed with unease at plotting the downfall of European dominance in the Far East together with an Asian power.[199]

---

[199] Matthäus/Bajohr (eds.), *Rosenberg Tagebücher*, p 400 (entry for 20 July 1941); 'Führerhauptquartier 18.12.1941, mittags. Gast: Reichsführer SS Himmler' and 'Wolfsschanze 5.1.1942 mittags. Gäste Reichsminister Dr. Todt, Sepp Dietrich, General Gause, Oberst Zeitzler H/Fu.'; both in: Jochmann (ed.), *Monologe*, pp 156, 179. Also Anton Joachimsthaler (ed.), *Christa Schroeder, Er war mein Chef. Aus dem Nachlaß der Sekretärin von Adolf Hitler* (Coburg: Nation Europa 1985), pp 131–2.

2

Hitler's Physical Health in Autumn 1941

Treatises on the progressive deterioration of Adolf Hitler's health during the war years have tended to have a particular focus: whether the onset of an incapacitating disease could have impaired his mental faculties to the point where it helps explain policies that were either barbaric or self-defeating. The society of post-war Germany was highly receptive to such theories. The idea of a charismatic ruler who took leave of his senses only after a number of years had passed might be seen as a partial exoneration of the millions of Germans who voted him into office in 1933, and then went on to pave the road to dictatorship and war in the months and years that followed.[1] Likewise, in more recent years, new accounts have become fixated on the need to debunk the notion that any moral judgement of the 'later Hitler' might have to be revised ever so slightly in the light of new findings about his health.[2]

The problem with this train of thought is twofold. To begin with, it tends to blot out the ideological world of the subject and the military prerogatives he himself had created. Moreover, it neglects the effect that the mere diagnosis of an illness, which was likely to lead to death or incapacitation at some point in the future, would have on the mind of someone already obsessed with the possibility of an untimely early death. Hitler lived in particular dread of cancer and in October 1937 and August 1939 spoke with astonishing candour to a small circle about the need to implement his expansionist agenda in the very near future. His fear was that in only a few years he might no longer be able to do so himself, and he could not bring himself to trust a successor with the task.[3] This backdrop is all the more relevant since most material witnesses agree in pointing to the period after mid-1942 as the time when evidence of physical deterioration and occasional mental instability began to mount up. By then, however, all the key decisions that would lead to the war's outcome had been made. From a military historian's point of view, the focus of research should really have been on the subject's likely knowledge of his condition all along; by

---

[1] This is the thinly veiled agenda of Johann Recktenwald, *Woran hat Adolf Hitler gelitten? Eine neuropsychiatrische Deutung* (Reinhardt: München & Basel 1963).

[2] Hans-Joachim Neumann and Henrik Eberle, *War Hitler krank? Ein abschliessender Befund* (Bergisch Gladbach: Gustav Lübbe 2009).

[3] Ian Kershaw, *Hitler 1936–1945: Nemesis* (London: Allen Lane 2000), pp 36–7, 228.

the second half of the war, the scale of his military blunders takes a back seat to the fact that by that stage, the strategic military initiative had passed for good to the enemy coalition.

2.1   General Health

Hitler's general health in the late summer and early autumn of 1941 was still good. He had suffered a minor shrapnel wound on the Western Front in World War I and a dislocated shoulder in the police charge in Munich that smashed his coup attempt against the Bavarian government in 1923. None of these left him permanently injured or in chronic pain. Between the late 1920s and mid-1930s, however, he developed a recurring form of stomach pain which generally manifested itself after meals and by the 1940s sometimes went hand in hand with constipation. By late 1936 he had also developed a persistent skin rash in both legs. His new personal physician, Dr Theodor Morell,[4] managed to cure the rash in a few months. Morell's attempts to alleviate the indigestion problem were successful in as much as they usually brought short-term relief; Morell was unable, however, to find a long-term therapy. With the benefit of hindsight, it can be surmised that Hitler was probably suffering from gastritis, a condition caused by the *Helicobacter* bacteria and sometimes worsened by stress.[5] It appears that Morell tentatively offered a diagnosis to that effect at some point in 1937–8 and most certainly kept advising changes in lifestyle that would have helped to ameliorate the symptoms, especially breaks from work, exercise and regular sleep patterns.[6] It goes without saying that Germany's strategic position would soon enough rule out the first recommendation, but the last two might have been addressed, at least up to a point. However, Hitler's aversion to exercise and his growing habit during the wartime years of

---

[4] Dr Theodor Morell (1886–1948) was a general practitioner who enjoyed considerable success as the medical counsellor of the rich and famous in Weimar Berlin. From early 1937 to April 1945 he served as Hitler's personal physician, even though he does not appear to have been on permanent standby at Führer's Headquarters until well into 1941. Fellow doctors both at the time and after the war criticised him for his indiscriminate use of intravenously administered drugs and his reluctance to seek advice from specialists with greater regularity than he did. While there is truth in these allegations, it needs to be kept in mind that Hitler was an awkward patient at the best of times, acquiescing in personal examinations only on a handful of occasions. Recent research is divided on whether Morell's panoply of drugs was harmful to his patient or not. Neumann and Eberle, *War Hitler krank*, tend towards the latter, while Norman Ohler, *Der totale Rausch. Drogen im Dritten Reich* (Köln: Kiepenheuer & Witsch 2015), makes a case for a powerful addiction to Eukodal – in addition to occasional helpings of morphine and cocaine – by the second half of 1944.

[5] Ernst Günther Schenck, *Patient Hitler. Eine medizinische Biographie.* (Düsseldorf: Droste 1989), pp 163, 374.

[6] See the account in Neumann/Eberle, *War Hitler krank*, p 142 which, however, lacks a source note.

tampering with his body clock by allowing briefings and staff talks to go on into the small hours of the morning, and then cap these with a couple of hours of small talk with secretaries and adjutants, would only make things worse.

His first serious health crisis, by contrast, was not the result of cumulative factors. Instead, it occurred a couple of weeks after shifting the location of his field headquarters to the mosquito-infested Wolfsschanze in East Prussia. After a major row with his foreign minister Ribbentrop – apparently about the wisdom of unleashing war with the USSR[7] – he either feigned or suffered (judgements differ) what seems to have been a minor heart seizure. For several days afterwards, he felt unwell and suffered from a recurring headache. He then nearly collapsed from a dizzy spell on 7 August 1941 and fell seriously ill with stomach pain and dizzy spells alternating with vomiting until 12 August. As a result, he was unable – an unheard-of occurrence – to attend the daily military briefings for a few days. By 17 August, he claimed to be fully recovered,[8] but Goebbels, visiting him on 18 August, found him still looking worn out and exhausted.[9] Even though some authors insist on describing this incident as 'unexplained',[10] it is likely that Hitler suffered from a bout of dysentery, a not uncommon ailment among the dwellers of the Wolfsschanze, not yet accustomed to the combination of mosquitoes attracted by the local swamps and the compound's initially quite basic hygiene.[11] The importance of this crisis, however, does not lie so much in the – unproven – impact it may have had on Hitler's ongoing quarrel with Oberkommando des Heeres (OKH) over the focus of the second phase of operations in the war against the USSR. More significantly, it may have given the first pointers to two potentially life-threatening medical conditions.[12]

---

[7] When first confronted with the plans for Barbarossa, Ribbentrop had been one of the few dignitaries of the Third Reich to temporarily question the wisdom of this decision. In the last days of July, the headlong advance of Army Group Centre in the direction of the Soviet capital suffered its first major reverse when it ran into unexpectedly strong resistance to the east of Smolensk. It appears that the clash between Hitler and his normally supine foreign minister was triggered by this event. On this incident, see the testimony by Adolf Freiherr Steengracht van Moyland and Ribbentrop before the International War Crimes Tribunal in 1946: *Trial of the Major War Criminals (TMWC) before the International Military Tribunal*, Vol. X (Nürnberg 1947), pp 113, 416–20. Also Michael Bloch, *Ribbentrop* (London: Bantam 1992), p 338.

[8] Morell's notes on this crisis can be found in Bundesarchiv-Koblenz (henceforth BA-Ko), N 1348/4 'Morell Auzeichnungen 1941'.

[9] Elke Fröhlich (ed.), *Die Tagebücher von Joseph Goebbels*, Teil II, Bd. 1 (München: KG Saur 1996), pp 255–72, esp. p 259 (entry for 9 August 1941).

[10] Fritz Redlich, *Hitler: Diagnosis of a Destructive Prophet* (Oxford: OUP 1998) p 235.

[11] The most comprehensive medical analysis of Hitler's near-collapse in August 1941 can be found in Schenck, *Patient*, pp 346–8, 361–4, 377–8.

[12] The best treatment of this controversy is to be found in David Stahel, *Operation Barbarossa and Germany's Defeat in the East* (Cambridge: CUP 2009) pp 273–9, 290–8, 339–44, 378–406.

2.2   Heart Condition

The extent to which his August illness had debilitated Hitler can be gleaned from the fact that for the first time he visibly gave in to Morell's badgering. On 14 August he submitted to have his electrocardiogram taken, which Morell then passed on – having omitted the patient's name – to Professor Arthur Weber, a major expert in the field. Taken in conjunction with the three other such examinations for which accurate dates exist (11 May 1943, 4 May 1944 and 24 September 1944), they show an obvious deterioration and growing risk of a coronary.[13] As far as the events of autumn 1941 are concerned, however, only the cardiogram taken in August that year is of any relevance. More to the point, any diagnosis suggested by it – either within the limitations of 1940s medical science or today – is less relevant than the extent to which Morell believed he had reason to be concerned and chose to pass this on to his patient.

Weber diagnosed a progressive left-ventricular hypertrophy and a mild asymptomatic myocardial ischemia. He recommended further cardiograms at regular intervals (every two weeks), but so far he saw no need to recommend a therapy.[14] This did not constitute a major cause for alarm, confirmed by a 2008 re-evaluation of the same cardiogram by a cardiologist, which led to the conclusion that the problem may have been even less serious than Weber thought.[15] We now need to turn to the question of how the patient was likely to have perceived this diagnosis. In a 1989 book, Ernst-Günther Schenck, the last contemporary witness with medical training to meet Hitler prior to his suicide, asserted that Morell did not discuss Weber's 1941 findings with Hitler.[16] In view of the fact that Schenck was never on Hitler's medical staff, such a statement should really have been supported by a footnote, which is lacking. Given the almost childlike curiosity Hitler often showed when confronted with new medical terms or diagnoses, which was likely to have increased many times over in the case of a novel examination like the electrocardiogram, Schenck's assumption is also highly implausible.[17]

There is, moreover, strong evidence suggesting that Morell did discuss the findings with his patient, though going out of his way to assuage any concerns about his long-term life expectancy. First, even though the covering letter that would have accompanied the 1941 ECG to Professor Weber appears to be lost, the letter mailed with the May 1943 ECG requests two separate reports: one for

---

[13] The 4 May 1944 readings were spoilt and are not preserved in Morell's records.

[14] For Professor Weber's letter to Morell see BA-Ko, N 1348/4 'Prof. Dr. A. Weber an Prof. Theo Morell (17.5.1943)'. It is also reproduced in Schenck, *Patient*, p 330.

[15] It was diagnosed as a probable microcirculation storation of myocardium in hypertension. See Neumann/Eberle, *War Hitler krank*, p 207.

[16] Schenck, *Patient*, p 334.

[17] For examples of this, see John Toland, *Adolf Hitler* (New York: Doubleday 1976), p 827, as well as David Irving, *Hitler's War, 1942–1945* (London: Papermac 1983), p 701.

Morell and another which 'I could show to the patient'.[18] While there is no evidence that he asked for the same arrangement in August 1941, it certainly seems likely. In addition, and more importantly, the entry for 17 December 1942 records at some length a conversation between him and his patient, which seems to have started innocently enough when Hitler enquired whether a drug Hermann Göring was taking for his low blood pressure might also be of use to him. As Morell explained that his problem was the opposite of Göring's (high blood pressure as opposed to low), the conversation turned to Hitler's heart condition in general. At this point, Morell all but admitted that he had kept the diagnosis 'coronary sclerosis' from him in 1941. In conjunction with an episode of extremely high blood pressure during the Russian counteroffensive in December 1941, it had caused him enough concern to begin administering a drug (iodine) to strengthen the heart.[19] Morell's rationale for not calling in a cardiologist appears to have been based on the perceived need to keep Hitler going at a time of crisis, along with a rather remarkable estimate of his own abilities – that he was likely to know best in any case.[20] Rather than blow up, Hitler seems to have agreed with this astonishing assessment much as he would do in October 1944, when allegations of professional misconduct ended with the sacking of Morell's accusers.[21]

As a final assessment, the only conclusion that can be drawn from the evidence currently available is that Hitler in November and December 1941

---

[18] 'Prof. Dr. med. Theo Morell (Führerhauptquartier) an Herrn Prof. Weber, Bad Nauheim (13.5.1943)'; in: Schenck, *Patient Hitler*, pp 330–1.

[19] BA-Ko, N 1348/5 'Morell notes (special entry for 17 December 1942)': 'Since I was on the subject of always giving him the most accurate picture of his condition, I referred to the existence of a coronary sclerosis and said this is why I have been giving him iodine for some time now. Subsequent electrocardiograms have confirmed my suspicion, I said. In many people this calcification occurs somewhat faster as a result of intensive hard work, but it usually starts at around forty-five. I added that as the blood vessels of the coronary artery narrow, he may get attacks of angina pectoris.' Nothing is known about the December 1941 incident Morell referred to in this conversation. It is inconceivable that Morell should not have kept a written record of such an event; the 1 September 1941–21 July 1942 gap in his notes on Hitler's health is probably due to losses caused in the last days of the war. On the likely fate of these (and other) papers missing from Morell's estate see Schenck, *Patient Hitler*, pp 162–72.

[20] BA-Ko, N 1348/5 'Morell notes (special entry for 17 December 1942)'.

[21] In September and October 1944 some of the consultants at Führer's Headquarters came to the conclusion that his deteriorating health could be traced back to the overdose of some of the drugs Morell administered. In conversation with Hitler, Morell freely confessed to having exceeded prescribed limits on occasions, but maintained that this had been inevitable in order to keep Hitler going at a time when Germany had the threat of utter collapse hanging over it. According to Morell's notes, Hitler concurred and even professed to be quite touched. On the whole controversy, see Eberle/Neumann, *War Hitler krank*, p 177–87.

did not have his decision-making powers impaired by the perception that his life was likely to be cut short by a major coronary in the near future.

2.3 Parkinson's Disease

From about autumn 1942 to the day he took his own life, Hitler's appearance began to deteriorate visibly in a manner that resembled an accelerated ageing process. This happened fairly gradually at first, but increased in his last year. His movements became slower and more deliberate, he acquired a stoop and his left hand began to tremble uncontrollably, an affliction that would eventually spread to the left leg. By 1945, he frequently required help in getting into and out of a chair; his facial expression was often described by witnesses as 'masklike'. On top of all of this, he found it increasingly difficult to sleep even fitfully without sedatives. Members of his retinue as well as visitors to Führer's Headquarters were equally struck by his condition. Those who penned their impressions of these encounters disagreed on specific details of his condition and on the extent to which he had been crippled by it or not, but they were almost unanimous in rejecting the notion that his mind was affected.[22] Morell was quite powerless to halt the progress of this affliction, the first symptoms of which he may have spotted as far back as 11 August 1941.[23] There were a few periods when the symptoms receded (most famously after the explosion of Stauffenberg's bomb on 20 July 1944[24]), but on the whole Hitler's condition kept worsening until the day he shot himself in his bunker under the Neue Reichskanzlei. For a time Morell appears to have suspected the long-term effects of a brief infection Hitler had contracted during a stay in his Vinniza HQ in July 1942. Most contemporary observers, however, tended to put it down to a combination of non-organic causes. As already mentioned, some of those in the know about Morell's therapy blamed him for overdosing Hitler with any number of drugs. This carried over into post-war allegations and was given new credence first in 1979, when two American psychiatrists put forward a theory that rested on chronic and persistent amphetamine abuse by Hitler, condoned by Morell over a prolonged period of time.[25] Later in 2015 Norman

---

[22] A compilation of testimonies to this effect can be found in Ellen Gibbels, 'Hitler's Nervenkrankheit'; in: *Vierteljahrshefte für Zeitgeschichte*, Nr. 2, 1994, pp 155–210, especially pp 169–86.

[23] BA-Ko, N 1348/4 'Morell notes (entry for 7 August 1941)': 'when outstretched, both hands show a tremor'.

[24] BA-Ko, N 1348/4 'Morell notes (entry for 29 July 1944)'.

[25] Leonard L. Heston and Renate Heston, *The Medical Casebook of Adolf Hitler* (London: William Kimber 1979), pp 104–42. Amphetamines were widely used in World War II by German servicemen in the field to fight off exhaustion. For an assessment of their side effects, see the recent account by a Luftwaffe pilot in Roderich Cescotti, *Fernflug. Erinnerungen 1919–2012* (Moosburg: NeunundzwanzigSechs 2012), pp 154–5. Assessing the quantity Hitler may have ingested at times is difficult in view of the

Ohler made a case for Hitler having become heavily dependent on the synthetic opiate Eukodal from July 1943 onwards.[26] Independently of this, it was felt both by Hitler and many of his closest collaborators that the main reason for his failing health was stress-related, since it could be plausibly traced to the deteriorating situation on all fronts and the friction this invariably caused with his senior military advisers.[27] Finally, some observers put the deterioration he showed after July 1944 down to the damage (physical or otherwise) done by Claus von Stauffenberg's bomb.[28] It goes without saying that these three theories were not mutually exclusive.

A possible organic cause was tentatively diagnosed for the first time on 7 April 1945. This came about in a manner that casts serious doubt on the professional skills of both Morell and his detractors. On that day, Hitler's eye doctor, Professor Walter Löhlein, came calling for the first time in thirteen months. His visit had been pencilled in since December, but a number of factors, such as Hitler refusing to be distracted in the planning of the Ardennes

conflicting information we have on the alleged amphetamine content of the Vitamultin chocolate treats which he appears to have wolfed down without any supervision on Morell's part. Schenck, *Patient*, pp 447–8, reached the tentative conclusion that in all likelihood only some of the chocolate treats came with added stimulant, while Ellen Gibbels, 'Hitler's Nervenleiden – Differentialdiagnose des Parkinson-Syndroms'; in: *Fortschritte der Neurologie, Psychiatrie*, 57. Jahrgang, Nr. 12, p 509, bases her analysis on each treat containing an equal (though minute) amphetamine dosage. Neumann/Eberle, *War Hitler krank*, p 153–60, devote eight pages to this question, without, however, solving the problem at the heart of it. Ohler, *Rausch*, pp 124, 282, is equally inconclusive.

26 Ohler, *Rausch*, pp 183–97, 218–47, 280–94. Ohler has also made a plausible case for the sudden cessation of the Eukodal supply (the factory producing it was destroyed in an air raid in late 1944) contributing to Hitler's dramatic deterioration in 1945. Eukodal is identical to the drug which has triggered the present-day prescription drug crisis in the USA. See Roland Lindner, 'Schneesturm und Seelenfinsternis'; in: *Frankfurter Allgemeine Zeitung* (30.4.2019), p 3.

27 It appears that by January 1945 Morell had come round to sharing this assessment, see BA-Ko, N 1348/5 'Morell notes (entry for 27 January 1945)'. Hitler's press spokesman Otto Dietrich was the first to promulgate this theory in the post-war years: Otto Dietrich, *12 Jahre mit Hitler* (Köln: Atlas Verlag 1955), pp 226–8.

28 A number of people from his entourage reached the same conclusion in the last months of the war or the initial period of peace. For the impressions of a *Gauleiter* who attended the last meeting of the senior NSDAP functionaries in the Neue Reichskanzlei on 24 February 1945: Rudolf Jordan, *Erlebt und Erlitten. Weg eines Gauleiters von München bis Moskau* (Leoni 1971), p 253–4. For a similar assessment see TB Goebbels, Bd. II.15, p 522 (entry for 16 March 1945). Both Göring and Jodl expressed the same opinion to Allied interrogators soon after their capture. See 'Sowjetisches Protokoll des Verhörs von Generaloberst Alfred Jodl, Kurort Mondorf, Luxemburg, 17. Juni 1945' and 'Sowjetisches Verhörprotokoll des Reichsmarschall Hermann Göring, Kurort Mohndorf, Luxemburg, 17. Juni 1945'; both in: Wassili Christoforow, Wladimir Makarow and Matthias Uhl (eds.), *Verhört. Die Befragungen deutscher Generale und Offiziere durch die sowjetischen Geheimdienste 1945–1952* (Oldenbourg: DeGruyter 2015) [= Veröffentlichungen des DHI Moskau, Bd. 6], pp 85, 132.

offensive, led to its postponement time and again. It was during this period in 1944–5 that Hitler's condition deteriorated most markedly and would have been positively shocking for a visitor like Löhlein, who had not laid eyes on him in over a year. After the check-up, the ophthalmologist raised the issue of Hitler's pitiful condition with Morell.[29] While there is no specific mention of a disease like Parkinson's in Morell's entry for 7 April, it is remarkable that eight days later he referred to the condition as *'Abart einer Schüttellähmung'*[30] and finally began treating his patient with the rudimentary therapy then available (injections of Harmin and drops of Homburg 680[31]). No long-term effects could be observed, since Hitler took his own life two weeks later.

If Hitler really did suffer from this insidious disease, the implications for his state of mind are difficult to overstate. Parkinson's disease is caused by the deterioration of dopamine-generating nerve cells in a brain area called the substantia nigra. This leads to symptoms of the kind shown by Hitler in 1943–5, but also disorders of speech, cognition, mood and thought. In the last stage of the disease, dementia generally precedes death. No effective treatment to alleviate the symptoms existed in the 1940s, meaning a life expectancy of less than ten years – with a rapidly deteriorating quality of life – from the time the first symptoms manifested themselves. The increasing frequency with which Hitler treated his entourage to outbursts of bad temper in the twilight of his regime could conceivably be traced back to Parkinson's, though it has to be said that the deteriorating war situation also provided reason enough for that. As far as his growing paranoia is concerned, the simple fact that the Stauffenberg plot had given him plenty to be paranoid about has to be factored in too.

The confusion and uncertainty about Hitler's condition in his last years carried over into post-war historiography. A case for Parkinson's was made as early as 1954 by the German neurologist Anton Edler von Braunmühl,[32] to be followed by a 1963 diagnosis which suggested that he was suffering from the long-term symptoms of *Encephalitis lethargica*,[33] a condition undistinguishable to the

---

[29] For Löhlein's visit, see BA-Ko, N 1348/5 Morell notes (entries for 6 and 7 April 1945) as well as the ophtalmologist's final report in BA-Ko, N 1348/4 'Augenuntersuchung des Führers vom 7. April 1945' (n.d.).

[30] The term *Schüttellähmung* ('shaking paralysis') encompassed both idiopathic Parkinson's as well as a number of other degenerative illnesses affecting the central nervous system in the German medical vernacular of the period. See entry for *Schüttellähmung* in: *Der Große Brockhaus*, Bd. 17 (Leipzig: Brockhaus 1934), p 70.

[31] BA-Ko, N 1348/5 'Morell notes (entry for 15 April 1945)'.

[32] Anton von Braunmühl, 'War Hitler krank?'; in: *Stimmen der Zeit* 79 (1954), pp 94–102. Braunmühl made a case for the disease being well advanced in Hitler's case, thus considerably impairing his intellectual capabilities by the second half of the war.

[33] Johann Recktenwald, *Woran hat Adolf Hitler gelitten?* A pandemic-like wave of this infection had swept through Europe from 1915 to 1925. It is commonly referred to as von Economo encephalitis after the Austrian neurologist Constantin von Economo who

layman from the idiopathic Parkinson's disease.[34] Over the years, the accusations against Morell and his overuse of some drugs, as well as attempts to diagnose a chronic sexual illness,[35] or various forms of insanity like schizophrenia,[36] have tended to obfuscate these early findings. Of Hitler's biographers, Joachim Fest in 1973 effectively capitulated before the mountain of contradictory evidence and refused to commit himself one way or another.[37] Three years later, John Toland opted to give the issue a wide berth and omitted it altogether.[38] In 1977, David Irving in his major work *Hitler's War*, while devoting considerable space to Hitler's deteriorating condition, did not dwell on a possible organic cause, instead implying that Morell's multitude of drugs were most likely responsible.[39] Three years later, in a smaller monograph on Hitler and his medical team, Irving was adamant that Hitler did not suffer from Parkinson's disease; instead, he attributed the dictator's physical decline to a blend of stress, after-effects of the Stauffenberg bomb and Morell prescribing a drug containing strychnine.[40] In 1978, Sebastian Haffner's highly influential *Anmerkungen zu Hitler* rationalised his condition in 1944–5 as the accumulated stress of five years of war, 'similar to Roosevelt's and Churchill's case'[41] – a rather remarkable statement which the author saw no need to revise in any of the countless reprints his book went through. As late as 1991, Alan Bullock considered the possibility of Parkinson's without, however, committing himself. The radical deterioration of Hitler's health in the last months of his life he put down to lack of rest and exercise and the stress-rich environment of Führer's Headquarters.[42]

---

first diagnosed it in detail. Patients affected by this condition tend to deteriorate and die within a timeline similar to Parkinson's.

[34] Even medical professionals have often struggled to tell the two conditions apart. See Gibbels, 'Differentialdiagnose', p 511.

[35] As early as May 1946 Göring speculated to one of his lawyers that Hitler may have suffered from syphilis. Werner Bross, *Gespräche mit Hermann Göring während des Nürnberger Prozesses* (Flensburg and Hamburg: Christian Wolff 1950), pp 223–4. A former Hitler confidant who fled abroad in 1937 was adamant that Hitler suffered from advanced syphilis; Ernst Hanfstaengl, *Hitler: The Missing Years* (New York: Arcade 1994 rp), p 123. Thus far, no evidence has emerged which might back up these speculations.

[36] For an early example of this, Wolfgang Treher, *Hitler-Steiner-Schreiber. Ein Beitrag zur Phänomenologie des kranken Geistes* (Emmendingen 1966).

[37] Joachim C. Fest, *Hitler* (London: Penguin 1982 rp), 671, 807.

[38] Toland, *Hitler*.

[39] David Irving, *Hitler's War, 1942–1945* (London: Papermac 1983 – unabridged rp of the 1977 edition), esp. pp 500–1.

[40] David Irving, *Wie krank war Hitler wirklich? Der Diktator und seine Ärzte* (München: Heyne 1980), pp 106, 126, 133.

[41] Sebastian Haffner, *Anmerkungen zu Hitler* (Frankfurt: Fischer Taschenbuch Verlag 2003), pp 170–1.

[42] Alan Bullock, *Hitler and Stalin: Parallel Lives* (London: Harper & Collins 1991), pp 886, 952.

It was only thanks to a major research project by Professor Ellen Gibbels, professor of neurology and psychiatry at the University of Cologne (1972–94), that this ambiguity was finally dispelled in the early 1990s. As well as interviewing the last survivors from his HQ staff and re-evaluating the written testimony of the post-war years, she gathered remarkable new evidence, which paradoxically had been seen many times before but never properly evaluated: weekly newsreels – the *Deutsche Wochenschau* – that featured appearances by Adolf Hitler from February 1940 to March 1945 (a total of 83[43]). These were analysed out of chronological sequence according to neurological precepts; in each case, a brief report summarising the findings – or lack of them – was produced. This process was complemented by comparing and contrasting his movements with those of a healthy male of the same generation for whom a large number of film images had been preserved (a professional actor). Over the course of nearly six years, this remarkable project yielded two publications in specialist medical journals,[44] a monograph,[45] a documentary[46] and a major article in a historical journal.[47] The evidence so painstakingly gathered pointed to what was most likely a case of Parkinson's disease of the idiopathic kind. Amphetamine abuse as a possible cause was firmly ruled out for two reasons. Amphetamine-induced shaking of the limbs would not have been limited to one side of the body and in any case would not have manifested itself when the affected limb was at rest. The likelihood of the illness' progress affecting his cognitive capability by 1944–5 could not be ruled out entirely, but based on the circumstantial evidence available seemed unlikely.[48] Increasingly frequent outbursts of temper and manifestations of paranoia during this period would certainly fit the symptoms of progressing Parkinson's. In view of the patient's known character traits and the

---

[43] For the years 1940 and 1941, only those newsreels showing Hitler in motion over a certain period of time were included in the sample. The 1942–5 period comprises every single appearance in front of the cameras.

[44] Ellen Gibbels, 'Hitler's Parkinson-Syndrom. Eine postume Motilitätsanalyse in Filmaufnahmen der Deutschen Wochenschau 1940–1945'; in: *Der Nervenarzt* 59 (1988), pp 521–8. Also: Ellen Gibbels, 'Differentialdiagnose'.

[45] Ellen Gibbels, *Hitler's Parkinson-Krankheit. Zur Frage eines hirnorganischen Psychosyndroms* (Berlin: Springer 1990).

[46] Ellen Gibbels, 'Hitler's Parkinson-Syndrom. Eine Analyse von Aufnahmen der Deutschen Wochenschau aus den Jahren 1940–45, Video-Produktion des Instituts für den Wissenschaftlichen Film (IWF) in Göttingen, 1992 (42 minutes)'. Since the closure of the IWF institute, the film has now become accessible under the same title in the Bundesarchiv (Koblenz), Bestand Film B/123530/1.

[47] Ellen Gibbels, 'Hitler's Nervenkrankheit'; in: *Vierteljahrshefte für Zeitgeschichte* Nr. 2/ 1994, pp 155–220.

[48] This is borne out by the fact that he managed to retain his excellent memory for dates and figures until the last days of his life. Gibbels, *Parkinson-Krankheit*, pp 19–28.

deteriorating war situation, it seems likely that these merely contributed to the mood swings, rather than being their sole cause.[49] The extent to which the progress of the disease contributed to Hitler's reluctance to evacuate untenable positions in a timely fashion in 1943–5, thus saving the German Army from suffering often avoidable casualties, is of course impossible to determine. Much more important is the question whether he could conceivably have known of his condition in time to affect in any way his 1941 decision-making process. He would, after all, have been conscious of the fact that he was not just living on borrowed time, but would not even be in a position to function effectively as a political and military leader for much of that limited period.[50] The clearest hint in that direction can be found in a statement he made in September 1941, in which he was adamant in ruling out war with the USA not just for the near future, but for his entire lifetime.[51] The events that transpired only three months later would seem to indicate a very abrupt change of heart, the reasons for which might not be limited to the strategic sphere.

[49] Mainstream academia has been remarkably slow in accepting this discovery and giving recognition to a non-historian for what was by any standards a major breakthrough. Marlis Steinert, *Hitler* (München: C. H. Beck 1994), p 555, was the first to give it its full due. Three years later, John Lukacs in an otherwise very erudite critical evaluation of all the major Hitler biographies published so far limited himself to mentioning Hitler's terminal disease in a footnote of one line that if anything made light of the condition. See John Lukacs, *The Hitler of History: Hitler's Biographers on Trial* (London: Weidenfeld & Nicholson 1997), p 75. Ian Kershaw in his seminal and deservedly praised two-volume biography saw Parkinson's as just one of several causes of Hitler's physical decline by autumn 1944, with an impact on a par with that made by stress and life style problems; Ian Kershaw, *Hitler 1936–1945: Nemesis* (London: Allen Lane 2000), p 728. The author of another scholarly biography omitted the issue altogether by briefly taking note of Hitler's deteriorating condition, but putting it down in the main to stress. He went on to imply that further physical decline in 1944–5 was a result of Count von Stauffenberg's bomb: Ralf Georg Reuth, *Hitler. Eine politische Biographie* (München: Piper 2003), pp 586, 616. A major new study focusing on the dictator's artistic inclinations, the influence they had on the way in which he perceived the world around him and how they even played a role in his political and military decision-making mentions Parkinson's only in a brief aside. This is all the more remarkable since the symptoms were likely to have contributed to his decision to avoid public speeches after 1942, a subject the author dwells on at some length. See Wolfram Pyta, *Hitler. Der Künstler als Politiker und Feldherr. Eine Herrschaftsanalyse* (München: Siedler 2015), pp 592, 640.

[50] A theory first put forward by the American neurologist Abraham Liebermann in 1996. See Abraham Lieberman, 'Adolf Hitler Had Post-Encephalitic Parkinsonism'; in: *Parkinsonism and Related Disorders*, Vol. 2 (1996), Nr. 2, pp 95–103. See also idem, 'Hitler's Parkinson's Disease Began in 1933'; in: *Movement Disorders*, Vol 12 (1997), Nr. 2, pp 239–40. Liebermann's research is limited by the fact that he was unable to examine sources and scholarship available only in German. As a result, Gibbels' exhaustive research, which preceded his own by several years, is not even mentioned in passing.

[51] 'Äusserungen des Führers zu Botschafter Abetz am 16.9.1941 (n.d.)'; in: ADAP, Serie D, Bd. XIII.2, pp 423–5.

Could Hitler conceivably have been given a diagnosis of his Parkinson's disease before Pearl Harbor? The overwhelming evidence appears to be against such a supposition. To begin with, his symptoms before the turn of the years 1941–2 were still relatively light and infrequent. Ellen Gibbels has detected the first possible manifestations in a newsreel from 7 May 1941, where his movements appear unnaturally slow at times. The next three newsreels in which Hitler appears are inconclusive, but by 4 October 1941 the slowed-down movement of his left arm is undeniable, an assessment confirmed by a newsreel that shows him during the Reichstag session of 11 December 1941 as well as attending a birthday gathering for army commander-in-chief, *Generalfeldmarschall* von Brauchitsch.[52] However, it needs to be kept in mind that these were still very mild symptoms that could be – and indeed were – attributed to other causes. When Morell repeatedly noticed a tremor in August 1941, this happened concurrently with Hitler's dysentery, which most probably was the real cause in this case, since it affected both hands. His worsening sleep problems Morell would invariably and plausibly put down to his patient's habit of refusing to keep regular working hours. More importantly, an examination of 1942 newsreels proves that the most telltale of Parkinson's symptoms – the rest tremor – did not in all likelihood manifest itself until June 1942 at the earliest.[53] It seems inconceivable that Morell would not have made a reference to an earlier, even tentative diagnosis along these lines as Hitler's deterioration took up more and more space in his notes in 1944–5. Finally, we have to examine the possibility that Hitler at some point received medical advice on the matter from a third party, which might have been closer to the mark than Morell's. According to the post-war account of Walter Schellenberg, head of Sicherheitsdienst foreign intelligence, a professor of psychiatry, Max de Crinis, confided in him in 1943 that according to his own assessment Hitler was suffering from Parkinson's disease. It is not entirely clear whether he reached this conclusion from witness testimony and newsreel pictures alone.[54] It can, however, be safely ruled out that this information ever reached Hitler, since his increasing exasperation with his condition (by late autumn 1944, bordering on desperation[55]) makes it inconceivable he would then have kept this from his doctor. On the contrary, Morell's written record proves conclusively that the doctor remained completely mystified and by late 1944 was inclined to agree with his patient's assessment that the worsening of his condition could be linked to stress factors – that is, bad news from any of

[52] Gibbels, 'Hitler's Nervenkrankheit', pp 166–7. The birthday party actually would have taken place well before the Reichstag session, since Brauchitsch turned 60 on 4 October.

[53] See the analysis made by Gibbels of the newsreel featuring his attendance of the funeral of a senior party functionary; Gibbels, 'Hitler's Nervenleiden', p 168.

[54] For a discussion of this see Schenck, *Patient Hitler*, pp 415, 436.

[55] BA-Ko, N 1348/5 'Morell notes (entry for 2 January 1945)'.

the fronts and/or a major clash with one of his senior officers.[56] There may, in fact, have been a grain of truth in this, since some of the symptoms of early to medium Parkinson's are still susceptible to positive or negative psychological influences. In Hitler's case, the relief he felt at surviving the Stauffenberg bomb plot and on receiving the news that the Ardennes offensive had managed to spring a complete surprise on the Allied High Command led to a marked, though only temporary easing of his tremor.

On balance, it appears highly unlikely that Hitler could have known of his condition prior to declaring war on the USA on 11 December 1941. It thus seems that a heightened awareness of his likely remaining life span in November 1941 did not play a role in influencing his decision.

---

[56] See BA-Ko, N 1348/5 'Morell notes (entries for 16 December 1944, 25 December 1944, 27 January 1945, 12 February 1945, 6 March 1945 and 2 April 1945)'. Reproduced in Gibbels, 'Hitler's Nervenleiden', pp 174, 178–9 as well as Schenck, *Patient Hitler*, pp 393, 397–8.

3

'All Measures Short of War': the German Assessment of American Strategy, 1940–1941

3.1 Introduction

In the small hours of 22 June 1941, Benito Mussolini, who was spending a few days at the seaside resort of Riccione, found himself roused from his bed by a valet. On the phone was his foreign minister and son-in-law, Galeazzo Ciano, who proceeded to read out a letter from Adolf Hitler, which the German ambassador had delivered to his residence only minutes before. In this document the German dictator was walking a tightrope. It was bad enough that the spate of disasters suffered by the Italian armed forces since early November 1940 had left the Duce with a badly bruised ego in need of careful handling. As a kind of sop, Hitler had made occasional attempts in the early months of 1941 to entrust him with tasks, like the Bordighera summit with Francisco Franco,[1] which while not of crucial importance to the Axis cause were not irrelevant either. However, for Mussolini to find himself now briefed on the impeding German invasion of the USSR, only hours before the world's media were informed, showed up these activities for what they were – window dressing. Little more than a façade remained of the Italo–German Axis Pact as an alliance among great-power equals.

The German dictator went to great lengths to explain and justify his 'sudden' decision to turn on his Soviet ally and listed various strategic and economic reasons that had 'forced' him to do so. One of these hinged on the USSR being an enemy power that lay within reach of Axis armies, British naval superiority notwithstanding. As far as the United States was concerned, the German dictator made a remarkable admission to his Italian counterpart: 'We simply have no way of removing America from the equation.'[2]

Self-evident though the admission may be, this is the one instance on record in which the German dictator was willing to express this fairly basic strategic reality in so many words. Just shy of six months later, he would

---

[1] On Bordighera, see Romano Canosa, *Mussolini e Franco. Amici, alleati, rivali: vite parallele di due dittatori* (Milano: Mondadori 2008), pp 398–407.

[2] 'Der Führer an den Duce (21.6.1941)'; in: *Akten zur deutschen auswärtigen Politik*, Serie D, Bd. XII.2 (Göttingen: Vandenhoeck & Ruprecht 1969), pp 889–92. Documents from this edition of records of the German foreign ministry will henceforth be quoted as ADAP.

think nothing of disregarding his own assessment. It stands to reason that his analysis of the challenges posed by American power had been subject to more than a few ups and downs. Accordingly, this chapter will attempt to analyse how the assessment of the American 'threat potential' evolved in Berlin in 1940–1.

3.2 The Deterioration and Collapse of Pre-War Relations

As early as 1933, an observer endowed with a sense of history might have described a future clash between the United States and the new Germany of Adolf Hitler as inevitable. While the United States had demonstrably attempted to foster and support the cause of democracy in Europe since at least 1848, the NSDAP was setting about dismantling the democratic structures of the Weimar Republic with a zeal and comprehensiveness that made Italy's (1922–6) and Japan's (1932–40) transitions to a one-party state appear downright gentle by comparison. While the USA had an – admittedly idealised – view of itself as a melting pot for immigrants from different ethnic backgrounds, the mere thought of blending races was anathema to National Socialist ideology. No other great power carried the idea of free trade as deeply embedded in its national consciousness as the USA, while Hitler's Germany was about to limit and regulate free trade with a view to husbanding foreign exchange and creating stockpiles of strategic raw materials. Finally, the USA had since the early 1920s invested considerable political capital in promoting the idea of global disarmament, while Hitler's first priority would be the expansion of the small Reichswehr bequeathed to him by the Weimar Republic into a juggernaut capable of taking on the armed forces of most of Europe.

What is surprising is that the tensions generated by such a multilayered ideological clash took so long to come to a head. The reasons for this were manifold. In the USA, isolationism had received an important boost in the years after 1918–19, when many Americans experienced first disappointment at the treaty signed at Versailles and then exasperation as most of their allies defaulted on the repayment of their wartime debts during the Great Depression. To fight the latter, the new Roosevelt administration decided on an unprecedented public-spending programme which in turn made it necessary to husband its political capital for domestic purposes, rather than foreign policy initiatives. The mid-1930s also witnessed a senatorial hearing chaired by Gerald P. Nye investigating the allegation that bankers and munitions producers had forced President Wilson's hand when the decision was made to declare war on Imperial Germany. While little of substance emerged, it reinforced the opprobrium that attached to the idea of the USA getting involved in overseas conflicts.

At the same time, a series of military interventions by Japan against a China crippled by civil war left the former nation in possession of a medium-sized empire in the Chinese northeast by 1935, constituting a clear violation of the Nine Power Treaty of 1922, according to which both Tokyo and Washington had guaranteed Chinese sovereignty. Geographical distance notwithstanding, Japan's series of invasions and annexations arguably constituted a more blatant challenge to US foreign policy than anything Hitler would do before March 1939 and hence would add to the uncertainties facing US policymakers in the 1930s.

In spite of this, US–German relations deteriorated visibly, with the parting of ways felt especially keenly in the economic area. By 1934, Germany was moving away from a free trade economy to one based on the principle of barter and clearing accounts. By 1935, exports from one country to the other had dropped by roughly 80 per cent in each case, and by October of that year both countries had cancelled each other's most favoured status. This process went hand in hand with trade wars which showed that the new German way of conducting foreign trade seemed to be working alarmingly well: US exporters found themselves virtually shut out from the Balkans while, adding insult to injury, German trade delegations managed to make surprising inroads into the United States' own back yard. Starting in mid-1934, German companies gained an increasing share of the Latin American market after having convinced a number of local governments and banks of the viability of the barter scheme.[3]

Roosevelt's famous Quarantine Speech of 5 October 1937 was determined as much by domestic priorities as those of foreign policy and appears to have been directed first and foremost against Japan and – to a lesser extent – Italy.[4] It singled out aggressor nations who had earned notoriety for their unwillingness to abide by international treaties and suggested a 'quarantine' to isolate them – without, however, giving any specifics of how or by whom this might be achieved. In Germany, the state-directed media had already delivered an unprecedented personal attack on the US President while reacting to a previous speech in mid-September. This may be the reason why on this occasion the reaction was muted. Hitler's assessment of US policy around this time is difficult to judge. In the mid to late 1930s he would still occasionally go on the record with statements indicating genuine admiration for US economic and technological achievements, thus echoing his views from a few years before;[5] at the same time, he was confident in

---

[3] Herbert Sirois, *Zwischen Illusion und Krieg. Deutschland und die USA, 1933–1941* (Paderborn: Ferdinand Schöningh 2000), pp 88–99.

[4] This was certainly the estimate of the German ambassador in Washington. See 'Der Deutsche Botschafter in Washington an das Auswärtige Amt (15.10.1937)'; in: ADAP, Serie D, Bd. I, pp 522–4.

[5] 'Rede vor Vertretern der deutschen Automobilindustrie (15.2.1936)'; in: Max Domarus (ed.), *Hitler. Reden und Proklamationen, 1932–1945*, Bd. I.2 (Wiesbaden: R. Löwit 1973), pp 576–9. Also Hildegard von Kotze (ed.), *Heeresadjutant bei Hitler 1938–1943*.

predicting that the USA would continue in its passive acceptance of German expansion.[6] The minutes of the gathering held at the Reichskanzlei on 5 November 1937 bear this out. The dictator had called a gathering with his foreign minister and his service chiefs to discuss Germany's strategic options over the next six to eight years. A number of possible contingencies (some of them quite improbable) were discussed, with the perceived need to invade and occupy Czechoslovakia in the near future being the first priority. Not one of the imagined conflicts, however, featured an intervention by the United States.[7] The reasons behind this are likely to have been twofold. In the USA, the President had just faced a harsh domestic reaction to the Quarantine Speech. Roosevelt found himself on the receiving end of a barrage of public and political criticism and had to qualify some of his statements a few days later. Isolationism in both Houses of Congress received an important boost.[8] It was obvious to any outside observer that the body politic of US society was not yet ready for even a verbal commitment to alliance politics, no matter how tentative. The impression this would have made on the German leader was compounded by the Rechenberg memorandum which came into his possession in October 1937. This document from the pen of a former German diplomat depicted the USA as still struggling from the effects of the Depression. Attempts by the New Deal to address this had only enjoyed a modicum of success and left the country deeply divided, with even a communist revolt alleged to be a definite possibility. German diplomats described this analysis as a grotesque exaggeration,[9] but since only the previous month the American economy had entered a new recession (the so-called Roosevelt Depression) that would last into 1939, for a time Rechenberg appeared to have the facts on his side.[10] Proof that Hitler took this seriously comes in the form of a comment the dictator made to one of his adjutants around this

---

    Aufzeichnungen des Majors Engel (Stuttgart: DVA 1974), pp 35–6 (entry for 5 September 1938).

[6] Ulrich Schlie (ed.), *Ulrich von Hassel. Römische Tagebücher und Briefe 1932–1938* (München: Herbig 2004), p 185 (entry for 19 April 1937).

[7] An excellent analysis of the issues discussed at the 5 November conference can be found in Ian Kershaw, *Hitler 1936–1945: Nemesis* (London: Allen Lane 2000), pp 46–51. The minutes which gave the conference its name (the Hoßbach memorandum) can be found in their entirety on www.ns-archiv.de/krieg/1937/hossbach (accessed 23 June 2020).

[8] Sirois, *Illusion*, pp 108–9.

[9] 'Aufzeichnung des Vortragenden Legationsrats Davidsen, Auswärtiges Amt (28.10.1937)'; 'Aufzeichnung des Vortragenden Legationsrats Freytag, Auswärtiges Amt (15.11.1937)'; in; ADAP, Serie D, Bd. I, pp 525–8.

[10] On the Roosevelt Depression, see Michael Hiltzik, *The New Deal: A Modern History* (New York: Free Press 2011). For a more detailed account of the Rechenberg affair, see Brendan Simms, *Hitler: Only the World Was Enough* (London: Allen Lane 2019), p 294.

time about the possibility of a communist takeover in the USA.[11] This as likely as not can be traced back to the lingering effects of the Rechenberg memorandum, but these appear to have dissipated by early 1939.

In March 1938 an event occurred which allowed Roosevelt to align ideological distaste and economic interest in his attempt to cast Germany as an entity beyond the pale. When Germany annexed Austria in the *Anschluß* of 12 March 1938 the reaction by the US media ranged from reluctant acceptance to open hostility. The Roosevelt administration signalled its acceptance, but reacted with outrage a few weeks later when Germany announced that it had no intention of honouring the foreign debt of the country it had just integrated into the Greater German Reich. An inkling of this attitude had already become obvious in October 1935, when the cancellation by the German government of the 1923 Treaty of Commerce had gone hand in hand with a unilateral lowering of the interest rate on the German debt. Reneging on the Austrian debt, however, constituted a transgression of a completely new kind. It brought out into the open a hostility which so far had been muted, and it was used by the US government throughout 1938–9 as an effective propaganda tool with which to beat the Third Reich whenever political expediency demanded it.[12]

In keeping with this shift in policy, the President used the Sudeten crisis as a way to test the public mood again, irrespective of the backlash he had endured in the aftermath of his Quarantine Speech. On 18 August, for the first time he gave a hint of how exactly the USA might go about checking the German march of conquest. Addressing an audience at Queen's University in Kingston, Ontario, he gave his 'assurance that the people of the United States will not stand idly by if domination of Canadian soil is threatened by any other Empire',[13] thus sketching out for the first time the concept behind the idea of hemispheric defence. The Munich agreement, which narrowly averted war and gave the Sudeten territories to Germany, was accepted by the administration, but in the clear knowledge that the underlying cause of tensions in Europe had not been removed. In the meantime, Ambassador Dieckhoff had been trying his best to convince his hosts that the annexations of Austria and the Sudetenland had been both justified and would lead to greater stability in Europe; simultaneously, he kept warning Ribbentrop not to take American neutrality for granted and to carefully nurture the good will of those parts of American society, who, while not outright pro-German, were still prepared to give the Third Reich the benefit of the doubt.[14] These efforts were dealt

---

[11] Fritz Wiedemann, *Der Mann der Feldherr werden wollte* (Velbert: Blick & Bild 1964), p 215. Wiedemann served on Hitler's staff from January 1935 to January 1939.

[12] Sirois, *Illusion*, pp 120, 132.

[13] Quoted in Sirois, *Illusion*, p 121.

[14] On Dieckhoff's ambassadorship throughout this period, see Sylvia Taschka, *Diplomat ohne Eigenschaften? Die Karriere des Hans-Heinrich Dieckhoff, 1884–1952* (Stuttgart: Franz Steiner 2006) [= Transatlantische Historische Studien, Bd. 25], pp 110–26.

a crippling blow by the events of 9–10 November, when an organised pogrom swept through most German towns and cities, leaving in its wake a hundred dead, plundered stores and torched synagogues. In the United States, public and official protest at these events reached an unprecedented intensity and unanimity. Most worryingly, according to Dieckhoff, even 'national circles, who are by definition anti-communist and in large part anti-Semitic, are now starting to turn away from us'. This included public figures such as former President Herbert Hoover, New York district attorney Thomas E. Dewey and newspaper magnate William Randolph Hearst, who had so far urged the government to pursue a less openly anti-German stance.[15] The most telling blow, of course, was the recall of the US ambassador in Berlin, Hugh Wilson, for consultations. Hitler retaliated a few days later by recalling Dieckhoff, leaving the running of the Washington embassy to caretaker envoy Hans Thomsen.

These events gave US–German relations a character that presaged the state of affairs that would later prevail between the USA and the USSR during the Cold War. In the weeks after the pogrom, the German media unleashed a campaign against the American government which focused on allegations of 'Jewish manipulations' of US government agencies and – slightly more plausibly – scathing criticism of President Roosevelt, who, it was alleged, was using European affairs to turn attention away from his flagging efforts to revive the US economy. These attacks were telling insofar as the state-controlled media of Nazi Germany had so far mostly refrained from personal attacks on the US President. In the USA, no such central directives to the newspapers were of course possible or, indeed, necessary. By early 1939, all major publications had come to regard German policies within a spectrum that ranged from robust scepticism to extreme hostility.[16]

The German annexation of the rump Czech Republic on 15 March 1939 provided proof that US–German relations really had entered a new phase. When envoy Hans Thomsen presented Secretary of State Cordell Hull with this latest fait accompli, he was faced with a blanket refusal on the secretary's part to acknowledge in any shape or form the latest deed of German aggression. In contrast to the US government's reaction to the Anschluß or the Sudeten crisis, Thomsen was informed that with regards to Czech affairs, the Roosevelt administration would go on dealing solely with the ambassador of that vanquished country. Just over four weeks later, Hitler made it clear that he certainly had no intention of even attempting to work towards better relations with the sitting US President. The latter had personally addressed the German Führer in a speech delivered on 14 April and virtually implored him to give a public pledge not to invade or occupy a series of European and Middle

---

[15] For Dieckhoff's reporting in these days see Taschka, *Diplomat*, pp 191–3.
[16] Sirois, *Illusion*, pp 170–5.

Eastern nations. Hitler made the most of this obvious display of weakness, and in one of his better speeches, which he gave to the Reichstag a fortnight later, he held up the American President to ridicule.[17] He no doubt did so in the knowledge that both Houses of Congress were unlikely to grant Roosevelt an extension of the Cash-and-Carry clause (see next section), which alone would have put him in a position to offer at least some assistance to the European democracies in case of war.

Even before the international situation had taken yet another turn for the worse, with Germany's occupation of the Czech Republic and the Memel territory, Joachim von Ribbentrop, in a rather bizarre move, had put his diplomats in Washington DC in a position where they found themselves increasingly shut out from the venues and events of diplomatic life in the American capital. Reacting to yet another speech by the American President which was critical of Hitler, he forbade them to accept invitations from American hosts, thus severely restricting them in the one activity they could still undertake: the collection of all kinds of intelligence. Fortunately for the Germans, Thomsen's two service attachés, being subordinate to the Oberkommando der Wehrmacht, were not bound by this directive and were able to continue in their work unperturbed. Army and air attaché, *Generalleutnant* Friedrich von Boetticher,[18] and naval attaché, *Vizeadmiral* Robert Witthoeft-Emden,[19] had held these posts since April and November 1933, respectively, when they arrived in Washington under the terms of an agreement negotiated by the Weimar Republic. The former in particular had managed to foster a network among senior US army officers, which would stand him in good stead for the remainder of his time in Washington. Ribbentrop relaxed his original ruling in November, but by then Germany's war of aggression had given many American hosts a reason to make the social boycott permanent. Virtually by default and, it would seem, with Thomsen's acquiescence, Boetticher soon grew into the role of a substitute ambassador,[20] who by March 1941 would often send off two

---

[17] The key passages of both speeches are reproduced in Detlef Junker (ed.), *Kampf um die Weltmacht. Die USA und das Dritte Reich 1933–1945* (Düsseldorf: Schwann 1988), pp 90–4.

[18] Boetticher, a gunner by trade, arrived in the USA while still a *Generalmajor*, but was quickly promoted to *Generalleutnant* on 1 October 1933. On 1 September 1940, he was elevated to the rank of *General der Artillerie* (full general). The latter rank in particular was wholly unusual for an officer in such a posting, *Oberst* (full colonel) or *Generalmajor* being more common.

[19] Witthoeft-Emden had still been a *Kapitän zur See* (equivalent to full colonel) on his arrival in the USA. He moved quickly up the promotion ladder, however, being made a *Konteradmiral* on 1 April 1935 and *Vizeadmiral* on 1 November 1937.

[20] A state of affairs essentially confirmed by the following communication from Thomsen to Permanent Secretary Weizsäcker. 'Botschaftsrat Thomsen, Washington an Staatssekretär von Weizsäcker (24. April 1940)'; in: ADAP, Serie D, Bd. IX, pp 188–9.

telegrams per day.[21] A visible manifestation of this was his growing habit of co-signing cables with the envoy Thomsen, forgetting to use the plural form in the text or at the very least make the odd reference to Thomsen's supposed co-authorship, a habit that eventually brought Ribbentrop's ire down on both of them.[22]

Boetticher, Witthoefft-Emden and, from June 1938, the new assistant air attaché, *Hauptmann* Peter Riedel,[23] were fortunate insofar as much of the intelligence they were after could be procured from open sources to a degree unthinkable in most democracies of the time, let alone any totalitarian regime.[24] Prior to Germany's invasion of Poland, American rearmament, such as it was, had been limited in scope and of unequal focus. Arguably the worst off was the regular army. Historically, a large standing army had always been regarded with suspicion in the USA and after the ending of World War I, many politicians called for its numbers to be reduced to pre-war levels (fewer than 100,000). The Congressional National Defense Act of June 1920 had in theory granted it a total strength of 298,000 men, to be complemented by a National Guard of 436,000,[25] but this was in fact never attained due to the

---

[21] Routinely, these were sent to the Auswärtiges Amt which would first decrypt them and then forward them to the military recipients. These could vary, but would generally include OKW *Ausland*, OKH *Attachegruppe* and the RLM *Attachegruppe* (the military intelligence/attaché departments of Oberkommando der Wehrmacht, Oberkommando des Heeres and Reichsluftfahrministerium, respectively). Though it was usually up to one of these departments to decide whether Halder or Keitel were to receive a personal copy, in a number of cases Boetticher took it upon himself to single out by name a particular senior recipient at the top, notably Army Chief of Staff Franz Halder or Luftwaffe Chief of Operations Hoffmann von Waldau. Communication from OKH or OKW to Boetticher also appears have taken place via the Auswärtiges Amt only, even in cases where speed was of the essence. For an insight into the mechanics of this process, PA/AA, StS USA, Bd. 5, 'Weizsäcker an Geschäftsträger persönlich ! (3.4.1941)', StS USA Bd. 6, 'Thomsen an Auswärtiges Amt. Geheime Reichssache (23.5.1941)' and BA/MA, RH 2/2942 'Oberkommando des Heeres, Attacheabt.V Gen.St.d.H. Nr. 1173/41 g.Kdos. an Auswärtiges Amt – Pol. I M z.Hd. Herrn Leg.Rat Kramarz (23.9.1941)'.

[22] 'Der Staatssekretär an die Botschaft in Washington (19. April 1940)', in: ADAP, Serie D, Bd. IX, pp 168–9.

[23] Peter Riedel, apart from being a former Lufthansa pilot and skilled glider pilot, also held a degree in engineering. Though Boetticher had been accredited as air attaché since July 1934, by 1938 the evolution of aviation technology left him increasingly out of his depth and overtaxed. To remedy this state of affairs, he was allowed to hire an assistant attaché more familiar with the technical side of air power.

[24] For a particularly vivid impression of this state of affairs, the reader is referred to the memoirs of Peter Riedel; Peter Simons, *German Air Attaché: The Thrilling Story of the German Ace Pilot and Wartime Diplomat Peter Riedel* (London: AirLife 1997), pp 48–58, 76–82.

[25] On the debate surrounding the National Defense Act, see David E. Johnson, *Fast Tanks and Heavy Bombers: Innovation in the US Army, 1917–1945* (Ithaca and London: Cornell UP 1998), pp 24–29, 50–53. Also Charles Reginald Shrader (ed.), *Reference Guide to United States Military History, 1919–1945* (New York: Facts on File 1994), pp 5–11, and

Figure 3.1 Envoy Hans Thomsen (second from right) and Attaché Friedrich Boetticher (second from left) are received by Hitler on their return from the USA. (ullstein bild/ ullstein bild via Getty Images)

assorted defence cutbacks of the Harding, Coolidge and Hoover administrations and the ravages of the Depression years.[26] By 1939, army strength had reached 190,000; a week after the beginning of World War II in Europe, President Roosevelt granted an expansion to 227,000.[27] This barely addressed the problem of an unfavourable ratio between officers and other ranks, with far too many of the former having spent too much time in command of companies and battalions that existed only on paper. As far as equipment was concerned, the army's infantry still had to do without a modern light air-cooled machine gun; its mechanised forces lacked a medium tank and the country's industry a factory which could have turned out such a tank in meaningful numbers. The Air Corps was slightly better off because of the perception in the months after the Munich agreement that superiority in the air had given the Germans a trump card in the talks. This ushered in a period of Presidential interest in

---

Edward M. Coffman, *The Regulars. The American Army 1898–1941* (Cambridge and London: Harvard UP 2004), pp 227–32.

[26] With an average strength of 180,000 throughout most of the inter-war years, the Guard considerably outnumbered the regular army. In terms of its share of the Federal budget, spending on the army reached an all-time low only in 1936. Coffman, *The Regulars*, p 416.

[27] Shrader, *Reference Guide*, p 5.

and benevolence towards the air arm. At a meeting with his top military aides on 14 November 1938, Roosevelt had envisaged an Air Corps of 20,000 planes; likely political opposition and military warnings that at present the country lacked factories in which to produce them, bases from which to operate them and men to fly and maintain them, cut this down to 5,500, granted by Congress in April 1939.[28] On the technical side at least and in contrast to 1917, American designers had already proven that they could deliver the goods. As far back as 1935, Consolidated had given the Navy a flying boat of unmatched range and dependability, and the Boeing B-17 four-engined bomber had revolutionised heavy bomber design; by early 1939, Lockheed and Bell were in the process of testing two new fighter prototypes of novel design and, it was hoped, great potential.[29] In contrast to these two, a recent improvement on the dated Curtiss P-36, the P-40, was more of a stopgap measure, but promised to be a dependable workhorse – as indeed it turned out to be. In view of the quickly deteriorating international situation Curtiss was the first company to benefit from this windfall, when it accepted a government contract for 524 P-40s on 26 April 1939.[30] While still a far cry from an Air Corps of 20,000 planes, the Curtiss contract represented a peacetime order of unprecedented size.

The US Navy had languished for a considerable period of time. Partly this was due to the Washington Conference of 1922 and the London Conference of 1930,[31] which had ushered in an era of internationally agreed limitations on the numbers and tonnage of capital ships and cruisers. More importantly, however, was the lack of funding. As a result of this, the US Navy was prevented from reaching the limits even of the treaty system, which would have given it parity with Great Britain. As a result, the Americans found themselves lagging badly behind the British: in 1932, the Royal Navy had fifty-two cruisers on its books, while the Americans had to make do with nineteen.[32] By the mid-1930s, the Japanese, who exploited the limits set by the treaty

---

[28] Geoffrey Perret, *Winged Victory: The Army Air Forces in World War II* (New York: Random House 1993), pp 34, 50.

[29] The Lockheed P-38 Lightning was a twin-engined, single-seater fighter of twin-boom design boasting unprecedented range. The Bell P-39 Airacobra was a more orthodox single-seater, single-engined interceptor. Uniquely, it featured an engine located behind the cockpit.

[30] On the evolution of the key American aircraft designs of the period, see Perret, *Victory*, pp 87–120.

[31] The Washington Treaty accorded the signatories ratios of 5 (UK):5(US):3(Japan). On the London Conference, see John H. Maurer and Christopher M. Bell (eds.), *At the Crossroads between Peace and War: The London Naval Conference in 1930* (Baltimore: Naval Institute Press 2014). For summaries of how the Treaty system affected the US Navy, see Robert Love, *History of the US Navy, Vol. 1, 1775–1941* (Harrisburg: Stackpole 1992), pp 524–83 and George W. Baer, *One Hundred Years of Sea Power: The US Navy, 1890–1990* (Stanford: Stanford UP 1994), pp 83–118.

[32] Baer, *Sea Power*, p 115.

system to the hilt and were helped by a treaty clause forbidding US fortifications west of Hawaii, enjoyed regional and in some cases overall numerical
superiority. The advent of the Roosevelt administration, after some initial
hesitation on the part of the new commander-in-chief, soon brought better
times: $238 million were appropriated under the new National Industrial
Recovery Act. By the end of 1933, Japan had left the League of Nations and
the idea of generating US employment through orders to shipyards was
accordingly given added momentum. On 27 March 1934 the Vinson–
Trammel Act authorising the replacement of obsolete vessels and the construction of new ships to treaty strength passed the Senate. The act authorised
construction of one aircraft carrier, six cruisers, sixty-five destroyers and thirty
submarines and contained a provision for the commensurate growth of naval
aviation.[33] Unlike previous naval bills of the 1920s, which had had only a very
gradual impact on account of the then prevailing political climate, funds were
soon forthcoming.[34] On 3 June 1936 a new Naval Act benefited from the
concurrent collapse of the treaty system. It provided for the construction of
two new aircraft carriers as well as the Navy's first battleships to be laid down
since 1921 – the USS *North Carolina* and USS *Washington*. Another act of
Congress, the Second Vinson Act, was passed in May 1938 against a backdrop
of increasing international tensions and facilitated an expansion of 20 per cent
over what the First Vinson Act had allowed.[35] This provided funding for four
battleships of the *South Dakota* class, a slight improvement over the *North
Carolinas*. The speed, protection and firepower which these ships combined
were all the more impressive since they had had to be designed with
a maximum beam in mind, which would allow them to pass the locks of the
Panama Canal. As a result of this burst of naval rearmament, the US Navy had
added three carriers,[36] eight light and six heavy cruisers,[37] sixty-one destroyers
and twenty-eight submarines to its inventory in the time that lay between

---

[33] Baer, *Sea Power*, p 130; Love, *US Navy*, pp 592–3. See also Thomas C. Hone, 'The
Evolution of the U.S. fleet, 1933–1941: How the President Mattered'; in: Edward
J. Marolda (ed.), *FDR and the US Navy* (New York: St Martin's Press 1998), pp 65–114,
esp. pp 78–9.

[34] Authorisation by Congress was only the first step towards the voting of funds, which
required a separate Appropriations Act. In a case typical of the pre-1933 climate, five
destroyers authorised in 1916 were not funded until 1932. See Dave McComb, *US
Destroyers 1934–45: Pre-War Classes* (Oxford: Osprey 2010), p 6.

[35] The beginning of the Sino–Japanese War (July 1937), the sinking of the gunboat USS
Panay off Nanking by Japanese dive-bombers (December 1937) and the annexation of
Austria by Germany. On the impact of the *Panay* incident, see Love, *US Navy*, pp 602–4.

[36] A fourth (the USS *Ranger*) already laid down under the Hoover administration and hence
not included in this count.

[37] Only two of the seven heavy *New Orleans* class cruisers are included in this count. The
others, though commissioned under Roosevelt, had been laid down under the Hoover
administration in 1931 and 1932.

Roosevelt's inauguration and the German invasion of Poland.[38] The new generation of super-battleships took rather longer to materialise due to their size and complexity; even so, four of them were in various stages of construction by September 1939. While a major improvement over the state of affairs which had prevailed in the previous fifteen years, it could not disguise two facts: the US Navy was only starting to make up for time lost in the 1920s and early 1930s and the forces available were as yet only able to deal with one strategic challenge at a time. Since 1921, the bulk of the fleet had been deployed in the Pacific, with little thought given to the possible emergence of an Atlantic challenger. Should the naval balance of power ever necessitate a fundamental re-evaluation of this focus, the navy would find itself severely short-changed.

In one of his last pre-war reports, envoy Thomsen estimated that a meaningful intervention by the US armed forces in a European war could be safely ruled out for the next year. If anything, this gave the army's and air corps' state of preparedness too much credit. The US Navy's greater potential was acknowledged, but the compelling need to keep most of its units in the Pacific was seen as a given, the current fallout between Tokyo and Berlin over the Molotov–Ribbentrop Pact notwithstanding.[39]

3.3   From Cash-and-Carry to Lend-Lease (September 1939–March 1941)

For Adolf Hitler, the first weeks of World War II provided a good indicator of how far his opponent in the White House was willing to go in thwarting him; it also gave him an insight into the range of instruments from which the President would choose to do so. From 1914 to 1917 America had extended considerable help to the Entente powers both in the form of credit as well as deliveries of munitions. The mood of the country in September 1939 would not allow the continuation of such a practice and had already paved the way with three Neutrality Acts.[40] The first of these had concerned a conflict that constituted a case of blatant aggression by one country on another (Italy's 1935 invasion of Ethiopia), where the risk of escalation was low to say the least. Even so, the mood created by the Nye hearings and a host of concomitant publications brooked no compromise. For Americans and their political representatives, avoiding entanglement in foreign conflicts had become a paramount political aim, irrespective of low risk and possible long-term benefit. The

---

[38] For a breakdown of these figures see Hone, *Evolution*, p 47.
[39] 'Thomsen an Auswärtiges Amt (28.8.1939)'; in ADAP, Serie D, Bd. VII, pp 314–5. Also 'Boetticher & Thomsen an Auswärtiges Amt (1.12.1939)'; in: ADAP, Serie D, Bd. VIII, p 369.
[40] For a comprehensive account of how the US Neutrality Acts came into existence see Ronald Powalski, *Toward an Entangling Alliance: American Isolationism, Internationalism and Europe, 1901–1950* (Westport: Greenwood 1991).

August 1935 Neutrality Act forbade both arms and ammunition exports; it also warned Americans that if they chose to travel on board ships of the belligerents, they did so at their own risk. Next year, the Neutrality Act of 1936 was both a continuation of the previous one, which expired in February 1936, and a further step towards retrenchment: it specified that loans or credits to all belligerents were now likewise prohibited. The logical successor to the 1936 Act was the 1937 Neutrality Act, passed in May that year, which incorporated changes made necessary by the outbreak of the Spanish Civil War.[41] On the face of it, this last act represented yet another tightening of the restrictive regime already in existence, since it carried no expiration date, covered civil wars, prohibited US shipping from carrying passengers or merchandise to ports of the belligerents and expressly forbade US citizens from travelling on belligerent ships. However, Roosevelt, who was increasingly concerned about the possibility of a European war, had gained some wiggle room: included was a clause limited to two years, allowing the President to permit arms shipments to belligerents if they paid for them in cash and carried them in their own ships (Cash-and-Carry).

On the outbreak of the Sino–Japanese War in July, Roosevelt refused to invoke the Neutrality Act on the pretext that neither side had formally declared war and for the obvious reason that only the Japanese would have benefited from a sudden cessation of American weapons' shipments to the region. This caused considerable irritation amongst isolationist congressmen and senators, who claimed that the spirit of the law was being undermined. Accordingly, they allowed Cash-and-Carry to lapse in May 1939 and proved reluctant to renew it on the outbreak of war in September. It took an impassioned plea from the President on 21 September, along with much backroom dealing, before a new Neutrality Act could finally be passed on 2 November 1939. It superseded the previous Neutrality Acts, held on to the spirit of its predecessors by barring American ships and citizens from entering war zones to be designated by the President and contained the all-important Cash-and-Carry clause. Since control of the sea lanes (the Baltic and Black Sea excepted) was exercised by the British and French navies, only the democracies could conceivably benefit from this ruling.

Much the same would eventually apply to the policing of a Neutrality Zone around the American continent, which all the governments of the Americas (Canada excepted) agreed to at a conference at Panama on 3 October 1939. The naval vessels of all nations at war were hereby instructed to refrain from belligerent acts while crossing what was quite a substantial body of water: while notionally limited to 483 km (300 miles), the inclusion of the US Virgin Islands and the

---

[41] On the role played by the Spanish Civil War in forming Roosevelt's perception of Axis aggressive designs, see Dominic Tierney, *FDR and the Spanish Civil War. Neutrality and Commitment in the Struggle that Divided America* (Durham, NC: Duke UP 2007).

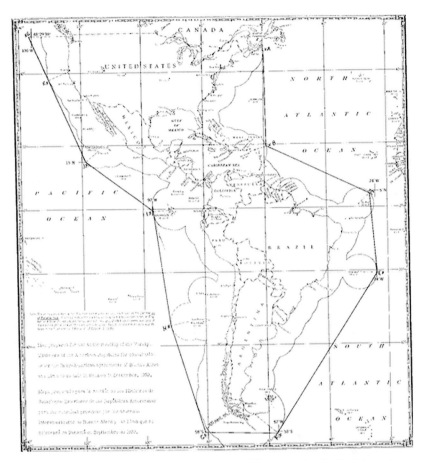

Map 3.1 The US Neutrality Zone: despite repeated badgering by the Seekriegsleitung, Hitler would waver only once in his determination to respect the boundaries of the US Neutrality Zone, proclaimed in October 1939 (Courtesy US State Department).

Brazilian archipelagos of St Paul and Trinidade had the effect of more than doubling the zone's depth across most of its length.[42] However, since Great Britain and France already possessed a number of base facilities in the Caribbean and the Guayanas, and the new zone did not propose to limit French

[42] A similar result was arrived at on the Pacific side of the continent. For a summary of how the limits of the Neutrality Zone were drawn, see 'Explanatory Note regarding Declaration of Panama Map (n.d.)'; in: *Foreign Relations of the United States Diplomatic Papers (FRUS) 1939, The American Republics*, Vol. 5 (Washington DC: US Government Printing Office 1957): history.state.gov/historicaldocuments/frus1939v05 (accessed 15 December 2019).

and British access to their possessions, this automatically placed the Germans at a disadvantage.[43]

In Germany all these events had been followed very closely, and with some concern. Despite the mocking language Hitler had recently adopted when referring in public to the USA and its President, a series of instructions and assessments from the early weeks of the war prove that the prospect of US intervention was a factor that was already very much part of the dictator's considerations. In mid-September, he urged his generals to find a way to hasten the fall of besieged Warsaw; far from fearing an Anglo–French move in the West, he instead stressed the need to terminate the campaign before the US Congress returned from its summer recess on 21 September.[44] In a directive from 9 October to Oberkommando der Wehrmacht he made it clear that 'even though the attempts by certain circles in the USA to push the continent in the general direction of an anti-German coalition are likely to get nowhere for the time being, they might still succeed at some point in the future. Here, too, time is likely to work against Germany'.[45]

The time factor also featured prominently in a harangue he delivered in a different context to a group of army officers on 23 November. Knowing that many of them were reluctant to go ahead with the invasion of Western Europe in the face of extremely harsh winter weather, he spoke of a diminishing window of opportunity for the Wehrmacht to initiate hostilities against the Anglo–French armies still in the process of forming up and re-equipping with new weapons systems; hence, he brooked no excuses aimed at putting off the attack until the spring. Three very similar – though not identical – sets of minutes of this address survive:[46] they all record open threats against anyone opposed to this course of action. One even has him questioning the nerve of the army's commander-in-chief, who was present during Hitler's speech.[47] The likely role to be played by various powers in the mid-term was mentioned by way of introduction, with Soviet Russia's loyalty to the new pact coming in

---

[43] Reiner Pommerin, *Das Dritte Reich und Lateinamerika. Die deutsche Politik gegenüber Süd- und Mittelamerika 1939–1942* (Düsseldorf: Droste 1977), pp 87–94, 113–16.

[44] Nikolaus von Vormann, *So begann der Zweite Weltkrieg. Zeitzeuge der Entscheidungen – als Offizier bei Hitler, 22.8.1939–1.10.1939* (Leoni: Druffel Verlag 1988), pp 121, 139. My thanks to Brendan Simms (Cambridge) for bringing this source to my attention.

[45] 'Denkschrift und Richtlinien über die Führung des Krieges im Westen (9.10.1939)'; in: Hans-Adolf Jacobsen (ed.), *Dokumente zur Vorgeschichte des Westfeldzuges 1939–1940* (Göttingen: Musterschmidt 1956), pp 4–21.

[46] *Trial of the Major War Criminals (TMWC)*, Vol. XXVI, pp 327–36; Helmut Krausnick and Harold C. Deutsch (eds.), *Helmuth Groscurth. Tagebücher eines Abwehroffiziers 1938–1940* (Stuttgart: DVA 1970), pp 414–18; '23.11, 12 Uhr: Besprechung beim Führer, zu der alle Oberbefehlshaber befohlen sind'; in: Gerhard Wagner (ed.), *Lagevorträge des Oberbefehlshabers der Kriegsmarine vor Hitler 1939–1945* (München: J.F. Lehmanns Verlag 1972), pp 49–54.

[47] TMWC, Vol. XXVI, p 329.

for particularly close scrutiny. He also raised the topic of the support extended by the US government to Britain and France; the first source described American support as 'not yet meaningful',[48] while the next one stressed a time lapse (between one and two years) before the support was likely to become 'much bigger and of greater scope'.[49] The contradiction inherent in this is more apparent than real and is in keeping with similar nuanced differences in both texts. Since the two statements are not mutually exclusive, it stands to reason that the first assertion was in all likelihood followed by the second one. The notes in the papers of Admiral Erich Raeder, head of the Kriegsmarine, recorded a further point, which is of interest since it gives us an idea of what yardstick Hitler was using to gauge American willingness to support the Allies. The way he saw it, as long as the existing neutrality legislation remained in place, America would be 'no threat to us'.[50] Very much in keeping with this estimate, in late January 1940 he finally decided to overrule the Seekriegsleitung's protests and insisted that the Kriegsmarine's raiders keep clear of the new Pan-American Neutrality Zone.[51]

In Washington, meanwhile, Thomsen and his staff were granted a brief respite by two unconnected events. First of all, the bungled Soviet invasion of Finland, which began on 30 November 1939, caused the USSR to be regarded in the eyes of the American public with equal or even greater loathing than Nazi Germany. For a few precious months, the German embassy no longer found itself in the daily glare of the US media spotlight. Concurrently, a cache of documents found among the files of the Polish foreign ministry was presented to the world's media in a series of official publications (the so-called *Weißbücher*) by the German government. They revealed the extent to which Roosevelt's ambassador in Paris, William Bullit,[52] had encouraged the Polish government to stand fast during the summer of 1939, thus contributing – according to Berlin's reasoning – to the Poles' reluctance to agree to a last-minute compromise and giving the lie to Roosevelt's claims to his countrymen that he had no intention of involving the USA in the war. The embassy was able to milk this for just over a week until the German invasion of Denmark and Norway pulled the rug from under them. As Thomsen had to report to the Wilhelmstrasse on 10 April, this move had most likely strengthened Roosevelt's position for re-election in November and also antagonised many Americans of Scandinavian stock who until now had been counted

---

[48] Ibid.
[49] Krausnick/Deutsch (ed.), *Tagebücher*, p 415.
[50] 'Besprechung beim Führer, zu der alle Obebefehlshaber befohlen sind (23.11.1939, 12 Uhr)'; in: Wagner (ed.), *Lagevorträge*, p 52.
[51] Pommerin, *Lateinamerika*, pp 113–16.
[52] On Bullitt's ambassadorship, see David Mayers, *FDR's Ambassadors and the Diplomacy of Crisis: From the Rise of Hitler to the End of World War II* (Cambridge: CUP 2013), pp 125–43, 249–59.

among the groups leaning towards isolationism.[53] Plans to have the revelatory incriminating documents translated into English, produced in a brochure and printed in large numbers still went ahead, but it was obvious that the latest events would rob them of much of the impact they might otherwise have had. While Boetticher and Thomsen undoubtedly considered this a setback, the German leader had by now reached a point where currying favour with parts of the US electorate was no longer a priority. In conversation with Joseph Goebbels on 8 April, he appeared to take the fact that the invasion of Scandinavia would increase the likelihood of US intervention in his stride. As he put it to the *Reichspropagandaminister*, US materiel help would only begin to make a difference in eight months' time, while an expeditionary army would not be ready for deployment before November 1941. By then, Germany had to be victorious.[54]

Though serious enough in its own right, the campaign in Norway became old news virtually overnight when the German invasion of Western Europe commenced on 10 May. By 15 May, it had become clear that the Allied defence had been completely outwitted by a concentrated armoured thrust through the Ardennes; a decisive German victory in the course of the next week or so seemed like a definite possibility. With this, one of the two pillars which had originally guaranteed the order of Versailles (the Royal Navy and the French Army) would be no more, opening up all sorts of mind-boggling possibilities. While disastrous in and of themselves, these momentous events also provided the US President with an unexpected opportunity to impress on an isolationist public the dangers of standing aside from the ongoing conflict. In a major speech to both Houses of Congress on 16 May, he asked for a defence budget for the next fiscal year (starting in July) of $1 billion. He also spoke of the need to physically occupy Greenland, Iceland and the Azores in order to guarantee the hemispheric security of the country. If one allows for the fact that only five weeks before, Congress had seen fit to slash the proposed defence budget of $1.5 billion by half, the political ramifications of Heinz Guderian's break-through at Sedan were nothing short of remarkable: the President in fact got $2 billion, to be raised to a total of $3 billion by the end of the next month.

The German attaché, who had to report on these events, stressed that the USA would not enter the war, irrespective of what some pundits had been predicting. He also dwelt at length on the mismatch between the funds voted and the means (training establishments and factories) available to actually produce the needed assets. There was some reason behind this, especially when the new British government asked for arms with which to re-equip the soldiers

---

[53] 'Der Geschäftsträger in Washington an das Auswärtige Amt (10. April 1940)', in: ADAP, Serie D, Bd.IX, pp 95–6.
[54] Elke Fröhlich (ed.) *Die Tagebücher von Joseph Goebbels*, Teil I, Bd. 8 (München: KG Saur 1998), p 41 (entry for 9 April 1940). Henceforth quoted as TB Goebbels.

of the British Expeditionary Force (BEF), who had escaped the Germans' clutches through the port of Dunkirk in little more than the clothes they stood up in. Making use of a little-known law from Great War days, and over the vocal opposition of some officers in the US Army,[55] Roosevelt ordered a substantial number of mothballed infantry weapons to be turned over to the British to help them ward off a possible invasion.[56] It was crucial help, but it also served to highlight the inadequacy of the US military–industrial complex of the time.

Both in Berlin and Washington, the next few weeks were spent assessing the extent of the Allied defeat as it unfolded and whether the British would still be willing to pursue the war at the end of it. The escape of the bulk of the BEF through Dunkirk ensured that the scale of their defeat would be just shy of catastrophic, and one month later the raid on the French Navy's base at Mers-el-Kébir showed that the British government was not yet in the mood for surrender. In Washington, this meant that Roosevelt could start to cast about for means with which to convince the general public that Britain's cause was worthy of continued support. He was aided in this by a mood change which indicated a polarisation among US voters. On the one hand was a sizeable minority, encompassing some genuinely pro-German, pro-fascist or anti-Semitic elements, but mostly made up of the considerable number of people who had been sufficiently impressed or even shocked by German successes into calling for a purely defensive strategy to defend the Western Hemisphere. On the other hand was a slowly growing majority, which began to show an inclination to support the enemies of the Axis powers with measures that would inevitably go beyond Cash-and-Carry. The former group counted among its supporters a number of eminent citizens like former President Herbert Hoover, Generals Robert E. Wood[57] and Charles P. Summerall,[58] newspaper magnates Robert McCormick and William Randolph Hearst, aviation legends Eddie Rickenbacker and Charles Lindbergh, former ambassador John Cudahy,[59] the three surviving children

---

[55] Or as then Major Walter Bedell Smith put it in light of a likely sudden American need: 'Everyone who was a party to the deal might hope to be found hanging from a lamp post'; Richard M. Leighton and Robert W. Coakley, *The War Department: Global Logistics and Strategy, 1940–1943* (Washington DC: Office of the Chief of Military History, Department of the Army 1955), p 35.

[56] Amongst them 25,000 Browning automatic rifles, half a million Enfield rifles, 895 75mm field guns and 129 million rounds of small arms ammunition. Ibid., p 33.

[57] Retired US Army brigadier; Chairman of Sears Roebuck & Co. (1939–1954).

[58] US Army Chief of Staff, November 1926–November 1930; President of The Citadel since 1931.

[59] Ambassador to Poland (September 1933–April 1937), Ireland (August 1937–January 1940) and Belgium and Luxembourg (January–July 1940). In April 1941, during his last visit to the German capital prior to returning to the USA, he secured interviews with Goebbels and Hitler.

of President Theodor Roosevelt[60] and architect Frank Lloyd Wright. It organised itself in the No Foreign Wars (June 1940–April 1941) and the America First (September 1940–December 1941) committees. The latter in particular achieved quite a mass following, but struggled to match the cohesion of the Committee to Defend America by Aiding the Allies under its founder and chairman, Republican newspaper editor William Allen White. The Committee turned into a very effective pressure group which, needless to say, enjoyed the full support of the Roosevelt administration.

Much more important, however, was the posture of the opposition Republican Party. The year 1940 would bring Presidential elections, and many Republicans had proven themselves to be vocal isolationists. It was of the highest significance that during a convention held in Philadelphia between 25 and 30 June, and thus overshadowed by the most recent Allied defeats in Western Europe, the party chose as its presidential candidate businessman Wendell Willkie, whose views on the war were virtually identical to Roosevelt's. Taking stock of this development, the German envoy admitted quite candidly that 'for us, Willkie's nomination is an unpleasant development'.[61]

Encouraged by these shifts in the political and public mood, the President was able to carry on with further measures to prepare Americans for the likelihood of war reaching their hemisphere. In order to put his government on a more bipartisan footing, he secured the services of two moderate Republicans for two key positions in his government. Henry Stimson and Frank Knox were respectively sworn in as secretaries of war and the navy on 10 and 11 July.[62] In the meantime, Congressman Carl Vinson of Georgia, in close cooperation with the White House, was putting the finishing touches to a bill which would define his long career as a legislator like no other. As the French collapse unfolded, Congress was getting ready to vote on the so-called Third Vinson Bill, which had been put before the legislators before the invasion of Western Europe. By that time, the 11 per cent increase in naval strength which had eventually been arrived at after much compromise, no longer reflected the critical situation of the Allied powers. On the day the President signed it into

---

[60] Theodore Roosevelt Jr. held the rank of a colonel in the US Army Reserve. He was a particular catch for the isolationist movement not just because he was a distant relative of the sitting President, but because he was widely known to have espoused progressive causes throughout most of his life. See Marc Wortman, *1941: Fighting the Shadow War* (New York: Atlantic Monthly 2016), pp 82–9, 182–4.

[61] 'Der Geschäftsträger in Washington an das Auswärtige Amt (28. Juni 1940)'; in: ADAP, Serie D, Bd. X, p. 41.

[62] The importance of this move is reflected in the tone of the cable sent by Boetticher and Thomsen to Berlin and in which they equate the accession of these two veteran politicians as a case of 'Jewdom now occupying key positions in the leadership of the US armed forces'. See 'Die Botschaft in Washington an das Auswärtige Amt (6. August 1940)'; in: ADAP, Serie D, Bd. X, pp 339–40.

law (14 June), the Germans were on the verge of a major strategic victory and the French a week away from signing an armistice. Accordingly, Vinson started work on the fourth bill to bear his name almost as soon as the third one had passed. He had stood out as an influential spokesman for naval expansion for much of the 1930s, but this latest boost to naval strength took naval expansion to levels (a 70 per cent increase) that would have been completely unthinkable only a few weeks before.[63] The backdrop was, of course, the need to see off simultaneous naval challenges from Japan and the European Axis, a prospect made particularly daunting by the lingering uncertainties that still surrounded the eventual fate of the French (and come to that, British) navies. On 16 July, Congress voted into existence the country's first Two-Ocean Navy, building on and at the same time vastly expanding the Naval Expansion Act of May 1938 and the Third Vinson Act of June 1940. The act authorised additional tonnage of nearly 280,000 tons for aircraft carriers and an increase of 12,000 naval aircraft over the 3,000 already voted in 1938. Cruisers, destroyers and submarines also benefitted, as did fleet auxiliaries, the category which had so far suffered the greatest neglect.[64] The supplementary budget needed to turn this paper fleet into reality would be passed by 6 September – by the standards of the American legislature, an all-time record.[65] The only drawback was that such an armada would take between three and four years to come into existence: new shipyards would need to be built before the keel of many of its ships could even be laid down, and there was a particular shortfall in trained crews. Coincidentally, only hours before he signed the bill into law, the President gave a speech in which he accepted his party's nomination for the presidency. The speech was another scathing attack, which while not mentioning Germany by name, openly referred to the 'totalitarian powers' as 'the enemy' with whom he would brook no compromise. He also reminded his listeners that he had been among the first of the world's statesmen to have warned of this danger to world peace. Ambassador Dieckhoff, commenting on these events from his Berlin exile, accused the President of 'political exhibitionism' and laid the blame for the continuation of this war squarely at his feet, but still advised his masters not to react to this

---

[63] Exploring the extent to which Vinson was mostly an instrument of the White House in this process or actually played a key part in determining the timing and scale of this vast step in naval rearmament lies outside the scope of this work. James F. Cook, *Carl Vinson: Patriarch of the Armed Forces* (Macon, GA: Mercer UP 2004) has argued that the 1940 Acts saw Vinson taking unilateral action that infringed on the constitutional prerogatives of the President.

[64] On the Third and Fourth Vinson Acts, see Dean C. Allard, 'Naval Rearmament, 1930–1941: an American Perspective'; in: Jürgen Rohwer (ed.), *Rüstungswettlauf zur See. 1930–1941* (Bonn: Bernard & Graefe 1991), pp 45–50.

[65] BA/MA, RH 67/49 'Telegramm Marine-Attache Washington Nr. 1904 vom 7.9.40. Betr.: Rüstungsstand der Luftwaffe und Marine in USA – Abschrift (10.9.1940)'.

'provocation' and to keep the German media muzzled. In his view, the great unresolved dilemma for the American President lay in squaring the militancy of such statements with his pledges to keep America out of the war for the remaining three and a half months of the Presidential race. Any German reaction to such polemics would be seen as foreign meddling in American politics and virtually guarantee thousands of votes for Roosevelt from uncommitted citizens.[66]

Only days later, even without the benefit of German meddling, the President gained another adherent. For more than a month, a debate over a British request for the delivery of a number of mothballed US Navy destroyers had been simmering away in the background. Even the German embassy had to admit that such a transfer was not fundamentally different from the half million rifles which had already been delivered to the British as an emergency measure in June and July.[67] In any case, existing laws specifically prohibited the delivery of warships to foreign powers and the mood in both Houses of Congress was very much against it. On 4 August, General of the Armies John J. Pershing, commander of the 1917–18 American Expeditionary Force (AEF), gave a speech over the radio in which he made a powerful case for the delivery of the vessels the British had asked for and also supported the idea of a peacetime draft, which was currently being debated in both Houses of Congress. The German envoy made light of the proposed destroyer deal, bracketing it with a recent statement of Secretary of the Treasury Henry Morgenthau, which had made the clearly absurd promise of monthly deliveries of 3,000 combat planes to the British.[68] When just under one month later, Roosevelt announced to the astounded American public that an expert opinion by the Department of Justice had found a way round the logjam by allowing the President to carry out a straight swap of fifty destroyers for bases in British territories in the Western Hemisphere, envoy Thomsen had to concede that this indicated how secure Roosevelt felt in his policy of support for the British.[69]

If there was still any positive news to be had for the Germans in these weeks, it lay in two areas. Despite some ominous rumours of the USA actually declaring war on the Germans, Thomsen and Boetticher felt confident in predicting that such a move was highly unlikely on account of the Japanese

---

[66] 'Aufzeichnung des Botschafters Dieckhoff (21.7.1940)'; in: ADAP, Serie D, Bd. X, pp 213–14.

[67] 'Der Geschäftsträger in Washington an das Auswärtige Amt (10.8.1940)'; in: ADAP, Serie D, Bd. X, pp 375–6.

[68] 'Die Botschaft in Washington an das Auswärtige Amt (6. 8.1940)'; in: ADAP, Serie D, Bd. X, pp 339–40. Also 'Der Staatssekretär an die Botschaft in Washington (8.8.1940)'; in: ADAP, Serie D, Bd. X, pp 363–4.

[69] 'Der Geschäftsträger in Washington an das Auswärtige Amt (3.9.1940)'; in: ADAP, Serie D, Bd. XI.1, pp 10–12.

threat and, more importantly, the opposition it was likely to encounter among the general public and its representatives in Washington.[70] Closely tied in with this was the issue of the lack of material and, more crucially, human assets that was currently limiting the speed with which American rearmament could progress. On 29 August, both German representatives took great pleasure in listing for their superiors in Berlin some of the problems US industry was currently encountering on its road to a wartime footing. A perennial lack of skilled labour was turning out to be the greatest obstacle by far, with the army arsenal at Philadelphia having announced 3,000 vacancies but managing to recruit only 98 workers. Most of the blue-collar workforce available was tied up in civilian jobs, which it was proving reluctant to leave. To solve this particular problem, Boetticher and Thomsen ventured to suggest, nothing less than dictatorial prerogatives for the President would suffice.[71] The German leader's prediction from a fortnight before that meaningful quantities of US help for Great Britain would not materialise 'for a long time yet' appeared to be borne out by the facts.[72]

American moves to confront the Third Reich took many forms, however. Congress granting permission to the President on 27 August to take the National Guard into Federal service for a year would not have shaken Boetticher out of his complacency,[73] but the passing of the Burke–Wadsworth Bill, which called for a full-blown draft, was a different matter altogether. When the House of Representatives passed it on 7 September, it gave the United States its first ever peacetime draft. It allowed for the yearly induction – starting the following month – of 900,000 men, more than doubling overall army strength at the stroke of a pen.[74] Unlike the National Guard, whose military skills even the open-minded Werner von Blomberg had belittled in his report on his 1930 visit,[75] a proper army of draftees was something a veteran European soldier like Boetticher could relate to. The cable to Berlin which assessed the consequences of this momentous change – it had undoubtedly been composed by the military attaché – was quite remarkable both for its brevity and the fact that it was rather muted in its tone.

---

[70] On 18 August, Thomsen even described such resistance as '*unwiderstehlich*' (insurmountable). See 'Der Geschäftsträger in Washington an das Auswärtige Amt (18. August 1940)'; in: ADAP, Bd. X, pp 418–19.

[71] BA/MA, RH 67/49 'Telegramm Washington Nr. 1843 vom 29.8.1940'.

[72] Klaus Gerbet (ed.), *Generalfeldmarschall Fedor von Bock. Zwischen Pflicht und Verweigerung. Das Kriegstagebuch* (München: Herbig 1995), p 165 (entry for 14 August 1940).

[73] Shrader, *Reference Guide*, p 6.

[74] Jonathan Kaufmann and Horst Kaufmann, *The Sleeping Giant: American Armed Forces between the Wars* (Westport, CT: Praeger 1996), p 173; Geoffrey Perret, *There's a War To Be Won: The United States Army in World War II* (New York: Random House 1991), p 29.

[75] BA/MA, RH 2/1825 'Generalleutnant Werner von Blomberg. Bericht über mein Kommando zu der Armee der Vereinigten Staaten (1.1.1931)', pp 95–9.

It ended with the following sentence: 'Over the course of 1941 and until the very latest the summer of 1942, the full readiness of an army of 1.2 million well-trained men endowed with high morale and armed with the best equipment will be a given. The same goes for a steadily growing air force of the first order.'[76]

In the following weeks, once the dust had settled on the momentous events of the spring and summer of 1940, Thomsen and especially Boetticher took stock of the Roosevelt administration's attempts to reposition itself in the new global order created by Germany's victories. In this, they were able to take heart from two things. First, as already stated, the USA faced a superhuman task in bringing its armed forces up to a level that would facilitate true hemispheric defence, to say nothing of large-scale intervention abroad. Second, Germany's quasi-ally Japan was finally stirring. In yet another attempt to cut off Nationalist China's links with the outside world, the Japanese government forced the French Vichy government to accept a partial occupation of northern Vietnam by the Imperial Army, thus severing the route from Haiphong harbour into Kumming province. The occupation was initiated on 23 September and promptly brought a US embargo on scrap metal exports in its wake. In and of itself only a moderately severe act of retaliation (exports of iron ore were still allowed to continue for a while[77]), it became yesterday's news much faster than anticipated, when on 27 September Berlin, Tokyo and Rome announced to the world that they had entered the Tripartite Pact – the first formal military alliance among the three powers. It purported to be a defensive alliance, which would be enacted the moment any of the signatories found itself under attack by a nation not yet involved in the current conflicts in China and Europe. Article 5 excluded the USSR from this arrangement, thus unambiguously expressing the treaty's anti-American agenda.[78]

Boetticher took these developments in his stride. He stressed how baffled the Americans had been left by the announcement of the Tripartite Pact, which was broadly accurate, though not without problems of its own.[79] As far as the embargoing of scrap iron was concerned, he seemed certain of two things. First, the Americans were unlikely to shift gear anytime soon and enact embargoes (especially on oil), which might have the potential to really cripple

---

[76] 'Die Botschaft in Washington an das Auswärtige Amt (14. September 1940)'; in: ADAP, Serie D, Bd. XI.1, pp 68–9.

[77] By the end of the year, iron ore, pig iron, ferro-alloys, nickel, copper and zinc had all been included in a licensing system which prioritised US needs and soon reduced exports to foreign countries other than the United Kingdom to a mere trickle. See Michael A. Barnhart, *Japan Prepares for Total War: The Search for Economic Security, 1919–1941* (Ithaca and London: Cornell UP 1987), pp 194–7.

[78] The full text of the treaty can be found in ADAP, Serie D, Bd. XI.1., pp 175–6.

[79] BA/MA, RH 67/49 'Telegramm Washington Nr. 2079 vom 28.9.1940. Wehrpolitische Wirkung des deutsch-italienisch-japanischen Vertrages'.

the Japanese economy. Second, even if they did, he was fairly confident the Japanese would resort to retaliatory measures which were likely to see them emerge victorious in view of the sufficient stockpiles they had been hoarding against such an eventuality. To judge by the question marks the recipient at OKH put against these optimistic assertions, this seems to have been one occasion where the general had failed to convince his superiors.[80] It appears he was then prodded for specifics, some of which he provided in a telegram on 4 October. Here, apart from giving figures for the scrap metal the Japanese would now have to forego, he finally had to admit that the extent to which Tokyo had managed to stockpile a number of key raw materials was 'a big mystery'.[81] Even so, he kept insisting in the following days, the American President could do little besides resorting to aimless hectic activity in his leadership circle and outright propaganda in order to cover up the 'mighty blow' delivered by Germany and its allies with their Tripartite Pact on 27 September.[82]

It was left to the assistant air attaché, Riedel, to bring to the attention of his superiors a morsel of information almost lost against the background noise of such momentous events. On 21 October, he reported on the state of the American aircraft industry and the problems still afflicting some types of plane. Above all, he drew his superiors' attention to the fact that in the last few days, the remaining problems with respect to a new taxation regime which had stood in the way of private companies accepting virtually unlimited government orders had finally been removed. For a start, most existing plants would now be considerably expanded, leading to a doubling of nationwide output per month to about 1,500 planes by July 1941.[83]

As October turned to November, the wild card in the deck for the Germans was the question of Roosevelt's re-election. It was, of course, an unprecedented event by virtue of the fact that he was running for a third term, even though his opponent Wendell Willkie's broad agreement with him on foreign policy took much of the sting out of it. On the campaign trail, Roosevelt had assured voters that his policy of supporting Britain was the safest way to keep the Germans at

---

[80] Ibid.

[81] BA/MA, RH 67/53 'Deutsche Botschaft. Der Militär- und Luftattache. Beurteilung eines vollen Warenembargos der Vereinigten Staaten gegenüber Japan (4.10.1940)'. Even though on this occasion he was unable to marshal any supporting evidence whatsoever, Boetticher's hunch turned out to be correct: Japanese scrap metal imports from the USA had in fact been so substantial (an average 1.7 million tons per year between 1937 and 1940) that the stockpile accumulated in Japan was enough to last for most of the war. See Edward S. Miller, *Bankrupting the Enemy: The US Financial Siege of Japan before Pearl Harbor* (Annapolis: USNIP 2007), pp 89–93.

[82] 'Die Botschaft in Washington an das Auswärtige Amt (9.10.1940)'; in: ADAP, Serie D, Bd. X.I, pp 232–4.

[83] BA/MA, RH 67/49 'Abt. Ausland/Abwehr. Vortragsnotiz. Betr.: Stand der amerikanischen Luftindustrie (21.10.1940)'.

bay, and hence America out of the war. Enough of the voters were convinced by this and by the prospect of an old hand in the White House in uncertain times to return him to the White House on 5 November, albeit it with a reduced majority in both the Senate and the House of Representatives. Despite an elaborate scheme to financially support the Willkie campaign,[84] the German leadership appears to have been more or less resigned to this outcome. If the dire prediction by the US ambassador to Bulgaria, George H. Earle III, that a re-election would be followed by an American declaration of war two days later,[85] was actually put before Hitler, he was left unimpressed by it. On the very eve of the American elections he held a conference with most of the army leadership in the Neue Reichskanzlei, during which he described US intervention in Europe as possible, though not likely to happen before 1942. If *Generaloberst* Franz Halder's notes are anything to go by, the looming US elections did not even rate a mention. Either Roosevelt's re-election was assumed as a given, or Willkie seen as just as hostile to the Axis.[86] Envoy Thomsen's assessment the day after the polls reflected this mood. In a report which bears the date of 6 November, he did not express the slightest surprise at the President's triumph. He also wrote that Roosevelt's main aim would continue to be 'to contribute to bring the totalitarian powers to their knees or, in case of the defeat of democracy's last bulwark in Europe, to resume and continue this fight from American soil'.[87]

Just over a week after Roosevelt's re-election, Hitler went on record for the first time as discussing the specifics of possible military action against the continental United States. During a conversation with Admiral Erich Raeder, he raised the desirability of one day seizing the Azores archipelago. The reason he gave was that this would give him 'the only possibility to attack America with a modern Messerschmitt bomber of 12,600 km [7,830 mile] range in case of that country entering the war; this would

---

[84] If an incomplete documentary record is to be believed, Göring's Mexico-based trouble-shooter, Joachim Hertslet, was able to dip into a fund of $5 million to support Willkie and a number of key personalities close to him, especially labour leader John L. Lewis. The use of intermediaries close to the isolationist camp, like oilman William Rhodes Davis, was a key element in this plan and has made it difficult to assess whether Willkie could have known, or at least suspected, where some of his monetary support was coming from. For a useful, though not yet exhaustive, account of this affair, see Dale Harrington, *Mystery Man: William Rhodes Davis, Nazi Agent of Influence* (Dulles, VA: Brassey's 1999), pp 137–61, esp. pp 144–55.

[85] PA/AA, Inland II g 337 'Der Chef der Sicherheitspolizei und des SD an den Reichsminister des Auswärtigen. Betr.: Haltung der USA und der Sowjetunion zur europäischen Lage (24.9.1940)'.

[86] Hans-Adolf Jacobsen (ed.), *Generaloberst Halder. Kriegstagebuch.* Bd. II (Stuttgart: W. Kohlhammer 1963), p 165 (entry for 4 November 1940).

[87] 'Der Geschäftsträger in Washington an das Auswärtige Amt (6.11.1940)'; in: ADAP, Serie D, Bd. XI.1, pp 402–4.

force the Americans to build an anti-aircraft arm for their own use, rather than helping Britain in that regard'.[88]

The long-term prospect of a US–German clash undoubtedly also inspired the all-out diplomatic effort by Hitler and Ribbentrop in October and November 1940 to convince the Franco regime in Madrid to join them in their war against the British Empire. A first step would see a joint German–Spanish attack on the British fortress of Gibraltar, to be followed by the Luftwaffe and Kriegsmarine setting up base facilities on one of the islands of the Canaries archipelago. The Spanish dictator ultimately declined, citing the devastation left by the recent civil war in his country. Belligerence would bring in its train a British blockade and a termination of the trickle of fuel and grain imports from the Western Hemisphere, which thus far had staved off economic collapse and widespread famine in Spain. While older scholarship has focused on the importance of Gibraltar as a thorn in the Axis side, more recently Norman Goda has made a compelling case for an alternative explanation. According to this, Gibraltar would have been but a means to an end, since its elimination would have allowed the Germans to cross to the African continent and establish a military presence in French Morocco.[89] The agenda behind this intended move is best described as one of 'hemispheric security' and was actually remarkably prescient. As the events of November 1942 would show, Morocco was indeed one of the more obvious points of entry where the as yet untested armed forces of the USA could hope to establish a sizable lodgement on the fringes of *Festung Europa*. Hitler was forced to respect the decision of his lukewarm fascist ally, but made a mental note to raise the issue again after the fall of the USSR.[90]

Whether by coincidence or not, it was around this time that Germany's intelligence gatherers redoubled their efforts to produce the raw data needed to gauge American mobilisation. Even the Sicherheitsdienst, whose reports had so far shown a tendency to focus on intelligence gathered among US expats, especially diplomats, now turned to the sort of research customarily done by Boetticher and Riedl in Washington. On 27 November and 2 December, it produced two voluminous reports on US rearmament in general and expansion of industrial plant in particular.[91] They confirmed in some detail what

---

[88] 'Seekriegsleitung I op 2486/40, Besprechung des Ob.d.M. beim Führer am 14.11.40, 13 Uhr'; in: Wagner (ed.), *Lagevorträge*, p 154. For a detailed analysis of the role accorded to the Me-264 in Hitler's ideas on confronting the USA, see the chapter on the Luftwaffe.

[89] Norman J. W. Goda, *Tomorrow the World: Hitler, Northwest Africa and the Path toward America* (College Station: Texas A & M UP 1998), pp 194–202.

[90] Goda, *Tomorrow the World*, pp 165–8.

[91] PA/AA, Inland II g, 337 'Der Chef der Sicherheitspolizei und des SD an den Reichsminister des Auswärtigen. Betr.: Amerikanische Luftrüstung (27.11.1940)'; ibid., 'Der Chef der Sicherheitspolizei und des SD an den Reichsminister des Auswärtigen (2.12.1940)'.

Riedl had already reported on 21 October: after receiving government guarantees which amounted to an underwriting of both existing and future orders by
the US government, many factories were now doubling or trebling in size.
A sudden outbreak of peace was not something the US administration
appeared to be willing to factor into its calculations. In contrast to
Boetticher's reports, which show a certain persistence in castigating
Roosevelt's 'Jewish' advisers while drawing attention to every short-term
obstacle in the Americans' way, those compiled by the Sicherheitsdienst were
driven by a wholly different approach. They tended to provide little in the way
of context, and neither judgement nor even predictions were offered. The facts
were laid out before the reader and allowed to speak for themselves.

By late November, both foreign and domestic observers began wondering
aloud how much longer Britain would be in a position to pay for US war
materiel, Cash-and-Carry, after all, laying equal stress on straight payment as
well as the means of transport. On 22 November, during one of his informal
press chats in the White House, Roosevelt was adamant in refuting any
rumours that his administration was contemplating extending either unlimited credit to Britain or providing UK-bound convoys with US naval escort.[92]
Further confirmation of this attitude came the German embassy's way on
30 November, when they learned from a dependable source that the British
ambassador Lord Lothian had been given a 'dressing down' in the White
House by the President, who felt increasingly badgered by British cries for
assistance. The same source, Thomsen reported, had identified Baruch and
Morgenthau (who, curiously enough, on this occasion were not vilified as
'bearers of Jewish influence') as the key element in advising the President to
make sure the British had spent every last bit of their cash before even
contemplating unlimited loans.[93]

Only seventeen days later, Roosevelt all but reversed his position when
during a press conference which was no doubt called to test the waters, he
hinted at a possible alternative: Britain would receive no credit, but should
be free to go on acquiring arms and munitions, provided they were manu-
factured in the United States. He likened this to allowing one's neighbour
the use of a garden hose in case of a fire breaking out in their home. The
Johnson Act, the President went on to add, would not be rescinded. On
29 December 1940 he explained the idea to American radio listeners, in
what would become one of his most famous Fireside Chats. He impressed
on his listeners the fallacy of believing in a compromise peace with the Axis
powers that could be both enduring and just. The corollary to this was to

---

[92] PA/AA, Inland II g 337, 'Der Chef der Sicherheitspolizei und des SD and den
Reichsminister des Auswärtigen (3.12.1940)'.
[93] 'Der Geschäftsträger in Washington an das Auswärtige Amt (30.11.1940)'; in: ADAP,
Serie D, Bd. XI.2, pp 627–8.

extend every conceivable support to Greece and China as well as to Britain and its Dominions, as the only countries actually fighting the aggressor states. In order to do so, the United States of America would have to turn itself into the 'arsenal of democracy'. With regards to the possibility of the USA actually becoming a belligerent, he stuck to the line he had used on the campaign trail: it was preferable that Europeans do the fighting now rather than Americans in the near future. It was perhaps significant, however, that in the key sentence he rejected the idea of 'sending armies to Europe', and thus did not specifically rule out other options, like allowing volunteer American airmen to serve in the RAF and one day even deploying US Navy destroyers to escort convoys. On neither of the two days did Roosevelt go into the specifics of how the embattled Allies were supposed to pay for this cornucopia of materiel, since it must have been clear to any observer even superficially conversant with military affairs that only a small fraction of military equipment delivered in 'garden hose fashion' would be returned intact at the end of the war. His State of the Union Address, which he delivered on 6 January 1941 (it became known as the Four Freedoms Speech), while still vague on the details, at least spelt out unambiguously that the real issue was the looming bankruptcy of Britain in the near future. He also suggested that payment for any deliveries taking place after Congress had passed new legislation on the matter would have to be deferred until well after the war and even then might have to be in kind.

Thomsen's commentary on these events is remarkable insofar as he does not seem to have grasped the full implications of what the President was proposing. After the 'garden hose' press conference, he emphasised that the stress put by Roosevelt on delivering finished products, rather than (as had been the case in World War I) mere monetary credit made perfect sense. In this way, even in the case of the British being defeated or forced into a compromise peace, in the following months the USA would be left immeasurably strengthened and in possession of the shipyards, factories and training facilities it was likely to need should it ever have to confront Germany on its own.[94] After the fireside chat of 29 December, Thomsen put to his superiors in Berlin that the address had primarily been aimed at putting the fear of God into his countrymen in order to ease the transition to a war economy, encourage Britain to fight on and manoeuvre the German government into a position where an outbreak of open hostilities could be blamed on Berlin.[95] The speech had been well received among the political class in Washington DC mainly because it was vague and offered few

---

[94] 'Der Geschäftsträger in Washington an das Auswärtige Amt (19.12.1940)'; in: ADAP, Serie D, Bd. XI.2, pp 755–6.
[95] 'Der Geschäftsträger in Washington an das Auswärtige Amt (31.12.1940)'; in: ADAP, Serie D, Bd. XI.2, pp 823–4.

specifics. As far as Thomsen was concerned, it offered little that was new ('*geringen Neuigkeitswerts der Rede*').[96] The envoy returned to this theme in the report he wrote on the State of the Union Address. According to Thomsen, Roosevelt's first priority at this stage was to concoct an alibi for his administration in case the British were to go down in defeat at some point in the next few months. This appeared a definite possibility for all sorts of reasons, not the least the fact that shipments to Britain were still very far from giving the besieged island nation a substantial safety margin with which to face a protracted German assault.[97] Boetticher's assessment, which he delivered on 10 January, at least made a brief reference to the impending change to Cash-and-Carry, but likewise failed to examine the full long-term implications of 'garden hose'– style deliveries of arms and munitions across the Atlantic.[98] That the two diplomats – both of them seasoned observers of Washington politics – should have failed fairly abysmally to realise the full implications of a looming and monumental sea change in the American government's attitude towards the war requires some explanation.

Rather unsurprisingly, both continued to take solace in the fact that American rearmament still had a lot of catching up to do. Apart from that, there is an undercurrent in their reports from those weeks that sees the Anglo–American alliance impaled on the horns of a dilemma: if British defeat at some point around mid-1941 were to be avoided, an American entry into the war was virtually unavoidable. Such an event, however, would mean a sharp drop in vitally needed American deliveries since the needs of the US armed forces would then take precedence to an even greater degree than was already the case. Hence, Roosevelt had to walk a thin line between preparing the American public for war on the one hand, and restraining the political forces thus unleashed on the other. It was thus in the President's interest to find ways which would ensure a long duration of the conflict, an interpretation supported by a contemporary Sicherheitsdienst report.[99] The new factor which appears to have occupied Thomsen's and, above all, Boetticher's minds more than before was Japan. The empire and the threat it posed to the Western

---

[96] Ibid.

[97] BA/MA, RH 67/49 'Thomsen an Auswärtiges Amt (6.1.1941)'. The notion that Roosevelt's chief concern might already lie in disassociating himself from a likely British defeat was emphatically rejected by the German admiralty. Werner Rahn and Gerhard Schreiber (eds.), *Kriegstagebuch der Seekriegsleitung 1939–1945. Teil A*, Bd. 17, (Bonn: Mittler und Sohn 1990), p 108 (entry for 9 January 1941).

[98] BA/MA, RH 67/49 'Amt Ausl./Abw – Telegramm Washington Nr. 74 vom 10.1.1941. Geheime Reichssache (15.1.1941)'. The document runs to nearly six pages of neatly typed script.

[99] PA/AA, Inland II g 338 'Der Chef der Sicherheitspolizei und des SD an das Auswärtige Amt. Betr.: USA-Gesandten Earle, Sofia und Montgomery – Aufenthalt in Budapest 10.1.1941 (16.1.1941)'.

possessions in East Asia had already played a part in earlier reports,[100] but after the signing of the Tripartite Pact, its stature had obviously been much enhanced in the eyes of German observers. The envoy stressed that a war on two fronts would cause an even sharper drop in deliveries to Britain than just a US–German conflict. Boetticher, in his report of 10 January, predicted (correctly, as it turned out) that Britain and the USA would attempt to exert pressure on Japan, without as yet resorting to open war, and he expressed some concern at this possibility. Where he differed from Thomsen was in his boundless optimism regarding the likelihood of British defeat, with nearly two pages of the report going into considerable detail about how exactly the USA would react in such a situation with a view to bringing over to its side the British Empire and the Royal Navy.[101] Such speculation is rather remarkable if it is placed in the military context of late December 1940 and early January 1941. While it is true that the Luftwaffe and Kriegsmarine were still in the process of inflicting grievous blows on Britain, Germany's Axis partner, Italy, was fast changing from dubious asset to outright liability, having suffered a series of humiliating defeats at the hands of the Greek Army, the Royal Navy's Fleet Air Arm and the Western Desert Force since early November 1940. These setbacks had been so devastatingly one-sided that they made the Italian armed forces appear completely dysfunctional and, moreover, they made the loss in the near future of the Italian protectorate Albania and Italy's colony Libya, a definite possibility.

A rather more realistic line was followed by Dieckhoff, the ambassador-in-exile. It appears that some people in Berlin had been impressed with the potential behind the latest Roosevelt scheme to get arms to Britain, and they had even expressed the view that having reached such a point, there was no longer a meaningful distinction between being at war with the USA or not. Dieckhoff appears to have felt compelled by their reactions to confront his superiors with a few home truths. He stressed that a United States openly at war with the Axis would sooner or later force most Latin American countries to follow suit, make a peace treaty with Britain virtually impossible and give the President war powers so sweeping that the ensuing mobilisation would allow for the equipment of both the embattled Allies and the US armed forces. This could only be countered by an adamant refusal to fall for provocations of any kind, thus denying Roosevelt the pretext he would need to ask Congress for

---

[100] See, for instance, Thomsen's report of 18 August 1940 which assesses the likelihood of an American declaration of war as low in view of the bulk of the US Navy being tied up in Oahu. 'Der Geschäftsträger in Washington an das Auswärtige Amt (18.8.1940)'; in: ADAP, Serie D, Bd. X, pp 418–19.

[101] BA/MA, RH 67/49 'AmtAusL. Abw – Telegramm Washington Nr. 74 vom 10.1.1941. Geheime Reichssache (15.1.1941)'.

a declaration of war.[102] Remarkably, Dieckhoff – whether because he feared being taken for an appeaser or because this reflected his true feelings – then went on to admit that there was a line in the sand, or rather water, the crossing of which would mean conflict. Should the USA abolish the exclusion zone around the British Isles which kept out US-flagged merchantmen, or should it even escort convoys into British ports, then all necessary 'consequences' would have to be foreseen. However, such a development, the ambassador went on, seemed 'highly unlikely' if the course of action recommended by him were to be adhered to.[103]

How was this contradictory reporting on US affairs received in Berlin? We are fortunate that a copy of a loose minute penned by *Staatssekretär* Ernst von Weizsäcker for Ribbentrop's benefit, and summarising recent reports from Washington, has survived to shed some light on this question. It needs to be remembered that Weizsäcker was widely regarded as a sophisticated old school diplomat who was wise in the ways of the world and hence would often despair at what passed for foreign policy under Hitler. Much of the text discusses the best manner with which to direct German propaganda aimed at the Western Hemisphere in the future. On the two really important points one would expect to feature prominently, the *Staatssekretär* basically followed the cue from his men in Washington. Roosevelt's proposal to allow the Allies purchase of armaments while putting off payment is not even mentioned, while a possible US entry into the war is seen as a threat only if it were to occur concurrently with a British collapse, thus putting Roosevelt in a position to offer 'protection' to both the Royal Navy and much of the British Empire.[104] If Weizsäcker was in any way concerned about US military and industrial potential and the consequences which the full mobilisation of either for the Allied cause might bring in its wake, the document does not betray it.

Once again, it is noteworthy that the reports produced by the Sicherheitsdienst of the SS show a greater tendency to take seriously the threat from the United States than the diplomats in the Wilhelmstraße. A mere ten days after the Lend-Lease Bill had been introduced into the legislative process, one of Reinhard Heydrich's senior subordinates submitted the SD's first assessment of the public debate in the United States on Roosevelt's proposed 'garden hose' scheme. Eschewing the torrent of abuse against 'Jews' and 'Jewdom' so common by now to Boetticher's telegrams, it gave a very factual assessment of the process so far, which came to the conclusion that public

---

[102] 'Aufzeichnung des Botschafters Dieckhoff (9.1.1941)'; in: ADAP, Serie D, Bd. XI.2, pp 883–5.

[103] Ibid. The fact that Dieckhoff used a rather cumbersome phrase ('all consequences pertaining to the spheres of diplomacy, war and propaganda') to drive home this point, suggests that he may not have had a fully blown military commitment by both sides in mind, but just a naval shooting war.

[104] 'Aufzeichnung des Staatssekretärs (16.1.1941)'; in: ADAP, Serie D, Bd. XI.2, p 930.

opinion appeared to be on the President's side and that his chances of getting the bill through both Houses appeared to be reasonably good, provided he agreed to a few compromises. Returning to their more traditional activity of eavesdropping on diplomats' conversations, the Sicherheitsdienst produced two further reports in quick succession, which attempted to capture the mood among US diplomats in Rome and Berlin. The first one echoed an earlier report, in which the US consul in Munich had said to an informer masquerading as an opposition monarchist that, in the event of further tensions between the two countries, Roosevelt would be able to ask for and get a declaration of war from Congress 'anytime'.[105] His counterparts at the Rome embassy were now on record as being pretty much resigned to a US entry into the war with or without a declaration of war; no individual or grouping existed within the USA that was currently capable of challenging the President's war policy.[106] Of particular interest is a note that Dieckhoff appended to the report, in which he described these comments as deliberate rumour-mongering aimed at demoralising the population of Axis countries.[107] The next report is much more extensive and summarises the content of several documents apparently purloined from the American diplomatic bag or photographed during a break-in at the Berlin embassy. The information found therein ranged from the highly sensitive (plans to relocate a large part of German industry to East Prussia in light of increased British air raids[108]), to the nonsensical (the invasion of Britain would be executed in April with the help of a fleet of troop-carrying submarines), to aspects which Boetticher had omitted from his optimistic tour d'horizon, especially the effect that Italy's eclipsing military fortunes were having on neutral opinion. Of particular interest to German readers must have been a reference to the imminent arrival of Boeing B-17 bombers in Britain. These were being delivered together with the revolutionary Norden bombsight, which had turned them into a weapons system of considerable potential and were intended – the report went on – to be used on long-range raids against Berlin. Finally, the possibility of a modus vivendi between Germany and the USA was ruled out unambiguously due to the incompatibility of both countries' economic systems.[109] It is impossible to tell how many of

[105] PA/AA, Inland II g 338 'Der Chef der Sicherheitspolizei und des SD an den Reichsminister des Auswärtigen (17.12.1940)'.

[106] PA/AA, Inland II g 338 'Der Chef der Sicherheitspolizei und des SD an den Reichsminister des Auswärtigen (20.1.1941)'. This in contrast to Boetticher, who kept pinning his hopes on the America First group and Charles Lindbergh in particular.

[107] PA/AA, Inland II g 338 'Note by Dieckhoff (23.1.1941)'.

[108] An idea put by Hitler to an audience of a select few in the Neue Reichskanzlei a fortnight earlier, thus indicating the US embassy had a source among the attendees. See 'Konferenz Hitlers mit führenden deutschen Militärs (9.1.1941)'; in: ADAP, Serie D, Bd. XI.2, pp 879–82.

[109] PA/AA, Inland II g 338 'Der Chef der Sicherheitspolizei und des SD an den Reichsminister des Auswärtigen (24.1.1941)'.

these reports were put before the dictator himself in those days, but for the moment he still appeared to be willing to take his cue from observers who stressed existing American weaknesses. On 22 January, he is on record as remarking to a group of military leaders that 'America, even if it should enter the war, does not constitute a major threat. Far more dangerous is the enormous bloc Russia.'[110]

The following weeks saw German observers busy themselves (in the embassy's case, rather belatedly) with reporting on the public and congressional debates that accompanied the legislative process of the so-called Lend-Lease Act. The Sicherheitsdienst preserved its lead, shooting off a whole batch of reports in the first half of February.[111] Again, the tone of these was remarkably more factual and level-headed than that which permeated Boetticher's missives. The author(s) went into considerable detail in summarising the testimony of key witnesses (ambassadors, military officers, publicists, historians) called to testify on Capitol Hill. While they stressed that the debate in the Senate posed the greater challenge to the administration, they did not express any hopes that the bill might actually be rejected by either of the two houses. This was borne out by the approval of Lend-Lease by the House of Representatives on 8 February.

This chimes with Thomsen's report of 23 February which looked back on how US public opinion had evolved since the Quarantine Speech of 1937. Both on that and a couple of other occasions, Roosevelt had actually found himself rebuffed when he had tried to nudge the American public in the direction of an anti-Axis policy. Taking stock of things now, a fortnight after the passage of Lend-Lease through Congress, Thomsen had to admit that blatantly partisan statements by government officials and legislators, which, according to him, 'were unashamedly aimed at accustoming the general public to the idea of war', were becoming an almost daily occurrence. Even

---

[110] Hans-Adolf Jacobsen (ed.), *Kriegstagebuch des Oberkommandos der Wehrmacht*, Bd. I (Frankfurt a.M.: Bernard & Graefe 1965), pp 274–5 (entry for 22 January 1941).

[111] PA/AA, Inland II g 338 'Der Chef der Sicherheitspolizei und des SD an den Reichsminister des Auswärtigen. Betr.: Weitere Stellungnahmen und Vorschläge zu dem lend-lease bill (5.2.1941)'; 'Inland II g 338 Der Chef der Sicherheitspolizei und des SD an den Reichsminister des Auswärtigen. Betr.: Weiterer Verlauf der Kongressberatungen über das Ermächtigungsgesetz (5.2.1941)'; 'Inland II g, 338 Der Chef der Sicherheitspolizei und des SD an den Reichsminister des Auswärtigen. Betr.: Vernehmungen über die "lend-lease bill" vor dem Senatsausschuss. Erklärung der Ausschussminderheit im Repräsentantenhaus (6.2.1941)'; 'Inland II g, 338 Der Chef der Sicherheitspolizei und des SD an den Reichsminister des Auswärtigen. Betr.: Verabschiedung der "lend-lease bill" durch das Repräsentantenhaus: Fortsetzung der Debatten im Senatsaussenausschuss (11.2.1941)'; 'Inland II g, 338 Der Chef der Sicherheitspolizei und des SD an den Reichsminister des Auswärtigen. Betr.: Wachsender Widerstand gegen das "lend-lease bill" im Senat, letzte Verhandlungen im Repräsentantenhaus vor Verabschiedung des Gesetzes (11.2.1941)'.

flagrant violations of previous pledges or international law, which would have caused a major scandal a year before, were now regarded as par for the course.[112]

Boetticher, in the meantime, was alternating between his usual bullishness and a rare moment of caution. While in mid-February a brief Far Eastern crisis triggered by the Dutch rejection of Japanese demands for economic concessions in the East Indies saw him harp on in an almost triumphalist fashion about American strategic overreach,[113] he adopted a more chastened tone a couple of days later in the context of a report on the projected arsenal of the US Army by mid-1941. The figures for tank production were still woefully inadequate, but those for artillery and infantry weapons were much more satisfactory. Some of these were admittedly modernised leftovers from World War I, but the Garand semi-automatic rifle pointed the way to a degree of sophistication no other army in the world would reach in the near future.[114] According to Boetticher, 'an underestimation of the output possible in 1941, especially in the second half of the year, would be problematic'. Criticism levelled at either the armaments industry or the US armed forces was after all often politically motivated and hence equally 'problematic'. The attaché was quick to point out, however, that he had always predicted this rise accurately.[115] A mere eight days later the general was his old ebullient self again. In a cable which, rather unusually, specified that Army Chief of Staff Franz Halder should also get a personal copy, Boetticher first worked himself into a proper rage – the first six sentences boasted no fewer than four references to 'Jewish influence' of one kind or another. This may well reflect his frustration over the manner in which both he and Thomsen had been caught napping by the emergence of Lend-Lease in early January, its easy passage through Congress, or both. Seeing the writing on the wall, Boetticher took care not to underestimate the problem again ('the empowerment which Roosevelt would receive on the bill's passage has never been given to any other President neither in time of peace nor war'). Then, however, rather predictably, he took solace in the fact that major deliveries would not be possible for at least a few more months and that the option of emptying the US Army's arsenals for Britain's benefit was not really on the table as long as Japan persisted in an even mildly hostile stance. Finally, even an increase in

---

[112] PA/AA, StS USA, Bd. 5, 'Thomsen an Auswärtiges Amt (23.2.1941)'.

[113] PA/AA, StS USA, Bd. 5, 'Boetticher und Thomsen an Auswärtiges Amt (15.2.1941)'; StS USA, Bd. 5, 'Boetticher und Thomsen an Auswärtiges Amt (16.2.1941)'. Though signed by both envoy and attaché, the language used – especially the repetitive reference to American 'bluffing' – makes it easy to identify the author as Boetticher.

[114] The Springfield Armoury was already turning out 560 per day in February 1941. See Leroy Thompson, *The M1 Garand* (Oxford: Osprey 2012), pp 30–1.

[115] PA/AA, StS USA, Bd. 5, 'Boetticher und Thomsen an Auswärtiges Amt (18.2.1941)'.

deliveries would still have to run the gauntlet of the Kriegsmarine's U-boats.[116]

What could have prompted Halder's sudden interest in the pace of US deliveries to Britain? Coincidentally or not, on 8 February – the very day that Lend-Lease was approved by the House of Representatives – the army chief of staff received a report as detailed as it was pessimistic from the OKW's *Wehrwirtschaft- und Rüstungsamt* on Germany's reserves of strategic raw materials. To Halder, who at the time was deeply engrossed in the preparations for the invasion of the Soviet Union, this was deeply unwelcome news and the passage of Lend-Lease through Congress may have thrown into further relief the inadequacies of his preparations for Barbarossa.[117] The head of the *Wehrwirtschafts-und Rüstungsamt* was ordered to prepare a sanitised version of his report to be submitted to Hitler and – it stands to reason – the army chief of staff took a sudden, if only passing, interest in the threat potential of the Lend-Lease Bill currently being debated in Washington. Boetticher did not disappoint. In two further cables sent on 2 and 4 March, he gave detailed figures on the shortfall of American powder production,[118] as well as on problems arising from an overall dearth of machine tools and shortages of copper, tin and aluminium.[119] The looming threat arising from a possible and sudden cessation of East Asian rubber shipments was also mentioned.[120] Finally, on 11 March, three days after Lend-Lease had been passed by the Senate, Boetticher sent another lengthy cable on the subject of 'America's entry into the war'. The distribution list gave Franz Halder as one of only three recipients.

This time, Boetticher returned to his favourite theme of American 'bluffing'. He insisted that there was no need to take American threats of war – veiled or otherwise – more seriously than in 1938, 1939 or 1940. Both the output of American industry and the psychology of the man in the street had by now been pushed to a threshold which might – given the right circumstances – make a declaration of war a practical proposition. However, the hostile stance of Japan, Germany's domination of continental Europe, shortage of merchant shipping tonnage and the lack of a modern air force all but ruled out such a course of action. The last two points might be rectified with time and hence Britain, China and the minor allies still had an important role to play, namely to keep the Tripartite powers busy until such time as the USA might actually enter hostilities with a minimum of risk. Boetticher conceded that Roosevelt's

---

[116] 'Die Botschaft in Washington an das Auswärtige Amt (26.2.1941)', in: ADAP, Serie D, Bd. XII.1, pp 132–5.

[117] On the events of those days at Oberkommando des Heeres, see the excellent account by Stahel. David Stahel, *Operation Barbarossa and Germany's Defeat in the East* (Cambridge: CUP 2009), pp 85–6.

[118] BA/MA, RH 67/49 'Telegramm aus Washington, Nr. 550 (2.3.1941)'.

[119] BA/MA, RH 67/49 'Geheimtelegramm aus Washington Nr. 565 (4.3.1941)'.

[120] Ibid.

possible reaction in the face of a serious incident might prove to be the wild card in this deck, but he was confident of the US Army's General Staff reining him in.[121] Though the United States as a major player is mostly absent from Franz Halder's personal war diary, he appears to have been sufficiently concerned about the disruption which a US entry into the war might have inflicted on his already shambolic timetable for Barbarossa that he took the unusual step of sending Boetticher a personal thank you note.[122]

As Thomsen had already elaborated on 9 March, irrespective of a lively debate on the Senate floor, Lend-Lease was never likely to fail because so many people in the United States agreed with the basic idea behind it. The best that Berlin could have hoped for would have been a watering down of the Bill by amendments limiting either the type of weapons systems deemed surplus to domestic requirements or the number of countries which could receive them.[123] The administration's supporters managed to block most of these attempts but had to accept a time limit of slightly more than two years on the law as well as a maximum ceiling for expenditure. Congress was also granted the right to withdraw the bill by a simple majority vote.[124] The maximum figure for expenditure was still to be determined in a separate debate, but Thomsen did not extend the slightest hope that the outcome of that vote might somehow hamstring Land-Lease. He was, of course, right not to. When the House of Representatives voted on the proposal to set a provisional maximum limit of $7 billion to Lend-Lease the response was nothing short of overwhelming, with 336 congressmen casting votes in favour, and a mere 55 against. The one proposed amendment that might have limited the impact of the Bill (excluding repairs to foreign naval vessels from Lend-Lease since such practice violated the 1939 Declaration of Panama) was rejected.[125]

What was the upshot of all of this as seen from Berlin? Based on the available evidence, it seems doubtful that even one of the staff officers and diplomats who supplied Hitler with intelligence on US affairs truly grasped the enormity of what they had just witnessed. As we have already seen, Thomsen initially

---

[121] 'Die Botschaft in Washington an das Auswärtige Amt (11.3.1941)'; in ADAP, Serie D, Bd. XII.1, pp 219–21. Even though co-signed by envoy Thomsen, the persistent use of the singular betrays the sole author to be once again Boetticher.

[122] PA/AA, StS USA, Bd. 5, 'OKH/Gen.St.d.H. an Gen.d.Art. v. Boetticher persönl. (1.4.1941)'. Though thanking the attaché both in his name and that of Army Commander-in-Chief Brauchitsch for his 'excellent' ('ausgezeichnet') work in general, Halder made a point of singling out the 'valuable' telegram No. 631 of 11 March for special praise.

[123] For a discussion of the proposed opposition amendments as seen from a German point of view, see 'Thomsen an Auswärtiges Amt (8.3.1941)' and 'Thomsen an Auswärtiges Amt (9.3.1941)', both in PA/AA, StS USA, Bd. 5.

[124] For a full text of the Lend-Lease Bill in its final form, see PA/AA, StS USA, Bd. 5, 'Thomsen an Auswärtiges Amt (13.3.1941)'.

[125] PA/AA, StS USA, Bd. 5, 'Thomsen an Auswärtiges Amt (25.3.1941)'.

failed to grasp the implications of Roosevelt's 'garden hose' approach to supplying Britain. Boetticher, meanwhile, after a brief moment of insecurity, was soon back at his old habit of applying a magnifying glass to every American weakness, and Weizsäcker appears to have been downright blasé about the whole thing. Ambassador Dieckhoff, in a report from 10 March, fell in line with Boetticher (something he had avoided so far) by stressing that some months would go by before the shipments made possible by the bill would actually make a difference to Britain's defences. Even so, he went on to say, the bill's propagandistic impact would be 'quite significant'.[126] After the Senate had passed Lend-Lease, Thomsen admitted that the effect would be a prolongation of the war.[127] This dovetailed with one of Boetticher's big themes: just about everything the Roosevelt administration did had to be seen under the aspect of its desperate need to 'play for time'. None of the memos and cables signed by these experts comes even close to conveying the enormity of the events and the simple fact that they were synonymous with a mortal threat to Nazi Germany. The only way to checkmate Lend-Lease lay in a total and irredeemable defeat of Britain in the near future, something that was not on the cards and had in fact just been rendered even more unlikely in light of Italy's military setbacks in Africa and Europe.

It appears that Hitler was much more alive to this threat than his diplomats. Exactly one week after the passage of Lend-Lease through the House of Representatives, he dwelt at length on the subject of American assertiveness and what might be done to check it. The way he saw it, Japan had to 'take possession of Singapore and all territories rich in raw materials which it might need for the continuation of the war, especially in case of an American intervention. The longer Japan hesitates, the stronger America will become, and Japan's task will be rendered more difficult. . . . All those military operations which Germany would like to see executed in the interest of its own struggle against England and possibly against America too, must be listed. In exchange for this, the Japanese must be granted generous access to Germany's military experience as well as given permission to build under license modern weaponry and equipment.'[128] The issuing of Directive 24 on future cooperation with Japan on 5 March was the automatic manifestation of this. In it, Hitler instructed his military and naval leadership to accommodate the Japanese wherever possible with a view to encouraging a move by Germany's new Tripartite partner, which would take the Americans' focus away from Europe. Interestingly enough, the ultimate aim was a timely British defeat in the Far East which would help Hitler to 'keep the USA out of the

---

[126] 'Aufzeichnung des Botschafters Dieckhoff (10.3.1941)'; in: ADAP, Serie D, Bd. XII.1, pp 213–14.

[127] 'Der Geschäftsträger in Washington an das Auswärtige Amt (9.3.1941)'; in: ADAP, Serie D, Bd. XII.1, p 207.

[128] KTB OKW, Bd. I, pp 328–9 (entry for 17 February 1941).

war'.[129] Once the President's signature turned Lend-Lease into a reality on 11 March, however, the German dictator entered a brief period (between three and four weeks) during which he clearly contemplated options which did not sit easily with the idea of keeping the USA out of the war. On 15 March he gave first instructions for the waters around Iceland to be included in the war zone where U-boats were free to sink on sight.[130] This measure was announced publicly ten days later and justified as a reprisal for Lend-Lease.[131] When during a briefing on naval affairs Admiral Raeder raised the issue of the US Neutrality Zone, the dictator promised to reconsider the problem posed by it and even suggested the possibility of ignoring it altogether; in such a case the Kriegsmarine would only be barred from US territorial waters. On 19 March, Hitler directed the Seekriegsleitung to look into the possibility of penetrating the main US Navy bases on the east coast with several U-boats with a view to repeating the feat of Günther Prien against Scapa Flow in October 1939 – his most unambiguous instruction to date with regards to how hostilities with the USA might be opened.[132] On 24 March, his inner circle was given a unique insight into how he read the latest developments. Talking to a small group made up of Speer, Keitel, Jodl, Borman and his army adjutant, Engel, any thought of just keeping the USA out of the war had obviously receded. He stated that 'the Americans have finally let the cat out of the bag; if one felt so inclined, it would be legitimate to interpret this as an act of war. He was now in a position to allow a war to break out without further ado. However, right now, it was not something he was keen on. The war with the US was sure to come sooner or later anyway. Roosevelt and the Jewish financiers have no other choice to than to strive for this war, since a German victory in Europe would mean enormous financial losses for the American Jews. It is merely regrettable that as yet no planes existed which could bomb American cities. This is a lesson he would like to teach the American Jews. To be sure, this new Lease Law would bring him additional major problems. He had now come to the conclusion that its success could only be prevented by ruthless naval warfare.'[133]

3.4 Inching towards War: April–December 1941

On the morning of 30 March 1941 slightly more than 100 senior Wehrmacht officers gathered in one of the halls of the Neue Reichskanzlei in Berlin. They

---

[129] 'Oberkommando der Wehrmacht, WFSt/Abt.L (I Op) Nr. 44 282/41 g.K. Chefs. Weisung Nr. 24 über Zusammenarbeit mit Japan (5.3.1941)'; in: Walther Hubatsch (ed.), *Hitlers Weisungen für die Kriegführung 1939-1945. Dokumente des Oberkommandos der Wehrmacht* (Koblenz: Bernard & Graefe 1983), pp 103–5.

[130] KTB Seekriegsleitung, Teil A (entry for 15 March 1941). See also 'Aufzeichnung des Botschafters Ritter (14.3.1941)'; in: ADAP, Serie D, Bd. XII.1 p 243.

[131] 'OKW/WFSt/Abt.L (IK Op) 44363/41 g.K. Chefs. (25.3.1941), Weisung des Oberkommandos der Wehrmacht (25.3.1941)'; in: ADAP, Serie D, Bd. XII.1, p 299.

[132] KTB Seekriegsleitung, Teil A, (entries for 19 and 22 March 1941).

[133] Kotze (ed.), *Aufzeichnungen Engel*, p 99 (entry for 24 March 1941).

included the service chiefs, a number of senior officers from assorted high commands as well as all the commanders-in-chief (together with their chiefs of staff) of the army groups, armies, *Panzergruppen*, air fleets and air corps which would invade the Soviet Union in June.[134] Before inviting them to lunch, Hitler addressed them for slightly more than two hours. No transcript of the speech survives, but Army Chief of Staff Franz Halder,[135] the commander-in-chief of Army Group Centre, *Generalfeldmarschall* Fedor von Bock,[136] the commander-in-chief of *Panzergruppe* 3, *Generaloberst* Hermann Hoth,[137] and Luftwaffe chief of operations *Generalmajor* Hoffmann von Waldau,[138] all took notes of some of the most important points either during or immediately after the presentation. At least half of the speech was dedicated to softening up the officers present for the kind of war they would have to fight in Russia: not an orthodox confrontation between regular armies, but a clash with the twin corrupting forces of communism and Jewdom. International law as it had been observed so far in the war against France and Britain would not just be out of place, but downright counterproductive ('A communist is no comrade before or after the battle'). As a milestone in the moral corruption of the Wehrmacht's senior officer corps, the speech has, of course, attracted the attention of numerous historians who have sought an explanation for the *Ostheer's* numerous crimes of commission and omission in Russia. Of equal, if not greater interest, are remarks with which Hitler prefaced his ideological tirade but which have received far less attention. By way of an introduction, the Führer looked back on the events of recent months, taking great care to explain both German setbacks (cancellation of Sea Lion) and more recent Italian ones. Mussolini's botched invasion of Greece received particular criticism because it occurred just in time to boost Roosevelt's anti-Axis agenda on the eve of the US presidential elections.

---

[134] Received wisdom had it until quite recently that between 200 and 250 officers must have attended this occasion, a figure in all likelihood introduced into the historical narrative by Walter Warlimont, *Im Hauptquartier der deutschen Wehrmacht 1939–1945* (Frankfurt a.M.: Bernard & Graefe 1962), p 175. In 2006 Johannes Hürter made a convincing argument that the number of attendees in all likelihood did not exceed 100. Johannes Hürter, *Hitlers Heerführer. Die deutschen Oberbefehlshaber im Krieg gegen die Sowjetunion 1941/42* (München: R. Oldenbourg 2006), p 3.

[135] KTB Halder Bd. II, pp 335–7 (entry for 30 March 1941).

[136] TB Bock, pp 180–2 (entry for 30 March 1941).

[137] BA/MA, RH 21–3/40 'Besprechung durch Führer am 30.3.1941 in Reichskanzlei' (n.d.) is a barely legible handwritten document which had escaped the attention of all previous researchers until Johannes Hürter presented it in his 2006 book. It has now been reproduced in full in Susanne Heim et al (eds.), *Sowjetunion mit annektierten Gebieten I. Besetzte sowjetische Gebiete unter deutscher Militärverwaltung, Baltikum und Transnistrien* (München: Oldenbourg 2011) [= Die Verfolgung der europäischen Juden durch das nationalsozialistische Deutschland 1933–1945, Bd. 7], pp 117–19.

[138] BA/MA, RL 200/17. Von Waldau's notes are briefer and only cover the first part of the presentation.

Hitler then moved on to a brief discussion of what sort of long-term hope might be motivating the British to hold out so persistently. According to Franz Halder's notes, Churchill was said to be betting everything on a Soviet and American intervention, while adding the rider that the US war economy would still take four years to reach peak performance, a prediction which, ironically enough, turned out to be quite accurate. Lack of shipping was also quoted as one reason holding back the projection of US power. Hermann Hoth's notes on the same passage were rather more elaborate. He made no mention of the USSR coming to Britain's help in any shape or form, instead just noting that everything boiled down to Britain's 'hope in America'. Apparently, Hitler also provided a reason why the US government should go to so much trouble in assisting Britain, namely its 'economic failure', an obvious reference to Roosevelt's only partial success in dealing with the Depression.[139] Hitler must have felt particularly vindicated in making this assessment, seeing that almost exactly eight years to the day earlier he had made a very similar prediction to Otto Wagener about Roosevelt's prospects of revitalising the US economy without resorting to an 'expansionist' foreign policy. This was followed by the clinching argument, one which also gives the lie to any speculation that the Hitler of 1940–1 could have been underestimating the United States. The world of 1941, he said, was dominated by just two centres: Berlin and Washington. And Britain had made abundantly clear where its choice lay.

What were the implications of this for German strategy? For the time being, US capacities were inferior to German ones,[140] a problem compounded by shipping shortages. As a result of this, Britain would have to hold out between twelve and eighteen months for US help to have a major effect.[141] Should such a state of affairs ever come about, Germany would have to redirect a major part of its resources towards expanding the capital ship element of its navy, and more importantly (he appears to have

---

[139] 'Grund für Amerika: Wirtschaftlichen Mißerfolg Roosevelt's ausgleichen'; See Hoth notes; in: Heim (ed.), *Sowjetunion*, p 118.

[140] Hitler's reference to 'our economic capacity' could of course have referred either to the economy of Germany or to Germany plus all the nations of Europe (whether Axis or just neutral) which to a greater or lesser extent were part of the Third Reich's economic sphere. Since in March 1941, this would have meant virtually the entirety of the continent (with the exception of Great Britain, Ireland, Iceland and Greece), the superiority alluded to would actually not have been entirely fanciful. The extent to which Europe's economic potential may have given Germany a brief period of parity with the Allied coalition is discussed in detail in Richard Overy, *Why the Allies Won* (London: Jonathan Cape 1995).

[141] It is probable that he arrived at this rough estimate by way of the information provided by Boetticher four days previously, see 'Der Geschäftsträger in Washington an das Auswärtige Amt (26.3.1941)'; in: ADAP, Serie D, Bd. XII.1, pp 300–2. In this telegram co-signed by Thomsen, the attaché had stated that the $7 billion just voted for Lend-Lease would take until the end of 1942 before they had a significant impact on Britain's defences.

mentioned this twice[142]) the air defence arm of the Luftwaffe. In order to make this feasible, Russia had to be crushed first.[143] The point about air defence is in all likelihood a reflection of Boetticher's numerous reports on the USA delivering Boeing B-17 bombers to the British while its own Air Corps barely had a handful. The reference to reviving in all but name the idea behind the Kriegsmarine's 1939 Z-Plan is more difficult to unravel, since it could be argued that British naval superiority in this department would still be the same a year hence even without any US assistance. The explanation could lie in Hitler's rather traditional view of sea power, which placed great premium on the number and size of a nation's battleships,[144] or the fear that a greatly strengthened US Navy would deter Japan from ever challenging the Western powers in the Far East, or both. This appears to be confirmed by another reference to the US rearmament process in Hoth's notes. Over the previous year, Boetticher had provided the German leader with countless examples of US industry being found wanting in its endeavour to meet the constantly growing orders of the US government. Hoth noted that Hitler described America's limitations as follows: (1) America's capacities being 'inferior to ours'; then (2) the 'length of building process of battleships' and (3) lack of merchant shipping tonnage. At the time of his speech the United States had six new battleships under construction capable of matching the German *Bismarck* class, two of them (USS *North Carolina* and USS *Washington*) only weeks away from commissioning.[145] While it is true that *North Carolina*'s construction had been beset with problems,[146] it is also true that *Bismarck* (*Tirpitz* was still months away from being ready for wartime service) had taken

---

[142] Hoth notes; in: Heim (ed.), *Sowjetunion*, p 118.

[143] A line of thinking confirmed by a private conversation he had with Alfred Rosenberg on 2 May. Jürgen Matthäus and Frank Bajohr (eds.), *Alfred Rosenberg. Die Tagebücher von 1934 bis 1944* (Frankfurt a. Main: S. Fischer Verlag 2015), p 383 (entry for 6 May 1941): 'I must take the responsibility for this step. Stalin is merely awaiting America's intervention.'

[144] An article Hitler wrote for the *Völkischer Beobachter* in 1930 on the subject of the London Conference of Naval Disarmament betrays considerable knowledge of and interest in naval affairs, down to the maximum beam allowed for capital ships by the locks of the Panama Canal. 'Die Hintergründe der Londoner Flottenkonferenz (29. Januar 1930)'; in: Klaus Lankheit (ed.), *Hitler. Reden, Schriften, Anordnungen. Band III.1* (München: K.G. Saur 1994), pp 42–54. He gave a self-critical appraisal of his previous fondness for capital ships, now somewhat dented by recent events in the Pacific, to Admiral Raeder on 29 December 1941. BA/MA, 'RM 7/133 Br.B.Nr. 1/42 g. Kdos.Chefsache. Besprechungsniederschrift vom 29. Dez. 1941 (1.1.1942)'.

[145] The USS *North Carolina* would commission on 9 April 1941, the USS *Washington* on 15 May 1941. Lawrence Burr, *US Fast Battleships 1936–47* (Oxford: Osprey 2010), p 45.

[146] A total of forty-one months elapsed between the laying down of the keel and commissioning. Delays incurred were partly due to persistent propeller shaft vibration which required extensive (and well publicised) sea trials. Ibid., pp 10–11.

even longer to complete.[147] The very brevity of Hoth's notes does of course allow for a slightly different interpretation, especially since the speaker's main intention was to impress on everybody the need for a timely defeat of the USSR. Hitler could have directed his audience's attention to the new American battleships being built because the first of their type represented something which the US Army and Air Corps – their exponential growth notwithstanding[148] – were as yet incapable of fielding: a fully worked-up weapons system capable of successfully challenging the best in the Axis armoury. The well-publicised teething problems experienced by *North Carolina* would have been seen by the German leader as an indicator of the approximate time frame within which this threat would fully develop. If the problems suffered by the first ship of this class were anything to go by, *North Carolina* and *Washington* would not be joined by their four sisters for another eighteen to twenty-four months.[149] Thus, it could be argued, time was still on Germany's side, but not for long.

It would be premature, however, to interpret the 30 March address as a clear-cut indication that the passing of Lend-Lease had provoked the German dictator sufficiently to factor in war with the USA as part of the ongoing conflict. Ten days after the gathering in the Neue Reichskanzlei, an entry in the Seekriegsleitung's war diary appeared to indicate the contrary. It recorded an exchange between Raeder and Hitler that in all likelihood took place during the gathering in the Reichskanzlei on 30 March and which concerned the practicality of integrating last-minute alterations to the designs of the new 'H' and 'J' battleship types. The dictator had insisted that these allow for the fact that construction of the new types was to be initiated as soon as possible 'after the cessation of hostilities'.[150] Since the US Navy would be the only conceivable remaining opponent for a victorious Kriegsmarine equipped with such behemoths, it stands to reason that a possible war with the USA was

---

[147] Most battleship classes built by European nations in the 1920s and 1930s took at least fifty to fifty-two months to complete, with sixty-five months not being unusual (the Italian *Littorio* class and the French *Dunkerque*). See H. P. Willmott, *Battleship* (London: Cassell 2002), pp 272–302.

[148] Between August 1939 and late March 1941, the aggregate strength of the US Army and Air Corps had increased from 210,000 to nearly 1.5 million officers and men. Shrader (ed.), *Reference Guide*, pp 5, 15; Johnson, *Fast Tanks and Heavy Bombers*, pp 144–5.

[149] This not unreasonable calculation was upset by the rapidity with which the successors of the *North Carolina* were handed over to the US Navy, the ironing out of the initial problems experienced with the first vessel of this type no doubt making a significant contribution in this regard: USS *Washington*, USS *South Dakota*, USS *Indiana*, USS *Massachusetts* and USS *Alabama* were commissioned after periods ranging from twenty-nine to thirty-five months. Burr, *Battleships*, pp 45–7.

[150] KTB Seekriegsleitung, Teil A (entry for 9 April 1941). The German term used ('*Kriegsende*', i.e. the end of the war as a whole, as opposed to a particular campaign) strongly implies a vanquishing of both Great Britain and the USSR.

estimated to be at least three years in the future after Germany had imposed its will on its current enemies.

In Washington, the month of April gave Boetticher the last opportunity to indulge in some major gloating at the expense of Roosevelt's attempts to keep the nascent anti-Axis coalition together. Neither he nor other German observers saw a threat to American rearmament in a recent wave of strikes affecting the US defence industry.[151] In the meantime, the military backdrop was nothing if not auspicious for the Germans. A foolish shift of focus in British strategy in the Mediterranean led to a fatal pause in operations in Libya and gave the Germans the opportunity to defeat the Western Desert Force in Cyrenaica (30 March– 13 April) as well as conquer Yugoslavia and Greece and throw the British expeditionary force which had just deployed to Greece into the sea (6– 30 April). The British breakthrough at Keren (Eritrea) on 27 March, which would lead to the unravelling of the Italians' defence of their isolated Ethiopian colony, had been long anticipated and so did not have nearly the same reverber- ations that the events in Libya and the Balkans had. It would, however, contrib- ute to bringing about a situation that would cause some embarrassment to the American President. As a result of the British breakthrough, the Italian Red Sea naval base of Massaua on the Eritrean coast was left exposed and, it stood to reason, would soon fall. Roosevelt seized this opportunity to announce that in the next few days he would rescind his proclamation from ten months before, which on Italy's entry into the war had declared the Red Sea to be a war zone from which US merchant vessels would henceforth be barred. The President stated explicitly that this would put the United States in a position to deliver war materiel to the new Yugoslav government, which had been constituted after the coup of 27 March had removed the pro-Axis cabinet.[152] Together with Greece, which had been fighting an Italian invasion attempt since October 1940, these two countries appeared to form an Allied bridgehead ready-made to receive a torrent of Lend-Lease shipments.

Needless to say, the speed with which both Yugoslavia and Greece were overwhelmed by the Wehrmacht – regardless of any illusions London and Washington may have had on the matter[153] – turned this promise into

---

[151] PA/AA, StS, USA, Bd. 5, 'Boetticher und Thomsen an Auswärtiges Amt (12.4.1941)'. Also BA/MA, RW 19/1568 'Oberkommando der Wehrmacht, Wehrwirtschafts- und Rüstungsamt Wi Ia H Nr.1163/41 g.K. (12.4.1941)'; PA/AA, Inland II g 339 'Der Chef der Sicherheitspolizei und des SD an das Auswärtige Amt. Betr.: Streiklage in den USA (15.4.1941)'; Inland II g, 339 'Der Chef der Sicherheitspolizei und des SD an das Auswärtige Amt (17.4.1941)'.

[152] PA/AA, StS USA, Bd. 5, 'Thomsen an Auswärtiges Amt (5.4.1941)'.

[153] The judgement on British policy in those days still varies, as is reflected in Klaus Schmider, 'The Mediterranean in 1940/41: Crossroads of Lost Opportunities?'; in: *War and Society*, Vol. 15 (1997), No. 2, pp 19–41, on the one hand, and Craig Stockings and Eleanor Hancock, *Swastika over the Acropolis. Re-interpreting the Nazi Invasion of Greece in World War II* (Leiden and Boston: Brill 2013), pp 543–87, on the other.

a mirage. Roosevelt had to publicly admit as early as 8 April that any help already on the way was not likely to arrive in time to retrieve the situation.[154] This setback for the Allied cause was magnified many times over by the neutrality pact which Japan signed with the Soviet Union on 13 April. Until now, American strategists had always been able to seek solace in the fact that Japan's enmity towards Russia was an unmovable factor in world politics. It had transcended both a world war where both countries had been nominal allies and a revolutionary regime change in Moscow in 1917. Both countries had clashed in two wars (1904–5, 1939) and one major 'incident' (1938), and the Japanese Army in particular defined its role largely by planning and training for the next war with Russia.[155] The Soviet Union had sent considerable assistance to Nationalist China in its struggle against the Japanese invaders since July 1937, with Soviet airmen making a particularly noteworthy contribution in stemming the tide of the Japanese onslaught.[156] The news that the Japanese appeared willing to postpone – if only for the short term – any hostile designs on Russia meant that Tokyo was now free to reconsider its military options in Southeast Asia.

Taking stock of this rapidly evolving situation, Boetticher on 16 April sent a telegram to Berlin which, it can safely be said, crossed the line that divides intelligence gathering from warmongering. Once again, he dwelt on the gap that still divided American ambitions on the one hand, and lack of means on the other. American promises of assistance had essentially doomed Greece and Yugoslavia; the campaign there had not bought the Allies any time, and promises of new merchant ships for Britain under the Lend-Lease scheme now threatened to compromise parts of the Two-Ocean Navy programme. Japan was brought into play several times. For instance, moves like the recent announcement of a US occupation of Greenland on 9 April were nothing but a fig leaf hiding the fact that the US President was fast running out of options, with the escorting of convoys the only move left open to him that might actually have a major impact. Boetticher, however, was adamant in ruling this out because of the US Navy's commitments in the Pacific. In short, America was in a fix because neither was it ready for war nor was it facing enemies (Japan and Germany, that is) who were willing to meekly await whatever fate the USA might have in store for them. Instead, Berlin and Tokyo 'would always be willing

[154] PA/AA, StS USA Bd. 5, 'Boetticher & Thomsen an Auswärtiges Amt (9.4.1941)'.
[155] Drea, *Imperial Army*, pp 125–221.
[156] For a good summary of Soviet military and financial help to China between 1937 and 1940, see Maochun Yu, *The Dragon's War: Allied Operations and the Fate of China 1937–1947* (Annapolis: USNIP 2006), pp 10–23. On the Soviet air war in China between December 1937 and January 1940, Mikhail Maslov, *Polikarpov I-15, I-16 and I-153 aces* (Oxford: Osprey 2010), pp 33–41, provides a succinct, though poorly sourced account.

to counter the cowardice and lack of daring so typical of Jewish-mercantilist thinking with their willingness to act'.[157]

Whether as a consequence of Jewish-mercantilist thinking or not, the subject of convoying was back on the agenda the very next day and would stay there until the eve of Pearl Harbor. In an article in the *Washington Times Herald*, several senators alleged that the Coast Guard, acting jointly with the US Navy's Neutrality Patrol, had already surreptitiously taken up convoying despite the government's pledges in this regard. Both the Secretary of the Navy and the Chief of Naval Operations had to refute these claims.[158] The US government, far from being intimidated by this renewed challenge, announced on 18 April that the old Neutrality Zone would from now on be renamed Security Zone and the patrol limit of the vessels policing it, expanded to roughly 3,000 miles (5000 km +) – well into the eastern half of the North Atlantic.[159] In addition, the Washington media were speculating about the government's attempts to secure a foothold in the Eastern Hemisphere by obtaining a lease of Irish ports in exchange for Lend-Lease;[160] at a more confidential level, Boetticher was copied into a report which summarised the gist of a conversation the Japanese ambassador to Spain had had with Roosevelt confidant, Admiral William D. Leahy (Chief of Naval Operations, January 1937–July 1939), the newly appointed US ambassador to Vichy.[161] During this exchange, Leahy was confident in predicting a US intervention in the war, though it was likely to be limited to the purely naval sphere, that is, convoy escort. The elimination of a quarter of the German U-boat force, he was alleged to have said, would be enough to avert a British defeat.[162] Attaché Witthoeft-Emden chose to take the allegation of close convoying in the *Washington Times Herald* with a pinch of salt,[163] but on 26 April Thomsen came to the conclusion that the 'never-ending' debate about convoying was not the result of unintended leaks but deliberate policy by the Federal government:[164] the idea being 'to get people used to the idea and, once the

---

[157] PA/AA, StS USA Bd. 5, 'Boetticher und Thomsen an Auswärtiges Amt (16.4.1941)'.

[158] BA/MA, RH 67/49 'Washington, den 17.4.1941, Nr. 1070 –Abschrift'; PA/AA, StS USA Bd. 5, 'Marineattache und Thomsen an Auswärtiges Amt (18.4.1941)'. The Neutrality Patrol may have plotted some sorties – especially after the operation by *Scharnhorst* and *Gneisenau* of February and March – so as to put its vessels in a position to provide a distant escort for some British convoys to the limit of the constantly expanding patrol zone. This is a subject that still needs to be examined in detail.

[159] Waldo Heinrichs, *Threshold of War: Franklin D. Roosevelt and American Entry into World War II* (Oxford: OUP 1988), pp 33, 46–47.

[160] PA/AA, StS USA, Bd. 5, 'Thomsen an Auswärtiges Amt (19.4.1941)'.

[161] On Leahy, see Phillips Payson O'Brien, *The Second Most Powerful Man in the World: The Life of Admiral William D. Leahy, Roosevelt's Chief of Staff* (London: Penguin 2019).

[162] PA/AA, StS USA Bd. 5, 'Heberlein an Auswärtiges Amt (24.4.1941)'.

[163] BA/MA, RH 67/49 'Telegramm aus Washington, den 17.4.1941, Nr. 1070 – Abschrift'.

[164] BA/MA, RH 67/50 'Geheimtelegramm aus Washington Nr. 1180 (28.4.1941)'.

moment of decision has arrived, be in a position which allows it to claim that it is only following what popular opinion demands of it'.[165] In light of the German dictator's reaction to Lend-Lease, it would only be logical to expect a similar reaction to the announcement of the expanded Security Zone which looked almost certain to overlap with the Kriegsmarine's expanded operational area. Rather remarkably, Hitler explained to Raeder on 20 April, he had decided against expanding Kriegsmarine operations as far as the edge of US territorial waters. While the reason he gave for this (it was important to capitalise on recent victories in the Balkans and North Africa[166]) had a certain plausibility, the fact remains that faced with an act of overt escalation by the US President, the German dictator had blinked first. From now until late November, German diplomacy and military strategy reverted to the priority which had dominated US–German relations prior to Lend-Lease: the Americans were to be kept out of the war at almost any cost.

On the 26 April Boetticher and Thomsen sent off another of their 'joint' cables, which is noteworthy on two accounts. First of all, the file copy in the papers of OKH's Attacheabteilung bears a note which says that a copy of this telegram was to be passed on to the head of OKW, *Generalfeldmarschall* Keitel.[167] A lot of well-known facts, especially on American lack of preparedness, were rehashed for the umpteenth time, but one genuinely new theme did emerge. According to the two diplomats, Roosevelt's often alluded to policy of playing for time did have a timeline. If by the autumn of that year, Britain had not succumbed to Germany's attacks, the American President would feel confident in stretching out the war for 'unlimited time', a concept which suited him both strategically as well as domestically, because it was only through the rearmament process that he had managed to breathe new life into the US economy.[168] Even though Boetticher did not say as much, such a conclusion was also supported by some of his own recent reports on subjects such as the expansion of the US explosive-producing plants or the setting up of the Chrysler Detroit Tank Arsenal, the first factory capable of mass-producing the US Army's first medium tank.[169] Until now, the attaché had limited himself to predicting a rise in US

[165] PA/AA, StS USA Bd. 5, 'Thomsen an Auswärtiges Amt (26.4.1941)'.
[166] 'Seekriegsleitung B.Nr.I op 515/41 g.Kdos.Chefs. Vortrag Ob.d.M. beim Führer am 20. April 1941'; in: Wagner (ed.), *Lagevorträge*, pp 217–21.
[167] BA/MA, RH 67/49 'Amt Ausland/Abwehr Abt. Ausland Nr. 1638/41 geh.I g – Abschrift von Telegramm aus Washington Nr. 1168 (28.4.1941)'.
[168] Ibid.
[169] PA/AA, StS USA Bd. 5, 'Boetticher und Thomsen an Auswärtiges Amt (12.4.1941)'. In this cable, Boetticher admitted that the explosives factories which were still under construction (40 per cent of the total) would in all likelihood come on line by October 1941. Production of the tank in question (the M3 Grant/Lee) did indeed start in August 1941, when the first thirty were handed over to the US Army.

armament output by mid-1941; this was the first time he tied this to a likely strategy on the part of the American government.

He further explored this issue in a lengthy cable dated 10 May. Taking his cue from a recent speech by Churchill, he described current Anglo–American priorities as: (1) securing the Middle East, (2) reinforcing Singapore and Malaya and (3) securing the South Atlantic 'narrows' between Natal (Brazil) and western Africa. Since only the first of these three was actually under attack by German forces, the timely reinforcement of the British Middle East Command with Lend-Lease weaponry was the first priority of the day. Otherwise, the Germans might be given a chance to advance into Egypt and even beyond, opening the possibility of a German–Japanese link-up. American military build-up in the Army and Air Corps would need until the end of 1942 before the two services could be considered 'wholly functional instruments of American imperialism'. In the meantime, the telegram concluded, the American government feared nothing more than the possibility that 'German and Japanese initiatives might produce premature decisions'.[170]

Concerns about a premature decision, though of a different kind, were apparently also harboured by the Australian prime minister, Robert Menzies. Travelling by flying boat from Britain to the USA, he had a one-day stopover at Lisbon. There, he appears to have repeated a statement by Churchill, which was then relayed to the German ambassador in the Portuguese capital. Churchill had allegedly said that he only wished for a US entry into the war around mid-1942, when Britain would be ready to go over to the offensive. At present, US neutrality meant both mounting Lend-Lease deliveries and an insurance policy against action by Japan in the Far East. To maintain this state of affairs, it was best that even the odd sinking of a US Navy vessel engaged in convoy escort should only be met with subdued protest.[171] A remarkable document, it certainly stands in contrast to the gist of most messages which Churchill sent the US President throughout the 1940–1 period and which all attempted – to a greater or lesser extent – to goad him into increasing US involvement in the war, lest it arrive too late to affect the bigger issue.[172] Such an unhurried

---

[170] PA/AA, StS USA Bd. 6, 'Boetticher und Thomsen an Auswärtiges Amt (10.5.1941)'. Rather unusually, this telegram was addressed to the head of OKW foreign intelligence as well as Halder and Hoffmann von Waldau personally and carried the highest level of secrecy.

[171] PA/AA, StS USA, Bd. 6, 'Huene an Auswärtiges Amt (13.5.1941)'.

[172] Warren F. Kimball, *Forged in War: Roosevelt, Churchill and the Second World War* (New York: William Morrow 1997), pp 35–126. Witness his attempt just a few months later to convince Roosevelt to deploy 'three or four' US Army divisions to Ulster in order to free up British forces for service elsewhere. Manchester Rylands Library, Auchinleck Papers, AUC 392, GB 133, 'Prime Minister to General Auchinleck (18.10.1941)'.

approach to coalition building chimes remarkably well with Boetticher's big theme which essentially reduced Roosevelt's policy to one of buying time at every opportunity. We know that Menzies spent the day he was left waiting in Lisbon as a guest of the Portuguese dictator Salazar and even went to see a bullfight.[173] Since it is unlikely that the Australian prime minister would have divulged sensitive information in a public setting, the most likely explanation is that one of his Portuguese hosts relayed the content of a private conversation to the Germans. In light of the impossibility of squaring such a statement with known British policy at the time, the possibility of a plant aimed at inciting the Germans into escalating the confrontation between the Kriegsmarine and the US Atlantic Fleet seems likely.

This morsel of high-level intelligence appears to have found its way to the Berghof by the most direct route and formed the backdrop (together with a Kriegsmarine proposal to relax the rules of engagement that the Rheinübung task force of the *Bismarck* and *Prinz Eugen* would be operating under in its upcoming sortie) to a conversation that took place there on 22 May. Talking to a small group of acolytes (Ribbentrop, Keitel, Raeder and Ambassador Hewel), Hitler for the first time appeared to be giving some serious thought to the strategic implications of bringing the USA into the war. The way he saw it, 'Japan's role in this was absolutely crucial. If she was still hesitant, it would be preferable to keep the US out of the war rather than to sink a few extra 100,000 GRT [gross register tonnage] in the Atlantic. Without the US, war would be over this year. With US intervention, it might still drag on for a number of years.'[174] The equanimity with which Hitler was willing to face the prospect of a few more years at war, at a time when the submarine arm was the only tool with which to conduct it, is positively bone-chilling even eighty years later. On the other hand, he was of course working from the assumption that the Soviet Union would have been successfully invaded and occupied by no later than September or October, thus facilitating the downsizing of the army and the expansion of the navy and air force already hinted at in his address of 30 March. This brief moment of hesitation notwithstanding, the *Bismarck*'s original orders, which had justified the task force's restrictive rules of engagement by pointing out that 'a US entry into the war must not be seen as something inevitable', were upheld.[175]

[173] Allan Martin, *Robert Menzies: A Life – Vol. 1: 1894–1943* (Melbourne: Melbourne UP 1993), pp 355–6.

[174] Institut für Zeitgeschichte (IfZ) ED 100–78 Tagebuch Walther Hewel (entry for 22 May 1941). Also KTB Seekriegsleitung, Teil A (entry for 22 May 1941).

[175] BA/MA, RM 7/1700 'Oberkommando der Kriegsmarine an Flotte, Gruppe West und Gruppe Nord (10.5.1941)'.

On 27 May, Roosevelt gave one of his fireside chats which German observers anticipated would be used to announce either the dismantling of the existing neutrality legislation, or the introduction of convoying, or both.[176] Seizing on the recent penetration of the waters around Greenland and Iceland by the battleship *Bismarck* and her consort, the heavy cruiser *Prinz Eugen*,[177] the President proclaimed an Unlimited National Emergency which built on the powers he had already assumed under the Limited National Emergency of September 1939. Together, they were to give Roosevelt the power to put under government control means of transport, factories and power stations working for the needs of the US armed forces. This also made permissible Federal intervention in labour disputes in a number of instances. In terms of domestic politics, this constituted yet another important power shift away from Congress, of the kind that had made the President such a controversial figure with the Right since 1933. However, in terms of what had been expected after the public debate on convoying of the previous months, it was seen as tantamount to temporary retrenchment.[178]

Irrespective of this, the next few days brought another hint of how Germany might find itself at war with the American war machine. Admiral Leahy's prediction of a purely naval shooting match for the time being no longer appeared to be an option. However, the first RAF squadrons equipped with American Curtiss P-40s flew their first combat sorties in the Middle East at the beginning of June:[179] a brief war against the French in Lebanon and Syria[180] was quickly followed by the first of a long series of clashes with the Axis air forces over the Western Desert.[181] Contrary to German speculation that the British were not at all keen on this type of aircraft, the US fighters went on to give a good account of themselves in both theatres.[182] Even more seriously, on 2 June 1941 Thomsen had reported from Washington that plans were afoot to

[176] The full text can be found in: Samuel I. Rosenman (ed.), *The Public Papers and Addresses of Franklin D. Roosevelt. 1941: The Call to Battle Stations* (New York: Harper & Brothers 1950), pp 194–5.

[177] For the well-known story of the chase for the *Bismarck*, see Graham Rhys-Jones, *The Loss of the Bismarck: An Avoidable Disaster* (London: Cassell 1999), pp 90–131.

[178] PA/AA, StS USA, Bd. 6, 'Thomsen an Auswärtiges Amt (28.5.1941)'; KTB Seekriegsleitung, Teil A (entry for 30 May 1941).

[179] No. 3 RAAF Squadron and No. 250 RAF Squadron were re-equipped with P-40s in March–April 1941, with No. 112 Squadron RAF following in June.

[180] The P-40s of No. 3 RAAF Squadron spearheaded a successful campaign against the French air services during the conquest of the French Levant by British Empire forces in June–July 1941. For a critical assessment of the P-40s' contribution to this Allied success, see Christian J. Ehrengardt and Christopher Shores, *L'aviation de Vichy au combat, tome II. La campagne de Syrie, 8 juin–14 juillet 1941* (Paris: Lavauzelle 1987), pp 158–70.

[181] Carl Molesworth, *Curtiss P-40: Long-Nosed Tomahawks* (Oxford: Osprey 2013), pp 43–9.

[182] PA/AA, StS USA Bd. 6, 'Boetticher an Auswärtiges Amt (12.6.1941)'.

supply Britain with large numbers of heavy B-17 and B-24 bombers which would then be used in a campaign to deliberately and systematically lay waste to the cities of the Reich.[183] The current output of these aircraft did not yet give cause for alarm, but the American car industry's skills at mass-production were a matter of record, and it was known to be in the process of retooling part of its production line for aircraft production. A total of eight new plants under construction were to be earmarked for bomber production only, with half their output being reserved for the Consolidated B-24, the newest American 'heavy', which had first taken to the skies in December 1939. A supplementary budget of $5 billion for the US Air Corps put before Congress in the first week of June was yet another indicator that the American administration had all but discarded from its calculations the possibility of peace breaking out in Europe.[184] When taken in conjunction with intelligence that a small, but growing number of US air crew were known to have been detailed for service with the Royal Air Force or Fleet Air Arm,[185] and that 7,000 Commonwealth airmen were being trained at US flight schools as part of the Lend-Lease scheme,[186] it gave a broad idea of the unprecedented steps the US government was willing to take to support a war which would not necessitate 'sending an expeditionary army abroad'.

Such an eventuality, it goes without saying, had repeatedly been dismissed by Boetticher, by referring to the 'cooler heads' at the General Staff (some of whom were personal acquaintances of his).[187] Putting to good use the intelligence provided by the attaché,[188] these seasoned professionals would almost

---

[183] PA/AA, StS USA, Bd. 6, 'Thomsen an Auswärtiges Amt (2.6.1941)'.

[184] BA/MA, RH 67/50 'Abschrift – Telegramm Washington Nr. 1721 vom 7.6.1941 (11.6.1941)'.

[185] BA/MA, RH 67/50 'Abt. Ausland. Nr. 1842/41 geh Ausl III d – Vortragsnotiz. Betr.: Flugzeuge (10.5.1941)'.

[186] PA/AA, StS USA, Bd.6, 'Thomsen an Auswärtiges Amt (12.6.1941)' which is essentially a verbatim repetition of the President's first preliminary report to Congress of all the goods and services rendered so far under Lend-Lease. Quite apart from benefits in terms of cost, this scheme also allowed flight training under far better conditions (no blackout, less congested skies and better flying weather) than would have been possible in the United Kingdom. For a history of the scheme see Gilbert S. Guinn, *The Arnold Scheme: British Pilots, the American South and the Allies' Daring Plan* (London: Spellmount 2007).

[187] The relationship between Boetticher and his US Army informants working in the Munitions Building is worthy of closer examination than is possible here. With some of them, genuine sympathy for Nazi Germany or deliberate play-acting to feed the general disinformation could be seen as possible motives for their closeness to a senior officer of a country repeatedly described as hostile by their commander-in-chief. The report of 13 June, where Boetticher quotes one of his informants as favourably comparing Adolf Hitler with Abraham Lincoln, could suggest either possibility. See PA/AA, StS USA, Bd. 6, 'Thomsen und Boetticher an Auswärtiges Amt (13.6.1941)'.

[188] On 4 September Boetticher went so far as to refer the General Staff's assessment as having been 'guided by me according to our precepts'. See PA/AA, Handakten Etzdorf.

invariably find ways to impress on President Roosevelt that the factors still limiting US strategic options (lack of shipping, the need to keep Japan in check and Britain supplied, the field army's lack of preparedness) made active intervention in Europe much too risky. Hence, American strategy in 1941 was little more than so much 'bluff', as he liked to put it. A rare challenge to this view was raised on 6 June by Ambassador Dieckhoff from his Berlin exile. In a loose minute he prepared for Ribbentrop, he emphatically expressed the opinion that Roosevelt's prevarication, though real enough, was almost entirely due to the existing uncertainties over the general public's willingness to go to war and Japan's possible course of action in Southeast Asia. Should a situation arise where both these concerns had been effectively neutralised, the President, Dieckhoff went on, would go to war at the first opportunity (*'lieber heute als morgen'*). He drove his point home by concluding that the USA in April 1917 had been even less well prepared for war than it was today, a fact which had not stopped President Wilson from taking the plunge.[189]

After Hitler's brief exposition of 22 May, another indicator of the extent to which the mounting evidence of American involvement in the European war was affecting his calculations can be found in two utterances he made in the immediate run-up to Barbarossa. Speaking to Joseph Goebbels on the evening of 15 June, he dwelt at length on the motives behind this momentous decision to launch Barbarossa. Over and above the fact that he suspected Stalin of playing a waiting game until Europe was thoroughly exhausted, there was also an American angle to invading the USSR. Japan would be encouraged to face up to the USA; Germany, having destroyed the USSR, would be in a position to demobilise a large part of its field army and redirect these men into industries that would allow it to expand its navy and air force. Only in this fashion would Germany be 'safe' from the USA.[190] In the letter he wrote to fellow dictator Benito Mussolini on 21 June informing him of the imminent invasion of the USSR by the Wehrmacht, he dwelt at length on the reasons which had compelled him to take this drastic step. Above all, he spoke of the pressure he found himself under for two reasons: the Soviet build-up of troop strength in the USSR's border districts on the one hand, and the mid-term impact which US Lend-Lease deliveries for the British Empire were going to have on the European balance of power on the other. It appears that the German leader had decided to take Boetticher's mantra about US inadequacies with a pinch of salt.[191]

On 4 July, Dieckhoff returned to the issue he had raised on 6 June. The occasion was a public appeal by the US Army Chief of Staff, General George

'Politische Berichte Washington. Meldung Mil.Att. Washington vom 4.9.1941 (9.9.1941)'.

[189] PA/AA, StS USA, Bd. 6, 'Zu dem Telegramm des Militärattaches in Washington Nr. 1655 vom 4. Juni 1941 (6.6.1941)'.

[190] TB Goebbels, Bd. I.9, p 378 (entry for 16 June 1941).

[191] 'Der Führer an den Duce (21.6.1941)'; in: ADAP, Serie D, Bd. XII.2, pp 889–92.

Marshall, that Congress abolish the legislation currently ruling out a deployment of the US Army outside the Western Hemisphere. The ambassador stressed that such a bold move flew in the face of Boetticher's constant mantra that the heads of the US Army could be relied on to act as a brake on any moves by President Roosevelt towards an even more proactive anti-Axis policy. This might have happened on a few occasions in the past, but with not nearly the frequency or consistency that warranted the sort of faith Boetticher put in it.[192] Even though Dieckhoff had not even mentioned it, the timing of Marshall's initiative was indeed remarkable because Germany's invasion of the USSR on 22 June had brought in its train a brief revitalisation of American isolationism. This surprising move appeared to give the lie to previous allegations that Hitler's first priority lay in conquering Britain and/or threatening the USA and also chimed with American anti-communism.

However, both Marshall's speech and an event following immediately afterwards soon proved that Roosevelt had reached a point where he felt that he was very much in a position to form public opinion by his actions, and not the other way around. On 7 July, elements of the First Marine Division, which had been earmarked for a descent on the Azores, began landing in Iceland. The Danish possession had been under British occupation since 10 May 1940, and with effect from 23 March of the following year the waters surrounding it had been included by Hitler in the war zone around Britain in which U-boats were allowed to sink on sight any merchant vessel. The Marines had come to relieve a large part of the British garrison on the island. When it was pointed out to the President at a press conference the following day that including Iceland in the concept of hemispheric defence really stretched the concept beyond breaking point, Roosevelt retorted that this latest move was dictated by military necessity, not 'vague' demarcation lines on a map which could not determine the

---

[192] Even though history would by and large bear out Dieckhoff's judgement, it needs to be stressed that Boetticher was not engaged in a wild goose chase. A number of US army officers of the period, like Lieutenant General Stanley Embick (US Army deputy chief of staff, May 1936–September 1938; commander Third Army, October 1938–September 1940); Lieutenant General Walter Krueger (commander VII Corps, June 1940–May 1941; commander Third Army, May 1941–February 1943); Lieutenant Colonel Truman Smith (military attaché in Berlin, August 1935–April 1939; 'Special Consultant' on Germany at the Intelligence Division of the General Staff, May 1939–September 1941), were known to harbour serious reservations about US participation in the conflict in general and intervention in the European war in particular. Even General George C. Marshall (US Army Chief of Staff, July 1939–November 1945) dithered on occasion in 1940–1, oscillating between a proactive and a mostly defensive strategy. See Mark A. Stoler, *Allies and Adversaries: The Joint Chiefs of Staff, the Grand Alliance and US Strategy in World War II* (Boston: Brill 2000), pp 10–15, 41–5, as well as Forrest C. Pogue, *George C. Marshall. Ordeal and Hope, 1939–1942* (New York: Viking Press 1966), pp 130–3, and David Kaiser, *No End Save Victory: How FDR Led the Nation into War* (New York: Basic Books 2014), pp 244–5.

limits of the nation's forward defence.[193] In Berlin, the Seekriegsleitung was quick to point out that this meant that the Americans were now in possession of an ideal base that would allow intervention by their air or naval forces at the very centre of the Battle of the Atlantic.[194] The fact that the Secretary of the Navy had announced that US Navy escorts would from now on convoy all Icelandic and US shipping which plied between the USA and Iceland, and had been deliberately vague on the rules of engagement which would govern their encounters with German surface or submarine raiders,[195] clearly indicated that incidents between the two navies were now virtually predetermined. Only a few days later, the Germans learned that American contractors had arrived in Northern Ireland to build bases for the British.[196] No effort was made to keep the project secret and the British government even openly admitted to the presence of the contractors.[197] To any Axis observer, it must have been obvious that these facilities would, once finished, almost certainly be turned over to the US Navy or Army Air Force,[198] thus facilitating the extension of the increasingly aggressive and disingenuous Neutrality Patrol into the Kriegsmarine's very own backyard.[199]

At the German embassy in Washington, the only discernible cloud with a silver lining lay in the actions taken by isolationist legislators on the Hill who had been galvanised by this burst of interventionist activity into mounting what would be their last stand. First, they challenged passage of the three bills put before Congress on 10 July, which called for the extension of the service of the class of conscripts drafted in September and October 1940, as well as for the deployability of these soldiers outside the Western Hemisphere. The latter in particular incited such unexpectedly vigorous resistance that the President quietly dropped it and decided to focus on winning support for the extension of the current draft.[200] With regards to the occupation of Iceland, isolationist senators and congressmen accused the government of having issued a secret shoot-on-sight order to the Atlantic Fleet, since without it convoying of any kind – even to a forlorn outpost like Iceland – would hardly make any sense.[201]

[193] PA/AA, StS USA, Bd. 7, 'Thomsen an Auswärtiges Amt (10.7.1941)'.
[194] KTB Seekriegsleitung, Teil A (entry for 8 July 1941).
[195] KTB Seekriegsleitung, Teil A (entry for 10 July 1941).
[196] John Blake, *Northern Ireland in the Second World War* (Belfast: Blackstaff Press 2000, rp of 1956 HMSO edition), pp 252–65, is the most comprehensive account of this project.
[197] KTB Seekriegsleitung, Teil A (entry for 19 July 1941).
[198] The US Army Air Corps had changed its name to US Army Air Force on 20 June 1941.
[199] For a more detailed treatment of the base building by US contractors in Ulster and Scotland, see below.
[200] PA/AA, StS USA, Bd. 7, 'Resenberg an Auswärtiges Amt (15.7.1941)'.
[201] Western Hemisphere Defense Plan 4 called for the escort of US and Icelandic shipping plying the route between Iceland and the USA and gave escort commanders considerable leeway in deciding whether a U-boat encountered in the general area did constitute a threat and should be engaged. British convoys were not to be escorted, but would be

Secretary of the Navy Frank Knox's deliberately obfuscating language cut no ice with senators like Burton K. Wheeler, and the President was forced to call a press conference on 18 July during which he restated his reasons for landing the Marines on Iceland and refused to be drawn on the subject of the rules of engagement issued to the Atlantic Fleet, since this would violate 'basic military precepts'.[202] An idea of the intensity of the opposition facing the President is given by the fact that in a cable dated 18 July, Thomsen referred openly to a very frank face-to-face talk he had had with 'the leading anti-interventionist Senator'. The latter had praised 'the calm dignity shown by the German government' and its refusal to be baited by 'American outrageousness'. He knew for a fact that the 'Führer's restraint' made 'Roosevelt absolutely livid'. If an incident could be avoided until the end of the year, the opposition would be strong enough to impress on the American people the 'egoistical nature of Britain's fight' and the 'the interventionists' lack of scruples'.[203] If previous communications are anything to go by, Thomsen usually made a point of communicating with isolationist legislators and other eminent isolationists through third persons to minimise their risk of exposure,[204] a sensible precaution validated by increasing indications that German diplomats were under surveillance by the FBI.[205] A personal meeting of the kind described, along with the frankness of the views exchanged, was more than just noteworthy, and it gives an idea of the bitterness some of Roosevelt's domestic opponents felt towards the President.[206]

Only three days later, Thomsen and Boetticher were forced to assess a crisis of a completely different kind, which forced all other issues to the sidelines.[207]

informed of routings and sailing times to allow them to hug the course of the US convoy, should they wish to do so. See Kaiser, *Victory*, pp 239–40.

[202] 'Confidential. Press Conference # 756, Executive Office of the President, July 18, 1941 – 10.50 A.M., E.S.T.'; in: www.fdrlibrary.marist.edu/_resources/images/pc/pc0120.pdf (accessed 2 July 2020). Also PA/AA, StS USA, Bd. 7, 'Thomsen an Auswärtiges Amt (18.7.1941)'.

[203] PA/AA, StS USA, Bd. 7, 'Thomsen an Auswärtiges Amt (18.7.1941)'.

[204] According to PA/AA, StS USA, Bd. 5, 'Boetticher & Thomsen an Auswärtiges Amt (27.4.1941)', Boetticher stayed in touch with Charles Lindbergh through an officer on the US Army's General Staff.

[205] For an example of the assistant air attaché, Riedel, finding himself tailed by the FBI during his honeymoon trip in July 1941 see Simons, *Air Attaché*, pp 104–12.

[206] The description of Thomsen's interlocutor as 'the leading isolationist spokesman' fits the profile of Senator Burton K. Wheeler, who invariably had more media attention directed at him because he was himself a Democrat. The previous spring, Roosevelt's unprecedented decision to run for a third term had robbed him of a promising bid for the White House.

[207] In the last week of July. the Germans managed to challenge American allegations of German involvement in a supposed coup plot in Bolivia by publishing a sworn affidavit by the attaché at the Bolivian embassy in Berlin. An event like this would normally have echoed in Boetticher's and Thomsen's reports for at least a week. See TB Goebbels, Bd. I.1, pp 141–2, 145–6 (entries for 29 and 30 July 1941).

So far, Roosevelt's policy of actively confronting Hitler in a step-by-step fashion had been met with at least a degree of opposition on the Hill, in the media and on the part of America First. To a large degree, this reflected the fact that many Americans by now tended to view the Great War as an instance where they had, against their better judgement, allowed themselves to be dragged into a conflict which did not concern them, a perception magnified many times over, as has already been mentioned, by the divisive peace treaty of Versailles and the sluggishness of their former allies in repaying their war debts. Moreover, many citizens of the United States – either by virtue of their family roots, studies abroad or military service with the AEF in 1917–18 – had a reasonable concept of and respect for Germany's military, economic and scientific potential. This was at least partly conducive to their reluctance to be dragged into another war against this country if it could at all be helped.

None of these factors, however, applied to Japan, with American appreciations of the Far Eastern power being in the main coloured by an inherently racist view. As such, an assertive or even aggressive foreign policy in the Pacific was something Americans from all political backgrounds could be relied on to heartily approve of.[208] So far, despite Japan's war of aggression against China,

---

[208] Testimony to this effect can be found in numerous contemporary sources which were carefully monitored by the Germans. See for instance PA/AA, Inland II g, 340 'Der Chef der Sicherheitspolizei und des SD an das Auswärtige Amt. Betr.: Meinungsäusserungen amerikanischer Diplomaten in Rom über die Lage im Fernen Osten (5.8.1941)'. According to the SD's source, one of the US diplomats at the embassy in Rome had stated the following: 'Botschaftssekretär Perkins spoke with contempt of the Japanese, who would occasionally make a nuisance of themselves, but need not be taken seriously as a real adversary.' In PA/AA, StS USA, Bd. 8, 'Thomsen an Auswärtiges Amt (27.8.1941)', the German envoy in Washington warned of the consequences of a Japanese move against the soon-to-be-independent Philippines: 'a war against Japan under these circumstances would be extremely popular here and would remove all lack of popular enthusiasm for a war at a stroke, which would also have consequences for the world war as a whole.' In November, the Abwehr recorded the following sentiments by the US assistant naval attaché at the Berlin embassy: 'The outbreak of war with Japan is something we expect from one day to the next. Japan's conditions . . . are unacceptable to us. Should the USA accept them, I would resign my citizenship in favour of an Argentine passport. Without oil, Japan's fleet is incapable of moving. I don't understand why the USA doesn't get on with initiating hostilities.' See BA/MA, RM 11/83 'Amt Ausland/ Abwehr an OKM-Attache-Gruppe/Ob.d.L.- Führungsstab Ic. Betr.: Äußerungen des K. Kpt. White, Gehilfe des USA-Marine- und Marineluftfahrtattaches (22.11.1941)'. A non-German observer of American mood swings – the Australian ambassador in Washington – broadly agreed with these assessments: 'It is a noticeable fact that the leading isolationists (Lindbergh, Wheeler, Nye) never refer to Japan at all – a reflection of what I believe to be the fact that this country would not listen to any appeasement vis-à-vis Japan'; in: Carl Bridge (ed.), *A Delicate Mission: the Washington Diaries of Richard G. Casey 1940–42* (Canberra: National Library of Australia), p 190 (entry for 14 October 1941). My thanks to Christopher Pugsley (Wellington) for drawing my attention to this source.

American support of that nation had been much less overt than in the case of the European allies. This was essentially due to two reasons. First of all, there was the concern over a spread of hostilities to Southeast Asia, where both the American protectorate of the Philippines and the virtual entirety of the world's rubber supply were hostages to fortune. In addition, Japan's mutation from a cooperative partner in the 1920s to aggressor nation had been much more gradual than in Germany and a number of its key decision makers were known to still favour a peaceful settlement of any existing differences with the United States. Even the ranks of the warmongers in Tokyo were divided, with some (mostly army) favouring an invasion of the Pacific provinces of the USSR, and others (mostly navy) more inclined to pick off some or all of the Western protectorates and colonies in Southeast Asia.

All these reasons had been powerful incentives for a carefully balanced policy which exploited the existing divisions among Japanese leaders, but on 24 July an event occurred which indicated its bankruptcy. On that day, the Japanese government announced its intention to occupy ten base areas in southern Indo-China ceded to them under a recent agreement with the French government. Unlike the occupation of the northern half of the colony the previous September, which had been rationalised in the context of the ongoing war in China (it cut off one of the last existing supply routes still open to the Kuomintang regime), this latest move was so obviously directed at acquiring a springboard for aggressive moves against Thailand and Malaya that the Roosevelt administration had to reconsider its options. On 26 July, the President announced the freezing of all Japanese assets in the United States, a measure which even Thomsen had to admit amounted to a 'radical operation'. Two days previously, in an address given to a group of civil defence volunteers who were visiting the capital with New York Mayor Fiorello La Guardia,[209] Roosevelt had gone to considerable lengths to justify this move and dwelt at great length on the patience shown so far by the US government. He even candidly admitted that supplying Japan with fuel until this point in time had to a large extent been tied to the fear that Tokyo might otherwise help itself to the Dutch East Indies.

The way Thomsen saw it, the measures just enacted, though unprecedented, were essentially a tool which the government would use if and when the situation in the Pacific deteriorated further. Accordingly, the German envoy was genuinely surprised when on 2 August the White House announced an oil embargo and the State Department complemented these two measures with a cancellation of all existing licences for exports of fuel products. This also affected licences already issued and contracts already paid for. The combined

---

[209] On 20 May 1941, La Guardia had been named head of the Office of Civilian Defense (OCD), a new office directly subordinate to the President. For the text of Roosevelt's address, see Rosenman (ed.), *Public Papers and Addresses*, pp 277–80.

effect of these measures was to cut Japan off from all oil exports. A clear hint that the US government was willing to renegotiate, but only with a view to satisfying the needs of a peacetime economy, could be gleaned from the fact that the baseline for any new deal would be Japan's oil consumption during the last year of peace in the Far East, that is, 1936.[210]

This would in theory still have allowed the export of a considerable quantity of oil to an extent apparently not realised by Thomsen.[211] However, the three-man working group of government officials (Assistant Secretary of State Dean Acheson, General Counsel Edward Foley, Assistant Attorney General Francis Shea) heading the newly created Foreign Funds Control Committee over the following weeks put so many obstacles in the way of Japanese embassy staff pleading with them over the release of just a fraction of the frozen funds that the scheme soon turned into the equivalent of a complete economic blockade.[212]

Observing these events from the German embassy, Boetticher did not appear to realise that a decisive corner had been turned. On 30 July, he returned to a theme which he had already dwelt on at the time of the US embargo on scrap metal in 1940: an economic war was a double-edged sword at the best of times and, in view of the need the USA currently had of Japanese shipping to help them transfer large quantities of rubber and tin from the East

---

[210] PA/AA, Handakten Ritter Japan, Bd. 18, Nr1 7634 'Thomsen an Auswärtiges Amt (2.8.1941, 02.54 h)'; ibid., 'Thomsen an Auswärtiges Amt (2.8.1941, 21.03 h)'.

[211] See the detailed figures provided by Miller, *Bankrupting the Enemy*, pp 174–6.

[212] The extent to which a small group of secondary officials was allowed to set policy absolutely key to American strategy in the summer of 1941 has baffled three generations of historians. President Roosevelt may have been out of the loop because he spent the first half of August travelling to and from the Placentia Bay summit with Churchill. Secretary of State Cordell Hull (aged 69 and in poor health) had let it be known on a number of previous occasions that he did not want his senior aides to bother him with too much detail and may only have been confronted with the true extent of the embargo during an interview with the Japanese ambassador on 4 September. To this day, no conclusive evidence has come to light suggesting that the President had intended such an outcome all along (the choice of the staunchly anti-Axis Acheson appears to support such an explanation) or, conversely, that he just balked at reversing his position in the face of public opinion at home and abroad, which was proving to be strongly supportive of such a move. Jeffrey Taliaferro, 'Strategy of Innocence or Provocation? The Roosevelt Administration's Road to World War II'; in: Jeffrey Taliaferro et al (eds.), *The Challenge of Grand Strategy* (Cambridge: CUP 2012), pp 193–223, has argued that Roosevelt must have acted in the knowledge that his actions were likely to bring about war. According to Kaiser, *Victory*, p 259, the answer to the riddle lies in the fact that: 'In the oil embargo decision, Roosevelt, as he so often did, chose the proper moment to yield to the blandishments of determined subordinates.' For an economic historian's view, the reader is referred to Miller, *Bankrupting the Enemy*, pp 191–204. See also Irvine H. Anderson, 'The 1941 De Facto Oil Embargo of Japan: A Bureaucratic Reflex'; in: *Pacific Historical Review*, Vol. 44, No. 2 (May 1975), pp 201–31, and Barnhart, *Japan Prepares for Total War*, pp 201–32.

Indies to increase the as yet insufficient stockpile, it might actually end up hurting Washington more than Tokyo. This was then followed up with the usual evisceration of an American policy supposedly based on mere 'bluff' and 'empty threats', but along the way the general allowed himself one very perceptive comment, which showed that occasionally he was also capable of analysis that went beyond a time span of three months. Returning to an earlier theme that President Roosevelt would as likely as not attempt to postpone war for a while yet, he added that in view of recent progress made by American industry the country might just about reach a preliminary state of readiness in spring 1942. This would make 'a two-front war with weak forces deployed on one front and concentration of the bulk of forces on the other front just about feasible'.[213] A few days later, encouraged by the news that the Japanese had indeed decided to cease merchant traffic to and from the USA, Boetticher was his old optimistic self again. The American strategic stockpile was still far too small, faith in Russian resistance obviously misplaced and the first reinforcements sent to the Far East just so much smoke and mirrors. American options were basically limited to moves like closing German consulates and relieving the British on Iceland.[214]

A few days after Boetticher's latest tirade, Joseph Goebbels was treated to an insider's view of American politics which is of relevance because the *Reichspropagandaminister* recorded his intention to have the gist of this exchange summarised for Hitler's benefit.[215] His guest that day was the former head of the US-based Transozean news agency who had just been deported from the USA after having all the branches of his office closed by presidential decree. After dwelling on the alleged influence of Jews on government policy in America and the fact that German-Americans had to be seen as a lost cause from the Third Reich's point of view, the conversation turned to the most critical subject. As Goebbels put it in his diary: 'At this moment it is not yet possible to say whether the US will enter the war or not. It is clear that Roosevelt wants it; he is merely awaiting a favourable opportunity. The only reason why he hasn't yet gone ahead with it is linked to the popular mood in the USA, which is against the war. But this is something which could change overnight.'[216]

A confirmation of this analysis was provided two days later, when both Houses of Congress had to vote on an eighteen-month extension of the service

---

[213] PA/AA, StS USA, Bd. 7, 'Boetticher & Thomsen an Auswärtiges Amt (30.7.1941)'. This telegram came with a distribution list that had Keitel, Halder and Luftwaffe chief of operations, Hoffmann von Waldau, as additional recipients.
[214] PA/AA, StS USA, Bd. 8, 'Boetticher & Thomsen an Auswärtiges Amt (7.8.1941)'; BA/MA, RH 67/50 'Amt/Ausland Abwehr. Abt. Ausland Nr. 9221/41 geh. Ig. Abschrift Telegramm Washington Nr. 2672 vom 9.8.1941 (12.8.1941)'.
[215] TB Goebbels, Bd. II.1, p 202 (entry for 9 August 1941).
[216] Ibid.

of the first class of the draft. The Bill had caused considerable discontent and irritation among conscripts and their families, who in turn brought pressure to bear on their representatives in Washington. It passed the Senate comfortably enough on 11 August but a considerable number of congressmen were up for re-election the following spring and feared the consequences of doing the government's bidding in the face of public opinion in their home states. A first vote gave the bill a comfortable majority, but then further congressmen approached the Speaker of the House one by one to change their votes. In the end, a total of sixty-five Democrat congressmen voted against the government, allowing the bill to squeeze past by a majority of exactly one vote.[217] If not an outright 'serious defeat', as Thomsen put it in a cable, it was certainly a major embarrassment for the President, the effect of which was magnified many times over by the fact that news of it reached him in the midst of his talks with Churchill in Newfoundland.[218]

Roosevelt's departure from Washington to meet the British prime minister at Argentia in Newfoundland (9–12 August 1941) had escaped Thomsen and Boetticher,[219] and the press release that proclaimed the Atlantic Charter agreed by the two leaders thus came as a genuine surprise. The charter's eight articles were powerful enough as a statement of general intent, with the sixth referring openly to the 'final destruction of Nazi tyranny' – a point not lost on the German dictator.[220] The signatories also pledged themselves to resist territorial expansion by undemocratic means, to defend the right of all peoples to freely choose their form of government, to facilitate access to raw materials the world over, to improve possibilities for economic advancement and ensure the safety of all nations and the freedom of the seas. However, the

---

[217] For allegations that the Speaker cut short the process to prevent a defeat for the administration, see the account in Doris Kearns Goodwin, *No Ordinary Time: Franklin and Eleanor Roosevelt – the Home Front in World War II* (New York: Simon & Schuster 1995), pp 267–9.

[218] J. Garry Clifford and Theodore A. Wilson, 'Blundering on the Brink, 1941: FDR and the 203–202 Vote Reconsidered'; in: J. Garry Clifford and Theodore A. Wilson (eds.), *Presidents, Diplomats and Other Mortals* (Columbia: Missouri UP 2007), pp 99–115, tends to downplay the gravity of this close shave by pointing out that a win for the opposition would not have been tantamount to the disbandment of most of the armed forces. While there is truth in this, it needs to be set against the impression the outcome of the vote left in London and Berlin.

[219] For comprehensive studies of the many facets of the summit, see Theodore A. Wilson, *The First Summit: Roosevelt and Churchill at Placentia Bay 1941* (Lawrence, Ks.: Kansas UP rev. ed. 1991) and Douglas Brinkley and David Facey-Crowther (eds.), *The Atlantic Charter* (New York: St Martin's Press 1994). A good summary can be found in William T. Johnsen, *The Origins of the Grand Alliance: Anglo–American Military Collaboration from the Panay Incident to Pearl Harbor* (Lexington: Kentucky UP 2016), pp 193–211.

[220] According to his Luftwaffe adjutant, Hitler showed signs of clear exasperation and was adamant in ruling out the outcome envisaged by the two Western leaders. Nicolaus von Below, *Als Hitlers Adjutant 1937–1945* (Selent: Pour le Merite rp 1999), p 287.

charter was fairly bland and non-committal where the specifics of a possible US intervention were concerned.[221] Churchill, already disappointed in his hope of moving the USA closer to a declaration of war, had sailed back to Britain under the impression that at the summit the President had committed to naval escorts for UK-bound convoys and a proclamation threatening war on Japan should it move against Dutch or British possessions in the Far East. The former move would materialise after a fashion four weeks later, but the latter initiative was so watered down by the US State Department as to turn it into an irrelevance.[222] Thus, envoy Thomsen actually had a point when he telegraphed Berlin on 14 August, stating that 'that the published record of the results achieved at the summit would certainly have been more impressive, if they had had positive decisions of far-reaching political and military importance to report'.[223] If nothing else, Argentia had certainly made a nonsense of Hitler's repeated musings about how a supposedly inevitable clash of interests between Great Britain and the USA would lead to a rift between both nations and eventually even an Anglo–German alliance. The roots of this bizarre idea can be traced back all the way to *Mein Kampf*, but coincidentally the dictator had dwelt on it with some insistence in July and August 1941.[224]

A loose minute on the summit was prepared by Ribbentrop for Hitler's benefit. By and large, it took its cue from the impressions collected by Thomsen and Boetticher in Washington, stressing that Roosevelt was momentarily being held in check by the lack of commitment on the part of the American public's silent majority and the concern over what the Japanese might do in Southeast Asia should American military focus shift decisively away from the Pacific. For good measure, the *Reichsaußenminister* added some idle speculation about the likelihood of an American entry into the war in case of a sudden Soviet collapse. What makes this minute a unique document is a casual aside

---

[221] Recent scholarly reassessments of the summit's results have tended to be critical. See John Charmley, *Churchill: The End of Glory – A Political Biography* (London: Hodder & Stoughton 1993), p 459. Also Clive Ponting, *Churchill* (London: Sinclair-Stevenson 1994), p 536; David Reynolds, 'Atlantic Flop'; in: Brinkley and Facey-Crowther (eds.), *Atlantic Charter*, p 129, and Kimball, *Forged in War*, p 103. Also Max Hastings, *Finest Years: Churchill as Warlord 1940–1945* (London: Harper Press 2009), p 199.

[222] Reynolds, 'Atlantic Flop', pp 138–9.

[223] PA/AA, StS USA, Bd. 8, 'Thomsen an Auswärtiges Amt. Für Staatssekretär ! (14.8.1941, 23.10 h)'. Following the new policy dictated by Ribbentrop, Thomsen and Boetticher reported on this event in separate cables. For Boetticher's rather more bullish impressions of the Placentia Bay summit, see PA/AA, Handakten Ritter Japan, Bd. 18, Nr. 7633 'Boetticher und Thomsen an Auswärtiges Amt (14.8.1941, 14.25 h)'.

[224] IfZ, ED 100–78 TB Hewel (entry for 11 July 1941); 'Führerhauptquartier 25.7.1941, abends'; and 'Führerhauptquartier, Nacht vom 8. auf 9.8.1941, Nacht vom 9. auf 10.8., 10.8.1941 mittags, 10.8.1941 abends, Nacht vom 10. auf 11.8.1941. H/Fu'; all in: Werner Jochmann (ed.), *Adolf Hitler. Monologe im Führerhauptquartier 1941–1944* (München: Orbis 2000), 47, 56. Hitler would occasionally return to this theme even after Pearl Harbor, see 'Wolfsschanze, 7.1.1942 abends. H/Fu'; in: ibid., pp 183–4.

Ribbentrop made while discussing the 'bluff and bluster' of Roosevelt's war policy. The American President, Ribbentrop elaborated for the Führer's benefit, was able to afford this rather cavalier approach to strategy 'because it is simply not possible to mount an attack on the United States on the hoof (*ohne weiteres*)'.[225] It has been established consensus among historians of the National Socialist regime for some time that among the political elite of the Third Reich, Hitler's foreign minister was by far the least suited either by intellect or temperament to fill out the position he had attained.[226] That even he should have been able to draw this rather simple, though no less vital, conclusion all by himself while it appears to have eluded the attaché in Washington for the last year constitutes a rather devastating indictment of the latter.

In the meantime, the prospect of a future combination of Anglo–American air power was a subject that simply would not go away. On 24 July, RAF Bomber Command unleashed a considerable part of its growing heavy bomber force against the two German capital ships still lying in French ports. *Gneisenau* was only bracketed by near misses, but *Scharnhorst*, which had recently moved to La Pallice, was hit from 15,000 feet by five bombs and sustained considerable damage. The raid was exceptional not just because of the numbers involved (149 bombers) but also because it took place in broad daylight. Eighteen of the bombers involved had been new four-engined aircraft, among them three B-17s recently arrived from the USA. Far from attempting to deny this, the American government actually allowed the story of American input to this success story to be spread far and wide, putting Boetticher in the unaccustomed position of having to explain a German setback.[227] An off-the-record briefing given by the British Under-Secretary of State for Air, Harold Balfour, to Washington journalists a fortnight later gave a broad idea of how the British intended to continue this type of warfare. According to Balfour, the only possible way to win this war would be by the use of heavy bombers against high-value targets, thus bringing German industry to a halt. An invasion of the continent would be superfluous and a US expeditionary army would only be needed in the Middle East.

---

[225] 'Aufzeichnung des Reichsaußenministers (17.8.1941)'; in: ADAP, Serie D, Bd. XIII.1, pp 266–8. Crucially, this document bears the stamp of Ambassador Hewel which confirms that it was put before Hitler.

[226] Wolfgang Michalka has described him as 'incapable and arrogant, capricious and unpredictable, extremely devoted to and dependent on Hitler'. Wolfgang Michalka, 'Joachim von Ribbentrop – vom Spirituosenhändler zum Außenminister'; in: Ronald Smelser and Rainer Zitelmann (eds.), *Die braune Elite. 22 biographische Skizzen* (Darmstadt: WBG 1989), pp 201–11.

[227] PA/AA, StS USA, Bd. 7, 'Thomsen und Boetticher an Auswärtiges Amt (26.7.1941)'. The damage to *Scharnhorst* was in fact inflicted by the new Handley Page Halifaxes of 35 and 76 Squadrons. Ken Merrick, *Handley Page Halifax: From Hell to Victory and Beyond* (London: Ian Allan 2009), p 21.

Figure 3.2 Churchill and Roosevelt at Argentia: even though the summit achieved little of immediate military substance, the public commitment by the head of state of a neutral country to the 'destruction' of another regime can safely be said to have been without precedent. (Bettman via Getty Images)

For once Boetticher, in relaying these statements, chose not to accompany them with his usual verbiage about Allied daydreaming – which in this case would actually have been fully justified – but added a page of figures detailing the current and expected output of American heavy bombers, as well as the factories currently being built or retooled for their production.[228] Five days later, he followed this up with a cable giving an even more detailed breakdown of US production of multi-engined aircraft. For the next nine months, he predicted an approximate production of 800 four-engined bombers (equally divided between the B-17 and the B-24), while by June 1943 a monthly total of 500 four-engined bombers was anticipated. He also worked on the assumption that the majority of these would find their way into service with the Royal Air Force and its affiliates.[229]

---

[228] BA/MA, RH 67/50 'Vortragsnotiz. Betr.: Schwere Kampfflugzeuge für den Angriff gegen Deutschland (14.8.1941)'.
[229] BA/MA, RH 67/50 'Telegramm aus Washington 17. August 1941, 4.36 h (18.8.1941)'.

An interesting insight into how these reports were interpreted by the Luftwaffe's leaders is given by two sources. A voluminous report, which was forwarded by the office of the *Generalluftzeugmeister* on 30 August, admitted to a major 'heavy bomber gap' between Britain and the USA on the one hand, and Germany on the other.[230] The authors of the report were particularly impressed by the Boeing B-17s operational ceiling, which they correctly linked to its engines being equipped with high-end turbo-superchargers. They expected a similar performance from the Consolidated B-24.[231] The projected production numbers were regarded as believable, and if anything 'on the low side'.[232] Together with the British Short Stirling and Handley Page Halifax bombers already serving in a few RAF squadrons, this meant that raids by heavy bombers 'in relatively large numbers' were likely to start occurring anytime soon,[233] with the performance of the two American aircraft in particular making a return to daytime raids more than likely.[234] A fortnight before, an entry into the Seekriegsleitung's war diary had forecast how such a development would affect the task confronting the Luftwaffe's fighter arm. On 13 August, a senior officer on Göring's staff, while stressing to his naval interlocutor that he was not relaying an official opinion, stated that US airplane deliveries to the United Kingdom would in all likelihood reach a 'seriously worrying' level as early as spring 1942. The Luftwaffe would struggle to maintain parity with a Royal Air Force engaged in such a steady growth process. To reverse such a development, incoming raids would have to be routinely decimated to the tune of 10 per cent – a near impossibility in the absence of a major technological advantage.[235]

The note of caution Boetticher had just sounded over the growth of Anglo–American air power was rather untypical for his reporting style. It might be put down to the influence of his assistant air attaché, Riedel, were it not for the fact

---

[230] BA/MA, RL 3/1833 'Lüftrüstungsvergleich Deutschland + Italien und Großbritannien + USA 1939–1943. Stand: 1. Juli 1941. Erster Teil'. The covering letter that accompanies the report bears the date 30 August 1941. Only seven recipients are listed, all of them part of the Luftwaffe's senior hierarchy.

[231] Ibid., pp 9–11, 117–19. To enhance performance at 16,000 feet and beyond, most aircraft engines of the time were equipped with mechanical superchargers to push more air into the cylinders. Unlike Britain and Germany, the USA had also done considerable research into turbo-superchargers, which used the engine's exhaust gases for the same process, but to enhanced effect. Elaborate tubing required for this process would limit turbo-supercharging mostly to the engines of heavy bombers and two fighters with spacious fuselages (the P-38 and the P-47). The author is indebted to Colonel Joseph Blandino of the Virginia Military Institute for his help in clarifying the story behind this aspect of aviation engine design to a humanities graduate completely ignorant of these matters.

[232] Ibid., p 8.

[233] Ibid., p 119.

[234] Ibid., p 9.

[235] KTB Seekriegsleitung, Teil A (entry for 13 August 1941).

that barely a fortnight later both he and Thomsen urged restraint yet again on a wholly unconnected issue. Answering to a query from Berlin, first Thomsen, then a day later Boetticher gave their estimate of a likely American reaction to a Japanese attack on the Philippines. The envoy's answer was considerably more succinct that Boetticher's and the latter once again could not resist the temptation of taking his readers along a detour detailing the extent to which US defence policy was based on little more than 'bluff'. They found themselves in agreement, however, on the key point: should a Japanese move into Southeast Asia also include the Philippines, war with the US would be the inevitable consequence. They also agreed in pointing out that such a move would be singularly gratuitous, since neither the bases nor military assets available there constituted enough of a threat to a Japanese move south to warrant such an attack.[236]

In the meantime, the Russo–German war continued to dominate the headlines. The first shipments of US war materiel to the Red Army under Cash-and-Carry were met with considerably more opposition from the US Army than those to Britain had in the early summer of 1940, seeing that a mere two months ago the beneficiary had itself aided and abetted Germany's wars of aggression. The fact that the US armed forces were by now engaged in an exponential growth which left precious little spare capacity made this even more controversial. Another contentious point lay in the President's refusal to invoke the Neutrality Act upon the outbreak of the Russo–German war. This had been justified by the White House on the grounds that Germany had omitted to declare war prior to initiating hostilities.[237] This loophole made it possible to sail US merchantmen into the new belligerent's harbours provided they did not infringe already existing war zones. In the case of the USSR, these did not of course extend to its Siberian ports, hostilities with the European Axis not having reached its Pacific territories. The only problem lay in the geography of the region which made it impossible to reach the main harbour of Vladivostok without skirting Japanese territorial waters.[238] Since the beginning of Barbarossa, Tokyo had repeatedly hinted that any attempt at establishing such a lifeline might bring into play the provision of the Tripartite Pact about mutual assistance. Accordingly, the envoy, Thomsen, spoke of a 'test case', when the first US tanker sailed for Vladivostok in late August. It arrived there on the 8 September unmolested, yet another event which appeared to suggest that the elements in the Japanese government favouring confrontation

[236] PA/AA, Handakten Ritter, Japan, Bd. 18, Nr. 7633 'Thomsen an Auswärtiges Amt (27.8.1941)'; StS USA, Bd. 8, 'Boetticher & Thomsen an Auswärtiges Amt (29.8.1941)'.

[237] Robert Huhn Jones, *The Roads to Russia: United States Lend-Lease to the Soviet Union* (Norman: University of Oklahoma Press 1969), p 36.

[238] See the map reproduced in Alla Paperno, 'The Unknown World War II in the Northern Pacific'; in: https://lend-lease.net/articles-en/the-unknown-world-war-ii-in-the-northern-pacific (accessed 23 June 2020).

with the USA were still in the minority. Even though not many deliveries of this kind were carried out pre-Pearl Harbor, what is noteworthy is that most of the German observers monitoring this traffic did so with little alarm; they tended to see it as a gauge that allowed them to read US resolve or Japanese lack of the same.[239] Its potential in breathing new life into a Red Army on the brink of defeat appears to have completely escaped them.

If de-escalation still appeared to be possible in the Pacific, an incident which occurred that same week on the other side of the world appeared to indicate that the time to exercise such options in the Atlantic was running out fast. In the early afternoon of 4 September, the destroyer USS *Greer*, which was operating in the waters off Iceland where the Western Hemisphere Security Zone as defined by the US administration overlapped with the Kriegsmarine's extended war zone, was informed by a British patrol bomber of the proximity of a U-boat which had just crash-dived in front of it. The USS *Greer* changed course, located the U-boat via sonar, then signalled to the bomber circling overhead the invisible position of the submersible off its starboard bow. The British pilot dropped his depth charges, which, however, failed to inflict any damage. The U-boat commander retaliated by rising to periscope depth and firing two torpedoes which failed to find their quarry. The destroyer in turn responded with a number of depth charge attacks which carried on into the late evening. U-652 escaped unscathed, but this being the first time that a German and a US vessel had engaged in combat, a line had clearly been crossed.[240]

Ever since the convoy taking the Marines to Iceland had set sail in early July, the US Navy's Atlantic Fleet had been issued a series of instructions that encouraged it to confront Kriegsmarine raiders which might constitute a threat to US convoy traffic to and from Iceland. These rules of engagement, however, tended to be ambivalent about the where and when. On the issue of intercepting Axis surface vessels, some clarity was finally achieved on 25 August, when the Atlantic Fleet was permitted to engage and destroy them if they had attacked shipping plying the Iceland–Newfoundland route or had done no more than to 'approach the lanes sufficiently close to threaten such shipping'.[241] On the very eve of the *Greer* incident, the Chief of Naval Operations both extended and clarified these rules of engagement: 'hostile forces will be deemed to threaten United States or Iceland shipping if they enter the general area of the sea lanes

---

[239] For examples of this, see KTB Seekriegsleitung, Teil A (entries for 8 September and 25 October 1941); PA/AA, StS USA, Bd. 8, 'Thomsen an Auswärtiges Amt (17.9.1941)'; StS USA, Bd. 9, 'Thomsen an Auswärtiges Amt (18.10.1941)'; StS USA, Bd. 9, 'Thomsen an Auswärtiges Amt (24.10.1941)'.

[240] The best account of this action is still the one to be found in Patrick Abbazia, *Mr. Roosevelt's Navy: The Private War of the US Atlantic Fleet, 1939–1942* (Annapolis: USNIP 1975), pp 223–32.

[241] Norton, *Open Secret*, p 73.

which lie between North America and Iceland or enter the neutrality zone of the Atlantic Ocean described in the Declaration of Panama' – in view of the vast expanse of sea covered by the latter, this amounted to a virtual carte blanche.[242] Thus, strictly speaking, the commanding officer of the USS *Greer* in passing on tactical intelligence to the British bomber had merely adhered to the long-standing practice of the Neutrality Patrol, though admittedly the circumstances made a misperception by the enemy unavoidable. However, since the US government failed to own up to either the role played by the British bomber or the fact that a set of new rules of engagement practically ordering American vessels to engage the Kriegsmarine had been issued only the day before, the *Greer* incident put the US administration in a position where it could claim that one of its vessels had become the victim of a wrongful attack. Initially though, the public reaction to the *Greer* incident was so muted as to quickly discourage any attempt on the part of the President to turn the destroyer into the Word War II equivalent of the USS *Maine*. Even among the openly interventionist newspapers only the *New York Times* advocated using the incident as a pretext for going to war.[243] A number of congressmen and senators pointed out that with the occupation of Iceland such incidents were only to be expected and that the destroyer could in any case have been legitimately mistaken for a British one, since it belonged to the same class as the fifty handed over to the Royal Navy the previous autumn.[244] Republican Senator George Aiken even openly doubted the veracity of the story put out by the government.

On the other side of the Atlantic, Hitler and Ribbentrop, once they were in possession of the U-boat's operational report,[245] decided on a two-track strategy: on the one hand, they upheld the U-boat arm's rules of engagement, which barred U-boats from engaging US Navy vessels beyond the limits of the old operations zone even when they were engaged in escorting British convoys.[246] On the other hand, once they realised that the story Roosevelt had fed to the media was so full of holes that a rare opportunity might present itself to embarrass the US administration, they instructed Thomsen in Washington to get in touch with American legislators known for their

---

[242] Ibid.

[243] PA/AA, StS USA, Bd. 8, 'Thomsen an Auswärtiges Amt (5.9.1941)'.

[244] The *Wickes* class destroyers were given their unique silhouette by four smoke stacks of identical size.

[245] U-652 radioed a brief report giving all relevant facts when asked to break radio silence for that purpose the following day. See KTB Seekriegsleitung, Teil A (entry for 5 September 1941).

[246] The set of orders allowed attacks on escorts while engaged in self-defence; once the enemy vessel had turned away, however, hostilities were to be terminated and not to be resumed. KTB Seekriegsleitung, Teil A (entry for 9 September 1941).

isolationist stance.[247] Whether by coincidence or as a result of this initiative, on 11 September Senators Gerald P. Nye and Bennett C. Clark entered a motion calling for the officers of the *Greer* to be interrogated before the Senate Naval Affairs Committee and the ship's log to be subpoenaed.[248] Only hours later, the President gave a major speech over the radio in which he addressed the problem posed by the Axis 'rattlesnakes of the sea'.[249]

In view of the lack of impact which the *Greer* incident had had, the President had been fortunate in that two further incidents had come to light in the intervening week. On 6 September, three survivors of the small steamer *Sessa* were rescued southwest of Iceland, thus bringing to light its sinking by *U-38* a week before, and on 7 September the *Steel Seafarer* was bombed and sunk by the Luftwaffe 322 km (200 miles) south of Suez.[250] Even Secretary Hull had to admit that the former ship's registry was doubtful,[251] and the latter vessel had been sent into a war zone with a freight of weapons for the British forces in Egypt after the US government had decided that it was safe for it to do so. However, together with the case of the four-month-old sinking of the *Robin Moor* and an alleged encounter of an American battleship with a German submersible 'in July',[252] they were all used as political ammunition to make a case for the US Navy taking a more proactive role in the Atlantic than before. For the first time, the President explicitly committed himself to defend the freedom of the seas – a term thus far avoided in public policy statements

---

[247] PA/AA, StS USA, Bd. 8, 'Ribbentrop an Thomsen (6.9.1941)'. The reference at the end of the cable to the interest shown by somebody 'in the highest position' is a clear allusion to Hitler.

[248] PA/AA, StS USA Bd. 8, 'Thomsen an Auswärtiges Amt (11.9.1941)'.

[249] Thomsen re-transmitted the entire text in the original English to Berlin; see PA/AA, StS USA, Bd. 8, 'Wortlaut Roosevelt-Rede (11.9.1941, 10.30 h)', 'Rooseveltrede erste Fortsetzung (11.9.1941, 10.30 h)', 'Rooseveltrede, 2. Fortsetzung (11.9.1941, 10.30 h)', 'Rooseveltrede – dritte Fortsetzung (11.9.1941, 10.30 h)', 'Roosevelt-Rede 4. Fortsetzung (12.9.1941, 01.54 h)', 'Rooseveltrede. Fünfte Fortsetzung (11.9.1941, 10.30 h)'. See also Rosenman (ed.), *Public Papers and Addresses*, pp 384–92.

[250] Jürgen Rohwer, *Chronology of the War at Sea 1939–1945: The Naval History of World War Two* (Annapolis: USNIP 2005), p 98.

[251] PA/AA, StS USA, Bd. 8, 'Thomsen an Auswärtiges Amt (9.9.1941)'.

[252] No U-boat had reported shadowing an American battleship during that month and thus the Germans immediately connected this accusation to *U-203*'s pursuit of the USS *Texas* on 20 June, see PA/AA, StS USA, Bd. 8, 'Oberkommando der Kriegsmarine, Neu B. Nr 1. Skl I. ia an das Auswärtige Amt z.Hd. von Herrn Gesandten Eisenlohr. Betr.: Zwischenfälle mit amerikanischen Schiffen. Bezugnahme auf das Telefongespräch zwischen Gesandten Eisenlohr und Graf Stauffenberg am 12.9.1941 (12.9.1941)'. Since the Germans never divulged this story, apparent American knowledge of it could easily have become yet another pointer towards a possible compromise of the U-boat arm's Enigma encoding machine, but this does not appear to have happened. The mix-up was only solved in 1975 when an American historian compared German records with the logs of the battleships then operating with the Atlantic Fleet. See Abbazia, *Roosevelt's Navy*, pp 174–6.

because of the memories it inevitably brought of the country's road to war in 1917. He was also adamant that the safe arrival of Lend-Lease shipments and possession of bases in places like Greenland, Iceland and Newfoundland gave the USA the right to protect shipping passing close by on their way to Britain, thus deliberately blurring the distinction between convoys headed for Iceland and those passing Iceland well to the south. Hence, due to the American interest in both these waters as well as the ships passing through them, Axis vessels encountered in this general area would from now on be attacked without warning. Even though Roosevelt went on to commit the US Navy to the protection of commercial traffic of all flags, he eschewed the use of the word 'convoy' and yet again would not be drawn on the geographical extent of the area thus covered, leaving the Seekriegsleitung with an estimate published by the Reuters News Agency as its best guess.[253]

On 15 September, Secretary of the Navy Frank Knox gave an address to the chapter of the American Legion in Milwaukee, which was unique in that it provided some badly needed specifics while at the same time further muddying the waters. After spending some time in explaining to his audience the original rationale behind Lend-Lease and linking the occupation of Iceland to the recent drop in British shipping losses, he declared that 'beginning tomorrow the American navy will provide protection as adequate as we can make it for ships of every flag carrying lend-aid supplies between the American continent and waters adjacent to Iceland'.[254] Convoying was thus strongly implied – though, yet again, not spelt out – and the reference to the waters adjacent to Iceland can be interpreted as a strong hint at the limited range of the Atlantic Fleet's escorts or the perceived need to provide isolationists with a sop, or both. Irrespective of what some pundits had hinted at in previous days,[255] the US Navy was for the moment choosing not to push its boats out much beyond its newly acquired base on the Arctic island. The outpost of Iceland had thus become a point on the map useful for temporarily obfuscating the potential impact of the new convoying policy, replacing the one started in July, which had been limited to a politically much less contentious traffic, merely aimed at keeping an American outpost resupplied.[256] The following day, the State

---

[253] KTB Seekriegsleitung, Teil A (entry for 13 September 1941). A calculation based at least in part on the previous growth rate of the Security Zone.

[254] PA/AA, StS USA, Bd. 8, 'Thomsen an Auswärtiges Amt (15.9.1941)', giving the key passages of the speech in the original English.

[255] Rear Admiral Yates Stirling Jr., the recently retired commandant of the Third Naval District, had stated that the change in strategy alluded to in the President's speech basically covered 'all the world's oceans'; KTB Seekriegsleitung, Teil A (entry for 16 September 1941).

[256] The ambiguity fostered by a terminology carefully calibrated to distract critical listeners in 1941 from the real issues has carried over into post-war historiography in quite a remarkable way. Distinguished historians of the late twentieth and early twenty-first centuries often fail to make the simple, but politically crucial distinction between

Department announced that after consultations with the Justice Department it had reached the conclusion that the 1939 Neutrality Act only forbade American merchantmen to sail into the ports of metropolitan Britain or those of its Dominions (Canada, Australia, New Zealand and South Africa). Its colonies were thus no longer affected by this restriction.[257] Finally, on 17 September, as anticipated by Hull in a speech the previous day, the first force of US Navy destroyers joined the UK-bound convoy HX-150 and escorted it to a mid-ocean meeting point (MOMP) where they handed it over to a Royal Navy escort.[258] In just a few days, the American administration had eroded large parts of the existing neutrality legislation while leaving its outer edifice in place.

The Atlantic Charter and the *Greer* affair belong to those stepping stones in the German–American 'Cold War' of 1940–1, where the paper trail provides us with proof of Hitler's interest in keeping abreast of the latest events of this slowly escalating conflict. Though it is not entirely clear whether he reacted to this by demanding more specifics on Roosevelt's preparations for war, the volume of intelligence generated in the following weeks certainly supports such a conclusion. On 19 September, Boetticher sent an extensive report on the creation of a new US government agency, the Supply Priorities and Allocation Board (SPAB), which would be tasked with systematically compiling data on the requirements of US civilian industry and the country's armed forces as well as those of its overseas allies, and allocating resources accordingly. Since the agencies which had preceded it had all failed rather signally in this task, a snide comment or two about this organisation's prospects would have been very much in keeping with the general's style of reporting. Instead, he described it as a development which pointed towards further 'considerable extension of industrial plant working for the war effort . . . in the very near future'.[259]

convoys headed 'to Iceland' on the one hand, and those to a 'point level with it' (and onwards to Britain or the USA) on the other. B. Mitchell Simpson III, *Admiral Harold R. Stark: Architect of Victory, 1939–1945* (Columbia: South Carolina UP 1989), pp 89–91. Also: Baer, *Sea Power*, pp 160–2; Clay Blair, *Hitler's U-boat War: The Hunters 1939–1942* (London: Weidenfeld & Nicholson 1997), pp 304, 315, 360; David J. Bercuson and Holger Herwig, *One Christmas in Washington: Churchill and Roosevelt Forge the Grand Alliance* (London: Weidenfeld & Nicholson 2005), p 33; Christopher M. Bell, *Churchill and Sea Power* (Oxford: OUP 2013), pp 226–7, and Kaiser, *Victory*, p 278.

[257] PA/AA, StS USA, Bd. 8, 'Thomsen an Auswärtiges Amt (16.9.1941)'.

[258] Something the Seekriegsleitung had been expecting since the *Greer* incident, irrespective of the reluctance of US government officials to mention convoys by name; KTB Seekriegsleitung, Teil A (entry for 9 September 1941). A further twenty-seven convoys (both east- and westbound) would be escorted in this fashion before Pearl Harbor. See Abbazia, *Roosevelt's Navy*, pp 255, 310.

[259] PA/AA, Handakten Etzdorf. 'Politische Berichte Washington. Meldung Mil.Att. Washington vom 19.9.1941 (23.9.1941)'. For the political debates which surrounded the creation of SPAB, the reader is referred to Maury Klein, *A Call to Arms: Mobilizing America for World War II* (New York: Bloomsbury Press 2015 pb), pp 196–207.

In the meantime, the Sicherheitsdienst of the SS had not been idle. Most of its previous reports based on eavesdropping on the conversations of US diplomats bore the signature of assorted SD bureaucrats of intermediate rank, but the covering letter addressed to *Reichsaußenminister* Ribbentrop that accompanied the latest SD intelligence scoop was signed on 26 September by *SS-Gruppenführer* Reinhard Heydrich himself.[260]

The report in question was of book-length size (175 pages), based at least in part on confidential sources, and gave an astonishingly detailed account of how far the mobilisation of the US economy had progressed in the last six months.[261] It covered subjects ranging from the order of battle of the growing services, the exponential growth of the aeronautical and shipping industries, problems of labour procurement, the extent to which the Federal government was regulating the economic life of the country, and the problems involved in stockpiling enough strategic raw materials. To allow the reader to contextualise different projects, most of them are itemised according to numbers ordered, cost incurred, labour force employed and cost to the Federal government. A big project like a new engine factory for the Wright Aeronautical Corporation in Lockland, Ohio (cost: $ 42,488,548) is singled out for being the most expensive government-bankrolled project of this kind so far, but the smaller fry ($175,000 for two industrial-sized refrigerators in Fort Bliss, Texas; $36,384 for improvements to the hangars at the USAAF base at Jacksonville, Florida[262]) is by no means neglected. In contrast to Boetticher, the author(s) of the reports limited their occasional criticism to relaying statements made by government, union or company spokesmen, who had themselves had some involvement with the projects in question. These usually referred to problems with industrial action or the delay in starting a strategic stockpile of raw materials, with rubber and tin singled out for special attention. Also mentioned were shortfalls in the production of steel and electricity and the failure to make the most of the available pool of unskilled labour. The report also dwells at some length on the weaknesses in terms of both quality and quantity of the anti-aircraft arm of both services and on the recent formation of the Civil Defence Corps tasked with dealing with the aftermath of enemy air raids.[263]

---

[260] PA/AA, Inland II g 340, Nr. 2645 'Der Chef der Sicherheitspolizei und des SD an den Herrn Reichsaußenminister von Ribbentrop (26.9.1941)'.

[261] PA/AA, Inland II g 477 a 'Aufrüstung der Vereinigten Staaten unter besonderer Berücksichtigung des Arbeitsmarktes der Rohstofflage und der Streiks (n.d.)'. The report's true importance only becomes apparent in conjunction with Heydrich's covering letter. Since the two were filed away separately and the letter does not mention the report by its title, finding a way of matching them up proved to be a daunting task to say the least. It was only thanks to the selflessness and high professional standards which are standard at the Politisches Archiv that this was made possible. Special thanks go to Dr Gerhard Keiper who played a key role in connecting these dots for me.

[262] Ibid., p 56, 89, 92.

[263] Ibid., 16–20, 58–64.

Since the report is not organised as an answer to a questionnaire, it has not been possible to establish whether these items reflected the priorities of the intelligence gatherers' paymasters. Overall, the tone is almost completely neutral, which is remarkable and, once again, sets the SD's work apart from Boetticher's increasingly hectoring style. While a number of difficulties are singled out for special attention, the author(s) are under no illusion that most of these will in due course be remedied.

The report appears to have been finished during the last week of June 1941, since the last date mentioned in it is 21 June. The three-month gap between that cut-off date and the day on which it was presented to Ribbentrop may have resulted from awaiting the arrival of additional morsels of information from the SD's more traditional sources of information, like break-ins at European embassies. The key question, of course, is whether the report's findings were ever put before Hitler. Unlike Stalin, he would have resisted the temptation of retiring to bed with a 175-page file and would in all likelihood have insisted on a verbal summary. If, as seems likely, the task fell to Walther Hewel, Ribbentrop's liaison at the *Führerhauptquartier*, there is a good chance that he would have seized the opportunity to do so with both hands. An exception among the Nazi elite, Hewel was a well-travelled man who had repeatedly attempted to impress on Hitler the foolhardiness of seeking a confrontation with the USA. The fact that he was on very good terms with Hitler – they had known each other since before the 1923 coup – would have ensured that he at least got a hearing. While there is anecdotal evidence to suggest that Hitler rejected out of hand a report on the expansion of the US aircraft industry couched in similar terms only a few weeks later,[264] it certainly seems that someone in the hierarchy of the Third Reich was impressed with *Aufrüstung der Vereinigten Staaten*, because just over two months later a second, even more detailed report organised along virtually identical lines was produced and submitted. This one ran to more than 270 pages and had separate chapters for subjects like the training of nursing personnel in the army or the building of housing for newly hired workers in the armaments industry. Since the last event referred to in the text bears the date 5 December, it seems unlikely that it reached the Wolfsschanze in time to play a role in Hitler's decision to join Japan in its war against the USA.[265]

The wartime events of the first three weeks of October gave Boetticher one last fleeting opportunity to impress on his American counterparts in the Munitions Building the unstoppable force of the Wehrmacht on the rampage. The British in North Africa were still biding their time, while in Russia

[264] BA/MA, ZA 3/264 'Die amerikanische Luftrüstung' by Justus Koch and Fritz Siebel (post-war deposition).
[265] PA/AA, Inland II g, 477 b and 477 c 'Die Aufrüstung der Vereinigten Staaten von Amerika im zweiten Halbjahr 1941 (n.d.)'.

Heeresgruppe Mitte, which had been reinforced with two fresh Panzer divisions and with a total manpower strength of a little less than 2 million, initiated its much awaited drive towards Moscow on 30 September. The dislocation of the Red Army units defending the approaches to the Soviet capital was already apparent in the first few days of the offensive, giving the lie to the estimates of the Soviet military mission in Washington that the Germans had shot their bolt and would soon find themselves on the receiving end of a major Soviet counterblow.[266] Hitler's speech of 3 October in the Berlin Sportpalast, during which he announced that the end of the USSR was just within reach, appeared genuinely plausible for about a fortnight, even though it may not have exercised quite the sort of mesmerising effect on Washington decision makers that Boetticher attributed to it.[267] Even so, it seemed unlikely that the pledge publicly entered into by Britain and the USA on 1 October – when at the conclusion of the Three Power Conference in Moscow they signed the First Protocol which promised regular monthly deliveries of weapons, raw materials and foodstuffs to the embattled USSR – could still reverse such a tide of defeat. Against this backdrop, it was easy for the German attaché to drive home his favourite theme about American strategic overstretch and the plethora of commitments which its arms industry was as yet in no way capable of meeting, a dilemma which only plenty of 'bluffing' could address.

In the meantime, President Roosevelt continued his step-by-step strategy of checkmating Hitler wherever he could, without bringing about a state of open war. The main obstacle still standing in his way was the neutrality legislation of 1939 which addressed a number of activities Americans were not allowed to engage in on behalf of any of the warring nations. The key passage forbade the shipping of any kind of goods in American-flagged ships into the harbours of belligerents (Article 2), thus reflecting the legislators' concerns about the kinds of incident which had brought the USA into the war in 1917. While it could be argued that countless laws and treaties implemented by the Roosevelt administration since the destroyers-for-bases deal of September 1940 had already violated the spirit, if not the letter, of the Neutrality Law many times over, the President realised that a frontal attack on this key piece of legislation was a different proposition altogether, calling for a careful and premeditated approach. The Seekriegsleitung noted that a professionally orchestrated propaganda campaign in favour of dismantling the law was already gathering pace by 26 September. Roosevelt himself went on the record stating that the law had been a cause for the spreading of the war throughout Europe since it had signposted for the dictators' benefit how far the United States would go in

---

[266] PA/AA, StS USA, Bd. 9, 'Boetticher und Thomsen an Auswärtiges Amt (8.10.1941)'.
[267] See especially PA/AA, StS USA, Bd. 9, 'Boetticher und Thomsen an Auswärtiges Amt (6.10.1941)'.

supporting the embattled democracies.[268] After lengthy deliberations with key legislators, the President decided that he would limit his assault on the law to rescinding Article 6, which ruled out the arming of American merchantmen, since this one could be regarded the least contentious in the light of recent sinkings. In a speech broadcast to the nation on 9 October, he again evoked the concept of the freedom of the seas to justify this move and expressed his hope that over the course of the debate on the floor of the House, the legislators themselves would come to realise that Article 2 would have to be amended along with Article 6.[269]

As President Roosevelt set about moving his country yet another step closer to becoming a full-blown ally of Britain in the glare of the world's media, the German government received intelligence which suggested that he had already taken much more sweeping steps in that direction under the cloak of secrecy. The informers the SD had in the social circle of US diplomats still on duty in their Rome embassy reported that the Newfoundland summit between Roosevelt and Churchill had in fact seen quite radical moves towards solving the practical issues involved in the day-to-day running of a military coalition fighting a global war. The meeting had allegedly witnessed the signing of an as yet secret military alliance which involved the creation of a joint high command and general staff and a clear division of operational responsibilities.[270] The latter, one of the sources (the US naval attaché) went on, would see the US Navy's Atlantic Fleet come under the command of the Royal Navy. At the same time, merchant traffic to and from the United Kingdom would become the sole responsibility of the United States, who would also provide the means for transatlantic escort in both directions. The bulk of the Royal Navy and Royal Air Force would thus be left in a position to concentrate their efforts against the main forces of the Axis powers. The report does not spell out whether such an arrangement might actually precede war with Germany, but in light of the fact that the Atlantic Fleet had begun escorting British convoys into mid-Atlantic the previous month, the implication is strong that it would.[271] Finally,

---

[268] KTB Seekriegsleitung, Teil A (entry for 26 September 1941).

[269] PA/AA, StS USA, Bd. 9, 'Fernschreiben an RAM über St.S. Zur gestrigen Botschaft Roosevelts an den Kongreß betr. Neutralitätsgesetz (10.10.1941)'.

[270] PA/AA, Inland II g 340 'Der Chef der Sicherheitspolizei und des SD an das Auswärtige Amt z.Hd. Herrn Amtsrat Schimake (9.10.1941)'.

[271] Ibid. These points have all been underlined in the copy held in the archives of the Auswärtiges Amt. These rumours may well have constituted the garbled echo of Anglo–American staff talks held in October 1940 and January–March 1941. In the first case, the British side had briefly suggested shifting the entire US Pacific Fleet (and hence, most US heavy units) to Singapore, leaving the Pacific under overall American, and the Atlantic, under British command. The ABC-1 talks of early 1941 had concluded with a tentative agreement that in case of the USA entering the war with Germany, the US Navy would assume operational control of all Allied units engaged in convoy escort throughout the Western Atlantic and that the US Navy's Asiatic Fleet based in Manila would come

the US Army was said to be in the process of training some of its units for deployment to Siberia, presumably to assist a retreating Soviet government in building a new front against a Wehrmacht engaged in pursuing the Red Army beyond the Ural Mountains.

This report constitutes an interesting mix of the plausible and the nonsensical. The setting up of a joint high command constitutes an eerily accurate premonition of the creation of the Combined Chiefs of Staff Committee during the Anglo–American Arcadia summit at Washington in December 1941 and January 1942.[272] Irrespective of whether the report was an Allied plant or merely reflected the kind of gossiping which underemployed American diplomats and officers would have indulged in during the autumn of 1941, what is important is that the SD's recipients at the Auswärtiges Amt took it very seriously indeed. Within forty-eight hours, it had been forwarded to Ribbentrop's office and given the highest level of security ('*Geheime Reichssache*').[273] Proof that Hitler himself was taking the time to follow these events very closely can be found in the minutes of Alfred Rosenberg's representative, Werner Koeppen, at Führer's Headquarters. In a message summarising what had been discussed over lunch on 17 October, he highlighted the joy Hitler had expressed at the resignation of the Japanese government of Funimaro Konoe the day before. Hindsight would suggest that the Führer was in all likelihood expressing relief at the fall of a government which in previous months had shown somewhat tepid enthusiasm for following an uncompromising pro-Axis policy; according to Koeppen's notes, however, the German leader was above all expressing the hope that the fall of the Konoe government would give US legislators hours away from voting on the repeal of Article 6 of the Neutrality Law some pause.[274]

Further proof – if any were needed – of Roosevelt's perfidy was not long in coming. As already mentioned, two senators had called into question the official account of the *Greer* incident and had demanded that the officers and crew of the destroyer be interrogated and the ship's log examined by the Senate Naval Affairs Committee. Even though the US Navy refused to bow to these demands, Admiral Harold Stark, the Chief of Naval Operations, in written testimony admitted that the *Greer* had in fact been cooperating with a British

---

under British 'strategic direction'. See Andrew Field, *Royal Navy Strategy in the Far East 1919–1939* (London and New York: Frank Cass 2004), p 116, as well as Johnsen, *Grand Alliance*, pp 118–87.

[272] Bercuson/Herwig, *Christmas in Washington*, pp 230–70.

[273] See the covering note to be found in PA/AA, Inland II g 340 'Aufzeichnung (11.10.1941)'.

[274] 'Sonnabend, 18. Oktober 1941. Mittagstafel 17.10.1941'; in: Martin Vogt (ed.), *Herbst 1941 im 'Führerhauptquartier'. Berichte Werner Koeppens an seinen Minister Alfred Rosenberg* (Koblenz: Bundesarchiv 2002) [= Materialien aus dem Bundesarchiv, Heft 10], pp 76–82, esp. p 78.

bomber and that the latter dropped four depth charges while the *Greer* had the U-boat locked in its sonar beam. These new findings were released to the public by the chairman of the Naval Affairs Committee, the Democrat senator, David Walsh, and inevitably caused a major stir, since they essentially confirmed the version put out by the German side immediately after the incident.[275] The timing of these new revelations could not have been less propitious for the President, since the vote in Congress on the amendment of the Neutrality Law of 1939 was only a few days away. However, in a manner reminiscent of the events which occurred immediately before the 'rattlesnakes' speech of 11 September 1941, when news of two sinkings arrived just in time to allow Roosevelt to generate outrage which was as yet lacking, the President was saved by the bell. In mid-October, the escorts of UK-bound convoy SC-48 were desperately trying to fend off a wolf pack which for once had been able to concentrate regardless of the intelligence provided to the Admiralty by Ultra. Five American destroyers escorting ON-24 were shifted to SC-48 on 16th when it was realised that the latter convoy was under more immediate threat. In the small hours of the 17th, one of their number, the brand new USS *Kearny*, found itself illuminated by the fire of a burning ship, thus presenting an easy target for *U-568*. *Kearny* took a torpedo hit which would have sunk most escorts but a combination of sound structural design and excellent seamanship on the part of the crew managed to save her. Eleven lives, however, had been lost.[276]

The news reached Washington with hours to spare before the vote in the House of Representatives. With no time to ascertain any details (the US Navy bulletin neglected to mention that the destroyer was hit while escorting a British convoy inside the German war zone), enough legislators allowed themselves to be swayed by this sudden event to spare the government another humiliation along the lines of the vote in August on the extension of the draft. A total of 259 congressmen voted in favour, 138 against rescinding Article 6 and the Bill was referred to the Senate. There, the government's case received an important boost when two days later the US steamer *Lehigh* was dispatched by *U-126* 121 km (75 miles) off the West African port of Freetown. In contrast to other US merchantmen which had recently fallen victim to the depredations of the Kriegsmarine or Luftwaffe, the *Lehigh* was not sunk inside the extended North Atlantic war zone that the Kriegsmarine had declared in March (*Sessa*), did not carry a cargo of arms and munitions for the British (*Steel Seafarer*) and was not Panama-registered (*Sessa*) or a recent acquisition from the British (*Robin Moor*). The sinking appeared to prove the government's case that even

---

[275] PA/AA, StS USA, Bd. 9, 'Thomsen und Witthoeft-Emden an Auswärtiges Amt (16.10.1941)'.

[276] On the battle for SC-48 see Blair, *The Hunters*, pp 368–71, as well as Abbazia, *Roosevelt's Navy*, pp 265–74.

going about one's lawful business in a completely transparent way no longer constituted a guarantee of safety on the sea lanes of 1941 and thus made for a compelling argument to arm all American merchantmen that sailed on routes outside the Western Hemisphere. The political pay-off was not long in coming: when the Senate Foreign Affairs Committee discussed the bill for the partial abolition of the Neutrality Law, one of the senators sitting on it, who had until now been well known for his isolationist stance, reversed his position and voted not just to support the bill, but to expand it to include the elimination of Articles 2 and 3 as well. The latter instructed the President to specify the war zones of an ongoing conflict, and by extension the ports located in them, while the former forbade US-flagged merchantmen to enter the ports specified in the above manner. Even though this in no way predetermined the Senate vote, Thomsen made no bones about the fact that the unexpected development was going to exercise 'a decisive influence' on the remainder of the debate both in the media as well as on the floor of the Senate.[277] Proof that these events were being very closely followed by Germany's key decision maker has come our way through a loose minute penned by Ambassador-in-exile Dieckhoff. In it, he referred to a summons requesting him to provide an analysis of the latest developments on Capitol Hill. Rather than forward the memorandum through proper channels to the Auswärtiges Amt, he was told to read it out over the phone to Walther Hewel, Ribbentrop's point man at Führer's Headquarters. Dieckhoff expressed his agreement with Thomsen's assessment on most issues, especially on the key role played by the timing and circumstances of the *Lehigh*'s sinking.[278]

Despite these important gains for the President's anti-Axis agenda, the Germans could still console themselves with what they perceived to be a major American credibility gap. This was confirmed after a fashion when only hours after the announcement of General Hideki Tojo's accession to the Japanese premiership, all US vessels currently plying Far Eastern waters were instructed to seek immediate refuge in the nearest port of a friendly nation, an embarrassment compounded many times over by the National Shipping Agency's announcement on 22 October that it was curtailing further sailings on the Vladivostok route.[279] This was clearly seen as a sign of weakness at a time when American–Japanese negotiations over the latter's occupation of Indo-China and large parts of China had just reached a critical impasse. Both the White House and the State Department were caught completely flatfooted by this, with their disjointed reactions contributing to the impression of an administration unsure of its priorities and lacking a strategy. Against such

---

[277] PA/AA, StS USA, Bd. 9, 'Thomsen an Auswärtiges Amt (22.10.1941)'; ibid., 'Thomsen an Auswärtiges Amt (25.10.1941)'.
[278] PA/AA, StS USA, Bd. 9, 'Dieckhoff an Staatssekretär Weizsäcker (27.10.1941)'.
[279] PA/AA, StS USA, Bd. 9, 'Thomsen an Auswärtiges Amt (24.10.1941)'.

a backdrop, Boetticher had every right to feel vindicated in his constant gloating: he drew Berlin's attention to the fact that the Americans were in no position to risk 'a Pacific conflict' since such an event was likely to cut them off from key raw materials (especially rubber),[280] thus effectively crippling their armaments programme. The way he saw it, it was only Japan's hostile presence just over the horizon which had stopped the US government from 'using the recent sinkings as a rallying cry for war, and turning the abolition of the Neutrality Law into the basis for a whole new agenda', a point which cannot have been lost on Germany's leaders fighting a two-front war.[281]

Even a press release by the newly created Supply Priorities and Allocations Board on 18 October had failed to give the attaché much pause. It described how a newly drafted Victory Program was expected to more than double the planned output of the US armaments industry by early 1944.[282] In his wire to Berlin giving the gist of the plan Boetticher dwelt on three points. As he saw it, the numbers of planes and motor vehicles listed in the Victory Program would require quantities of rubber which would only be available if Southeast Asia remained at peace, thus practically ruling out the idea of a confrontation with Japan right from the start. In a bigger sense, it pointed to the timeline constraining American strategic options, since it appeared to make clear that the Americans would not be in a position to make a meaningful contribution on the field of battle before the autumn of 1943. Last, the Victory Program was essentially a sales pitch to encourage the British and the Soviets not to desist in their fight against the Germans.[283] It appeared to be yet another confirmation of a point he made time and again over the previous months: that the one and only American strategic priority of 1941 was to buy time.

Unlike Boetticher, the officer heading the OKW's war economy office showed a greater inclination to take a closer look at the value of the currency the Americans were using to purchase themselves extra time. In an extensive

---

[280] PA/AA, Handakten Etzdorf, 'Politische Berichte Washington. Meldung Mil.Att. Washington vom 23.10.1941 (26.10.1941)'. The issue of US industry's desperate need for unlimited tin and rubber supplies from Asia had already been touched on in a wire one week earlier. See Ibid., Handakten Etzdorf. 'Politische Berichte Washington. Meldung Mil.Att. Washington vom 15.10.1941 (18.10.1941)'.

[281] PA/AA, StS USA, Bd. 9, 'Boetticher und Thomsen an Auswärtiges Amt (22.10.1941)'.

[282] The Victory Program's real title was 'Joint Board Estimate of the United States Over-all Production Requirements' and had been submitted to the President in September. It was supposed to deliver 125,000 planes and 'tens of thousands of tanks' by the turn of the year 1943–4. As far as plane production was concerned, the figure of 125,000 turned out to be remarkably accurate, with the total production for the years 1942 and 1943 coming to 132,000 (150,500 if the 1941 production is included). See Stoler, *Allies*, pp 45–50 and James Lacey, 'World War II's Real Victory Program'; in: *Journal of Military History*, Vol. 75 (July 2011), pp 811–34.

[283] PA/AA, Handakten Etzdorf. 'Politische Berichte Washington. Meldung Mil.Att. Washington vom 23.10.1941 (26.10.1941)'.

report dated 22 October, *Generalmajor* Georg Thomas of the *Wehrwirtschafts-und Rüstungsamt* explored the extent to which the Anglo–American commitment made to the Soviet government on 1 October could actually be honoured.[284] At no point does the document imply that the recent military defeats suffered by the Red Army east of Kiev and at Vyazma/Bryansk had dealt the Soviet state a mortal blow and that little more than mopping up remained to be done. The report makes unambiguously clear that meaningful quantities of goods could only come from the USA, with the British role limited to making short-term deliveries for a few months until American mobilisation picked up the slack. Both the merchant shipping and the port facilities needed to make the Anglo–American relief effort a practical proposition were available, with Vladivostok and the railway line servicing it named as the most obvious point of entry.[285] All of this was of course conditional upon the American government's willingness to at least temporarily reduce either Lend-Lease shipments to Britain (probable) or the quota reserved for its own armed forces (less likely) in order to allocate a sizeable share to the USSR. Even allowing for American shortages in a number of areas, the author of the report was convinced that the USA could make an important contribution to the Soviet war effort. With regard to wireless sets, rubber tyres, aviation petrol, aluminium, molybdenum and copper, the report predicted that in the long term the USA would be able to satisfy Soviet needs in their totality. In light of the destruction or dislocation of much of its war industry, however, the USSR had a great need for short to mid-term deliveries of planes, tanks, artillery ammunition and machine parts. Here, the rub lay in defining what exactly the mid-term constituted. Unlike Boetticher, who since mid-1940 had repeatedly implied that American production figures were perpetually a year or more away from turning a truly decisive corner,[286] the author of this report was incapable of finding much solace in the graphs of American factory output. In light of a November 1940 statement by President Roosevelt that he was contemplating setting aside up to 50 per cent of US armaments production to supply the needs of Great Britain and its Dominions,[287] this meant that in the current month of October a maximum of 450 combat planes, 200 tanks and 30 anti-tank guns could conceivably have been reserved for export. The problem lay in the fact that by May 1942 reliable estimates saw these figures

---

[284] BA/MA, RM 7/94 'Wehrwirtschafts- und Rüstungsamt Abt.Wi Nr. 3409/41 gKdos. Beurteilung der Möglichkeiten einer materiellen Unterstützung Rußlands durch die angelsächsischen Mächte – Abschrift (22.10.1941)'.

[285] Ibid.

[286] PA/AA, Handakten Etzdorf, USA, 'Mittel- und Südamerika. Betr. Vereinigte Staaten von Amerika. Notiz. Die Aufrüstung des Heeres und der Heeresluftwaffe (26.8.1940)'; BA/MA, RH 67/ 50 'Telegramm Washington Nr. 953 vom 8.4.1941 (10.4.1941).

[287] Susan Dunn, *A Blueprint for War: FDR and the Hundred Days that Mobilized America* (New Haven: Yale UP 2018), p 14.

increase to 650 combat planes, 450 tanks and 120 anti-tank guns. The report further illustrated this by pointing out that if the US government were to set aside for the USSR its entire export quota, the damage inflicted by the German occupation of the most developed part of European Russia would be largely negated.[288]

Irrespective of such chastening forecasts, the fact remained that the President did not appear to be making much progress in eroding the main obstacle to his strategy: the rather tepid enthusiasm the man in the street was showing to fight in another European war. Evidence of this could be found in the manner in which the administration came clean about the circumstances surrounding the USS *Kearny's* torpedoing. Even though by 22 October, rumours were already making the rounds that Admiral Stark had testified to a closed Senate hearing that the destroyer had been engaged in escorting a convoy, the President in his Navy Day speech on 27 October, while openly calling for US participation in 'the destruction of Hitlerism', was far more cautious when it came to the specifics of achieving the aforementioned destruction. Thus, he delivered an impassioned plea for the abolition of the 1939 Neutrality Law while at the same time clinging to the old concept of Atlantic Patrol. At the same time, he blurred – no doubt deliberately – the lines between the arming of merchantmen in general, granting them permission to sail into British ports and providing them with a US Navy escort while they did so. Only once did he unambiguously make a case for escorted convoys, and only in the context of providing US merchantmen with US Navy protection.[289] When pressed on the matter of the USS *Kearny* the following day, he did admit that she was chasing a U-boat when torpedoed, but would not go further. Only on the 29th, twelve days after the vessel was hit, did Secretary of the Navy Frank Knox finally admit that the *Kearny* had been defending a convoy when she was torpedoed.[290] In view of the fact that the secretary had announced as far back as 15 September that the US Navy would start escorting convoys forthwith, such hesitation betrayed a remarkable residual concern over the public's reaction to the navy's participation in a shooting war.

Barely two days later, an event occurred which rendered these concerns redundant. While escorting eastbound convoy HX-156, the old destroyer USS *Reuben James* was torpedoed and sunk by *U-552* in the early morning of

---

[288] BA/MA, RM 7/94 'Wehrwirtschafts- und Rüstungsamt, Abt. Wi Nr. 3409/41 gKdos. Beurteilung der Möglichkeiten einer materiellen Unterstützung Rußlands durch die angelsächsischen Mächte – Abschrift (22.10.1941)',

[289] PA/AA, StS USA, Bd. 9, 'Thomsen an Auswärtiges Amt (27.10.1941'): 'Our American merchant ships must be protected by our American navy. It can never be doubted that goods will be delivered by this nation whose navy believes in the tradition of "Damn the torpedoes. Full speed ahead."' For the full text, see Rosenman (ed.), *Public Papers and Addresses*, pp 438–45.

[290] PA/AA, StS USA, Bd. 9, 'Thomsen an Auswärtiges Amt (29.10.1941)'.

31 October 1941. More than two-thirds of its crew, including all of the officers, were killed.[291] The manner in which the aftermath of this incident played itself out in Washington over the following days suggested an increasing polarisation of American society about these issues, though this did not manifest itself in the only form which could have checkmated the President's strategy: a political deadlock between the legislature and the White House. When the news reached the American capital, most commentators were still shell-shocked by a revelation which the President had included towards the beginning of his Navy Day speech. In this he had alleged that he was in possession of documents proving German plans to invade, occupy and carve up the entirety of Latin America and also abolish all religious creeds on a global scale.[292] Public criticism of these clearly preposterous claims, which in fact were the result of a plant by British intelligence's MI6, was at first slow in coming.[293] Thomsen interpreted this as yet another indicator of the extent to which the government had managed to intimidate its opponents into keeping their thoughts to themselves out of fear that they might be branded as Nazi sympathisers.[294]

However, news of the sinking of the USS *Reuben James* as well as the ongoing debate in the Senate over the dismantling of the Neutrality Law inevitably led to a wider discussion, which soon saw the government on the defensive. First, Roosevelt's refusal to publicise the documents supposedly proving German designs on Latin America led to increased criticism, and even the German government's formal rejection of these claims for once was given plenty of headline space.[295] The sinking of the *Reuben James* and, one day before it, the torpedoing of the navy tanker USS *Salinas*,[296] did not lead to a sense of outrage and calls for war; instead the majority of the public appeared to be gripped with apathy and some senators even criticised the

---

[291] The best account of the events of that night is to be found in Abbazia, *Roosevelt's Navy*, pp 293–308.

[292] Rosenman (ed.), *Public Papers and Addresses*, pp 439–40.

[293] The MI6 station in New York had become quite adept at inserting the 1940s equivalent of 'fake news' into the US news cycle, which in this particular case appears to have happened with Roosevelt's collusion. See Henry Hemming, *Our Man in New York: The British Plot to bring America into the Second World War* (London: Quercus 2019), pp 163–72, 253–9. The crudity of the claims made in the Navy Day speech stand in contrast to the sophistication normally shown by MI6 in planting bogus intelligence. It can only be explained by the desperate military position of the USSR in October 1941.

[294] PA/AA, StS USA, Bd. 9, 'Thomsen an Auswärtiges Amt. Vorabdruck! (29.10.1941)'.

[295] PA/AA, StS USA, Bd. 9, 'Thomsen an Auswärtiges Amt (2.11.1941)'. An investigation by the Auswärtiges Amt had already reached the preliminary conclusion that the map was not of German origin by the end of the month; PA/AA, Handakten Luther. Schriftverkehr N-Sch. 'Mitteilung für Herrn Gesandten v. Rintelen (31.10.1941)'.

[296] The *Salinas* was torpedoed while sailing in westbound convoy ON-28. Despite sustaining two torpedo hits, there were no fatalities among her crew. Abbazia, *Roosevelt's Navy*, pp 283–91.

President for putting the vessel in harm's way with his ambiguous orders. Thomsen himself appeared surprised at the harsh language used on the floor of the Senate, with some legislators accusing the President of having the fallen sailors' 'blood on his hands'.[297] The White House hit back by publishing the exchange of notes between Berlin and Washington over the sinking of the *Robin Moore* in an attempt to prove that American trade was not likely to enjoy safe passage anywhere in the world, whether outside or inside the German war zone. In trying to plead the government's case, the *New York Times* concluded that 'American defensive waters' had thus already been violated as far back as May 1941.[298] Since the steamer had been sunk off the coast of Liberia near the equator such a line of argument clearly smacked of desperation; together with the government's lack of transparency in presenting the facts of the *Greer* and *Kearny* incidents, it meant that the cases of the *Reuben James* and *Salinas* would not be enough to generate cries for war, the large number of casualties sustained on the former notwithstanding.

In the meantime, a completely different attempt by the administration to generate public support for the Allied cause was running into similar trouble. On 30 October, the President had publicly committed himself to extending Lend-Lease assistance to the embattled USSR, an option not specifically ruled out in the original piece of legislation. This move was supported by a media campaign aimed at painting the embattled USSR in more acceptable colours to a viscerally anti-communist American electorate, with eminent public citizens roped in for this purpose. However, public statements like that by a former ambassador to Moscow that Stalin's purges had essentially been aimed at eliminating future fifth columnists were met with either hilarity or outrage across a broad political spectrum.[299] The Archbishop of Cincinnati fared only slightly better when he reinterpreted the anti-communist encyclical of Pope Pius XI (1922–39) as being directed only against the Soviet regime, not its people.[300]

Despite these public relations setbacks, the administration was able to score two important victories on 7 November. One was the extension of Lend-Lease to the USSR. Though technically it only required a written instruction to the newly created office of the Lend-Lease administrator stating that the continued survival of the USSR was deemed to be 'vital to the defence of the United States',[301] this measure nevertheless constituted a political hot potato with the potential to galvanise the isolationist camp. More crucially, on the same date the Senate also approved the repeal of Articles 2, 3 and 6 of the Neutrality Law

[297] PA/AA, StS USA, Bd. 9, 'Thomsen an Auswärtiges Amt (5.11.1941)'.
[298] PA/AA, StS USA, Bd. 9, 'Thomsen an Auswärtiges Amt (3.11.1941)'.
[299] PA/AA, StS USA, Bd. 9, 'Thomsen an Auswärtiges Amt (1.11.1941, 15.58 h)'.
[300] PA/AA, StS USA, Bd. 9, 'Thomsen an Auswärtiges Amt (1.11.1941, 12.04 h)'.
[301] Rosenman (ed.), *Public Papers and Addresses*, pp 481–2.

of 1939, thus effectively turning it into an empty shell. Thomsen put this down to the fact that the torpedoings of the *Reuben James* and the *Salinas* had helped the administration after all, since they would have made a number of legislators more inclined to support a warlike course of action and less amenable to listen to the voices advocating caution. While probably true in a few cases, there is no denying the fact that the events of the last months appeared to support the rationale behind Lend-Lease: with Britain backed into a corner and the USSR on the brink of collapse, even the greatest sceptic had to admit that it made eminent sense to bring war materiel to those still fighting, and in doing so put off a military confrontation with Germany either indefinitely or until such time as all three services were prepared to face the Wehrmacht unassisted. Should the House of Representatives – as appeared likely – follow the example of the Senate this would have serious consequences. To Thomsen, this 'would give the President such far-reaching powers that a declaration of war would become a virtual irrelevance. He would be able to wage an undeclared war according to his wishes without having to fear the censure of Congress.'[302] In Berlin, *Reichspropagandaminister* Joseph Goebbels on 12 November after poring over a report assessing the shifting mood in the USA, reached a rather different conclusion. Roosevelt would in all likelihood seize on the next incident to sever diplomatic relations between Washington and Berlin, with a declaration of war as the next logical step. It is interesting that Goebbels did not rate a state of open hostilities between both countries as 'a virtual irrelevance', but was ready to admit that it was likely to bring 'enormous disadvantages' in its wake.[303]

Important though it was, the vote in the Senate still had to be sealed by the House, since the lower chamber had so far only approved the rescinding of Article 6. Roosevelt and his Secretary of State were clearly concerned about the outcome of the vote, because they both resorted to the unusual measure of each addressing an open letter to Speaker of the House Sam Rayburn and the majority leader, John McCormack. In his message, the President stressed that a defeat would weaken the position of the Allies and cause 'rejoicing in the Axis nations'. Remarkably, he also dwelt on the domestic front, which was currently witnessing a major labour dispute in the coal-mining industry. Without spelling it out in so many words, he hinted at the possible need to break the strike by deploying Federal troops in order to keep the steel industry going. Such a move might not have the popular backing needed if the House had shown a visible lack of support for the Allied cause so desperately in need

---

[302] PA/AA, StS USA, Bd. 9, 'Thomsen an Auswärtiges Amt (8.11.1941)'.
[303] TB Goebbels, Bd.II.2, p 279 (entry for 13 November 1941). Note: the diary entries always give a chronicle of the previous day's events. It has not been possible to ascertain the provenance of the aforementioned report with certainty. BA-Lichterf, NS 5/VI 37204 'Kultur und Wissenschaft im Ausland, Nr. 7 (12.11.1941)', produced by the *Deutsche Arbeitsfront's* research institute, appears to be a possible match.

of the products of American industry. In his letter, as befitted the country's foreign minister, Cordell Hull dwelt on the changed international situation since November 1939, when the Neutrality Law was first passed. Back then, the Germany of Adolf Hitler still appeared to be safely contained. Two years later, Germany's armed forces were in the vanguard of 'a worldwide movement of invasion under Hitler's leadership and which is now moving steadily in the direction of this hemisphere and this country'. Britain and the Atlantic sea lanes linking it to the USA were described as the linchpin of Allied defence. The German naval campaign to 'drive our ships from high seas and ships of all nations from most of the North Atlantic' would leave it exposed and vulnerable.[304]

Despite the fact that the bill had enjoyed considerable support not just from the White House, but also the Senate, the vote on 13 November turned out to be a surprisingly close-run thing. Articles 2, 3 and 6 were rescinded by 212 ayes against 194 nays. As Ambassador-in-exile Dieckhoff in Berlin was quick to point out, this meant that less than half of the total number of legislators notionally available (the House in the early 1940s had 435 seats) had actually supported the administration. His impassioned plea notwithstanding, Roosevelt's key piece of legislation was only saved by the fact that twenty-nine congressmen had been absent during the vote, whether by their own free choice or not.[305] Interestingly enough, neither Thomsen nor Dieckhoff chose to interpret this as an indication that the isolationist movement was gaining its second wind, with the former in fact fearing that the government's persistent hounding of America First by the FBI might cause its current leader to resign.[306] Instead, the reasons behind the close vote were linked to a temporary falling out between the administration and the ordinarily ultra-loyal Democrats from the states of the old South.[307] In late September, Ambassador Dieckhoff had predicted that a dismantling of the neutrality legislation would inevitably lead to a rise 'in armed incidents which would in turn affect the prevailing mood' among the American public. Any residual reluctance to enter the war 'would be eroded until such time that the President would be in a position to sooner or later ask Congress for a declaration of

---

[304] Thomsen transmitted the text of both letters verbatim to Berlin, see PA/AA, StS USA, Bd. 9, 'Thomsen an Auswärtiges Amt (14.11.1941)'.

[305] PA/AA, StS USA, Bd. 9, 'Fernschreiben an RAM über St.S. Zur gestrigen Abstimmung des Repräsentantenhauses über die Neutralitätsgesetz-Vorlage (14.11.1941)'.

[306] The evening after the vote, Thomsen cabled Berlin that the embassy was already in touch with Lindbergh through intermediaries with a view that he replace the incumbent, General Robert E. Wood. PA/AA, StS USA, Bd. 9, 'Thomsen an Auswärtiges Amt (13.11.1941)'.

[307] PA/AA, StS USA, Bd. 9, 'Thomsen an Auswärtiges Amt (13.11.1941)'. According to Thomsen, the Southern congressmen were concerned by the President's reluctance to break the ongoing coal miner's strike by using force, thus jeopardising the rearmaments programme.

war'.[308] In their assessments of this latest development, Thomsen and
Boetticher did not address this possibility in so many words, though it cannot
be ruled out that they were taking it for granted. Instead, they focused on the
short to mid-term consequences which this sea change was likely to have for
the Axis powers. The arming of merchantmen was by far the most innocent,
since not nearly enough artillery pieces were readily available to arm even
a fraction of the US merchant navy. The fact that most decks would need to be
reinforced to withstand the recoil of a deck gun meant another delaying
element.[309]

In the Pacific, the gutting of the Neutrality Law meant that in the case of
a Japanese move against the British or Dutch colonial empires, the USA would
not automatically become dependent on the services of neutral shipping to get
out as much rubber and tin as they could while this was still feasible. Two days
after the vote in the House, Thomsen in fact stressed that as matters stood now
the US government had all conceivable incentives not to back the Japanese into
a corner. War in the Far East was likely to be of considerable duration, would
leave the US Navy hopelessly stretched and was likely to sabotage what might
well be a war-winning strategy for the USA: 'to defeat Germany by superior
factory turnout and delivery of war materiel' to Britain and its allies.[310] He was
right of course to stress that the theatre of war most directly affected by the
gutting of the Neutrality Law was the Atlantic. Over the past seven months, the
President had first found a way to allow American-flagged merchantmen with
American crews to sail into Suez, thus providing key assistance to the embattled Eighth Army; the ports of the British colonial empire followed a few
months later, with only Britain itself and the Dominions classed as belligerents
in the traditional sense and thus forbidden to American ships. Even with this
barrier out of the way, it was unlikely, in the light of an overall dearth of
tonnage, that an avalanche of American merchantmen would be headed for
British ports anytime soon, Thomsen reflected on 15 November. The mid to
long-term threat lay in the fact that the moment American shipping became
more than a minority presence in eastbound convoys, US Navy escorts and
planes were soon likely to follow. As luck would have it, fresh intelligence on
the progress made with the construction of two bases by American contractors
in Scotland and Ulster reached the Germans in these very days, and contributed to an intelligence assessment that the US Navy was introducing convoy
escort on the last leg to British ports.[311] In a separate cable, Boetticher even
forecast a situation where such an American bridgehead might play a crucial

---

[308] PA/AA, StS USA, Bd. 8, 'Fernschreiben an RAM (24.9.1941)'.
[309] PA/AA, StS USA, Bd. 9, 'Thomsen an Auswärtiges Amt (15.11.1941)'.
[310] PA/AA, StS Japan, Bd. 5, 615 'Thomsen an Auswärtiges Amt (15.11.1941)'.
[311] PA/AA, StS USA, Bd. 9, 'Thomsen an Auswärtiges Amt (15.11.1941)'; KTB
Seekriegsleitung, Teil A (entries for 10, 25 and 28 November 1941).

role in allowing Roosevelt to pour in reinforcements to prevent a British moral collapse, possibly even leading to an outright occupation of Great Britain.[312] Such a scenario was obviously only a few steps away from the concept of the unsinkable aircraft carrier, the establishment of which would eventually enable American and British Empire forces to invade the European continent on 6 June 1944. A few sources from the second half of 1941 exist which prove that the Germans had given this idea some thought from a relatively early period; the evidence available, however, does not suggest that it was a threat they accorded a high priority. Hitler, for one, repeatedly stressed that the prospect of a major amphibious descent on Western Europe left him unconcerned.[313] Arguably the first document to dwell on this problem was a cable which Thomsen sent on 19 August. It summarised rumours which had been making the rounds in the wake of a confidential briefing during which Roosevelt had informed a number of congressmen about what had transpired at the Argentia summit. An isolationist newspaper alleged that the prime minister and the President had agreed on the paramount need to keep the Red Army in the fight and to mobilise a large US expeditionary force which would be used to stage a major amphibious landing in either 1942 or 1943. Furthermore – in contrast to what many British strategists were claiming in those weeks – an Anglo–American consensus had been reached that strategic bombing would never suffice to bring Germany to its knees.[314] Barely two months later, Boetticher had sent a memo on the subject which allegedly reflected the thinking of some of his contacts in the Munitions Building. According to him, they predicted that an expeditionary force attempting a major landing on the shores of German-dominated Europe would find itself facing a Dunkirk-like fate. The sheer number of defenders, the lack of shipping and the certainty of Luftwaffe counterstrikes appeared to doom such an endeavour. Should the British ask for US support for such an operation, only small elements of the US Army and Army Air Force would be made available and even their deployment appeared a doubtful proposition in light of the overall dearth of shipping and other priorities in the Pacific.[315] The possibility of Boetticher being spoon-fed tainted intelligence has already been referred to, but the pessimistic assessment he relayed to Berlin did indeed reflect a fairly broad consensus in civilian and military circles in the United States at the time. A report by the attaché, dated 8 September, quoted at length from a recent letter to the editor of the *New York Times*. In it, a retired US army officer, who had played a key role in organising

---

[312] PA/AA, StS USA, Bd. 9, 'Boetticher und Thomsen an Auswärtiges Amt (15.11.1941)'.
[313] TB Goebbels, Bd. I.9, p 120; (entry for 1 February 1941); 'Hoth notes (30.3.1941)'; in: Heim (ed.), *Sowjetunion*, pp 117–9; TB Goebbels, Bd. I.9, p 300 (entry for 9 May 1941); ibid., Bd. II.1, p 262 (entry for 19 August 1941).
[314] PA/AA, StS USA, Bd. 8, 'Thomsen an Auswärtiges Amt (19.8.1941)'.
[315] BA/MA, RM 11/83 'Oberkommando des Heeres, GenStdH/Attacheabt. (OvD) Nr. 1263/ 41 gKdos. an den Leiter des Nachrichtendienstes (19.10.1941)'.

the move of the AEF from the USA to France in 1917–18, highlighted a number of the logistical challenges encountered in the process, despite the fact that it was underpinned by the communications network of a friendly great power. The chances of replicating such a feat while simultaneously repelling massive enemy counter-attacks struck the author as 'doubtful'.[316] In early November, the US military attaché in Bucharest had been careless enough to unburden himself to an informant sympathetic to the Axis cause, and in doing so, he had declared an amphibious landing in German-occupied Europe to be 'technically impossible'. He supported this by quoting an array of figures relating to manpower and shipping tonnage and rejected out of hand a comparison with the deployment of the AEF in 1917–18. In contrast to the days of the Great War, no friendly host nation would be standing by to provide functioning ports, railroads and a great deal of food and military kit besides.[317] Former President Herbert Hoover expressed his agreement in a public speech given on 19 November. At the heart of his argument was the contention that the current war could only be decided militarily in the Allies' favour with a major amphibious descent on the European continent. Since he deemed this to be an impossible endeavour, he accused Roosevelt of leading the country into an unwinnable war.[318] Unbeknownst to the Germans, Lieutenant Colonel Truman Smith, the former military attaché at the Berlin embassy, also echoed these assessments. In a fifty-three-page manuscript finished at approximately the same time, he based his calculations on an imminent Soviet defeat. With a large part of the German field army redeployed to defend Western Europe against a major amphibious oper-ation, he worked out that the force needed for such an endeavour would have to number – over and above a British contribution of 1 million – somewhere between 12.5 and 15.5 million men,[319] a figure high enough to render the whole idea well-nigh unfeasible in the eyes of most decision makers in 1941.[320]

If a major amphibious descent on Western Europe was a distant and even far-fetched prospect, the threats born out of Anglo–American cooperation over the last sixteen months must still have seemed alarming enough. Both the army in metropolitan Britain and the Home Fleet had been given important material help in their direst hour of need. Lend-Lease had come next, and

---

[316] PA/AA, Handakten Etzdorf. 'Politische Berichte Washington. Militärische Nachrichten vom 8.9.1941 (11.9.1941)'.

[317] PA/AA, StS USA, Bd. 9, 'Gerstenberg und v. Killinger an Auswärtiges Amt (7.11.1941)'.

[318] TB Goebbels, Bd. II.2, p 326 (entry for 21 November 1941).

[319] Even though Smith was willing to mentally set aside a million men for a possible Pacific war, the stated figure does not even allow for the manpower needs of the US Navy or the Marine Corps.

[320] Smith appears to have penned 'The Truth about an AEF' during the period between the battle of Kiev and the Pearl Harbor raid. The manuscript remained unpublished. For an analysis, see Henry G. Gole, *Exposing the Third Reich: Colonel Truman Smith in Hitler's Germany* (Lexington: Kentucky UP 2013), pp 263–6.

partly as a result of it, other forms of assistance were taking shape. Naval patrolling by the US Navy was now complemented by convoy escort, with the prospect of this kind of activity soon covering the approaches to British home waters too. The Eighth Army was being reinforced with American-built tanks, bombers and fighter planes, with the Red Army standing to benefit from this scheme too if it could just stay in the fight for a few more months. Closer to home, the possibility of a major strategic air war waged by US-trained airmen in US-produced bombers was turning into a real prospect. To coordinate all these measures, the creation of an Anglo–American joint high command appeared to be under serious consideration. The last barrier which might conceivably have proved an obstacle to some of these schemes – the neutrality legislation – had been left standing, but as an empty shell.

The second half of November brought an event which must have gone a long way to drive home the ultimate consequences of all these moves. On 18 November, the Eighth Army began its long awaited offensive (Operation Crusader) aimed at relieving Tobruk and dislodging Rommel from Cyrenaica. The Luftwaffe, the Regia Aeronautica and Vichy's Armee de l'Air had already encountered US-built planes in British service, and this operation would witness the biggest concentration of US-supplied air power yet (ten out of forty-five squadrons).[321] However, what set Crusader apart from previous operations was the deployment of the US Army's first modern combat tank – the M-13 Stuart – in such numbers that even a tactical virtuoso like Rommel would be left facing an insoluble dilemma.[322] Hitler's reaction is instructive, because we have a record of the comments he made on the subject both before and after the event. On 23 and 24 October, he had belittled the new American tank in conversation with a number of hangers-on at the Wolfsschanze, describing it as inferior to comparable Panzers.[323] Barely a month later this assessment appeared to be confirmed by events on the ground, when in the early stages of Crusader a brigade of Stuarts was wiped out in the battle fought for possession of the airstrip at Sidi Rezegh. Having received intelligence of this clash both from the units on the ground and – via Boetticher – from American sources,[324] the dictator concluded that the Stuart's

---

[321] Christopher Shores, Giovanni Massimello and Russell Guest, *A History of the Mediterranean Air War 1940–1945, Vol. 1: North Africa, June 1940–January 1942* (London: Grub Street 2012), pp 292–3.

[322] Three hundred of the Eighth Army's force of 738 tanks were Stuarts. Since Rommel's force of 386 tanks included 210 obsolete types (Italian makes and Panzer IIs), his position bordered on the hopeless. Martin Kitchen, *Rommel's Desert War* (Cambridge: CUP 2009), pp 146, 149.

[323] 'Freitag, 24. Oktober 1941' and 'Sonnabend, 25. Oktober 1941'; both in: Vogt (ed.), *Herbst 1941*, pp 98–9, 105.

[324] PA/AA, Handakten Etzdorf. 'Politische Berichte Washington. Generalstab des Heeres, Abt. Frd. Heere West/ A. Meldung Mil.Att. Washington vom 26.11.1941 (29.11.1941)'.

key vulnerability lay in its thin armour, thus seemingly validating his hunch from a month ago. Rather remarkably, he impressed on Goebbels the absolute need to keep this insight a secret; the German media, he went on, must on no account be allowed to gloat about it. It was preferable that the Americans go on producing an inferior design for as long as possible.[325] It was obvious that the dictator was confident that US industry was capable of turning out tanks much superior to the Stuart.

Whatever short-term relief Hitler and his generals may have drawn from the British (and by extension, American) setback at Sidi Rezegh is likely to have been snuffed out by the arrival of a US military mission attached to the British Middle East Command. Under the command of Brigadier Russell Maxwell, it was tasked with coordinating the assembly, distribution and servicing of US-built tanks, trucks and planes arriving in theatre as well as the training of their new crews. Such a move, which took Anglo–American cooperation yet another step beyond what legal opinion of the time might still have described as 'neutral', could have been expected to be executed under a cloak of secrecy. Instead, it was accompanied by a veritable PR campaign on both sides of the Atlantic.[326] It was obvious that the Americans were there to stay.

On 4 December, Boetticher, who always took considerable pride in the intelligence he was able to elicit from his contacts in the Munitions Building, was as flabbergasted as the rest of political Washington when the morning editions of the *Chicago Tribune* and the *Washington Times Herald* appeared with headlines announcing the leaking of 'FDR's secret war plans!' They quoted extensively from a nineteen-page document bearing the title *Ultimate Requirements Study: Estimate of Army Ground Forces* by Lieutenant Colonel Albert C. Wedemeyer of the War Plans Division. It was but a part of the armed services' much larger Victory Program,[327] and concerned itself mainly with the likely manpower demands the US Army would have to meet in a total war with Germany; it was accompanied by a covering letter from the President directing the General Staff to lay the groundwork of a tenfold expansion of army manpower. A copy found its way into the hands of Senator Burton K. Wheeler, who in turn shared it with the *Chicago Tribune*.[328] The study foresaw a likely opening of hostilities by April 1942, followed by an extended bombing campaign against selected targets of the German war economy like

---

[325] TB Goebbels, Bd. II.2, pp 379, 399–400 (entries for 28 and 30 November 1941).

[326] For German assessments of the Maxwell mission, PA/AA, StS USA, Bd. 10, 'Boetticher & Thomsen an Auswärtiges Amt (23.11.1941)'; and BA/MA, RM 7/3381 OKM, 3.Abt. Skl. 'FH B Nr. 32/41 D Fremde Handelsschiffahrt. Bericht Nr. 32/41 (25.11.1941)'.

[327] The Victory Program in its entirety is reproduced in Steven T. Ross (ed.), *American War Plans 1919–1945*, Vol. 5 (New York: Garland: 1992), pp 143–298.

[328] On the circumstances of the leak, see Thomas Fleming, *The War within World War II: Franklin Delano Roosevelt and the Struggle for Supremacy* (London: Perseus Press 2011), pp 1–48.

the synthetic fuel factories and a major landing on the European continent at some point after June or July 1943. The armed forces needed for such an endeavour would come to a total of 10,045,658 men divided along the following lines: 6,745,658 men for the Army, 2,050,000 for the Army Air Force, 1,100,000 for the Navy and its air arm, and 150,000 for the US Marine Corps. Five million from all services would make up the force which would carry out the major amphibious operation at the centre of the plan.[329] The intention was to carry out the scheme irrespective of how British and Soviet arms were doing; in fact, it was taken as a given that a defeated Red Army would in all likelihood have retreated into Siberia by mid-1942 and would thus be removed from the equation. The Japanese would not be subject to a land campaign by American forces. Instead an economic and naval blockade, together with increased support for the Chinese, would keep them from aiding the European Axis.[330]

Once Roosevelt's and Stimson's reactions made it clear that the leaked document was authentic, Boetticher, unruffled by the prize piece of intelligence that had eluded him, soon reached the conclusion that it bore out his long-standing assessment that American strategy was all about winning time. He criticised it mainly for failing to discuss possible German countermoves and for its blithe disregard of a possible joint Japanese–German action.[331] What is noteworthy is that Boetticher, even though he may have found himself in agreement with some of the more general criticism articulated by the American media,[332] did not bother to discuss the feasibility of the mechanics involved. It is of course perfectly possible that the events that followed Pearl

---

[329] To put this in context, it is important to remember that on the day the *Chicago Tribune's* article appeared, the US Army totalled 1,644,000 men, with the Army Air Force contributing a further 297,103, the Navy 274,427 and the US Marine Corps 65,881 officers and men. See Shrader, *Reference Guide*, pp 5, 11, 14–16. The biggest peacetime military establishment of the period was that of the USSR, with the Soviet Army and Navy of June 1941 (including both services' air arms) totalling 5,373,000 men. Ewan Mawdsley, *Thunder in the East: The Nazi–Soviet War 1941–1945* (London: Hodder Arnold 2005), p 30.

[330] The text of the *Washington Times Herald* article was translated and telegraphed to the Auswärtiges Amt in two lengthy wires by the Deutsches Nachrichtenbüro. See PA/AA, StS USA, Bd. 10, 'Deutsches Nachrichtenbüro – Eigendienst (5.12. und 6.12.1941)'. In the normal run of things, translating and sending news items of such importance would have been a task for the embassy staff, and the delay incurred in sending the second half is certainly unusual. If the embassy also sent its own translation, it is no longer extant in the files of the Staatssekretär's office. An entry in Joseph Goebbels' diary appears to confirm that the full text was not available in translation in Berlin before the evening of the 6 December at the earliest. See TB Goebbels. Bd. II.2, p 446 (entry for 7 December 1941).

[331] PA/AA, StS USA, Bd. 10, 'Boetticher und Thomsen an Auswärtiges Amt (5.12.1941, 00.18 h)'.

[332] The points raised concerned mainly the cost of the mobilisation described. PA/AA, StS USA, Bd. 10, 'Thomsen an Auswärtiges Amt (6.12.1941, 18.11 h)'.

Harbour left him without much time to do so. On the other hand, he may have struggled with an ominous sensation: the sheer unprecedented scale of the scheme and the added fact that he personally knew and respected some of the individuals who had had a hand in putting it together.[333]

Hitler did refer to the scoop published in the *Washington Times Herald* and the *Chicago Tribune* in the speech he gave to the Reichstag between 15.00 and 16.30 on 11 December 1941. In this allocution, he gave his reasons for declaring war on the USA, citing amongst other things the openly hostile stance of the US Navy in the Atlantic and the various articles published in the isolationist dailies. Even so, the likelihood that the revelation of the US Army's study on manpower requirements played a role in pushing him over the edge is low. As will be made clear in the following chapter, the dictator's fundamental decision to join Japan in a war against the USA almost certainly took place around 21–23 November. The only piece of circumstantial evidence contradicting this is a note by Ambassador Dieckhoff bearing the date 2 December recording the fact that he had just been ordered by Ribbentrop to work on new ways in which Germany might support the American isolationists.[334] In the light of a supposedly imminent war with the USA this would have to be seen as a truly bizarre waste of effort; however, the long history of Japanese empty promises regarding their willingness to join the European Axis may have made for a considerable reluctance on the part of many German government departments to believe that this time Tokyo really would take the jump.[335]

3.5   Conclusion

The intelligence picture of the United States as it was being relayed to Hitler offered short-term reassurance and plenty of reasons for long-term disquiet. The former could be traced back to the fact that with the important exception of parts of the Navy, the United States had to start from scratch to mobilise its

---

[333]   See BA/MA, RH 2/2942 'Boetticher an von Tippelskirch (1.2.1937)'. In this private letter to a fellow officer at OKH, Boetticher referred to the then captain Wedemeyer in terms which suggest feelings of strong sympathy or even friendship.

[334]   PA/AA, StS USA, Bd. 10, 'Richtlinien für die Beeinflussung der öffentlichen Meinung in den Vereinigten Staaten (2.12.1941)'.

[335]   In the briefing for a rather more select audience (senior NSDAP functionaries) which he gave on the following day in his private quarters of the Neue Reichskanzlei, the revelations printed in the *Herald* and the *Chicago Tribune* were mentioned either only very briefly or not at all. See TB Goebbels, Bd. II.2, pp 494–500 (entry for 13 December 1941). For the theory that Hitler was swayed in his decision-making at the last minute by the scoops published in the *Herald* and the *Tribune*, see Fleming, *World War II*, p 35. While I disagree with Thomas Fleming's interpretation of events as they transpired on the German side, he has made a plausible argument for Roosevelt being behind the leak of the War Plans Division document in order to goad Hitler into joining the Japanese in their imminent initiation of hostilities.

armed forces and industrial potential to meet the Axis challenge. This problem was compounded when from 27 September 1940 Japan openly allied itself to Germany and Italy, creating a strategic dilemma for US policymakers which Boetticher kept harping on about to the point of saturation. An aggressive Japan meant a likely move on Malaya and the Dutch East Indies, thus effectively turning the entirety of America's supply of natural rubber into a hostage to fortune. The considerable isolationist feeling, which pervaded large parts of American society and gave way only slowly, constituted an important obstacle to the administration's attempts to address all or at least some of these problems.

The flipside to this fairly favourable picture (for Germany) lay in Roosevelt's success in convincing voters and legislators alike that a third way between war and acquiescence existed: it was called 'all measures short of war' and implied active help for all the regimes (even ones that were not outright democracies) already fighting the aggressor states. In a best-case scenario this might render a war with Germany redundant or, at the very least, put it off until such time as the odds might favour America. In the meantime, the army and the air services in particular underwent a tenfold expansion in size to make up for the years of penury in the 1920s and 1930s, a course of action approved of by the majority of US citizens, many isolationists included.

A programme like this might arguably have been best served by keeping a low profile, but in the eighteen months that lay between the fall of France and Pearl Harbor, the President kept referring to the Tripartite powers in general and Germany in particular in terms normally associated with exchanges between countries already at war. This culminated in the Atlantic Charter which spelt out the agenda (the destruction of the Third Reich), followed by the double leak of key data from the Victory Program in October and Wedemeyer's War Plans Division paper in December, both of which described the instrument of the agenda: air power amounting to 125,000 planes and armed forces totalling 10.5 million men. Stimson's admission that the planned expansion of the US armed services was genuine confirmed that the Atlantic Charter was to be taken seriously. In the eyes of Hitler, this would have been but the backdrop to the intelligence that was reaching him from countless experts on American affairs (whether US citizens who served as sources of information for Abwehr and SD or Germans familiar with the country): almost without exception they agreed that Roosevelt, should he feel the right moment had come, could take the country to war any time he wanted. In the meantime, the polarisation of American society meant that the America First Committee, which alone might have been able to sabotage the President's policy, grew in numbers, but became increasingly marginalised from the country's political mainstream. Hitler does not appear to have put much faith in the committee's effectiveness; in fact, his reactions to the passing of the Lend-Lease Bill prove that from a fairly early stage, he was more inclined to factor in the USA as a major belligerent than were the diplomats of the Auswärtiges Amt reporting on these events.

Boetticher's reporting, though usually correct in the short to mid-term, was terribly flawed because on only one occasion did he stop to consider when the USA might arguably have reached a point in its mobilisation where his boss in Berlin could be said to 'have missed the bus'. Unlike Ribbentrop he does not even appear to have pondered the problem of how Germany might go about waging war on America once a state of war had been declared. In contrast to Boetticher's perennial habit of producing an endless record of American shortcomings and flaws, the Sicherheitsdienst' compilations strongly suggested – if only by implication – that by the summer of 1941 it was already too late for Germany to pose a mortal threat to the USA.

There are some indications that Roosevelt at least as late as September was still labouring under the delusion that a war against Germany could and should be won by the British and Soviet armies alone, with America limiting itself to providing material help, escort for convoys and possibly at a later point in time air power to strike strategic targets.[336] What would Hitler's reading of the situation have been based on? The events that surrounded the passing of Lend-Lease offer proof that he was more alert to the threat posed by the United States than Thomsen, Boetticher or even Dieckhoff. The US President, when it came to aiding and abetting Britain and its allies, had consistently managed to outmanoeuvre all domestic opponents like America First. Despite Britain's declining military fortunes, popular revulsion at assisting communist Russia and major embarrassments over the *Greer* and *Kearny* incidents, not one major move that took the USA closer to belligerent status had been defeated in even one of the two Houses of Congress, a process culminating in the dismantling of the 1939 Neutrality Law. This raised the spectre of US merchantmen delivering their cargo directly into British ports; if the past pattern was anything to go by, the close escort provided by US Navy vessels to a point south of Iceland would soon enough be extended to cover the entire route. It is, of course, possible that the dictator would have drawn some consolation from the fact that US resources did not allow a great deal of power projection across the Atlantic, but hardly likely. Proof of this can be found in his statement from November 1939 in which he had expressed unambiguously the importance that he attached to the very existence of the American Neutrality Laws: as long as they remained in existence, the USA would be 'no threat' to Germany.

At the same time, Boetticher and Thomsen, with varying degrees of insistence, kept harping on one theme: that the one major Achilles heel of the United States was its need for more time. An unexpected beginning of hostilities

---

[336] On this point see Stoler, *Allies*, pp 57–8, and Johnsen, *Grand Alliance*, p 240. This interpretation was but a reflection of how many leading pro-interventionists saw the likely evolution of US participation on the Allied side. See Stoler, *Allies*.

against Japan was, they believed, likely to bring a series of calamities for the USA in its wake. The Lend-Lease programme at the very least would collapse immediately, and the US Navy, still two years away from completing the Two-Ocean programme, would find itself hopelessly stretched. Moreover, in the case of war breaking out in the Pacific, America's only source of natural rubber would be rendered inaccessible, possibly permanently. By implication, postponing hostilities could only mean one thing: the American position was likely to become more unassailable than at present, with enough vessels joining the navy to allow for offensive operations in two oceans, a growing economy that would allow the equipment of the US armed forces as well as that of assorted allies and the availability of a natural rubber substitute that would lessen the impact of the spread of hostilities to Southeast Asia.

4

Forging an Unlikely Alliance: Germany and Japan, 1933–1941

4.1 Introduction

On the late evening of 7 December 1941, the German dictator learned the news of Japan's attack on Pearl Harbor while at his Wolfsschanze HQ in East Prussia. His reaction, as recorded by some of his senior aides, betrayed both genuine surprise and overjoyed relief. He even made a point of rushing over to the building housing the OKW staff to break the news to Keitel and Jodl in person. The former would insist in his memoirs that even 'the most skilled actor' could not possibly have feigned the kind of surprise Hitler was exhibiting. The inevitable conclusion was that he must have been completely ignorant of Japan's preparations for war.[1] Hitler's reaction that evening has raised a number of important questions that all have a bearing on his decision to join his Far Eastern ally in its fateful course of action. For openers, his foreign minister had just spent the last five months attempting to convince the Japanese to join the Germans in their war against the USSR. It is certainly noteworthy that Hitler seemed happy enough to join the Japanese in an entirely different conflict. Was the decision to follow Japan into war a wholly spontaneous one, as the manner of his reaction that evening appeared to suggest? It must be kept in mind that Japan's whirlwind-like conquest of Southeast Asia in just under five months still lay in the future;[2] this begs the question what specific expectations he tied to a Japanese alliance.

4.2 From Hitler's Rise to Power to the Tripartite Pact

From 1934 onwards, Hitler's dismantling of the Versailles order was assisted by a number of external factors. First and foremost was the loathing with

---

[1] The accounts left by four witnesses of this event all coincide in the key points. Otto Dietrich, *12 Jahre mit Hitler* (Köln: Atlas 1955), p 85; Walter Warlimont, *Im Hauptquartier der deutschen Wehrmacht 1939-1945. Grundlagen. Formen. Gestalten* (Frankfurt a.M.: Athenäum 1964), p 221; Wilhelm Keitel, *Mein Leben. Pflichterfüllung bis zum Untergang* (Berlin: edition q 1998 rp), p 343, and, Institut für Zeitgeschichte (IfZ), ED 100-78, 'Tagebuch Walther Hewel (entry for 8 December 1941)'.

[2] A fact historians of the period almost never dwell on. For a rare exception, Evan Mawdsley, *World War II: A New History* (Cambridge: CUP 2009), p 207.

which the USSR was regarded by virtually all the nations of Europe, thus removing a key component of any potential anti-German coalition from the start. Second were the differences between Great Britain, France and Italy, who as signatories of the 1919 treaties would have had to block German expansionism at an early stage. The fleeting consensus established among them at the Stresa Conference (April 1935) took a blow when Britain broke ranks to sign a bilateral treaty limiting German naval rearmament and was then shattered by Italy's invasion of Ethiopia. The third factor was the reluctance of most governments to see a repeat of the events of 1914; hence, the early transgressions of the new German government were met with considerable forbearance, a fact that Hitler knew how to exploit by giving repeated assurances that he too was interested in peace.[3] Against such a backdrop, it is hardly surprising that he managed to get away with the occasional blunder, the botched coup against Austria's Dollfuß regime being the most egregious such instance.[4]

To an even greater extent than Italy, Japan should have been the most obvious partner in crime for Berlin, its annexation of Chinese Manchuria in 1932 giving it impeccable credentials as an up-and-coming revisionist power. However, on this issue the newly minted Führer ran into genuine opposition from a large coalition of interests ranging from the Reichswehr to big business, Foreign Minister Neurath and the chairman of the Four Year Plan, Hermann Göring. They all pointed to the paramount importance of preserving good Sino–German relations, which allowed the Germans to barter key raw materials for high-tech products (especially weapons) without dipping into the Reichsbank's foreign exchange reserves. Despite the occasional reminder to the Auswärtiges Amt that relations with Tokyo must not be neglected,[5] the dictator went along with this and even put up with the continued presence of a German military mission with Chiang Kai-shek's Kuomintang Army.

The first breakthrough came when Joachim von Ribbentrop, then one of the NSDAP's troubleshooters for foreign affairs, negotiated the Anti-Comintern Pact which the German and Japanese governments signed in November 1936. Officially limited to thwarting the designs of the Communist International, it came with an annex that committed both parties to abstain from signing major treaties or alliances with the USSR and to maintain neutrality in case Moscow

---

[3] For an excellent analysis of the issues underlying the policy of appeasing Germany, see Tim Bouverie, *Appeasing Hitler: Chamberlain, Churchill and the Road to War* (London: The Bodley Head 2019).

[4] Kurt Bauer, 'Hitler und der Juliputsch 1934 in Österreich. Eine Fallstudie zur nationalsozialistischen Aussenpolitik in der Frühphase des Regimes'; in: *Vierteljahrshefte für Zeitgeschichte* 2/2011, pp 193–227.

[5] Hartmut Bloß, 'Die Zweigleisigkeit der deutschen Fernostpolitik und Hitler's Option für Japan 1938'; in: *Militärgeschichtliche Mitteilungen* 1/1980, pp 55–92, esp. p 64; BA/MA, RM 11/68 'Attachebericht, betrifft: Ankauf von Luftschiffen durch Japan (9.1.1935)'. My thanks to Dr Sander-Nagashima for drawing my attention to this source.

were to attack either of them. However, the hostility with which it was met in many Western capitals gave the Japanese emperor and Japanese parliament (Diet) pause. As a result, much of the political momentum it was supposed to generate was quickly lost.

The outbreak of the Sino–Japanese War in July 1937 soon became the kind of problem that could put German foreign policy in an untenable position. The Japanese field army initiated hostilities without referring back to Tokyo, and upon encountering fierce resistance compounded this blunder by the slaughter of much of the civilian population of Nanking in December 1937. For the first six weeks of the war, German media coverage adhered to strict neutrality, but from mid-August newspaper editors received instructions from Joseph Goebbels' ministry to systematically minimise Japanese transgressions and war crimes.[6] Hitler ached to do more than that, but was still held back by economic realities. In October 1937, he first forbade arms shipments to China, only to allow them to be resumed surreptitiously a few days later by shipping them through Singapore.[7] Smarting from this climbdown, he allowed the Auswärtiges Amt to attempt to broker a peace deal, while he privately professed to put his faith in a Japanese victory.[8] When the Japanese government publicly rejected the idea of negotiations on 16 January, the point became moot. Hitler expressed his willingness to recognise the Japanese puppet state of Manchukuo and after the so-called Weekend Crisis of May 1938, redoubled his efforts to get closer to his fellow revisionist power by ordering the return of the German military mission serving with Chiang Kai-shek.

On 3 November 1938, the Japanese prime minister, Fumimaro Konoe, proclaimed the notion of a New Order in East Asia, under the auspices of which Tokyo might be willing 'not to reject' the notion of negotiating with the Kuomintang after all. Such ambiguity was compounded when six weeks later the prime minister initiated talks not with Chiang Kai-shek, but his deputy Wang Jingwei who had just defected from the capital Chungking. As if these sudden shifts in policy were not irritating enough by themselves, Konoe abruptly resigned his premiership in early January 1939, thus advertising the fact that he lacked faith in any of them.

In the meantime, German–Japanese relations had entered a state of limbo. Hitler, who had repeatedly expressed the hope that Japan might one day help

---

[6] Stefan Hübner, 'National Socialist Foreign Policy and Press Instructions, 1933–1939: Aims and Ways of Coverage Manipulation Based on the Example of East Asia'; in: *International History Review*, Vol. 34, No. 2 (June 2012), pp 271–91.

[7] 'Aufzeichnung des Legationsrats von der Heyden-Rynsch (22.10.1937)'; in: *Akten zur deutschen auswärtigen Politik*, Serie D, Bd. I (Baden-Baden: Imprimerie Nationale 1950), pp 626–7, 629–30. This edition of records of the Auswärtiges Amt will henceforth be referred to as ADAP.

[8] Elke Fröhlich (ed.), *Die Tagebücher von Joseph Goebbels*, Teil I, Bd. 4 (München: KG Saur 2000), p 429 (entry for 30 November 1937). Henceforth quoted as TB Goebbels.

Germany in tackling the USSR, was increasingly keen on the idea of expanding the existing Anti-Comintern Pact into a proper treaty of military assistance, and this was mirrored by the attitude of the Japanese Army. The emperor, the navy and the ministries of foreign affairs and finances were only willing to entertain such thoughts with regards to an anti-Soviet treaty and opposed extending it to the Western powers. In this manner, negotiations between Berlin and Tokyo continued throughout the autumn of 1938 and into 1939.

The Japanese government repeatedly tried to square the circle presented by domestic opposition to such an alliance by putting forward various drafts, which would have diluted Japan's obligation to come to the assistance of its ally in case of hostilities breaking out between the European Axis on the one hand, and Great Britain and France on the other. A thoroughly exasperated Ribbentrop rejected this idea time and again, pointing out that this would have wrecked the desired deterrence effect such a pact was supposed to have on all possible challengers.[9] The possibility of future US belligerence was occasionally touched on during the talks, but Ribbentrop insisted that the value of an alliance between Tokyo and the European Axis lay in its potential to deter, rather than incite, American intervention in another great-power war.[10] In the end, only Berlin and Rome committed themselves to a treaty of military assistance on 22 May, while talks with the Japanese continued in a desultory fashion.

The vexing issue of the Sino–German swapping of weapons for wolframite, which had continued on the quiet,[11] cannot have been conducive to creating an atmosphere that might facilitate a breakthrough. However, it paled into insignificance beside the news broadcast all across the world on 24 August. The day before, Germany had signed a non-aggression pact with its mortal enemy the Soviet Union, which would free it to invade Poland. This constituted a flagrant violation of both the letter and the spirit of the Anti-Comintern

---

[9] See Gerhard Krebs, *Japans Deutschlandpolitik 1935–1941. Eine Studie zur Vorgeschichte des Pazifischen Krieges* (Hamburg 1984), pp 262–89, for a thorough analysis of these negotiations.

[10] The seed for the idea that Berlin was already plotting war against the USA as early as May–June 1939 was sown by the prosecution at the Nürnberg trials. See *Trial of the Major War Criminals (TMWC)*, Vol. 2 (Nürnberg 1947), pp 296–7. However, of the documents frequently put forward to support this claim, neither 'L'ambasciatore a Berlino, Attolico, al ministro degli esteri, Ciano (16.6.1939)'; in: I Documenti Diplomatici Italiani (DDI), Serie 8, Vol. XII (Roma 1953), pp 211–15, nor 'Der RAM an die Botschaft in Tokio (17.6.1939)'; in: ADAP, Serie D, Bd. VI, pp 615–17, support the notion that Ribbentrop was trying to interest the Japanese in an offensive alliance against the USA.

[11] The available evidence suggests that Göring had actually gone behind Hitler's back in facilitating further deals with China. See Alfred Kube, *Pour le merite und Hakenkreuz. Hermann Göring im Dritten Reich* (München: Oldebourg Verlag 1987), pp 168–9. According to Bloβ, 'Fernostpolitik', pp 59–61, 85, more than half of the wolframite which reached Germany in 1939 prior to the outbreak of war originated from China.

Pact, made even worse by the simultaneous events playing themselves out on the edge of Japan's continental empire. Here, a border war that had been raging since May between the Kwantung Army garrisoning Manchuria and the Soviet forces deployed in Mongolia was decided when the Red Army in a few days enveloped and destroyed the Twenty-third Division of the Imperial Japanese Army (IJA). The fact that this was a campaign fought over the exact ground, and against the very enemy, that the army had spent the last thirty-plus years preparing for, made this an unqualified disaster.[12] The government might have weathered this particular setback, but not the craven betrayal by its German ally. As was to be expected, it fell from power, and one of the key criteria for picking a new prime minister was his dislike of the very idea of a German alliance.[13] The Japanese foreign ministry (the Gaimusho) made a point of recalling the well-known Germanophile Hiroshi Oshima from his post as ambassador in Berlin and German–Japanese relations entered a brief ice age. To make matters even worse, since June Japan had also gratuitously antagonised the United Kingdom by blockading the British concession at Tientsin over a trifling issue, thus compounding its isolation.[14] In Berlin, Hitler had to concede that a Japanese intervention on the side of Germany was now only likely if Tokyo felt it might be able to do so with 'a minimal effort'.[15]

The eight months that followed arguably gave Japan its last best chance to end the China conflict and mend fences with the Western powers. However, the hardening attitude of the US State Department to the Japanese escalation of the war in China meant that the cancellation of the bilateral Treaty of Commerce and Navigation announced in August 1939 became effective in late January 1940. This was enough to indicate that a point had been reached where it was no longer an option simply to take up again relations with the USA where they had been left off pre-1937. In early 1940, Japan was thus in a position where, having antagonised both the USA and the United Kingdom, it was left without allies and fighting an unwinnable war on the Asian continent. The number of troops (850,000) tied down by that conflict also virtually ruled out the possibility of ever resuming hostilities with the USSR along the

---

[12] The most extensive account of this campaign is still Alvin D. Coox, *Nomonhan: Japan against Russia* (Stanford, CA: Stanford UP 1985). The elements of the Imperial Japanese Army Air Force (IJAAF) supporting the army on the ground were defeated more gradually, but almost as comprehensively. On this little-known aspect of the campaign, see Dimitar Nedialkov, *In the Skies of Nomonhan: Japan versus Russia, May-September 1939* (Manchester: Crecy Publishing 2011).

[13] Edward J. Drea, *Japan's Imperial Army: Its Rise and Fall, 1853–1945* (Lawrence: Kansas UP 2009), p 207.

[14] For an up-to-date summary of the Tientsin affair, see Daniel Todman, *Britain's War: Into Battle, 1937–1941* (London: Allen Lane 2016), pp 170–7.

[15] 'Denkschrift und Richtlinien über die Führung des Krieges im Westen (9.10.1939)'; in: Hans-Adolf Jacobsen (ed.), *Dokumente zur Vorgeschichte des Westfeldzuges 1939–1940* (Göttingen: Musterschmidt 1956), pp 4–21.

Manchurian border. On 30 March 1940 Chiang's former deputy Wang was belatedly sworn in as 'acting President' of a new Chinese government in occupied Nanking, but the Japanese failed to extend to him any political concessions worthy of the name, or for that matter diplomatic recognition.[16] Chiang, needless to say, did not see this as an incentive to take up negotiations, which is what some Japanese decision makers appear to have hoped for. In the meantime, the war droned on.

In the end, the Japanese were rescued from the insoluble strategic dilemma their own inconsistent policies had created by events that took place on the far side of the world. Starting on 9 April 1940, the Germans initiated a series of campaigns which after two and a half months would leave them as the uncontested masters of continental Europe. British expeditionary forces were ejected from Norway, Belgium and France, having had to leave all of their weapons behind. The main units of the French field army were defeated and either taken prisoner or forced to demobilise under the stipulations of an armistice signed on 22 June. Britain was left isolated and expecting an invasion. In contrast with most campaigns of a comparable scale during World War I, the Germans did not suffer losses even remotely commensurate with the spectacular damage they had inflicted.[17]

The fact that the colonial powers of Southeast Asia had either been vanquished (The Netherlands, France) or militarily paralysed (Britain) changed the strategic picture in the Far East overnight. The government of Hirota Koki had first contemplated possible military expansion into Southeast Asia in a policy document in August 1936, and none of its successors had ever repudiated it. Now the possibility of acting on this idea appeared suddenly to have become feasible. In order to seize the opportunity, however, the Japanese government elites, still struggling to come to terms with stalemate in China and defeat in Mongolia, would have to execute nothing short of a strategic about-turn.

On the face of it, the Japanese government seemed nothing if not keen. As early as 15 April 1940 the mere rumour of an imminent German invasion of The Netherlands had compelled Foreign Minister Hachiro Arita to express his country's 'interest' in the future of the Dutch East Indies. This declaration was met with a forceful rebuttal by US Secretary of State Cordell Hull two days later, which stated unambiguously that Washington would not tolerate the

---

[16] For a good summary of the events surrounding Wang's defection and his attempts to establish himself as a credible partner of the Japanese, see Rana Mitter, *China's War with Japan, 1937–1945: The Struggle for Survival* (London: Allen Lane 2013), pp 201–18.

[17] The German conquest of northern and western Europe has been the subject of many important titles. The most recent ones are Karl-Heinz Frieser, *Blitzkrieglegende. Der Westfeldzug 1940* (München: Oldenbourg 1996) as well as Geirr H. Haarr, *The Battle for Norway, April 1940* (Annapolis: USNIP 2009) and *The Battle for Norway, April–June 1940* (Annapolis: USNIP 2010).

hostile occupation of any area in Asia that was of importance to American industry.[18] Realising that his initiative had been somewhat premature, Arita temporarily back-pedalled, but on 29 June returned to the fray. By that time, Western Europe had fallen, France had signed an armistice and Britain's position appeared to be untenable. Thus emboldened, Arita declared on Japanese radio that the time had come for the nations of Asia to 'cooperate and minister to one another's needs for their common well-being and prosperity'. Such a process would eventually lead to the establishment of a 'single sphere on the basis of common existence'. This sphere, it went without saying, would of course have to 'be led by the Japanese and free of Western powers'.[19]

As the Germans were to find out many times over, such a seemingly unambiguous statement from a senior Japanese spokesman did not necessarily mean that rhetoric would be matched by military action in the near future. Had Tokyo in the summer of 1940 been in a position to implement improvised plans for a Far Eastern Blitzkrieg to mirror the European variety, the consequences could have been earth-shattering. Needless to say, the perpetual logjam of political forces in Japan and the uniquely ponderous decision-making mechanisms available to the Japanese government were never going to produce such a dramatic decision.[20] In light of the unprecedented opportunities which appeared to beckon, the army showed itself surprisingly amenable to the idea of neglecting the theatres of war (China and Russia) it was historically linked to; provided Japan acted quickly, it appeared feasible to descend on Southeast Asia while sparing the Philippines, thus avoiding a US intervention. Rather surprisingly, the fly in the ointment was provided by the navy. A series of war games and conferences which began even before the French had surrendered soon led to a fairly unanimous consensus that an invasion of the Dutch East Indies carried with it an exceedingly high likelihood of war with the United States, a risk most of the senior officers were not yet ready to face.[21] Against such a backdrop, it is no surprise that the government of Admiral Yonai limited itself to demanding from the British and French governments that they stop any supplies from reaching Chiang Kai-shek's embattled forces through Burma and Vietnam,[22] while the army and navy

---

[18] 'Thomsen an Auswärtiges Amt (18.4.1940)'; in: ADAP, Serie D, Bd. IX, pp 161–2.
[19] As quoted in Francis Pike, *Hirohito's War: The Pacific War, 1941–1945* (London: Bloomsbury 2015), pp 91–2.
[20] The diary kept by the Lord Keeper of the Privy Seal (effectively the emperor's chief advisor on foreign affairs) offers illuminating examples in that regard. See Koichi Kido, *The Diary of Marquis Kido, 1931–1945* (Fredrick, MD: University Publications of America 1984), p 250 (entry for 30 July 1940) and p 251 (entry for 10 August 1940).
[21] On this, see Akira Iriye, *The Origins of the Second World War in Asia and the Pacific* (London: Longman 1987), p 102; Sadao Asada, *From Mahan to Pearl Harbor: The Imperial Japanese Navy and the United States* (Annapolis: USNIP 2006), pp 235–9.
[22] The French agreed to the presence of a forty-man-strong Japanese inspection team, which was granted permission to search trains headed for China for contraband; the

began drawing up plans for a possible descent on Southeast Asia in the future. Other officers demanded a non-aggression pact with the USSR in order to cover Japan's back during a probable campaign in the south. Most importantly, the Japanese military, as soon as the scope of the German victories in Europe became obvious, endeavoured to get into Hitler's good books. The German dictator, however, spent June and July cold-shouldering the fellow revisionist power in the hope that the threat of invasion would make the British amenable to the idea of a compromise peace. Only when the Churchill government failed to oblige did Hitler finally acquiesce. In the meantime, the Japanese Army and Navy, in a rare moment of consensus, had brought down Yonai's government in order to expedite closer relations with Germany.[23] They then returned Prince Konoe to the premiership on 22 July.

This was an important development since he had begun his first government with a clear agenda to create a more militarised state and compounded this by escalating the war in China and announcing to the world Japan's intention to create a New Order in the Far East. One of his first acts as premier was to sign a cabinet order on 27 July stating that he would seek both a settlement of the war in China as well as a treaty with the Dutch East Indies that facilitated their economic exploitation by Japan. Should diplomatic negotiations aimed towards that end fail to produce a satisfactory result, an aggressive move against the Dutch colony would be carried out in the foreseeable future.[24] The more ambitious schemes discussed in army and navy circles since early July were soon discarded, mainly because the different factions within the armed forces failed to come to an agreement on the specifics of such an operation, especially with regards to the possibility of a US intervention. Consensus on a move into northern French Indo-China, however, was soon established since this would put Japan in a position to increase pressure on China by opening up a new front along the Vietnamese–Chinese border, establishing air bases in the French colony and permanently cutting the Hanoi–Kumning railway bringing supplies to Chiang Kai-shek's armies. The ensuing negotiations between Tokyo and the new French government dragged on throughout August and much of September, a fact all the more remarkable in light of the colony's limited

British in mid-July consented to a temporary closure of the Burma Road. Drea, *Imperial Army*, p 210.

[23] The key source on Yonai's fall from power is Kido, *Diary*, p 244 (entry for 8 July 1940). For slightly differing interpretations of this event, see Iriye, *Origins*, pp 100–3; Gordon M. Berger, 'Politics and Mobilization in Japan'; in: Peter Duus (ed.), *The Cambridge History of Japan, Vol. 6: The 20th Century* (Cambridge: CUP 1989), p 143 (henceforth CHJ).

[24] 'Imperial Conference, September 19, 1940'; in: Nobutaka Ike (ed.), *Japan's Decision for War: Records of the 1941 Policy Conferences* (Stanford: Stanford UP 1967), p 11. Also: Berger, 'Politics and mobilization'; in: CHJ, Vol. 6, p 143.

military assets.[25] What is important to note in the context of this work is the fact that throughout most of this period, German support for Tokyo's demands was lukewarm at best.[26] However, by the time the Japanese started to take over their newly assigned base areas after 23 September, the diplomatic situation had started to change.

By late August, the British refusal to cave in had led Hitler to send envoy Heinrich George Stahmer to Tokyo; assisted by ambassador Eugen Ott, Stahmer endeavoured to take the Japanese up on their previous offer. In this manner, the favourable conjunction of French defeat, British resistance and a Japanese decision to turn south finally brought about the signing of the first treaty of military alliance between the two countries, together with Italy, on 27 September. Even though the text stated quite clearly that it was to be defensive in nature, it still sent out a clear political signal: the three countries were to render military assistance to each other as soon as one of them found itself under attack 'by a country not currently involved in the present war'. Since Article 5 of the text excluded the USSR from this definition, it left the United States as the only conceivable enemy of the new alliance.[27] On the face of it, the combination of a joint revisionist agenda, German military success and sheer chance had finally brought about circumstances that allowed Japan and the European Axis to agree on a joint strategy. However, the first doubts about Japan's commitment were not long in coming. The day after the signing, the spokesman for the Gaimusho in Tokyo took it upon himself to declare to the *New York Times* that the pact did not, in fact, 'entail an automatic pledge' to declare war in case of an armed clash between one of the signatories and a hostile power.[28] Since on the eve of the signing, the two German envoys had succumbed to some last-minute blackmail on the part of the Japanese foreign minister which led to the watering down of the concept of mutuality at the heart of the treaty,[29] this was in fact a reasonable interpretation. This peculiar

---

[25] The best account of the negotiations leading up to the Japanese occupation of northern Vietnam is John E. Dreifort, *Myopic Grandeur: The Ambivalence of French Foreign Policy toward the Far East, 1919-1945* (Kent and London: Kent State UP 1991) pp 195–213.

[26] 'Vermerk des Vortragenden Legationsrats Knoll (4.9.1940)'; in: ADAP, Serie D, Bd. XI.2, p 17.

[27] The text of the treaty is reproduced in: ADAP, Serie D, Bd. XI.1, pp 175–6.

[28] 'Die Botschaft in Rom an das Auswärtige Amt (4.10.1940)'; in: ADAP, Serie D, Bd. XI.2, pp 222–3.

[29] With less than a day to go before the announced signing ceremony would go ahead in Berlin, Matsuoka claimed that the Japanese emperor had given his consent on the condition that Japan's pledge to join Germany in a war against the USA be considerably weakened. Conscious of the importance Ribbentrop attached to the treaty, the two diplomats caved in. This was done by an exchange of notes that stressed the German obligation to come to Japan's aid should it find itself under attack by the USA, while doing no such thing for the reverse scenario. Two good accounts of this remarkable development are Theo Sommer, *Deutschland und Japan zwischen den Mächten 1935-1940. Vom*

arrangement was given an extra twist by the decision on Stahmer's part to keep this morsel of information to himself; Ott, when realising this in June 1941, made a belated (and it appears, rather half-hearted) attempt to enlighten Ribbentrop, though it is unclear whether this information ever reached the foreign minister.[30]

In the meantime, Japanese prevarication would be met by increasing exasperation on the part of German and Italian spokesmen who kept refuting claims that the Tripartite Pact was somehow a 'fair weather treaty'. The lack of an unambiguous commitment to the alliance on the part of Tokyo reflected conflicting opinions on the topic in Japanese government circles. However, dissenting voices from within the Tokyo establishment were not mollified by the fact that the pact had effectively been gutted before it was even signed. An example of this can be found in an intelligence report from the head of the Reichssicherheitshauptamt (RSHA), Reinhard Heydrich, which found its way into Ribbentrop's in tray a fortnight later. It referred to a confidential source in Rome who had reported that the Japanese ambassador in the Italian capital, when first discussing the proposed treaty with the Italian foreign minister, Galeazzo Ciano, had criticised the idea in such blunt terms that Ciano had been forced to show him the door and report the matter to his superiors.[31] It was obvious the new alliance was not off to a flying start.

4.2.1   The Japanese System of Government in the Run-up to Pearl Harbor

On 29 June 1941 the Japanese naval attaché in Berlin, Commander Yokoi, sent a coded message to his superiors in Tokyo on the subject of the recent German invasion of the USSR which offers a unique glimpse of the inner workings of Japanese government machinery.[32] First, Yokoi made an unfavourable comparison between the awkward silence emanating from Tokyo on the subject of Operation Barbarossa and the speed with which Ribbentrop had agreed with Hitler and Ciano over the telephone to recognise the Japanese puppet state of Nanking China. He then went on to stress that such a silence was incomprehensible in view of the fact that his superiors had been, according to him, in the picture about the imminent German invasion of the USSR since mid-April. To

---

Antikominternpakt zum Dreimächtepakt (Tübingen: Paul Siebeck 1962), pp 394–449 and Krebs, Deutschlandpolitik, pp 466–87.

[30] Sommer, Deutschland und Japan, pp 437–9.

[31] 'SS-Gruppenführer Heydrich an Reichsaußenminister v. Ribbentrop (5.10.1940)'; in: ADAP, Serie D, Bd. X.1, p 226.

[32] 'Bericht des japanischen Marineattaché in Berlin, Kapitän zur See Yokoi an den stellvertretenden Marineminister und den stellvertretenden Admiralstabschef (29.6.1941)'; in: Berthold J. Sander-Nagashima, Die deutsch-japanischen Marinebeziehungen 1919 bis 1942 (unpublished Ph.D., Hamburg University 1998), pp 604–6. The message was intercepted by American signals intelligence, but not translated until April 1946.

the modern-day historian, this message is remarkable on two counts. For a start, the mere idea that states with a government structure as byzantine and chaotic as that of 1940s Germany and Italy could be seen as exemplary by any outsider raises the question of what sort of a yardstick he might be using to reach such a conclusion. Furthermore, Japanese sources confirm that the Japanese ambassador in Berlin informed his superiors about the growing likelihood of a Russo–German war on 16 April; a number of further warnings, each more unambiguous than the previous one, were to follow; when 22 June came, the Japanese government still managed to act shocked and surprised by the event. Bizarre failures in sharing and evaluating intelligence such as this have earned the Japanese government structure of the period post-war epithets such as 'unsophisticated, parochial, fragmented, adamantine, spasmodic and often vague and waffling to boot'.[33] This was to play a far from negligible role in the critical months of 1941 which saw the ripening of the German–Japanese alliance.

By the late 1930s, Japan's constitutional structure bore only a passing resemblance to that of any other developed nation on the planet. On paper, the constitution of 1899 offered a number of similarities with that of Imperial Germany, in that the military were directly subordinated to the monarch and that the latter held a number of important prerogatives (to declare war, for example, and ratify international treaties) over parliament, which in any case was only in session for fewer than three months a year. Parliament's most powerful instrument was the passing of the budget; should it refuse to do so, last year's budget was simply implemented a second time. By 1918, it had become customary for the prime minister to be an appointee from one of the two main political parties (the Seiyukai and the Minseito), which dominated the Lower House or Diet. On the face of it, it was a reasonably successful compromise in power sharing between the elites of a previous era and those of the new period.[34]

There, however, the similarities with other developed countries ended. Even though democratic and socialist ideas found acceptance among a number of intellectuals after World War I and universal suffrage for all males aged twenty-five and over was introduced in 1925, these were not reliable indicators of modern Japan's successful transition to becoming a pluralistic society. One of the foremost reasons standing in the way of such an evolution was a series of economic and financial disasters. Hard on the heels of a financial panic in 1921, on 1 September 1923 a major earthquake and ensuing firestorm devastated

[33] Alvin D. Coox, 'Japanese Net Assessment in the Era before Pearl Harbor'; in: Williamson Murray and Allan R. Millett (eds.), *Calculations: Net Assessment and the Coming of World War II* (New York: The Free Press 1992), pp 258–98, esp. p 298 (quote).
[34] On the pre-1932 constitutional structure of Japan, see Taichiro Mitani, 'The Establishment of Party Cabinets, 1898–1932'; in: CHJ, Vol. 6, pp 55–96.

a large part of the urban areas of Tokyo and Yokohama. The aggregate human and financial loss made this the worst natural disaster in the history of modern Japan. In April 1927, the collapse of a bank led to yet another financial crisis which meant that the country would be in even worse shape to withstand the impact of the Great Depression of the early 1930s than most other great powers. More than any other segment in Japanese society, the small farmers were devastated by this, a fact which was to have important political consequences, since many army officers had important ties to this group and from now on felt compelled to take up its case. Against this backdrop of penury, the Japanese ruling classes might have been expected to seize any chance to downsize the armed forces with both hands.

The agreement reached at the Washington conference on naval disarmament (November–December 1921) had saved Japan from what would have been a ruinous arms race and secured for it conditions which effectively left the western Pacific at its mercy in case of a US–Japanese war.[35] Astonishingly, on their return the architects of the agreement soon found themselves in a situation where they were ostracised by many of their peers; the professional advancement of officers associated with them was blocked. Vice Admiral Kato Kanji, the leading spokesman of the faction opposing the treaty, voiced his antagonism in such a blunt and open manner in a public forum that this move alone would have discredited his cause in any Western military establishment. Not so in Imperial Japan: while he was reprimanded, support for the pact which he had criticised progressively crumbled, with its supporters growing fewer and fewer in number as the decade wore on. The Japanese delegation accepting a similar compromise on cruisers and assorted other vessels at the London conference in 1930 led to similar reverberations. By 1931, elements within the army were ready to move from grumbling to mutiny when the Kwantung Army, tasked with protecting the railway zone and military bases Japan had obtained in southern Manchuria as a result of the Russo–Japanese War, staged a terrorist incident which it used as a pretext to initiate the occupation of the province. Far from culminating with the arrest and trial of the miscreants, the ensuing political crisis led to the fall of the government in Tokyo.[36]

Of even greater importance is the fact that the next government to be formed, in May 1932, was one of 'national unity' under a retired officer, with just a handful of portfolios going to party politicians. This state of affairs endured till the end of the war; the role of the parties was further eroded by key ministries taking over relief and public-spending tasks which until now

[35] A good account of the Washington conference can be found in Asada, *Mahan to Pearl Harbor*, pp 47–95.
[36] Drea, *Imperial Army*, pp 166–71.

had been in the hands of local party political bosses.[37] On 12 October 1940 all parties were disbanded and reconstituted under the banner of the Imperial Rule Assistance Association (IRAA), thus turning Japan into the notional equivalent of a one-party state.[38] A newly created Central Planning Office – a ministry in all but name – was created with a brief to implement reforms across the entire government structure, which would do away with fiefdoms standing in the way of total mobilisation. Initially, opposition to all these measures was subdued, mainly because of the perceived need not to break ranks at a time when the fight against economic depression and then the war with China created a requirement for extraordinary measures. Partly because of this, the media were allowed to retain a measure of freedom wholly unthinkable in regimes organised along truly totalitarian lines like Germany or the USSR.[39]

On the face of it, Japan appeared to be turning into militaristic dictatorship where everything was being geared towards the prosecution of total war. The façade of national solidarity, however, hid important cracks, which would seriously impede a smooth prosecution of a total war. Though the two military services had become without a doubt the most important players on the eve of Pearl Harbor, the influence they could wield was limited by a deeply rooted antagonism towards each other, a fact which did not stay hidden from foreign observers. A case in point occurred in July 1936 when the German naval attaché was informed by one of his Japanese counterparts that the navy did not really object to clandestine German weapons shipments to China as long as they were kept abreast of their scale and timings as a matter of professional courtesy![40] Not even the compelling need for intra-government cooperation in wartime was enough to fundamentally change this dynamic. The joint Imperial General Headquarters, set up in November 1937, not only excluded cabinet ministers, but even the emperor from its deliberations.[41] Truly joint meetings between the service chiefs or their chiefs of staff were rare, leaving much of the routine liaison work in the hands of bureau and division chiefs. Accordingly

---

[37] On the erosion of the parties' power, see Berger, 'Politics and Mobilization'; in: CHJ Vol. 6, pp 105–17.

[38] A number of politicians had themselves suggested this as far back as 1934–5 in the hope of salvaging some of their influence, if not outright power. See ibid.

[39] For examples of the friction this disparity in media management would occasionally cause in German–Japanese relations in the run-up to war, see The 'Magic' Background of Pearl Harbor (MBPH), Vol. 2, Appendix., Doc. 562, 'Berlin to Tokyo (12.5.1941)' and Doc. 562 a, 'Berlin to Tokyo (12.5.1941)'; Vol. III App., Doc. 825, 'Berlin to Tokyo (13.8.1941)', Doc. 826 'Berlin to Tokyo (13.8.1941)' and Doc. 878, 'Berlin (Oshima) to Tokyo (13.10.1941)'; PA/AA, StS Japan, Bd. 5, 613 'Ott an Auswärtiges Amt (9.10.1941)'.

[40] Sander-Nagashima, Marinebeziehungen, p 371.

[41] Both the emperor as well as some cabinet ministers had routinely attended the IGHQ sessions held during the wars of 1894–5 and 1904–5.

many of these younger officers of medium rank ended up with a degree of influence that belied their rank.[42]

Direct consultation between the country's civilian and military leadership on matters of foreign affairs increasingly took place within the confines of the so-called Liaison Conference. This comprised the prime minister with the ministers of finance, foreign affairs, the army and the navy as well as the two service chiefs, and it met irregularly. Since it was not a constitutional organ, its findings had to be confirmed by the cabinet and, in exceptional cases, an Imperial Conference under the nominal chairmanship of the emperor. Notwithstanding this caveat, as the country's international position grew increasingly precarious in 1941, the conference became the forum for discussions whose outcome ultimately determined the government's decision to go to war.[43]

Failure to achieve a consensus was most visible (and damaging) at the strategic level. Periodic reviews between the army and navy consistently ended with further confirmation that the two services were incapable of reaching an agreement on the most basic strategic priorities for the future. In light of the country's limited resources, a war with either the USA or the USSR should have been seen as a daunting prospect, even in a best-case scenario, but the diverging strategic outlooks of both services made a clear prioritisation of war planning against just one of the two giants impossible. Instead, year after year, both the United States and Russia (more often than not expected to be fighting in a probable alliance with Britain and/or China) were described as enemies, who would in all likelihood have to be fought concurrently, a clear impossibility given the shortage of resources.[44]

Internal schisms within the services, however, were almost as crippling as divisions between soldiers and civilians. In the case of the navy, they mostly reflected antagonisms which arose from the London and Washington treaties,[45] as well as branch rivalries (especially between the naval general staff and the navy ministry), not uncommon in Western military establishments. The army, however, was a different case. Initially, tensions among its senior officers were a reflection of rivalries between Samurai clans who had

---

[42] On the inner workings of IGHQ, see Drea, *Imperial Army*, pp 192–4, and Gerhard Krebs, *Japan im Pazifischen Krieg. Herrschaftssystem, politische Willensbildung und Friedenssuche* (München: IUDICUM 2010) [= Monographien aus dem Deutschen Institut für Japanstudien, Bd. 46], pp 45–9.

[43] For a more detailed discussion on the nature of the Liaison and Imperial Conferences, see Ike (ed.), *Decision for War*, pp XV-XVII; Krebs, *Japan im Pazifischen Krieg*, pp 45–7.

[44] On this, see Drea, *Imperial Army*, pp 137–41, 181–9.

[45] This particular problem had become a moot point by 1936, when the treaties lapsed. Since those officers who had spoken up for the treaty system had always been a minority, it had been a comparatively straightforward task to block their advance and force them into retirement. See Sander-Nagashima, *Marinebeziehungen*, pp 371–7.

either sided with or defied the emperor during the civil wars of the 1860s and 1870s. The two main clans whose intervention ensured imperial victory – the Satsuma and the Choshu – found themselves at daggers drawn in a rivalry involving control of the three key positions within the army bureaucracy: the general staff, the war ministry and the inspectorate of military education.[46] After World War I this rivalry was progressively eclipsed – though not completely superseded – by the claim to power of two groupings of field grade officers intent on doing away with such an obvious system of regional patronage detrimental to military effectiveness.

Both interest groups became involved to a greater or lesser degree in the debates of the 1920s and 1930s about strategic priorities and domestic politics. The former revolved around the issue of how to re-equip the army for a future war. The adherents of a short war (the Imperial Way faction) wanted an army strong in numbers which would be able to strike a devastating first blow and tended to focus on the USSR as the most likely enemy; a lack of technology and firepower would be compensated by elan and willpower which as they saw it had already carried the day in the war against Tsarist Russia in 1904–5. Their main rationale for this thinking was that Japan would never be able to compete on an equal footing with the more developed nations likely to wage war against it; hence any attempt at fighting a protracted war along the lines of World War I was doomed anyway. Their opponents of the Control faction refused to accept this and pressed for a smaller army to free funds for modernisation.[47]

By 1935 Imperial Way had reached a measure of ascendancy, but then matters came to a head with the assassination on 12 August 1935 of Lieutenant General Nagata Tetsuzan, a senior Control faction officer, by a lieutenant colonel of Imperial Way. Even though assassinations of civilian politicians (including one prime minister) by cadets or junior officers had become an alarmingly frequent occurrence since 1930, Nagata's murder caused widespread outrage in military as well as civilian circles. Hard on the heels of this came an attempted coup in Tokyo by junior officers and NCOs of the Guards division who sympathised with Imperial Way (26–29 February 1936). This went hand in hand with the murder of the Lord Privy Seal, the finance minister and General Watanabe Jotaro, the inspector of military education. A harsh reaction came from the one individual still in a position to rein in the army – the emperor himself. Hirohito was initially faced with the fact that even some members of the imperial family sympathised with the plotters and that loyal army units in the Tokyo area showed a marked reluctance to engage the rebels, thus leaving him with the prospect of crushing

---

[46] Drea, *Imperial Army*, pp 10–46.

[47] For a more detailed account of the history of these two factions and the groupings that attached themselves to them, see the excellent account in Drea, *Imperial Army*, pp 146–81.

the coup with the navy alone. It took him three days to break the logjam and force the surrender of the rebels.[48] Considerably more than a hundred plotters were tried and fifteen of them executed. Just as importantly, numerous senior officers known to be supporters of Imperial Way were forcibly retired or sidelined in the aftermath of the rebellion. While this brought a degree of temporary calm to the internal affairs of the army,[49] it should not be equated with the restoration of civilian government, especially since in May the army re-instituted its former right to appoint war ministers from a pool of active duty general officers.[50]

Together with the perpetual failure to establish an inter-service consensus, clashes like the February coup, which would have been unthinkable in the military establishments of any other developed country in the world at the time, all but ensured that the armed forces would never become the sole power broker in Japanese society. Between 1936 and 1940, attempts to enforce a war economy which allowed the state sweeping powers to control access to raw materials and labour were contested by business interests, part of the senior bureaucracy and the residual power of the Diet. The last initiative launched by the Central Planning Office before the war was defused in December 1940 in a compromise which left the firebrands in the army, who had hoped for the introduction of state management of private industry, far from satisfied.[51] Fumimaro Konoe, the prime minister who had originally espoused an agenda that would allow the military and their supporters to create the structures of a more streamlined state, thus stayed true to his erratic nature. Possibly as a sop to the military, he had previously allowed the reintroduction of party deputy ministers in the ministries to lapse;[52] in April 1941, on the other hand, he initiated a major purge of the pro-military reformist elements in the Central Planning Office for alleged 'communist tendencies'.[53]

This brief summary must suffice to illustrate that predicting the course of Japanese policy in 1940–1 was a daunting one at the best of times. For Western observers still struggling to acquaint themselves with the cultural subtleties of a fundamentally alien society, it must have bordered on the impossible. The Japan of the time was a bizarre hybrid between the dictatorial and the demo-cratic. The power of the Diet had been much reduced, but it was still in

---

[48] The most detailed account of events in and around Tokyo in those days is provided by David Bergamini, *Japan's Imperial Conspiracy* (London: Heinemann 1971), pp 621–59.

[49] Drea, *Imperial Army*, pp 179–81.

[50] Drea, *Imperial Army*, p 184.

[51] Berger, 'Politics and mobilization'; in: CHJ Vol. 6, pp 126–31, 144–8.

[52] Ibid., p 152.

[53] For the hidden agendas at work in this case, see Krebs, *Deutschlandpolitik*, pp 550–75; Michael A. Barnhart, *Japan Prepares for Total War: The Search for Economic Security, 1919–1941* (Ithaca and London: Cornell UP 1987), pp 200–1, 550–75; Krebs, *Japan im Pazifischen Krieg*, pp 170–1.

existence; unlike the German or Italian case, no charismatic leader had emerged to claim its powers for himself. Though Japan was nominally a one-party state by October 1940, the IRAA never came remotely close to commanding the power and influence of the CPSU or the NSDAP. Senior bureaucrats had been invested with considerable power since 1932, but were split between those with a revolutionary agenda and more conservative elements. Elements in the army had repeatedly meddled in the affairs of the state in a manner more reminiscent of most Latin American republics, with the leading role played by officers of medium and even junior rank suggesting alarming discipline issues.[54] The government, while historically committed to an anti-Russia strategy, had sent close to a million men to fight a gratuitous war in China, which it struggled to finish either by political or military means. In theory, such a situation called for a strong prime minister, but many of the incumbents of the 1936–41 period are best described as nonentities; Prince Fumimaro Konoe came closest to having a power base transcending more than one faction, but on important issues he repeatedly turned out to have the consistency of a weather vane. All of the various power brokers constantly invoked the name of the emperor whose prerogatives were ill-defined and almost never exercised in full, the putting down of the 1936 military rebellion being the most important exception. Finally, and most importantly, any major decision like a treaty or even a declaration of war, would require a consensus to be reached between political forces barely on speaking terms and not above keeping important information from each other.

4.3   The Inscrutable Allies: Early Problems of the German–Japanese Alliance (October 1940–June 1941)

The early months of the Tripartite Pact soon revealed signs that the treaty was the diplomatic equivalent of a house built on sand. Quite apart from the different gloss which Japan and its European partners put on the commitment to come to each other's aid in case of an American transgression, there was the matter of mutual economic assistance. A key article of the pact stressed that all parties should endeavour to give each other access to the latest advances in high technology and raw materials that the other partner or partners might be lacking. This appeared to set the stage for a mutually beneficial exchange of German weapons technology for Asian rubber and wolframite in much the same way as had occurred with China. As far back as August, the Japanese had offered to undertake major purchases in the Dutch East Indies on behalf of Germany and had renewed that offer after the signing of the Tripartite Pact. A loose minute penned five weeks later by the head of the trade department of

---

[54] For a more detailed analysis of this issue than is possible here, see Danny Orbach, *Curse on This Country: The Rebellious Army of Imperial Japan* (New York: Cornell UP 2017).

the Auswärtiges Amt, *Ministerialdirektor* Emil Wiehl, however, cast serious doubt on the feasibility of the sort of scheme that had worked so well with China. To begin with, the weapons and machinery demanded by Japan were to a large extent already spoken for since the Soviet government had made virtually identical demands in the treaties that followed the Molotov–Ribbentrop Pact.[55] As far as deliveries from the Far East were concerned, Wiehl's note stressed that a problem of a more political nature had arisen. The German ambassador in Tokyo had found himself 'upbraided' by the Japanese deputy foreign minister for having had the temerity to suggest that a shipment of Indo-Chinese rubber promised by the French be taken to Manchuria on Japanese ships. According to the minister, such a deal should have been submitted to the Japanese government, since otherwise it violated the spirit of the Tripartite Pact, which after all had the division of the world into spheres of influence as its guiding principle.[56] Wiehl felt that this was quite out of the question where deals with countries not ruled by Japan were concerned; French Indo-China might constitute a borderline case, but even here the sale of rubber had been agreed at a time when Japan had yet to intervene in the French colony. Finally, it should be intimated to the Japanese that their wishes would be addressed and a trade delegation sent to Tokyo 'after' all pending issues had been addressed, thus introducing a subtle note of blackmail into the proceedings. As far as Asian deals were concerned, 'the idea that we should ask the Japanese for permission every time we have some deal pending' was clearly out of the question as far as both the Dutch and the French colonies were concerned.[57]

This logjam continued into early 1941, with the Germans taking the line that they should be free to conduct business in areas not actually under Japanese rule; for good measure, Wiehl asked Ott on 2 December to remind the Japanese that countries currently involved in hostilities against Germany were allowed to proceed completely unhindered in their dealings in Indo-China and were thus given a preferred status that placed them above Germany.[58] By January, German industry was faced with a serious rubber shortage which put a completely different gloss on the proceedings thus far. On 21 January, Hitler himself was forced to intervene to inject a sense of urgency into the negotiations;[59] the deterioration in relations between the two allies can be gleaned from the fact that the next day, Wiehl wired to the embassy in Tokyo instructions that the Japanese habit of referring to their area of

[55] 'Aufzeichnung betreffend Wirtschaftsbeziehungen mit Japan (15.11.1940)'; in: ADAP, Serie D, Bd. XI.2, pp 489–91.
[56] Ibid., p 490.
[57] Ibid., p 491.
[58] 'Aufzeichnung des Staatssekretärs (29.11.1940)'; in: ADAP, Serie D, Bd. XI.2, p 622, fn 2.
[59] 'Der Botschafter in Tokio an das Auswärtige Amt (14.1.1941)'; in: ADAP, Serie D, Bd. XI.2, p 905, fn 6.

influence as the Greater Asian Sphere (rather than Greater Far East Asian Sphere) was inadmissible and should not be adopted in embassy communications.[60]

This unedifying spectacle took place against a curious backdrop which stood in contrast to the squabble about rubber shipments. On 13 December, the Gaimusho announced the appointment of General Hiroshi Oshima as ambassador to Berlin. A veteran diplomat, Oshima was widely known to be rabidly pro-German and had been one of the string-pullers who facilitated the passage of the Tripartite Pact.[61] Six days later, the recently appointed foreign minister Yosuke Matsuoka accepted a previous invitation by Ribbentrop to join him and Hitler for high-level talks in Berlin, aimed, as he put it, 'at making a strong gesture in favour of the Tripartite Pact'.[62] Matsuoka, though raised in the USA, was thoroughly committed to the idea of an alliance with Germany and appeared to be unfazed by the recent setbacks suffered by Hitler's ally, Mussolini. He was uncharacteristically blunt and open for a Japanese, traits which had landed him in trouble in the world of Tokyo politics on more than one occasion, but were likely to stand him in good stead when dealing with the high and mighty of the Third Reich.[63] If the comments he made to fellow government officials in January and February are a reliable indicator, one of the reasons for travelling to Europe when he did was a perceived need to engage in some serious negotiations with the Germans before they had the time to defeat Britain – an event the Japanese foreign minister appears to have felt was if not quite imminent, then certainly not a long way off.[64] While a cynic might dismiss Oshima's appointment and Matsuoka's visit as the equivalent of a cheque sure to bounce in the near future, another event which took place that very week finally suggested that there might after all be some substance to the new alliance between the two improbable partners.

Apart from regular warships, the surface element of the Kriegsmarine also deployed nine converted merchantmen as camouflaged raiders to prey on Allied merchant traffic. Experience from World War I indicated that steamers converted to the task hurriedly after having been caught on the high seas by the outbreak of war tended to have only a marginal impact due to their limited

[60] 'Der Leiter der Handelspolitischen Abteilung an die Botschaft in Tokio (22.1.1941)'; in: ADAP, Serie D, Bd. XI.2, p 966.

[61] 'Der Botschafter in Tokio an das Auswärtige Amt (13.12.1940)'; in: ADAP, Serie D, Bd. XI.2, p 721. Oshima had previously served in Berlin, first as attaché (1934–8), then as ambassador (1938–9).

[62] 'Der Botschafter in Tokio an das Auswärtige Amt (19.12.1940)'; in: ADAP, Serie D, Bd. XI.2, pp 756–7'.

[63] Eri Hotta, *Japan 1941: Countdown to Infamy* (New York: Alfred Knopf 2013), pp 57–75, is excellent on Matsuoka.

[64] James William Morley (ed.), *The Final Confrontation: Japan's Negotiations with the United States, 1941* (New York: Columbia UP 1994) [= Japan's Road to the Pacific War, Vol. 6], p 10.

speed, range and armament.[65] Hence, the World War II Kriegsmarine took care to pick the right sort of vessels from among the German merchant fleet and then went to great trouble converting them for the task in hand. *Atlantis*, under the command of *Kapitän zur See* Bernhard Rogge, formed part of the first wave of raiders to put to sea and would become the most successful. On 11 November 1940 she stopped and searched the Singapore-bound SS *Automedon* in the Indian Ocean. By a stroke of amazing luck, the German boarders discovered a strong room which, among other items, contained a trunk with confidential mail for the British Far East Command.[66] Two of the documents were copies of Chiefs of Staff Committee reports, dated 31 July and 7 August, which had been submitted to the British cabinet for discussion on 15 August. Both documents stressed British weakness in general and in the Far East in particular. Accordingly, they were adamant in ruling out any assistance to either French Indo-China or Thailand should either of these find themselves under Japanese attack; the Dutch East Indies could count on a degree of help, but only if they met the attack with force of their own.

Far more remarkable than the capture itself was the speed with which this prize was passed on to the Japanese. Rogge handed the documents to an officer who took them into Kobe in a tanker previously captured by *Atlantis*.[67] Within hours of the prize's arrival on 4 December, the documents were being perused by the German naval attaché in Tokyo, who sent them on to Berlin with a courier travelling on the Trans-Siberian Railway. At the same time, he urged his superiors at the Seekriegsleitung to allow him to share a copy he had made with the Japanese admiralty. Permission was granted after five days and thus Wenneker was able to hand a copy to Vice Admiral Nobutake Kondo, Deputy Chief of the Naval General Staff on 12 December.[68]

From the day this intelligence coup became known after the war, historians have debated to what extent it predetermined the direction of Japan's road to war, the loss of many Japanese policy documents in 1945 making it exceedingly difficult to arrive at a definitive answer.[69] The time which would pass until the actual outbreak of hostilities (a full year), the fact that northern French Indo-China had already been occupied by the Japanese since September without provoking a war with Britain, the absence of any reference in the documents to

---

[65] John Walter, *The Kaiser's Pirates: German Surface Raiders in World War One* (London: Arms & Armour 1994).

[66] On the circumstances of the seizure see the detailed account by Eiji Seki. Seki, *Mrs Ferguson's Tea Set – Japan and the Second World War: The Global Consequences Following Germany's Sinking of the SS Automedon in 1940* (Folkestone: Global Oriental 2007), pp 58–74.

[67] Ibid., p 82.

[68] Ibid., p 87.

[69] By far the most sophisticated examination of this problem can be found in Sander-Nagashima, *Marinebeziehungen*, pp 478–88.

the all-important American posture, as well as the fact that Britain's unique moment of weakness in the summer of 1940 had by then long since passed, all would appear to put a major question mark against any assumption that the *Automedon* papers were a key factor in the process which led to the eventual forming of a consensus for war among Japan's elites. On the other hand, a discussion of the intelligence scoop did feature in the Liaison Conference of 27 December. It is difficult to see how it could have failed to play a major role in the preliminary planning for an invasion of Indo-China and Thailand contained in the government paper *Summary of Measures to Be Taken against French Indo-China and Thailand* of 30 January.[70]

Of far greater importance for the purposes of this study is the causal link between the sharing of the captured cabinet papers with the Japanese and a marked change in the German attitude towards its Far Eastern ally. The first piece of evidence pointing towards a fundamental rethink by the German leadership of Japan's options can be found in the minutes of a briefing Raeder, gave for Hitler's benefit on 27 December. It is important to realise that in the five such meetings held since the signing of the Tripartite Pact, Japan had not even featured as an item on the agenda.[71] This day, however, Raeder, all of a sudden went out of his way to highlight Britain's weakness in the Far East and the strategic reverberations which would follow from a Japanese seizure of Singapore; even a credible threat to this pillar of British power in the Far East would go a long way towards easing the pressure on the Axis navies in the Atlantic and the Mediterranean.[72] The minutes do not reflect whether Raeder shored up his arguments by marshalling the evidence captured on the *Automedon*, but it is difficult to conceive how he could have failed to do so. Hitler for the moment showed himself cautious and expressed an opinion that in all likelihood, the Japanese would not 'do anything decisive for the moment'.[73]

Hitler's initial scepticism notwithstanding, from January 1941 onwards the Auswärtiges Amt and the Seekriegsleitung, convinced that the intelligence Rogge had delivered to Kobe signposted a war-winning strategy for their new ally, began a campaign to convince the Japanese that the time had come to strike against Southeast Asia in general and Singapore in particular. A lengthy memo by the Seekriegsleitung dated 14 January constitutes the

---

[70] Seki, *Automedon*, p 93. See also Morley, *Final Confrontation*, p 64.
[71] On 26 September, 14 October, 4 and 14 November and 3 December. Though the Tripartite Pact was only signed on 27 September, the meeting held the previous day was included in the count, since by then all the negotiations preceding the signature had been concluded.
[72] 'Seekriegsleitung Iop 2/41 Vortrag Ob.d.M. beim Führer am 27.12.40, 16 Uhr'; in: Gerhard Wagner (ed.), *Lagevorträge des Oberbefehlshabers der Kriegsmarine vor Hitler 1939–1945* (München: J. F. Lehmanns 1972), pp 171–5.
[73] Ibid.

first evidence of this.[74] The *Automedon* papers are not mentioned in so many words, but in every other respect the author positively gushed with enthusiasm at the prospect of Japan joining the Axis march of conquest. An intervention against Malaya would mean that the British would have to relocate many naval assets currently wreaking havoc in the Mediterranean. Even the Americans being dragged into such a war held little fear for the author since as a result of such an event, they would struggle to assist the British in the Battle of the Atlantic. Accordingly, Japan ought to be 'encouraged to seize any conceivable initiative in the Far East'.[75] The only concern voiced by the author no doubt reflected the recent disappointments over Italy's contribution to the Axis cause. He thus hedged his bets by pointing out that lack of fuel, a threat from Russia or the diversion in China might force the Japanese to conduct the war in a lackadaisical fashion. A contemporary report from naval intelligence was an interesting indicator that radically diverging opinions within the same service were not a uniquely Japanese feature. The author(s) identified a number of Achilles heels in Japan's armed forces and finished on a downright pessimistic note: Tokyo was unlikely to enter the war before the prospect of an imminent German victory became a lot more clear-cut than at present.[76]

A week later, Ott and the service attachés at the embassy at Tokyo staged an elaborate two-day war game to assess Japan's chances of success in a forthcoming operation in Southeast Asia. On 31 January, the ambassador summarised their findings for Ribbentrop's benefit. Japan's prospects were assessed as good, but a US entry into the war appeared to be likely irrespective of the strategy it chose. On the political front, he took care to stress the fact that only a 'minority group' amongst Japanese diplomats and admirals were openly advocating an immediate strike against Singapore while giving US possessions a wide berth; moreover, the Japanese government was extremely unlikely to commit itself to one course of action or the other as long as Germany had not defeated the United Kingdom.[77] Naval Attaché Paul Wenneker dwelt at length on the different scenarios the war game had entailed in a separate report a few days later. It refers to the captured War Cabinet papers by name and is the first German document of the period which unambiguously describes the Western possessions of Southeast Asia as the primary Japanese military target should

[74] BA/MA, RM 7/253a 'Seekriegsleitung 1/Skl. Iop 46/41 Chefs. An Herrn Admiral Dr. h.c. Groos. Eigenhändig (14.1.1941)'.
[75] Ibid., p 13.
[76] BA/MA RM 7/253a 'Oberkommando der Kriegsmarine. 3. Abt. Seekriegsleitung. Geheim! Fremde Marinen (Nachrichtenauswertung) Nr. 2 (23.1.1941)'. This report alludes to 'recently captured material of the enemy powers' in referring to the state of Singapore's defences.
[77] 'Der Botschafter in Tokio an das Auswärtige Amt. Für Herrn Reichsminister des Äußeren (31.1.1941, 05.40 h)'; in: ADAP, Serie D, Bd. XI.2, pp 1024–5.

tensions escalate with the USA over the current war in China.[78] The military potential of the British, Dutch and US forces available in the region is assessed as low. What is even more remarkable about the report is the level of detail it goes into in discussing likely American reactions to Japanese intervention in any (or all) of the colonies and protectorates of the region,[79] along with the daunting challenges facing the US Pacific Fleet in making a crossing from Pearl Harbor to Singapore while passing through a region dotted with Japanese bases. Despite such bright prospects, Wenneker reached a fairly devastating conclusion at the end. US participation in the war would lengthen the conflict and render a peace deal incomparably more complicated. Japan becoming a belligerent would close a loophole in the British blockade and, finally, the Dutch East Indies would in all likelihood be lost to Germany in case of a complete Japanese victory – an interesting sidelight on the levels of exasperation in the German embassy over Japanese attitudes to German trade with this region. Thus, Wenneker finished his report on a note which stood in contrast to the optimistic forecast he had given for Japanese operational success: 'There can be no doubt that it can only be of advantage for Germany, that Germany and Italy should achieve total victory over England through their own means and without a Japanese intervention, thus allowing the Tripartite Pact to play its allotted role as an instrument of war prevention.'[80]

There is strong circumstantial evidence that Ott's report was immediately passed on to Hitler, since it is the most logical explanation for his curious comment to Joseph Goebbels on 31 January that 'Japan's navy was superior to the American one'.[81] Such a statement was not entirely divorced from the realities of 1941, but only if one allows for intangible factors like the considerable gap in effectiveness between American and Japanese torpedoes as well as the superior training of the Imperial Japanese Navy for night fighting. In view of the fact that these factors were as yet unknown even to most experts, the statement has a startling quality to it, especially coming as it does from somebody endowed with a considerable knowledge of naval hardware.[82] It would only appear to make sense in the context of the war game Ott presided

---

[78] BA/MA, RM 7/253a 'Deutsche Botschaft. Der Marineattache. B.Nr. 75/41 g.Kdos an das Oberkommando der Kriegsmarine M-Att., z.Hd. Herrn Korv.Kpt. Besthorn. Betr.: Der Eintritt Japans in den europäischen Krieg. Möglichkeiten und Auswirkungen (3.2.1941)'.

[79] The war game had assessed three different scenarios: a Japanese occupation of southern Vietnam; a descent on Singapore, North Borneo and Hong Kong; and, last, a simultaneous seizure of Singapore and the Philippines.

[80] Ibid., p 11.

[81] TB Goebbels Bd. I.9, pp 120–1 (entry for 1 February 1941).

[82] The following comments were recorded by after the war by a historian attached to OKW's Military History Department: 'He was endowed with the most remarkable memory. His knowledge of the firepower and military effectiveness of individual naval vessels was staggering. He could also recite from memory the muzzle velocity of individual gun

over in Tokyo, which was most likely held during 28 and 29 January 1941.[83] Rather than addressing the alleged superiority of the Japanese Navy over the American one in general, it had focused on ferreting out the challenges the US Pacific Fleet would face in the scenario the German war-gamers had deemed to be most likely, and hence relevant: a hypothetical attempt by the main body of the US Pacific Fleet to come to the aid of the Western forces fighting Japanese invaders over possession of the East Indies. Even more importantly, Hitler in the same conversation had also expressed his utter confidence that Japan would 'immediately intervene' on Germany's side should the USA open hostilities against the Third Reich.[84] This would seem to confirm that he was genuinely ignorant of the last-minute dilution of the Tripartite Pact undertaken by Stahmer and Ott.

While Raeder did not yet share the dictator's confidence in Japan's commitment to the letter and spirit of the Tripartite Pact, he was – in contrast to Wenneker – inclined to see it as a development that was to be welcomed. In an extensive report compiled for Hitler and dated 4 February, the Seekriegsleitung had gone to a great deal of trouble in assessing Japan's potential and limitations as an active ally.[85] The recent reports by Wenneker and Ott are not alluded to, but are likely to have influenced its findings. With a view to the near future, the opinion was expressed that Japan should support its fellow allies in a manner similar to that practised by the USA vis-à-vis Britain. Thus, it was expected that the Japanese should support German surface raiders both logistically and by the provision of intelligence and, for good measure, resupply the beleaguered Italian forces in Somalia by running the British blockade. Japan openly joining its Tripartite partners in the ongoing war might be conditioned by its willingness to make a full commitment – something which the war in China and tensions with the USSR might make questionable. Should such obstacles be removed, however, Japanese participation was to be welcomed because it would force the US leadership to relocate not just the bulk of its navy, but even its army and air force to check the Japanese onslaught. A war in the Pacific would also force Britain to shift at least some of its assets away from the Mediterranean and Middle East to defend Singapore. Overall, from the German point of view, such a development would clearly favour Germany:

---

calibres.' See BA/MA, MSG 2/11357 '4 Jahre als Forscher an der Kriegsgeschichtlichen Abteilung des OKW, 1941–1945, Dr. phil. Habil. Claus Grimm', p 9.

[83] Ott's report was wired to Berlin from the embassy on 31 January at 05.40 (30 January 1941, 22.40, German time).

[84] TB Goebbels, Bd. I.9, p 121 (entry for 1 February 1941).

[85] 'Seekriegsleitung I op 112/41 Vortrag des Ob.d.M. beim Führer am 4.2.1941 nachm (n.d.), Anlage 1'; in: Wagner (ed.), Lagevorträge, pp 190–6. The minutes note that Raeder handed Hitler a copy of the report for his perusal; it is highly likely he also gave him a verbal summary. If Hitler made any comments, they are not included in the minutes. See ibid., p 185.

'the sum of the benefits outweighed any disadvantages'.[86] This assessment is all the more remarkable since the author of the report still harboured some residual doubts about the capability of the Japanese armed forces to either dispose of the British position in Singapore or inflict major losses on the US Pacific Fleet.[87] The entire assessment was predicated throughout on a hypothetical situation where a US–German war had already broken out and Japan faced the choice (moral or legal) of coming to the aid of its Tripartite partner or withdrawing into neutrality. The possibility of Japan initiating hostilities on its own was apparently seen as improbable.

While Ott's report of 31 January had probably served as a catalyst to rekindle Hitler's interest in Japan's potential as an ally, this development needs to be contextualised by referring to recent military events. On 27 December, the dictator had still appeared somewhat tepid in the face of Raeder's sales pitch, but the days and weeks that followed were marked by a dramatic deterioration of Italy's military situation. To begin with, the Italians formally approached their ally the very next day asking for the deployment of German Army units to help them shore up the front in southern Albania, which was being invaded by the Greeks. Such a plea for help was unprecedented and made a complete nonsense of Mussolini's much-trumpeted concept of *guerra parallela*, which had had as its underlying rationale the preservation of the Mediterranean and North Africa as Italy's exclusive sphere of influence.[88] Things did not yet appear quite as dire in eastern Libya, since there the invading British Western Desert Force had only just crossed the Egyptian border and now faced the prospect of lengthy siege operations against the well-fortified port cities of Bardia and Tobruk. When the former fell after a brief fight on 5 January, it soon became clear that Tobruk was likely to follow in due course. Hitler decided to send a small armoured force to Libya to allow the Italians to at least hang onto a toehold around Tripoli,[89] and he summoned Mussolini to the Berghof for talks in order to establish a framework for Axis cooperation in the Mediterranean which would somehow still salvage a fragment of Italian pride.[90] The German dictator's sudden interest in Japan's naval potential may

[86] Ibid., 195. Unlike many other German documents from the period, this report does not dwell on the impact that the loss of the rubber-producing colonies of Southeast Asia would have on the US economy.

[87] Prospects for an attack on Singapore were assessed as not 'entirely devoid of hope', thus falling somewhat short of a ringing endorsement. Ibid.

[88] MacGregor Knox, *Mussolini Unleashed 1939–1941: Politics and Strategy in Fascist Italy's Last War* (Cambridge: CUP 1982), pp 134–230.

[89] 'Der Führer und Oberste Befehlshaber der Wehrmacht OKW/WFSt/Abt. L Nr 44018/41 g.K. Chefs. Weisung Nr. 22. Mithilfe deutscher Kräfte bei den Kämpfen im Mittelmeeraum (11.1.1941)'; in: Walther Hubatsch (ed.), *Hitler's Weisungen für die Kriegführung 1939–1945. Dokumente des Oberkommandos der Wehrmacht* (Koblenz: Bernard & Graefe 1983), pp 93–5.

[90] Knox, *Mussolini*, pp 231–5.

to some extent have been informed by intelligence from the *Automedon* papers, but it was certainly given a sense of urgency by the realisation that a replacement needed to be found for Germany's main ally.

War prevention is not a concept most historians would normally associate with the name of Joachim von Ribbentrop, but towards the end of the month he found himself unwittingly following in Wenneker's footsteps. On 10 February, Ott had relayed to him a statement from Japanese Foreign Minister Matsuoka, who had referred to the possibility of an attack on Singapore, but in the context of a war waged against both Anglo-Saxon powers.[91] Ribbentrop, still faithful to Hitler's idea of keeping the USA out of the war for the time being, thus found himself in the curious position of having to preach the gospel of de-escalation to the new Japanese ambassador when the latter presented his credentials to him at his private residence, Fuschl.[92] In a talk lasting several hours, Ribbentrop insisted on three separate occasions that the Japanese armed forces should focus their efforts on initiating operations against Singapore to the exclusion of other targets.[93] Provided they studiously avoided touching US territory on their march of conquest, the Japanese would probably reap all the benefits of a major war without actually having to fight one. He even went so far as to suggest that Matsuoka should be the bearer of an unambiguous decision for war along these lines during his upcoming visit to Germany. When the conversation touched on a couple of topics which in the past had left German diplomats confused and exasperated, Oshima sheepishly admitted that 'Japanese policy often did not speak with one voice'. Thus encouraged, even before Oshima had left the building Ribbentrop sent off a telegram requesting Ott to admonish the Japanese foreign ministry for the obviously tepid commitment of their ambassador in Washington to the idea of the Tripartite Pact.[94]

The weeks prior to Matsuoka's arrival in Berlin saw German–Japanese relations in a state of flux. The political will on the German side to turn the Tripartite Pact into an active military alliance was very much in evidence, but so were the difficulties that would have to be surmounted along the way. Already on 15 February, Hitler had stressed the need to give the Japanese every support for an operation against Singapore. He put forward the idea of far-reaching strategic cooperation and scolded the Kriegsmarine for its reluctance to share military secrets with the new ally. He felt confident in ruling out

---

[91] 'Der Botschafter in Tokio an das Auswärtige Amt. Für Herrn Reichsminister des Auswärtigen (10.2.1941)'; in: ADAP, Serie D, Bd. XII.1, pp 59–60.
[92] 'Niederschrift über die Unterredung des Herrn Reichsaußenministers mit Botschafter Oshima in Fuschl am 23. Februar 1941 (23.2.1941)'; in: ADAP, Serie D, Bd. XII.1, pp 114–24.
[93] Ibid., pp 118–20.
[94] 'Der Reichsaußenminister an die Botschaft in Tokio (24.2.1941)'; in: ADAP, Serie D, Bd. XII.1, pp 126–7.

an about-turn on the part of Tokyo; furthermore, the Japanese could be trusted with safeguarding German secrets more 'than any other people'.[95] Twelve days later, Ribbentrop urged Ott in Tokyo that the Japanese government needed to be persuaded with 'all the means at your disposal' to initiate an operation against Singapore at the earliest opportunity.[96] On 5 March, Hitler issued his Directive No. 24 on 'cooperation with Japan', which stressed the need for cooperation with Japan in order to keep the USA out of the war.[97] This was followed five days later by an OKW directive which ordered all Wehrmacht commands to extend every conceivable courtesy to a Japanese delegation which had just arrived in Germany with a view to acquainting themselves with the latest German weapons technology. While these developments appeared encouraging enough they need to be contrasted with the underbelly of the German–Japanese relationship. The idea of sharing technological secrets came in for renewed criticism by the Seekriegsleitung on 22 February; as recorded in the central war diary, both Japan's tepid commitment to the alliance thus far as well as the Anglophile sentiments still prevailing in parts of the Imperial Navy warranted a fundamental rethinking of such a policy.[98] As far as Hitler's directive was concerned, it spoke of the need to encourage a Japanese move against Singapore but at the same time forbade any reference to the upcoming invasion of the USSR; in view of the fact that such a morsel of information might actually have encouraged a Japanese move south, this was a crucial omission which the Seekriegsleitung had warned against on 3 March.[99] A report dated 13 March in which Wenneker summarised a recent conversation with the Deputy Chief of the Naval General Staff, Nobutake Kondo, likewise made for sobering reading: Kondo had had to admit that an operation against Singapore was still in preparation but would only be carried out when no other options remained, since such a move carried with it the possibility of bringing the United States into the war as well. If in such a case, the US Navy decided to bide its time and, rather than seeking a big

[95] Hans-Adolf Jacobsen (ed.), *Kriegstagebuch des Oberkommandos der Wehrmacht, Bd. I: 1.8.1940–31.12.1941* (Frankfurt a.M. 1965), p 328 (entry for 17 February 1941). The entry makes reference to a comment made by Hitler on 15th.

[96] 'Der Reichsaußenminister an die Botschaft in Tokio. Für den Herrn Botschafter persönlich (27.2.1941)'; in: ADAP, Serie D, Bd. XII.2, p 150. By early March, OKW was already assuming an 'imminent' Japanese entry into the war which would be followed by a campaign prioritising the occupation of Singapore 'with all available means'. Werner Rahn and Gerhard Schreiber (eds.), *Kriegstagebuch der Seekriegsleitung 1939–1945. Teil A, Bd. 19,* (Herford & Bonn: Mittler & Sohn 1990), (entry for 3 March 1941).

[97] 'Oberkommando der Wehrmacht WFSt/Abt. L (I Op) Nr. 44 282/41/g.K.Chefs. Weisung Nr. 24 über Zusammenarbeit mit Japan (5.3.1941)'; in: Hubatsch (ed.), *Weisungen,* pp103–5.

[98] KTB Seekriegsleitung. Teil A (entry for 22 February 1941).

[99] KTB Seekriegsleitung, Teil A (entry for 3 March 1941).

fleet action, put its faith in unrestricted submarine warfare, this could result in a decade-long conflict. Provided the Americans continued to show their previous willingness to sell oil to Japan, there was certainly no pressing need for such radical moves. Such momentum as had been generated by the capture of the cabinet papers appeared to have spent itself, a fact Wenneker put down to the recent rash of disasters suffered by Germany's Axis partner Italy.[100]

Another factor which severely limited Japan's strategic options was the war with China. On 18 March Propaganda Minister Joseph Goebbels reflected on the findings of a report sent to him from Shanghai by a member of the local NSDAP branch. In words which were eerily reminiscent of the briefing that travel writer Colin Ross had given for Hitler's benefit exactly one year earlier, he described the Japanese situation as virtually hopeless both on account of the military stalemate and Tokyo's failure to either find a political compromise or at least invest a puppet ruler with more than token authority. In the meantime, the commitment of the Japanese Army to this vast theatre of war had reached such proportions that the mere idea of initiating hostilities against a great power elsewhere appeared highly questionable.[101] While Goebbels would in the normal run of things not have concerned himself with such matters, this instance is of importance not just because he noted his approval with the gist of the report, but also because he had a summary typed up and forwarded to Hitler.[102]

In the run-up to Matsuoka's visit a number of German officials attempted to find a way to add their input to the agenda of the forthcoming talks. The by now thoroughly exasperated Wiehl produced a lengthy report on 21 March which addressed recent problems of German–Japanese cooperation and appeared to seriously call into question the very foundations on which the Tripartite Pact rested. When set against the China of Chiang Kai-shek, Wiehl wrote, Imperial Japan had turned out to be a major disappointment as a trading partner. In virtually all parts of occupied China, German trade was either being displaced by Japanese government agencies which claimed a monopoly for themselves or was subject to conditions inferior to those granted to British or American competitors. German requests for the Japanese to act as go-betweens for purchases of raw materials in the Dutch East Indies or Bolivia had more often than not been met with delaying tactics

---

[100] BA/MA, RM 7/253 'Der Marineattache an das Oberkommando der Kriegsmarine M Att. z.Hd. Herrn K.Kpt. Besthorn (13.3.1941)'. As it happened, a shift in American strategy towards the Atlantic (Plan Dog) had just brought in its wake a considerably enhanced role for unrestricted submarine warfare in case of conflict with Japan. For a discussion of the consequences, see the excellent monograph by Joel Ira Holwitt, *'Execute against Japan': The U.S. Decision to Conduct Unrestricted Submarine Warfare* (College Station: Texas A & M UP 2009), esp. pp 84–138.

[101] TB Goebbels Bd. I.9, pp 192–3 (entry for 18 March 1941).

[102] Ibid., p 193.

or outright refusals on account of alleged shipping constraints.[103] As far as the vexed issue of trading directly with semi-independent countries or colonies in the Japanese sphere of influence was concerned, Wiehl was even willing to concede defeat, since wartime conditions meant that Germany was likely to be dependent on Japanese support for some time yet. Conversely, the Japanese were far from reticent about making the most of the privileged position to be enjoyed by their trade in Germany, while demanding monetary credit and free access to new patents. The only bright spots in recent weeks had been a willingness on the Japanese side to help finally with the shipments of Indo-Chinese rubber to Manchuria and the sale of whale oil. The former had taken a personal intervention by Adolf Hitler, the latter had only been possible because German buyers had been able to outbid a British offer.[104]

In contrast to Wiehl, who can safely be said to have been overwhelmed by the grime and dirt proliferating in the engine room of the Tripartite Pact, three other individuals had a more sensitive issue in mind. First was the Kriegsmarine commander-in-chief, Erich Raeder. During a briefing for the dictator on 18 March which covered a wide range of topics, the admiral also touched on the subject of Matsuoka's visit.[105] Waiting till the other attendees had left the room, he warned Hitler that according to the head of the Japanese naval mission which had recently arrived in Germany, Matsuoka was likely to raise the subject of the USSR. He then went on to suggest to Hitler that he brief the Japanese foreign minister on 'the intentions towards Russia'.[106] Two memos produced by German diplomats on the subject of German–Japanese relations were also aimed at remedying the omission which lay at the heart Hitler's 5 March directive and which would play an increasingly important role in the next three months. On 24 March, *Staatssekretär* Ernst von Weizsäcker produced a minute for Ribbentrop which highlighted the two points on which everything would hinge in the talks with the Japanese foreign minister. With a view to bringing Japan into the war against Great Britain, he cautioned against investing too much hope in the leverage to be extracted from continued German support for Japan's China policy or concessions like the surrender of any German claims on the Dutch East Indies or the pre-1914 South Pacific empire, which had little more than symbolic value anyway. In his judgement, Japan's willingness or not to enter the war basically rested with further German military successes against Britain and little else besides.[107] A more sensitive

[103] 'Aufzeichnung über deutsch-japanische Wirtschaftsfragen für die Besprechung mit dem japanischen Außenminister (21.3.1941)'; in: ADAP, Serie D, Bd. XII.1, pp 270–2.
[104] Ibid., p 270.
[105] 'Vortrag des Ob.d.M. beim Führer am 18.3., 16.00 h'; in: Wagner (ed.), *Lagevorträge*, pp 201–6.
[106] Ibid., 206.
[107] 'Aufzeichnung des Staatssekretärs. Vertraulich (24.3.1941)'; in: ADAP, Serie D, Bd. XII.1, p 287.

matter was Matsuoka's current policy of reconciliation with the USSR, an option for which he had actually received some German encouragement in the recent past. In light of the planned invasion of the USSR, Weizsäcker drew attention to the need for someone to have 'an open word' with him during his Berlin stay in order to prevent the loss of political credibility he might otherwise suffer in Japanese government circles.[108]

A note penned by Ambassador Ott, who had travelled to Germany a few days ahead of Matsuoka, touched on the same subject. It began with a summary of recent conversations with Admiral Kondo and the army chief of staff, General Hajime Sugiyama, on the subject of Japanese war preparations. Both indicated that their respective services would be ready for war by late May provided it would be possible to ensure Soviet passivity in the Far East through a diplomatic agreement.[109] The pessimism shown by Admiral Kondo in early March now appeared to be less in evidence. If nothing else, these shifts provide further confirmation of the challenge faced by Western diplomats attempting to make sense of Japanese statements of intent. Most importantly, Ott, in much the same vein as Weizsäcker, drew attention to the fact that any ambiguity over Russia might well be seized on by some Japanese decision makers to block the road to war. Hence, it should be 'hinted' to Matsuoka that developments in the very near future might in all likelihood dispose of this problem in a thoroughly unexpected fashion.[110]

Unbeknownst to Ott or Weizsäcker, exactly such a hint came crashing down to earth the very next day, hours before Matsuoka's arrival in Berlin. In a conversation Oshima had with Hermann Göring, Hitler's designated successor and commander-in-chief of the Luftwaffe, the latter enthused over the long-term prospects of the Tripartite Pact, Japan's unique chance to seize Singapore and the assured success of a renewed attempt on the part of the Luftwaffe to wrest control of the air from RAF Fighter Command in order to facilitate an amphibious invasion.[111] After that, the next step was clear: 'First we will defeat England and next the Soviet [Union], and in the policy of ours there is no change. In this connection let me state that you Japanese will have to cooperate with us for a long time.'[112]

Matsuoka's stay in Europe was a prolonged one. Travelling on the Trans-Siberian Railway, he broke his trip for two days in Moscow where he discussed the possibility of a Russo–Japanese neutrality pact with Stalin and Molotov; he duly arrived in Berlin on the evening of 26 March. His stay in the German capital was interrupted by a trip to Rome (31 March–3 April) from where he

---

[108] Ibid.

[109] 'Stichworte zur Lage Japan. Für den Herrn RAM (25.3.1941)'; in: ADAP, Serie D, Bd. XII.1, pp 298–9.

[110] Ibid.

[111] MBPH, Vol. I, Doc. 328, 'Berlin (Oshima) to Tokyo (26.3.1941)'.

[112] Ibid.

Figure 4.1 Yosuke Matsuoka on his arrival in Berlin, March 1941. (Keystone/ Stringer/Hulton Archive via Getty Images)

returned to Berlin for more talks, finally leaving on 6 April. Even though on the face of it, this marathon of meetings did not achieve a great deal and in fact may well have ended up by wrecking the last best chance for Germany and Japan to coordinate a joint strategy for 1941, it offers the historian a unique glimpse into the dynamics governing German–Japanese relations prior to Barbarossa. The mere fact that this was the first and last occasion, Hitler would have to discuss future strategy with a key Japanese decision maker before Barbarossa reduced communications between both sides to the air waves justifies analysing them in some detail. The first round of talks between the two foreign ministers took place on the morning of 27 March and was of a preparatory nature, since Matsuoka was scheduled to meet Hitler later that same day. Even so, Ribbentrop took it upon himself to explain the current military situation in great detail, attempting to put a positive gloss on recent Italian defeats and highlighting – amongst other things – the soon-to-be-expected growth of the U-boat fleet.[113] US support for Britain was mentioned while stressing its limitations, both as regards the quantity as well as the quality

---

[113] 'Aufzeichnung über die Unterredung zwischen dem RAM und dem japanischen Aussenminister Matsuoka in Anwesenheit der Botschafter Ott und Oshima in Berlin am 27. März 1941 (31.3.1941)'; in: ADAP, Serie D, Bd. XII.1, pp 310–15, esp. 310.

of the equipment the Americans would be able to share with Britain and its Dominions. Italian setbacks in North Africa had to a large extent been compensated for by the arrival of a German expeditionary force.[114] Hence, the war could no longer be lost by Germany. It goes without saying that the success of the talks hinged to a considerable degree on the German leaders showing themselves willing to follow the advice dispensed by Weizsäcker and Ott and drop a 'hint' as to Germany's future intentions towards the Soviet Union. Allowing for the standards of diplomatic subtlety which prevailed even under the Third Reich, Ribbentrop did not do too badly. He initially referred to the relationship with the USSR as 'correct, but not too friendly' and followed this up with a passing reference to some 'recent unpleasantness'. Before moving on to the subject of the desirability of a Japanese move against Singapore, he finished off on a fairly blunt note: 'Should Russia one day adopt a posture which could be seen as a threat to Germany, the Führer would smash Russia. Everybody in Germany was confident that such a campaign would end with an absolute victory of German arms and the complete destruction of the Russian army and its state. The Führer is convinced that should it be necessary to execute such an operation, Russia would have ceased to exist as a great power.'[115]

If the minutes of Matsuoka's talk with Hitler that same day are anything to go by, the hint dropped by Ribbentrop did not register. Working through an interpreter, the German leader found himself in a position where many of the rhetorical instruments he normally used in challenging interviews were beyond his grasp.[116] Instead, he had to impress his guest with factual content. He rehashed much of the information on the military situation already passed on by Ribbentrop, but was cunning enough not to repeat the nonsensical promise 'that the war could no longer be lost'; instead, he shrewdly hinted at the possibility of the conflict ending with a political compromise, which would leave Japan facing a considerably reinforced Western military and naval presence in the Far East in a couple of years' time.[117] He then went on to encourage Japan to move against Britain in the Far East using similar arguments to those marshalled by Ribbentrop. The most revealing comments by far, however, were two references to the German field army. Initially referring

---

[114] Ibid., p 311.

[115] Ibid., pp 312–13 (quotes).

[116] Until recently, a scholarly examination of Hitler's strengths and weaknesses as a negotiator was very much a desideratum. See now the excellent Karl-Günther Zelle, *Mit Hitler im Gespräch. Blenden-überzeugen-wüten* (Paderborn: Ferdinand Schöningh 2017).

[117] 'Aufzeichnung über die Unterredung zwischen dem Führer und dem japanischen Außenminister Matsuoka in Anwesenheit des Reichsaußenministers sowie der Botschafter Ott und Oshima am 27.3.1941 (1.4.1941)'; in: ADAP, Serie D, Bd. XII.1, pp 317–24, esp. p 320 (quote).

to the 160 to 180 divisions he had available against Russia 'in case of any emergency', he then mentioned almost in passing three paragraphs later – as recorded in the minutes – that 150 of those were already deployed on the Soviet border.[118]

In the final part of the exchange, Matsuoka candidly admitted that he was not yet able to promise a Japanese operation against Singapore on account of too many cabinet members being against such a move. He also summarised the approach he had used in his talks with Stalin in a manner which must have struck the two Germans as bizarre in the extreme. According to Matsuoka, Japan and the USSR shared plenty of common ground in view of the adherence of old Japanese families to something he called 'moral communism', which essentially constituted an attempt to return to the old ways, now corrupted by Western and liberal influences.[119] It must have seemed obvious to Hitler and his foreign minister that many more hints would have to be dropped before Matsuoka boarded his train again.

The next exchange between the two foreign ministers took place on 28 March and, if anything, witnessed a display of even greater candour;[120] in light of the fact that the latter was a commodity usually in extremely short supply where German–Japanese relations were concerned, this should have augured well for the future. Even though Ribbentrop, in his attempt to sell Matsuoka the idea of an offensive against Singapore, repeated many of the arguments made before (especially with regards to the USA not being in a position to effectively retaliate against such a move), he also went one important step beyond what he and Hitler had promised so far: in planning for a move south, the Japanese should put any concerns about the USSR out of their minds because 'Germany would strike immediately should Russia attempt to make any kind of move against Japan.'[121] When prodded by Matsuoka on a possible German course of action after a British collapse, Ribbentrop stressed that Germany did not have 'the slightest interest in going to war against the United States', a statement which appeared to satisfy his interlocutor. With regards to the future of Japanese relations with Moscow, Matsuoka did not shrink from making a highly revealing statement which bore out numerous reports filed by German diplomats in the past year or so: 'Japan was waiting for the final German victory in the Balkans. Without the good offices of Germany there was really no chance for Japan to bring about a permanent improvement of Russo–Japanese relations.'[122] He even asked

---

[118] Ibid., pp 319–20.
[119] Ibid., pp 323–4.
[120] 'Aufzeichnung über die Unterredung zwischen dem Reichsaußenminister und dem japanischen Außenminister Matsuoka am 28. März 1941 (31.3.1941)'; in: ADAP, Serie D, Bd. XII.1, pp 334–7.
[121] Ibid., p 334.
[122] Ibid., p 336.

Ribbentrop's opinion on a possible Russo–Japanese neutrality pact, while at the same time being adamant in ruling out Russian membership in the Tripartite Pact. The German foreign minister expressed scepticism about this, but in the minutes it is difficult to elucidate which of the two issues he was referring to;[123] thus it cannot be ruled out that the seeds of a misunderstanding may have been sown at this point.[124] The dialogue ended with Matsuoka expressing a confidence in the Singapore option (failure to act 'would reduce Japan to the status of a third-class power'[125]), which had not been there before.

The last exchange between the two men prior to Matsuoka's departure for Rome took place on the 29 March and appears to have been considerably more extensive. Ribbentrop again went to considerable lengths to convince his colleague of the unique opportunity that a move against Singapore would constitute for Japan. In order to lay to rest any residual concerns on Matsuoka's part, he had rather bizarrely gone to the trouble of quizzing the Kriegsmarine commander-in-chief, Admiral Erich Raeder, about the potential of the US Navy's submarine arm, and received the comforting information that US submersibles were of 'lousy' quality;[126] accordingly, they had limited potential to wreak any havoc from bases in the Philippines on the lifelines of a Japanese task force supporting operations around Indo-China or Malaya. Much more important (and in light of his position as foreign minister, relevant) were his comments on the future of German–Soviet relations. Matsuoka at one point gingerly touched on the possibility of Germany pulling off another diplomatic about-turn like the 1939 non-aggression pact.

---

[123] Ibid., p 336.

[124] Both a German and a Japanese source appear to support this theory. See '20th Liaison Conference, April 22, 1941'; in: Ike (ed.), *Decision for War*, p 23, and PA/AA, StS Japan, Bd. 4, Nr. 608 'Ribbentrop an Botschaft Tokio (5.7.1941)'. See also the passing comments made by *Staatssekretär* Ernst von Weizsäcker in two private letters he wrote on 11 and 14 April, respectively. Leonidas Hill (ed.), *Die Weizsäcker-Papiere 1933–1950* (Frankfurt a.M.: Propyläen 1974), pp 245–7.

[125] 'Aufzeichnung über die Unterredung zwischen dem Reichsaußenminister und dem japanischen Außenminister Matsuoka am 28. März 1941 (31.3.1941)'; in: ADAP, Serie D, Bd. XII.1, p 337.

[126] 'Aufzeichnung über die Unterredung zwischen dem RAM und dem japanischen Außenminister Matsuoka in Berlin am 29. März 1941 (31.3.1941)'; in: ADAP, Serie D, Bd. XII.1, pp 340–6, esp. p 342. Since the US submarine force of the period was going through a period of transition which saw the phasing out of the obsolete 'V' and 'S' types from the 1920s, with the bulk of the Philippines-based flotilla still being made up of the latter type, Raeder actually had a point of sorts. Much more relevant (though unbeknownst to him) would be the exploder problems afflicting US torpedoes. Attempts to get to grips with this problem were seriously botched, and as a result the first twenty months of unrestricted warfare against Japanese shipping would, to a large extent, turn out to be a wasted effort. See Anthony Newpower, *Iron Men and Tin Fish: The Race to Build a Better Torpedo during World War II* (Westport and London: Praeger 2006).

Ribbentrop was adamant in ruling out such a course of action and instead stressed 'that the largest part of the German Army was already in position along the eastern borders of the Reich' and that 'a conflict with Russia was within the realms of possibility'. In mentioning recent differences of opinion with Moscow over the future of Finland and Bulgaria, Ribbentrop went even further: 'in light of the circumstances just described, it is certainly possible that a conflict between Russia and Germany might come about fairly quickly'.[127] A few paragraphs down, however, he felt the need to emphasise that such a contingency should by no means distract Japan from its main mission, namely a strike against the fortress of Singapore. This was in fact so important that just this once, the Japanese government might even see the benefit of keeping the Kwantung Army on a very short leash: 'Should the Russians pursue an irresponsible policy and force Germany to strike, the current mood in the China army [Kwantung Army] might make it imperative to prevent that army from striking unilaterally against Russia. Japan would help the common cause the most if it did not allow anything to distract it from the operation against Singapore.'[128]

Against such a backdrop of global strategy, Ribbentrop must have felt downright churlish bringing up the odd subject thrown up by the as yet imperfect mechanics of the Tripartite Pact: the vexed rubber issue simply refused to go away, and for a few minutes the two foreign ministers found themselves discussing issues such as the tonnage of blockade runners and the need for their continued use to complement the Trans-Siberian Railway, a subject Matsuoka found himself singularly ill-prepared to discuss in any detail. It may have been due to Matsuoka's desire to close the subject that he made assertions ('Matsuoka answered that Japan was in dire need for its own reconstruction and the development of China of cooperation with Germany'), which were so at odds with the reality on the ground that Ribbentrop must have wondered to what extent his guest was being kept abreast of developments.[129] Towards the end of the conversation, Ribbentrop, with remarkable lack of tact and poor judgement, reminded Matsuoka that the heaviest burden for the conduct of the war had thus far rested on Germany's shoulders and that he expected Japan to acknowledge this fact at some point.[130]

---

[127] 'Aufzeichnung über die Unterredung zwischen dem RAM und dem japanischen Außenminister Matsuoka in Berlin am 29. März 1941 (31.3.1941)'; in: ADAP, Serie D, Bd. XII.1, pp 340–2 (quotes).

[128] Ibid., p 345.

[129] Ibid., pp 343–4.

[130] Fatalities suffered by Japan in its forty-four-month war in China would by that point in time have numbered around 170,000, and hence about three times the number of dead suffered by the Wehrmacht in its whirlwind conquest of Poland, Scandinavia and western Europe. Edward Drea and Hans van de Ven, 'An Overview of the Major Military Campaigns during the Sino–Japanese War, 1937–1945'; in: Mark Peattie,

Rather remarkably, he referred to Russia in this context using terminology which strongly suggested that the Soviet empire was already a belligerent ('Furthermore, Russia's main weight was well known to lie on the European side').[131] On this slightly bizarre note, the two men went their separate ways.

On Matsuoka's return from the Italian capital, where he spoke to the Italian king and Mussolini, as well as the Pope, the Berlin talks were resumed on 4 April. Either Hitler or Ribbentrop must have decided that enough hints had been dropped on the subject of likely Soviet belligerence and opted to lay off this topic for the moment; Matsuoka's summary of his conversation with Mussolini and the Duce's assessment of the United Sates as 'enemy no. 1', while the USSR was only 'enemy no. 2', as well as Matsuoka's agreement with this, may well have highlighted to the two Germans that their strategy of subtle persuasion had not got them very far as yet.[132] This was followed by a very emphatic plea on the Japanese foreign minister's part that Germany needed to be more forthcoming in sharing some of the high technology that underpinned its underwater warfare against Great Britain. Even though Matsuoka felt fairly confident of deterring the United States from intervening on Britain's behalf in case of Japan making a move against Singapore, the Japanese Navy was insistent on being given access to German technology in case such a war were to escalate and bring in the United States.[133] Hitler responded that he would see to this and attempted to assuage Matsuoka's concerns about US intervention in a number of ways. He pointed out that Germany's current position completely ruled out an American amphibious descent on the European continent – a theme he would return to time and again in 1941. The merchant tonnage available to the Anglo–American powers was subject to constant attrition and German soldiers were 'as a matter of course' superior to their American peers.

This outpouring about German military virtues might have been seen by any interlocutor as routine propaganda fare, but what followed gave the talk a completely new dimension. When Matsuoka explained that a majority of Japan's decision makers were still hesitant about taking the war into Malaya and the Dutch East Indies out of fear of a possible US intervention, the German dictator said that he was prepared to intervene 'immediately in case of

Edward Drea and Hans van de Ven (eds.), *The Battle for China: Essays on the Military History of the Sino-Japanese War of 1937–1945* (Stanford: Stanford UP 2011), p 42.

[131] 'Aufzeichnung über die Unterredung zwischen dem RAM und dem japanischen Außenminister Matsuoka in Berlin am 29. März 1941 (31.3.1941)'; in: ADAP, Serie D, Bd. XII.1, p 346.

[132] 'Aufzeichnung über die Unterredung zwischen dem Führer und dem japanischen Außenminister Matsuoka in Anwesenheit des Reichsaußenministers und des Staatsministers Meissner in Berlin am 4. April 1941 (4.4.1941)'; in: ADAP, Serie D, Bd. XII.1, pp 374–8, esp. 374.

[133] Ibid., p 376.

a conflict [*im Konfliktfalle*] between Japan and America'. In light of the American agenda to undermine the Tripartite Pact by challenging its component countries one after another, nothing else made sense.[134] Since Ribbentrop had just assured Matsuoka on 27 March that a US entry into the war was something to be avoided 'by any means', this revelation was certainly remarkable. At this point, Matsuoka would have been expected to enquire exactly what set of circumstances were covered by Hitler's definition of 'in case of conflict', especially since the hypothetical scenario under discussion as likely as not would have entailed a staggered American intervention with concomitant gradual escalation of hostilities. If the Japanese foreign minister quizzed Hitler on this absolutely crucial point, the minutes do not reflect it. Instead, he went on digressing about how current Japanese policy was taking the empire closer and closer to war with the United States. While the overall situation still favoured Japan, many of its key decision makers hesitated to take the plunge and in fact opposed Matsuoka. Hitler commiserated, pointing out that he too had found himself in similar situations in 1935 and 1936, when he had to enforce his view over numerous doomsayers in order to introduce conscription and reincorporate the Rhineland. Seeing how he had been rewarded for his steadfastness back then, he would not 'hesitate for a moment to immediately react to any widening of the war, be it by Russia, be it by America'.[135]

In light of the fact that Matsuoka had arguably been offered the diplomatic equivalent of a blank cheque not once, but twice over, the two Germans must have felt rather let down by the Japanese foreign minister's concluding remarks. Allowing them what must have been (for Westerners) a unique glimpse of the engine room of Japanese policymaking: 'As a result of this, he had to explain to him the regrettable fact of life that he (Matsuoka) in his capacity as Japanese foreign minister would not be in a position to share with anyone in Japan a single word of what he had discussed with the Führer and the *Reichsaußenminister* about his plans. To do so would seriously harm his interests in political and financial circles. ... Under these circumstances, he was in no position to say when he would be able to brief the Japanese prime minister or the emperor on the aforementioned issues.' He would have to wait for a particularly 'propitious opportunity' to do so and even then there would a real possibility that the ensuing political process would lead to no tangible result whatsoever. He even went so far as to insist that communications on the subject should not be entrusted to coded telegram for fear that something might leak out at the Japanese end.[136]

---

[134] Ibid., p 376 (quotes).
[135] Ibid., p 377.
[136] Ibid., pp 377–8 (quotes). After the war, Ribbentrop's interpreter would describe Matsuoka's comments as 'surprisingly candid and highly unusual for exchanges of this kind'. Paul Schmidt, *Statist auf diplomatischer Bühne. Erlebnisse des Chefdolmetschers im Auswärtigen Amt mit den Staatsmännern Europas* (Bonn: Athenäum 1950), p 533.

Figure 4.2 Hitler receives Matsuoka in his Reichskanzlei apartment. The Berlin talks between Matsuoka and his hosts were the only instance when Hitler appeared momentarily to divert from his strategic priority to keep the USA out of the war. (ullstein bild/ullstein bild via Getty Images)

On 5 April, the Berlin talks came to an end with an interview between the two foreign ministers. While the previous conversations had seen revelations of crucial importance this one constituted something of an anticlimax. Conversation kept drifting between subjects which either had only a marginal bearing on German–Japanese relations (the imminent invasion of Greece and Yugoslavia in particular[137]) or were just downright bizarre (the role of intellectuals in modern societies or Ribbentrop's assertion that the post-war Third Reich would seek to emulate the old traditions of the Holy Roman Empire). Once the conversation moved on to rather more down-to-earth topics, the German foreign minister, rather than taking his cue from Hitler's veiled threat that Germany might have to settle for a compromise peace if Japan did not join it in hostilities against Britain, chose to be adamant in ruling out a such a course of action and bluntly restated his absolute confidence in

---

[137] 'Aufzeichnung über die Unterredung zwischen dem RAM und dem japanischen Außenminister Matsuoka in Berlin am 5. April 1941 (7.4.1941)'; in: ADAP, Serie D, Bd. XII.1, pp 388–92, esp. pp 389–90.

Germany's victory – if Japan chose to join in now this outcome would be merely 'accelerated'. Such a glaring inconsistency on a rather important matter appears to have registered with Matsuoka, since the minutes record him as insisting on this point.[138] The conversation concluded with both men assuring each other about the fact that all the key personnel in their respective ministries were actively supportive of the Tripartite Pact; any waverers had been weeded out, a possible reference to the stir caused by the reaction of Japan's ambassador in Rome the previous September. On this note, the two men concluded their exchange.

Had anything of substance been achieved in ten days of talks? Both sides had agreed that it was in their interest to keep the USA out of the war if possible. The potential enormity of Hitler's unexpected pledge to stand by Japan should the USA decide to 'widen' the current war stood in glaring contrast to the instructions of Führer's Directive No. 24 a mere four weeks before, which had stated that the key rationale of enhanced cooperation with Japan was to keep the USA out of the war. Provided this pledge was actually articulated as unambiguously as the minutes suggest,[139] it can only be explained in the context of the Lend-Lease Bill which President Roosevelt had signed into law on 11 March and which the dictator correctly judged to be a major step towards war by the world's biggest democracy. Allowance should also be made for the fact that at this time the German dictator was still confident of defeating the USSR by mid-August; even in the case of a US–Japanese war breaking out in the meantime and in turn leading to a German declaration of war on the USA, the as yet extremely limited resources available to the US Army and the two US air services all but ruled out an American intervention on a meaningful scale in Europe or the Middle East. But for the conscientious work of the stenographer this key moment in history (the first time the German dictator spoke of committing himself to a war of choice against the USA) could easily have been lost, since it does not appear to have registered with Matsuoka and may well have been lost in translation.

Matsuoka's remarkable candour, both as far as his own isolated position in cabinet and Japan's determination to tie further moves to German battlefield successes were concerned, was not echoed by the Germans being forthright with him about Operation Barbarossa. Whether it was because the dictator felt a sense of unease at this or because he still had Weizsäcker's warning nagging away at him, Hitler made one last attempt to square the circle by steering Matsuoka in the right direction without completely giving the game away. When his guest called on him on 6 April to bid him goodbye, Hitler finished their conversation by impressing on him that 'on his return to Japan, he could

---

[138] Ibid., pp 390–1.
[139] For a sceptical assessment, see Gerhard Krebs, 'Deutschland und Pearl Harbor'; in: *Historische Zeitschrift* Bd. 253 (1991), pp 313–69, esp. pp 316–17, 366.

not tell his emperor that a conflict between Germany and the USSR could be ruled out'. The interpreter even translated this sentence twice in order to rule out misunderstandings.[140] Whether even greater honesty (or bluntness) on the German part would have prevented Matsuoka from signing the Russo–Japanese Neutrality Pact on his return trip on 13 April is of course impossible to say. Reflecting on what was by any standards a major diplomatic success on his way back to Japan, Matsuoka gave no indication that he suspected that momentous events were about to call into question the strategic rationale behind the new détente in Russo–Japanese relations.[141] If Oshima had – as stands to reason – shared with him the content of his talk with Göring, it is likely that Matsuoka reached the conclusion that a Russo–German war would occur only after the defeat of Great Britain and hence probably not before the spring of 1942. Göring's additional comment about the need for Japan and Germany to remain allies 'for a long time' may have reinforced this perception.[142]

Judged by the yardstick which Ribbentrop appears to have set himself – an immediate Japanese attack on Singapore which avoided US possessions – the Berlin talks must be judged to have been a failure. A report sent by the German naval attaché in Tokyo while Matsuoka was still making his way back on the Trans-Siberian Railway revealed that he had encountered the Deputy Chief of the Naval General Staff, who was exultant over both the signing of the pact with Russia and the recent German successes in North Africa, which looked likely to cut the Suez Canal route in the very near future.[143] Even so, he admitted that the Japanese leadership was extremely unlikely to seize an opportunity which in the consensus of most senior leaders still carried with it a very high likelihood of a US intervention and a ten-year-long war. It appeared 'very doubtful whether Japan would prove equal to such a siege'.[144]

Truly fundamental doubts about Japan's potential as an alliance partner assailed a Kriegsmarine officer who in April 1941 chaperoned a delegation of Japanese naval officers touring German naval bases and research facilities.

---

[140] Since no official record exists of this brief exchange, the only source is the post-war testimony of the interpreter: see Schmidt, *Statist*, p 537. Insofar as many of his wartime reminiscences were borne out by minutes from his own hand published in the 1960s and 1970s his reliability has to be rated highly.

[141] Hotta, *Japan*, pp 65–8, for a good impression of Matsuoka's mood during the return trip to Japan.

[142] MBPH, Vol. I, Doc. 328 Berlin (Oshima?) to Tokyo (26.3.1941).

[143] BA/MA, RM 11/77 'Deutsche Botschaft. Der Marineattache. An das Oberkommando der Kriegsmarine M-Att., z.Hd. Herrn Korv.Kpt. Besthorn. Betr.: Unterhaltung mit dem Vizechef des Admiralstabes, Vizeadmiral Kondo (17.4.1941)'. The offensive by Erwin Rommel's recently arrived *Deutsches Afrikakorps* had originally only been conceived as a reconnaissance in strength; it was launched on 24 March and upon meeting little effective resistance grew into a full-fledged offensive.

[144] Ibid.

Quite apart from the fact that the Japanese officers appeared to have a rather unilateral concept of the idea of 'sharing' information, leading to some exasperation on the German side, the head of the delegation, Vice Admiral Naokuni Nomura, expressed views on the Japanese Navy's readiness for war which appeared to render all of Matsuoka's promises moot. According to him, the possibility of an operation against Singapore still required extensive examination and in any case a Japanese naval war against the Anglo-Saxon powers would in all likelihood have to wait until 1946 if it was to have any prospect of success. On 21 April, Nomura explained the rationale behind this timeline to Seekriegsleitung Chief of Staff Kurt Fricke. The latter appears to have been quite forceful in expressing this disagreement and described the idea of postponing hostilities for another five years as a serious 'strategic error', since by then Germany would have long concluded its drive for conquest and be engaged 'in other tasks'.[145] A Japanese campaign to expel the Western powers from Asia would thus face the undivided might of the United States or even an Anglo–American coalition.[146] Unbeknownst to Nomura, the mere suggestion of putting off hostilities by half a decade could not but raise hackles on the German side, since it was uncomfortably close to the timeline that had been quoted by Benito Mussolini when he had temporarily declined to join Hitler in his war in August 1939.

Matsuoka got back to Japan on 22 April and put the idea of a strike against Singapore before the Liaison Conference which convened on 3 May. It is likely that he felt empowered by his diplomatic success in Moscow to make a case for a move against Singapore straightaway, despite his prediction in Berlin that he might have to bide his time on this.[147] He then went on to plead for Japan joining Germany in a war against the USA if Washington's increased patrolling activity in the Atlantic should lead to a clash with the Kriegsmarine. The fact that he had the nerve to put this to a US journalist five days before it was discussed at the Liaison Conference on the 8th,[148] is unlikely to have helped his case:[149] this was definitely a step too far for the other attendees, who were more used to seeking consensus at a glacially slow pace. The support he counted on from Konoe and the emperor failed to materialise, leaving him isolated among his peers and facing an adamant refusal.[150] However, news of this reverse had not even reached Berlin when a message from Ott arrived on the 5th which appeared to make a complete nonsense of the Berlin summit. Ever since mid-April, a diplomatic initiative had been gathering momentum, which had the potential to undermine the philosophy behind the Tripartite Pact. Behind this

---

[145] KTB Seekriegsleitung, Teil A (entry for 22 April 1941).
[146] Ibid.
[147] '21st Liaison Conference, May 3, 1941'; in: Ike (ed.), *Decision for War*, pp 24–7.
[148] KTB Seekriegsleitung, Teil A (entry for 5 May 1941).
[149] '22nd Liaison Conference, May 8, 1941'; in: Ike (ed.), *Decision for War*, pp 27–31.
[150] Morley, *Final Confrontation*, p 76.

was one Japanese officer along with a Japanese and two American civilians, with links to government circles, but devoid of any official licence to engage in diplomatic activity.[151] This foursome (soon known as the 'John Doe associates') had managed to introduce a document into the almost dormant negotiation process between Tokyo and Washington, with the collusion of Ambassador Kichisaburo Nomura in Washington. It was phrased in such a way that it might suggest to a not overly attentive reader that it actually constituted an official American diplomatic initiative. In the past, Nomura's peculiar behaviour had been put down to sheer gullibility (he was a retired admiral with little experience as a diplomat) or his well-known zeal for somehow preserving the peace in the Pacific, or both.[152] Older scholarship has stressed that those Japanese naval leaders in the know received this initiative with even greater scepticism than their army peers;[153] however, recent research has uncovered evidence that Nomura did in fact act on instructions from the naval leadership in Tokyo while the Gaimusho were at least initially kept out of the loop.[154]

The paper suggested a series of radical measures to defuse the current tension in the Far East. The Japanese side would subscribe to the principle of Chinese sovereignty as well as the Open Door principle. The US government would recognise the satellite status of Manchuko, and Japan would recognise the independence of the Philippines. The two governments of Chiang Kai-shek and his former deputy, Wang Jingwei, would be reconstituted as one, upon which Japanese troops would leave China. In the South Pacific, Japan would limit itself to expansion by peaceful means in return for which the USA would help it acquire key resources and would resume the Treaty of Commerce.[155] US Secretary of State Hull had stressed to Nomura that even wholesale acceptance of these ideas would probably not suffice to meet US expectations and insisted on attaching to it a document of his own, the so-called Four Principles. These highlighted US expectations that in future Tokyo would commit to a policy that would respect the territorial integrity of all nations, the principle of non-interference in the affairs of other countries and the principle of economic equality, while pledging not to alter the status quo in the Pacific by other than peaceful means. Nomura for his part failed to stress

---

[151] Father James M. Drought and Bishop James E. Walsh had access to the Postmaster General, while Tadao Ikawa and Colonel Hideo Iwakuro had the ear of Prime Minister Konoe.

[152] Robert J. C. Butow, *The John Doe Associates: Backdoor Diplomacy for Peace, 1941* (Stanford: Stanford UP 1974); Morley, *Final Confrontation*, pp 20–105.

[153] Barnhart, *Japan Prepares for Total War*, p 205.

[154] Peter Mauch, 'A Bolt from the Blue? New Evidence on the Japanese Navy and the Draft Understanding between Japan and the United States, April 1941'; in: *Pacific Historical Review*, Vol. 78, No. 1 (2009), pp 55–79.

[155] The document is reproduced in full in Ike (ed.), *Decision for War*, pp 287–91.

adequately to his superiors that the document – soon to be known as the Draft Understanding – did not reflect official US policy,[156] and he took great care to deflect attention away from the Four Principles, rather than stressing their importance. He appears to have done so in the expectation that at this point the navy minister in Tokyo would seize the moment, admit to the special part played by the navy in facilitating this initiative and put the case for the proposal to his peers at the Liaison Conference – a step he failed to undertake, thus robbing the initiative of vital momentum.[157] This comedy of errors once again highlights the dysfunctional nature of Japanese government structures of the time. Matsuoka, who according to new research appears to have realised the Draft Understanding's dubious authorship almost as soon as it was put before him,[158] showed himself deeply sceptical right from the start, professing that such a treaty must on no account violate the spirit of the Tripartite Pact. He took an inordinate time in drawing up a counterproposal, the conditions of which virtually ruled out a meeting of minds. Prime Minister Konoe – true to form – had initially been a sceptic himself, but came to see the benefit behind the Draft in the same way that Army Minister Tojo did. As Matsuoka proceeded to dismantle it, Konoe failed to bring his minister to heel, claiming that he enjoyed too much popularity with a large segment of the public.[159]

Historians have tended to give this episode its due attention because an argument can be made that this exchange, irrespective of the screwball nature in which it came about, did generate some diplomatic activity, which might just have led to a positive outcome. It can be argued that the impact it had on the stability of the Tripartite Pact was far more important. Had Ribbentrop known that the original Draft Understanding was the work of poorly coordinated interlopers who enjoyed only tepid support from one of the power groupings in Tokyo, he would no doubt have rested easy. Instead, it is fair to say that from the moment the German foreign minister was informed of this development until the day when Ambassador Oshima formally requested German assistance for a war against Britain and the USA, he spent much of the intervening period (just shy of seven months) in permanent damage-control mode. Ott first passed on a summary of the Draft Understanding on 5 May. It summarised just some of the key points of

[156] Ike (ed.), *Decision for War*, pp XXII; Hotta, *Japan*, pp 69–71. Hull's role in this affair has been interpreted in different ways. Tsunoda Jun, 'On the So-called Hull-Nomura Negotiations'; in: Hilary Conroy and Harry Wray (eds.), *Pearl Harbor Re-examined: Prologue to the Pacific War* (Honolulu: University of Hawaii Press 1990), pp 89–95, sees him as ignorant as his Japanese opposite number; according to Morley and Hotta, he was at least broadly familiar with the manner in which the initiative had developed. See Morley, *Final Confrontation*, p 9, and Hotta, *Japan*, pp 69–71.

[157] On the reasons, see Mauch, 'Bolt from the Blue', pp 75–7.

[158] Hotta, *Japan*, p 71.

[159] Mauch, 'Bolt from the Blue', p 78.

the Draft,[160] but described it with a term (a *'Geheim-Entente'* between both nations) guaranteed to bring up the most nefarious associations in the mind of any German of Ribbentrop's generation. If acted on, it had the potential to neutralise the Far East while allowing the US government to carry on with its strategy of 'all measures short of war' to assist the British Empire.

By the end of the day, Matsuoka forwarded to Berlin a copy of his preliminary answer to the Draft Understanding in which he had impressed on Hull the strength of the Axis position in terms even Ribbentrop could not have improved on: the confidence of the European Axis in their victory was unshakeable and US intervention in any shape or form futile (if it achieved anything at all, it would be the 'prolonging of the war' and possibly even the 'eventual downfall of modern civilisation').[161] If this was supposed to mollify Ribbentrop, it failed abysmally. After waiting for a few days,[162] he subjected Matsuoka to a five-page broadside pleading with him to see through the obvious American ploy which might just give the US President a unique chance to weaken the Tripartite Pact and convince the anti-interventionists in his country of the feasibility of his anti-German policy. That Ribbentrop was genuinely shaken can be gleaned from the fact that he did not shy away from confronting Matsuoka with a scenario where both Italy and Germany might conceivably go down in defeat – less than five weeks after he had explained to his Japanese opposite number not once, but several times over, that Axis victory in Europe was practically preordained.[163] Should such a catastrophic event come about, Japan would soon find itself isolated and its every strategic move checkmated by a superior coalition of powers. Only the steadfast refusal of American wooing could help prevent such an outcome. He finished by virtually imploring Matsuoka not to engage in further exchanges with the US government without him having been given the opportunity to comment on their content first.[164]

This hope was dashed soon enough when on 14 May Ott and Matsuoka had what must have been a fairly undiplomatic exchange even by the standards of the period. The previous day Matsuoka had sent an answer to Hull without first running it past Ribbentrop. Ott was presented with the text which, amongst other

---

[160] The points were: (1) a mutual pledge not to enter the European war on one's own initiative; (2) the USA to use its good offices to bring about a Sino–Japanese peace; (3) normal economic relations to be restored and even expanded; (4) both sides to guarantee the current status of Manchuko and the Philippines. See PA/AA, StS Japan, Bd. 3, 604 'Ott für Reichsminister. Citissime. (5.5.1941)'.

[161] PA/AA, StS Japan, Bd. 3, 604 'Ott für den Reichsaußenminister. Citissime! (5.5.1941)'.

[162] The reasons for this are unclear. He may have awaited background briefings such as the one submitted by the former ambassador in Washington. See PA/AA, StS Japan, Bd. 3, 605 'Dieckhoff für den Herrn Reichsaußenminister (10.5.1941)'.

[163] PA/AA, StS Japan, Bd. 3, 605 'Ribbentrop an Botschaft Tokyo (11.5.1941)'.

[164] Ibid.

things featured a troubling reference to 'foreign ideas or ideologies' as well as a paragraph that effectively accepted the existing US policy of assisting any nation in the current European war as long as it did not resort to 'any aggressive measure' in doing so. Apart from objecting to the overall tone, the German ambassador complained that it read like a draft for a treaty which was merely lacking a signature. A document of such importance surely should have been run past Berlin first.[165] Matsuoka pleaded with him for some trust, but when Ott persisted in voicing his fundamental disagreement, the Japanese foreign minister turned the tables on him by changing tack. He reminded Ott that only about a fortnight ago he had pledged to stand by Germany in case of a Russo–German war breaking out;[166] even though this had been at a time when such a possibility still seemed remote, the Japanese foreign minister felt that it entitled him to up-to-date briefings on the state of German–Soviet relations. He pointed out to Ott that according to his sources, six German divisions were now in position in Finland and Stalin had just been presented with an ultimatum. Accordingly, he would be 'extremely grateful to the German government, if he could be kept informed of Germany's intentions, in order to put him in a position to act accordingly'.[167] Ott refused to be drawn and instead referred Matsuoka to what had been discussed about this general subject in Berlin. In the final paragraph of his telegram, he described the 'crisis' of Japanese foreign policy as the result of American plotting which, assisted by Ambassador Nomura in Washington, had managed to draw in 'Anglophiles, defeatists, the navy and even part of the army' in order to sow the seeds of discord among Japanese decision makers.[168] In further communications, Ribbentrop and Ott seemed almost resigned to the possibility of a US–Japanese treaty along the lines suggested by the Draft Understanding.[169] Ribbentrop betrayed his growing anxiety in rather undiplomatic fashion by insisting yet again on the need to be kept informed of any communications even before they happened; Matsuoka would only promise to do so if and when circumstances allowed, a clear sign that his patience was starting to wear thin.[170]

---

[165] PA/AA, StS Japan, Bd. 3, 605 'Botschaft Tokyo für Herrn Reichsaußenminister. Citissime! (14.5.1941)'.

[166] This verbal commitment cannot be found among the Auswärtiges Amt records dealing with German–Japanese relations of the first half of May 1941. However, proof of a communication to that effect from Ott to Ribbentrop can be found in a telegram from Oshima, in which he makes a reference to being shown the document in question by Weizsäcker. See MBPH, Vol. II App., Doc. 531, 'Berlin (Oshima) to Tokyo (19.5.1941)'.

[167] PA/AA, StS Japan, Bd. 3, 605 'Botschaft Tokyo für Herrn Reichsaußenminister. Citissime! (14.5.1941)'.

[168] Ibid.

[169] PA/AA, StS, USA, Bd. 3, 605 'Ribbentrop an Botschaft Tokyo. Für Botschafter persönlich (15.5.1941)'.

[170] PA/AA, StS Japan, Bd. 3, 605 'Ott für Herrn Reichsaußenminister. Citissime! (18.5.1941)'.

This exasperation is also evident in a rather remarkable exchange of telegrams between Matsuoka and his ambassador in Berlin. On 19 May, Oshima sent three lengthy telegrams which, as regards both their content and their tone, marked him out as the sort of envoy who ends up becoming a spokesman for the interests of his host country rather than his own. In the first, he virtually accused his superior of showing 'apparent disinterest' on account of his failure to ask him to provide an up-to-date perspective on German officialdom's possible views on the ongoing US–Japanese talks.[171] In the second message, he informed Matsuoka that it had been Ribbentrop who had kept him abreast of the discussions about the Draft Understanding talks since 3 May by sharing telegrams from Ott with him, the contents of which Matsuoka had expressly asked to be kept confidential.[172] The third telegram was basically an exhortation to reject American entreaties, not to abandon the expansion into Southeast Asia and stand by the European Axis. Any other options would just 'invite suspicion and contempt of our friends'.[173] Matsuoka – no doubt through clenched teeth – congratulated the ambassador on 'the superlative trust' which Ribbentrop had shown towards him.[174] He was quite adamant, however, in rejecting German interference; as he put it to the ambassador, 'We do not have, on every occasion, to run to Germany and Italy and ask their advice, do we?'[175]

This series of exchanges is important not only for what it tells us about the chronic inability of Germany and Japan to find a consensus on strategic matters that was more than extremely fleeting in nature. They also provide the backdrop to the increasing reluctance shown by the Gaimusho over the following months to share sensitive information with Oshima and help us contextualise one of the few utterances on record on the matter by Germany's supreme warlord. He had been kept informed by his foreign minister of the exchanges with Tokyo over the Draft Understanding and had even shown some willingness to be less doctrinaire about the interpretation of the Tripartite Pact than Ribbentrop.[176] On the afternoon of 22 May 1941 he conferred with Ribbentrop, Raeder and Keitel on the subject of US belligerence in general and the possibility of the US Navy taking up convoying for the British in particular. Walther Hewel, who was also present, jotted down the

---

[171] MBPH, Vol. II App., Doc. 530, 'Berlin to Tokyo (19.5.1941)'.
[172] MBPH, Vol. II App., Doc. 531, 'Berlin (Oshima) to Tokyo (19.5.1941)'.
[173] MBPH, Vol. II App., Doc. 532, 'Berlin (Oshima) to Tokyo (19.5.1941)'.
[174] MBPH, Vol. II App., Doc. 534, 'Tokyo (Matsuoka) to Berlin (24.5.1941)'.
[175] MBPH, Vol. II App., Doc. 535, 'Tokyo (Matsuoka) to Berlin (24.5.1941)'.
[176] While Ribbentrop was adamant in his rejection of the mere notion of US–Japanese talks, Hitler (probably realising that he was in no position to enforce a certain course of action on Tokyo) signalled his acceptance to Oshima. See MBPH, Vol. II App., Doc. 531, 'Berlin (Oshima) to Tokyo (19.5.1941)' and '25th Liaison Conference, May 22, 1941'; in: Ike (ed.), *Decision for War*, p 41.

following excerpt for his private diary: 'Führer still doubtful on his posture towards America, since it is impossible to "look into Roosevelt's soul". If he wants war, he will find any way, even if we are in the right from a legal point of view. Japan is the key factor. If it is still vacillating, it is preferable to keep US out of the war than possibly sink a few extra 100,000 GRT. Without USA war would be over this year. With USA, many more years.'[177] The notes taken by Raeder's adjutant at the meeting add additional nuance to this source: not only was the dictator concerned about American might, but also conscious of the lukewarm nature of Japan's commitment to the alliance with Germany. He predicted that in case of a US–German clash in the Atlantic leading to war, Japan would only enter hostilities if Germany was clearly in the position of the wronged party.[178] As if to confirm the Führer's doubts, the very next day Wenneker was informed by Admiral Kondo that the momentum behind the idea of an assault on Singapore had spent itself; the possibility of such an operation was no longer even a subject for debate (*'nicht einmal mehr zur Debatte steht'*).[179] The fact that only three days later the attaché was allowed to address a crowd of 25,000 in a major sports stadium and exhort them – in keeping with the spirit of Tsushima – to march on Southeast Asia at the earliest opportunity no doubt raised a few eyebrows in Tokyo's diplomatic community, but was still only a poor substitute for the real thing.[180]

The next event to test the stability of the Tripartite Pact was not long in coming. On 27 May, the American President delivered a radio address in which he was widely expected to announce the introduction of convoying by the US Navy. Instead, he used the Allied defeats of the previous weeks as a backdrop to warn of further aggressive designs by the Axis, leading inevitably to moves against the nations of the Western Hemisphere and indeed the 'toppling of the democratic order in the entire world'. He then went on to proclaim a State of Unlimited National Emergency which enhanced the powers of the Federal government with a view to mobilising the country's assets more effectively. What was noteworthy was the complete omission of even a passing reference to the Far Eastern crisis, thus advertising to the world that the Roosevelt administration still deemed Japan capable of political redemption. A statement by a Japanese government spokesman on the morning of the 30th, that the American point of view was at least

---

[177] IfZ, ED 100–78, 'TB Hewel (entry for 22 May 1941)'. 'Japan' underlined in the original German.

[178] 'Geheime Kommandosache. Anlage 1: Das gegenwärtige Problem der Seekriegführung im Atlantik im Hinblick auf die Haltung der USA (Mai 1941)'; in: Wagner (ed.), *Lagebesprechungen*, p 236.

[179] BA/MA, RM 12/II 249 'Kriegstagebuch Marineattache Japan (entry for 23 May 1941)'.

[180] The audience which had turned out for the occasion was made up of members of naval associations as well as serving men and officers of the IJN. BA/MA, RM 12 II/249 'Kriegstagebuch Marineattache Japan (entry for 26 May 1941)'.

'understandable',[181] appeared to provide yet another indication that an important faction in Tokyo was in the process of considering options that did not involve the Tripartite Pact. On the evening of the same day – whether as a reaction to this gaffe or not – Ribbentrop sent a lengthy telegram to Ott in which, in a manner downright demeaning by the standards of the Third Reich, he instructed him to seek common ground with Matsuoka. He stressed the need to find something that would allow a coordinated public relations offensive by Germany, Italy and Japan against the latest Roosevelt speech. Given the experiences of the last fortnight, he appeared to realise that Tokyo might feel disinclined to consider a public joint statement or even separate proclamations; should Ott get that impression, he should merely settle for a curt acknowledgment by telegram of any proclamation the German government might see fit to issue on its own.[182] For a foreign minister long used to getting his way by a blend of bluster and threats, the experience must have been unsettling. It was echoed in the candour with which both he and Hitler ranted about the fractured Japanese system of government to their visitor Mussolini two days later. Their diatribes revealed not just exasperation but, insofar as it pinned their hopes for the future of the Tripartite Pact on the political survival of two individuals (Matsuoka and ambassador Oshima), also a measure of desperation.[183] The dictator and his foreign minister may still have been oblivious of the fact that Stahmer and Ott had allowed themselves to be bluffed by Matsuoka into effectively gutting the treaty in 1940, but they appear to have realised nonetheless that Japanese adherence to it was highly conditional and completely dependent upon the right set of circumstances.

On 4 June, Ott had to report that Matsuoka was indeed averse to issuing a joint statement. Matsuoka tried to point to the futility of such a move in light of the American President's well-known skills as a political operator, but on being prodded by Ott eventually admitted that he could not afford to make such a move while still awaiting Washington's response to the Japanese proposal for a neutrality accord from a few weeks before. He professed not to believe in the eventual success of the negotiations, but the number of decision makers in cabinet who did forced him to at least go through the motions.[184] This rebuff cannot have lifted Ribbentrop's mood, but it was as nothing compared with the telegram Ott sent two days later. In it, the war in China was revealed to be the 'elephant in the room' which currently dominated Japan's strategy more than any other factor. The factions clamouring either for

---

[181] PA/AA, StS Japan, Bd. 3, Nr. 605 'Ott an Auswärtiges Amt (30.5.1941)'.

[182] PA/AA, StS Japan, Bd. 3, Nr. 605 'Ribbentrop an Ott. Für Missionschef persönlich (30.5.1941)'.

[183] 'Aufzeichnung über die Unterredung zwischen dem Führer und dem Duce in Anwesenheit des RAM und des Grafen Ciano auf dem Brenner am 2. Juni 1941, Füh.34 g. Rs. (3.6.1941)'; in: ADAP, Serie D, Bd. XII.2, pp 783–92.

[184] PA/AA, StS Japan, Bd. 3, 606 'Ott an Auswärtiges Amt. Citissime (4.6.1941)'.

compromise or escalation as a means to terminate the conflict were currently deadlocked; rumours about American intervention and a possible Russo–German clash compounded this problem and contributed to paralysing the Japanese government's already very sluggish decision-making processes.[185] Under these circumstances, the Japanese willingness to engage the United States in talks should not come as a surprise; the Singapore strategy tentatively agreed to in Berlin was accordingly shunted aside. Even more worryingly, Ott reported that Matsuoka had hinted that the mood in cabinet appeared to call into question Japan's commitment to the letter and the spirit of the Tripartite Pact. Should a German–American war result from one of the countless US 'measures short of war' in aid of Britain, a lot would depend on the exact circumstances of the case. Paradoxically, the willingness to aid Germany in case of a Russo–German conflict appeared to be marginally bigger, the lack of a treaty-based commitment to do so notwithstanding.[186]

As for the fading possibility of keeping the USA out of the war for good, Matsuoka insisted with his inimitable candour that there was really only one move: 'a rapid invasion of England'. The Japanese foreign minister also repeated his previous complaint about being kept in the dark about any German designs on the USSR; speaking to Ott, he urged him to stress the need for Ribbentrop to brief him in some detail, since an invasion of the USSR could in any case be construed as a violation of the spirit, if not the letter, of the Tripartite Pact. This in turn would give an opportunity to those Japanese decision makers opposed to further escalation to call for a repeal of the treaty, which was fast turning into a major obstacle to re-establishing tolerable relations with the United States.[187] A report sent by Wenneker on 10 June added a few extra nuances, but they were all bad. According to the information shared by one of his Japanese counterparts, Japan's joining a US–German conflict would depend not on the exact circumstances of the casus belli, but solely on the Japanese strategic priorities at the time. In the meantime, the two services had for once managed to reach a consensus on strategy. Both an attack on Singapore and – in case of a German invasion of the Soviet Union – a Japanese move against the USSR had definitely been ruled out. In the case of the former contingency, both the defences of the British base as well as the 'inevitability' of US intervention made it appear highly ill-advised.[188] In Berlin, the Seekriegsleitung's diarist concluded that the prospects of Japan actually standing by Berlin in case of a US–German conflict appeared to be looking 'dubious in the extreme'.[189]

---

[185] PA/AA, StS Japan, Bd. 3, 606 'Ott an Auswärtiges Amt. Citissime. An RAM (6.6.1941)'.
[186] Ibid.
[187] Ibid.
[188] BA/MA, RM 12 II/249 'Kriegstagebuch Marineattache Japan (entry for 10 June 1941)'. Only three months before, Vice Admiral Kondo had judged a US intervention in such a case as merely 'possible'.
[189] KTB Seekriegsleitung, Teil A (entry for 13 June 1941).

As far as the coming German invasion of Russia was concerned, it appears that Ott had been kept in ignorance of the fact that the Japanese ambassador in Berlin and his attachés were well abreast of German planning for the invasion of the USSR. As far back as 16 April, Oshima had shared with Tokyo in two lengthy telegrams the intelligence which thus far had come his way. In the first, he gave the gist of several conversations he had had in recent days with Ambassador Ott (2 April), *Staatssekretär* Weizsäcker (4 April), Ribbentrop (10 April) and *Legationsrat* Stahmer (14 April). The foreign minister had indicated the possibility of a Russo–German war even if the USSR refrained from attacking Japan and justified this by recent British attempts to bring Stalin over to the Allied side, something allegedly borne out by the Soviet posture during the crisis over Yugoslavia. He also coincided with Stahmer in pointing out that the Wehrmacht was currently fully equipped for a major land campaign while the aero-naval siege of Great Britain would in any case still take several months in producing results. Hence, an attack on the USSR seemed like an attractive option.[190]

The second wire essentially gave Oshima's analysis of these impressions.[191] While he conceded that Germany's war on Britain's communications might have stalled, he readily accepted the explanations offered by his hosts in every regard and on occasions appears even to have embroidered on them.[192] He foresaw no risks in such a campaign and went out of his way to highlight the strategic opportunities which the collapse of the USSR would bring for Japan. Finally, he failed to clarify one contradiction. While in the first telegram, he had stated that a Japanese participation was something Germany 'might possibly wish', the second one stated quite clearly that 'I do not think she expects us to make a simultaneous attack on them.'[193] In three further communications dated 24 April, 6 May and 14 May, Oshima was somewhat more circumspect about predicting war with certainty, though he made it clear that

---

[190] 'Botschafter Oshima an Außenminister Konoye (16.4.1941)'; in: Andreas Hillgruber (ed.), 'Japan und der Fall "Barbarossa"'. Japanische Dokumente zu den Gesprächen Hitlers und Ribbentrops mit Botschafter Oshima von Februar bis Juni 1941', in: *Wehrwissenschaftliche Rundschau* Bd. 18 (1968), pp 326–9. Fragments of this message are also reproduced in Morley, *Final Confrontation*, pp 84–5, 123.

[191] On account of its length, it was sent in four parts. MBPH, Vol. I, Docs. 366, 367, 368 and 369 (all 16.4.1941).

[192] Especially his references to the Luftwaffe's strength of '20,000 planes of the latest model' (a five-fold exaggeration) and the Army's '250 divisions of highly mechanised troops'. See MBPH, Vol I, Doc. 367, Berlin (Oshima) to Tokyo (16.4.1941). Intelligence of this kind, rather than being rejected out of hand, found a number of eager recipients in Tokyo, with the army general staff circulating an estimate of Luftwaffe strength of 60,000 (this one, presumably, included second-line aircraft) by early June; Alvin D. Coox, 'Japanese Foreknowledge of the Soviet–German War, 1941'; in: *Soviet Studies* 23 (4) April 1972, pp 554–72, esp. p 565.

[193] MBPH, Vol. I, Doc. 369, 'Berlin (Oshima) to Tokyo (16.4.1941)'.

military preparations were gathering pace and the decision over war and peace lay in the hands of Hitler alone, not Stalin.[194] This was complemented by two more warnings on 9 May. In one, a senior German source (most likely Ribbentrop) impressed on Oshima that Germany was not engaging in a game of 'demonstrated bluff' in order to merely extort concessions from Stalin.[195] In the other, the consul in Vienna was confident in predicting 'war with the USSR about June' since this would allow the Germans to seize the Ukrainian harvest.[196] Matsuoka's initial reactions to this torrent of intelligence reflected the apprehension he must have felt at the prospect of seeing his most important achievement so far (the Neutrality Pact with the USSR) called into question. On 27 May, he emphatically denied to Oshima that he had recently promised Ott Japanese participation in a possible Soviet–German war, stressing that he had merely expressed a 'personal opinion'.[197] A day later, he went a step further and ordered Oshima to express to Ribbentrop his expectation that Germany 'insofar as is possible, will avoid a military clash with the Soviet [Union]'.[198]

In the meantime, Oshima kept relaying summaries of the intelligence piling up in the in tray of his Berlin office. A lengthy message to Tokyo dated 30 May betrayed residual doubts still besetting him despite all the evidence before him. It stressed that 'the overthrow of England' was still the Third Reich's main war aim. The ambassador then pointed to possible moves in the direction of the USSR, the Mediterranean, the Middle East and even the area around Dakar as possible strategic options for the Germans.[199] However, he also made clear which of these options appeared to be the most likely: he described Soviet–German tensions as 'an inevitable development', the 'adjustment' of which had to be seen as an 'indispensable element in the new order of Europe'. The ongoing war with Britain need not preclude the annihilation of the USSR 'within a short period'.[200] On the evening of 4 June, Oshima sent three telegrams giving the gist of his talks with Hitler and Ribbentrop over the course of the last forty-eight hours. The first was a one-liner bluntly stating: 'Both men tell me in every probability war with Russia cannot be avoided.'[201]

---

[194] MBPH, Vol. I., Doc. 370, 'Berlin (Oshima) to Tokyo (24.4.1941)' and Doc. 377, 'Berlin to Tokyo (6.5.1941)' as well as MBPH, Vol. II App, Doc. 555, 'Berlin (Oshima) to Tokyo (14.5.1941)'.

[195] MBPB, Vol. I, Doc. 364, 'Berlin to Tokyo (9.5.1941)'.

[196] MBPH, Vol. I, Doc. 378, 'Vienna (Yamayi) to Tokyo (9.5.1941)'.

[197] MBPH, Vol. II App., Doc. 537, 'Tokyo (Matsuoka) to Berlin (Koshi) (27.5.1941)'.

[198] MBPH, Vol. II App., Doc. 538, 'Tokyo (Matsuoka) to Berlin (28.5.1941)'; Krebs, Deutschlandpolitik, p 539.

[199] MBPH, Vol. II App., Doc. 556, 'Tokyo to Nanking, Shanghai, Tientsin, Peking and Hsinking (Circular). Message from Berlin 619 on 30 May (3.6.1941)'.

[200] MBPH, Vol. II App., Doc. 557, 'Tokyo to Nanking, Shanghai, Tientsin, Peking and Hsinking (Circular). Message from Berlin 619 on 30 May (3.6.1941)'.

[201] MBPH, Vol. II App., Doc. 645 'Berlin (Oshima) to Tokyo (4.6.1941)'.

In his conversation with Hitler on 3 June, the dictator justified turning on Stalin by pointing to the USSR's increasingly antagonistic attitude in a number of areas, with its alleged support of the vanquished Yugoslav state featuring prominently.[202] Oshima also came away with the impression that Hitler desired a Japanese participation in the upcoming operation and had even justified this by invoking the Tripartite Pact.[203] Ribbentrop in a separate conversation the following day had said that war was not yet 'a certainty', but then went into considerable detail to disabuse his visitor of any notions that peace might still be preserved. As for the options which would present themselves to Japan as a result of these events, Ribbentrop still gave priority to a Japanese expansion into Southeast Asia but suggested the possibility of Tokyo's participation in the fight against the USSR in case 'the equipment' available appeared to make this more practical.[204]

Taking stock of the momentous intelligence which had just been shared with him, Oshima added his own analysis: irrespective of the weak attempt on the part of Ribbentrop to hedge his bets, the mere fact that a head of state had gone to the trouble of summoning a foreign ambassador to impart such intelligence made 'the outbreak of a Soviet–German war seem in all likelihood unavoidable'. Showing remarkable prescience, he also stressed how in this particular case an ideological agenda and strategic considerations reinforced each other, making reconsideration even more unlikely. Hostilities would in all likelihood erupt abruptly and without having been preceded by diplomatic negotiations or the issuing of an ultimatum.[205]

On 7 June another telegram arrived from the Berlin embassy warning of the fact that transit of goods via the Trans-Siberian Railway would 'soon be

---

[202] Here, Hitler was exaggerating for effect and putting the worst possible gloss on Russian actions; while it is true that Soviet–German relations had deteriorated between January and April 1941, after the rapid fall of Yugoslavia the Soviet government had gone out of its way to satisfy almost every conceivable German wish. See Gabriel Gorodetsky, *Grand Delusion: Stalin and the German Invasion of Russia* (New Haven and London: Yale UP 1999), pp 202–315.

[203] 'Botschafter Oshima an Außenminister Matsuoka (5.6.1941)'; in: Hillgruber (ed.), 'Fall Barbarossa', p 333–6. Since the Tripartite Pact was framed in such a way that it specifically ruled out any commitments against the USSR this argument does not hold water. His good German notwithstanding, Oshima may have misunderstood Hitler on this particular point. The obvious source which might clarify this issue (the minutes taken on the German side by Walther Hewel) appears to have been lost during the war. See IfZ, ED 100–78 'TB Walther Hewel (3.6.1941)'. In Tokyo, Marquis Kido merely recorded 'an indirect demand' by Hitler that Japan join in the attack on the USSR. Kido, *Diary*, p 279 (entry for 6 June 1941).

[204] MBPH, Vol. II App., Doc. 645 'Berlin (Oshima) to Tokyo (4.6.1941)' and Doc. 646 'Berlin (Oshima) to Tokyo (4.6.1941)'.

[205] 'Botschafter Oshima an Außenminister Matsuoka (5.6.1941)'; in: Hillgruber (ed.), 'Fall Barbarossa', pp 335–6.

impossible'.[206] On 12th, Oshima warned Tokyo that Ott had just forbidden German nationals residing in Japan from returning to Germany via Siberia,[207] and two days later he reminded his superiors that previous German attacks had not been preceded by the issuing of an ultimatum; he also berated them for leaving him without instructions in the face of an imminent strategic upheaval.[208] On 18th, he described the outbreak of war as 'imminent', without however betraying any anxiety about Germany's prospects. In fact, he expressed confidence that the invasion of the USSR would be followed within a few weeks by an amphibious assault on Great Britain.[209] The last warning he sent summarised yet another exchange with Ribbentrop. The foreign minister had gone to almost ridiculous lengths to kill off a rumour making the rounds in Berlin's diplomatic community about Russo–German talks. According to Ribbentrop, Soviet Ambassador Dekanozov had indeed made an appearance at the Auswärtiges Amt, but the matter had been expeditiously dealt with by *Staatssekretär* Ernst von Weizsäcker without yielding anything of substance.[210]

The first time this deluge of warnings led to a preliminary re-assessment by the Japanese of their existing options appears to have been in a meeting of the bureau chiefs of the army general staff on 15 May, which reached the conclusion that Russo–German hostilities were unlikely to break out soon.[211] Even Oshima's message summarising his briefing by Hitler and Ribbentrop on 3 and 4 June at first failed to make a major impact. Such sluggishness for once does not appear to have had the dysfunctional nature of the Japanese leadership structure as its only cause. Both Foreign Minister Matsuoka and War Minister Tojo at first refused to believe in an outbreak of war without the preliminaries of a diplomatic crisis; on 6 June the former gave the emperor an evaluation of the likelihood of a Russo–German clash that came close to being misleading (he described the odds of war breaking out as 60:40 against).[212]

The Liaison Conference held on the following day represented a crucial shift insofar as Matsuoka finally appeared to accept the increasing likelihood of a German attack on the USSR, but still clung to the idea that any such move would be preceded by an ultimatum and, hence, a degree of forewarning. The chiefs of staff of both services, however, refused to discuss the subject ('they did not regard it as urgent'), thus postponing further discussions.[213] A meeting of

---

[206] MBPH, Vol. II App., Doc. 606, 'Berlin (Oshima) to Tokyo (7.6.1941)'.

[207] MBPH, Vol. II App., Doc. 648, 'Berlin (Oshima) to Tokyo (12.6.1941)'.

[208] MBPH, Vol. II App., Doc. 659, 'Berlin (Oshima) to Tokyo (14.6.1941)'.

[209] MBPH, Vol. II App., Doc. 613, 'Berlin (Oshima) to Tokyo (18.6.1941)'.

[210] MBPH, Vol. II App., Doc. 652, 'Berlin (Oshima) to Tokyo (20.6.1941)'.

[211] Coox, 'Japanese Foreknowledge', p 562.

[212] Kido, *Diary*, p 279 (entry for 6 June 1941); Krebs, *Deutschlandpolitik*, p 540.

[213] '28th Liaison Conference, June 7, 1941'; in: Ike (ed.), *Decision for War*, pp 46–7.

division and bureau chiefs of both services on 10 June,[214] and the Liaison Conference of the 16th, likewise failed to produce any binding results, Matsuoka's plea to finally address the issue notwithstanding.[215] It stands to reason that this was because the army general staff was focused on the impending takeover of French Indo-China and possibly because contradictory reports from the Japanese embassy in Moscow, which was limited to fewer sources than Oshima, mostly reflected Stalin's desire to keep the peace.[216] By the time Oshima on 17 June sent yet another summary of a conversation with Ribbentrop in which the foreign minister had been adamant in ruling out the possibility of negotiations, the Japanese government's room for manoeuvre had dwindled to virtually nothing.[217] When on the eve of the German invasion of the USSR, Konoe felt the need to offer his government's resignation, this was met with a retort by the Keeper of the Privy Seal that also amounted to a scathing indictment of the crisis management shown by the government: 'The present pending war between Germany and the Soviets should come as no surprise. Ambassador Oshima had been informed, though informally, about the attitude of Germany toward the Soviets, thus leaving much time for the government to take measures to cope with the situation.'[218]

In the meantime, a development of a completely different nature presaged a Japanese move away from reconciliation with the USA. On 10 June, one of Oshima's counsellors revealed to the Germans that the Japanese armed forces (as opposed to merely one of the services) had plans to establish a sizeable presence in southern Vietnam and Cambodia, putting them in a position to threaten Thailand, Malaya and the Philippines.[219] Even though technically only an extension of the state of affairs already in existence in northern Vietnam, it meant a clear step towards extending by violent means the new Co-Prosperity Sphere at the expense of some or all of the Western possessions in Southeast Asia. The proponents of this move had managed to sell it to the key decision makers as something unlikely to bring about war with the USA while at the same time improving Japan's economic and strategic position in the

---

[214] Morley, *Final Confrontation*, p 119.

[215] '31st Liaison Conference, June 16, 1941'; in: Ike (ed.), *Decision for War*, pp 53–6.

[216] MBPH, Vol. II App, Doc. 609, 'Moscow to Tokyo (15.5.1941)'; Doc. 610, 'Tokyo to Washington (17.5.1941)'. As Soviet–German relations deteriorated, Ambassador Tatekawa conceded the possibility of a clash, but even then insisted that such an event would be preceded by the presentation of 'certain important demands on Russia'. See ibid., Doc. 639, 'Moscow (Tatekawa) to Tokyo (7.6.1941)'.

[217] Morley, *Final Confrontation*, pp 133–7.

[218] Kido, *Diary*, p 284 (entry for 21 June 1941). See also PA/AA, Handakten Ritter Japan 18 'Ott an Auswärtiges Amt. Für Reichsaußenminister. Citissime! (3.7.1941)', where Ott passed on Matsuoka's thanks to Ribbentrop for having been informed in a timely enough manner of the impending outbreak of hostilities.

[219] PA/AA, StS Japan, Bd. 3, Nr. 606 'U.St.S.Pol.Nr.526. Für Herrn Reichsaußenminister (10.6.1941)'.

region. It was supposed to deter the Western powers while at the same time putting the armed forces in a position to move against the Western possessions in the region should the need to do so arise.[220] Virtually on cue, the collapse of the Japanese–Dutch trade talks in Batavia the following day appeared to provide the sort of political scenario bound to increase the likelihood of such a move.[221] Matsuoka spend most of June opposing this scheme on the grounds that it was a dangerous half-measure; since it was bound to mortally antagonise the Anglo–American powers, it only made sense if it included plans for an immediate second-phase movement from the newly acquired Indo-Chinese bases into Thailand, Malaya and the Dutch East Indies.[222] On 21 June Matsuoka indicated in conversation with Ott his commitment to the Indo-China operation demanded by the military with a view 'to move against the Dutch East Indies',[223] though he would not in fact give up his opposition to the plan for another week. The ambassador was unaware of this split in the Liaison Conference, but even if he had been aware, it is doubtful he would have put too much stock by either of the two options. In light of the gap which had soon opened up between the Japanese foreign minister's enthusiasm as expressed during his Berlin visit and the definite lack of the same on the part of the rest of the government, even French Indo-China may not have seemed like a sure bet.

Within hours of the beginning of Barbarossa, the Matsuoka who in late May had emphatically denied any previous pledges on his part to stand by Germany in case of a war between the Third Reich and the USSR was a changed man. With almost puppy-like enthusiasm, he promised Ott to blockade Vladivostok against US attempts to bring in military supplies and even promised to go to war against the USA should Washington intervene on the side of the USSR. With regards to the Russo–German war, and quite irrespective of the fact that Germany had not formally asked for any assistance, he expressed his opinion that Japan would not be able 'to stay neutral for long'.[224] As good as his word, during a marathon of Liaison Conferences and cabinet meetings that took place between 25 June and 1 July, he argued for a strike against the USSR and

---

[220] Eri Hotta, 'Japanese Policy, Thinking and Actions'; paper delivered at the Five Days in December conference of the Centre on Geopolitics, Peterhouse, Cambridge (28.9.2019).

[221] PA/AA, StS Japan, Bd. 3, 606 'Ott an Auswärtiges Amt (12.6.1941)'; 'Ott an Auswärtiges Amt (14.6.1941)'. The talks had collapsed over the Dutch insistence on limiting ship-ments of oil, rubber and tin to pre-war levels and insisting on verifiable guarantees that would rule out any trans-shipments to Germany; they were also adamant in limiting the influx of Japanese settlers.

[222] '29th Liaison Conference, June 11, 1941'; '30th Liaison Conference, June 12, 1941'; '35th Liaison Conference, June 28, 1941' and '36th Liaison Conference, June 30, 1941'; all in: Ike (ed.), *Decision for War*, pp 47–53, 68–75.

[223] PA/AA, StS Japan, Bd. 3, Nr. 606 'Ott an Auswärtiges Amt. Für Reichsaußenminister (21.6.1941)'.

[224] PA/AA, StS Japan, Bd. 3, Nr. 606 'Ott an Auswärtiges Amt. Für Herrn Reichsaußenminister (23.6.1941)'.

for the move on Indo-China to be cancelled or at least postponed.[225] With Konoe apparently failing to offer any opinions whatsoever, Matsuoka should have found himself preaching to the converted. Instead, he faced a fairly unreceptive audience, mostly reluctant to wreck the inter-service consensus so laboriously reached, which called for a limited move against southern French Indo-China only. To make matters worse, the Minister for War and the Army Chief of Staff were in receipt of contradictory intelligence on the likelihood of Soviet survival beyond the summer months.[226] Predictable opposition by the navy to a shift to a decidedly continental strategy as well as concerns over the number of troops already tied up in China added further weight to the case for Indo-China.[227]

In the meantime, German Far Eastern policy had undergone a radical shift, which though fully on a par with the signing of the Molotov–Ribbentrop pact of 1939, thus far has not received the scholarly attention it clearly deserves. On 17 June, Oshima had already reported to Tokyo that Ribbentrop had for the first time indicated unambiguous interest in a Japanese contribution to the imminent war against the USSR.[228] On the morning of 28 June, Ott sent a telegram to Berlin in which he explained that a consensus was evolving within ruling circles in Tokyo that favoured the occupation of southern Indo-China.[229] At the same time, he warned his superiors in the Auswärtiges Amt that while this would shift everybody's attention south and away from Manchuria and Vladivostok, the momentum thus generated was unlikely to be strong enough to carry Japanese strategy all the way to Singapore. Thus, he felt justified in questioning the rationale of German foreign policy especially in light of the fact that Ambassador Oshima was now said to be pushing for a Japanese contribution to Germany's 'anti-Bolshevik' crusade.[230]

Irrespective of whether Ott had hit a nerve with Ribbentrop or whether this was a case of two 'great' minds thinking alike, by evening Ott had an answer which virtually demanded Japanese participation in Barbarossa. This sudden change of direction not only ran contrary to the estimate Hitler himself had given to Admiral Raeder in April,[231] and a gathering of senior army officers in

---

[225] An unprecedented five Liaison Conferences were held over a period of six days. For a summary of the points discussed, see Coox, 'Japanese Net Assessment', pp 288–98, as well as Hotta, *Japan*, pp 128–30.

[226] Coox, 'Japanese Net Assessment', pp 281–8, 297.

[227] On opposition by the navy, see '32nd Liaison Conference, June 25, 1941'; in: Ike (ed.), *Decision for War*, pp 56–60. The distraction posed by the war in China featured prominently in '34th Liaison Conference, June 27, 1941' as well as '36th Liaison Conference, June 30, 1941' in: ibid., pp 64–7, 70–5.

[228] Krebs, *Deutschlandpolitik*, p 541.

[229] PA/AA, Handakten Ritter Japan 18, Nr. 7635 'Ott an Auswärtiges Amt (28.6.1941)'.

[230] Ibid.

[231] Hitler had stressed to Raeder that the Soviet–Japanese neutrality pact was a development which should be welcomed, since in blocking Japan's path to Vladivostok, it made

the Neue Reichskanzlei a fortnight earlier,[232] it also made a complete nonsense of every diplomatic move undertaken by Berlin since the capture of the *Automedon* papers. In typical Ribbentropian fashion extreme hyperbole ('The war between Germany and Soviet Russia ... will have as a consequence the final struggle solution of the Russian question in its totality') went hand in hand with rather questionable logic (a 'quick' victory was expected 'shortly', but for Japan to simply bide its time and attack a prostrate Russia would 'impair Japan's political and moral position considerably').[233] Victory over China, a later move against Southeast Asia as well as the deterrence of the USA would all be greatly facilitated by first vanquishing the USSR.[234] As a show of good will, the German foreign minister had already the previous day promised to immediately break off relations with the Nationalist China of Chiang Kai-shek and recognise the puppet regime of Wang, a move the Japanese had been insisting on for months.[235] According to Ribbentrop's post-war recollections, directing Japan's expansionist agenda away from the East Indies and against the USSR had been his idea alone. He claimed that Hitler in fact reproached him for this initiative, since he preferred to finish off the USSR on his own while the Japanese readied themselves for a strike against Singapore.[236]

4.4 The Road to War (July–December 1941)

In Tokyo, the second half of 1941 was ushered in by an event that would come to be regarded as the key turning point in Japan's long and winding road to war. Unlike the routine Liaison Conferences, Imperial Conferences gathered

---

a strike against Singapore that more likely. See 'B.Nr. I op 515/41 gKdos.Chefs Vortrag Ob.d.M. beim Führer am 20. April 1941'; in: Wagner (ed.), *Lagevorträge*, pp 217–21.

[232] This was the last briefing given to the commanders-in-chief of the armies and army groups of the *Ostheer* prior to the beginning of the invasion of the USSR. See Klaus Gerbet (ed.), *Generalfeldmarschall Fedor von Bock. Zwischen Pflicht und Verweigerung. Das Kriegstagebuch* (München: Herbig 1995), pp 193–4 (entry for 14 June 1941). Henceforth quoted as TB Bock. Here, the dictator made it clear that 'active help by Japan was not to be expected'.

[233] PA/AA, Handakten Ritter Japan 18, Nr. 7635 'Ribbentrop an Ott. Citissime (28.6.1941)'.

[234] Ibid.

[235] 'Bericht des japanischen Marineattaches in Berlin, Kpt. z.S. Yokoi an den Stellvertretenden Marineminister und den stellvertretenden Admiralstabschef (29.6.1941)'; in: Sander-Nagashima, *Marinebeziehungen*, pp 604–6. Sino–German relations continued at a clandestine level, mostly through intermediaries in Switzerland. Chiang appears to have seen in this an insurance against the possibility of German victory in Europe. See Nele Friederike Glang, 'Germany and Chongqing: Secret Communication during WW II'; in: *Intelligence and National Security*, Vol. 30, No. 6 (2015), pp 871–89.

[236] Joachim von Ribbentrop, *Zwischen London und Moskau. Erinnerungen und letzte Aufzeichnungen* (Leoni: Druffel-Verlag 1961), p 248.

much more infrequently and were chaired by the emperor himself. In the normal run of things, they served the purpose of rubber-stamping important decisions previously arrived at in other bodies.[237] By virtue of receiving the Tenno's seal of approval, a major policy decision was elevated to a new constitutional plane. To reverse a process set in motion by an Imperial Conference constituted a major challenge, since it was akin to admitting that the emperor had been ill advised or even in error.

On 2 July, the Imperial Conference confirmed the decision on the direction of Japanese strategy arrived at during numerous debates at the cabinet and Liaison Conference levels. Rather remarkably, Army Chief of Staff Hajime Sugiyama and President of the Privy Council Yoshimichi Hara chose this occasion to vote for an invasion of the Soviet Far East at the earliest opportunity. Matsuoka expressed the same sentiment, but in a more non-committal way than on the previous days.[238] None of this was enough to overturn a decision already made for submission to the emperor. Hence, imperial assent to carry on with the takeover of southern French Indo-China was duly obtained. In addition, it was decided to reinforce the Kwantung Army but to give the order to cross into Soviet territory only in the case of a large-scale retreat by Soviet troops or of signs of an impending collapse of morale that promised to make this a risk-free endeavour. Previous scholarship has tended to focus on the political dynamics that led to the convocation of the conference and the question of whether the emperor – who remained silent throughout – could or should have intervened. For the purposes of this study, the key issue is how the results were presented to Japan's Tripartite allies. The next day, Matsuoka summoned both the German and Italian ambassadors and handed them identical notes for their foreign ministers.[239] This communication gave a summary of what had transpired the previous day which, while not wholly misleading, gave it a peculiar nuance. The move on Indo-China was announced and the preparations made in Manchuria for an invasion of the USSR stressed. The fact that the Japanese leadership had made an invasion of Siberia conditional upon a near-collapse of the USSR was conveniently omitted. An expert cynic might have reached that conclusion all the same by reading between the lines, but Ott in early September would still insist to his superiors in Berlin that the conference of 2 July had originally prioritised a move against the Soviet Union.[240]

---

[237] For a more detailed discussion of the differences between the two bodies, see Krebs, *Japan im Pazifischen Krieg*, pp 45–9.

[238] 'Imperial Conference, July 2, 1941'; in: Ike (ed.), *Decision for War*, pp 77–90.

[239] PA/AA, Handakten Ritter Japan, Bd. 18, 'Ott an Auswärtiges Amt. Für Reichsaußenminister (3.7.1941)'.

[240] PA/AA, Handakten Ritter Japan, Bd. 18, 'Ott an Auswärtiges Amt. Citissime (4.9.1941)'. The German admiralty was much quicker in realising the fallacy of the Japanese pledge, see KTB Seekriegsleitung, Teil A (entries for 7 and 13 July 1941).

As for Ribbentrop's sudden 180-degree turn of 28 June, he could not have known how the Imperial Conference would turn out. The fact remains, however, that in light of the damage the Molotov–Ribbentrop Pact of 1939 had done to German standing in Japan, the German foreign minister must have had at least an inkling that another about-turn of the kind might come at a hefty political price. It thus stands to reason that he weighed his options carefully; if he really found himself in disagreement over this with Hitler,[241] concerns over the course of the campaign can be safely ruled out as a reason. The first four weeks of the war saw the Germans riding the crest of a wave that seemed to be carrying them to victory.[242] Only with the series of battles fought east of Smolensk from the last week of July and throughout August did the Red Army manage to slow down appreciably the momentum of Army Group Centre, the *Ostheer*'s most important formation.[243] Concern over Allied aid shipments can likewise be ruled out, since in such a case it would have made far more sense to hold Matsuoka to his earlier promise of blockading access to Vladivostok and requesting specifics as to how this might be done, something Ribbentrop would not do till September. The only military source that appears to indicate an interest on Hitler's part is an entry in the personal diary of Fedor von Bock, *Heeresgruppe Mitte*'s commander-in-chief. In it he paraphrased a conversation he had on 25 July with the head of OKW, *Generalfeldmarschall* Wilhelm Keitel. Here an interest in a Japanese offensive against Vladivostok is voiced but it is unclear whether this reflects an interest on the part of Hitler, Keitel or (most likely) Bock, whose forces were just beginning to feel the strain of more than four weeks of uninterrupted fighting.[244]

---

[241] Ribbentrop's reasoning on this crucial issue has received barely any treatment from his biographers. Michael Bloch, *Ribbentrop* (London: Bantam Press 1992), omits it altogether while Stefan Scheil, *Ribbentrop. Oder: Die Verlockung des nationalen Aufbruchs* (Berlin: Duncker & Humblot 2013), p 311, assumes that concern on his part over Germany's odds in the struggle with the USSR compelled him to act unilaterally and without Hitler's knowledge. The source quoted to back this up (Ribbentrop's telegram to Ott from 28 June 1941), however, fails to support such a sensational claim. Peter Herde, *Italien, Deutschland und der Weg in den Krieg im Pazifik* (Wiesbaden: Franz Steiner 1983) [= Sitzungsberichte der Wissenschaftlichen Gesellschaft an der Johann Wolfgang Goethe Universität Frankfurt am Main, Bd. XX, Nr. 1], pp 45–6, marshals a greater array of sources to make a case for a nuanced disagreement between Hitler and Ribbentrop.

[242] Though quoted almost ad nauseam, the entry in Franz Halder's diary which claims that the campaign had 'in essence been won in fourteen days' is still the best insight into the mood that reigned on the German side in those days. Hans-Adolf Jacobsen (ed.), *Generaloberst Halder Kriegstagebuch*, Bd. III (Stuttgart: W. Kohlhammer 1964) p 38 (entry for 3 July 1941).

[243] On the battle of El'nia, see the analysis in David Stahel, *Operation Barbarossa and Germany's Defeat in the East* (Cambridge: CUP 2009), pp 285–412.

[244] TB Bock, pp 230–1 (entry for 25 July 1941). After Keitel explained to him how the US Navy presence around Iceland had led to the U-boats being put 'on a leash', he made his

In the absence of a military explanation it seems reasonable that Ribbentrop's motive was political. The factor that above all others had governed Germany's relations with Japan since early May was the fear of Tokyo and Washington reaching an accord that would turn the Tripartite Pact into little more than an empty shell. It could be argued that, since the German government had received the first warnings about the planned Japanese occupation of southern French Indo-China as early as 10 June, this should have allowed it to rest easy in the knowledge that a further deterioration of relations between Washington and Tokyo was imminent. However, the nature of Japanese policymaking made a last-minute cancellation or postponement of such an endeavour at least as likely as its prompt execution, even after Matsuoka personally pledged himself to the idea on 21 June. The nearest thing to a reliable forecast of Japanese intentions appeared to be Ott's telegram of 6 June, which indicated that a move against Singapore was out of the question, while a move against the USSR was just about within the realms of possibility.[245] In the meantime, Ribbentrop remained as apprehensive as ever about Japan's loyalty to the pact, a fact that became painfully obvious with the frantic wire he sent to the Tokyo embassy on 10 July. Not only was he convinced that he was being kept in the dark about the goings-on at the Washington talks, he also quizzed Ott in all seriousness about whether he had any evidence pointing towards an American–Japanese collusion that would have encouraged Roosevelt to give the occupation of Iceland (7 July) the go-ahead.[246]

If Hitler or Ribbentrop were still harbouring such doubts four days later, when they hosted Oshima at Führer's Headquarters, they made sure to keep them to themselves.[247] Three weeks into the campaign, and having inflicted a maximum of disruption on the first strategic echelon of the Red Army, Hitler was positively brimming with pride in the Wehrmacht's latest achievements. With the exception of Soviet armour, the enemy was belittled and all contributors on the Axis side showered with lavish praise. Any attempts to turn Japan into a belated ally in the war against the USSR were ambiguous at best. On the one hand, the German dictator predicted an effective end to the campaign in

---

feelings plain: 'That's exactly what we did in the Great War and I fear that in much the same manner as happened then, the Americans will manage to find another excuse. The Japanese seize the moment to establish themselves in Indo-China, but are less than enthusiastic about the idea of attacking Russia, which is what we are hoping for!'

[245] PA/AA, StS Japan Bd. 3, 606 'Ott an AA. Citissime. Für RAM (6.6.1941)'.

[246] PA/AA, Handakten Ritter Japan 18 'Ribbentrop an die Botschaft in Tokyo. Für Botschafter persönlich (10.7.1941)'.

[247] 'Aufzeichnung über die Unterredung des Führers mit Graf Oshima in Anwesenheit des Reichsaußenministers im Führerhauptquartier am 14. Juli 1941, von 17 bis 19 Uhr. Geheime Reichssache Füh 42/41 (15.7.1941)'; in: ADAP, Serie D, Bd. XIII.2, Anhang II, pp 829–34.

six weeks, spoke of units that were already being disengaged from the front and stressed that he was in no need of 'support'. On the other hand, a little later he described the destruction of the USSR as 'the political legacy' of Germany and its Far Eastern ally,[248] which was key to 'keeping the US out of the war'. As far as the United States was concerned, he opted for a twin-track strategy. Obviously irked by the US occupation of Iceland (it was mentioned twice), he stressed that a confrontation with that country was 'unavoidable anyway' and dropped a couple of hints about the futility of appeasing the USA by not blockading Vladivostok.[249] He capped this by stating bluntly that in light of the threat that the USA and the USSR posed to the Tripartite partners 'they should be annihilated together'.[250] Possibly sensing that even a pro-Axis zealot like Oshima would struggle to sell such a scheme to his superiors in Tokyo,[251] he back-pedalled two paragraphs later when he put it to the Japanese ambassador that 'merely keeping the USA out of the war would very much depend on the annihilation of the USSR'. Even so, he still managed to return to his original theme by making it unambiguously clear that 'if it became necessary to fight the USA, it might as well happen under his leadership'.[252]

All things considered, Hitler's attempt – if it can be called that – to convince Oshima of the need for Japan to join the Wehrmacht in the destruction of the USSR was not nearly as unambiguous as the instructions Ribbentrop had sent to Ott on 28 June; it is best described as confusing and contradictory. This is also reflected in the message the Japanese ambassador sent to Tokyo that same evening. Here, the German dictator is recorded as describing the USA and the USSR as joint enemies of Germany and Japan, but without making any specific demands for a Japanese participation in Barbarossa. He did, however, express concern over the ongoing talks between Washington and Tokyo and urged on his guest 'that Japan clearly express its attitude with the Tripartite Pact as its basis'.[253] If one accepts the notion that Germany's recent attempts to woo Japan into joining the anti-Soviet coalition were driven by the hidden agenda of sabotaging a détente in US–Japanese relations, Hitler's ambivalent behaviour during the meeting with Oshima becomes intelligible. He was both worried that Tokyo and Washington might end up mending fences and

---

[248] Ibid., p 834.

[249] Ibid., p 832.

[250] Ibid., p 833.

[251] See the American intercept of Oshima's report of this conversation, in which he twice described Hitler's attitude towards Japan and the Tripartite Pact as indicative of his character as 'a very idealistic person'. MBPH, Vol. II App., Doc. 599, 'Berlin (Oshima) to Tokyo (17.7.1941)'.

[252] 'Aufzeichnung über die Unterredung des Führers mit Graf Oshima in Anwesenheit des Reichsaußenministers im Führerhauptquartier am 14. Juli 1941, von 17 bis 19 Uhr. Geheime Reichssache Füh 42/41 (15.7.1941)', p 834; in: ADAP, Serie D, Bd. XIII.1, p 834.

[253] MBPH, Vol. II App., Doc. 599, 'Berlin (Oshima) to Tokyo (17.7.1941)'.

infuriated by the recent US occupation of Iceland. At the same time, he was genuinely convinced that the campaign against the USSR had turned a decisive corner. An impending collapse of the Soviet state, however, carried with it the risk that a Japanese intervention would not be rated as a full-blown act of aggression in Washington. Much as the USSR had done in 1939, when it had postponed its invasion of Poland until the last possible moment, Tokyo might be left in a position where it would be able to pick up the spoils without making an irreversible commitment to the Tripartite cause. This was something the dictator would have been keen to avoid.

Within the next seventy-two hours, however, three separate events would cast a pall over the present state of the Tripartite Pact, never mind its future. A renewed German–Japanese clash over the apportioning of Indo-Chinese rubber would not in itself have constituted a newsworthy item, were it not for the fact that this time the Japanese Navy felt sufficiently aggrieved to temporarily deny all German merchant vessels berthing rights, thus throwing into disarray the resupply of merchant raiders currently on operations in the Far East.[254] Rather more seriously, Ott was apprised of the fact that – as suspected by Ribbentrop – the Americans had indeed sent an answer to the latest Japanese counterproposal as early as 21 June.[255] The German foreign minister, to his considerable irritation, discovered that the revised proposed draft treaty contained yet another innocuous-sounding phrase which was tantamount to watering down a key article of the Tripartite Pact.[256] Addressing this grievance was bound to be tricky, since only two days before the entire Japanese cabinet had resigned (on the eve of a major military operation, no less), thus once again underlining the simple fact that fathoming the ways of Japanese politics was not something given to most Westerners. When it reconstituted itself two days later without the

---

[254] BA/MA, RM 11/77 'Oberkommando der Kriegsmarine, Seekriegsleitung 1. Abt. Skl. Ic 15816/41 g.Kdos an Ausw. Amt z.Hd. von Herrn Leg.Rat Kramarz. Betr.: Leihweise Überlassung von Rohgummi an Japan (22.7.1941)'.

[255] The failure on Matsuoka's part to immediately share the contents of this telegram with Ott and enhance his pro-German credentials by doing so is difficult to explain. Since in the same exchange, Hull had also hinted that somebody like the acting Japanese foreign minister was not the best man to entrust these negotiations to, it is perfectly possible that Matsuoka was acting out of hurt vanity or even genuine concern that Konoe might take this hint as his cue to effect a change. See PA/AA, StS Japan, Bd. 4, 608 'Ott an Auswärtiges Amt. Für Herrn Reichsaußenminister (14.7.1941)', where the German ambassador describes Matsuoka during an interview they had on 8 July as 'insecure and hectic, which, as I hear, is tied to concerns over his personal position'. Note: the copy extant in 'Handakten Ritter' is a garbled message missing more than half its content.

[256] 'Notiz für dem Herrn RAM (18.7.1941)'; in: ADAP, Serie D, Bd. XIII.1, pp 142–6. While the Tripartite Pact stressed the fact that the treaty was intended to deter countries not involved 'in the current European conflict' (that is, the USA) from intervening in it, Hull changed this to 'it is intended to contribute to the non-spread of the current war'.

pro-German Matsuoka,[257] it brought home to the Germans the limits of their existing leverage in Tokyo, reducing both Ott and Ribbentrop to the reading of tea leaves.[258] Hitler spend an entire day fuming at the inability of his diplomats to provide him with up-to-date intelligence of this crisis;[259] it is doubtful that Ott's tentative conclusion (offered four days later), that the composition of the cabinet and its ties to pro-Western financial circles indicated a tactic of 'wait and see', reassured him in any way.[260]

The spectacular sacking of a pro-Axis hawk like Matsuoka notwithstanding, the decision to land in southern Vietnam and Cambodia was announced on 24 July. Since Konoe had disregarded an eleventh-hour proposal by Roosevelt to comprehensively neutralise French Indo-China – and hence block the supply routes to China – in exchange for Japan desisting from the operation,[261] it appeared that Hitler and Ribbentrop's anxiety had been misplaced. Irrespective of the fact that Ott thought of that operation as a half-measure, it triggered an extremely harsh American reaction in the form of a near-total trade embargo, plus freezing of assets, which caught both Germans and Japanese (and, it might be added, quite a few Americans) completely by surprise. The German envoy in Washington in his first reports in fact seriously underestimated the consequences of the measures enacted and only came to realise their full extent on 2 August. However, these were not developments Ribbentrop could possibly have foreseen; hence it is reasonable to assume that his attempt – with some feeble support from Hitler – to talk the Japanese into becoming partners in Operation Barbarossa served the purely political purpose of sabotaging the possible détente between Japan and the United States.

A Japanese aggression against the USSR, while far less likely to bring the USA into the war than the invasion of Malaya or the Dutch East Indies, would certainly have been regarded in Washington as a clear signal that Japan was willing not just to stand by the Tripartite Pact, but to expand its remit.[262] Such

---

[257] The reasons for Matsuoka's fall from power were varied and can mostly be traced back to the fact that too many power brokers inside and outside the Japanese cabinet had come to regard him as a loose cannon. The best analysis of these events can be found in Krebs, *Deutschlandpolitik*, pp 545–7.

[258] PA/AA, StS Japan, Bd. 4, 609 'Aufzeichnung an den Herrn Reichsaußenminister zur Vorlage beim Führer. Betrifft: Lage in Japan nach Rücktritt des Kabinetts (18.7.1941)'; Handakten Ritter, Japan 18 'Ribbentrop an Gesandtschaft in Tokio (21.7.1941)'.

[259] H. D. Heilmann (ed.), 'Aus dem Kriegstagebuch des Diplomaten Otto Bräutigam'; in: Götz Aly et al (eds.), *Biedermann und Schreitischtäter. Materialien zur deutschen Täter-Biographie*: (Berlin: Rotbuch Verlag 1987), pp 123–87, esp. pp 136–7 (entry for 16 July 1941).

[260] PA/AA, 'Handakten Ritter Japan 18 Ott an Auswärtiges Amt. Citissime! (20.7.1941)'.

[261] Hotta, *Japan*, pp 144–7.

[262] As borne out by an assessment arrived at in the German admiralty: 'It is not yet foreseeable whether the aim of German policy to arrive at a point where a move against Russia by Japan will lead to her indirect positioning against England and the USA will actually succeed.' KTB Seekriegsleitung, Teil A (entry for 24 July 1941).

a move would without a doubt immediately have doomed any attempt at building a *Geheim-Entente* between Japan and the United States. This explanation finds further support in the fact that, throughout the summer and early autumn, the envoy and military attaché in Washington would repeatedly make a case in their cables for a Japanese takeover of Southeast Asia while deliberately sparing the Philippines. Even when they described various attempts on their part to convince Japanese embassy staff of this option,[263] they were never admonished by Ribbentrop to follow a new party line. Since such a move – even if it did not lead to a US–Japanese war – would have ruined the possibility of any understanding between Tokyo and Washington even more comprehensively than an invasion of Siberia, it would have suited the German agenda just as well.

On the face of it, the mere occupation of southern Indo-China and the ensuing economic siege of Japan by the Western powers appeared to have achieved the same end as any other strategic option open to Tokyo; indeed this was exactly the assessment arrived at by one of Hitler's senior henchmen.[264] However, it is important to realise that the growing estrangement between Tokyo and Washington did not automatically translate into an increasingly harmonious relationship between the two main partners of the Tripartite Pact. On 25 July, Ott and his military attaché sent a rare joint wire to Berlin detailing the influx of Japanese reservists to bolster the strength of the Kwantung Army in Manchuria. While the build-up was impressive on paper, the two diplomats stressed that the odds of Japan's most important uncommitted military force marching off to do battle anytime soon were pretty low. Army Chief of Staff Okamoto Kiyotomi had 'repeatedly' stressed to them in conversation that Japan would not 'make a move before German forces had reached the

---

[263] PA/AA, Handakten Ritter Japan, Bd. 18 Nr. 7633 'Thomsen an Auswärtiges Amt (27.8.1941)'; StS USA, Bd. 8, 'Boetticher & Thomsen an Auswärtiges Amt (29.8.1941)'; Handakten Etzdorf. Politische Berichte Washington. 'Meldung Mil.Att. Washington vom 3.9.1941 (3.9.1941)'; StS Japan, Bd. 4, 612 'Thomsen an Auswärtiges Amt. Cito! Für Herrn Staatssekretär (17.9.1941)'; ibid., 'Boetticher & Thomsen an Auswärtiges Amt. Citissime! Geheime Reichssache. Für O.K.W. Ausland. Für O.K.H. Attache-Abteilung und R.L.M. Attache-Gruppe (21.9.1941)'; ibid., Handakten Etzdorf, 'Politische Berichte Washington. Meldung Mil.Att. Washington vom 11.10.1941 (13.10.1941)'.

[264] TB Goebbels, Bd. II.1, p 127 (entry for 26 July 1941): 'For us it is much more convenient that Japan should pick a fight with the USA than engage in military operations in another theatre of war. As long as Japan stays in the game as a force potentially hostile to the US, I do not think we have to fear any decisive moves on the part of the US.' Note: even though 'another theatre' could conceivably be a reference to a renewed escalation of operations in China, the supreme indifference of the German government to such a course of action strongly suggests Goebbels was referring to a Japanese strike against eastern Siberia.

Volga'.[265] Ott's first interview with the new Japanese foreign minister, Admiral Teijiro Toyoda, was similarly disheartening. While on 23 June, Matsuoka had not hesitated to promise Ott a quarantine of Vladivostok,[266] his successor Toyoda, while not ruling out such a move, hedged his bets by pointing out that 'he was not yet familiar with the details which had a bearing on the issue'. Once he had undergone a (brief) process of familiarisation, he made clear his position at the Liaison Conference of 1 August: a move against the USSR was out of the question and Japan would abide by the recent Neutrality Pact, a valuable morsel of information he shared with the Soviet ambassador on the 5th. Quite independently of Toyoda and his ministry, the army general staff's Soviet intelligence section had reached similar conclusions;[267] on 7 August, the Gaimusho impressed on its rabidly pro-German subordinate Oshima that according to its assessment, the Soviet regime and its remaining armed forces were likely to suffer further defeats but at the same time were still deemed capable of executing an orderly retreat beyond the Urals, thus effectively blocking the Trans-Siberian Railway for the foreseeable future.[268] In contrast to the habits prevailing in Matsuoka's times, Ott was given no indication of this major shift in Japanese strategy.

While these events might still be regarded as the kind of speed bump that inevitably goes hand in hand with a change in government, they occurred against a backdrop that once again served to highlight the dysfunctional nature of the Japanese decision-making process. On 4 August, the Japanese military attaché in Berlin, Lieutenant General Ichiro Banzai, called on Oberkommando des Heeres. According to the notes summarising the exchange he had with his German hosts, he had been sent there by the Japanese Army Chief of Staff with the specific mission of briefing the German military leadership on a strategy on which government and army had for once established a firm consensus.[269] While drawing attention to the fact that Japan would not simply be able to disengage from the China theatre of operations, he described in some detail how the Kwantung Army was being reinforced to a total of sixteen full-strength divisions. He would not be drawn on a date for the initiation of

[265] PA/AA, StS Japan, Bd. 4, Nr. 609 'Ott & Kretschmer an Auswärtiges Amt. Citissime! Zugleich für O.K.W. und O.K.H. (25.7.1941)'. Also KTB Seekriegsleitung, Teil A (entry for 29 July 1941).

[266] PA/AA, StS Japan, Bd. 3, 606 'Ott an Auswärtiges Amt. Citissime! (23.6.1941)'.

[267] Morley, *Final Confrontation*, pp 155–7.

[268] MBPH, Vol. III App., Doc. 806, 'Tokyo to Berlin (7.8.1941)'.

[269] PA/AA, Handakten Ritter Japan 18 'Aufzeichnung über den Besuch des japanischen Militärattaches, Generalleutnant Banzai, begleitet von Major Endo, bei OQ IV am 4.8.1941 in Jägershöhe (5.8.1941)'. The insert emphasising that this initiative had the support of both government and army in Japan is both underlined and features an exclamation mark.

hostilities against the USSR, but made clear that it was merely a matter of deciding the when, not the if.[270] What must have seemed like a wholly unexpected gust of fresh air to his audience had, according to their visitor, been made possible by Ambassador Oshima threatening Tokyo with his resignation.[271] According to another source, Banzai indicated that operations might start in September and lead to the fall of Vladivostok by November. The operation against British Malaya would follow at some point after that.[272] That Deputy Foreign Minister Amau had told Ott in Tokyo the same day that 'in his personal opinion, an immediate entry into the war by Japan [against the USSR] was the right thing to do' would certainly have been conducive to suggesting to Berlin that a corner had finally been turned.[273]

What at first glance appeared to be a major breakthrough for Ott's diplomacy of the last five weeks was soon called into question by the more routine contradictory 'chatter' of Tokyo politics. Vice Admiral Naokuni Nomura of the military commission of the Tripartite Pact had a lengthy conversation with *Konteradmiral* Groos on 6 August during which he stated with remarkable candour that it was really up to Germany to defeat the USSR as well as Great Britain and follow this up by considerably increasing the strength of its surface fleet before Japan could make a move – in 1946.[274] Only towards the end of the conversation did he reluctantly concede that a joint strategy against the Soviet Union might have something to commend it, without however going into any specifics.[275] Ott reported on 9 August that the Japanese government was still wanting 'clear leadership' and reluctant to undertake what to him was 'the next logical step', that is, either an invasion of Thailand or the USSR.[276] According to Ott, even the army did not seem overly keen: a general he described as a 'former firebrand' had explained to him in detail that the gradual retreat of Soviet forces to the European Front was as yet so minor that an invasion was

[270] Ibid.
[271] Four weeks previously, Oshima had indeed asked for his relief on grounds of ill health; the Japanese foreign ministry virtually had to beg him to remain at his post, see MBPH, Vol. II App., Doc. 732, 'Tokyo to Berlin (5.7.1941)'. This appears to indicate that there was at least a kernel of truth to Banzai's account; then again, he may just have used the story of Oshima's threatened resignation – of which the Germans may at least have heard rumours – to bolster the Japanese Army's standing in the eyes of the Wehrmacht.
[272] KTB Halder III, pp 152–3 (entry for 4 August 1941).
[273] KTB Seekriegsleitung, Teil A (entry for 4 August 1941).
[274] BA/MA, RM 7/94 'Abschrift zu B.Nr.1. Abt.Skl 1 17934/41 g.Kdos. Unterredung mit Vizeadmiral Nomura am 6.8.1941 (n.d.)', p 4. Even after more than seventy years, the document makes for an entertaining read on account of the colourful language of the marginal comments of Kurt Fricke, Seekriegsleitung chief of staff, which are an eloquent testament to the exasperation that many German senior officers by now felt towards their Tripartite partner. It is reproduced in full in Sander-Nagashima, *Marinebeziehungen*, pp 614–22.
[275] Ibid.
[276] PA/AA, Handakten Ritter Japan 18 'Ott an Auswärtiges Amt (9.8.1941)'.

out of the question.[277] A report by the German consul in Manchuria made for equally depressing reading. On 13 August, he reported that the visiting deputy foreign minister had ruled out both an invasion of the USSR and a takeover of Southeast Asia. So as he was concerned, Japan's role as Germany's ally should be limited to maintaining a certain level of tension in the area of the Pacific.[278] A spokesman for the Kwantung Army was quite specific in promising an imminent challenge to the USSR over Vladivostok's role, but expressed disbelief at the mere notion of a war with the USSR. Southeast Asia he described as a different issue; provided Germany conquered Egypt in winter, Japan would not hesitate to strike.[279]

In faraway Washington, envoy Thomsen chimed in on 21 August: in a précis of discussions with the Japanese military attaché that he prepared for OKH, he described both the officer in question, as well 'as all Japanese in general', as highly susceptible to American 'hints' that Tokyo would be well advised to await another major German strategic success, like a successful landing in Britain or the fall of the Middle East, before it made a major move of its own.[280] By the middle of August, a point had been reached where of all the promises the Japanese government had made to its German ally over the past few months, virtually every one had been contradicted or qualified so often as to render them meaningless, driving Oshima to the point of offering his resignation for the second time in four weeks.[281] Only a serious challenge to the Soviet and US governments over the use of Vladivostok appeared likely to pass muster, since recent weeks had seen not just a number of Japanese spokesmen stressing this point,[282] but also reports from Washington indicating a growing American reluctance to challenge Japan on this issue.[283]

How was this thoroughly confusing intelligence picture received in Berlin? Oshima at one point informed the Gaimusho that he had received information from a source at OKH or OKW that Hitler had allegedly expressed his determination to join Tokyo in a war against America should an armed clash (even an accidental one) lead to such a conflict, but this is not borne

---

[277] Ibid.
[278] PA/AA, StS Japan, Bd. 4, 610 'Wagner an Auswärtiges Amt (13.8.1941)'.
[279] Ibid.
[280] PA/AA, StS Japan, Bd. 4, 610 'Thomsen & Boetticher an Auswärtiges Amt. Geheime Reichssache (21.8.1941)'.
[281] MBPH, Vol. III App., Doc. 812, 'Tokyo to Berlin (12.8.1941)'.
[282] PA/AA, Handakten Ritter Japan 18 'Ott an Auswärtiges Amt (16.8.1941)'.
[283] PA/AA, Handakten Ritter Japan 18 'Thomsen an Auswärtiges Amt (12.8.1941, 01.18 h)'; StS Japan, Bd. 4, 610 'Thomsen an Auswärtiges Amt (12.8.1941, 12.52 h); StS USA, Bd. 8, 'Boetticher & Thomsen an Auswärtiges Amt (21.8.1941)'. Even this appreciation was too sanguine, since unbeknownst to the Germans, the Japanese leaders only took an interest in Vladivostok-bound traffic from the USA because of concerns that it might be a cover for setting up bases for US naval and air forces on Soviet Far Eastern Territory. 'Imperial Conference, September 6, 1941'; in: Ike (ed.), *Decision for War*, pp 133–63, esp. pp 146, 153.

out by any German sources.[284] Rather, throughout the month of August, both OKW and Hitler continued to express confidence in the Japanese joining Barbarossa with a consistency not seen before. A mere two days after Banzai's visit, Walter Warlimont, in a comprehensive evaluation of strategic options, referred to the Japanese intervention as something 'foreseeable' and indeed 'important' in light of the likelihood of the Anglo–American powers using Far Eastern ports to funnel aid to the embattled USSR.[285] On 18 August Hitler expressed to Joseph Goebbels his 'conviction' that Japan would attack the USSR, adding wistfully that this would even happen irrespective of whether the *Ostheer* had reached Moscow or not.[286] This is noteworthy on two counts. It was the first time the dictator appeared to express a genuine interest in a Japanese contribution on purely military grounds. At the same time, he showed a cavalier disregard of the main theme to be found in virtually all reports filed by German observers since the beginning of the year: in these, a Japanese move against either the USSR or one or all of the Western powers was nearly always linked to the condition that Germany first bring Britain or the USSR to the brink of collapse. At the time, a long quarrel with OKH over operational priorities, a bout of dysentery and the gradual realisation that defeating the Red Army would constitute a much bigger challenge than previously anticipated had left Hitler thoroughly exhausted.[287] Operations had momentarily stalled along most fronts and the spectacular victory over the Kiev grouping still lay nearly a month in the future. It is highly unlikely that every report summarising the latest mood swings among the Japanese leadership was run past him, especially since Ribbentrop, keen to get back into the Führer's good books after a clash between the two over the wisdom of invading

---

[284]   MBPH, Vol. III App., Doc. 808, 'Berlin (Oshima) to Tokyo (14.8.1941)'. The term 'General Headquarters' as used by Oshima could be a reference to either OKW or OKH. For a sceptical assessment of this supposed promise, see Krebs, 'Pearl Harbor', pp 322–3.

[285]   BA/MA, RM 7/258 'Abt. Landesverteidigung-Chef Nr. 441339/41 g.K.Ch. Kurzer strategischer Überblick über die Fortführung des Krieges nach dem Ostfeldzug (6.8.1941)'.

[286]   TB Goebbels, Bd. II.1, p 263 (entry for 19 August 1941).

[287]   The language he used to unburden himself to Goebbels was, quite literally, unprecedented: 'The past weeks had seen a number of critical moments. It was obvious that we have seriously underestimated the fighting power and equipment of the Soviet armies. We were not even close to having an accurate picture of what was available to the Soviets. This led to our misjudgements. The Führer had estimated the number of Soviet tanks at 5,000, when it turned out they had around 20,000. As far as planes were concerned, we estimated they had around 10,000, while in reality they had 20,000. ... The Führer is angry for having allowed himself to be deceived in such a fashion about the potential of the Bolsheviks.' Ibid., pp 260–1. Note: On the eve of the German attack, the Red Army had available a total of 22,600 tanks; the air arms of both services totalled 20,000 planes. See Evan Mawdsley, *Thunder in the East. The Nazi–Soviet War 1941–1945* (London: Hodder Arnold 2005), p 47. This constituted a rough fivefold superiority over the force with which the Germans invaded the USSR.

the USSR, was admonishing his subordinates not to add to the dictator's 'concerns'.[288] In light of Hitler's daily dealings with OKH it seems likely that either Halder or Brauchitsch, not knowing what was really transpiring in Tokyo, had informed him of the cheerful tidings Banzai had brought during his visit on 4 August. Thus, while Hitler may indeed have been pinning his hope on 'phantom allies' on this occasion,[289] his expectations at least had a grounding in fact – albeit a fact limited to the lifespan conferred on it by the quicksands of Tokyo power politics. Four days later, Admiral Erich Raeder was treated to the same estimate. Hitler was 'convinced that Japan would carry out the attack on Vladivostok, as soon as their dispositions were finished. Their current restraint can be traced back to the need to finish their preparations in an undisturbed fashion and preserve the element of surprise for the attack'.[290]

While Hitler and Raeder were pondering issues of strategy, two messages were making their way from Tokyo to Berlin that would make a complete nonsense of these ruminations. Ambassador Ott reported that Japanese resolve to bar American tankers known to be crossing the Pacific from access to Vladivostok appeared to be flagging. As for Japan's future course of action, the navy was said to be dead set against an invasion of the USSR, the main reasons given being the fear of Anglo–American intervention and the near-impossibility of actually joining hands with the Germans along the Trans-Siberian Railway in the near future.[291] This, in turn, caused parts of the army to waver, since the navy's air arm would be needed in any operation against Vladivostok. What with Konoe being unwilling to provide strong leadership, Ott despaired of things ever moving in the right direction. Characteristically, a reassuring comment by Foreign Minister Toyoda that Tokyo and Washington were not currently engaged in negotiations was marked with a big question mark in the file copy.[292]

Almost simultaneously, a message in two parts from the naval attaché arrived at the Seekriegsleitung. It was briefer and more to the point. Referring to his source as 'naval officers in senior positions', he stated that Japan was definitely not going to move against the USSR. In light of the expected Russian collapse and the lack of accessible raw materials in eastern Siberia, the premature execution of such a move would leave Japan just as

---

[288] 'Note by Staatssekretär Ernst von Weizsäcker (6.9.1941)': 'It is absolutely necessary, since he has temporarily been affected in his health by his life as a bunker dweller (which is strictly confidential) to spare him any concerns. He, Ribbentrop, has grown into the habit of bringing him only good news'; in: Hill (ed.), Papiere, p 267.

[289] Stahel, Operation Barbarossa, p 402.

[290] 'Vortrag Ob.d.M. beim Führer in Wolfsschanze am 22. August 1941 nachm. (26.8.1941)'; in: Wagner (ed.), Lagevorträge, pp 277–83, esp. p 283.

[291] PA/AA, Handakten Ritter Japan, Bd. 18 'Ott an Auswärtiges Amt. Citissime! (22.8.1941)'.

[292] Ibid.

isolated as it was now. It followed logically that Japan would not interfere with US supplies to Vladivostok either.[293] The second part referred to the specifics of the move south that the navy was trying to impose on the government. Before the end of the year, Thailand would be occupied following the pattern of 'peaceful' coercion used in the staggered invasion of French Indo-China. Only after the new position had been consolidated would army and navy execute an invasion of the Dutch East Indies and the Philippines together with a blockade of Singapore. Wenneker stressed that a consensus for such a plan between government, army and navy did not as yet exist, and was indeed unlikely (*'fraglich'*) to come about.[294]

It is likely that Ribbentrop had not yet seen either of the two messages when he received Ambassador Oshima on 23 August at his private residence. The foreign minister kept pressing Oshima on the issue of a Japanese entry into the war, with arguments that ranged from the plausible (Germany would be able to turn on Britain the faster the USSR collapsed, an event he himself had to admit was unlikely to occur in 1941) to the utterly ludicrous (self-restraint on the part of Japan would be tantamount to self-destruction; while Germany was capable of achieving these aims on its own, it would be 'nicer' to accomplish them together).[295] Quizzed by Ribbentrop on the subject of Japanese–American talks, Oshima rather revealingly admitted that, in view of his well-known opinion on this subject, 'Tokyo was no longer in the habit of sharing much information with him'. According to the minutes, the US shipments to Vladivostok were mentioned only briefly.[296] Giving another astonishing proof of his lack of tact, Ribbentrop finished the conversation by pointing Oshima to a recent German victory over a body of Soviet troops supposedly equal in number to the forces facing the Kwantung Army in Siberia.[297] Displaying an almost wilful ignorance of the rough treatment the Japanese Army had experienced at the hands of the Soviets at Nomonhan in the summer of 1939, the German foreign minister told his guest that disposing of such a force 'really was not all that difficult'.[298]

---

[293] BA/MA, RM 7/253 a 'Fernschreiben von Marineattache Tokio. Abschrift Marinenachrichtendienst (22.8.1941, 18.33 h)'.

[294] BA/MA, RM 7/253 a 'Fernschreiben von Marinattache Tokio (22.8.1941, 22.11 h)'.

[295] 'Aufzeichung über die Unterredung des Herrn Reichsaußenministers mit dem japanischen Botschafter General Oshima in Steinort am 23. August 1941 (23.8.1941)'; in: ADAP, Serie D, Bd. XIII.2, Anhang IV, pp 839–41.

[296] Ibid., p 840.

[297] Ribbentrop was referring to the fall of Gomel to *Armeegruppe* Guderian and 2. *Armee*, which had netted the capture of more than 80,000 prisoners and 500 artillery pieces. See David M. Glantz, *Barbarossa Derailed: The Battle for Smolensk, 10 July–10 September 1941*, Vol. 1 (Solihull: Helion 2010), pp 367–405.

[298] 'Aufzeichnung über die Besprechung des Herrn Reichsaußenministers mit dem japanischen Botschafter General Oshima in Steinort am 23. August 1941 (23.8.1941)'; in: ADAP, Serie D, Bd. XIII.2, Anhang IV, p 841.

The scant attention paid to Vladivostok should not be seen as an indication that Ribbentrop treated this subject lightly. Proof of this can be found in a lengthy message that was sent to Ott in the small hours of the 25th, which constituted Ribbentrop's reaction to Ott's and Wenneker's wires of the 22nd; two of six pages were exclusively devoted to the issue of Vladivostok-bound transports from the USA and how Japan might stop them. The rest of the message detailed the near-catastrophic losses suffered by the Red Army and how this presented Japan with the unique opportunity of quickly disposing of the Soviet threat in its rear. This would put it in an ideal position to carry on with its expansion in Southeast Asia unmolested, especially since speeding up the Soviet collapse would facilitate the redirection of the German war effort against Britain, thus ruling out any substantial British reinforcements of its Far Eastern possessions. In light of the barely half-ready state of the American air services and army, Ribbentrop was confident in ruling out an American intervention against Japan at this stage, an assessment supported by envoy Thomsen in Washington.

Ribbentrop's efforts notwithstanding, the next fortnight saw another rash of headlines which appeared to suggest that Germany was losing more and more diplomatic leverage in Tokyo. On the 28th, the Gaimusho published an appeal to President Roosevelt by Konoe to resume negotiations, which found a considerable echo in the American press. The broadcast merely reinforced a message delivered by Ambassador Nomura to the White House twenty days earlier, which had suggested a summit meeting between the two leaders. The Germans had no way of knowing about the message delivered to the White House, but taking their cue from speculation in the US media, they strongly suspected it.[299] Ott, on presenting himself at the Gaimusho, was first referred to Toyoda's deputy and upon returning the next day treated with considerable reserve by the minister, who refused to let him see the text of Konoe's original message. The contrast with Matsuoka's way of doing business could not have been starker. In the meantime, further confirmation of the Japanese Army's refusal to initiate hostilities against the USSR arrived, soon to be followed by news of the first US tankers making landfall in Vladivostok.[300]

In Ribbentrop's eyes such a barrage of news items must have driven home the apparent futility of any attempt at ever binding Japan closer to its European allies, but by a bizarre coincidence 3 September witnessed three events that appeared to presage the exact opposite. At a Liaison Conference that day Konoe, always true to character, at the last minute shied away from putting forward a daring proposal involving the wholesale withdrawal of Japanese troops from China.[301] The same gathering, however, passed a mobilisation

---

[299] KTB Seekriegsleitung, Teil A (entries for 29 and 30 August 1941).
[300] PA/AA, Handakten Ritter 18 Japan 'Thomsen an Auswärtiges Amt (30.8.1941)'.
[301] Hotta, *Japan*, pp 162–72.

plan with a view to initiate hostilities against the Western powers towards the end of October; the emperor voiced misgivings, but eventually gave his reluctant approval at another Imperial Conference, which convened three days later.[302] Lastly, 3 September was the day President Roosevelt rejected the idea of a summit meeting unless a number of key issues – like a Japanese retreat from China – had previously been agreed on by both sides.[303] The Germans no doubt would have been elated had they been in the know about what had transpired at the Liaison Conference. Ott, who as far as can be ascertained was completely ignorant of the conference decision, nonetheless came to some very prescient conclusions in a telegram he dispatched on the 4th. After giving his superiors further confirmation of the army's reluctance to engage the USSR, he added that the navy's increasing willingness to 'move south' might just compensate for that, even though the Japanese admirals appeared rather obstinate in refusing to contemplate the possibility of fighting the British while deliberately avoiding a clash with the USA.[304] Ott did not put much store by the prospects of the latest talks in Washington on account of an 'insurmountable clash of interests'. He felt that public opinion was getting more and more agitated, with a return to the rash of assassinations of senior politicians of the early to mid-1930s a definite possibility.[305] He put this down to 'the failure of the third Konoe cabinet to provide the strong leadership called for in light of the existing political problems of a domestic and foreign nature. The government shows a clear tendency to avoid any kind of decision, while attempting to play off the activist groups against each other in order to paralyse them.'[306]

While this assessment appeared to suggest that the German government was in a position to adopt a waiting attitude, that same day an event took place on the far side of the world which was virtually guaranteed to keep Ribbentrop's attention fixated on the slightest rumble emanating from Tokyo politics. Ever since the US Navy started to expand the radius and rules of engagement of vessels engaged in its Neutrality Patrol, the possibility of a clash between German and American warships had been at the centre of deliberations about the future of the Tripartite Pact in Tokyo, Berlin and Washington.

[302] 'Imperial Conference, September 6, 1941'; in: Ike (ed.), *Decision for War*, pp 133–63. Also Kido, *Diary*, p 304 (entry for 6 September 1941).

[303] Hotta, *Japan*, p 169.

[304] PA/AA, Handakten Ritter Japan 18 'Ott an Auswärtiges Amt (4.9.1941)'.

[305] On 15 August, cabinet minister Kiichiro Hiranuma had been assaulted and shot six times in his residence. The attack was probably triggered by Hiranuma's frequent meetings with US Ambassador Joseph Grew. See Hotta, *Japan*, p 177. The extent to which some Japanese decision makers in 1941 may have been motivated to acquiesce in a course leading to war out of sheer fear for their lives, rather than imperialist zeal, is given surprisingly short shrift in most histories of the Pacific War. For a rare exception, see Morley, *Confrontation*, pp 235, 243.

[306] PA/AA, Handakten Ritter Japan 18 'Ott an Auswärtiges Amt (4.9.1941)'.

The Germans had been quite adamant that if such an incident led to a German–American war, Japan was bound by treaty to join them, while the Japanese pronouncements on the topic had been equivocal at best. On the American side, such a scenario was viewed with some concern, if not by the President, then certainly by the heads of the US Army and Navy who doubted that their services were prepared to deal with the challenge of a two-ocean war. On 4 September, *U-652* and the destroyer USS *Greer* clashed not far off Iceland in the area where the war zones declared by both countries overlapped. Even though no blood was drawn, it was clear that further incidents would probably follow soon, especially when the American President on 11 September announced that the US Navy's rules of engagement would be relaxed in order to put it in a position to deal with 'the rattlesnakes of the sea'. Since in the same speech, which was essentially one scathing expression of vituperation against the European Axis, Japan was not mentioned even in passing,[307] the stakes over Japan's allegiance to the pact were automatically raised yet again, giving Ribbentrop another incentive to keep his finger on the pulse of Japanese politics.

Hitler's pronouncements on the topic, meanwhile, were somewhat equivocal. As already discussed, the comments he made in mid-July to Oshima on the desirability of Japan joining Germany for Barbarossa were ambiguous at best. The month of August had been punctuated with remarks which appeared to indicate that he was taking a genuine interest in a Japanese participation in Barbarossa, but between 6 and 10 September he is on record as repeatedly stressing the need to stop pressuring Tokyo, because he did not want to give his ally the impression that their intervention was vital to German strategy.[308] A remark he made to the German ambassador to Vichy on 16th was of similar ilk. With the USSR vanquished, Europe would achieve total autarky and from that point onwards, he, Hitler, 'couldn't care less about America'.[309] Quite apart from the fact that he would by now have received intelligence which clarified any confusion that as likely as not had arisen over Lieutenant General Banzai's rash pledges to invade Siberia, this reassessment was no doubt also influenced by the changing military situation in Russia. While most of August had been marked by a number of important, but far from decisive, successes in the northern and southern sectors and a situation dangerously close to stalemate in the centre, things were definitely looking up in early September. On the 8 September, 18. *Armee* reached Slisselburg on Lake Ladoga, thus cutting off Leningrad from all rail and road communication to the Russian

---

[307] PA/AA, StS Japan, Bd. 4, 611 'Thomsen an Auswärtiges Amt (12.9.1941)'.

[308] 'Note by Weizsäcker (6.9.1941)'; in: Hill (ed.), *Papiere*, p 268. Also 'Auszug aus den Notizen des Vertreters des Auswärtigen Amtes beim OKH (8.9.1941)'; in: ADAP, Serie D, Bd. XIII.1, p 381 and KTB Halder III, p 219 (entry for 10 September 1941).

[309] 'Äusserungen des Führers zu Botschafter Abetz am 16. September 1941'; in: ADAP, Serie D, Bd. XIII.2, pp 423–5.

hinterland.[310] On the same day, *Armeegruppe* Guderian's 3. and 4. *Panzerdivision* effected a crossing of the River Seim in northeastern Ukraine, thereby fulfilling a key condition for the encirclement (achieved on 15th) and destruction of the large grouping of armies under General Michail Kirponos in the Kiev area.[311] Within a few days, movement had returned to the Eastern Front and conditions been created for a major victory over the Red Army; thus it may seem paradoxical that on 23 September he expressed the 'hope' to Joseph Goebbels that Japan might join in after all. Moreover, he did this while positively exulting over the recent successes east of Kiev, hence his turn of phrase that the opportunity to 'partake of the inheritance' would tempt the Japanese into taking the plunge.[312]

The most plausible explanation of this apparent inconsistency is to be found in the reason behind Germany's wooing of Japan. Rather than reflecting the perceived need of Japanese help to defeat the Red Army,[313] it was always first and foremost a ploy to torpedo the sort of détente between Tokyo and Washington that Ribbentrop feared was constantly lurking around the corner. Hitler, while going along with this, would occasionally allow the day-to-day business of running the biggest land campaign in military history to intrude on his reflections about Japan. Hence, his August musings undoubtedly reflect a brief, but real concern over a stalemated front and the hope that Japanese intervention might contribute to solve this logjam. The comments made to Goebbels on 23 September, on the other hand, in all likelihood betray the lurking suspicion that Roosevelt's deliberate sparing of Japan in his speech of 11 September, together with a possible US initiative to detach Japan from the Axis which Thomsen in Washington had warned about on 17th (see later in this chapter), might mean that German diplomacy had, after all, failed in its endeavour to sow discord between Americans and Japanese – hence the hope that a Japanese attack on eastern Siberia might achieve the same result.

In the meantime, Ambassador Ott in Tokyo was kept busy trying to ascertain the prospects of a Japanese–American agreement. The Japanese ambassador to the Court of St James, who was in Tokyo on his annual holiday, described such a political sea change to him as 'impossible', but inevitably this reassuring assessment was followed by irritating questions about the next German victory, which might indicate to Japan that a decisive corner had

---

[310] According to Halder, Hitler had already expressed himself to be completely satisfied with the progress in *Heeresgruppe Nord's* sector as early as 5 September: 'Leningrad: Aim achieved. From now on to be treated as a sideshow.' KTB Halder III, p 215 (entry for 5 September 1941).

[311] David Stahel, *Kiev: Hitler's Battle for Supremacy in the East* (Cambridge: CUP 2012), pp 209–11.

[312] TB Goebbels, Bd. II.1, p 484 (entry for 24 September 1941).

[313] This is the theory put forward by Peter Longerich, *Hitler. Biographie* (München: Siedler 2015), p 792.

finally been turned in Europe (in this case, the timeline for a German advance beyond the Caucasus and into the Middle East).[314]

For Ott, finding himself questioned every step of the way by Japanese who were, in effect, constantly admonishing Germany to find a way to win the war for them must have been exasperating, but visits to the Gaimusho were settling into a pattern that was worse. As a matter of course, Toyoda would make a point of excusing himself and leave his deputy Amau to conduct negotiations with Ott. Only when the latter insisted quite emphatically on being allowed to speak to the foreign minister himself would he be given a hearing. This did not mean that a great deal was achieved, however. Under pressure to ascertain the Japanese reaction to Roosevelt's 11 September speech, Ott confronted Amau with the rumour that Roosevelt had sent an answer to Konoe's offer to negotiate of 28 August. Amau confirmed this, stressed that negotiations thus far had been of only a general nature, but still refused to share the text with Ott.[315] Insult was added to injury when the ambassador finally met Toyoda two days later and was told that he could not let him have the text 'since he needed Roosevelt's permission for that'. Ott's retort wondering whether he thought that Roosevelt would have any qualms about sharing the same correspondence with Churchill must have scored a point, since Toyoda abruptly changed the subject and accused Germany of isolating Japan from the outside world on account of an as yet undefeated USSR still controlling the Trans-Siberian Railway.[316] Towards the end of their conversation, and no doubt anxious to toss Ott any kind of bone, Toyoda resorted to barefaced lying by claiming that Japan was still in the process of negotiating the cessation of American oil shipments to Vladivostok.[317]

In Germany, another exchange of views between admirals Groos and Nomura likewise failed to produce a meeting of minds. After sitting down to discuss a Japanese intelligence report on the Newfoundland summit meeting, recriminations soon followed. Nomura insisted that the Washington talks were just a way of stringing the Americans along; Japan had every intention of staying loyal to the Tripartite Pact.[318] When Nomura brought up the subject of the blocked Trans-Siberian Railway, Groos answered that if Japan was in a hurry to reopen that route, it could see this as an incentive to assist its

[314] PA/AA, StS Japan, Bd. 4, 611 'Tokyo an Auswärtiges Amt. Geheim! (5.9.1941)'.

[315] PA/AA, StS Japan, Bd. 4, 611 'Ott an Auswärtiges Amt. Citissime! (12.9.1941)'.

[316] 'Der Botschafter in Tokio an das Auswärtige Amt. Citissime. Geheime Reichssache (13.9.1941)'; in: ADAP, Serie D, Bd. XIII.1, pp 401–3.

[317] The previous month, Toyoda had expressed his concern over US shipments to the Soviet ambassador, but only if they included ammunition. See MBPH, Vol. III App, Doc. 903, 'Tokyo to Berlin (15.8.1941)'.

[318] BA/MA, RM 12 II/250 'Kriegstagebuch Marineattache Tokio. Eingang Telegramm Matt 3923 gKdos (entry for 25 September 1941)'. The exchange summarised in this telegram had taken place on 12 September.

German ally in bringing about a speedier conclusion to the Russian war. Nomura would not take that one lying down. He did concede that Japan's options were restricted on account of the unresolved war in China but, in return, pointed to the recent drop in sinkings by U-boats in the North Atlantic and made an unflattering comparison between the situation of the *Ostheer* in Russia and that of the Imperial Japanese Army in China. He also expressed the opinion that only the 'destruction of Russia's armed forces and the occupation of her industry and mines' would allow Germany to turn against the Western allies and, hence, benefit Japan. To that, an exasperated Groos snapped back 'that not everything could come exclusively from Germany'.[319]

The Washington embassy also found itself increasingly involved in these days. The Japanese attaché, Major General Saburo Isoda, called on Boetticher on 15 September and again on 20 September, to have a frank exchange about Japan's odds in a war against the USA.[320] Boetticher attempted to impress on him the limitations of US military and economic potential at this moment in time, but bemoaned the proclivity of Japanese observers to be taken in by any morsel of alleged fact picked up in a newspaper, especially as regards the growth of American air power. In any case, both he and envoy Thomsen were in agreement that a Japanese move into Southeast Asia which bypassed the Philippines would have an excellent chance of presenting the USA with a fait accompli, provided the export of rubber and tin were allowed to carry on much as before.[321] Despite such excellent prospects, the German embassy was concerned that the lack of decisiveness shown by the Japanese and the concurrent German successes in Russia would tempt the Americans into mounting a diplomatic offensive aimed at bringing about a Japanese defection from the Tripartite camp. A likely approach would be to bait Tokyo with a substantial concession at the 'cost of Holland or England or China'. Only by handing the Japanese Borneo or Celebes would it possible to 'maintain a Russian military presence in Siberia'.[322] Little did Thomsen

---

[319] Ibid.

[320] PA/AA, StS Japan, Bd. 4, 612 'Boetticher & Thomsen an Auswärtiges Amt. Citissime. Für OKW-Ausland und für OKH-Attache-Abteilung. Betreffend japanische Einstellung zu Amerika. Geheime Reichssache (16.9.1941)'; ibid., 'Boetticher & Thomsen an Auswärtiges Amt. Citissime! Geh. Reichssache. Für O.K.W. Ausland. Für O.K.H. Attache-Abteilung und R.L.M. Attache-Gruppe (21.9.1941)'.

[321] Ibid.

[322] PA/AA, StS Japan, Bd. 4, 612, 'Thomsen an Auswärtiges Amt. Cito! Für Herrn Staatssekretär (17.9.1941).' Four days previously, Boetticher had articulated similar thoughts; as he put it, ceding Borneo to the Japanese while 'maintaining the façade of Dutch sovereignty' might be the indicated move to reach an American 'understanding with Japan'. PA/AA, Handakten Etzdorf, 'Politische Berichte Washington. Bericht Mil. Att. Washington vom 13.9.1941 (15.9.1941)'.

know that the conclusions being arrived at in the White House pointed in exactly the opposite direction.[323]

In much the same vein, Ott appears to have been completely ignorant of what went on behind the façade of impassivity he always encountered in his interviews with Toyoda. On 18 September, the first orders went out to the field headquarters of the Imperial Japanese Army (IJA) to start pre-positioning fuel dumps, shift divisions and prepare provisional air strips. The aim was to be in a position to invade Thailand and the Southeast Asian colonies of the Western powers near the end of October.[324] The Japanese kept Berlin in ignorance of these developments by the simple expedient of keeping any meaningful information from their rabidly pro-German ambassador in Berlin. On 4 September, as already mentioned, a despondent Oshima was embarrassingly frank to Weizsäcker in admitting that the Gaimusho was by now bypassing him with increasing frequency. According to his interpretation, this state of affairs was a direct consequence of the numerous cables he had sent to Tokyo in which he had admonished his superiors not to compromise the Tripartite Pact. Weizsäcker took pity on the ambassador ('he appeared somewhat crushed') and tried to console him by pointing out that surely sooner or later 'the military instincts of the Japanese people' would reassert themselves.[325] Over the following weeks, Oshima would continue venting his frustrations at Germans and Japanese alike, but to no avail.[326]

On 2 October, Ambassador Nomura's attempts to facilitate the summit meeting desired by Konoe were dealt another blow when Secretary Hull handed him a note listing American demands: the secretary stressed the importance of his Four Principles, demanded a preliminary commitment to a retreat of Japanese troops from China and Indo-China and urged Nomura to reconsider Tokyo's position vis-à-vis the Tripartite Pact.[327] This virtually ruled

---

[323] The results of a fact-finding mission to Moscow by Harry Hopkins in late July 1941 convinced the President that Russia had a chance of holding out against the Wehrmacht. Accordingly, keeping the pressure on Japan in order to deter any moves by the Kwantung Army against Vladivostok had become a key element of American strategy in the late summer and autumn of 1941. See Waldo Heinrichs, 'The Russian Factor in Japanese–American relations, 1941'; in: Conroy/Wray (eds.), *Pearl Harbor Re-examined*, pp 163–78.

[324] Morley, *Final Confrontation*, pp 199–206. The Navy's pre-deployment had already been concluded.

[325] 'Der Staatssekretär an die Botschaft in Tokio. Für Botschafter persönlich (16.9.1941)'; in: ADAP, Serie D, Bd. XIII.2, pp 421–2. For a remarkable admission by senior Japanese officers to the German air force attaché in Tokyo that Oshima's reporting was by now regarded as so one-sided that it had led to a loss of credibility of reports emanating from German sources in general, see PA/AA, StS Japan, Bd. 4, 612 'Gronau & Ott an Auswärtiges Amt. Geheim! Für R.L.M. Attache-Gruppe (22.9.1941)'.

[326] MBPH, Vol. III App., Doc. 844, 'Berlin to Tokyo (20.9.1941)'; PA/AA, StS Japan, Bd. 5, 613 'Notiz für den Herrn R.A.M. Geheim! (11.10.1941)'.

[327] '57th Liaison Conference, October 4, 1941'; in: Ike (ed.), *Decision for War*, pp 179–81.

out the sort of progress that Roosevelt had insisted on if he was to meet with the Japanese prime minister.

In contrast to Nomura, who was trying to avert a war, Ott in Tokyo was doing his best to instigate one, but with the same conspicuous lack of success as his Japanese colleague in Washington.

A record of a lengthy discussion Ott had with three Japanese generals is interesting on two counts: both for what he made of it and for what it reveals about a shift in perception on his part. As far as the war against the USSR was concerned, the residual power of the Red Army continued to impress the Japanese officers: they expressed their conviction that even after a Soviet retreat beyond the Urals and with Japan joining Germany as a belligerent, the conflict ultimately would have to be resolved by a negotiated peace.[328] Ott, though fully aware that even Japanese newspapers were by now openly pleading for a political solution to the struggle of giants in the west,[329] described such ruminations as 'bizarre'; the plans laid out by the army for an invasion of Southeast Asia struck him as so inadequate that they appeared likely to compromise the success of the operation. Hence, he assumed 'that the current government will attempt to further postpone a move to the south'. At the same time, he criticised his interlocutors for 'shying away' from the subject of war with the USA, since the Japanese leadership was only willing to contemplate such a conflict in 'an extreme emergency'.[330] Ott insisted that he had carried on preaching the gospel of war against the USSR, but the possibility of a joint war against the USA appeared much more relevant to him: 'There is a growing sensation here that war with the United States is unavoidable, hence it is of the greatest importance that Japan should partake of the decision about when it should be waged jointly'.[331] In contrast to Boetticher and Thomsen, who over the last few months had insisted over and over again that a Japanese move against Southeast Asia should spare the Philippines and avoid a clash with the USA, Ott failed to discuss such a possibility even in passing.

Reluctance over confronting the USA was not in evidence two days later, when Ott's subordinate Wenneker spoke to Captain Maeda of the naval general staff. Maeda described American demands for a Japanese withdrawal from China and Indo-China as unacceptable and sketched out the campaign

---

[328] 'Ott an Auswärtiges Amt. Citissime. Für Herrn Reichsaußenminister (4.10.1941)'; in: ADAP, Serie D, Bd. XIII.2, pp 497–500. The Japanese officers in question were Lieutenant General Hideki Tojo (minister for war), General Hajime Sugiyama (chief of the general staff) and Lieutenant General Kiofuku Okamoto (head of military intelligence).

[329] KTB Seekriegsleitung, Teil A, (entry for 2 October 1941). See also TB Goebbels, Bd. II.2, pp 67, 88 (entries for 2 and 10 October 1941).

[330] 'Ott an Auswärtiges Amt. Citissime. Für Herrn Reichsaußenminister (4.10.1941)'; in: ADAP, Serie D, Bd. XIII.2, p 499.

[331] Ibid.

plan being hatched in his headquarters. He was emphatic in describing the seizure of Manila, and hence war with the USA, as 'an unavoidable necessity'. In fact, the problems arising out of a siege of Singapore appeared to give him more pause than the looming confrontation with America.[332] Maeda's seemingly gratuitous insistence on including the USA in the growing list of Japan's enemies did nothing more than reflect the emerging consensus in the Japanese leadership. Between 5 and 7 October, the question was addressed for the last time in a number of formal and informal meetings. Konoe himself suggested the idea of excluding US possessions from the Japanese campaign plan against Southeast Asia to Army Minister Tojo. Rather characteristically, and no doubt still feeling a little shaken from a recent attempt on his life, he failed to put the full weight of his office behind it.[333] One of the navy's bureau chiefs, Commander Oka Takazumi, brought up the same idea at a joint army–navy meeting, but found himself in a minority of one. Tojo himself insisted on deferring to the consensus that had gradually emerged in the Japanese admiralty since May 1940 and passed up a final chance to question its wisdom in late October.[334]

On 9 October, two important events occurred. In Berlin, government spokesman Otto Dietrich announced at a press conference that Operation Taifun (the envelopment of the bulk of eight Soviet armies to the southwest of Moscow) by Army Group Centre was reaching a successful conclusion, which would lead in turn to the collapse of the USSR in the days following. According to at least one contemporary – albeit non-military – source, the timing of this announcement was tied to the expectation that it would encourage Japan to initiate hostilities against the Western powers in the Far East.[335] While possible, this theory clashes with evidence clearly indicating that from mid-September onwards, Hitler's interest in bringing Japan into the war during the period in question was waning. On the same day in Tokyo, Maeda and Wenneker met again. Apparently, the full implications of what his Japanese interlocutor had shared with him three days before had failed to register fully with Wenneker, because he seemed surprised or even shocked at what Maeda

---

[332] BA/MA, RM 12 II/250 'Kriegstagebuch Marineattache Tokio (entry for 6 October 1941)'. The passage discussing the problems arising out of an operation against Singapore (not Manila) was marked by Wenneker with an exclamation mark.

[333] Four assailants brandishing pistols had jumped on the running boards of his car as it left his villa on 18 September. Bergamini, *Imperial Conspiracy*, p 790, has speculated that Konoe himself may have staged the incident, but the previous attempt on Hiranuma's life does highlight the very real risks political moderates (very much a relative term in the Japan of the period) exposed themselves to whenever they tried to slow the rush to war.

[334] Morley, *Final Confrontation*, pp 212–17; '62nd Liaison Conference, 27 October 1941'; in: Ike (ed.), *Decision for War*, pp 190–3.

[335] Rudolf Semmler, *Goebbels: The Man Next to Hitler* (London: Westhouse 1947), pp 55–6 (entry for 11 October 1941). Semmler was an aide to Joseph Goebbels who kept a personal diary.

suggested to him this time. A formal resolution by the Liaison Conference to propose a wartime alliance to Berlin was still over a month in the future, but the lack of such a commitment does not appear to have deterred Maeda in any way. With truly un-Japanese candour, he asked the German attaché what Berlin's reaction was likely to be once Japan attacked the United States: would a German declaration of war follow suit, and if so, would Germany make a separate peace, if having vanquished its enemies in Europe, hostilities in the Pacific were still ongoing?[336]

Wenneker could not but draw attention to the fact that the Tripartite Pact was defensive in nature and hence did not cover such a contingency. With regards to the possibility of a separate peace, he pointed out that the well-documented hostility of the USA made this more than unlikely. Maeda, possibly sensing he had unsettled the German attaché, reassured him that his enquiries were 'exclusively of a private nature'.[337]

Wenneker must have discussed the points raised by Maeda with Ott, since a couple of them were incorporated into a lengthy telegram the latter sent to Ribbentrop on 11 October. While insisting that he was still trying to sell the Japanese the idea of joining the Germans in their war against the USSR, he discussed at length the increasingly open preparations on the part of the Imperial Japanese Navy for the invasion of Southeast Asia. He appeared to rate this service higher than the army and did not foresee major problems with achieving the objectives it had set itself. The decision to include the Philippines in the campaign plan was noted, but not criticised.[338] What did give Ott pause, however, were two other points. The preliminary decision to mount an elaborate siege of Singapore, rather than to storm it, appeared to indicate a lack of resolve and had to be seen as a 'bad omen'. Even more seriously, he was not convinced that the 'activist elements' in the navy had the political clout to impose this campaign plan, the execution of which he judged to be 'vital to Japan'. Failing that, more hesitation, compromise and eventually postponement loomed. He finished his telegram by basically telling Ribbentrop that it was time to ditch the old strategy. If Germany had a serious interest in having Japan's forces deployed in a manner that went beyond that of a fleet and army 'in being' (held back with a view to tying down a similar number of enemy forces), Tokyo needed to be included in 'joint planning for the next campaign phase against the Anglo-Saxons'.[339]

---

[336] BA/MA, RM 12 II/250 'Kriegstagebuch Marineattache Tokio (entry for 9 October 1941)'. Wenneker's sense of astonishment can be gleaned from the fact that the paragraph making reference to Japan initiating hostilities is marked with an oversized exclamation mark.

[337] Ibid.

[338] PA/AA, StS Japan, Bd. 5, 613 'Ott an Auswärtiges Amt. Für Herrn Reichsaußenminister (11.10.1941)'.

[339] Ibid.

Ott had every reason to be concerned, since the sort of hesitation he had alluded to would still manifest itself as late as October 1941 in the most unlikely personalities. War Minister Hideki Tojo repeatedly rejected Konoe's half-hearted attempts to convince him of the need to yield to some of the American demands. On 4 October, he had even expressed his conviction to a gathering of army division and bureau chiefs that Japan should not hesitate to go to war with the USA, irrespective of Germany joining it or not.[340] In private conversation, however, he too occasionally expressed concern at the prospect of a war with the USA, on at least one occasion practically pleading with Navy Minister Oikawa to own up to his service's material inferiority to the Americans; only this would allow him to force the radicals in the army to reconsider Japan's strategic position.[341]

Back in Berlin, the news coming in from Russia was opening up glittering vistas. On 16 October, one of Ribbentrop's aides held out to Oshima the promise of a campaign that would sweep through the Caucasus in winter and take the war into Iraq and Iran.[342] Seekriegsleitung Chief of Staff Kurt Fricke, for his part, had managed to repress the exasperation which Admiral Nomura's comments about perhaps joining Germany in 1946 had caused him. After a brief meeting with his Japanese counterpart, he sat down to compile for him a lengthy memorandum discussing Japan's strategic options. He was most emphatic in stressing, Boetticher-style, the incomplete state of American mobilisation and hence Roosevelt's reliance on bluff to see him through the next three to four years.

Unlike Ribbentrop, who had first, with great pomposity insisted on the 'inevitability' of a German victory in his talks with Matsuoka, only to hysteric-ally impress on the Japanese the possibility of an Axis defeat when news reached him of the talks brokered by the 'John Doe associates', Fricke dis-played considerably greater skill in playing the same hand. Building on the argument he had already put to Nomura in April, he pointed out that the time to join Germany on its march of conquest was now, since by 1945 or 1946 a victorious Third Reich would have defeated its enemies and would be busy rebuilding Europe according to its dictates; the German people, no matter how sympathetic they might be to Japan, would hardly feel inclined to take up arms again to support their Far Eastern ally in acquiring territory which had already been theirs for the taking in 1941.[343]

Unlike Ott a few days before him, Fricke was also utterly unambiguous about the direction a Japanese war should take. The way he saw it, an attack on

[340] Krebs, *Japan im Pazifischen Krieg*, pp 187–200.
[341] Ibid., p 201; Morley, *Final Confrontation*, p 217.
[342] MBPH, Vol. IV App., Doc. 730, 'Tokyo to Hsinking, Peking, Nanking and Shanghai. Message from Berlin 1250 (23.10.1941)'.
[343] BA/MA RM 7/253a 'Der Chef des Stabes der Seekriegsleitung. Vertraulich! (15.10.1941)', p 82 (post-war pagination).

the USSR was entirely unjustified for three reasons. The Red Army was a broken reed, American supplies coming in through Vladivostok were 'utterly irrelevant' while sheer distance and residual Soviet strength were a combination that made a German–Japanese link-up on the Trans-Siberian Railway within a reasonable time frame highly unlikely. Such a campaign would, however, tie up enough Japanese army units to rule out other strategic options.[344] Hence, Japan should seize the Dutch and British colonial empires to the south where the tin mines and rubber plantations needed by American war industry were essentially hostages to fortune. Such a move would either force the Americans to opt for a policy of détente or stampede Roosevelt into a premature conflict, with the US Navy looking at the prospect of fighting a campaign thousands of kilometres from its main bases while still leaving many units committed to the Atlantic. Fricke was honest enough to admit that such a strategy would also suit German strategy.[345] All things considered, the Fricke memorandum was one of the more intelligent and comprehensive strategic examinations of German–Japanese cooperation to come out of this period. Even though Nomura claimed to have forwarded the gist of it to Japan, it probably came too late to influence the very brief debate on the Japanese side about the desirability of conquering Southeast Asia while giving USA possessions a wide berth.[346]

The day after Fricke finished his memorandum, Konoe resigned from the premiership. The reason was his perennial failure to establish a consensus within his government for continued talks with the USA;[347] by this move he fulfilled with almost eerie accuracy a forecast by the emperor.[348] His departure made way for the much anticipated and much talked about forming of a military-led cabinet. Admirals and generals had held the position of prime minister before, but always after having left the service. Konoe's successor was Lieutenant

---

[344] Ibid., p 74.

[345] Ibid. pp 78–80. Michael Salewski, *Die deutsche Seekriegsleitung 1935–1945, Bd.1* (Frankfurt a.M.: Bernard & Graefe 1970), pp 505–7, gives a completely misleading rendering of this key exchange by alleging that Fricke attempted to goad Japan into going to war against both Britain and the USA.

[346] BA/MA, RM 7/253a Handwritten thank you note appended to the original document (31.10.1941). The extent to which Fricke's assessment influenced the thinking of some Japanese decision makers is impossible to ascertain. The Liaison Conference's decision to reject any (hypothetical) German demands for a Japanese declaration of war on the USSR in exchange for Germany going to war against the USA was reached on 27 October; based on the chronology of events, it is certainly possible that it was informed by Fricke's emphatic dismissal of the USSR as a power still to be reckoned with. '62nd Liaison Conference, October 27, 1941'; in: Ike (ed.), *Decision for War*, pp 190–3.

[347] Kido, *Diary*, pp 313–14 (entry for 16 October 1941); Krebs, *Japan im Pazifischen Krieg*, p 206.

[348] Kido, *Diary*, pp 254–5 (entry for 15 September 1940): 'As for Prince Konoye, His Majesty was afraid he might slip off as usual if the situation became difficult, and he honestly hoped that Konoye would share his joy and sorrow with him.'

General Hideki Tojo, the former minister for war; not only did he stay on the active list, he also got a promotion to full general into the bargain. While in the post-1945 world, his very name would become a byword for mindless militarism, in October 1941 his appointment came with a brief from the emperor to start with a clean slate and reconsider all of Japan's options, the evacuation of conquered territories included. Older scholarship has tended to disregard this as a sham aimed at convincing any waverers that the new government was really trying its best to safeguard peace in the Pacific,[349] but more recent research has tended to take this seriously. The very fact that somebody like Tojo had been given this mission could be seen as indication of such an agenda, since in contrast to the weak-willed Konoe he was widely regarded as having the toughness to impose such an unpopular solution on a recalcitrant officer corps. A visible sign that the new prime minister may indeed have been supportive of a last-minute compromise was his appointment of the pro-peace diplomat Shigenori Togo as foreign minister and the decision to retain for himself both the ministries of army and internal affairs. This gave him control over the instrument he would need – the police – to quell disturbances that might erupt in the wake of the signing of an unpopular agreement.[350]

In mid-September, a German report on the Japanese Army had given a description of the Japanese system of government which was as accurate as it was unflattering: 'on account of the lack of a strong leader and the extreme clashes of vested interests, the cabinets change with great frequency. Policy, both domestic and foreign, is practised for the moment and is always directed towards the lowest common denominator.'[351]

The question before the Germans was, quite simply, what the Tojo government's 'lowest common denominator' was likely to be. They turned to their friend Oshima for help. In a brief exchange with Weizsäcker he described the new cabinet as 'a satisfactory step in the right direction'. Even so, it still lacked homogeneity on account of the presence of some individuals – he singled out Togo – and a reshuffle would be required in about three months. A military move against Russia was not to be expected from it.[352] Hours later, Oshima was quizzed at greater length by one of Weizsäcker's aides. He described the new cabinet as a compromise solution, which reflected the simple fact that

---

[349] Bergamini, *Imperial Conspiracy*, pp 794–5, 801–2; Barnhart, *Japan Prepares for Total War*, p 234.

[350] A view supported in recent years by Keiichiro Komatsu, *Origins of the Pacific War and the Importance of 'Magic'* (Richmond: Curzon 1999), pp 290–2; Hotta, *Japan*, p 220; Krebs, *Japan im Pazifischen Krieg*, pp 210–11, 216–17.

[351] PA/AA, Handakten Ritter, Bd. 17, 'Nr. 7632 Oberkommando des Heeres, Generalstab des Heeres. O Qu IV/Abt.Fr.H.Ost (III). Nr. 1695/41 g.kdos. Geheime Kommandosache. Die japanische Kriegswehrmacht. Stand: 1.9.1941 (17.9.1941)'.

[352] PA/AA, StS Japan, Bd. 5, 613 'Fernschreiben an Reichsaußenminister, Sonderzug (10.10.1941)'. The date given is obviously a typo.

fundamental change in Japanese politics was only possible if executed gradually. He also admitted that the talks with the USA would in all likelihood continue for the time being.[353] Even though Tojo might adopt a tougher stance towards the USSR, a war with Stalin seemed unlikely; as for a move against Southeast Asia, he was confident in ruling it out altogether. As far as his own opinion was concerned, Oshima in his inimitable way spoke of the desirability of Japan's armed forces moving both north and south. However, even this uncompromising Germanophile for once invoked the same theme with which Japanese officers and diplomats had been driving their German counterparts to distraction for nearly a year: further German operations against Great Britain, Oshima helpfully suggested, might well serve as a catalyst for a Japanese decision to execute a move south.[354]

On the same day, Admiral Nomura was quizzed by Groos on the same subject. In two pages of notes he typed up after the interview, Groos showed himself satisfied that the Japanese admiral was finally showing an 'increased approximation' towards the ideas he and Fricke had repeatedly put to him in recent weeks. When pressed for specifics as to the new cabinet's course of action, however, he appeared as clueless as Oshima had been. He went through every conceivable option without giving any indication whether one appeared to be closer to realisation than the others. Even so, Groos must have felt that progress had been achieved. He told Nomura that 'the main point was that Japan should be ready to choose a course of action' and very graciously conceded that the 'choice of main effort' was, of course, Japan's alone.[355] The German admiral must have felt downright churlish in bringing up, towards the end of their exchange, the vexed rubber issue, which in the meantime had raised its head again.[356]

---

[353] PA/AA, StS Japan, Bd. 5, 613 'Erdmansdorff an Gesandten von Rintelen über Büro RAM (18.10.1941)'.

[354] Ibid.

[355] BA/MA, RM 7/253a 'B.Nr. 1 Skl. 24039/41 gKdos. Unterredung mit Vizeadmiral Nomura am 18.10.1941. Abschrift (n.d.)'.

[356] Paradoxically, Japan's seizure of the rubber-rich province of South Vietnam had exacerbated the issue of rubber supply, rather than easing it. This move had brought in its wake a temporary refusal by Thailand to sell rubber to Japan as well as a clash between Vichy and Japan as to whether the Americans should still be allowed to purchase Indo-Chinese rubber. The German position was rendered untenable by the fact that they were still allowed to purchase rubber in Thailand, but were dependent on the Japanese for transport. See PA/AA, StS Japan, Bd. 5, 613 'Ott & Wohltat an Auswärtiges Amt (15.10.1941)'; ibid., 614 'Ott an Auswärtiges Amt (20.10.1941)'. On the Thai–Japanese relationship in the last months of peace, see Nigel Brailey, 'Thailand, Japanese Pan-Asianism and the Greater East Asia Co-Prosperity Sphere'; in: Saki Dockrill (ed.), *From Pearl Harbor to Hiroshima. The Second World War in Asia and the Pacific, 1941–45* (London: Macmillan 1994), pp 119–33.

Ott in Tokyo was marginally less optimistic. In a cable he sent on 20 October he took stock of recent events and noted that the new government would without a doubt raise Japan's value as a 'factor of tension' in the Far East. As to the possibility of the country actually initiating hostilities against either the USSR or the West, this was still to be determined by the armed forces finally reaching a consensus and overwhelming the forces preaching moderation, neither of which was as yet a foregone conclusion.[357]

In the meantime, the meetings between Ott's subordinate Wenneker and Commander Maeda of the Japanese admiralty were becoming something of a regular fixture. On 15th, Maeda had gone out of his way to share with Wenneker some recent fruits of the codebreaking efforts of the Imperial Japanese Navy (IJN);[358] when the two men met again on 24th, Maeda again raised the subject of a US–Japanese war. Wenneker answered in pretty much the same vein as he had before, attempting to be both encouraging and evasive at the same time. Unlike Boetticher in Washington a couple of weeks before, he did not attempt to dissuade his Japanese interlocutor from including the Philippines in the Japanese plans of conquest; rather, he pointed out that in case of a war between Japan and the USA, the ensuing drop in US shipments to Britain would be welcome to Germany, 'since this war would be decided not in Russia, but on the Atlantic'.[359]

The key question, of course, was the impression the change in government had made at the Wolfsschanze. On the day Tojo was made premier, the German dictator had expressed some hope that this might at least give US legislators, hours away from voting to rescind parts of the Neutrality Act, some pause for thought.[360] A mere three days later, however, he gave Goebbels

---

[357] 'Der Botschafter in Tokio an das Auswärtige Amt. Citissime (20.10.1941)'; in; ADAP, Serie D, Bd. XIII.2, pp 546–7.

[358] BA/MA, RM 12 II/250 'Kriegstagebuch Marineattache Tokio (entry for 15 October 1941)'. At the time, both the IJN and IJA intelligence branches intercepted and read some of the State Department's radio communications, see Ken Kotani, *Japanese Intelligence in World War II* (Oxford: Osprey 2009), pp 14, 72. The decrypted message Maeda shared with Wenneker was a summary of the Three Powers Conference held in Moscow in the last days of September. Some of the points alluded to in this document, however – an Anglo-American proposal that Stalin grant Siberia political autonomy to ensure against a Soviet capitulation west of the Urals; a Russian proposal that parts of the Caucasus, Turkey, Iran, Iraq and Syria be turned into an Armenian state to act as buffer zone between British and Russian zones of influence – are so downright bizarre as to defy belief. In light of the well-documented Japanese interest in a German–Soviet compromise peace, the possibility of a plant intended to convince the Germans that the USSR had reached a point where its leadership might even consider a peace treaty involving the loss of large swathes of territory cannot be ruled out.

[359] BA/MA, RM 12 II/250 'Kriegstagebuch Marineattache Tokio (entry for 24 October 1941)'.

[360] 'Sonnabend, 18. Oktober 1941'; in: Martin Vogt (ed.), *Herbst 1941 im 'Führerhauptquartier'. Berichte Werner Koeppens an seinen Minister Alfred Rosenberg* (Koblenz 2002) [= Materialien aus dem Bundesarchiv, Heft 10], pp 76–9.

instructions on the gloss the media should put on the news from Japan, which speak for themselves. As the *Reichspropagandaminister* put it in his personal diary the following day: 'The Führer hasn't much confidence in the new prime minister General Tojo and has asked for the greatest restraint to be exercised in the coverage of this news item by the German media. The way he sees it, the forming of this cabinet is merely a bluff aimed at pulling the wool over our eyes by mollifying us or, alternatively, to goad America into making a firm commitment in its negotiations.'[361] An unflattering report by Heydrich's SD to the Auswärtiges Amt on the new government's agenda does not appear to have been the cause of this, since Ribbentrop had refused to forward it to Hitler.[362] In all likelihood, the dictator's low opinion was formed by the assessments offered by Oshima on 18 October; together with the ongoing negotiations in Washington they underpinned Hitler's opinion of the new Japanese leader for the next four weeks.[363] Ernst von Weizsäcker at the Auswärtiges Amt was kept abreast of this assessment by his sources, but he put a different gloss on it: the way he saw it, the dictator was actually fearful of a Japanese move against the USSR. This would contribute little to the imminent collapse of the Soviet state, but might stand in the way of a compromise peace between Germany and the United Kingdom.[364] A few days later, in a lengthy conversation with the Italian foreign minister, Galeazzo Ciano, which covered a wide range of subjects, Japan was mentioned but once. According to the stenographer, Hitler made a passing remark that Japan's time as a partner of the Axis powers surely 'would come one day'.[365] Since in the preceding paragraph he had pointed out to Ciano that the issue of the looming confrontation between Europe and America would have to be left to a 'later generation',[366] it is reasonable to

---

[361] TB Goebbels, Bd. II.2, p 151 (entry for 21 October 1941).

[362] PA/AA, Inland IIg 440 'SS-Obergruppenführer Heydrich an Reichsaußenminister von Ribbentrop (18.10.1941)'. The report originated from a source close to the US embassy; it highlighted alleged intentions of the Tojo government to react to a Soviet collapse by turning the entirety of Siberia into one or several satellite states and offer them protection from 'a German attack'. Ribbentrop saw in this a transparent US attempt to sow dissent between Berlin and Tokyo and refused to pass it on, see ibid., 'Unterstaatssekretär Luther an SS-Obergruppenführer Heydrich (4.11.1941)'. It goes without saying that this estimate could nonetheless have reached the dictator by a different route.

[363] Oshima's opinion would have carried special weight far transcending his Germanophilia, as he had known Tojo since their time as officer cadets in 1902–5. The various pronouncements in favour of war which Tojo had made in the last weeks of the Konoe government, however, had all occurred behind closed doors and it is extremely unlikely that Oshima, much less Hitler, could have learned of them.

[364] 'Note by Weizsäcker (21.10.1941)'; in: Hill (ed.), *Papiere*, p 274.

[365] 'Aufzeichnung über die Unterredung zwischen dem Führer und dem Grafen Ciano im Hauptquartier am 25. Oktober 1941'; in: ADAP, Serie D, Bd., XIII.2, pp 563–70, esp. p 567.

[366] Ibid.

assume that as far as a Japanese contribution to the current war was concerned, he was not holding his breath.

Two days later, in an interview with Seekriegsleitung Chief of Staff Kurt Fricke, he exhibited a bluntness that suggests he had actually exercised diplomatic restraint while in Ciano's company. Hitler agreed with Fricke's assessment of the essential futility of having Japan go to war in order to block access to Vladivostok; now the time had come for Tokyo to move south. Either way, the whole point was probably moot anyway: as he put it to Fricke, he took 'the new Japanese government to be too uncommitted and disinclined to be in any way proactive'.[367]

Hitler's hunch was apparently confirmed in the next two cables sent by Ott. He expressed the opinion that the new government appeared to lack 'a clear agenda'. When he approached the new foreign minister to ask for Japan's support in the matter of the progressive dismantling of the US Neutrality Act, the reaction he received very much followed the pattern set by Toyoda and Amau: procrastination was followed by a barrage of probing questions on Germany's next move in its war against Britain.[368] Tojo's reputation as a hardliner notwithstanding, everything appeared to be business as usual at the Gaimusho.

If Ott's dealings with his Japanese counterparts appeared to be settling into an ever-more predictable routine, those of his naval attaché, Wenneker, were marked by startling revelations every week. Unbeknownst to the two diplomats, a seventeen-hour-long Liaison Conference (1–2 November) had finally reached the irrevocable decision to go to war with the Western powers by the end of the month unless negotiations in Washington produced a breakthrough.[369] The Kriegsmarine officer had no way of knowing this, but when Maeda told him on the evening of 3 November that the decision for war with the USA was 'as good as made' and that the campaign to seize Southeast Asia would start before the end of the year, he was for once receiving information that reflected actual reality, rather than a Japanese interlocutor's wishful thinking.[370] He went over the details of the campaign plan for the second time and intimated that the government would soon approach Berlin to propose both a military alliance against the USA and mediation to settle the Russo–German war. Furthermore, he gave away a morsel of information that showed

---

[367] 'Führer hält (. . . .) die neue japanische Regierung für noch zu laurig und wenig aktions-freudig'; in: KTB Seekriegsleitung, Teil A (entry for 28 October 1941). This barbed comment is not to be found in the set of minutes used in the Wagner edition.

[368] PA/AA, StS Japan, Bd. 5, 614, 'Ott an Auswärtiges Amt. Citissime! Geheim! Vorabdruck (28.10.1941)'; Ibid., 'Ott an Auswärtiges Amt. Geheim. Citissime! (31.10.1941)'.

[369] '66th Liasion Conference (November 1st, 1941)'; in: Ike (ed.), Decision for War, pp 199–207.

[370] BA/MA, RM 12 II/250 'Kriegstagebuch Marineattache Tokio (entry for 3 November 1941)'.

a willingness to lay his cards on the table, which was without precedent in the thirteen-month tortuous history of the Tripartite Pact. Hostilities, Maeda told Wenneker, would be initiated without the slightest regard for Germany's progress (or lack thereof) in Russia. Even allowing for the fact that Maeda appears to have been under the impression that the fall of Moscow, and hence the toppling of Stalin, were but a matter of time,[371] this was candour of a kind virtually never seen in German–Japanese relations. A weary Ott conceded that the new government appeared to be showing a greater willingness to confront the West than its predecessor. However, mindful of the countless snippets of intelligence from respectable sources that had crossed his desk over the past year, all of which had had it on good authority that Japan was weeks away from joining Germany in its war against the West, the USSR or both, he noted that he was relaying this intelligence only, not vouching for its content.[372]

Had he been privy to some of the correspondence between Foreign Minister Togo and his ambassadors, he would have found ample confirmation for his scepticism. Well into the second half of November, Japanese diplomats were exchanging telegrams that foresaw the likelihood of continued Soviet resistance, whether to the west or the east of the Urals.[373] Much like Commander Maeda had done, they also reflected at length upon the desirability of brokering a peace treaty between the two warring giants.[374] Only Oshima appeared willing to unerringly keep the faith in these days, pointing out to Togo that Alfred Rosenberg's appointment as plenipotentiary for the occupied parts of the USSR indicated that Germany was moving from a purely 'military' to a 'political' phase of its campaign.[375]

It is unlikely that Ribbentrop would have been surprised at any of this. As long as Americans and Japanese were still going through the motions of negotiating in Washington, the German foreign minister was kept in a constant state of heightened anxiety. The attempt by Japanese Foreign Minister Togo to breathe new life into the talks by sending a special envoy, Saburo Kurusu, to the American capital to serve as advisor to Ambassador

---

[371] Ibid.

[372] PA/AA, StS Japan, Bd. 5, 614 'Ott an Auswärtiges Amt. Citissime! Geheim (5.11.1941)'. Wenneker's telegram can be found in BA/MA RM 7/253a 'Fernschreiben von Marineattache Tokio. Für O.K.M., O.K.W.-Ausland (5.11.1941)'.

[373] MBPH, Vol. IV App., Doc. 719, 'London to Washington (16.10.1941)'; ibid., Doc. 783, 'Hsinking to Hong Kong (6.11.1941)'; ibid., Doc. 790, 'Tokyo to Washington. Circular. Report on European conditions. Secret (11.11.1941)'.

[374] MBPH, Vol. IV App., Doc. 721, Hsinking to Tokyo (n.d.; late November 1941); ibid., Doc. 817, Tokyo to Berlin (21.11.1941). Even the *Draft Proposal for Hastening the End of the War against the United States, Great Britain, The Netherlands and Chiang* (15.11.1941), which spelled out Japan's strategic priorities in the upcoming conflict, devoted some space to the possibility of fostering a German–Soviet peace; Ike (ed.), *Decision for War*, pp 244–9.

[375] MBPH, Vol. IV App., Doc. 796, 'Berlin to Tokyo (21.11.1941)'.

Nomura alarmed Ribbentrop sufficiently to reconsider the tactics he had used over last few months.

If the account in Ribbentrop's memoirs is to be believed, encouraging Tokyo one week into Barbarossa to join Germany in its war of aggression against the USSR, rather than initiate hostilities against the British and Dutch in Southeast Asia, had been his idea alone and had caught Hitler by surprise. While the dictator went along with it, his commitment to this notion appears to have been somewhat lukewarm and eventually became tied to the momentum achieved by the *Ostheer* in Russia at any given time. Since the primary agenda behind the scheme was to sabotage any rapprochement between Tokyo and Washington, rather than achieving a particular military outcome, the strategy was moot anyway. On 3 November, however, envoy Hasso von Etzdorf, the Auswärtige Amt's liaison at Oberkommando des Heeres, recorded a comment by Hitler which appeared to make a complete nonsense of German policy towards Japan since the capture of the *Automedon* papers. It was best, the dictator said, that Japan should stay out of the war altogether, since otherwise the signing of a peace deal would be made much more complicated.[376] As already mentioned, the same motives had been imputed to Hitler by Ernst von Weizsäcker in an attempt to rationalise the dictator's negative reaction to the possibility of Japan joining Germany in its war against the USSR.[377] Exactly what sort of intelligence had suggested to Hitler that either Britain, the USSR or a putative successor regime to Stalin's might be ready to talk peace in the very near future has remained a mystery to this day.

At the time, the German dictator would have been aware of the basic parameters dominating Japan's military options: a move into Vladivostok and eastern Siberia was by now virtually ruled out on account of plummeting temperatures.[378] As far as a move to the south was concerned, Ott's telegrams sent on 4 and 11 October, giving the gist of recent conversations with Prime Minister Tojo, Sugiyama and Maeda cannot have left him in any doubt that planning for an invasion of the entirety of Southeast Asia (that is, including the Philippines) had reached an advanced stage.

---

[376] PA/AA, Handakten Etzdorf, 'Schreibmaschinen-Umschriften aus Aufzeichnungen VAA (3.11.1941)'. At least two tentative peace probes appear to have been underway in Europe in late October and early November, even though, according to the key monograph on the subject, they were the result of the actions of unauthorised individuals that achieved a temporary echo only on account of 'British misperceptions'. See Ulrich Schlie, *Kein Friede mit Deutschland. Die geheimen Gespräche im Zweiten Weltkrieg 1939–1941* (München & Berlin: Langen Müller 1994), pp 343–50. Etzdorf's note appears to indicate that this assessment may require qualification.

[377] 'Note by Weizsäcker (21.10.1941)'; in: Hill (ed.), *Papiere*, p 274.

[378] As far back as August, Ribbentrop had requested Oberkommando des Heeres to provide him with dates indicating when the drop in temperature would make campaigning in Manchuria first more cumbersome, and finally impossible. See PA/AA, Handakten Etzdorf, 'Schreibmaschinen-Umschriften aus Aufzeichnungen VAA (7.8.1941)'.

That this was met by a sense of unease in Berlin can be gleaned from an instruction Ribbentrop issued to his subordinates on 4 November. He instructed them to collect a number of samples of recent cables from the Washington embassy providing circumstantial evidence that a move by Japan against Southeast Asia which bypassed the Philippines would not be met by an American declaration of war; a summary of these should then be sent to Ambassador Ott in Tokyo.[379] The following day, Ott relayed Wenneker's impressions of his most recent exchange with Maeda, which as was stressed earlier, had been of truly unprecedented candour.[380] This was complemented a couple of days later by a rare snippet of up-to-date intelligence which Foreign Minister Togo had decided to share with Oshima in Berlin. In this communication, Togo had relayed the recent impressions of Ambassador Nomura in Washington, who until now had been emphatic about the American willingness to enter the war against Germany if the circumstances seemed right. The muted American reaction to the torpedoings of the USS *Kearney* and USS *Reuben James*, however, had now forced him to reconsider this assessment.[381]

Finally, on 9 November 1941, Ribbentrop dispatched a cable to Ott which effectively demanded of him yet another about-turn and also provided positive proof that his previous policy of inciting Japan to join the Russo–German war had definitely not been an end in itself. Japan, he explained, should seize the moment and strike out for the south since the one factor that had allowed the Americans to intimidate Japan (continued Soviet resistance) was fading fast and US arms production had as yet only been able to provide Britain, China and the USSR with 10 per cent of the promised goods.[382] Echoing Thomsen's warning of 17 September, he advised his allies against accepting a territorial compromise that would never satisfy its needs for 'living space'. Provided it took care to spare US possessions on its march of conquest, Southeast Asia was its for the taking. Both the incomplete state of US base facilities in the Pacific and the growing number of US Navy units deployed in the Atlantic practically ruled out a US intervention in such a case.[383] Wenneker put this case to Maeda in their next meeting on 13 November. The Japanese officer, however, was adamant in ruling out a campaign plan that bypassed the Philippines. Even if a US intervention was not forthcoming straightaway, it was sure to follow in the aftermath of the Japanese conquest of the general area; operating from bases in the Philippines, US forces would then be in a position to interdict the

[379] PA/AA, StS Japan, Bd. 5, Nr. 614 'Loose minute signed by Woermann (4.11.1941)'.

[380] PA/AA, StS Japan, Bd. 5, Nr. 614 'Ott an Auswärtiges Amt (5.11.1941)'.

[381] PA/AA, StS Japan, Bd. 5, Nr. 614 'Aufzeichnung (7.11.1941)'.

[382] 'Der Reichsaußenminister an die Botschaft in Tokio (9.11.1941)'; in: ADAP, Serie D, Bd. XIII.2, pp 622–3.

[383] Ibid.

logistical lifelines of Japan's forces in the East Indies.[384] Ribbentrop then sent one of his envoys to interview Oshima.

Expecting reassurances on the topic of conflict limitation from a certified warmonger like the Japanese ambassador may have smacked of desperation, but without any prodding by his German visitor Oshima appears to have sketched out a campaign plan that would spare the Philippines. This would have constituted priceless information had the ambassador not added the by now inevitable rider that the 'deliberations and intentions of his government' were completely unknown to him and he was thus only able to share his private opinion.[385]

The next telegram to arrive from the Tokyo embassy indicated to Ribbentrop that his attempt to resume his pre-Barbarossa strategy of edging the Japanese in the general direction of Singapore had come too late. Ott said that the head of military intelligence, General Kiofuku Okamoto, had called on him with information that echoed Maeda's earlier requests. The talks in Washington would almost certainly fail to yield any results, war was sure to come and it would involve the United States. Ott's Japanese interlocutor had even added, no doubt tongue in cheek, that this constituted a good opportunity for Germany, since Japan was ready to move south long before the *Ostheer* had had an opportunity to reach, let alone breach, the Caucasus.[386] The ambassador's attempt to suggest a strategy that would spare the Philippines had been brushed aside with the same arguments used a few days earlier by Maeda. It is to Ott's credit that, apart from pointing out the blindingly obvious (that an attack by one of the signatory nations on the USA was not covered by the Tripartite Pact), he also urged Ribbentrop to consider asking for something in return. Both a smoother processing of German rubber shipments and a blockade of Vladivostok could fall under this heading.[387]

Even though another exchange between Nomura and Groos indicated that the Germans' idea of what kind of campaign the Japanese were planning to fight was sketchy in the extreme, and the will of Japanese representatives based in Berlin to address this issue equally underdeveloped,[388] events now gathered speed.

---

[384] BA/MA, RM 12 II/250 'Kriegstagebuch Marineattache Tokio (13.11.1941)'.

[385] PA/AA, StS Japan, Bd. 5, 615, 'Fernschreiben an den Herrn Reichsaußenminister über Büro RAM (17.11.1941)'.

[386] 'Ott an Auswärtiges Amt. Citissime. Für Reichsaußenminister (18.11.1941)'; in: ADAP, Serie D, Bd. XIII.2, pp 652–4.

[387] Ibid.

[388] Some of the ideas put forward by Nomura (he accorded priority to a strike into Burma in order to cut off China's supply route to the exterior, while expressing the hope that such a move might be possible without bringing a British declaration of war in its train) raise the question whether he was really so ill-informed or whether this has to be seen as a desperately incompetent attempt at spreading disinformation. BA/MA, RM 7/253a 'Anlage zu 1. Skl 26999 Kdos. Unterhaltung mit Vizeadmiral Nomura am 20.11.1941 (n.d.)'. A report from the German embassy had filled in some of the blanks but had left

It goes without saying that the key to further developments lay in the mind of the German leader, who only a fortnight previously had ruminated on the desirability of keeping the Japanese out of the war in order to facilitate a compromise peace. A comment he made on 19 November chimed rather well with this. While being briefed by Army Chief of Staff Franz Halder on a variety of subjects just after noon he expressed the opinion that recent developments (he mentioned alleged social unrest in Britain) pointed towards 'the realisation that both enemy groupings are incapable of annihilating each other, thus leading to a compromise peace'.[389] This statement has been frequently misinterpreted as Hitler despairing of ever defeating the Red Army, a conclusion that clashes with any number of statements made by him and his senior aides in the weeks after the victory achieved during the Taifun operation.[390] In 1983 Peter Herde suggested a different interpretation: he concluded that this comment could only have referred to the emerging Anglo–American coalition, not the prostrate USSR, and that it essentially encapsulated the dictator's first reaction to Ott's telegram of the 18th, which had provided final confirmation of Japan's determination to go to war against the USA.[391] It is difficult to argue with the first point, but the second one constitutes a major problem. It is theoretically possible that said missive could already have reached him (the telegram was decoded at the Auswärtiges Amt at 06.10), but it leaves us with the problem of a Hitler as resigned to the thoroughly alien idea of a compromise peace (a notion he only ever referred on a couple of occasions) as he had been on 3 November. Surely, the announcement that a major ally was about to join the European Axis could not but have forced him to undertake a fundamental reassessment of the strategic options before him.

---

key questions (especially if and how Singapore would be attacked) unaddressed. See PA/ AA, StS Japan, Bd. 5, 615, 'Kretschmer & Ott an Auswärtiges Amt. Citissime! (21.11.1941)'.

[389] KTB Halder III, p 295 (entry for 19 November 1941). An admission made even more remarkable by the fact that only a few days earlier Churchill had used the Lord Mayor's Banquet speech to publicly pour scorn on the very idea of a peace deal with Nazi Germany or even a successor regime. See KTB Seekriegsleitung, Teil A (entry for 11 November 1941).

[390] Krebs, *Deutschlandpolitik*, p 601; Bernd Wegner, 'Warum verlor Deutschland den Zweiten Weltkrieg? Eine strategiegeschichtliche Interpretation'; in: Christian Müller & Matthias Rogg (eds.), *Das ist Militärgeschichte! Festschrift für Bernhard Kroener* (Paderborn: Ferdinand Schöningh 2013), pp 103–21, esp. pp 108–9; Lars Lüdicke, *Hitlers Weltanschauung. Von 'Mein Kampf' bis zum 'Nero-Befehl'* (Paderborn: Ferdinand Schöningh 2016), p 170. Enrico Syring, 'Hitlers Kriegserklärung an Amerika vom 11. Dezember 1941'; in: Wolfgang Michalka (ed.), *Der Zweite Weltkrieg. Analysen, Grundzüge, Forschungsbilanz* (München: Piper 1989), pp 683–96, is ambivalent on this point.

[391] Herde, *Weg in den Krieg*, p 75.

Such a reaction is very much in evidence forty-eight hours later. Joseph Goebbels, who over the previous weeks had repeatedly echoed Hitler's negative judgement of Tojo in his personal diary,[392] was left singularly unimpressed by vocal calls for war that had been emanating from the Japanese media. The extraordinary session of the Diet that took place between 17 and 20 November appeared to bear out this point of view. There the new Tojo government, in attempting to make a case for continued negotiations with Washington, was confronted with a unanimous resolution that harshly criticised its supposed lack of resolve in defending the Greater Co-Prosperity Sphere.[393] Tojo was forced to issue a statement stressing his government's willingness to assert Japan's rights in the Far East. Hence, the *Reichspropagandaminister* was left not a little surprised when, on calling on the dictator on 21 November, he found him quite upbeat at the prospect of Japan joining Germany in its war against the Western allies 'in the near future'.[394] Goebbels, who would not have been privy either to Ott's telegram of the 18th, summarising Okamoto's offer of an alliance against the Anglo–American powers, or to the fact that Ribbentrop had sent an affirmative answer,[395] was not convinced.

The evidence before us, circumstantial though it may be, seems to indicate that in the days prior to the afternoon of 19 November, Hitler, while confident of having crippled the USSR, felt himself to be at his wits' end about how to effectively challenge a Britain currently on the ascendant in the Mediterranean, benefitting from the recent drop in sinkings in the North Atlantic and receiving ever-growing quantities of American material support. The last factor was magnified many times over by the gutting of the Neutrality Law (voted on by Congress on 13 November), since it would allow US merchantmen to deliver their cargoes straight into British ports. It took the latest news from Tokyo to lift his spirits and banish all thoughts of compromise peace from his head, the many 'false starts' in the history of the Tripartite Pact notwithstanding.

As if to bear out Goebbels' persistent scepticism, a telegram from Ott arrived on the 24th which was ambiguous at best. He had received Lieutenant General Okamoto on the 22nd, who had expressed gratitude and relief at the German government's offer to stand by Japan in a war with the USA and sought clarification on whether the German telegram of the previous day also covered the contingency of Japan unilaterally initiating hostilities against the USA, as opposed to a clash that came about as a result of Japan first making a move

---

[392] TB Goebbels, Bd. II.2, pp 214, 223–4, 234, 239–40, 299, 304, 308–9 (entries for 1, 2, 5, 6, 16, 17 and 18 November 1941).

[393] The anti-American slant of many speeches held during the Diet session was not challenged by any of the deputies present. See PA/AA, StS, Japan, Bd. 5, 615 'Ott an Auswärtiges Amt. Citissime! (21.11.1941)'.

[394] TB Goebbels, Bd. II.2, p 339 (entry for 22 November 1941).

[395] PA/AA, StS Japan, Bd. 5, 615 'Ribbentrop an die Botschaft in Tokio. Geheime Reichssache (21.11.1941)'.

against Britain or The Netherlands. At the same time, he was strangely evasive when questioned about the topic of a Japanese attack on the Philippines and insisted that the ongoing negotiations in Washington were not tied to a time limit.[396] He also suggested to the German ambassador that future negotiations on the topic of a war alliance between the two countries should bypass Togo. To a seasoned observer of Tokyo politics like Ott this could mean but one thing: 'a decision on the question of a move against the south has not yet been made'.[397]

A sudden turn of events in Washington would contribute to dispel any lingering doubts about Japanese intentions. The Tojo government had allowed its two Washington envoys to table two different proposals. One – referred to as Proposal A – involved a staggered retreat of Japanese forces from Indo-China and most of China over a period of twenty-five years. The timeline alone more or less guaranteed that it would be a non-starter. The second (Proposal B) was intended to de-escalate the situation by temporarily returning to the state of affairs that had prevailed prior to the Japanese invasion of southern Indo-China. Accordingly, agreement on this proposal would entail a pledge by both parties not to make any further armed advances into any part of Asia, an American promise to desist from any action that might hinder 'efforts for peace by both Japan and China' as well as the resumption of trade with the Dutch East Indies and US oil sales. A Japanese offer to immediately pull back from southern Indo-China was to be made only 'as occasion demands'.[398] The two key issues that had been blocking the talks so far (the war in China and Japan's alliance with Berlin) were to be shelved for the moment. Despite concerns over the freedom of action this might accord Tokyo, President Roosevelt expressed interest in such an option when the two Japanese envoys took it upon themselves to immediately extend the offer of a retreat from southern Indo-China. Only last-minute British and Chinese protests,[399] as well as revelations from diplomatic decrypts which indicated that Japan was preparing the next stage of its military aggression while still negotiating in Washington,[400] caused Hull to reject this

---

[396] PA/AA, StS Japan, Bd. 5, 615 'Ott an Auswärtiges Amt. Für Herrn Reichsaußenminister (23.11.1941)'. In this fashion, both the Japanese and the Americans (through their codebreaking efforts) were aware that the Washington talks would be broken off on 29 November (later extended to 1 December). Only the Germans were kept in ignorance of this vital fact.

[397] Ibid. Togo had in fact asked the army leadership to stand in for the Gaimusho since in his opinion, 'it would be awkward for me as Foreign Minister to talk directly with Germany through Ambassador Oshima while I am negotiating with the United States'. See '68th Liaison Conference, November 15, 1941'; in: Ike (ed.), Decision for War, pp 244–7.

[398] The two proposals are reproduced in 'Imperial Conference, November 5, 1941'; in: Ibid., pp 208–39, esp. pp 209–11.

[399] For a discussion of the ambiguity of the British position in those days, see Komatsu, 'Magic', pp 318–20.

[400] The extent to which the Japanese position at the talks was doubly compromised by both American foreknowledge of Kurusu's and Nomura's negotiating tactics as well as

idea. On 26 November he presented the two envoys with a note which not only demanded full compliance with all American demands of the past months, but was also couched in terms that may well have led to increased tension.[401] The two envoys were still able to secure an interview with the President on the following day, but nothing of substance came out of this meeting.

Delivery of the Hull Note, as it came to be called, was followed by a press conference which the secretary of state gave for media representatives and in which he confirmed rumours that Japan was preparing an invasion of Thailand in the very near future.[402] Thomsen had to admit that nothing indicated the kind of territorial compromise he had warned about on 17 September, aimed at pacifying Japan at the expense of China or The Netherlands. At the same time, the German envoy was at a loss to predict Roosevelt's next move.[403] Barely a fortnight earlier, he had been quite emphatic in describing a US–Japanese war as an 'open-ended adventure', which would deprive America of the chance to 'defeat Germany through superior production and export of war materiel'.[404] Now, the 'tone and arrogance of American demands' had created a situation that constituted the 'the extreme limit of what could still be described as bluff'.

On the other side of the world, Ott was still far from convinced. As late as 27 November, he reported to Berlin that while both the media and government spokesmen were becoming more assertive in their statements, some evidence still pointed towards a compromise. What he found most striking was the fact that even rumours about a wholesale retreat from China and preparations being made to that end were not being rejected out of hand by his sources in the Japanese armed forces.[405]

On the same day, Oshima was received by Hitler in the Neue Reichskanzlei together with the foreign ministers of the member states of the Anti-Comintern Pact. What passed between them was not recorded, but Oshima had only hours before received assurances from Togo that the Japanese envoys

---

a number of misconceptions arising out of mistranslations of the Magic intercepts is discussed in Komatsu, 'Magic', pp 247–347.

[401] Previous US communications dealing with the same topic had always discriminated between Chinese territory annexed in 1931–2 and Chinese territory occupied since July 1937, something which the Hull Note failed to do, thus creating the impression that Hull might expect Japan to evacuate Manchuria too. President of the Privy Council Hara raised this inconsistency with the other decision makers attending the Imperial Conference of 1 December, without, however, managing to slow the momentum towards war. The extent to which this point could have made the difference between war and peace was much debated by post-war historians. 'Imperial Conference, December 1, 1941'; in: Ike (ed.), Decision for War, pp 262–83, esp. p 279.

[402] PA/AA, StS Japan, Bd. 5, 615 'Thomsen an Auswärtiges Amt. Citissime! (27.11.1941)'.

[403] Ibid.

[404] PA/AA, StS Japan, Bd. 5, 615 'Thomsen an Auswärtiges Amt (15.11.1941)'.

[405] PA/AA, StS Japan, Bd. 5, 615 'Ott an Auswärtiges Amt. Cito! (27.11.1941)'.

were still persevering in the Washington talks 'with a dauntless attitude'; at the same time, he insisted that he would stand by the Tripartite Pact.[406]

The exchanges that made history occurred the following day. First, Hitler received Oshima for a forty-minute talk in the Reichskanzlei. No record of the meeting survives in German files and the telegram to Tokyo giving its gist was only discovered in 1991.[407] Oshima explained that the German leader had immediately enquired about the state of US–Japanese negotiations in Washington. While he assured his Japanese guest that the European conflict was as good as won, growing US hostility made it absolutely necessary for both Germany and Japan to prepare to actively resist American encroachments. On two separate occasions when Hitler pressed the ambassador on a particular point, the hapless diplomat had to admit that 'he had no information'. Oshima finished the telegram by asserting that Germany would support Japan should the latter find itself embroiled in a conflict with the USA.[408] Provided the message is an accurate account of what passed between the two men, it is certainly noteworthy that Hitler does not yet appear to have taken an imminent Japanese entry into the war for granted. This finds a degree of confirmation in the comment he made to the foreign ministers of Italy and Spain the following day. In this conversation he forecast that the war might escalate in the near future as a result of a US–German clash, rather than any moves on the part of Japan.[409]

Late in the evening of the 28th, it was up to Ribbentrop to quiz Oshima in greater detail. This promised to be a crucial exchange, since as yet no unambiguous Japanese response to the German offer of 21 November to join Japan in its upcoming war had been forthcoming. Luckily, what passed between the two men was recorded for posterity not once, but twice over. The German set of minutes, while incomplete, has the advantage of being the work of a professional stenographer working on the spot; Oshima had to record his account for Tokyo from memory. By his own standards, the ambassador showed a greater than average willingness to question some of Ribbentrop's assumptions; the *Reichsaußenminister* found himself increasingly at a loss to produce a plausible scenario for Britain's defeat, even assuming the imminent downfall of the USSR. The truly bizarre aspect of the talks, however, revealed

---

[406] MBPH, Vol. IV App., Doc. 824, 'Tokyo to Berlin (27.11.1941)'. The dignitaries had gathered in Berlin for the renewal of the Anti-Comintern Pact on the evening of 27 November. Since Japan was not in a position to send a foreign minister, Oshima had to do the honours instead.

[407] Reproduced in full in: Krebs, 'Pearl Harbor', pp 367–9.

[408] Ibid.

[409] 'Geheime Reichssache Füh. 58a g.Rs. Aufzeichnung über die Unterredung zwischen dem Führer und dem italienischen Außenminister Graf Ciano sowie dem spanischen Außenminister Serrano Suñer in Anwesenheit des RAM und des Botschafters v. Stohrer in Berlin am 29.11.1941 (30.11.1941)'; in: ADAP, Serie D, Bd. XIII.2, pp 736–7.

itself when Ribbentrop quizzed Oshima on the US–Japanese negotiations and was told by his guest that he 'had received no official word'.[410] It soon became painfully clear that Ribbentrop, who was privy to the gist of Okamoto's and Maeda's preliminary talks with the diplomats of the German embassy in Tokyo, was more up-to-date on the latest Japanese position than Oshima was. Thus, the German foreign minister found himself in the strange position of having to egg Oshima on ('he did not believe that Japan would be able to avoid the confrontation with the US'),[411] while the latter was left making a case for the sort of war Ribbentrop himself had recommended as recently as 9 November, but with one key difference: while the German foreign minister had attempted to sell his allies the idea of a campaign plan that would spare US protectorates in the South Pacific, Oshima now sketched out a campaign plan that would be limited to Thailand and the Dutch East Indies, while sparing both American *and* British possessions. Should London react to such a move, hostilities would of course spread to its possessions too. The ambassador mentioned the USA only in passing since 'he did not believe' that the Americans would react militarily to a Japanese occupation of Thailand and Borneo.[412] Ribbentrop, who by that point must have had in mind Ott's recent warnings about continuing Japanese prevarication, then showed himself willing to settle for something far smaller by dusting off his old scheme of an exclusion zone barring US merchant vessels from Vladivostok. After Oshima rejected this with a transparent excuse,[413] the foreign minister finished the conversation by thrusting upon his guest the statement that in case of Japan entering a war against the USA, 'Germany, of course, would join the war immediately.'[414] Since Oshima lacked the most basic information he would have needed to contextualise this unbidden pledge, it is difficult to see what the conversation had achieved.

The levels of absurdity reached in this exchange may well serve as a symbol for the main problem of German–Japanese relations in 1939–41: while both sides fundamentally agreed on their right to 'living space' at the expense of others and even shared a common set of enemies, a chronic inability to synchronise their cycles of aggression, so to speak, almost doomed their alliance. In this case the outbreak of war was only days away and even the most preliminary exchange about a possible military alliance that might supersede the Tripartite Pact had yet to take place.

[410] MBPH, Vol. IV App., Doc. 822, 'Berlin to Tokyo (29.11.1941)'.
[411] 'Aufzeichnung über den Empfang des japanischen Botschafters Oshima durch den Herrn RAM am 28.11.1941 abends. Geheime Reichssache RAM 58'; in: ADAP, Serie D, Bd. XIII.2, pp 708–10.
[412] Ibid., pp 709–10.
[413] Ibid., 710. Oshima claimed that drifting Soviet mines had turned out to be too great a hazard, forcing the Americans to terminate these supply runs.
[414] MBPH, Vol. IV App., Doc. 822, 'Berlin to Tokyo (29.11.1941)', p A-383.

It took another Liaison Conference in Tokyo on 29 November and a total of forty-eight hours before Togo finally saw fit to send his ambassador a series of telegrams which would have enlightened him as to what Ribbentrop had been trying to tell him on the late evening of the 28th. The first missive stated unambiguously that the Washington talks had effectively collapsed and spoke of the need to move troops into parts of Southeast Asia to forestall impending Allied moves. After that, 'war may suddenly break out . . . through some clash of arms'. As if to make up for lost time, the telegram ended with the words that 'war may come quicker than anyone dreams'.[415] The second part appears to have contained the Japanese demand that its allies join it in its war against the USA based on the spirit, if not quite the letter, of the Tripartite Pact; it also listed the key points to be included in a proper military alliance that would seal such an agreement, especially the need for a clause not to agree to a separate peace.[416] The third and final part of the telegram made it clear that Japan would not be able to yield to any German demands that it turn on the USSR, thus depriving Oshima of critical room for manoeuvre.[417] Two further telegrams gave a rather peculiar summary of why the talks had failed, which the ambassador was expected to share with his German hosts. According to this précis, it was Japan's selfless resistance to the insistent American demand that Japan ditch the Tripartite Pact that had led to the collapse of the Nomura–Hull talks.[418]

Ott, in the meantime, found himself left out of the loop. In a conference with Togo on the 30th, the Japanese Foreign Minister stopped well short of describing the Washington talks as a failure and merely hinted at his expectation that in such an eventuality the Axis powers 'would stand by Japan'. He did, however, use the opportunity to slip in yet another comment about the desirability of a compromise peace with a Russian successor regime after the fall of Moscow.[419]

Over the next three days, the race to war entered a bizarre hiatus which was, of course, more apparent than real. Thomsen in Washington did not foresee a Japanese move that would go beyond Thailand and in fact gave more thought to war in the Pacific breaking out as a result of an American aggression;[420] he all but ruled out such a move in a separate message, in which he stressed again the American dependency on rubber imports from Southeast Asia, since substitutes in sufficient quantity were still a few years in the future.[421] For

---

[415] MBPH, Vol. IV App., Doc. 825, 'Tokyo to Berlin (30.11.1941)'.
[416] Even though this part was lost, its contents can be extrapolated from subsequent communications. See Herde, *Weg in den Krieg*, p 82.
[417] MBPH, Vol. IV App., Doc. 826, 'Tokyo to Berlin (30.11.1941)'.
[418] MBPH, Vol. IV App., Doc. 828, 'Tokyo to Berlin (30.11.1941)'; ibid., Doc. 829, 'Tokyo to Berlin (30.11.1941)'.
[419] PA/AA, StS Japan, Bd. 5, 615, 'Ott an Auswärtiges Amt. Citissime! (30.11.1941)'.
[420] PA/AA, StS Japan, Bd. 5, 615, 'Thomsen an Auswärtiges Amt. Cito! (3.12.1941)'.
[421] PA/AA, StS USA, Bd. 10, 615, 'Thomsen an Auswärtiges Amt (4.12.1941)'.

his part, Ott reassured Berlin that the position of those Japanese decision makers who had always made a case for compromise had been considerably weakened by the impact of the Hull Note; on the other hand, military operations might be limited to Thailand only, with further moves dependent on the development of the international situation.[422] Oshima thus found himself in the unaccustomed position of being better informed than any of his counterparts, so that turning Hitler's and Ribbentrop's assorted pledges to join Japan in a war against the USA into reality fell finally to him, Togo's man on the spot in Berlin. When he was received by Ribbentrop on the evening of 1 December, he was told that Hitler had left Berlin and could not be contacted.[423] Only on 3 December, when an increasingly anxious Oshima revisited him, did the German foreign minister hint in broad terms at the German dictator's absence at or near the Russian Front.[424] The combination of the Japanese government's peculiar obsession with putting off an approach to Germany until the last possible moment with Hitler's unheralded trip to the Ukraine had produced a situation in which the complicated campaign plan for the simultaneous invasion of Southeast Asia and attack on Pearl Harbor threatened to overtake diplomatic negotiations with Berlin and Rome, thus reducing Oshima's room for negotiation to virtually nothing. By seeing off the new Tripartite alliance to such a bumbling start, the Japanese government had handed Germany's leaders a major potential advantage in the negotiations. Japan thus briefly found itself in a situation of being a virtual supplicant before a partner whose trustworthiness was still being questioned by some of its decision makers. On 5 November, Yoshimichi Hara at the Imperial Conference had pointed out that embracing Germany as an ally meant shackling the empire to an ally whose well-known racist ideology would lead it to betray Tokyo sooner or later, possibly by joining an anti-Japanese entente of 'the white powers'.[425]

Upon Hitler's return from the Ukraine to Rastenburg in the afternoon of 4 December, Ribbentrop was given the go-ahead to turn the Tripartite Pact into a proper military alliance along the lines suggested by Oshima.[426] By now the window of opportunity to do so with some calm was fast closing, but it is important to remember that the Germans only had the sketchiest idea of Japan's war plans and were completely ignorant of the planned Pearl Harbor

---

[422] PA/AA, StS Japan Bd. 5, 615 'Ott an Auswärtiges Amt. Citissime! Für Herrn Reichsminister (3.12.1941)'.

[423] MBPH, Vol. IV App., Doc. 831, 'Berlin to Tokyo (2.12.1941)'.

[424] MBPH, Vol. IV App., Doc. 833, 'Berlin to Tokyo (3.12.1941)'. For Hitler's visit to the headquarters of 1. Panzerarmee and Heeresgruppe Süd, see the chapter on operations in Russia.

[425] 'Imperial Conference, November 5, 1941'; in: Ike (ed.), Decision for War, p 237.

[426] It has been impossible to determine the exact time at which Ribbentrop got in touch with Hitler to brief him on Oshima's proposal. If on his return, the dictator took time off for a nap, it may well have been late afternoon. See Mawdsley, December 1941, pp 109–10.

strike. As regards timing, the latest intelligence update they received came from one of Wenneker's contacts in Tokyo, who on 6 December promised the opening of hostilities against both Britain and the United States 'by Christmas'.[427] The negotiations proceeded pretty smoothly, with only a few minor differences of opinion to be ironed out, but the mere act of exchanging several drafts between the three capitals was bound to consume time, with poor radio communication between Europe and Japan adding to the problem. A few hours before news of the strike on Oahu reached Berlin, Oshima was instructed by Togo to tell Ribbentrop 'that Japan is expecting Italy and Germany to go to war against Britain and America before this agreement is officially signed'.[428] By the evening of the same day, both Hitler and his foreign minister who, at least in the case of the latter, had still harboured some residual doubts about Japan's willingness to do more than invade Thailand,[429] were informed that Japan had just initiated hostilities in a manner strongly suggesting an absolutely irrevocable commitment.

Since at this point the only treaty binding Germany to Japan was the original Tripartite Pact, which ruled out assisting a nation that had initiated hostilities, Hitler could in theory have added last-minute demands, like a blockade zone around Vladivostok. This did occur to Ott when he was informed by Togo of the Pearl Harbor strike,[430] and it did not, in fact, constitute an unreasonable demand in exchange for a declaration of war on the USA. Some last-minute blackmail of this kind would, of course, have gone a long way towards bearing out the sort of misgivings voiced by Hara a month previously. That the dictator eschewed this option is yet another indicator that he did not as yet perceive the news from the Russian Front as warning of a serious crisis.

His insistence on the clause forbidding separate peace agreements, on the other hand, seems downright quaint, coming as it did from a ruler who never signed an accord he would not have been happy to break at a moment's notice. The most plausible explanation for his emphasis on this point also allows us to make sense of his apparent failure to even consider the possibility of simply sitting out the beginning of the Pacific conflict and giving himself some time to consider his options. Quite apart from the need not to upset the possibly brittle and hence ephemeral consensus for war in Tokyo, he had to consider the

---

[427] BA/MA, RM 12 II/250 'Kriegstagebuch Marineattache Tokio. Rücksprache Freg.Kpt. Shiba (entry for 6 December 1941)'.

[428] MBPH, Vol. IV App., Doc. 840 (7.12.1941).

[429] Instructions from his office to continue seditious work among German-Americans appears to indicate that Ribbentrop did not yet believe in the outbreak of war between Japan and the Western powers in the near future. See PA/AA, StS USA, Bd. 10 'Richtlinien für die Beeinflussung der öffentlichen Meinung in den Vereinigten Staaten (2.12.1941)'.

[430] 'Der Botschafter in Tokio an das Auswärtige Amt. Citissime (9.12.1941)'; in: ADAP, Serie D, Bd. XIII.2, pp 805–7.

possibility that the Allies might decide to buy off the Japanese by allowing them to keep some of their initial conquests, a possibility Thomsen and Boetticher had warned about in mid-September.[431] Apparently oblivious to the outrage that the sneak attack on Oahu had caused in the USA, the possibility that the allies might decide to buy off Berlin's fickle ally, even after the latter's initiation of hostilities, had Hitler and Ribbentrop genuinely concerned until about the turn of the year.[432]

In the end, the treaty was signed in Berlin on 11 December 1941, minutes before Hitler began reading out his declaration of war on the USA to the assembled deputies of the Reichstag. Against all the odds, Germany and Japan had finally managed to become allies.

4.5 Conclusion

The long and tortuous road chosen by Japan's elites to take their country into war has been the subject of many scholarly studies, the majority of which have focused on the deterioration of US–Japanese relations in 1940–1. *Staatssekretär* Weizsäcker in a private letter claimed to have predicted the course of events as far back as 1938 – namely, that Japan would choose to actively join Germany in its endeavour to overturn the Versailles order by violent means once a consensus among its leaders had been reached that the moment was right and not one day sooner.[433] Even so, the German side of the story is still relevant for what it tells us about Hitler's reasoning about global warfare. The fact that the Japan of the period was a society where assorted government officials and military officers had more or less openly preached the desirability of a war of aggression against the West since April 1940 should have made such a meeting of minds a foregone conclusion. In practice, however, Ribbentrop in Berlin and Ott in Tokyo must have felt most of the time that they were engaged in a fool's errand.

To begin with, the road to a German–Japanese alliance was cratered with the potholes provided by a uniquely opaque and contradictory decision-making process on the Japanese side. Even at the best of times this was utterly

---

[431] PA/AA, Handakten Etzdorf, Politische Berichte Washington. 'Bericht Mil.Att. Washington vom 13.9.1941 (15.9.1941)'; ibid., StS Japan, Bd. 4, 612, 'Thomsen an Auswärtiges Amt. Cito! Für Herrn Staatssekretär (17.9.1941)'.

[432] Sources pointing in this direction are: PA/AA, Handakten Ritter 17, Nr. 7631 'Für den Vortrag beim Führer über die militärische Vereinbarung mit Japan (30.12.1941)'; 'Wolfsschanze 31.12.1941/1.1.1942, nachts. H/Fu.'; in: Werner Jochmann (ed.), *Adolf Hitler. Monologe im Führerhauptquartier 1941–1944* (München: Orbis 2000), pp 178–9; see also 'Aus dem Notizbuch von Hitlers Historiographen (13.2.1942)'; in: Marianne Feuersenger, *Im Vorzimmer der Macht. Aufzeichnungen aus dem Wehrmachtführungsstab und Führerhauptquartier* (München: Herbig 1999), pp 106–10.

[433] 'Note by Weizsäcker (11.4.1941)'; in: Hill (ed.), *Papiere*, pp 245–6. See also Weizsäcker, *Erinnerungen*, p 326.

dependent on the establishment of a consensus between the key power centres in Tokyo and sometimes even between factions within those. Even a clear-cut and unambiguous statement of intent (Banzai's visit to OKH in August 1941 comes to mind) could well be nothing more than a fleeting manifestation of an ongoing process of fermentation which in any case might not reach further than one power centre – in this case, the army. At the same time, Ribbentrop was conscious of the fact that Japan's field army in particular by now enjoyed such a reputation for taking unilateral action in open defiance of the government that any attempt at a joint strategy between Tokyo and Berlin might easily be upset by elements of the Kwantung Army deciding to strike ahead of time or at the wrong enemy.

To make an already farcical situation even worse, Matsuoka through a sleight of hand had sown the seeds of distrust by effectively turning the Tripartite Pact into a fair-weather treaty where Japan was concerned. This would probably have been bad enough even if a consensus had been established by both sides to adhere to a strict code of silence where this matter was concerned. Instead, this clause was liberally referred to by Gaimusho spokesmen in their statements to the Western media, causing considerable consternation and exasperation in Berlin and Rome. The armed forces, on the other hand, did their best to hide their own internal struggles from the Germans by making half-baked commitments to the Axis cause, which were then hedged with absurd demands that the Wehrmacht should first land in Britain or invade Egypt. Last, but not least, the one Japanese decision maker (Matsuoka) who had come closest to consistently making a case for an alignment with the Axis powers was unceremoniously dismissed from the cabinet in July 1941. In light of such inconsistencies, the Germans eventually reached the conclusion that their would-be allies were probably seeking a better deal from the West. In the first such instance (the so-called John Doe talks), a diplomatic initiative that lacked any real backing was seen as a genuine threat. In the second case, a mere supposition (Thomsen warning Berlin about an American offer to swap parts of the East Indies for Japanese cooperation) substituted for fact.

Under these circumstances, it was by no means a foregone conclusion that Berlin and Tokyo would end up as allies and it is impossible to deny the key role played by the German dictator who, after some hesitation, provided something like consistency to the entire process. Throughout the 1930s, his interest in Japan, while genuine, had been of a pragmatic nature and he had showed some inclination to sacrifice it to other options as evidenced by the signing of his pact with Stalin or his cold-shouldering of Tokyo while there appeared to be a chance of the British seeking a compromise peace after Dunkirk. It is only after this possibility became exceedingly remote and the armed forces of Fascist Italy turned from dubious asset into catastrophic liability that German attempts to 'activate' Imperial Japan as a military ally acquired a consistent theme. Only once do these appear to have taken the form of directing Japan's potential for aggression against the USA, when the signing of the Lend-Lease Bill into law incited Hitler to extend an offer to go to war against the USA if Japanese expansion into Southeast Asia were to meet with a violent reaction from Washington. Since this offer met with no Japanese response, by May the dictator merely described Japan's role in forging an Axis strategy against the USA as 'key', without however making clear whether he preferred Tokyo to play the role of aggressor or deterrent.

Such musings had to take a back seat to damage control when it appeared that a US–Japanese deal might be possible. Hence the seemingly abrupt change of strategy of 28 June 1941, which attempted to redirect Japanese aggression against the USSR. It was undoubtedly favoured by Ambassador Ott's telegram of 6 June, which was adamant in ruling out an aggressive move by Tokyo against any Western combination, even if Germany were to be the wronged party in an incident with the USA.

A war against the USSR, on the other hand, might just about be seen as both acceptable and viable. Even if Ribbentrop's post-war account that he unilaterally initiated this change in policy is correct, there can be no doubt that the dictator ultimately went along with it. The assumption that Ribbentrop could have carried out this initiative behind Hitler's back, thus suggesting a fundamental dissent at the top of the Nazi state,[434] is untenable. Even assuming he had had the sheer nerve to keep up such a charade over a period of more than four months, it presupposes a degree of control over proceedings at Führer's Headquarters that Ribbentrop never had. To begin with, a number of senior military figures were also copied into a sizeable fraction of the reports emanating from the embassy in Tokyo; the extent to which they discussed their contents with Hitler would have been completely outside the foreign minister's control. Moreover, for such a scheme to work, he would at the very least have had to be sure of the active collusion of the point man of the Auswärtiges Amt on Hitler's staff responsible for submitting incoming diplomatic messages to the dictator;[435] since Walther Hewel was a NSDAP veteran of the 1923

---

[434] This is the view put forward both in Andreas Hillgruber, *Deutsche Großmacht- und Weltpolitik* (Düsseldorf: Droste Verlag 1978), p 216, and Bernd Martin, *Japan and Germany in the Modern World* (Oxford: Berghahn 1995), pp 245, 251.

[435] The log kept by Hewel (PA/AA, R 27487, 'Betr. Botschafter Hewel. Vorlagen beim Führer vom Januar 1940 bis April 1942') indicates that a wide spread of missives from German ambassadors and envoys was regularly submitted to Hitler for his perusal, even though usually with a minor delay (two or three days) after their receipt at the Auswärtiges Amt. Instructions given by the dictator and entered into the log indicate that Hewel either gave an verbal summary for the dictator's benefit or that Hitler himself skim-read at least some of the documents.

coup with far closer ties to Hitler than to Ribbentrop, this would have been a very doubtful proposition to say the least.[436]

The month of August arguably did see Hitler manifesting his interest in Japan joining the war against the USSR, with a consistency that suggested an agenda going beyond a scheme to ruin a US–Japanese détente. This undoubtedly reflected his concern over the stalemate in front of *Heeresgruppe Mitte*, proof of which can be found in the suddenness with which he gave instructions to ease off on the Japanese government once the military situation improved markedly in the days after 8 September. It is noteworthy that this growing remoteness between Tokyo and Berlin was mirrored by the dictator's declining interest in the possibility of confronting the USA. Documentary evidence of this can be found throughout the period of mid-September to mid-November, thus calling into question the notion that the October offensive against the Red Army grouping at Vyasma-Bryansk and the subsequent drive on Moscow were in any way dictated by a desire to galvanise the Japanese into action by further diminishing Soviet power. This culminated in the period of late October and early November when Hitler appeared to be downright hostile to the idea of Japan's participation in the war, since this might make a peace deal more difficult. Over and above the fact that he may well have been under the impression – mistaken or not – that such an entreaty might be feasible, during this period he would still have drawn strength from the series of spectacular victories scored over the Red Army between mid-September and mid-October. When the first days of November brought mounting evidence that Japan might finally take the plunge and go to war against all Western powers in the Pacific, Hitler's and Ribbentrop's first reaction – even at the risk of damaging German credibility by yet another about-turn – was to restrain the Japanese from extending their war of aggression to the USA.

By the third week of November, however, the political situation had changed. By gutting the Neutrality Act both Houses of Congress ensured not just British survival but Britain's offensive potential for the foreseeable future. With London's position considerably strengthened, a compromise peace was made that much less likely. As far back as November 1939, Hitler had clearly stated that the dismantling of the existing Neutrality Laws would have to be regarded as the ultimate tripwire indicating that war with the USA was inevitable.[437] Until then, his expressed preference was for Japan to direct its aggression against British possessions in Southeast Asia (December 1940–June 1941), then the Soviet Union (July–October 1941), then Britain again (November 1941). Throughout this period, with the sole exception of the

---

[436] On the Hewel-Ribbentrop relationship, see Ulrich Schlie (ed.), *Albert Speer. Die Kransberg-Protokolle 1945* (München: Herbig 2003), pp 237–8.

[437] '23.11., 12 Uhr: Besprechung beim Führer, zu der alle Oberbefehlshaber befohlen sind'; in: Wagner (ed.), *Lagevorträge*, pp 49–55, esp. p 52.

exchange with Matsuoka on 4 April, the dictator and his foreign minister had actively and consistently attempted to steer Japan away from confrontation with the USA. When faced with the passing of the revised neutrality legislation by both Houses of Congress, Hitler was so dumbfounded for a few days that he even began to return to the theme of a compromise peace which, while unlikely enough to begin with, had now been all but ruled out by Washington's new stance. In such a situation the Japanese offer to join Germany in its war must have seemed like a godsend, especially since it must have been painfully obvious to all German decision makers that none of the military successes Japanese spokesmen had always insisted on as dowry for a military alliance (a landing in Britain, the fall of Egypt, the breaching of the Caucasus) would be forthcoming for quite some time yet. Even so, the litany of half-baked promises that had reached the German leader from Tokyo throughout the year must have left him with an important element of residual doubt about this latest offer. This explains his overjoyed reaction on the evening of the 7th: not only had the Japanese finally thrown down the gauntlet, they had done so in a manner that indicated a serious commitment.

Facing the Same Dilemma: the US and German Quest for Rubber

5.1 Introduction

In the last days of 1941, Adolf Hitler shared some of his thoughts on the situation created by his recent declaration of war on the USA with his Luftwaffe adjutant, Nicolaus von Below.[1] The way he saw it, plans for a resumption of offensive operations against the USSR would proceed irrespective of this strategic upheaval. To the Americans, 'the endangered US possessions in the South Seas, such as the Philippines, constituted a higher priority than the war in Europe'. The American government would be forced to follow this order of priorities by the 'decisive role' played by concerns over a subject disconnected from matters of political prestige or military strategy: the preservation of the US economy's access to rubber grown in Southeast Asia.[2] That the German dictator should view the Far Eastern theatre of war in such a light is a wholly new insight; thus far, he had rationalised some major operations with the need to seize or secure access to raw materials for Germany.[3] The case of Far Eastern rubber appears to indicate that he was equally capable of integrating natural resources into a strategy of denial.

5.2 The Role of Rubber in the Second Industrial Revolution and the Role of the Plantation System

Natural rubber is found in the form of a milky latex produced by more than 100 wild-growing plants ranging from vines to trees. A hydrocarbon polymer, it was first examined scientifically by the French explorer François Fresneau,

---

[1] BA/MA, N 745/4 'Was ich als Hitlers Luftwaffenadjutant erlebte (aufgezeichnet im Winter 1949/49)'. This manuscript is virtually identical with the memoirs first published by Below in 1980. Two brief paragraphs discussing Hitler's thinking on his declaration of war on the USA, however, were omitted from the published edition. They are used here for the first time.

[2] Ibid. The choice of words ('gefährdet', i.e., 'endangered') implies quite strongly that the outcome of the campaign for the Philippines still hung in the balance. This suggests a date prior to Manila being declared an 'open city' (26 December 1941), since this event would have indicated that the battle had clearly turned against the Americans.

[3] Swedish iron ore in the case of the invasion of Norway, Soviet oil in the planning of the second summer campaign against the USSR.

who spent several years in the 1740s touring Spain's American colonies.[4] For the next eighty years its uses would be limited and its potential at first largely unrecognised. This was at least in part due to its inherent limitations. Even though it was known that exposing it to heat and smoke turned the milk into a malleable mass, this mass would invariably turn soft at high temperatures and hard at low ones, quite apart from giving off an unpleasant smell. It was only the discovery of vulcanisation in 1839 that gave the world a finished product of much improved tensile strength, shelf life and tolerance to changing temperatures. For the next three decades the new commodity's uses remained limited until the simultaneous advent of electricity and a new type of wheeled transport caused rubber to become an indispensable item to both industrial progress and military success. The introduction of the bicycle on a large scale from the 1870s led to a first spike in demand, but this was as nothing when compared to the voracious demand unleashed by the invention and then large-scale marketing of the motor car in the following decades. When solid tyres were progressively replaced by the pneumatic tyre from the 1890s onwards,[5] this led to yet another increase in demand, since the latter needed more rubber than the former. In a parallel development, both electrical and telegraph cables crisscrossing first countries and then continents were in need of insulation in order to ensure a long working life.

Around the turn of the century, the demands of the industrialised nations were mostly met by the Amazon territories of Brazil, Peru and Bolivia, along with Mexico and the Congo Free State.[6] The rubber being exploited came from the *Hevea brasiliensis* tree (or in the case of the Congo, the *Landolphia owariensis* vine), growing wild. *Hevea* trees took a while (five to seven years) to reach maturity, when they could safely be tapped, but they soon proved superior to all other plants for the quality and quantity of their yield. Periodic political unrest in Brazil in the years after the proclamation of the republic (1889) coincided with the discovery that planting *Hevea* trees in Malaya allowed unprecedented economies of scale; while in Brazil a range of predators and parasites (especially South American leaf blight, *Mycrocyclus ulei*) made short work of any attempt to bunch the trees together in big

---

[4] For the gradual process of discovery of natural rubber by the Europeans, see John Loadman, 'Der Baum der weint. Vom Blutgummi zum Plantagenkautschuk'; in: Ulrich Giersch and Ulrich Kubisch (eds.), *Gummi. Die elastische Faszination* (Ratingen: Dr. Gupta 1995) pp 32–47.

[5] A pneumatic bicycle tyre was first licensed in 1888, with a design suited for motor cars following in 1895.

[6] Between 1905 and 1913 Mexican rubber tapped from the *guayule* plant accounted for 19 per cent of US demand in 1910 alone. This project eventually came to grief as result of the Mexican revolution of 1911 and the civil wars that followed it. See Mark F. Finlay, *Growing American Rubber: Strategic Plans and the Politics of National Security* (New Brunswick, NJ: Rutgers UP 2009), pp 22–9.

plantations, the different ecosystem in Malaya posed no such obstacles. As a result, rubber exports from Southeast Asia (mostly Malaya) went from 821 tons in 1900 to 50,000 tons in 1913. Brazil found itself relegated to second place, despite the fact that its share increased from 26,323 tons to 39,000 tons over the same period.[7]

The explosion in demand created by World War I should have given naturally grown rubber a last chance to defend its share of the market, but by 1920 the balance sheet was unambiguous: Brazilian exports in that year were stuck at 23,616 tons and those of the Congo at fewer than 5,000 tons, while Malaya had exported 174,322 tons. Crucially, the British success with introducing *Hevea* had found imitators in the region. In 1920 the Dutch East Indies exported 75,522 tons and Ceylon 39,532, with French Vietnam and Thailand also beginning to join in.[8]

The 1920s and 1930s saw further exponential growth fuelled by the motorisation of all developed societies, which even the Great Depression failed to dent more than briefly. On the downside, rubber prices stayed erratic throughout much of this period. The rubber-producing countries attempted to counter this by two schemes. The first one, the informal Stevenson Restriction Scheme (1922–8), enjoyed a measure of success in 1924 and 1925 but on account of a failure to get the Dutch to participate led only to an increase in the Dutch East Indies' share in annual rubber production. May 1934 saw a renewed effort, with government representatives of all rubber-producing countries signing The Hague Treaty. It was rather more successful in putting a check on overproduction because, as an intergovernmental treaty, it had the force of law behind it.[9] Both agreements – the Stevenson Scheme and The Hague Treaty – incentivised consumer countries to invest in an industry dedicated to the large-scale reclaiming of old rubber and recycling it into new tyres, a development that would have important consequences in wartime.

By 1940, wild-growing rubber had become an irrelevance. The Dutch East Indies produced 537,465 tons, and in so doing drew almost exactly level with Malaya. Vietnam, Thailand and Northern Borneo/Sarawak totalled 188,106 tons. Contributions from Brazil, Liberia and Congo all hovered around 10,000

---

[7] Howard Wolf and Ralph Wolf, *Rubber: A Story of Glory and Greed* (New York: Covici Friede 1936), p 136. Also G. L. Wallace, 'Economic and social aspects of the industry'; in: P. Schidrowitz and T. R. Dawson (eds.), *History of the Rubber Industry* (Cambridge: W. Hefer & Sons 1952), p 329, Austin Coates, *The Commerce in Rubber: The First 250 Years* (Oxford: OUP 1987), pp 161, 164 and Wilhelm Treue, *Gummi in Deutschland. Die deutsche Kautschukversorgung und Gummi-Industrie im Rahmen weltwirtschaftlicher Entwicklungen* (München: F. Bruckmann 1955), p 121. Unless otherwise stated, figures given are in long tons (=1,008 kgs).

[8] Figures according to G. L. Wallace, 'Statistical and economic outline'; in: Schidrowitz and Dawson (eds.), *History*, pp 337–45, esp. p 329.

[9] On the negotiations that led to The Hague treaty, see Coates, *Commerce*, pp 274–9.

tons. Virtually the totality of the global production for 1940 (1,388,001 tons) came from Southeast Asia.[10] For the nations outside the orbit of the Tripartite Pact, the idea of unlimited access to this cornucopia was something they now took for granted. Only the USSR enjoyed a measure of autarky, its first synthetic rubber factory having come on line in 1936.[11]

5.3 The German Quest for Autarky

No country entered World War II better prepared for a world without natural rubber than Germany. The seeds for this development had been sown in 1914, when on account of the short-sightedness of its general staff it found itself fighting an open-ended war while under blockade. The first reclaim facilities alone would never have been enough to rescue Germany from this predicament, since reclaimed rubber still required the admixture of 10–30 per cent fresh rubber. Last-minute imports from neutral countries and booty seized in occupied countries or even on the high seas played a key role in helping the Germans stave off a total collapse. Even so, by 1918 most army trucks were left running on metal or wooden contraptions for wheels, which by churning up roads materially contributed to the slowing down of the German spring offensive of that year.[12]

The ingenuity of German scientists had nonetheless led to the development of the world's first synthetic rubber, giving the country's leaders a brief glimpse of future possibilities. Methyl rubber was extremely costly and laborious to produce and moreover too leather-like to be used for tyres.[13] Instead, most of the 2,500 tons produced were earmarked for insulating the batteries of the U-boats that fought in the First Battle of the Atlantic.[14] The limited use of this methyl rubber and its high price, however, meant that any further work on it was discontinued when the war ended.

It was only gradually resumed in 1925, when the newly created IG Farben chemical-industry conglomerate decided to return to the drawing board and

[10] All figures according to Wallace, 'Statistical and Economic Outline', p 329.

[11] After years of research, Dr Sergei Vasiljevich Lebedev had developed a process that allowed the production of polybutadiene in industrial quantities. Though its qualities were not equal to those of natural rubber, the finished product could be used for car tyres. The contribution of Soviet synthetic rubber to Allied victory is a subject still awaiting scholarly investigation. For German estimates of Soviet wartime production, see IWM, Speer Collection, FD 4479 'Vortragsnotiz SU-Kautschukversorgung 1942/43'; ibid., 'Kautschukversorgung 1942/43. Gemeinsame Beurteilung Wi-Amt/Wi-Ausl. VI u. Ic (16.12.1942)'.

[12] David Zabecki, *The German 1918 Offensives: A Case Study in the Operational Level of War* (London: Routledge 2006), pp 86–8.

[13] Gottfried Plumpe, 'Industrie, technischer Fortschritt und Staat. Die Kautschuksynthese in Deutschland 1906–1944/45'; in: *Geschichte und Gesellschaft* 9 (1983), pp 564–97.

[14] Ibid., p 572.

retrace the steps taken by one of its subsidiaries (Bayer Leverkusen) just before and during the war. The temporary success of the Stevenson Restriction Scheme in keeping prices up played a role in this. The extreme limitations of methyl rubber meant that research had to start almost from scratch.[15] Progress was largely facilitated by the discovery of a chemical process whereby coal and lime were brought together and turned into calcium carbide. A number of chemical processes were then needed to turn it first into acetylene and then the all-important butadiene, the basic raw material of synthetic rubber. Adding sodium (natrium in German, hence the acronym Buna: butadiene–natrium) in the final stage would produce a straight butadiene polymer of rubber-like qualities. The entire process was also feasible with the oil derivate, naphtha, used instead of coal. Even though a patent was taken out as early as June 1929, several more years of experiments were needed before the final product – automobile tyres made of the general-purpose Buna-S – could be presented at the Berlin Automobile Fair of early 1936. This was a copolymer which combined butadiene (75 per cent) and styrene (25 per cent).[16] This development gave the Germans a slight edge over the Soviet product and placed them well ahead of the American competition.[17] Even though in 1931 two American corporations had announced the imminent commercialisation of two synthetic rubbers named Thiokol and Neoprene, these two products lacked the resilience and tensile strength necessary for use in tyre production. It was only their high resistance to petrol, oil and solvents that allowed the American products to secure a niche market in the following years.

In Germany, enthusiasm for the new tyres was at first limited. In the early 1930s, many of their properties still marked them out as inferior to those made of natural rubber; the armed forces drew attention to their high production cost and for a time came close to stonewalling the entire project. Hitler's unambiguous stance, however, brooked no compromise: he made a point of announcing the beginning of work on the first of three rubber plants in a major public speech in February 1936; he also rejected the idea of creating a stockpile because such a scheme was fraught with too many uncertainties.[18] It is important to stress that at that time many IG Farben scientists still harboured

[15] Ibid., p 574, describes the original synthetic rubber as 'a dead end'.
[16] For the chemistry of Buna production, see Sigrid Koch, 'Buna wird zum Symbol eines Triumphs der Chemie'; in: Giersch and Kubisch (eds.), Faszination, pp 116–25, as well as P. T. Bauer, The Rubber Industry: A Study in Competition and Monopoly (London: Longmans 1948), pp 287–91.
[17] Even though of similar composition, the addition of styrene gave German Buna-S a slight advantage in quality over Soviet tyres made of polybutadiene rubber.
[18] 'Rede vor Vertretern der deutschen Automobilindustrie (15.2.1936)'; in: Max Domarus (ed.), Hitler. Reden und Proklamationen 1932–1945, Bd. I (Wiesbaden: R. Löwitt 1973), pp 576–9. For a discussion of the viability of a stockpiling scheme, see Plumpe, 'Kautschuksynthese', pp 594–5.

important residual doubts about the technological viability of the entire scheme.[19] IG Farben was nonetheless given the right economic incentives and soon two major factories at Schkopau and Hüls began large-scale production of Buna. Using feedback from the as yet not entirely satisfied army, IG's laboratories continued the search for improvements, and already by 1939, 22,400 tons were being produced, with the long-term aim being a yearly output of 170,000 tons. Production peaked in 1943 at 118,700 tons, with the 1944 production still coming to a respectable 103,400 tons, damaging air raids on the factories notwithstanding.[20] This gave a total amount of Buna to satisfy – though only just – most of the needs of Germany's armed forces and the economy supporting them. On the downside, Buna suffered from a number of limitations. Rubber products containing Buna could be recycled only once,[21] thus severely limiting the potential of the recycling branch of the German rubber industry, which had played so crucial a role in 1914–18. Buna's poor strength under high temperatures meant that it could not be used for heavy truck or aircraft tyres, leading to heavy trucks being phased out of the Wehrmacht's inventory.[22] Car tyres made out of 100 per cent Buna were trialled from early 1941 on, but with decidedly mixed results.[23] For most other products, a constant supply of fresh rubber was needed because the new compound required an admixture of the natural product for reasons of quality. However, the reserve available on the war's outbreak (17,815 tons), the booty captured during the 1940 Blitzkrieg (7,500 tons), rubber imported between September 1939 and June 1941 via the Trans-Siberian Railway (50,000 tons plus) as well as the tonnage brought in on surface or submarine

[19] Ibid., pp 581–4.
[20] Figures for 1940, 1941 and 1942 were 40,900, 70,600 and 100,500 tons respectively. See ibid., p 592.
[21] BA/MA, RW 19/1467 'OKW/Wi Rü Amt Kautschuk und die Versorgungslage im Kriege (März 1941)'.
[22] Ibid. This limitation was common to all Buna-type synthetic rubbers of the 1930s and 1940s. Only in 1954 did the pooling of German wartime research with American innovations produce a type of synthetic rubber that could take the place of the best natural rubber used for airplane and heavy truck tyres; see Jochen Streb, 'Technologiepolitik im Zweiten Weltkrieg. Die staatliche Förderung der Synthesekautschukproduktion im deutsch-amerikanischen Vergleich'; in: Vierteljahrshefte für Zeitgeschichte Bd. 50 (Juli 2002), pp 367–98, esp. p 394. In the present day, the sole advantage of natural rubber over the synthetic variety is a slightly higher resistance to freezing temperatures, which accounts for its use in winter tyres. Johannes Winterhagen, 'Rund erneuert. Der Reifen der Zukunft muss vor allem energieeffizient sein'; in: Frankfurter Allgemeine Zeitung – 'Technik und Motor' supplement (6.11.2012).
[23] Werner Rahn and Gerhard Schreiber (eds.) Kriegstagebuch der Seekriegsleitung, Teil A, Bd. 24 (Herford: Mittler & Sohn 1991) (entry for 20 August 1941). See also Paul Erker, Vom nationalen zum globalen Wettbewerb. Die deutsche und amerikanische Reifenindustrie im 19. und 20. Jahrhundert (Paderborn: Ferdinand Schöningh 2005), pp 428, 439–45.

blockade runners from the Far East until 1944 (44,495 tons) was enough to satisfy this particular need.[24] The last, arguably most serious, drawback was its lack of secrecy. Before Hitler's rise to power, American scientists had been able to catch a glimpse of the chemistry that made Buna possible.

5.4   The US Quest for Autarky

The search for alternatives to Southeast Asian plantation rubber in the United States was the direct result of the Stevenson Restriction Scheme of the 1920s. American individuals and companies explored a number of possible alternatives. While blessed with only limited success, this process still played an important role: it meant that by the time the USA found itself confronting a rubber famine almost overnight in 1942, a number of possible substitutes had already been explored and ruled out.

By far the most successful attempt to alleviate America's dependency on Far Eastern rubber had come in the form of Washington's reaction to the 1920s Stevenson cartel. Coordinated and supported by Secretary of Commerce Herbert Hoover, the rubber industry invested heavily in reclaim facilities of the kind that had played such a crucial role in supplying Imperial Germany with at least a minimum of rubber. In 1921 41,400 tons of reclaimed rubber were processed. By 1928 the output already totalled 223,000 tons.[25] The experience thus gained would prove invaluable in stretching US reserves in 1942–3.

Attempts that took place around the same time to find a plant that could be safely grown in the USA or at least in the Americas all, however, ended in failure. For reasons that have never been made entirely clear, no attempt was ever made to resume in Mexico the large-scale growing of *guayule*, which had served US needs rather well before 1913.[26] Instead, two American tycoons of the period attempted to grow the plant with the demonstrably highest yield – *Hevea* – outside the USA. Blocked by Philippine domestic politics and British influence from establishing themselves in Southeast Asia, Harvey Firestone in 1925 chose Liberia in Africa, and Henry Ford three years later a site by the Tapajos river in Brazil. The former project was hobbled by the extreme underdevelopment of the country, but could at least count on the fact that leaf blight had yet to appear in Africa.[27] The *Hevea* trees planted by Firestone

---

[24] Figures according to Treue, *Gummi*, pp 284–94 and BA/MA, RW 19/1467 'OKW/Wi Rü Amt, Kautschuk und die Versorgung im Kriege (März 1941)'.

[25] G. L. Wallace, 'Statistical and Economic Outline'; in: Schidrowitz and Dawson (eds.), *History*, p 337.

[26] Finlay, *American Rubber*, pp 132–9.

[27] William G. Clarence Smith, 'Rubber Cultivation in Indonesia and the Congo from the 1910s to the 1950s: Divergent Paths'; in: Ewout Frankema and Frans Buelens (eds.), *Colonial Exploitation and Economic Development: the Belgian Congo and the Netherlands*

were yielding 12,000 tons of rubber by 1942.[28] The Ford enterprise (name Fordlandia) had the shadow of leaf blight hanging over it from the start, while lacking a remedy that might help it get past that obstacle. Even when the blight *Mycroclus ulei* made its first appearance in 1935, Ford persevered and even expanded the project. A second outbreak of blight in 1940–1 finally inflicted such damage that no meaningful yield was achieved before the end of the war.[29] Paradoxically enough, the PR campaign unleashed by Ford when the project first ran into trouble in the early 1930s had the effect of convincing a number of outside observers (German ones included) that it was not only viable, but likely as not destined by 1950 to break the monopoly on the trade held until then by the Southeast Asian plantations.[30]

At the same time, experiments had taken place to find or breed a plant that could thrive in the USA. The project that came closest to a qualified success involved inventor Thomas Alva Edison and the goldenrod wildflower (*Santiago leavenworthii*). The plant was native to southern Florida and enjoyed the major advantage that it could be harvested after only a year. In the end, the project foundered when it was discovered that no means to harvest it mechanically would become available and that the plant, contrary to expectations, would not thrive in the remainder of the old South.[31] Together with the collapse of the Fordlandia project, the failure to domesticate goldenrod drove home the realisation that the USA would not be able to grow meaningful quantities of rubber in the continental USA or adjoining territories.

The last – and most improbable – avenue of research in America's quest for rubber was initiated one year after the vanguard of Henry Ford's planters arrived in the Brazilian rainforest. In the Germany of 1927, the IG Farben conglomerate was engaged in a major project aimed at the large-scale hydrogenation of coal – that is, to extract petrol from it. In this they were supported by contemporary gloomy predictions on the likely limit of the planet's oil reserves, which in September 1926 were given the official seal of approval when the Federal Oil Conservation Board estimated that the world's last barrel was

Indies Compared (London: Routledge 2013), pp 193–210. My thanks to my colleague Edward Flint for bringing this source to my attention.

[28] Bauer, *Industry*, p 306.

[29] The most comprehensive account of Ford's attempt to grow rubber in Brazil makes no mention of leaf blight featuring in the planning discussions prior to the establishment of the plantation. Greg Grandin, *Fordlandia: The Rise and Fall of Henry Ford's Forgotten Jungle City* (London: Icon Books 2010). Research sponsored by the US government into cross-breeding resistant *Hevea* strains did not begin until 1940. See Michael Langford, 'South American Leaf Blight of *Hevea* Rubber Trees'; in: US Department of Agriculture, Washington DC. Technical Bulletin No. 882 (January 1945), pp 1-31.

[30] See Jünger, *Kautschuk*, pp 170, 179. It is difficult to gauge whether this favourable assessment was coloured by the fact that Ford's anti-Semitism made him a kind of persona grata in the Germany of the period.

[31] Finlay, *American Rubber*, pp 74–106.

likely to be pumped in 1932.[32] Despite this (for them) promising backdrop, the technological challenges were draining IG Farben's coffers, and hence a strategic partner with big cash reserves needed to be sought out. The choice fell on Standard Oil of New Jersey (the future Exxon), one reason being that this company had an interest in putting off the feared oil shortage. It would do this by making sure that even the most low-grade oil, such as shale, which so far had been excluded from the refinement process on account of its poor yield, could be exploited. Fuel hydrogenation promised to do this to an unprecedented degree of effectiveness. In November 1929, in exchange for $35 million in shares, the IG gave up all its rights to fuel-hydrogenation technology outside Germany. A joint company was set up to administrate the exploitation of the patents and the sharing of technology that arose from the partnership. Almost as an afterthought, IG also put Buna on the table: since it seemed obvious that Germany would – if ever – only mass-produce it from coal, the company saw no harm in letting the Americans have the patent provided they limited research and production to the oil-based variant. In due course, this deal was sealed too. Had either side hesitated for just a few months, it is possible nothing would have come of these momentous developments: on 3 October, a major new oilfield (soon dubbed the Black Giant) had been discovered in east Texas.[33] Within weeks, confirmation of its unprecedented size made a nonsense of the rationale behind large-scale hydrogenation as far as Standard was concerned.

As for the Buna part of the deal, the Great Depression caused prices for Far East rubber to drop precipitously, making synthetic rubber the least of Standard's priorities for the moment. In the long term, however, the fact that Standard held the patent for what was at the time the world's only general-purpose synthetic rubber meant that other companies in the USA still interested in developing such a product had to find a way of settling with Standard, or risk legal action. The extent to which this arrangement really hindered the development of general-purpose synthetic rubber in the USA in the run up to Pearl Harbor is as yet an unresolved question.[34] As far as this account is

---

[32] Daniel Yergin, *The Prize: The Epic Quest for Oil, Money and Power* (New York: Simon & Schuster 1991), p 222; Diarmuid Jeffreys, *Hell's Cartel: IG Farben and the Making of Hitler's War Machine* (London: Bloomsbury 2008), p 110.

[33] Yergin, *The Prize*, pp 244–6.

[34] For a preliminary assessment, see Davis R. B. Ross, 'Patents and Bureaucrats: US Synthetic Rubber Development before Pearl Harbor'; in: Joseph R. Frese and Jacob Judd (eds.), *Business and Government: Essays in 20th-Century Cooperation and Confrontation* (New York: Sleepy Hollow Press 1985), pp 119–56. William M. Tuttle is the one historian who has made the most unambiguous case for a delay actually occurring, because of Standard adopting a twin-track strategy: the threat of legal action for patent infringement was complemented by extending the prospect of cooperation to prospective partners like Goodrich or Goodyear as soon as IG Farben delivered all the secrets of the Buna process. This would have led to widespread hesitation to engage in research of their

concerned, however, it is of the utmost importance, because it served the Germans as a tripwire system, giving them at least an approximate idea of how far American research in this area had progressed. Complementing this was the increasing urgency with which Standard began to plead with IG from late 1937 for the technical know-how that would put meat on the bones of the Buna patent. In an amazing piece of sophistry, IG's representative Fritz ter Meer took refuge behind the letter of the original 1929 contract and insisted the Americans first hand over the know-how to a recently developed special-ised synthetic rubber called Butyl. He then proceeded to string them along until September 1939, when IG made an accomplice of Standard by handing over several thousand patents for safekeeping during the war. Even then, the details of the Buna process were not included.[35] Under the conditions of the original contract, IG would in fact have been perfectly justified in refusing point-blank to hand over the Buna know-how. However, as ter Meer explained to a delegation from Göring's Office of the Four Year Plan on 21 March 1938, this would in all likelihood have a counterproductive effect.[36] As the develop-ment of Neoprene and Butyl indicated, the Americans already had much of the know-how needed for developing synthetic rubbers unassisted.[37] Under the circumstances, it was much preferable to go on holding out the hope of imminent German assistance rather than goading them into making a maximum effort of their own by slamming the door in their face.

It is undeniable that this strategy enjoyed a measure of success. A few months into the war Standard, by now resigned to the idea of proceeding unassisted, attempted to interest a few tyre companies in joining a cartel to

own. See William M. Tuttle Jr., 'The Birth of an Industry: The Synthetic "Rubber Mess" in World War II'; in: *Technology and Culture* Vol. 22 (1981), Pt 1, pp 35–67.

[35] In his otherwise excellent account of US–German corporate cooperation in the 1930s, Gerhard Kümmel asserts that by November 1938 the Reichswirtschaftsministerium stated that it had no objections to IG Farben handing over all the details of the Buna process to the Americans should they wish to do so; Kümmel, *Transnationale Wirtschaftskooperation und der Nationalstaat. Deutsch-amerikanische Unternehmensbeziehungen in den dreißiger Jahren* (Stuttgart: Franz Steiner 1995), p 178. This would mean that IG Farben took it upon itself to withhold the remaining secrets of the Buna process for the following ten months. Regrettably, this remarkable claim is not supported by a source reference.

[36] Joseph Borkin, *The Crime and Punishment of IG Farben*, chap. 4 ('The Marriage of IG and Standard Oil under Hitler'), esp. fn 11:. www.bibliotecapleyades.net/sociopolitica/socio pol_igfarben02.htm (accessed on 9 June 2020).

[37] The extent to which this assessment was also informed by the fact that Goodyear only a month before had handed IG's New York office a synthetic tyre made in the Goodyear laboratories is difficult to say. In August 1937, Goodyear had received a 454 kg (1,000 lb) sample of Buna-S and Buna-N and this may have sown doubts in ter Meer's mind as to whether the rubber used on the tyre in question had actually been made in the USA; 'Goodyear Statement to the Special Committee of the United States Senate Investigating the National Defence Programme, n.d. (spring 1942)'; in: Frank Howard, *Buna Rubber: The Birth of an Industry* (New York: D. van Nostrand 1947), p 286.

produce and market tyres based on the Buna formula. This offer was rejected as unattractive, especially since it was too obviously aimed at establishing a permanent hegemony of the oil giant over any prospective partners. Goodrich and Goodyear proceeded with their own research without Standard's blessing. On 5 June 1940 Goodrich introduced the Ameripol tyre to the nation. Ameripol was made from oil-based butadiene and was different from Buna-S only insofar as methyl methacrylate replaced styrene. It shared with the original German product most of its strengths and limitations (especially the need to mix it with at least 30 per cent natural rubber). Importantly, however, the introduction of Ameripol was not just a one-off publicity stunt, but came with a small plant that could produce 2,000 tons of synthetic rubber a year. The accompanying PR campaign coincided with the news of the impending fall of France; Goodrich could hardly have wished for a more auspicious moment to highlight the potential strategic importance of its new product.[38]

5.5   The American Attempts to Close the Rubber Gap as Seen through German Eyes: A Window of Opportunity?

For German observers, to keep track of American's growing anxieties about the rubber situation pre-Pearl Harbor was a fairly straightforward task. Most of the economic and political issues that had a bearing on the importation, stockpiling and processing of rubber and other critical raw materials were the subject of press statements,[39] Senate debates and conferences hosted by interest groups; the upshot of these was then discussed at great length in the country's media. As early as January 1939, Walter Lipmann, arguably the country's most influential syndicated columnist, drew attention to the fact that Japan's march of conquest threatened the lifeline that linked the USA to its key suppliers of 'rubber and other necessary materials'.[40] That he should have done so even before Japan had extended its war against China to the islands (Hainan and the Spratleys[41]) from which such an interdiction might have been at least theoretically possible makes this statement all the more remarkable.

---

[38] On the introduction of Ameripol see Erker, *Wettbewerb*, pp 472–4; Peter J. T. Morris, *The American Synthetic Rubber Research Programme* (Philadelphia: Pennsylvania UP 1989), p 9.

[39] A joint army–navy report from 1940 listed fourteen raw materials deemed to be of 'strategic' importance: antimony, chromium, coconut shell char, manganese, manila fibre, mercury, mica, nickel, quartz crystal, quinine, rubber, silk, tin and tungsten. Some of these could also be procured from parts of the globe unlikely ever to be reached by the Axis (South Africa for chromium, Gold Coast for manganese), and not one had to be imported into the USA in such huge quantities as rubber. See 'The Strategic and Critical Materials' (Washington, Army and Navy Munitions Board 1940).

[40] As quoted in Jonathan Marshall, *To Have and Have Not: Southeast Asian Raw Materials and the Origins of the Pacific War* (Berkeley: California UP 1995), p 62.

[41] In February and March 1939, respectively.

Over the following months, such warnings became more and more frequent until they were finally echoed by the US government. When in April 1940 the Japanese, seeking economic concessions in the Dutch East Indies, attempted to exert pressure on the Dutch government in The Hague, Secretary of State Cordell Hull let it be known on the 17th that any such attempt would 'endanger the peace and security, not just of the Dutch East Indies, but of the whole Pacific region'. The German envoy took careful note of this, stressing that the country's dire need of rubber and tin was such that even the most isolationist legislator would turn a blind eye to such belligerent talk.[42] An impassioned plea by Secretary of Commerce Harry Hopkins, a Roosevelt confidant, at a cabinet meeting on 10 May was very much in the same vein. Warning that the German invasion of Western Europe was likely to turn the rubber-producing colonies of France and The Netherlands into hostages to fortune, he stressed the need for emergency purchasing to create an enormous strategic stockpile.[43] It appeared that the US government was willing to take the issue very seriously indeed.

Such a promising start notwithstanding, the Roosevelt administration's track record in achieving autarky in rubber proved to be chequered to say the least. On the one hand, though the Japanese had backed down in April, their two-phase takeover of French Indo-China after the fall of Paris should have been enough to keep the subject on the agenda. On the other, many government departments showed little willingness to even acknowledge the likelihood of an imminent rubber crisis. However, pressure groups such as the Council on Foreign Relations kept stoking the fires of debate through their own in-house journals. Nor did the debate remain a specialist's preserve. Mass circulation dailies and weeklies like *Time*, the *New York Times*, the *Washington Star*, the *Washington Post* and the *San Francisco Chronicle* soon began publishing articles on the subject of US dependency on East Asian imports and in virtually every case singled out two raw materials for special attention: rubber and tin.[44] In the case of the latter, US dependence on imports was in the region of 80 per cent, and the one existing mine outside the Far East, in Bolivia, while difficult to develop, at least was safely out of Axis hands.[45] In the case of rubber,

---

[42] 'Der Geschäftsträger in Washington an das Auswärtige Amt (18. April 1940)', in: *Akten zur deutschen auswärtigen Politik (ADAP)*, Serie D, Bd. IX, (Frankfurt a.M.: P. Keppler 1962), pp 161–2.

[43] Jonathan W. Jordan, *American Warlords: How Roosevelt's High Command Led America to Victory in World War II* (New York: Penguin 2015), p 14.

[44] For a comprehensive assessment of contemporary articles, see Marshall, *Have and Have Not*, pp 66–104.

[45] A fact that did not stop the Sicherheitsdienst from developing Bolivian sources (in all likelihood, inside the country's National Bank) to get a clearer picture of the growing American interest in that country's tin mines. See PA/AA, Inland II g 337 'Der Chef der Sicherheitspolizei und des SD an das Auswärtige Amt z.Hd.d. Leiters der Abteilung

however, the Asian share of overall imports stood at 98 per cent.[46] Moreover, the attempt to develop alternative sources in the 1920s and 1930s had met with little success.

Despite the less than encouraging Brazilian precedent, the US government re-examined the possibility of establishing *Hevea* plantations in the Western Hemisphere. To any discerning observer, the fact that the Roosevelt administration, irrespective of the events that had transpired by the Tapajos, should be willing to bankroll expeditions by the Department of Agriculture into assorted Latin American countries, in order to assess their feasibility for the planting of new *Hevea* strains bred by the department, could hardly have been seen as anything other than a measure of desperation.[47] This was especially so since, even in the unlikely event of such an endeavour being crowned with success, five to seven years would be needed before any such source would start to make a meaningful contribution to the US economy.

By comparison, the first attempts to develop factories capable of turning out general-purpose synthetic rubber on a large scale were half-hearted at best. The PR campaign unleashed by the Goodrich Company to introduce its Victory Tyres made of Ameripol rubber (June 1940) made it clear that the government had in fact an option: it could establish a new industry either in cooperation with Standard Oil or by going into partnership with one of its competitors. Moreover, research carried out by the Carbide and Chemicals Corporation had revealed that Buna's key ingredient, butadiene, could also be distilled from grain alcohol.[48] After Standard had failed to reach an agreement with Goodrich and Goodyear, the spotlight fell on a scheme by which the US government in August 1940 agreed to bankroll and supervise the erection of four rubber factories, where tyre producers would start turning out synthetic rubber tyres according to the formula (Standard's or Goodrich's) they preferred. This very promising (and to a German observer, worrying) beginning was fatally watered down when seven months later the initial proposal involving four facilities capable of turning out 100,000 tons a year was changed to one setting up four pilot plants with a maximum production capacity of 10,000 tons.[49] The reason for this abrupt change appears to have been the attitude of new Secretary of Commerce Jesse Jones, who was also the head of the Reconstruction Finance Corporation (the Rubber Reserve's overseeing

Deutschland, Herrn Gesandten Luther. Betr.: Zinnproduktion in Bolivien – Abkommen Boliviens mit England und den USA (15.1.1941)'.

[46] Maury Klein, *A Call to Arms: Mobilizing America for World War II* (New York: Bloomsbury Press pb 2015), p 78.

[47] Finlay, *American Rubber*, p 133; Langford, 'Leaf Blight', pp 1-31.

[48] Streb, 'Technologiepolitik', p 375.

[49] 'Statement of the Goodyear Company to the Special Committee of the United States Senate Investigating the National Defence Programme, n.d. (spring 1942)', in: Howard, *Buna Rubber*, p 287–8.

body). He looked askance at the idea of bankrolling projects for private industry and had, moreover, just made a major political investment in allowing the large-scale purchase of rubber from Dutch and British planters in Southeast Asia to create a strategic reserve.[50] All this dithering was widely reported in the US press, and even though Jones and other conservatives had their critics, the majority of opinion at the time tended towards putting off a major investment into what was, after all, a technology barely out of its testing phase.[51] The low price of Asian rubber in 1940–1 no doubt contributed to the reluctance of both government and industry to sink major sums into a technology the dire need for which was not yet clear to more than a minority among Washington's legislators, public servants and journalists.[52]

For the next year or so, Fritz ter Meer's tactic of delaying the development of a viable synthetic rubber industry in the USA appeared to have taken on a bizarre life of its own. Even now, when it must have been blindingly obvious to all concerned that further cooperation with IG would at best be forthcoming only after a complete German victory in Europe and only on the terms of a victorious Third Reich, neither government nor industry could bring itself to focus on the need to find a rubber substitute, should Southeast Asia one day become the scene of momentous events mirroring those which had just swept away the peacetime order in Europe. Even when a senior member of Roosevelt's cabinet drew attention to the US dependence on Asian rubber and tin in a public speech,[53] he did so in the context of arguing for a US foreign policy that would check Japan's advance into French Indo-China and possibly beyond, rather than making a case for finding an alternative source that would decrease US industry's dependence on plantation rubber. All this complacency is rendered all the more astonishing by the record of a round of secret talks held between US and British senior officers in Washington in February 1941. On 24 February, the American representatives professed to be remarkably relaxed at the prospect of losing most of Southeast Asia for a period of time to the Japanese should war break out in the Pacific. Such a loss would be more 'psychological than substantive' they explained to their undoubtedly astonished British counterparts.[54]

---

[50] Ross, 'Patents and Bureaucrats', pp 121–3.

[51] See the August 1940 issue of *Fortune*, as quoted in Finlay, *American Rubber*, p 136.

[52] Or as Davis Ross put it rather flippantly in 1985: 'More likely, however, is the conclusion that no company (including Standard) gave much of a hoot nor holler for the Buna-S patent and know-how prior to the middle of 1941.' Ross, 'Patents and Bureaucrats', p 143. Klein, *Call to Arms*, p 234–8, stresses lethargy and inconsistency on the part of the government officials involved, the President included.

[53] A fact carefully recorded by the Germans. See KTB Seekriegsleitung, Teil A (entry for 25 July 1941).

[54] William T. Johnsen, *The Origins of the Grand Alliance: Anglo–American Collaboration from the* Panay *Incident to Pearl Harbor* (Lexington: Kentucky UP 2016), pp 143–4.

On 11 September 1941, however, an event occurred that appeared to indicate that US rubber policy – the government's procrastination notwithstanding – was starting to move in the right direction: on that day, Standard Oil filed charges against the Goodrich and Goodyear companies for violation of its patents.[55] The timing is of enormous importance because it would have signalled to anybody watching from Berlin that, whatever Standard's reasons for waiting over a year to do so, events had reached a point whereby an American synthetic rubber industry might finally be evolving against all the odds and irrespective of anything the custodian of the IG patents might have been able to do to slow down this process. From this moment on, a unique strategic advantage held by Germany would progressively be reduced with every passing month.

In view of the American administration's foot-dragging in the matter of synthetic rubber, the one area which was likely to put off the day of reckoning was the establishing of a large strategic stockpile in the manner suggested by Harry Hopkins in May 1940. In this, the US government came closest to a qualified success: in September 1939, rubber stocks held in the USA totalled 160,000 tons, or the equivalent of three months' worth of consumption. Attempts to substantially improve on this did not really get underway until the autumn of 1940 and even then did not proceed smoothly. At first, the Dutch and British had to be convinced to essentially scrap the Restriction Scheme of 1934 and fling open the doors of their warehouses.[56] A final decision as to which government agency should be tasked with coordinating this effort was not reached until March 1941, when the Rubber Reserve Company was empowered to do so. Once this was settled, enough ships had to be found to carry the bulky merchandise across the Pacific. At the peak of this endeavour, ships were ordered to dock in west coast ports so that the rubber they were carrying could be unloaded onto freight trains with destinations for the eastern seaboard or the Midwest (where most of the country's rubber industry was concentrated), thus increasing costs, but also improving the turnaround time for each vessel.[57] By the eve of Pearl Harbor, the stockpile had increased to 673,000 tons despite a belated start.[58] This mountain of rubber together with the maximum use of reclaim facilities saved both the United States and the British Empire from a major rubber famine in 1942–3.

In the meantime, all the belated attempts by the US government to insure against a possible reduction of rubber imports were being carefully monitored by a number of German observers who appeared to take a much greater

[55] Howard, *Buna Rubber*, pp 171–2, 289.

[56] For some of the diplomatic exchanges that preceded this see the correspondence compiled in: *Foreign Relations of the United States, 1940, Volume II: General and Europe* (Washington 1957), pp 276–88.

[57] Marshall, *Have and Have Not*, pp 51–53.

[58] Marshall, *Have and Have Not*, p 50.

interest in this issue than their Japanese counterparts.[59] A report by General Friedrich Boetticher, the military attaché at the embassy in Washington, dating from as far back August 1940, is noteworthy in this regard.[60] Even though it also discusses problems in the American production of steel and aluminium, a full six of its eleven pages are devoted to the – as yet far from pressing – rubber shortages facing US industry. Boetticher was rightly dismissive of the potential of plantations outside Southeast Asia and drew attention to the fact that attempts to build a strategic reserve were only just gathering pace. Output of synthetic rubber was described as negligible for the time being (1,700 tons in 1939), but with an increase to 10,000 tons promised for 1940. Should the USA find itself cut off from Asian supplies, even rationing would only guarantee a rubber supply of seven to ten months.[61] It appears he was pressed for more specifics on the subject, because five months later he narrowed down the time period during which the USA would be able to get by without imports to between eight and nine months. More importantly, the likely output of synthetic rubber for 1941 is given as a 'maximum of 5,000 tons', though given twelve to eighteen months' notice, industry spokesmen were reasonably confident of achieving an expansion to 100,000 tons.[62] On 21 April 1941 the attaché dwelt at length on the problems the Rubber Reserve Company was experiencing in creating a large enough strategic reserve (total rubber holdings in the USA were given as 350,000 tons). Lack of shipping and a persistently high level of civilian consumption were identified as the causes.[63] A report on the planned erection of the four pilot plants for synthetic rubber followed on 21 May 1941,[64] with another one a week later stressing the as yet inadequate stocks of imported rubber.[65]

Four weeks later, these reports were fleshed out with intelligence acquired straight from the horse's mouth. The House Armed Services Committee had been

---

[59] The marginal priority accorded this issue by the Japanese leadership can be gleaned from the fact that Emperor Hirohito – who received regular briefings on matters of strategy and national security – had to take it upon himself to raise the issue of US rubber stocks with one of his senior aides in late September 1941. The way in which he phrased the question indicates that so far it had not featured in any previous briefing. Koichi Kido, *The Diary of Marquis Kido, 1931–1945* (Fredrick, MD: University Publications of America 1984), p 307 (entry for 29 September 1941).

[60] BA/MA, RH 67/53 'Deutsche Botschaft. Der Militär- und Luftattache. Strategische Rohstofflage der Vereinigten Staaten (16.8.1940)'.

[61] Ibid.

[62] BA/MA, RH 67/49' Telegramm aus Washington (4.2.1941)'.

[63] BA/MA, RH 67/49 'Washington, den 21. April 1941 (21.4.1941)'. Of the 350,000 tons available on US soil, only 150,000 were held by the Rubber Reserve Company.

[64] BA/MA, RH 67/50 'Boetticher/Thomsen an OKH Attacheabteilung und für RLM-Attachegruppe (21.5.1941)'.

[65] BA/MA, RH 67/50 'Oberkommando des Heeres/Attacheabteilung (zbV) Gen.St.d.H. (28.5.1941)'. It is noteworthy that the sentence discussing insufficient rubber stocks is underlined several times and highlighted by an oversize exclamation mark.

carrying out an investigation into the problems the US economy was experiencing in gearing up for wartime conditions. A summary published for public consumption is a good indicator of the extent to which German intelligence gatherers in the USA were able to draw from open sources, since it gave Boetticher and envoy Hans Thomsen a unique insight into how the Americans perceived their own inadequacies in the early summer of 1941.[66] Even though it dwelt at length on issues like 'lack of coordination' and an overall 'lack of urgency' holding back US mobilisation in general, more than half the text concerned itself with the prospect of an imminent rubber crisis. According to the author of the report, excessive consumption by the US car industry, the wholly inadequate scale of the beginnings of a synthetic rubber industry,[67] the delay in starting a stockpiling programme and problems with the efficient coordination of shipping sailing to and from the Far Eastern territories now under Japanese threat were all conspiring to cripple US readiness in the case of a major crisis. It is noteworthy that a further telegram from the embassy a few weeks later neglected even to mention most of the aforementioned issues and instead zeroed in on the one on which everything hinged: the synthetic rubber industry, Thomsen elaborated, was still a few years from becoming fully operational.[68]

In the meantime, the Kriegsmarine began to take an interest in the subject too. On 11 August 1941 the Seekriegsleitung's war diary recorded that American attempts to create a strategic stockpile had so far covered the likely needs of a fully mobilised war industry (without regard for civilian needs) for two years – a rather generous estimate.[69] Only nine days later, the war diarist qualified that last entry by adding that stocks appeared to be lower than originally estimated, without, however, giving figures.[70] As far as the Luftwaffe is concerned, it needs to be kept in mind that much of the paper trail generated by its top commands did not survive the war, but a report produced by the *Generalluftzeugmeister*'s office in August on the strengths and weaknesses of German, Italian, British and American air power offers a good cross-section on account of its sheer length.[71] Five of its 174 pages discuss the US rubber industry. The section on rubber makes clear the degree to which the Americans were dependent on Far Eastern imports and does not foresee any

---

[66] PA/AA, StS USA, Bd. 7, 'Thomsen an Auswärtiges Amt (30.6.1941)'.

[67] 'The four plants that have been authorised to be built by government funds and operated by private industry are at best pilot plants that cannot produce results in appreciable quantities for some years to come.' Ibid. The original scheme, which had called for a yearly output of 100,000 tons, had just been scaled down to 10,000 in March 1941.

[68] PA/AA, StS Japan, Bd. 4, 610 'Thomsen an Auswärtiges Amt (12.8.1941)'.

[69] KTB Seekriegsleitung, Teil A (entry for 11 August 1941).

[70] KTB Seekriegsleitung Teil A (entry for 20 August 1941).

[71] BA/MA, RL 3/1833 'Der Generalluftzeugmeister Nr. 1123/41 g.Kdos. (30.8.1941) Luftrüstungsvergleich Deutschland + Italien und Großbritannien + USA 1939–1943 Stand: 1. Juli 1941. Erster Teil'.

problems in that regard. The fledgling synthetic rubber industry, on the other hand, lacked 'any decisive weight' since its currently diminutive output was unlikely to substantially increase in 1942. Even if existing plans to expand production to anywhere near the planned quota of 80,000 tons were to be crowned with complete success – something the author is confident in ruling out for the time being – this would amount only to a month's production.[72]

Of all the reports received in Germany on the subject as the date of Pearl Harbor neared, one produced by naval intelligence, dated 28 November 1941, was the most specific as far as production estimates were concerned. It gave a fairly accurate assessment of the short to mid-term prospects of the USA achieving autarky in this crucial area.[73] Its estimate of the reserve accumulated by late 1941 (613,000 tons) erred slightly on the conservative side, but it tended to give the fledgling US synthetic rubber industry rather too much credit (the estimate of 26,000 tons produced in 1941 was definitely on the high side and failed to highlight the all-important figure for general-purpose Buna rubber: a miserly 9,450 tons[74]). Most crucially, it emphasised that an important increase in synthetic rubber production was to be expected for the next year (80,000 tons – as it turned out, a considerable overestimate). When seen against the backdrop of likely yearly consumption (600–800,000 tons), however, it was estimated that for the time being the USA would remain heavily dependent on imports from East Asia. Further confirmation of this can be found in the last reports on the American economy that conceivably could have come to the attention of Hitler before he declared war on the United States. On 4 December, the Wehrmacht's War Economy Office estimated that provided imports of raw materials were not to cease, nothing would stand in the way of an increased mobilisation of the US war economy. The strategic stockpile of natural rubber at its current level, however, was unlikely to last beyond autumn 1942.[75] On the very same day, envoy Thomsen, reporting from Washington against the backdrop of the crisis caused by the collapse of the diplomatic talks between Japan and the United States, saw no need for undue concern. An attack by Japan on the USA could be safely ruled out and thus the ball was really in the Americans' court. However, he insisted, the initiation of hostilities by Washington was extremely unlikely, the warmongering headlines of many dailies notwithstanding. A war with Japan would not be a 'walk in the park', especially since it was likely to interdict access to raw materials of vital importance to

---

[72] Ibid., pp 62–5.
[73] BA/MA, RM 7/256 'Abschrift aus "Fremde Marinen" Nr. 40 v. 28.11.1941'.
[74] Tuttle, 'Birth of an Industry', pp 35–67.
[75] BA/MA, RW 19/1568 'Oberkommando der Wehrmacht. Wehrwirtschafts- und Rüstungsamt Wi Ia H Nr. 3839/41 g K Geheime Kommandosache! Die wehrwirtschaftliche Lage des Auslandes [September/Oktober/November] (4.12.1941)'.

the American economy. Substitutes for these were being trialled but would not be available in plentiful quantities for a few more years – an obvious reference to Goodrich's incipient Buna-S production.[76]

5.6   Southeast Asia as Seen from the Berghof

The first official report penned by a German observer that emphasised both the critical importance of Southeast Asia to the US economy as well as the capacity of the Japanese armed forces to successfully execute a war of conquest in that area bore the date, 4 October 1940. In a telegram analysing possible US reactions to the recent Japanese occupation of northern Indo-China, Attaché Boetticher pondered the likely consequences of an all-encompassing economic embargo of Japan by the US government. He reached the conclusion that such a move might prompt the Japanese to seize Southeast Asia, an escalation the USA would be largely powerless to counter with the military assets currently available.[77] Four months later, *Konteradmiral* Paul Wenneker, the naval attaché at the embassy in Tokyo, pondered the same topic. He stressed US dependence on the Asian rubber (90 per cent of total imports) and Asian tin (76 per cent of total imports), correctly assessed Dutch and British weaknesses in their respective colonies and was sceptical about the chances of a timely US intervention stemming a Japanese advance.[78] It is difficult to assess the impact information of this kind had on the mind of Adolf Hitler over the course of 1941, especially since the circumstantial evidence available indicates very strongly that throughout much of this period he was busy plotting the attack on the USSR or attempting to goad Japan into attacking Britain; the thought of war with the USA was mostly framed as something to be avoided unless a certain set of circumstances made it all but unavoidable. However, the key role played by rubber in his decision-making process of November and December 1941 is certainly discernible. In his conversation with Ambassador Oshima on 28 November 1941, Ribbentrop almost straightaway asked the diplomat when Japan would be in a position to block the region's exports of rubber and oil to the USA – the fact that the diplomat had not even indicated when and how his country would make its next expansionist move in the region does not appear to have deterred

---

[76] PA/AA, StS USA, Bd. 10, 'Thomsen an Auswärtiges Amt (4.12.1941)'.

[77] BA/MA, RH 67/53 'Rüstung und Wirtschaft. Beurteilung eines vollen Warenembargos der Vereinigten Staaten gegenüber Japan (4.10.1940)'. Boetticher's list of likely Japanese targets included the US protectorate of the Philippines, thus leaving no doubt that he had military, not political checkmate in mind.

[78] BA/MA, RM 7/253a 'Deutsche Botschaft. Der Marineattache an das Oberkommando der Kriegsmarine M.-Att. Betr.: Der Eintritt Japans in den europäischen Krieg. Möglichkeiten und Auswirkungen (3.2.1941)'.

him.[79] In the original draft of his memoirs, Hitler's Luftwaffe adjutant, Nicolaus von Below, specifically referred to Hitler explaining his decision to declare war on the USA by the fact that a Japanese move south would cripple US decision-making because of the need to prioritise the protection of Washington's only plentiful supply of rubber.[80]

It goes without saying that the importance of substitutes to a modern twentieth-century war industry without access to overseas markets had been impressed on Hitler's mind on many an occasion. In fact, it is probably fair to say that he was more familiar with the key issues than most statesmen of his time, Germany's vulnerability in this regard during World War I having left a deep impression on him.[81] His keen interest, developed in the 1920s,[82] in boosting the German car industry in general and motorising the German army in particular could not but have served notice on him that such steps, crucial though they may have been, would make a German economy devoid of easy access to oil and rubber even more vulnerable to wartime blockade than it had been in 1914–18. Thus, it is hardly surprising that as early as September 1932 he had already spent an evening discussing the need for fuel hydrogenation with two senior IG managers in Munich.[83] Within weeks of his accession to power he was stressing both publicly and at cabinet meetings the need to increase the number of motor vehicles in use in Germany by means as diverse as tax breaks, the building of a highway network and the sale of fuel refined from the small amounts of oil found in German soil. In contrast to most of his ministers and senior aides, who if anything were ready to support such measures with a view to facilitating troop transports or reducing the blight of unemployment, the new dictator was adamant that the potential inherent in the car industry justified making it an end in itself.[84]

---

[79] 'Geheime Reichssache. RAM 58. Aufzeichnung über den Empfang des japanischen Botschafters Oshima durch den Herrn RAM am 28.11.1941 abends (n.d.)'; in: ADAP, Serie D, Bd. XIII.2, pp 708–10.

[80] BA/MA, N 745/4 'Was ich als Hitlers Luftwaffenadjutant erlebte (aufgezeichnet im Winter 1948/49)'.

[81] 'Führerhauptquartier 18.10.1941, abends. Gäste: Prof. Speer, Prof Breker. H/Fu.'; in: Werner Jochmann (ed.), *Adolf Hitler. Monologe im Führerhauptquartier 1941–1944* (München: Orbis 2000), pp 93–4.

[82] See his remark about the phenomenon of 'general global motorisation' which he described as 'a question of incalculable importance for the future' (*'eine Angelegenheit von einer gar nicht abzumessenden Zukunftsbedeutung'*) in his *Second Book*. Gerhard L. Weinberg, Christian Hartmann, Klaus A. Lankheit (eds.), *Hitler. Reden. Schriften. Anordnungen. Februar 1925 bis Januar 1933. Band II A. Aussenpolitische Standortbestimmung nach der Reichstagswahl Juni-Juli 1928* (München: K.G. Saur 1995), p 84.

[83] Jeffreys, *Cartel*, p 137.

[84] 'Vermerk des Oberregierungsrats Willuhn über einen Vortrag des Generaldirektors der Deutschen Reichsbahngesellschaft zur Frage des Wettbewerbs zwischen Reichsbahn und Kraftverkehr am 16. März 1933, 12.30 h'; 'Besprechung mit führenden Industriellen, 29. Mai 1933, 16.15 h'; both in: Karl-Heinz Minuth (ed.), *Akten der Reichskanzlei 1933–1938*.

The major stumbling block for such a project was the dearth of domestic oil and the total lack of home-grown rubber. Procuring either in quantity would soon deplete the Reichsbank's exiguous foreign exchange reserves; as it was, the country's ongoing frantic rearmament programme was only made viable by what Hitler himself called the 'wizardry' of the head of the Reichsbank, Hjalmar Schacht.[85] Against this backdrop, self-sufficiency had a lot to commend it: 1933–5 was spent in negotiations with IG Farben to determine the question of how to ensure a steady supply of rubber for Germany in the event of another major war. After weighing the relative pros and cons of stockpiling natural rubber and producing untried substitutes, Hitler in February 1936 publicly committed himself to the industrial-scale production of Buna-S at a time when the formula for the compound had only passed the first tests indicating the strength and durability that would be required of it in a military context.[86] From a strictly fiscal point of view, it was of course a ruinous undertaking and together with the mining of low-yield German ores caught the eye of Economics Minister and Reichsbank President Schacht. While originally supportive of Buna, he became a sceptic when the sheer scale of the project became apparent in September 1936. He confronted the regime's new troubleshooter for economic affairs, Hermann Göring, but ended up resigning in disgust as minister after a power struggle of a year.[87] Even though Hitler does not appear to have intended this outcome originally,[88] it nevertheless marked a sea change in the evolution of his regime into a truly totalitarian state.

Over the following years, the dictator was kept in the loop whenever it looked as if the small strategic stockpile of natural rubber available in Germany at any given time might drop to unacceptably low levels, since only he could approve the release of funds or the diplomatic initiatives needed to alleviate this scarcity. A case in point was in early 1941 when, despite the booty secured

---

Die Regierung Hitler. Teil I: 1933/34, Bd. 1 (30. Januar bis 31. August 1933) (Boppard am Rhein: Harald Boldt 1983), pp 225–31, 506–27.

[85] '22.4.1942, mittags', in: Henry Picker (ed.): *Hitler's Tischgespräche im Führerhauptquartier* (Propyläen: München 2003), pp 327–31.

[86] 'Rede vor Vertretern der deutschen Automobilindustrie (15.2.1936)'; in: Domarus (ed.), *Reden und Proklamationen* Bd. I.2, pp 576–9.

[87] For Schacht's evolving views on substitute production, see Plumpe, 'Kautschuksynthese', pp 583, 586, as well as Hans-Erich Volkmann, 'Die NS-Wirtschaft in Vorbereitung des Krieges'; in: Wihelm Deist et al (eds.), *Ursachen und Voraussetzungen des Zweiten Weltkrieges* [= Das Deutsche Reich und der Zweite Weltkrieg, Bd. 1] (rev. ed., Frankfurt a.M.: Fischer TB 1989), pp 336–7 and Christopher Kopper, *Hjalmar Schacht. Aufstieg und Fall von Hitlers mächtigstem Bankier* (München: Hanser 2006), pp 306–23.

[88] See the excellent analysis of the Schacht/Göring clash in Alfred Kube, *Pour le merite und Hakenkreuz. Hermann Göring im Dritten Reich* (München: R. Oldenbourg 1987), pp 151–63, 185–94.

in Western Europe[89] and an all-time high output of Buna in December (4,471 tons), reserves fell to a dangerous low. *Generalfeldmarschall* Wilhelm Keitel briefed Hitler on 13 January 1941 that Germany faced a major rubber supply crisis. Staving it off was not just a question of money; valuable political leverage would be sacrificed by asking the Vichy government to release a part of the Indo-Chinese rubber crop and ship it to the Manchurian port of Darien, from where it would reach Germany on the Trans-Siberian Railway.[90] Japanese cooperation was of course essential to turn the logistical side of this plan into a practical endeavour; previous Japanese reticence about allowing the use of their ships for the transfer of German rubber for fear of compromising their neutrality suggested this would not be as straightforward a proposition as it might seem. In this instance, the German initiative in approaching the Vichy government led to the Japanese predictably objecting to this intrusion in their sphere of influence and demanding a cut of the deal, thus necessitating further negotiations which eventually led to a full-blown diplomatic crisis between the two would-be allies.[91] It is thus difficult to conceive of a situation where the crucial importance of a wartime source of rubber would have been far away from Adolf Hitler's mind for more than a few weeks in 1941. Another indication of this are his repeated musings between August and November 1941 about planting 100,000 hectares (about 250,000 acres) of rubber trees in the occupied southern regions of the USSR in order to alleviate Germany's perennial rubber shortage.[92]

At the same time, the importance of the East Indian plantation rubber to the economies of the West may have been impressed on his mind at more or less the same time in a manner that was both more impressionistic and more personal. One of the few people among his entourage who repeatedly dared to contradict him and yet stay on friendly terms with him was Walther Hewel, the

---

[89] A large part of which had to be shared with the economies of the newly occupied countries and the new Italian ally, which had joined Germany on 10 June.

[90] For these events, see BA/MA, RW 19/1467 'OKW/Wi Rü Amt, Kautschuk und die Versorgungslage im Kriege (März 1941)'.

[91] The frictions over rubber between the newly minted allies are covered in: PA/AA, Handelspolitische Akten Wiehl, Bd. 2. 'Beutner (Rio de Janeiro) an Auswärtiges Amt (28.1.1941)'; KTB Seekriegsleitung, Teil A, (entry for 23 May 1941) and 'Aufzeichnung betr. Kautschukverhandlungen und allgemeine Wirtschaftsverhandlungen in Tokio (20.8.1941)'; in: ADAP, Serie D, Bd. XIII.1, pp 279–81.

[92] 'Führerhauptquartier, 2.8.1941, abends H/Fu'; 'Führerhauptquartier, 17.9., mittags, abends und in der Nacht zum 18.9.1941 H/Fu'; 'Führerhauptquartier 13.10.1941, mittags. Gast: Reichswirtschaftsminister Funk. H/Fu'; all in: Jochmann (ed.), *Monologe*, pp 53, 63, 78. See also the dictator's passing comment on the topic in Paul Fröhlich and Alexander Kranz (eds.) *Tagebuch des Chefs des Stabes beim Chef der Heeresrüstung und Befehlshaber des Ersatzheeres 1938 bis 1943* (entry for 29 November 1941) (forthcoming). Hitler's repeated references during those months to 'rubber trees' are too vague to infer what sort of plant he could have been referring to. Trees of the *Hevea* type – the most prevalent of the period – are unlikely to have prospered in the climate of the Ukraine or Caucasus.

representative of the Auswärtiges Amt at Führer's Headquarters. This was almost certainly down to the fact that, as a nineteen-year-old student, Hewel had taken part at Hitler's side in the attempted Beer Hall Putsch of November 1923. He had engaged the Bavarian police in a firefight and then owned up to this fact in the following trial, thus greatly enhancing his already considerable National Socialist credentials. After serving his sentence together with Hitler, Hewel spend a year in the United Kingdom, learning the language and going into business, and then moving on to the Dutch East Indies. Here, he spent the years 1927–35 working for the Anglo-Dutch Plantations of Java Ltd. as a manager of assorted tea and rubber estates.[93] Back in Germany, Hewel was recruited in 1936 by Joachim von Ribbentrop, the NSDAP's new foreign affairs' 'expert', first as the head of his department for British affairs and then as his liaison man at Führer's Headquarters, a task he fulfilled – barring an interruption of nearly half a year in 1944[94] – from March 1938 until the end of the war.

Most contemporary observers coincided in describing Hewel as a happy-go-lucky individual who managed to keep a distance from the snake pit of Führer's Headquarters' court politics by staying on good terms with most key players.[95] He became something of a fixture at the late evening social gatherings, when he used to regale Hitler and his guests at headquarters with anecdotes of his time in the Indies;[96] partly as a result of the increasing exasperation they both came to share with Foreign Minister Ribbentrop, the period 1940–1 is regarded as the one where Hewel and Hitler grew closest. We are thus left with the paradox that Hewel, who was one of the few of Hitler's paladins who tried to stop the race to war in 1939 and apparently also warned of the danger inherent in challenging the USA,[97] may well have unwittingly provided his lord and master with the one piece of information that appeared to give the decision to confront the USA the guise of feasibility. It is certainly

---

[93] On Hewel's early life, see Enrico Syring, 'Walther Hewel – Ribbentrop's Mann beim 'Führer''; in: Ronald Smelser et al (eds.), *Die braune Elite. 21 weitere biographische Skizzen* (Darmstadt: WBG 1993), pp 150–65, esp. 150–6.

[94] Hewel spent six months convalescing from serious injuries suffered in an airplane crash in April 1944.

[95] Hewel appears to have made a habit of treating everybody with respect and politeness, even the employees of the Berghof who were used to be treated with disdain by the high and mighty of the Third Reich. See Rochus Misch, *Der letzte Zeuge. Ich war Hitlers Telefonist, Kurier und Leibwächter* (München: Piper 2008, 2013 pb), pp 134, 162.

[96] Institut für Zeitgeschichte (IfZ), ED 100–78 'Tagebuch Hewel (entry for 22 February 1941)'.

[97] The key source for Hewel's insistence in warning Hitler about both British and American potential is one of the first post-war interrogations of Albert Speer. Ulrich Schlie (ed.), *Albert Speer. Die Kransberg-Protokolle 1945. Seine ersten Aussagen und Aufzeichnungen (Juni-September)* (München: Herbig 2003), pp 232, 237 (7.9.1945). See also Syring, 'Hewel', pp 155–7.

difficult to conceive of a situation in which Hitler could have failed to become familiar with most of the economic and political pitfalls of plantation rubber in the 1930s, while having had Walther Hewel by his side for nearly four years on an almost daily basis.

5.7 Beyond Pearl Harbor

The disaster that befell the Allies during the winter of 1941–2 in the Far East appeared to bear out Adolf Hitler's gamble to bring the Japanese into the war by siding with them against the Americans. Within hours of the Japanese initiation of hostilities, Attaché Boetticher made the accurate prediction that even the introduction of convoying would not allow the Americans to continue shipping rubber from Asia in any meaningful quantities; the growth of the USA's strategic stockpile had effectively been terminated overnight.[98] A few days later, General Walter Warlimont of the *Wehrmachtführungsstab*, in a remarkably sober and level-headed report reviewing Axis and Allied options in the near future, foresaw both the likelihood of the fall of Southeast Asia as well as the long-term consequences such an event was likely to bring in its train: 'As far as the economic area is concerned, it seems doubtful whether the Anglo-Saxon Powers will be in a position to cope with the termination of the supply of rubber and tin from Malaya and the Dutch East Indies on which their economies are so heavily reliant'.[99] Subsequent events would appear to bear out the first part of this optimistic forecast: from December 1941, the rubber-producing colonies or nations of the Far East fell like ninepins before the onslaught of the Japanese armed forces: Thailand within a day of being invaded in the early hours of 8 December 1941; northern Borneo and Sarawak by 19 January 1942; Malaya with the fall of Singapore on 15 February 1942; and the Dutch East Indies over the course of a seven-week campaign, which culminated with the capitulation of the Dutch and assorted Allied forces on Java on 9 March 1942. At the same time, the crippling of the US Pacific Fleet's battleships, as well as the fall of Manila and Bataan, firmly ruled out the possibility of an Allied return to Southeast Asia within the foreseeable future. The events of these months have usually been associated in historians' minds with the loss of four Allied capital ships,[100] and with the

---

[98] PA/AA, Handakten Etzdorf. 'Politische Berichte Washington. Meldung Mil.Att. Washington vom 7.12.1941 (11.12.1941)'.

[99] 'WFSt./Abt.L (I K op) Nr. 44 2173/41 g.K. Chefs. F.H.Qu. (14.12.1941)'; reproduced in: Michael Salewski (ed.), *Die deutsche Seekriegsleitung 1935–1945. Band III: Denkschriften und Lagebetrachtungen 1938–1944* (Frankfurt am Main: Bernard & Graefe 1973) pp 249–61, esp. p 251. A file copy for Oberkommando des Heeres can be found in the Bundesarchiv/Militärarchiv under RH 2/1521.

[100] USS *Oklahoma* and USS *Arizona* were destroyed in the Pearl Harbor raid on 7 December 1941; HMS *Prince of Wales* and HMS *Repulse* were sunk by land-based

surrender of two sizeable bodies of Western troops in Singapore and Bataan, but the loss of the bulk of the world's rubber-producing territories constituted a far more serious blow to the Allied cause. At a stroke, the Japanese found themselves controlling more than 90 per cent of the world's supply of natural rubber. During the following years, strenuous attempts by the Allied powers to revitalise all the sources still available fell well short of what would have been needed to meet even a sizeable fraction of the combined needs of the economies and armed forces of the United States and the entirety of the British Empire: in 1943, Ceylon – the only rubber-producing Asian colony not to fall to the Japanese juggernaut – would yield just over 100,000 tons,[101] all of Africa in the region of 50,000 tons and Brazil 23,000 tons.[102] US peacetime imports of natural rubber in 1939 had totalled 592,000 tons,[103] which is barely an indicator of wartime needs, because at that time Great Britain and its Dominions were still self-sufficient, the country was just beginning to emerge from a major economic slump in 1937–8 and the US armed forces were only in the initial phase of that expansion that would put them in a position to actively confront the Axis powers from mid-1942. Seen against this backdrop, even the enormous rubber reserve of 673,000 tons,[104] accumulated at the eleventh hour by the Rubber Reserve Company, would do little more than buy the Federal authorities some time (depending on the extent of rationing, slightly under or over a year) in order to come up with a permanent solution. Obviously, synthetic rubber constituted the only viable option.

Despite this, the first nine months after Pearl Harbor saw not just a continuation, but arguably an increase in the foot-dragging and inconsistency that had crippled US rubber policy in 1940–1. This has gone down in US

IJN torpedo bombers on 10 December 1941, while on a sortie to intercept the Japanese invasion fleet bound for Malaya.

[101] Further proof of the priority that the German leadership accorded to the continued denial of natural rubber to the Allies can be found in an entry in the Seekriegsleitung's war diary, which discusses suggestions by OKW for future action against key vulnerabilities of the Allied war effort. Ranked on a par with the interdiction of convoy traffic to Murmansk and Archangelsk is the 'elimination of the island of Ceylon by the Japanese as the last remaining supplier of natural rubber'. See KTB Seekriegsleitung, Teil A (entry for 20 April 1942).

[102] See the figures in Henry Guttmann, *Die Rohstoffe unserer Erde. Das materielle und geistige Potential der Welt* (Berlin: Safari 1952), p 276. The Liberian total of this was 14,000 tons; the Congo's approximately 10,000 tons. See Bauer, *Rubber Industry*, p 306. Frantic attempts to maximise natural rubber yields in colonial Africa led to a return to exploitative measures usually associated with an earlier phase of European imperialism. See Eric T. Jennings, *Free French Africa in World War II: The African Resistance* (Cambridge: CUP 2015), pp 179–99.

[103] BA/MA, RH 67/53 'Deutsche Botschaft. Der Militär- und Luftattaché. Strategische Rohstofflage der Vereinigten Staaten (16.8.1940)'.

[104] It completely dwarfed the German reserves of September 1939, which stood at barely 15,000 tons.

history simply as the rubber 'mess'.[105] The major companies tasked with producing synthetic rubber had signed a written commitment to share knowledge and pool their patents as early as 19 December 1941. They went on to agree to a scheme which, while generous, saw an intrusion by the Federal authorities into their sphere of operation unprecedented in US history: the fifteen planned factories were to be built at the state's expense, and then leased back to the companies operating them for a nominal fee and a limited period of time. Prices for the rubber produced were fixed, though costs incurred by the companies in running the factories were to be borne by the Rubber Reserve Company.[106] From the record of Adolf Hitler's late evening table talks, we know that he followed with great interest the belated American attempts to finally shift gear on synthetic rubber production. On the evening of 7 January 1942 he stated: 'England and America now want to build a synthetic rubber industry. This means not just the erection of factories, but also unimaginable quantities of coal. The problem will reach a critical point in six months.'[107] Further confirmation of his interest in the matter comes from another source. His press spokesman, Otto Dietrich, in memoirs written immediately after the war, alludes to Hitler's habit of belittling reports that pointed to a growing Anglo–American production miracle in the year after Pearl Harbor. According to his train of thought, such a rise in production would always be impeded by a dearth of key raw materials now mostly in Axis hands, with dwindling rubber reserves in particular severely limiting the number of jeeps, trucks and planes, which after leaving the assembly plants could be put – quite literally – on wheels.[108] Such thoughts have until now, been dismissed as the ravings of a dictator increasingly prone to shutting out bad news, but at least in the case of rubber production, they should be seen against the backdrop of the not inconsiderable knowledge on the subject he had acquired during the 1930s.

At the same time, many US government agencies tasked with providing direction were at first found wanting. To begin with, there is some evidence that the sheer speed with which the Japanese gobbled up all of Southeast Asia left many government officials in a state of genuine shock. According to the

---

[105] Several scholars have produced detailed accounts of the events of those months in Washington. Arguably the most succinct accounts can be found in Tuttle, 'Birth of an Industry', pp 35–67 and Finlay, *American Rubber*, pp 171–97.

[106] Streb, 'Technologiepolitik', p 386–7.

[107] 'Wolfsschanze, 7.1.1942, abends H/Fu.'; in: Jochmann (ed.), *Monologe*, p 184. It is difficult to ascertain what exactly he meant by 'critical point'. It could be that he simply underestimated either the amount of rubber hoarded in US warehouses or the capacity of US industry to reclaim used rubber and was thus left under the impression that synthetic rubber would have to start making up for a major deficit as early as mid-1942.

[108] Otto Dietrich, *12 Jahre mit Hitler* (Köln: Atlas Verlag 1955), pp 116–17. For a similar assessment, see TB Goebbels, Bd. II.4, pp 56–7 (entry for 6 April 1942).

testimony of one of them, even though many decision makers had accepted the likelihood of such a Japanese move, virtually no one had foreseen the possibility of it bringing a long-term strategic upheaval in its wake.[109] At the same time, there can be little doubt that throughout the spring and summer of 1942, the Roosevelt administration failed to exercise the leadership called for to address the rubber crisis.[110] This left a total of eight competing Federal agencies (the Rubber Reserve Company, the Reconstruction Finance Corporation, the War Production Board, the Office of Petroleum Coordinator, the Office of Defense Transportation, the Price Administrator, the Board of Economic Warfare and the Department of Agriculture[111]), two senatorial committees, assorted congressmen, special interest groups and the media to find a solution to the sudden loss of most of the US pre-war rubber supply. While Standard Oil found itself in the limelight for its dealings with IG Farben, an equally vicious debate flared up over the respective merits of producing the butadiene needed for synthetic rubber either from grain (which could be turned into alcohol) or oil. This controversy was widely perceived to pit the quintessential 'man in the street' – in this instance, the Midwest farmer – against the interests of the big oil corporations, and hence appealed to the imagination of a public already traumatised by the Pearl Harbor attack. The delay this produced for the production of US rubber is hard to gauge. While it is true that most of the synthetic rubber factories had to be built from scratch, for a number of months in 1942 rubber output was hindered more by lack of butadiene than by lack of factory capacity.[112] At the same time, U-boat successes at sea had led to more and more goods being shifted by road and rail, with the result that the US transport network was under severe strain during exactly these months. It was only after President Roosevelt belatedly asked Bernard Baruch, who had overseen the mobilisation

[109] US Attorney General and Roosevelt confidant Robert Jackson had the following to say on the subject in his posthumously published memoirs: 'I had heard repeatedly in Cabinet meetings that a war with the Orient would not amount to much, that our Navy "would knock Japan out of the water" in no time. I think Secretary of the Navy Frank Knox had said a number of times that it would only take maybe six months. At any rate, when questions had arisen such as stockpiling rubber, Knox, with great assurance, had said that our naval forces in the Pacific were so superior to those of Japan that we would have a very brief interruption of our rubber supply.' See John Q. Barrett (ed.), 'That Man': An Insider's Portrait of Franklin D. Roosevelt (Oxford: OUP 2003), p 104.

[110] Tuttle, 'Birth of an Industry', pp 35–67; Klein, Call to Arms, pp 404–5, 407–9.

[111] Thomas Fleming, The War Within World War II: Franklin Delano Roosevelt and the Struggle for Supremacy (London: The Perseus Press 2001), p 155.

[112] This allegation was first made by Frank Howard, who had played a key role in Standard's negotiations with IG Farben, in his 1947 book Buna Rubber. Since he himself had been accused in 1942 of delaying the development of an American synthetic rubber industry, it may sound like special pleading. The impact of the 1942 scarcity of butadiene has, however, been independently confirmed, see Peter J. T. Morris, The American Synthetic Rubber Research Program (Philadelphia: Pennsylvania UP 1989), pp 14–15.

of the US economy in 1917–18, to provide an assessment of the current rubber crisis that a government strategy finally became more discernible. In his report, which he presented on 10 September 1942, Baruch urged the rationing of rubber and gasoline, made a case for both alcohol and oil to be used for the production of synthetic rubber and recommended the appointment of a rubber 'tsar' with plenipotentiary powers. Even so, by the end of the year, the USA had produced only 22,400 tons of synthetic rubber, of which a mere 3,700 tons were Buna-S type rubber which could be used for tyres,[113] thus bearing out the prognosis which had featured in the *Generalluftzeugmeister*'s report of 30 August 1941. Such a production figure was little more than a drop in the proverbial bucket, a fact gleefully recorded in a confidential report produced by Joseph Goebbels' propaganda ministry. It quoted a congressional spokesman as describing the 1942 shortfall in synthetic rubber production as *'eine arge Klemme'* ('a tight spot') for the entire American war effort, unless a solution was found soon;[114] this assessment was confirmed by an American manager writing after the war. To him, the bungled attempts of 1940–2 to create a Buna industry constituted nothing less than 'a scandalous, a complete, a nearly catastrophic foul up'.[115] It appeared as if Hitler's gamble of cutting off America from its main source of rubber before its industry could develop a synthetic alternative in large enough quantities might still come off.

The details of what happened next are outside the scope of this study and will only be given in the briefest summary. Suffice it to say that once given a clear direction and a set of priorities to work with, US industry outdid itself in truly unprecedented manner. Since the Germans were the pioneers of synthetic rubber manufacture, a comparison with their output can serve as a yardstick. Germany's Buna production evolved in a fairly steady manner from the 3,500 tons produced in 1937 (the year the contract for production was signed by IG Farben and the German government), to the 5,700 tons of 1938, and on to the 22,400 tons of 1939. Once truly industrial quantities were produced, the growth rate inevitably slowed down, but did not yet level off: 40,900 tons in 1940, 70,600 tons in 1941, on to 100,500 tons in 1942 and 118,700 tons in 1943.[116] US industry, on the other hand, faced the challenge of making a truly major leap to compensate for time lost in the 1930s. Whether by coincidence or not, this happened as soon as the Baruch Committee produced a strategy and butadiene production finally picked up. While in 1942 American industry had produced a mere 22,400 tons, 1943 saw all fifteen projected factories come on line with the production of 234,3000 tons (of which

---

[113] Bauer, *Rubber Industry*, p 296.
[114] BA-Lichterf., R 55/792 'Ministerium für Volksaufklärung und Propaganda. Abteilung Propaganda-Auswertung. Die Lage in USA, Nr. 12. Stichtag 15.1.1943'
[115] As quoted in Klein, *Call to Arms*, p 509
[116] All figures according to Plumpe, 'Kautschuksynthese', p 592.

Figure 5.1 Fitting a tyre to the landing gear of a Boeing B–17 heavy bomber in 1945. By that time, the dire rubber supply forecasts of 1942 were but a distant memory. (Anthony Potter Collection via Getty Images)

184,800 were the crucially important Buna-S type rubber).[117] As far as Buna-S was concerned, this constituted a more than fortyfold increase in production. This was the rough equivalent of one and a half times the German output at its very peak that same year. Even though an astonishing achievement which few people could have foreseen, it turned out to be barely enough to meet the combined civilian and military needs of the Western allies until the end of the war. Even after the defeat of Germany had considerably eased the pressure of demand, the Chiefs of Staff Committee in a July 1945 draft telegram to Southeast Asia Command warned that the 'conversion to synthetic has been pushed to the furthest extent possible'. Since demand continued to outstrip supply, however, there existed a real 'possibility of a breakdown [in] early 1946'. Hence, Allied strategy needed to prioritise the retaking of at least some of the rubber-producing territories lost in 1941–2.[118]

---

[117] Figures according to Treue, *Gummi*, p 262 and Bauer, *Rubber Industry*, p 296. Figures for the German output are given in metric tons.

[118] TNA, CAB SO/96C.O.S. (45) 490 (o). 'Chiefs of Staff Committee. Rubber position of the United Nations. Note by the War Office (23.7.1945)'. My thanks to my colleague Tim Bean for drawing my attention to this source.

5.8 Conclusion

The manner in which plantation rubber production had evolved in the inter-war years, alongside the head start enjoyed by German industry in 1940–1 in the production of substitutes, had created a situation whereby the US economy gearing up for war found itself in an unexpectedly vulnerable position. As if this were not enough, very few people in the US capital seem to have had any concept that a Japanese move against Southeast Asia could deny the West more than 90 per cent of the world's rubber production in one fell swoop and for a period that could prove more than transitory. At the same time, the feeble American attempts to engage in even small-scale production of synthetic rubber were carefully monitored by the Auswärtiges Amt, the SD and all three German armed services.

As yet, no document has come to light that would give us a record of the German dictator connecting all these dots in the months before Pearl Harbor, but it is difficult to see how he could have failed to do so. From his first weeks in government, the need to boost the motorisation of German society had been one of his top domestic priorities, the dearth of locally available oil and rubber notwithstanding. Together with the procurement of other expensive substitutes, this had led the German economy into a near-insoluble fiscal dilemma and brought about the resignation of a key player of the early regime. In the unlikely event that he did not already have a clear idea of the Southeast Asian dimension of this issue, it is difficult to believe that he would not have become thoroughly familiarised with it in his countless conversations with Walther Hewel. It is probably fair to say that regardless of any intellectual curiosity, sheer necessity would have given him an understanding of raw materials and their substitutes that any other leader of the 1930s and 1940s would have struggled to match. The USA, as Ribbentrop had put it to him, might be virtually immune to orthodox military defeat and conquest. A strategy of denial, however, had the potential to either paralyse much of US war-making potential before it had even left the factories or force the USA into throwing the bulk of its half-ready armed forces into a campaign to contest the Japanese invasion of Southeast Asia.

6

The Crisis of the German War Economy, 1940–1941

6.1 Introduction

On 28 November 1941 the German minister for munitions production, Dr Fritz Todt, met with Walter Rohland, both deputy CEO of Vereinigte Stahlwerke and one of Todt's key collaborators. The latter had just returned from an inspection trip to the rear area of Heinz Guderian's 2. *Panzerarmee* in Russia; there, both the worn-out state of German equipment and the rugged dependability of captured Soviet tanks had left him deeply worried.[1] Todt and Rohland were supposed to meet Hitler at a conference on tank design in the Neue Reichskanzlei the following day at noon, and the minister felt it incumbent on him to allow his subordinate to give the dictator a 'warts and all' summary of his impressions. Accordingly, he arranged for a preliminary meeting that would precede the conference. Apart from himself and Rohland, only generals Brauchitsch and Guderian would be in attendance.[2]

Hitler, whose foreign minister, Ribbentrop, had spent much of the evening of the 28th practically goading the Japanese ambassador into initiating hostilities against the USA without delay, was thus given a chance to reconsider his own options while the Japanese task force was already on its way to Ohau. The fact that Rohland was introduced by Todt is particularly important, since the minister boasted impeccable political credentials, his membership in the NSDAP dating back to 1923.

At the meeting with Hitler, Rohland spoke at length about the impressions he had gathered during his recent trip and added that, in light of the problems German industry was experiencing in keeping up with the combined output of British and Soviet tank production, the full mobilisation of US heavy industry would inevitably spell doom. Todt then weighed in and demanded that the war be brought to an end by seeking a compromise peace, since a military victory appeared to be less and less

---

[1] Walter Rohland, *Bewegte Zeiten. Erinnerungen eines Eisenhüttenmannes* (Stuttgart: Seewald 1978), pp 75–7.

[2] Ibid., p 77. In the end, Guderian was delayed and did not take part.

likely. Hitler demurred, saying that the conversation on this topic would have to be continued at a later date.[3]

This exchange was the second time in a month that the dictator found himself confronted with evidence, put to him by a senior subordinate, that Germany was waging a war completely beyond its means, its recent victories notwithstanding. In light of this, his decision to escalate the war a fortnight later appears downright irrational and offers important support to the contention that by the autumn of 1941 he had become someone who was either guided by unswayable ideological obsessions or hell-bent on bringing about his own obliteration.

Hitler's perception of Germany's economic situation in the late autumn has as yet not been the subject of a major examination. The rise and fall of the German war economy has been covered by a number of historians, but insofar as they have tied in its history with particular moments that could be seen as decisive in strategic terms, they have tended to emphasise Germany's lagging output as the key factor bedevilling much of the economy between mid-1940 and mid-1941.

This is, indeed, justified as there can be little doubt that a shortfall of key military equipment played an important role in denying Germany victory over Britain in 1940–1 and the USSR in 1941–2. The reasons behind this, however, are far from clear, especially since output in most weapons systems did not peak until 1944,[4] despite round-the-clock Allied air raids; it stands to reason that the regime had taken an inordinate time to fully mobilise the economy,

---

[3] Ibid., p 77–8. Such an account would appear to be seriously self-serving, but the key point (Hitler having the idea of a compromise peace put to him) is, in fact, validated by another source. More on this below.

[4] Production figures for key weapons systems suggest that the German war economy peaked between August 1944 and January 1945. August 1944 witnessed the highest-ever output of armoured personnel carriers (1,038) and heavy Flak guns (787), while September saw that of fighter planes (3,375) and V-1 cruise missiles (3,419). A record production of *Nebelwerfer* rocket launchers (1,273) in October was followed in November by the absolute production peak both for heavy artillery pieces (391) and tanks/self-propelled guns (1,780), while December witnessed the maximum output for heavy anti-tank guns (273), light artillery pieces (979), mortars (4,287), machine guns (31,339), submachine guns/assault rifles (78,271) and Würzburg radar sets (400). Finally, U-boat and light Flak production crested in January 1945 with a total of 36 and 1,668, respectively, being handed to the Wehrmacht. When set against production at the turn of the years 1941–2, these figures constituted a twofold (submarines) to tenfold (light artillery) increase. See Rolf-Dieter Müller, 'Albert Speer und die Rüstungspolitik im totalen Krieg'; in: Bernhard Kroener et al (eds.), *Organisation und Mobilisierung des deutschen Machtbereichs. Kriegsverwaltung, Wirtschaft und personelle Ressourcen 1942–1944/45* (Stuttgart: DVA 1999) [= Das Deutsche Reich und der Zweite Weltkrieg, Bd. 5/2], pp 275–773, esp. pp 570–1, 585, 590–1, 599, 620, 622–3, 631 and 639 as well as Lutz Budrass, *Adler und Kranich. Die Lufthansa und ihre Geschichte 1926–1955* (München: Karl Blessing 2016), p 379.

when the opportunity to do so under much less trying circumstances had presented itself in 1939–41.

Soon after the war, economic historians Burton Klein and Alan Milward reached the conclusion that the underperformance of the German economy in the first two and a half years of war had been the result of a deliberate strategy. Making maximum use of Germany's head start in the 1930s arms race and striving not to inflict too many privations on the German population, the idea of a Blitzkrieg economy had taken hold. Germany would fight its war in spurts, winning a series of brief but victorious campaigns. The pauses between each land grab would be used to re-equip the armed forces for the next one; a full and permanent mobilisation of the civilian economy for war could thus be avoided.[5] This theory came under sustained criticism in the 1980s by a number of historians, Richard Overy and Rolf-Dieter Müller chief among them. They both essentially argued that as yet no documentary evidence supporting the Klein–Milward theory had come to light. On the contrary, the paper trail of the first months of the war would suggest that orders for a comprehensive mobil-isation had been issued and that the German civilian population was subjected to quite considerable privations; where consumer industry was allowed to carry on uninterrupted, it did so under the proviso that a disproportionate share of its products would go to the armed forces.[6] A clear focus on ammuni-tion production prior to the invasion of Western Europe appeared to indicate a set of priorities on the part of the German leadership formed by the experi-ence of World War I. What was expected was a campaign which as likely as not would be long, drawn-out and heavily reliant on firepower and attrition, not speed. Research by Karl-Heinz Frieser and Adam Tooze into the army's force structure and the extent of economic mobilisation have provided abundant confirmation of this.[7]

The reasons behind the lacklustre performance of the German war economy in 1939–41 appeared to lie elsewhere. Both Overy and Müller argued that the never-ending turf wars in Berlin over control of the economy resulted in a lack of clear and effective leadership and as such were the most important obstacle standing in the way of an optimum factory output. Only the appointment of Albert Speer as minister of armaments production would lead to centralisation at the top and delegation at the level of production management, thus leading to the production miracle of 1944. In addition, Overy pointed to the number of major projects, which in 1939 were still months or even years away from

[5] Burton H. Klein, *Germany's Economic Preparations for War* (Cambridge, MA: Harvard UP 1959); Alan Milward, *The German Economy at War* (London: Athlone Press 1965).

[6] Richard Overy, *War and Economy in the Third Reich* (Oxford: Clarendon 1995 pb), pp 259–314.

[7] Karl-Heinz Frieser, *Blitzkrieglegende. Der Westfeldzug 1940* (München: Oldenbourg 1996), pp 30–41; Adam Tooze, *The Wages of Destruction: The Making and Breaking of the Nazi Economy* (London: Allen Lane 2006), pp 338–47.

reaching completion, but of considerable importance if the German economy was to achieve the sort of depth it would need to persevere in a great power conflict. The Nibelungenwerke tank factory at Linz, the Salzgitter foundry which specialised in the smelting of poor-yield ores, the Flugmotorenwerke Ostmark aircraft-engine plant, the Stahlwerke Braunschweig metalworks and the synthetic rubber factory at Auschwitz/Monowitz are easily the best known because they were created from scratch; however, the expansion of several existing airplane and tank factories was equally, if not more, important. While some of the new projects would effectively turn out to be white elephants,[8] the long-term effect of this last-minute burst of industrial expansion would provide the Wehrmacht with the means to stave off collapse in 1944. In addition to these enterprises, a number of major military projects were only half-finished at the start of the war (the Westwall fortifications, the battleships *Bismarck* and *Tirpitz*). Their doubtful military value notwithstanding, they would continue to tie up labour urgently needed elsewhere for several months.

In the early 1990s, Bernhard Kroener argued for a compromise between the two schools of thought by drawing attention to the fact that in at least one case (the war against the USSR) the German leadership had indeed made a deliberate choice to limit the arms and munitions output destined for the army prior to a major campaign. However, he contradicted Milward and Klein by stressing that this move was driven by a strategic agenda (a planned surge in production for the Kriegsmarine and Luftwaffe) rather than a domestic one.[9]

Overy's point about a German war economy still in the final stages of construction in 1939–41 was further developed by Adam Tooze in 2005–6.[10] Having made allowance for this factor, and working from a different set of statistics from his predecessors,[11] Tooze reached the conclusion that output during the period in question had actually been good and that the bureaucratic battles among the numerous military and civilian leaders tasked with overseeing the war economy were effectively little more than a distraction.[12] He also found himself in agreement with Overy that mobilisation of the female workforce had been satisfactory and did not constitute a major missed opportunity. The contribution of Speer's management to the peak of production in 1944 was

---

[8] The Auschwitz/Monowitz facility fell to the Red Army in early 1945 without producing a single ton of synthetic rubber. Tooze, *Wages*, pp 445–6

[9] Bernhard Kroener, 'Der "erfrorene Blitzkrieg". Strategische Planungen der deutschen Führung gegen die Sowjetunion und die Ursachen ihres Scheiterns'; in: Bernd Wegner (ed.), *Zwei Wege nach Moskau. Vom Hitler-Stalin Pakt zum 'Unternehmen Barbarossa'* (München: Piper 1991), pp 133–48.

[10] Adam Tooze, 'No Room for Miracles: German Industrial Output in World War II Reassessed'; in: *Geschichte und Gesellschaft* Bd. 31 (2005), pp 439–64. Also Tooze, *Wages*.

[11] Tooze, 'No Room for Miracles', pp 444–57.

[12] Tooze, *Wages*, p 432

put down to a number of issues, with mass use of slave labour (a factor not yet in play in 1939–40) every bit as important as improved methods of production.

This chapter does not propose to address the unresolved issues between these different schools of thought. Rather, an attempt will be made to assess when and how the German dictator would have been in a position to realise that the coming together of the unremitting intensity of hostilities in the East, on the one hand, with the gradual drop-off in weapons output that became evident over the course of summer and autumn 1941, on the other, had the potential to derail his plans for victory over the USSR, and hence call into question any plans for turning on the USA.

6.2   The Burden of Shifting Priorities: September 1939–June 1941

Several statements by Hitler in the months before the invasion of Poland indicate that while he was hoping to settle his next move with a short sharp war, he was not banking on so happy an outcome. Instead, he stressed the duty of the political leadership to prepare the country's economy for the possibility of a war lasting ten to fifteen years.[13] The crisis preceding the invasion of Poland saw the drafting of a directive for a comprehensive mobilisation of the German economy. It was held back while the Western powers had not yet shown their hand, but issued the day France and Great Britain declared war.

The German economy at the time was a hybrid: while individual enterprises were allowed to make a profit and issue shares, the new regime's priorities could not but leave a deep imprint on German economic life. Both the cost-intensive development and production of a range of synthetic substitutes aimed at rendering Germany invulnerable to a blockade and the constraints imposed on hard-currency-dominated free trade had the effect of distorting the dynamics usually governing a capitalist economy. German entrepreneurs learned to cope and even benefit from this system – only in a handful of cases did the regime turn to coercive measures like incarceration and/or expropriation.[14]

At least on paper, a perfectly satisfactory structure to guide the transition to a war economy was already in place on the first day of the war. The *Ministerrat für die Reichsverteidigung* (Ministerial Council for the Defence of the Reich) was to coordinate the work of both the civilian *Generalbevollmächtigter für*

---

[13] 'Bericht über eine Besprechung am 23. Mai 1939 (n.d.)'; in: *Akten zur deutschen auswärtigen Politik (ADAP)*, Serie D, Bd. VI (Baden-Baden: Imprimerie Nationale 1956), pp 477–83.

[14] Aviation pioneer Hugo Junkers had his factory seized in 1933, while in 1937 the steel conglomerates, Vereinigte Stahlwerke, Hoesch and Krupp, had to sign over important mining rights to the new state-run Reichswerke Hermann Göring. On the Junkers case, see Lutz Budrass, *Flugzeugindustrie und Luftrüstung in Deutschland* (Düsseldorf: Droste 1998), pp 320–35; the case of the steel companies is discussed in Tooze, *Wages*, pp 230–9.

die Wirtschaft (Walther Funk) and the Oberkommando der Wehrmacht's *Wehrwirtschaft- und Rüstungsamt* (*Generalmajor* Georg Thomas), which oversaw the running of the civilian and military parts of the war economy, respectively. The fact that the *Ministerrat* was chaired by Hermann Göring, head of the Four Year Plan agency for economic coordination and No. 2 in the regime, should have guaranteed that all the decisions made in the council's meetings would be followed to the letter. The *Ministerrat's* attempt to uphold an artificial separation between factories producing for civilian and military needs, while problematic, was not nearly as harmful as the fact that Göring only made a perfunctory attempt to exercise effective control. Following a behavioural pattern which would soon become routine, he soon lost interest in his new position,[15] thus creating a vacuum at the top of the German war economy, which different players would endeavour to fill of their own accord. Every once in a while, Göring would make a show of taking up the reins again and resume issuing directives, but since all concerned knew that nothing permanent would come of these bursts of activity, they had no lasting effect.[16] Funk, for his part, showed himself consistently anxious not to antagonise his mentor Göring and also found himself increasingly out of his depth as the war wore on. Hence he was happy to take his cue from others and play a secondary role in the running of the war economy;[17] Thomas lacked both the rank and access to Hitler to make his weight count.[18] Moreover, Thomas' commanding officer, OKW Chief of Staff *Generaloberst* Wilhelm Keitel lacked both the expertise and temperamental inclination to impress on Hitler the need for a centralised coordination of the war economy. Only by virtue of the fact that OKW oversaw the allocation of raw materials to factories carrying out

---

[15] While older scholarship has tended to put Göring's incapacity for consistent work down to extreme laziness and fondness of the good life, recent research has found evidence that he had wrestled with serious doubts about Germany's prospects in another major European conflict as far back as 1938. The outbreak of war then brought about successive bouts of depression which left him increasingly listless and incapable of fulfilling his duties. Karl-Günther Zelle, *Hitlers zweifelnde Elite. Goebbels-Göring-Himmler-Speer* (Paderborn: Ferdinand Schöningh 2010), pp 91–174.

[16] For a brief history of the *Ministerrat's* activities in 1939, see Paul Fröhlich, '*Der unterirdische Kampf'. Das Wehrwirtschafts- und Rüstungsamt 1924–1943* (Paderborn: Ferdinand Schöningh 2018), pp 311–20.

[17] On Funk, see Willi A. Boelcke, *Die deutsche Wirtschaft 1930–1945. Interna des Reichswirtschaftsministeriums* (Düsseldorf: Droste 1983), pp 185–9, as well as Ludolf Herbst, 'Walther Funk – Vom Journalisten zum Reichswirtschaftsminister'; in: Ronald Smelser et al (eds.), *Die braune Elite II. 21 weitere biographische Skizzen* (Darmstadt: WBG 1993), pp 91–102.

[18] Fröhlich, *Kampf*, p 269. The first time the two men met in wartime was in December 1940; since this occurred in the context of a major reception for key personnel engaged in the running of the economy, it is unlikely Thomas would have had the opportunity to discuss any of the problems hampering production in any kind of detail. See Rolf Dieter Müller, 'Die Mobilisierung der deutschen Wirtschaft für Hitlers Kriegführung'; in: DRZW 5/1, p 538.

military orders were Thomas and Keitel in a position to exercise a degree of leverage. This state of affairs gave what should have been secondary players like the armed services' top procurement officers, General Friedrich Fromm (army), *Generaladmiral* Karl Witzell (Kriegsmarine) and *Generalfeldmarschall* Erhard Milch (Luftwaffe), unexpected elbow room.

The resulting arrangement suffered its first crisis when higher than expected ammunition usage during the Polish campaign conjured memories in Hitler's mind of the ammunition crisis of late 1914. Since ammunition production was in fact far from satisfactory in the winter of 1939–40, a new player was brought into the game: as of 7 March 1940 Fritz Todt, an engineer by trade and veteran of the NSDAP, was made *Reichsminister für Bewaffnung und Munition* with a brief to coordinate production of all types of army ordnance.[19] He had a flying start, in that by early March the mobilisation of the last reserves of raw materials and foreign exchange had already ushered in a big boost in factory output; this was clearly not his doing, in spite of which he was perceived by many as the driving force behind the hike in production, enhancing his reputation.[20] Göring correctly saw Todt's installation as a challenge to his position as chairman of the *Ministerrat*; the fact that Todt was on very good personal terms with Hitler no doubt made this even more grating. Göring lost no time stressing that the newcomer was to be in control of production only, not allocation of labour and raw materials. Despite this first check, the wily Todt, making good use of his access to Hitler,[21] expanded his remit as opportunities arose. By the end of the year, he had added tank production to his empire by entrusting industrialist Walter Rohland with coordinating the production of all armoured fighting vehicles.[22]

The events of May and June 1940 put the German leadership in a position where they could not avoid a radical reassessment of strategic and, hence, production priorities. A directive signed by Hitler on 13 July 1940 gave clear priority to the air force and navy in general and to the production of the new Junkers 88 bomber and U-boats in particular. Before this new set of priorities had the time to make themselves felt, however, Hitler's decision of 28 July to prioritise production of Flak guns

---

[19] Todt had previously overseen important building projects for the new regime, the Autobahnen and the Westwall fortifications chief among them; see Franz W. Seidler, *Fritz Todt. Baumeister des Dritten Reiches* (München: Herbig 1986), pp 97–238. Since his status as a civilian had caused occasional clashes with the army over the Westwall project, Göring invested him with the rank of a *Generalmajor* in the Luftwaffe in October 1939.

[20] Tooze, *Wages*, p 352.

[21] In 1944, General Thomas, reflecting on the events of 1940–1, described Todt's habit of briefing Hitler while increasingly bypassing Keitel. IWM, Speer Collection, FD 386/46 'Grundlagen für eine Geschichte der deutschen Wehr- und Rüstungswirtschaft (mid-1944)'. In contrast to the paper trail created by Speer, Todt does not appear to have put a major effort into recording the gist of these meetings.

[22] Rohland, *Bewegte Zeiten*, pp 70–1; Müller, 'Mobilisierung', pp 529, 541.

Figure 6.1 OKW's *Generalfeldmarschall* Wilhelm Keitel in conversation with Hitler. By a process of elimination, the dysfunctional structure of the German war economy in 1939–41 left Keitel as the point man tasked with delivering unpalatable evidence to Hitler of the mismatch between ends and means in Germany' s war production. It was a role he was temperamentally ill-suited to fulfil. (Evans/ Stringer/Hulton Archive via Getty Images)

put a question mark against it.[23] His decision to turn on his Soviet ally then forced a temporary refocusing on army production. In order to facilitate this, an order dated 28 September directed the army to temporarily release up to 300,000 soldiers from its ranks. The majority of these hailed from the metalworking trade and would – or so the logic of the decree claimed – produce the weapons they themselves would take to the field with them in spring. The impact of this measure was limited by a number of factors, not the least of which was the ineffective allocation of labour and raw materials throughout the German war economy. Attempts to tackle this problem by creating a system of prioritisation soon led to all three services clogging up the system by allocating top priority to any number of projects.[24] This

---

[23] For a more detailed discussion of the rationale driving the production of Flak guns in 1940–1, see the chapter on the Luftwaffe.

[24] BA/MA, RW 19/199 'Oberkommando der Wehrmacht Wi.Rü.Amt/Stab I b 5, Nr. 1943/ 41 gKdos. Wirtschaftlicher Lagebericht Nr. 21. Mai 1941 (10.6.1941)': 'The considerable rise in orders categorised as belonging to priority S or SS has led to the remainder of production being disadvantaged with regards to allocation of labour and transport. As a consequence, factories have started to put off or even refuse any orders outside the top priority system.'

problem was compounded by a frequent tendency on the part of the armed services to place an order and shift the raw materials needed for it to a shipyard or factory, irrespective of the latter being ready to process the order in the near future. When delays were incurred, the armed services' adamant refusal to release the raw materials for other orders often led to copious quantities of copper or iron being left immobilised and unused, sometimes for months on end.[25] Factory managers repeatedly colluded in this by pulling the wool over the eyes of visiting inspectors, whose task it was to match raw material stocks against orders. To compound matters, the existing pricing system, which was based on the actual costs of earlier production runs, constituted a major disincentive for plant managers to explore ways to rationalise the production process on their own initiative.[26] This meant, in effect, that by the time the last of the workers released from the field army returned to their units in April 1941, production in some areas (especially tanks) had met expectations, but a sizeable gap had opened up in others. More importantly, even before the beginning of Operation Barbarossa, the first orders went out directing industry once more to prioritise production for the Luftwaffe and (to a lesser extent) the Kriegsmarine.[27] In contrast to the planning that had preceded the invasion of Western Europe, no allowance was made for the next major operation to go on beyond a certain date – in this case, September 1941.

6.3   The Growing Gap between Means and Ends:
May 1941–January 1942

A month before the invasion of the USSR, Hitler asked Keitel and Todt to join him at his summer retreat in Berchtesgaden to take stock of what had been achieved by the whirlwind activity of the last few months. Even though not a verbatim account of what passed between the three men, the memo compiled afterwards is a crucial source for assessing how the German dictator was judging the performance of a war industry that at the time still fell short of

---

[25] BA/MA, RW 19/654 'Die wehr- und rüstungswirtschaftlichen Maßnahmen im Jahre 1941', pp 437–8.

[26] The Reichsluftfahrtministerium, which introduced a fixed-price system that allowed aircraft producers to pocket the difference made through gains in efficiency in March of 1937, was the exception to the rule. See Lutz Budraß, Jonas Scherner and Jochen Streb, 'Demystifying the German "Armament Miracle" during World War II: New Insights from the Annual Audits of German Aircraft Producers' [= Economic Growth Centre, Yale University, Centre Discussion Paper No. 905, January 2005], pp 1–40, esp. 23–4. Available at www.econ.yale.edu/growth_pdf/cdp905.pdf (accessed 21 March 2016).

[27] 'BdF und OBdW, betrifft: Rüstung (20.6.1941)'; in: Martin Moll (ed.), Führer-Erlasse 1939–1945 (Stuttgart: Franz Steiner 1997), p 178.

firing on all cylinders.[28] Unsurprisingly, the main bone of contention was the terms under which servicemen 'loaned' to industry would be returned to their units or allowed to stay there. On the subject of war production, Hitler expressed displeasure with the production figures for some weapons and calibres, which appeared to lag behind the available production potential. This was all the more frustrating since production of a number of ammunition types had already been considerably scaled back in order to achieve higher output elsewhere. He also proved his eye for detail and memory for figures by chiding his interlocutors for including items such as unserviceable ammunition among the figures presented.[29] By far the most prescient comment, however, concerned a subject that would not really become an issue until the large-scale attrition suffered by the army during Barbarossa became apparent. Without specifying a particular weapons system, he noted that many of the existing pieces of equipment were overly sophisticated (*überzüchtet*),[30] which in turn meant that both their production and maintenance made excessive demands of the skills of the workers in the factories and service personnel in the field. He stressed that a return to 'more robust and primitive designs' was called for in all three services.[31]

The full importance of this statement will become clear in due course. For the moment, suffice it to say that it gives us an insight into the dictator's thoughts on the subject at a time of minimum military stress: barring the Battle of Britain, the Wehrmacht could look back on a string of successes without precedent in modern history and little appeared to indicate that the next endeavour would follow a fundamentally different pattern.

The first weeks of fighting in the western USSR appeared to confirm German expectations and the directive confirming the shift away from production of most army requirements was issued on 13 July 1941. Flak gun production was supposed to be exempt from this, as was tank production; in the latter case the idea behind this was the creation of a major pool of armour, which would

---

[28] IWM, EDS Mi 14/463 '(III) OKW Wi Rü Amt/Rü (IIa). Nr. 1714/41 g.K. Aktennotiz über die Besprechung bei Chef OKW, Reichskanzlei Berchtesgaden am 19.5.1941 (21.5.1941)'. The meeting with Hitler had taken place on the 18th. For a detailed contemporary analysis of German war production between September 1940 and March 1941, see BA/MA, RW 19/822 'Oberkommando der Wehrmacht Wi Rü Amt/Rü (IIa). Bericht über die Leistungen auf dem Gebiet der materiellen Wehrmachtrüstung in der Zeit vom 1.9.40 bis 1.4.41 (10.7.1941)'.

[29] Hitler's gift for memorising figures repeatedly allowed him to catch out senior officers in briefings. For another example, see Hildegard von Kotze (ed.), *Heeresadjutant bei Hitler 1938–1943. Aufzeichnungen des Majors Engel* (Stuttgart: DVA 1974), p 112 (entry for 4 October 1941).

[30] Hitler used the term '*Waffen und Gerät*', which in military German also encompasses items of a non-lethal nature, like trucks and field kitchens.

[31] IWM, EDS Mi. 14/463 (III) 'OKW Wi Rü Amt Rü (IIa). Nr. 1714/41. Aktennotiz über die Besprechung bei Chef OKW Reichskanzlei Berchtesgaden am 19.5.1941 (21.5.1941)'.

equip a force that would invade the British-dominated Middle East through Turkey and the conquered Caucasus in early 1942.[32] In the meantime, the mundane task of routinely replacing rifles, trucks and howitzers lost in the fight against the Red Army would become progressively more difficult as the campaign wore on.

Even though this radical shift away from army-centred production should have freed up raw material and labour on a huge scale, it must be remembered that the new plans were nothing if not ambitious. The air force interpreted the original focus on the Ju-88 rather loosely and looked to quadruple its size under the so-called *Göring-Programm*. The new mechanised force would see Panzer divisions increase from twenty to thirty-six, and motorised infantry divisions from nine to eighteen; the new force would require a total of 15,444 tanks. Since by mid-July fewer than half of the approximately 4,000 tanks currently engaged in Russia were expected to last more or less undamaged to the end of the campaign,[33] this meant the production of more than 13,000 tanks in slightly over half a year. In the meantime, the Flak programme which had originated in July 1940 saw a further increase. For its part, the navy insisted that all sorts of ancillary services only marginally connected to the U-boat arm enjoy the same top priority as the production and repair of submersibles;[34] the same went for the construction and particularly labour-intensive upkeep of its capital ships,[35] the recent disastrous ending of the *Bismarck* sortie notwithstanding.

Early deliberations among representatives of the armed services, OKW and Todt's ministry soon arrived at the conclusion that most of the production figures demanded in Hitler's directive of 13 July were quite simply out of reach. The Luftwaffe's demands were easily the most outlandish, but the others were equally predicated on pre-Barbarossa calculations that had assumed a Soviet collapse by mid-September at the latest, allowing the disbandment of fifty infantry divisions and the freeing up of up to a million workers.[36] Shortage of

---

[32] 'BdF und OBdW, betrifft: Panzer-Programm im Rahmen der Umrüstung des Heeres (13.7.1941)'; in: Moll (ed.), *'Führer-Erlasse'*, pp 181–3.

[33] IWM, Speer Collection, FD 5450/50 'Aktenvermerk über die Sitzung des Panzerausschusses am 17.7.41'.

[34] For Todt's exasperation over this, IWM, Speer Collection FD 5450/45 'Dr. ing. Fritz Todt an Generalfeldmarschall Keitel (30.7.1941)'.

[35] Even though only two were still under construction (the carrier *Graf Zeppelin* and the cruiser *Seydlitz*), many of the existing ship types were notorious for the number of man-hours required to service and refit their steam-turbine engine plant after each sortie. For a contemporary assessment of this technological Achilles heel, see Wilhelm Treue, 'Entwurf einer Denkschrift über den Flottenaufbau 1926–1939, n.d.' (early 1943); in: Wilhelm Treue et al (eds.), *Deutsche Marinerüstung 1919–1942. Die Gefahren der Tirpitztradition* (Herford: Mittler & Sohn 1992), pp 41–181, esp. pp 91–112.

[36] BA/MA, RW 19/177 'OKW Wi Rü Amt/Rü (IIa) Nr. 2747/41 g.Kdos. Niederschrift. Besprechung Chef OKW mit den Wehrmachtteilen am 16.8.1941 über 'Die Auswirkung

labour was also behind a drop-off in coal production with a concomitant impact on steel output, which put yet another question mark against the wish list encapsulated in Hitler's directive.[37]

In the run-up to a major meeting with Keitel, Thomas and the service chiefs had a series of talks in which they arrived at figures they believed to be within the bounds of feasibility. Seeing that the Luftwaffe had just asked for the equivalent of four times the yearly German output of aluminium,[38] it was no surprise that it had to take the most substantial hit, with plane production slashed to the figures needed to keep up (barely) with its losses; in the mid to long term, Luftwaffe production managers, Erhard Milch and Ernst Udet, suggested a doubling (rather than quadrupling) of effectives as the aim they would strive for.[39] The army had already given some thought to how it would cope with the post-Barbarossa structure. The expected monthly production of 2,000 tanks was to be slashed first to 900, then 650. However, equipping the new motorised force for the Middle East not just with tanks, but with the assorted vehicles needed to ensure the mobility of all its ancillary parts, would require the *Entmotorisierung* (demotorisation) of all remaining infantry divisions.[40] The Flak programme, in the meantime, had been declared out of bounds, even though this called into question the production of heavy artillery for the new motorised and mechanised army of 1942.[41] Needless to say all these readjustments were still predicated on a defeat of the USSR occurring if not quite within the time frame predicted,[42] then only a few months later.

Coming face-to-face with such a dramatic mismatch between ends and means could, of course, have turned into a catalyst for dramatic changes of

der Richtlinien des Führers vom 14.7.41 sowie die Durchführbarkeit der sich daraus ergebenden Schwerpunkt-Programme' (18.8.1941)'.

[37] Ibid.

[38] BA/MA, RW 19/559 'Wi Rü Amt/Stab. Aktenvermerk über die Chefbesprechungen bei GFM Keitel vom 14.-16.8.41 (17.8.41)'.

[39] BA/MA, RW 19/559 'Wi Rü Amt/Stab Aktenvermerk über die Chefbesprechungen bei GFM Keitel vom 14. – 16.8.41 (17.8.41)'. In the meantime, it was accepted that the wear and tear aircraft were routinely exposed to in Russia meant that not many would be in condition to resume operations elsewhere on the conclusion of Barbarossa.

[40] IWM, Speer Collection, FD 5450/45 'Ausführungen zu den Besprechungsunterlagen vom 17.7.41 für die Vorbereitung der Durchführungsbestimmungen zu o.a. Verfügung (n.d.)'; BA/MA, RW 19/1970 'Rü II a Nr. 2418/41 g.Kdos. Aktennotiz über die Besprechung bei WFSt/L (II Org) am 17.7.41 (19.7.1941)'.

[41] BA/MA, RW 19/1970 'Niederschrift über die Besprechung beim Chef des Waffenamtes mit den Wehrmachtteilen am 7.8.1941 (8.8.1941)'.

[42] Even though it does not appear that a new estimate for the date at which a Soviet collapse would occur was ever issued, an OKW document from mid-July speculated about the need to postpone the planned restructuring of the army to 'late December'. IWM, Speer Collection, FD 5450/45 'OKW Nr. 1714/41 g.Kds. WFSt/Abt. L (II Org) Ausführungen zu den Besprechungsunterlagen vom 17.7.41 für die Vorbereitung der Durchführungsbestimmungen zu o.a. Verfügung (n.d.)'.

one kind and another. Instead, a three-day conference held in mid-August culminated in an exhortation by Keitel that every service find ways to focus the resources allocated to it by 'ruthlessly' cancelling less important projects. Failing that, he threatened, he and Todt would not hesitate to intervene and slash orders over the services' objections. It would be a mistake, however, to overrate the spirit of cooperation on display here. Within days of this meeting Keitel was commenting to Thomas that he had no intention of making good on this threat since he was 'concerned that in such case, he would not receive the necessary support from *Reichsminister* Todt'.[43] Cooperation along similar lines with Göring was likewise ruled out, since this might mean delegating important powers to the agency of the Four Year Plan.[44]

It is difficult to assess the extent to which the dictator fully appreciated the waste and friction being generated by this kind of management and the extent to which this might become a large enough obstacle to block his path to victory. The consensus of scholarly opinion is that he had only an incomplete grasp of the intricate inner workings of the German war economy; on those occasions when he did grapple with economic issues, it would usually be in the context of boosting flagging production figures of a particular weapons system.[45] Neither Keitel nor Göring were temperamentally inclined to point him in the direction of wider problems of a more systemic nature. Todt, who was both more forthright and technically competent, had an inclination to deal with problems as they arose, rather than demand reforms that might shake the existing system to its core.[46] Thus, it comes as no surprise that a directive issued by Hitler on 11 September did little more than echo Keitel's previous exhortations; it also alluded to the new joint control of war production supposedly exercised by OKW and Todt's ministry.[47] More importantly, the overall thrust of production priorities did not change. While the Luftwaffe had had to accept a major aluminium cutback, it was still given a sizeable steel allocation with which to build or expand the factories, flight schools, air bases and Flak units that would underpin the totality of the enormous Luftwaffe of the *Göring-Programm*. The army, on the other hand, was left with less than half the steel it had asked for.[48] Hitler, for his part, got personally involved in

---

[43] BA/MA, RW 19/2334 'Geheime Kommandosache. Aktenvermerk über Vortrag beim Chef OKW im Führerhauptquartier am 30.8.1941 (2.9.1941)'.

[44] Ibid.

[45] Seidler, *Todt*, p 246; Müller, 'Mobilisierung'; in: DRZW Bd. 5/1, pp 550, 627, 650, 687; Bernhard Kroener, *'Der starke Mann im Heimatkriegsgebiet'. Generaloberst Friedrich Fromm. Eine Biographie* (Paderborn et al: Ferdinand Schöningh 2005), p 406.

[46] Rohland, *Bewegte Zeiten*, p 81.

[47] BA/MA, RM 7/94 'Der Führer und Oberste Befehlshaber der Wehrmacht Nr. 340/41 g.Kdos. Chef OKW. Abschrift von Abschrift (11.9.1941)' Also reproduced in Moll (ed.), *'Führer-Erlasse'*, pp 197–8.

[48] BA/MA, RW 19/1971 OKH 'Der Chef der Heeresrüstung und Befehlshaber des Ersatzheeres an den Chef des Oberkommandos der Wehrmacht (18.9.1941)'.

Figure 6.2 Aircraft designers Willy Messerschmitt (far left) and Ernst Heinkel (second from left) join Hitler and Fritz Todt (far right) at a pre-war reception. The years 1939 and 1941 saw the failure of two attempts to expand the Luftwaffe to the point which would have elevated it to the position of the Wehrmacht's senior service. (ullstein bild/ullstein bild via Getty Images)

pushing Flak gun production a mere month after OKW had reached the conclusion that such a course of action would leave the new mechanised force bereft of heavy artillery.[49]

It goes without saying that the continuation of the priorities set by the July 1941 directive was predicated on a Soviet defeat – or at the very least, paralysis – setting in by October or November 1941. For about a fortnight around mid-October 1941, this appeared to be a reasonable expectation. The Red Army had suffered further shattering defeats at the battles of Vyazma-Bryansk and the Sea of Azov; the Soviet capital was rocked by instances of open dissent, plunder and the spectacle of officials fleeing the city. This had an immediate effect on the planners of the German war economy. A loose minute in the papers of Thomas's office records a promise by Göring to Hitler that in

[49] BA/MA, RW 19/822 'Der Reichsminister für Bewaffnung und Munition Nr. M 5467/41 (19.9.1941)'; ibid., 'Der Chef des Oberkommandos der Wehrmacht an Chef Wi Rü Amt (19.9.1941)'; ibid., 'Reichsminister Dr. ing. Fritz Todt an General der Artillerie Ritter v. Leeb (23.9.1941)'.

due course up to a 100,000 blue-collar workers would be released from the army in the east and distributed among the factories with the highest priority.[50] For a brief moment, the sentiment behind an angry retort Hitler had made to Keitel a few days earlier, that 'he failed to understand how the war economy could be short of raw materials, now that he had conquered all of Europe',[51] appeared to be borne out by the facts.

Such illusions did not dissipate overnight. On 23 October, OKW issued a twenty-page directive on the preliminaries of switching the war economy round again. While stressing that it was up to Hitler to determine when exactly operations against the Red Army had reached the mopping-up phase,[52] it did not deviate from the existing priorities: army demobilisation would affect rather fewer than the fifty divisions planned for, but the structural changes in favour of a greatly enhanced Panzer arm, the navy and – above all – the Luftwaffe were left unchanged. Hence the next weeks would see the release of 50,000 factory workers from the army.[53] One of the handful of individuals in the German leadership unconvinced by these forecasts was *Generaloberst* Friedrich Fromm of the *Ersatzheer* (Home Army). On 26 October, he finished a document that effectively called into question the German Army's capacity to carry on with the war if the raw material allocations were left in place and even implied the need to seek a negotiated peace. He circulated copies to Halder, Todt and Keitel.[54] Keitel's reaction was by far the most illuminating. In a handwritten comment in the margins of the document he recorded the fact that he had shown this document to Hitler; he also questioned the need for the shift to army production Fromm had insisted on, since the Red Army's waning powers of resistance did not warrant such a change in focus.[55]

The events of the first half of November (an operational hiatus before Moscow, and in far-off Washington the dismantling of US neutrality legislation) led to a gradual reassessment of options, but as yet no admission that Germany was facing a major crisis of war production. In a letter that Keitel wrote to Funk on the 5th of the month, the head of OKW admitted in a roundabout sort of way that hostilities in Russia were not likely to end

---

[50] BA/MA, RW 19/1914 'Ro Ib. Aktennotiz (18.10.1941)'.
[51] BA/MA, RW 19/165 'Kriegstagebuch Wi.Rü.Amt/Stab. Besprechung General v. Hanneken beim Amtschef mit Chef Ro. (13.10.1941)'.
[52] IWM, Speer Collection, FD 5450/45 'Oberkommando der Wehrmacht WFSt/Abt. L (II Org), 2200/41 g.K.dos. (23.10.1941)'.
[53] Ibid.
[54] For a comprehensive discussion of the circumstances which surrounded the issuing of this document, see Bernhard Kroener, 'Zwischen Blitzsieg und Verhandlungsfrieden. Der Chef der Heeresrüstung und Befehlshaber des Ersatzheeres fordert im Herbst 1941 die Beendigung des Krieges'; in: Wolfgang Elz and Sönke Neitzel (eds.), *Internationale Beziehungen im 19. und 20. Jahrhundert. Festschrift für Winfried Baumgart zum 65. Geburtstag* (Paderborn et al: Ferdinand Schöningh 2003), pp 341–60.
[55] Ibid., p 356.

soon. At the same time, he reminded the civilian minister that the production priorities dictated by Hitler remained unchanged: the U-boats, the Luftwaffe, the enhanced Panzer arm as well as a 'considerably boosted Flak programme', to say nothing of various civilian projects, all had to be given the same top priority.[56] The obvious implication was that the Red Army, while still in existence, was no longer in a position to pose an active threat.

Two days later, the gist of a long meeting between Göring and around thirty government ministers, company CEOs and representatives of the armed forces was broadly similar. Essentially Göring's swansong as notional supreme coord-inator of the wartime economy, the points he failed to dwell on were as interesting as those at the centre of his exhortations. The central theme of the gathering was the overall rationalisation of production to facilitate the implementation of the inflated and contradictory priorities Hitler had set the German economy.[57] Göring specified a number of instances where, according to him, either labour or raw material was being systematically wasted, while contrasting this with the threat to Germany posed by the gigantic US war economy, which was only just starting to shift into higher gear.[58] The war in Russia, on the other hand, was mentioned only in passing. There was one brief and rather equivocal reference to possible American truck deliveries to the USSR;[59] at the same time, the fall of the Caucasus and the return of a large number of demobilised servicemen from Russia were referred to in the manner of a foregone conclusion.[60]

It soon became clear that, in spite of Göring's exhortations, any attempt at rationalising the process by which human and material assets were to be shifted to individual plants in Germany would come too late to prevent the contradictions in the July directive from revealing themselves. A glimpse of these could be found in an entry in the *Wehrwirtschafts- und Rüstungsamt's* war diary of 21 November. It admonished the field army, which was starting to run desperately short of some ammunition types, to make do with the available

---

[56] BA/MA, RW 19/822 'Der Chef des Oberkommandos der Wehrmacht an Herrn Reichsminister Funk. Geheime Kommandosache (5.11.1941)'.

[57] BA-Lichterf., R 3112/99 'Bericht über die Sitzung beim Reichsmarschall am 7.11.1941 – Dauer von 15 Uhr 30 bis 19 Uhr (8.11.1941)'. Among those attending were the ministers Funk and Todt and the generals Milch, Udet, Fromm and Thomas. Note: this report used to be filed under R 25.

[58] 'As repugnant as the American [sic] was to him at a personal level, his achievements in the technical sphere (engines and aircraft) were impressive.' See ibid., p 5.

[59] Ibid., p 2, refers to a quote by Stalin which allegedly held out the hope of US motor vehicle deliveries to compensate for the factories lost to the Germans. Since the next sentence makes clear that US production was not expected to peak until 1943, it is not clear whether US deliveries to the USSR of the kind described are seen as feasible or likely to make a major difference.

[60] Ibid., pp 3, 6 and 8.

resources, while at the same time noting the need to raise with Keitel the issue of the Luftwaffe's first call on resources.[61]

The following day, Todt, Thomas and their staffs held a meeting which had been specifically called to discuss Fromm's demands. The armaments minister – his notional rank as a Luftwaffe general notwithstanding – called for the army to be given additional copper from the air force's share and then went on to describe the Luftwaffe's expansion programme as 'not feasible', since none of the human and material resources needed for it were available.[62] A directive by Keitel issued two days later unwittingly drove home that very point. Referring to a previous conversation with the dictator, the OKW chief reduced the number of workers who by virtue of their age group or skill sets would be exempt from the draft.[63] While it was clear that the war was going to drag on for some time yet, the question of who would build the new weapons all services were clamouring for remained unanswered.

An opportunity to raise this welter of inconsistencies with Germany's supreme warlord presented itself on 29 November. Prior to a two-hour meeting on tank production with a number of key players of the German armaments industry, Hitler met privately, as described at the beginning of this chapter, with Fritz Todt and Walter Rohland, fresh from his tour of the Eastern Front. According to Rohland's post-war account,[64] both he and Todt stressed to Hitler that an American entry into the war was sure to spell doom for the Wehrmacht. Rohland's post-war assertion, that Todt even insisted Hitler should seek to end the war by a negotiated peace,[65] finds a degree of corroboration in a turn of phrase used by the dictator later that afternoon when he chaired the meeting on future tank design. Using words that echoed his remark to Keitel from six weeks earlier, he stressed that 'he would never capitulate on account of raw material shortages. The very thought was utterly ridiculous. He disposed of the entirety of Europe.'[66] All other points on the agenda, however, involved tank design rather than grand strategy, and here Hitler was in a position to show off his considerable knowledge of the subject. To begin with, he was at pains to qualify reports about the growing superiority of Allied armour. He argued that

---

[61] BA/MA, RW 19/259 'KTB Stab Wi Rü Amt (entry for 21 November 1941)'.

[62] BA/MA, RW 19/166 'Besprechung Reichsminister Dr. Todt beim Amtschef mit Chef Rü und Chef Ro (22.11.1941)'.

[63] IWM, EDS Mi 14/433, '(II) Oberkommando der Wehrmacht WFSt/Abt. L (II Org) Nr. 3600/41 g. Betr.: Schutz der Spezialbetriebe und Sicherstellung des Ersatzbedarfs zur Erhaltung zur Erhaltung der Schlagkraft der Wehrmacht (24.11.1941)'.

[64] Walter Rohland, *Bewegte Zeiten*, pp 77–8

[65] Ibid., p 78.

[66] Paul Fröhlich and Alexander Kranz (eds.), *Tagebuch des Chef des Stabes beim Chef der Heeresrüstung und Befehlshaber des Ersatzheeres 1938 bis 1943* (entry for 29 November 1941) (forthcoming). This edition of the war diary of Fromm's office promises to be a treasure trove of insights into the reasons behind Germany's stunted mobilisation effort.

within a year or two, the widespread use of the hollow charge was likely to confer a major advantage on the defence in armoured warfare.[67] Such a development would, in fact, favour Germany since by then it would be in possession of all the territories it could reasonably expect to seize and hence be able to settle down for a prolonged defence. In the meantime, additional technological solutions would have to be sought to prevent the Allies from making the most of their numerical superiority. He dwelt on the intricacies of modern armour and shell design in a manner that indicated his knowledge of the subject, but then moved on to a subject he had first broached in May that year: the need for much greater standardisation of all German motor vehicles, thus making production in the factory and maintenance in the field a much smoother process. Such a move, he argued, was made more difficult by the proclivity of German designers for producing vehicles of extremely high quality (and cost) which did not, however, reflect the time most of them would actually last in frontline service. He then extended this point to weapons in general by pointing to a new type of machine gun: a design which was more simple to build and less wasteful of man-hours and raw materials had actually turned out to be superior to the models that came before it.[68]

The directive issued under his name on 3 December was an accurate reflection of these deliberations: it started off with the assumption that both as regards raw materials and qualified labour, the German war economy had hit a glass ceiling. Hence a major effort at rationalisation was called for as the only way to boost production. Existing designs should be simplified, new ones conceived with the idea of mass production rather than labour-intensive high-quality workmanship (*Werkmannsarbeit*). In order to reach this goal, the input from civilian engineers was to be actively sought.[69] Even though the general thrust of the directive anticipated the idea behind many of the Speer reforms, it

[67] BA/MA, RW 19/822 'Besprechung am 29. November 1941, 12.00–14.00 Uhr. Ort: Reichskanzlei (7.12.1941)'. The hollow charge had been designed to compensate for Germany's limited access to tungsten ore which was needed to produce hardened armour-piercing shells. For an introduction to this subject, see Rolf-Dieter Müller, '"Für Hitler war Uran nur ein Metall". Wie aus einem Geschoß für den Notfall dennoch eine Waffe für den Masseneinsatz wurde'; in: *Frankfurter Allgemeine Zeitung*, 'Die Gegenwart' supplement (21.2.2001).

[68] BA/MA, RW 19/822 'Besprechung am 29. November 1941, 12.00–14.00 Uhr. Ort: Reichskanzlei (7.12.1941)'. Although he did not refer to it by name, the dictator undoubtedly had in mind the new Maschinengewehr (MG) 42, which was weeks away from entering field service. Made of stamped sheet metal, it was cheaper to produce both in terms of cost and man-hours than its predecessor, the MG 34, while boasting greater ruggedness and superior firepower. See Chris McNab, *MG 34 and MG 42 Machine Guns* (Oxford: Osprey 2012), pp 14–21.

[69] IWM, EDS Mi 14/433 '(II), Der Führer und Oberste Befehlshaber der Wehrmacht. Wi Rü Amt/Rü (IIa) Nr. 3750 41 g.Kdos. Vereinfachung und Leistungssteigerung unserer Rüstungsproduktion (3.12.1941)'. Also in Moll (ed.), *'Führer-Erlasse'*, pp 210–12.

constituted nothing new, the main points having already been raised by Hitler at the Berghof meeting of 18 May. The dictator undoubtedly drew strength from the fact that a mere five months before the attack in the West, the German armed forces had faced a similar shortfall of equipment and ammunition in far more daunting circumstances: back then, the German empire was limited to the Czech half of Czechoslovakia and a rump Poland while the British and French field armies were growing stronger with every passing day; an all-out attack on them in spring appeared to constitute the last chance to score a decisive success. The surge in production which ensued appeared to prove that the problem had been one of management and resource allocation.[70] By comparison, in November 1941 Germany ruled most of Europe, had forced the British to retreat from the Continent on three occasions and had brought the USSR to the brink of defeat. The problems in effectively allocating raw materials were thus eerily similar to those of early 1940, but the pressure to do so far less.

It comes as no surprise, then, that the directive of 3 December failed to address the main bugbear of German production planning: a production line hopelessly clogged by too many projects boasting the highest priority. Neither the meeting at the Reichskanzlei nor the directive that followed it conveys the image of a leader increasingly aware of a looming crisis and starting to contemplate new and truly radical solutions. The need for the latter was openly discussed in a memo prepared by Thomas for Keitel on 9 December. In it, he described the army's desperate need for munitions and cautiously put the question whether the 'changed situation in the East' warranted a shift in priorities. The focus of the paper also made it clear that in light of recent developments, the navy's call on resources should take a back seat to those of the army. It was, however, inevitable that some sort of sacrifice be made, since the cupboard was completely bare.[71] The most specific concession made thus far by OKH was a pledge to release 20,000 blue-collar workers and 50,000 coal miners from the field army by 15 December. The fact that Thomas made no reference to this promise in his memo may be because he already suspected nothing would come of it. A conference at Walter Warlimont's office two days later revealed that the promise, while not quite empty, had just had an important qualifier attached to it: the workers would be released as soon as the units they belonged to were sent on furlough.[72]

In the days after 14 December, the contradictions at the heart of the German war effort – a huge field army fighting an increasingly open-ended campaign and supported by a dysfunctional command economy – finally came to a head.

---

[70] Tooze, *Wages*, pp 338–53; Fröhlich, *Kampf*, pp 323–44

[71] BA/MA, RW 19/822 'Wehrwirtschafts- und Rüstungsamt Rü II. Vortragsnotiz für Chef OKW. Geheime Kommandosache (9.12.1941)'.

[72] BA/MA, RW 19/2071 'Vermerk über Besprechung bei WFSt/L am 11.12.41 mit AHA und Stabschef HRüstungsamt (11.12.1941)'.

The catalyst was the series of blows that had been raining down on *Heeresgruppe Mitte* since 6 December. Though these appeared to be of manageable proportions for the first week or so, starting on 14 December a series of local crises began to merge into a big one that threatened to engulf the entire army group. With few reserves available to shore up the front, Hitler turned to Fromm for help. The latter seized the moment to make a comprehensive case for a reversal of the July directive, which had privileged the Kriegsmarine and Luftwaffe with regards to labour and raw-material allocation, and demanded a doubling of the army's quota of iron. In a meeting with Keitel and Fromm at the Wolfschanze on 23 December, the dictator tried to put a positive gloss on things by pointing to recent Japanese successes and the problems these would bring for the Allies. Fromm was unimpressed. Despite the fact that Thomas and Keitel had finally seen fit to raise the army's share of raw materials only a couple of hours earlier, Fromm reminded Hitler that the field army would not be demobilising a single division, much less fifty, and hence would need to be re-equipped to pre-Barbarossa levels.[73] Tanks were available, but with regards to any other type of motor vehicle as well as a number of artillery ammunition types, the situation was dire. The war economy would have to be turned around by '180 degrees rather than merely 90'. Hitler acknowledged this and promised to free up factory space and man-hours by stopping the preferential treatment enjoyed thus far by the two other services. He also insisted that the *Ostheer* would have weathered the worst of the storm in about a fortnight.[74] The minutes do not record Fromm's answer to that statement.

The following days saw a further dramatic deterioration in the situation of *Heeresgruppe Mitte*. Between 20 December 1941 and 10 January 1942 several Soviet attacks tore into its northern flank held by 9. *Armee*; others widened the gap between 4. *Armee* and 2. *Panzerarmee*. Stalin was sufficiently emboldened by these developments to order a general offensive along the entire front on 5 January, an overambitious undertaking that would ultimately doom the Soviet winter offensive.[75]

Hitler, faced with the most existential crisis of his regime so far, issued a stream of orders to his front commanders to hold their ground regardless of the cost. As far as grand strategy was concerned, however, he showed a remarkable reluctance to follow through on the promises he had given Fromm on 23 December. On 3 January 1942 the war diarist of Thomas's headquarters noted with concern that while production plans for the navy

---

[73] BA/MA, RH 14–4 'Stab OKH Nr. 1441/41 g.Kdos. Betr.: Notizen über den Vortrag des Chef H Rüst und B d E beim Führer und Obersten Befehlshaber der Wehrmacht im Führerhauptquartier am 23.12.1941 (28.12.1941)'.

[74] Ibid.

[75] For a summary of these events, see Klaus Reinhardt, *Die Wende vor Moskau. Das Scheitern der Strategie Hitlers im Winter 1941/42* (Stuttgart: DVA 1972), pp 226–43.

and air force were being radically curtailed, the original scheme for a greatly enhanced Panzer arm had had only minor alterations made to it, giving it a current notional strength of thirty Panzer and twenty motorised divisions. Such a move, the entry went on, had definitely taken place 'against the will of the Wirtschafts- und Rüstungsamt'.[76]

Fromm – though not usually an ally of Thomas – had also noticed with concern that Hitler seemed to be dragging his feet on this matter. By 10 January his chief of staff grew increasingly restless, especially when he heard from a staff officer at Führer's Headquarters that the matter was currently in Keitel's hands and that it was pointless to expect the weak-willed OKW chief to press the matter with Hitler.[77] Even though the dictator did ultimately sign a new directive clarifying future production priorities later that same day, his reluctance to do so over eighteen days still requires an explanation. He must have realised that curtailing production for the navy, air force and Panzer arm in the manner desired by Fromm was likely to wreck his grand strategic design beyond redemption. At the same time, many of the heavy weapons which a new production effort would provide for the army would not reach the front for at least a couple of months.[78] With Hitler apparently still clinging to the hope that the Soviet offensive was a week or two from spending itself, redirecting production away from the other two services and towards the army might end up damaging the overall effort without delivering any short-term benefits. While impossible to prove, it seems likely that the widening of the Soviet offensive ordered by Stalin on 5 January – even though ultimately unsuccessful – helped Hitler to focus and discard any lingering illusions about the short-term nature of the threat the *Ostheer* was facing.[79]

6.4   Conclusion

There can be little doubt that the German war economy underperformed in a number of areas in the eighteen months between the fall of France and the collapse of Operation Barbarossa. It can safely be stated that the reasons behind this played a major role in determining the outcome of the war and

---

[76] BA/MA, RW 19/166 'Kriegstagebuch Wi Rü Amt Stab (entry for 3 January 1942)'.

[77] BA/MA, RH 14–4 'Kriegstagebuch Bef.d.E. u. Chef d.Heer.Rü. (entry for 10 January 1942)'.

[78] A dilemma the nature of which had just been highlighted by Thomas' staff in a memo from that same date; see BA/MA, RW 19/1776 'Wehrwirtschaft- und Rüstungsamt Rü (IIa) Nr. 4010/41 g.Kdos. Die Forderungen an die Rüstung unter Berücksichtigung der Lage im Dezember 1941 (23.12.1941)'.

[79] Rolf-Dieter Müller has argued that the directive of 10 January did not constitute a true turning point because as yet no central organ capable of actually enforcing it was in existence. This begs the question of whether this would have been as obvious to Hitler on the day in question as it became to a historian two generations later. See Müller, 'Mobilisierung'; in: DRZW Bd. 5/1, pp 658–68.

hence it is only reasonable that the debate about them will continue for some time, the number of scholarly titles already produced on the subject notwithstanding. As with the other chapters in this book, the problem is not one of determining the causes of a particular problem, but of one individual's perception of them.

The German economy of the time has been aptly described as a 'loosely articulated system of cartels and business groups'.[80] It was essentially a hybrid economy, with its capitalist and command elements kept in a precarious balance. Hitler's eye for detail and prodigious memory were certainly of some assistance in evaluating factory output but he appears to have possessed only a rudimentary understanding of the inner workings of the system created by Schacht and Göring in the 1930s; hence he must have struggled to anticipate how it would stand up under the strains of war. There is certainly some evidence to indicate that the system – if it can be dignified with such a term – of steering a war economy by attempting to loosely coordinate the wishes and priorities of several power brokers at times had him as confused as many bystanders.[81] If for much of the period under discussion nobody – not even Todt, who was probably best suited to this – took the trouble of drawing Hitler's attention to the problems likely to arise from fighting a prolonged war in such a fashion, it was undoubtedly because of the complacency born of the spectacular victory in Western Europe. Only by August 1941 did the evidence begin to mount that the Russian campaign would not be finished by the end of the year. Hitler realised this, but only in an operational context. If he arrived at any conclusions pertaining to war production, he appears to have kept them to himself. Of his economic chieftains Keitel, Göring and Funk would have been temperamentally disinclined to turn themselves into bearers of ill tidings which might or might not come to pass, and Thomas lacked access to the dictator. Todt may – for all we know – have raised the issue in one of his numerous private conversations; Hitler's recorded comments about having conquered virtually all of Europe and the obvious economic benefits to be derived therefrom, gives us an approximate idea of how he is likely to have brushed off such an awkward question.

The key sources of late November and early December give us glimpses of a dictator who, while realising that not all is well, is not overly concerned either. The directive of 3 December betrays no apprehension over the fact that

---

[80] Tooze, *Wages*, p 189.

[81] In a report he prepared after the war for his American captors, Speer's deputy Karl-Otto Saur spoke of Hitler's surprise upon realising in early July 1942 (!) that *Generaloberst* Friedrich Fromm was not merely tasked with running the army's recruiting and training establishments, but that he was also responsible for the *Waffenamt* and hence involved in the design and production of countless weapon types. IWM, Speer Collection, FD 3049/ 49 (Karl-Otto) Saur. '17. Zwischenbericht über den Stand der Arbeiten an der Kartei des Technischen Amtes (25.8.1947)'.

Heeresgruppe Süd had just suffered an important reverse and that *Heeresgruppe Mitte's* advance was slowing to a crawl. Rather than question the priorities set down in the July directive in a fundamental way, he merely ordered a series of measures that were expected to be conducive towards a process of general rationalisation of the production process. It goes without saying that this reflected the prevailing mood at OKW and OKH, where after Vyasma-Bryansk most senior officers had reached the conclusion that the Red Army, while still capable of localised counterstrikes, was no longer in a position to pose a major challenge to the positions attained by the *Ostheer*. Proof of this can be found not just in the tone of operational assessments from those days, but also in the fact that the release for the benefit of civilian industry of 70,000 soldiers currently still campaigning in Russia was still being contemplated until 11 December 1941. It took the dramatic deterioration of the military situation in the days following 14 December to bring about a fundamental reassessment.

The End of Blitzkrieg? Barbarossa and the Impact of Lend-Lease

7.1 Introduction

In the late morning of 9 December 1941 the commander-in-chief of *Heeresgruppe Mitte, Generalfeldmarschall* Fedor von Bock, had an extended telephone conversation with the army's chief of staff, *Generaloberst* Franz Halder. Most of the time was spent discussing the impact of the Red Army's winter offensive, which had started on 5–6 December, against Bock's army group. Bock expressed genuine alarm and drew attention to the fact that Heinz Guderian, one of his army commanders, had openly referred to his men as losing confidence in the high command's capacity to handle the crisis.[1] Halder intimated that he considered Guderian's concerns overblown and that the current situation could be explained as follows: 'The enemy has been forced by the pressure we brought to bear in recent days to deploy formations which had been resting or forming up in the rear with a view to deploy them only in 1942. We have to summon our last strength to see off these attacks. I suppose that they will continue until the middle or end of the month and then die off.'[2]

Irrespective of whether Halder's assessment reflected cockiness or just poor intelligence, its proximity in time to Hitler's declaration of war on the USA raises issues absolutely key to understanding the context of the Third Reich's last (and ultimately fatal) act of horizontal escalation. Even in the days before the start of the Red Army's offensive, the *Ostheer* had already seemed committed, virtually open-endedly, to keeping the bulk of its elite army formations in this theatre of operations.[3] After 5 December, a series of reverses pointed not just towards a continuing stalemate, but even the possibility of a major military reverse. This added a major question to the long-planned redirection of key resources (especially skilled labour) away from a shrinking field army and into

---

[1] BA/MA, RH 19 II/122 'Heeresgruppenkommando Mitte, Kriegstagebuch Ia (Ferngespräch OB HGr Mitte-Gen.Oberst Halder, 11.15 h)'.

[2] Ibid.

[3] In November 1941, nineteen out of twenty-one Panzer divisions, thirteen out of fourteen motorised divisions, five out of six mountain divisions and both airborne divisions were still deployed in Russia.

Figure 7.1 Hitler at an OKH briefing flanked by Halder (right) and Brauchitsch (left): in 1941, Hitler would have received most of his information on the war in Russia from either Army Commander in Chief, *Generalfeldmarschall* Walther von Brauchitsch, or Halder. (CORBIS/Corbis Historical via Getty Images)

factories and shipyards that would boost Germany's aeronaval strength for the coming confrontation with Great Britain and its covert ally, the USA. Against such a backdrop, dragging another great power into the war would appear an utterly reckless decision.

At the time, most of the communications between the German leader and the senior field commanders in Russia still ran through Oberkommando des Heeres (OKH) and its two top men: army commander-in-chief, *Generalfeldmarschall* Walther von Brauchitsch, and the army chief of staff, *Generaloberst* Franz Halder. In 1940–1 the former would on average brief Hitler about army affairs once or twice a week in detail as well as staying in touch with him over the telephone. Day-to-day briefings were in the hands of Oberkommando der Wehrmacht's (OKW) General Alfred Jodl, but even he depended on material collected and forwarded to him by OKH.[4] Halder would

---

[4] Nicolaus von Below, *Als Hitlers Adjutant 1937–1945* (Selent: Pour-le-Merite 1997 rp), p 282; Geoffrey Megargee, *Inside Hitler's High Command* (Kansas: Kansas UP 2000), pp 80–1, 162.

sometimes accompany Brauchitsch to these meetings, but generally he stayed in the background;[5] very much in keeping with Prussian military tradition, he was in charge of actually running the operations of the field army on a day-to-day basis. To what extent the two officers in pursuing their own agenda attempted to hoodwink Hitler during the planning stages of Barbarossa has already been the subject of an excellent new analysis by David Stahel.[6] This chapter will establish whether something similar could have happened in late 1941, thus skewing the dictator's perception of the global balance of power as a result of the intelligence reaching him from the Russian theatre in November and December 1941.

7.2   Winning Oneself to Death: the Progress of Barbarossa, June–October 1941

It could be argued that if there was ever a moment in which Nazi Germany stood an even remote chance of defeating the Red Army in a straight military confrontation, then the summer of 1941 was probably it. Relative to all the other armed establishments in the world, the Heer and the Luftwaffe were close to achieving a unique peak in effectiveness. Building on the modern training of its command cadres in the Reichswehr of the Weimar Republic, on limited but very much up-to-date combat experience in the Spanish Civil War and a long history of devolved command doctrine,[7] the two services had achieved a series of stunning victories when operating jointly between 1939 and 1941; moreover, the operational experience gained in winning their victories had not come at a major price in blood. This meant that, in contrast to the second half of the war, units had continuously gained in fighting proficiency without having to suffer commensurate attrition, bound eventually to reverse this process. A residual reluctance in unleashing the new Panzer divisions and thus maximising their potential had still been in evidence during the campaign in the West, but this could be attributed to growing pains. The relationship between Hitler and his senior generals, while hardly harmonious, could still be described as good; insofar as conflict had arisen on a few occasions, it always involved issues of a technical, rather than fundamental nature (such as the political aims of the war currently being waged).

---

[5] Proof of Brauchitsch's key role in this period can be found in 'Note by Weizsäcker (14.1.1942)'; in: Leonidas Hill (ed.), *Die Weizsäcker-Papiere 1933–1950* (Berlin: Propyläen 1981), pp 285–6.

[6] David Stahel, *Operation Barbarossa and Germany's Defeat in the East* (Cambridge: CUP 2009).

[7] The impact which the fabled *Auftragstaktik* actually had on the field of battle has only recently received the scholarly attention it deserves. See Marco Sigg, *Der Unterführer als Feldherr im Taschenformat. Theorie und Praxis der Auftragstaktik im deutschen Heer 1869 bis 1945* (Paderborn: Ferdinand Schöningh 2014).

The Red Army, on the other hand, had been undergoing a process whereby lessons it could have learned in the conflicts of the 1930s were negated for all sorts of reasons.[8] The regime's purges of the officer corps (1937–41), regardless of the damage these purges inflicted,[9] encouraged a mindset among the survivors in which independence of thought was, to say the least, discouraged. Moreover, the officer class was left in a condition where it was ill prepared to meet the challenges that went hand in hand with the expansion of the field army from early 1939 onwards. The disaster of the war against Finland (November 1939–March 1940) led to some important self-criticism and the relegation of the political commissars to an advisory role, but the first setbacks in June and July 1941 saw the prompt return of the dual-command system and all the baleful consequences resulting from it. The Spanish Civil War and German victory over France provided valuable lessons on the future role of armour in conventional warfare, but in the Russian case these led first to the ill-advised disbandment of major mechanised units, only to witness their hasty reconstitution as oversized mechanised corps in the wake of the events of May and June 1940. The Red Army at that stage simply lacked the experience, command skills and radio technology to effectively operate formations with a nominal strength of 1,031 main battle tanks, thus rendering such formations highly vulnerable to German encirclements. This made a nonsense of the sophisticated 'deep battle' manoeuvre warfare theory first devised in the mid-1930s. The flaw was rendered downright fatal by the regime's unwillingness to consider – even temporarily – a commitment to a doctrine of defensive warfare. Time might have ameliorated some of these problems and would also have been highly welcome in allowing the introduction of a new generation of combat aircraft,[10] along with main battle tanks, into the order of battle. Of the

[8] Soviet soldiers and airmen saw more action in conventional warfare against a wider range of enemies than the armed forces of any other country of the period: the Spanish Civil War (1936–8), the Sino-Japanese War (1937–40), the Changkufeng Incident (July–August 1938), the Nomonhan War (May–September 1939), the Soviet–Polish War (September 1939) and the Winter War against Finland (November 1939–March 1940). For an excellent analysis of the Soviet experience in these conflicts, see Alexander Hill, *The Red Army and the Second World War* (Cambridge: CUP 2017), pp 77–168.

[9] In light of new evidence on the continuing purge of the officer class into 1941 (especially in the Army Air Force), it no longer seems appropriate to bookend the beginning and end of this murderous phenomenon between the more commonly used dates, 1937 and 1939. See Evan Mawdsley, *Thunder in the East: The Nazi–Soviet War 1941–1945* (London: Hodder Arnold 2005), pp 20–2.

[10] The Yakovlev Yak-1 was the only Soviet single-engine fighter that compared well with recent types of Western and German fighters; however, only twenty pilots had qualified on this type by 22 June. The heavily armoured Ilyushin Il-2 Sturmovik strike aircraft and the fast Petlyakov Pe-2 light bomber were excellent designs which would go on to provide invaluable close air support for the Red Army; as with the Yak-1, neither of the two types would be available in quantity before 1942. For more on this subject, see Christer Bergström, *Barbarossa: The Air Battle, July–December 1941* (London: Ian Allan 2007),

latter, the superlative T-34 and KV-1 were already available in some quantity on 22 June,[11] but some units had only just received them and, accordingly, had to go into battle with barely trained drivers or the wrong type of ammunition.

The static defensive line that hugged the old state border (the Stalin Line), and which might have been an important asset to an army grappling with doctrinal issues and faced with a mobile adversary constantly searching for open flanks, had largely been stripped of its assets in order to equip a similar structure, still under construction, which followed the new border acquired in the wake of the annexations of Lithuania, eastern Poland and Bessarabia.[12] This meant that neither of the two fortified zones was manned or complete on the day of the German invasion. Last, but not least, an intervention by Stalin in October 1940 had prioritised the build-up of Red Army forces in Ukraine at the expense of the units in White Russia and the Baltics.[13] Since the *Schwerpunkt* of the German invasion would be aimed at White Russia, this distribution of forces contributed to the unhinging of Soviet defensive dispositions. The most important asset of the USSR at the start of Barbarossa was a state system geared since its inception to mobilising the country's population en masse, albeit quite often for the most hare-brained of enterprises. In the early summer of 1941, this meant that in the first eight days of the war, nearly 5 million reservists were called to arms, thus at a stroke almost doubling the manpower available to the Soviet armed forces.

Rivers of ink have been spilt on why Stalin, countless warnings from many sources notwithstanding, allowed himself to be surprised by the German invasion. A number of plausible explanations have been put forward, all of which would have been reinforced by his certified paranoid nature: his refusal to believe that Germany would wantonly initiate hostilities in the east while Britain still stood unbowed, his obsessive fear that either Britain or a cabal of German generals was trying to goad him into making the first move against his as yet ally, Adolf Hitler, or – conversely – that he was so focused on launching a pre-emptive strike of his own that he neglected basic defensive precautions. In recent times, Evan Mawdsley has argued that Stalin at some point probably did accept the possibility of a

pp 11–13, 26, 128 as well as Von Hardesty and Ilya Grinberg, *Red Phoenix Rising: The Soviet Air Force in World War II* (Lawrence: Kansas UP 2012), pp 13–33.

[11] 832 medium T-34s and 433 heavy (47.5 tons) KV-1s. See Hill, *Red Army*, p 220; Robert Forczyk, *Panzerjäger vs KV-1* (Oxford: Osprey 2012), p 27.

[12] On this often underrated subject, see Robert Tarleton, 'What really happened to the Stalin Line?, parts 1 and 2'; in: *Journal of Soviet Military Studies*, Vol. 5 (June 1992), No. 2, pp 187–219 and *Journal of Slavic Military Studies*, Vol. 6 (March 1993), No. 1, pp 21–61 as well as Neil Short, *The Stalin and Molotov Lines: Soviet Western Defences 1928–1941* (Oxford: Osprey 2008).

[13] For the possible reasons behind this move, see Richard W. Harrison, 'Soviet Planning for War, 1936–1941: The "Preventive Attack" Thesis in Historical Context'; in: *Journal of Military History* 83 (July 2019), pp 769–94.

German attack but took solace in the fact that the two major strategic echelons covering the districts to the west of Moscow afforded him plenty of security, irrespective of some units' shortcomings.[14] In light of the numbers involved (109 divisions for the first echelon, 62 divisions for the second[15]) and the fact that the Soviet dictator did not show symptoms of shock until the fall of Minsk on 29 June, this line of argument has a lot to commend it.

Discussion of the early drafts of Operation Barbarossa saw Hitler and Chief of Staff Franz Halder engaged in a battle of wits over strategic priorities.[16] This was never satisfactorily resolved and arguably contributed to the operation's failure. Put simply, Halder wanted to prioritise the capture of the Soviet capital while the dictator, who expressed concern over the open flanks of Army Group Centre that would result from such a strategy, made this move contingent upon the previous capture of Leningrad and (possibly) of most of the Ukraine. Rather than openly confronting the Führer over this issue and making an unambiguous argument for Moscow, Halder and Brauchitsch at some point decided to go along with Hitler's concept in the hope that further developments would either render the whole point moot (because of a Soviet collapse) or make Hitler more amenable to their point of view. In the meantime, the chief of staff stuck to his idea that a drive on Moscow had to be the cornerstone of the campaign. However, besides making sure that a key passage in the Führer's Directive No. 18 for Barbarossa was given an ambiguous turn of phrase, he did nothing overt; whenever Hitler in the following months stressed the need to pause once Smolensk had been reached and detach a large part of Army Group Centre's armour for a drive on Leningrad, he kept tight-lipped, thus allowing the issue to fester.[17]

The failure to reach an early consensus on strategic priorities was compounded by the challenge the *Ostheer* and its Axis allies encountered upon initiating hostilities with the USSR. The problems that would arise out of the need to use dirt roads and re-gauge most railway lines had – to some extent –

---

[14] Mawdsley, *Thunder*, pp 32–7. See also Mawdsley, '"Crossing the Rubicon": Soviet Plans for Offensive War 1940–1941'; in: *International History Review*, Vol. 24 (2003), no. 4, pp 818–65.

[15] The first echelon held positions 10–100 km (6–60 miles) from the borders of East Prussia, German-occupied Poland and Romania, with the second being staggered back by about 320–400 km (200–250 miles), respectively. See the map in Christopher Bellamy, *Absolute War: Soviet Russia in the Second World War* (London: Macmillan 2007), p 180.

[16] The so-called Marcks and Lossberg studies made different allowances for the challenges which space and terrain might pose to the operation. However, neither questioned the feasibility of defeating the Red Army by early autumn at the latest. For an analysis of both papers, see David Stahel, *Barbarossa*, pp 39–54.

[17] The most comprehensive and detailed analysis of this conflict is to be found in ibid., pp 39–69, 76–95.

Figure 7.2 Wrecked Soviet aircraft, June 1941: the first three days of Operation Barbarossa saw Soviet plane losses on a scale which would have meant the obliteration of any other air service then in existence. (ullstein bild/ullstein bild via Getty Images)

been foreseen, but the hope placed in capturing enough Russian-made rolling stock proved to be over-optimistic,[18] thus leading to a logistics crisis by the second half of July. Over and above this problem, the challenges inherent in defeating the Red Army had been badly underestimated. As regards quantity – the sheer number of tanks, planes and trained men that the Soviet regime was able to draw on – German intelligence estimates had been off the mark by a factor of 100–200 per cent. In terms of both overall fighting proficiency and command and control, these forces were markedly inferior to their German counterparts, but they were able to make up for these deficiencies by a willingness to stand their ground and endure appalling privations.

A month or so into the invasion the full potential of the Wehrmacht as well as its limitations in the context of the Russian battle space were revealing

---

[18] Hans-Adolf Jacobsen (ed.), *Generaloberst Halder. Kriegstagebuch. Tägliche Aufzeichnungen des Chefs des Generalstabes des Heeres 1939–1942*, Band III. (Stuttgart: Kohlhammer 1964), p 144 (entry for 2 August 1941): 'Russian rolling stock not in plentiful supply. We have only been able to capture a small number and most of these are not ready for use. Things are particularly bad with regards to locomotives; those available are all in bad need of an overhaul.' Henceforth quoted as KTB Halder.

themselves. The three air fleets (*Luftflotten* 1, 2 and 4) allocated to *Heeresgruppen Nord* (North), *Mitte* (Centre) and *Süd* (South), respectively, had scored the most spectacular success by far. In return for minimal losses they accounted for a total of 3,900 aircraft destroyed in the air and on the ground in the first three days of the war – a estimate which recent research has actually revealed to be on the low side.[19] On the ground, operations would be dominated by the presence of the Panzer groupings (*Panzergruppen*) on the one hand, and the Luftwaffe's elite close air-support formation, *Fliegerkorps* VIII, on the other. The former were made up, on average, of four or five Panzer divisions and a couple of *Panzergrenadier* divisions. Fully mechanised and motorised and boasting the highest proficiency levels of inter-arms cooperation of any armed force in the world at the time, they constituted the mailed fist of German mechanised warfare. In a manner similar to the invasion of Western Europe, their task was to surge ahead of the roadbound infantry armies, penetrate the enemy front line and cut off a large chunk of the opposing force. Since Army Group Centre was allocated two such formations, enveloping the enemy was a much easier task for it than for the two other army groups, who were only allocated one apiece.

In the case of the northern theatre, the sheer rate of advance by *Heeresgruppe Nord* (*Generalfeldmarschall* Wilhelm Ritter von Leeb) bears testimony to both the potential and the limitations of the *Ostheer*'s way of war. After a mere four days, one of *Panzergruppe* 4's two corps had seized a bridgehead across the Divina, almost half the distance to Leningrad. By 14 July, *Panzergruppe* 4 had reached a position less than 100 km (60 miles) from the USSR's second city and appeared ready to seize it. However, logistical problems, threats to its exposed right flank and the need to allow at least some roadbound infantry formations to catch up meant that it stayed in place until 8 August. The *Panzergruppe*'s lightning advance had been an impressive achievement by any standards; even so, it failed to net a substantial number of prisoners along the way.[20]

The task of *Heeresgruppe Mitte* (*Generalfeldmarschall* Fedor von Bock) was greatly facilitated by the fact that its first mission consisted of pinching off a major salient in the area of Bialystok where the Soviet first strategic echelon had established a major troop concentration. Working in close conjunction, *Panzergruppen* 2 (Heinz Guderian) and 3 (Hermann Hoth) had accomplished this task by 30 June. It is indicative of future problems that three days into the invasion, a row broke out among the senior commanders of the army group about the wisdom of extending the arms of the encirclement until the land bridge between the Divina and Dnepr rivers had been reached, regardless of

---

[19] Bergström, *Air Battle*, pp 11–28, esp. p 23.
[20] Robert Kirchubel has been particularly critical of Leeb's generalship in this context. See Robert Kirchubel, *Operation Barbarossa: The German invasion of Soviet Russia* (Oxford: Osprey 2013), pp 357–61.

threats to flanks and the likelihood of a number of Red Army soldiers escaping from the pocket. Both the intelligence collected at the time about the extent of Soviet disruption and latter-day historical research have indicated that this might have been viable.[21] Hitler broke the deadlock by expressing a preference for the more conservative solution, thus limiting the 'bag' and leaving the leaders of the two *Panzergruppen* in particular with the feeling that they had been robbed.

A second, even bigger encirclement was sealed off to the east of Smolensk on 27 July. Heinz Guderian immediately clamoured for permission to seize the next objective, preparatory to establishing yet another encirclement. By now, however, the priorities to be weighed in such an instance were making themselves felt. Leaving the bulk of the Panzer formations to 'guard' the cut-off enemy force meant forfeiting further operational opportunities; allowing the mechanised formations to race off without waiting for the roadbound infantry to catch up would permit large numbers of the besieged enemy to break out and rejoin their forces. By late July the rest of *Heeresgruppe Mitte* was already a week behind the Panzer forces, turning this choice into a real dilemma. In addition, the Red Army almost immediately initiated a series of assaults by mechanised forces to relieve their besieged comrades at Smolensk, which left *Heeresgruppe Mitte* fighting on two fronts. Even though poorly coordinated by German standards, these assaults indicated that the comparatively easy successes enjoyed by the *Ostheer* in its first four weeks in Russia were now a thing of the past.

In the south, *Heeresgruppe Süd* (*Generalfeldmarschall* Gerd von Rundstedt) would theoretically have had the chance to pull off a massive envelopment, since its two launching pads (occupied southeastern Poland and northern Romania) meant that the Soviet defenders of Galicia were caught in a vice. A major concentration of Red Army mechanised formations in the region,[22] along with the limitations imposed by the absence of a second *Panzergruppe*, meant that throughout much of June and early July, the Soviet defenders had to be gradually pushed back into the Ukraine, their front still largely intact. The sheer disruption inflicted in the first ten days of fighting and poor Red Army recovery assets meant that Soviet losses in armoured vehicles were very high.[23] Even so, it was not until the first week of August that the German army group

---

[21] For a pithy discussion of the issues involved, see Stahel, *Operation Barbarossa*, pp 159–79.

[22] A total of eight new mechanised corps fielding more than 4,400 main battle tanks, among them a disproportionate number of KV-1s and T-34s. See Robert Forczyk, *Tank Warfare on the Eastern Front, 1941–1942* (London: Pen & Sword 2015), pp 29–37. Also Aleksei Isaev, *Dubno 1941: The greatest tank battle of the Second World War* (Solihull: Helion 2017), pp 29–38.

[23] For conflicting interpretations of the early fighting in Galicia, see Forczyk, *Tank Warfare*, p 64 and Isaev, *Dubno*, pp 192–203.

Figure 7.3 Wrecked KV-1 tank: even though in June 1941 the Red Army already fielded an important number of heavy T-34 and KV-1 tanks, deficiencies in training and support services limited their impact. (ullstein bild/ullstein bild via Getty Images)

managed to cut off a sizeable chunk of the Soviet defenders and annihilate them at the battle of Uman.

The last days of July saw the German leadership taking stock of the successes achieved so far. The conclusions reached were basically a reflection of the realisation that the continuous resistance put up by the Red Army and the growing depth and width of the battle space would make necessary a series of smaller and more localised operations. At the same time, it meant that the ambiguities of *Führerweisung* No. 18 could no longer be papered over. The ensuing acrimonious debate between Hitler, Halder and some of the field commanders over the order of strategic priorities no doubt contributed to the length of the pause in operations in the northern and central sectors throughout much of August, a fact that has dominated the historical narrative of Operation Barbarossa for decades. Only more recent research has highlighted the fact that *Heeresgruppe Mitte*, in particular, was put under such pressure by a series of Soviet spoiling attacks that the task of replenishing its units, thoroughly exhausted after the dash of June and July, was made considerably more laborious and time-consuming. It is to the nature of some of these attacks that we must now turn.

Heeresgruppe Nord resumed its drive on Leningrad on 8 August, but soon enough ran into trouble. *Generaloberst* Ernst Busch's 16. *Armee*, which advanced on the right, became the target of a major Soviet counter-attack on 12 August. More than twenty Red Army divisions under Lieutenant General Nikolai Vatutin found the gap between two of Busch's corps, forced the Germans to retreat 50 km (30 miles) and retook a major town (Staraya Russa) on the fifth day of the offensive. While *Generalfeldmarschall* Wilhelm Ritter von Leeb, commander-in-chief of *Heeresgruppe Nord*, was at first inclined to dismiss this move as 'irrelevant',[24] Hitler was sufficiently spooked to redeploy a *Panzerkorps* as a countermeasure; twenty-four hours later Leeb concurred and demanded further reinforcements,[25] while describing the experience as 'nerve-testing' in his personal diary.[26] Soviet 34th Army, which had been the spearhead of the operation was eventually cut off by a mechanised counterstrike and destroyed, but only after the German corps fixing the attacking Russians in place was forced to use its sappers as fighting infantry.[27] An enemy counter-attack on such a scale was a new experience for *Heeresgruppe Nord*. Having lost more time in this fashion, Leeb's men did not reach the approaches of Leningrad until 8 September. Rather than storming the USSR's second city, operational priorities in other theatres forced them to settle down for a long siege rather than taking it by storm.

Generalfeldmarschall Fedor von Bock, the commander-in-chief of *Heeresgruppe Mitte*, found himself fending off a whole series of increasingly well-coordinated Soviet attacks even after the Soviet high command's attempts to relieve the Smolensk pocket had come to nought with the collapse of the Red Army units cut off in that encirclement (6 August). Weakened by the detachment of key units from his command to the northern and southern sectors,[28] Bock's infantry armies soon found themselves on the receiving end of a series of attacks by Timoshenko's Western Front and Giorgii Zhukov's Reserve Front, ultimately aimed at recovering Smolensk and destroying the German forces in their path. Timoshenko's attacks emanated from an area about 100 km (60 miles) to the northeast of Smolensk;[29] Zhukov's were aimed at reducing a salient 60 km (40 miles) across, which had formed farther south

---

[24] KTB Halder III, p 176 (entry for 14 August 1941).

[25] KTB Halder III, pp 177–8 (entry for 15 August 1941).

[26] Georg Meyer (ed.), *Generalfeldmarschall Wilhelm Ritter von Leeb. Tagebuchaufzeichnungen und Lagebeurteilungen aus zwei Weltkriegen* (Stuttgart: DVA 1976), p 332 (entry for 15 August 1941). Henceforth quoted as TB Leeb.

[27] KTB Halder III, p 185 (entry for 18 August 1941).

[28] *Fliegerkorps* VIII and elements of *Panzergruppe* 3 were shifted to Leeb's command to assist with operations against Leningrad. *Panzergruppe* 2 remained under his command but was increasingly tied up fighting a series of engagements which ultimately led to the fall of Gomel, to the south.

[29] The frequency with which the town of Dushkovina featured in these engagements has led to these battles being called the 'Dushkovina offensive'.

around the town of El'nia, possession of which gave the Germans a bridgehead on the east bank of the River Desna.[30] Every major push by one of the two Fronts was on average carried out by at least ten divisions and supported not just by superior artillery but a resurgent Red Air Force, which was establishing a major presence over the battlefield. For slightly more than a month, Timoshenko and Zhukov kept hammering away at the defending German armies (9. *Armee* in the north, 4. *Armee* to the south[31]). Despite suffering higher losses than they inflicted, they severely mauled an infantry division to the point that it had to be pulled out of the line. They defeated – an unheard-off first – a counter-attack by 7. *Panzerdivision* and inflicted such losses on all the other German divisions involved that the replenishment they were supposed to be undertaking for the next phase of operations was seriously called into question.[32] Bock, who throughout this period struggled to keep at least one division in reserve for emergencies, repeatedly expressed concern over 9. *Armee*'s capacity to hold the line against Timoshenko's attacks,[33] and soon despaired of ever returning to a war of manoeuvre.[34] On 28 August he made it clear to the Army Chief of Staff that, should the Russians keep up the pressure, the collapse of his entire army group was a real possibility.[35] Even the notoriously unflappable Halder grew increasingly concerned at this.[36] No doubt with a heavy heart, he agreed on 2 September to relinquish the El'nia salient;[37] regardless of its intended use as a springboard for the expected push against Moscow, the losses involved in defending it had become untenable. Despite this retreat, the fighting farther north around Dushkovina (described by

---

[30] An exchange between Hitler, Halder and Bock exemplified the Germans' realisation that the El'nia position would in all likelihood invite a whole series of counter-attacks: KTB Halder III, pp 146, 152 (entries for 3 and 4 August 1941).

[31] The El'nia sector was under 2. *Armee*'s command until 22 August, when 4. *Armee* took over. KTB Halder III, p 187 (entry for 18 August 1941).

[32] Despite the size of the forces involved, the Soviet summer offensives which followed on the fall of the Smolensk pocket had only received the sketchiest historical analysis until the advent of the twenty-first century. Stahel, *Barbarossa*, pp 306–99 was the first major analysis based on German primary sources. David Glantz, *Barbarossa Derailed: The Battle for Smolensk, 10 July–10 September 1941*, Vol. 1 (Solihul: Helion 2010), pp 406–575, as well as Glantz, *Barbarossa Derailed: The Battle for Smolensk, 10 July–10 September 1941*, Vol. 2 (Solihul: Helion 2012), pp 162–363, 504–49, is mostly based on Soviet sources, a number of which of which are reproduced in the two volumes.

[33] See the numerous entries in his personal diary: Klaus Gerbet (ed.), *Generalfeldmarschall Fedor von Bock. Zwischen Pflicht und Verweigerung. Das Kriegstagebuch* (München: Herbig 1995), pp 234, 243, 247, 253, 254, 257, 259, 261, 265, 266, 267 and 269 (entries for 29 July, 8 August, 12 August, 20 August, 21 August, 23 August, 26 August, 28 August, 1 September, 2 September, 3 September and 4 September 1941).

[34] Stahel, *Operation Barbarossa*, pp 394–95.

[35] KTB Halder III, p 202 (entry for 28 August 1941).

[36] KTB Halder III, pp 182, 193 (entries for 17 and 22 August 1941).

[37] KTB Halder III, p 211 (entry for 2 September 1941).

Halder as 'furious attacks in the style of major World War I battles'[38]) went on regardless for several days, with an OKH staff officer, Hellmuth Stieff, still expressing concerns over the viability of retaining Smolensk as late as 5 September.[39]

In the meantime, a situation not dissimilar to that experienced by 4. *Armee* had developed with *Heeresgruppe Süd*. The two weeks following the battle at Uman mostly involved a pursuit of the forces of the Southwest Front under Mikhail Kirponos, but starting on 23 August, III. *Panzerkorps* found itself facing a situation broadly similar to that at El'nia. Having seized a crossing over the Dnepr at Dnepropetrosk,[40] it spent the following three weeks fighting the Ukrainian city's Soviet defenders for possession of the bridgehead. Even though the urban battle space favoured the Red Army, it was above all their superiority in artillery and the sheer ferocity of their counter-attacks that put the Germans on the back foot throughout much of the battle and repeatedly threatened to force them to retreat back across the Dnepr.[41] Evacuation was considered, but Halder, who had just signed off on the retreat from El'nia, would not hear of it. Only the collapse of the Soviet position in central Ukraine by mid-September rendered the point moot. In a manner similar to El'nia, most of the divisions involved in the fighting emerged seriously worn out and with little to show for their efforts.

Thus while it is fair to say that the month of August had witnessed a strategic hiatus at the *Führerhauptquartier*, with Halder and Brauchitsch plotting ways to convince the dictator to give priority to a drive on Moscow, the intensity of the fighting showed no sign of abating. Hitler, for his part, took three weeks to reach a decision on the next maximum effort. While the key players in both OKH and OKW were still clinging to the hope of finishing the campaign in 1941 by driving on Moscow, he had reached the conclusion that the campaign would undoubtedly run into 1942. Hence, on 22 August, he expressed his intention of prioritising the capture of natural resources that might enable the Red Army to rebuild over the winter of 1941–2.[42] This made a shift of focus to the central and eastern Ukraine

---

[38] KTB Halder III, p 214 (entry for 5 September 1941).

[39] 'Letter from Oberst Helmuth Stieff to his wife (5.9.1941)'; in: Horst Mühleisen (ed.), *Hellmuth Stieff. Briefe* (Berlin: Siedler 1991), pp 126–28. Stieff usually found ways to convey letters to his wife and sister in ways which bypassed military censorship, thus allowing him considerable displays of candour.

[40] On this little-known battle, see Stahel, *Kiev 1941*, pp 139–43, 198–204 and Adrian Wettstein, *Die Wehrmacht im Stadtkampf 1939-1942* (Paderborn: Ferdinand Schöningh 2014), pp 142–68.

[41] KTB Halder III, p 195 (entry for 24 August 1941).

[42] 'Studie (22.8.1941)'; in: Hans-Adolf Jacobsen (ed.), *Kriegstagebuch des Oberkommandos der Wehrmacht*, Bd. I (Frankfurt a.M.: Bernard & Graefe 1965), pp 1063–8.

unavoidable.[43] The success of recent operations by Heinz Guderian's *Panzergruppe* 2 aimed at pre-empting a possible Red Army drive into the southeastern corner of *Heeresgruppe Mitte*'s position no doubt contributed to this decision, since it provided the *Ostheer* with an ideal jumping-off point for an operation aimed at meeting *Panzergruppe* 1 in the eastern Ukraine, thus cutting off Kirponos' grouping of armies. This decision – its spectacular success notwithstanding – has arguably become the most notorious in the long litany of World War II's 'what if?' case studies.[44] *Heeresgruppe Mitte*'s seemingly narrow failure outside Moscow in early December has long been regarded as proof of the 'fact' that both the Soviet capital and the USSR would have succumbed to the *Ostheer* if a major effort had been unleashed against it a month sooner than actually was the case (30 September).[45] Rather more important for the purposes of this study is another decision – or rather conclusion – reached by the Führer in the second half of August, which undoubtedly also contributed to his decision to prioritise the Ukraine.

All three army groups were by now operating behind schedule. Just as seriously, a combination of logistical constraints as well as the ferocity of Soviet resistance made clear that, in contrast to what the 1940 operational studies for the invasion of the USSR had envisaged, it would not be possible to continue Barbarossa without reducing at least one army group sector to a secondary theatre; key assets from that group, such as a *Panzergruppe* and *Fliegerkorps* VIII, would have to be shifted to the others. None of Hitler's 1941 directives spell this out in so many words, but his 22 August memo, along with an OKW study from early September which clearly reflects his thinking on the issue,[46] are both quite unambiguous about the inevitable consequences: short of an unexpected collapse of its government structure, the USSR and its armed forces would not be defeated by the end of 1941; planning for the continuation of the war into 1942 would have to commence forthwith. Accordingly, the first obvious step was to deny the USSR as many of its remaining economic assets

---

[43] For a detailed analysis of the tug of war which ensued at Führer's Headquarters over this issue, see Stahel, *Barbarossa*, pp 189–90, 228–30, 240–5, 338–44, 375–79, 392–401, 424–38.

[44] For an example, see David Downing, *The Moscow Option: An Alternative Second World War* (London: Greenhill Books 2001).

[45] Until quite recently, scholarly opinion had tended to follow the opinion put forward by the majority of surviving German generals who were emphatic in branding this decision as the height of folly. Recent years have seen the emergence of a new school of thought inclined to 'side' with the German dictator on this particular issue. See Stahel, *Operation Barbarossa*, p 438 as well as Stahel, *Kiev 1941*, pp 350–2.

[46] 'Der Chef des OKW an den Reichsmarschall und Oberbefehlshaber der Luftwaffe, den Oberbefehlshaber der Kriegsmarine, den Oberbefehlshaber des Heeres und an den Reichsaußenminister (1.9.1941)'; in: ADAP, Serie D, Bd. XIII.1, pp 345–53. According to a covering letter, the memorandum had met 'with the Führer's approval'.

that might put it in a position to regenerate its battered armed forces on a significant scale.

7.3 'By Mid-December, Winter Calm Will Have Descended on the East': the Final Phase of Barbarossa, November–December 1941

7.3.1 Heeresgruppe Nord: *Sealing off Leningrad*

From 18 September onwards, *Panzergruppe* 4, LVII. *Panzerkorps*, the Luftwaffe's VIII. *Fliegerkorps* and much of *Heeresgruppe Nord*'s heavy artillery were gradually moved from the front outside Leningrad to take part in the drive on Moscow. [47] This meant that by early October *Generalfeldmarschall* von Leeb's army group found itself relegated – this time permanently – to fighting a poor man's war. Supported by the weakest of the three *Luftflotten*, it was reduced to a mere two army commands (16. and 18. *Armee*) fielding a total of twenty-seven divisions, only two of which (8. and 12. *Panzerdivisionen*) were mechanised.[48] Rather than taking Leningrad by storm,[49] 18. *Armee* was now tasked with putting the Soviet Union's second city under close siege while also keeping watch on a nearby lodgement of Soviet troops at Oranienbaum, opposite the Kronstadt naval base. At the same time, 16. *Armee* was supposed to strive for a link-up with Finland's Karelian Army to the east of Lake Ladoga. Of those two objectives, the former at least seemed feasible in terms of time and space, but already on 25 September 1941 Leeb made it clear that he had issued orders to his command to temporarily stand down and adopt a defensive posture, a move he justified by the dwindling assets still available to him.[50] This meant that Leningrad would be left outside the range of most of the *Heeresgruppe*'s artillery pieces and that the totality of 18. *Armee* and its ten divisions would be tied up for the next twenty-eight months manning the ramparts of a siege operation destined to keep in check a city defended by a numerically superior garrison supported by the guns of the Red Banner Baltic Fleet. Plans to improve the siege lines in order to render the city's position untenable were soon drawn up,[51] but they were compromised by the

---

[47] 'By mid-December, winter calm will have descended on the East': see TB Leeb, p 393, fn 549 (entry for 18 November 1941).

[48] BA/MA, RH 19 III/771 'Heeresgruppenkommando Nord, Ia an O.K.H. Op. Abt. Betr.: Beurteilung der Lage für die Abwehr im Winter (4.11.1941)'.

[49] The chances of such a move have been assessed as good by some historians, provided *Panzergruppe* 4 had been allowed to stay with *Heeresgruppe Nord* for another week or two. The most comprehensive and sober assessment of this controversy is offered by Wettstein, *Stadtkampf*, pp 172–5.

[50] BA/MA, RH 19 III/766 'Heeresgruppe Nord, Ia Nr. 2214/41 g.Kdos. Fernspruch an Major v. Rumohr, 19.45 h'.

[51] BA/MA, RH 19 III/766 'Armeeoberkommando 18, Abt. Ia Nr. 4592/41 g.Kdos. Betr.: Gedanken über die Fortsetzung der Operation (22.9.1941)'.

Map 7.1 The progress of Operation Barbarossa, June–December 1941.

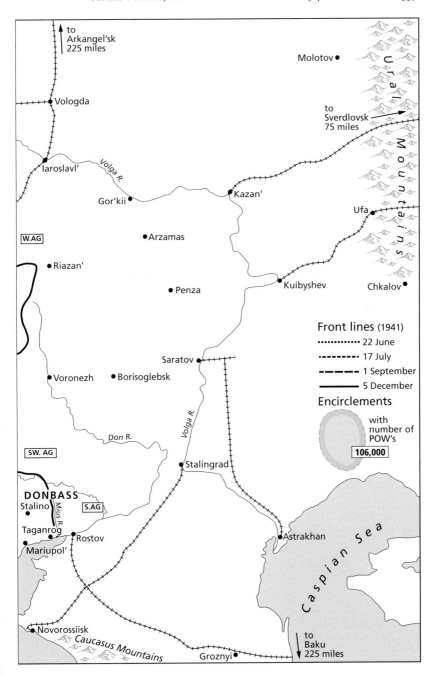

to
Arkangel'sk
225 miles

Molotov

Vologda

to
Sverdlovsk
75 miles

Iaroslavl'

Volga R.

Gor'kii

Kazan'

Ufa

W.AG

Arzamas

Riazan'

Penza

Kuibyshev

Chkalov

Front lines (1941)

············ 22 June
– – – – – – 17 July
— – — – — 1 September
———— 5 December

Saratov

Encirclements

Voronezh Borisoglebsk

with
number of
POW's

Volga R.

106,000

Don R.

SW. AG

Stalingrad

DONBASS
Stalino

S.AG

Taganrog

Rostov

Mariupol'

Astrakhan

Caspian Sea

Novorossiisk

Caucasus Mountains

to
Baku
225 miles

Groznyi

Ural Mountains

persistence with which the besieged kept probing 18. *Armee*'s lines for weak spots. Even the long-term option of starving out the city was a doubtful prospect, as Leeb himself had pointed out on 25 September: supplies could still be run in across Lake Ladoga and the defenders retained a sizeable arable hinterland in the form of the isthmus north of the city between Ladoga and the Baltic, which the Finns had thus far refused for political reasons to invade.

After a brief hiatus, both Hitler and Leeb looked for options that might allow the *Heeresgruppe* to achieve one or more of its objectives before the onset of winter. The elimination of the Oranienbaum bridgehead was the least ambitious, a link-up with the Finnish Karelian Army to the east of Lake Ladoga the most. On 2 October, Hitler suggested what could be described as a compromise solution: a drive on the communication hub, Tichwin, to the east.[52] Such a move would have the effect of sealing Leningrad's isolation from the outside world by cutting the railway line which served the terminal at Volkhov, from where goods were unloaded and ferried across Lake Ladoga. Leeb's main concern over such an operation was the fact that the problems posed by the terrain in that region (much of it covered by dense forests, crisscrossed by rivers and dotted with swamps) would be magnified many times over by the rainy season which was about to start. The advance would be channelled into the few available roads and become easy to block as a result.[53]

A few days later, the spectacular encirclement by *Heeresgruppe Mitte* of the Red Army forces defending the approaches to Moscow (Operation Taifun) led to OKH reconsidering its options. *Heeresgruppe Nord* was ordered to concentrate the few units left to it under 16. *Armee*'s command, preparatory to striking out to the southeast in the direction of Borovici. There, they would meet halfway an offensive by *Heeresgruppe Mitte*'s *Panzergruppe* 3 who would be approaching from Kalinin.[54] If successful, this bold stroke would lead to a shortening of the German front line and also cut off a large part of the Novgorod Front with its four armies. Leeb's staff immediately drew up plans detailing the forces required for each operation,[55] but on 14 October the scheme to meet *Panzergruppe* 3 somewhere around Borovici was postponed and the plan to seize Tichwin confirmed.[56] Even though, far to the south, elements of *Panzergruppe* 3 had entered Kalinin that very day, the ferocity of Soviet resistance there and a tenuous logistical lifeline suggested that the German plan to cut off the Novgorod Front would suffer

---

[52] TB Leeb, p 368 (entry for 2 October 1941).
[53] TB Leeb, p 369 (entry for 3 October 1941).
[54] BA/MA, RH 2/1327 'OKH, Gen.St.d.H./Op.Abt. Nr. 41 452/41 g.Kdos. an Heeresgruppe Nord (8.10.1941)'.
[55] BA/MA, RH 19 III/766 'Heeresgruppenkommando Nord, Ia an O.K.H./Op.Abt. (11.10.1941)'.
[56] TB Leeb, p 375 (entry for 14 October 1941).

some delay.[57] However, 16. *Armee* was instructed to tie down the Soviet forces in front of it with raids and spoiling attacks, a clear indication that OKH was still holding out some hope for their scheme to be implemented later on. On 16 October, the operation against Tichwin was initiated by 16. *Armee*. The forces involved were rather small (XXXIX. *Armeekorps* with two mechanised, two infantry and one motorised divisions), but as Leeb had repeatedly stressed to OKH, the terrain and state of the roads would not, in any case, have made an advance by a more substantial force practical.[58] After the crossing of the Volkhov river, the bulk of XXXIX. *Korps* headed off towards the northeast; its left flank was guarded by two divisions of I. *Armeekorps* which advanced north on both sides of the Volkhov river.

On 26 October, Leeb flew to the Wolfsschanze to confer with Hitler and Brauchitsch. His personal diary is silent on what brought about this sudden summons, especially at a time when everybody's attention at the Wolfsschanze was likely to have been fixated by the vistas opening up outside Moscow and beyond Kharkov. It is likely that the event behind this conference was the deterioration of the German position at Kalinin. Here, the attempt by the lead elements of *Panzergruppe* 3 to move beyond the city in order to effect a link-up with 16. *Armee* had effectively ground to a halt in the face of fierce Soviet resistance.[59] It is, of course, impossible to assess the extent to which this reverse was preying on Hitler's mind when he met Leeb, but the fact of the matter is that, not for the last time in the autumn 1941, the Führer ended up urging caution while one of his senior officers insisted on one last throw of the dice.

On his arrival at the Wolfsschanze, Leeb was first briefed by army commander-in-chief Brauchitsch. The latter appeared broadly supportive of Leeb's demands that he be allowed to pursue both the push on Tichwin and a major operation to destroy the Oranienbaum bridgehead; from the minutes it is not clear whether he briefed him in detail on the crisis at Kalinin, but a hint by Brauchitsch that the pincer operation against the Novgorod Front was being reconsidered appears to have gone straight over Leeb's head. Afterwards, both men proceeded to discuss things with Hitler, who proved to be a much more sceptical interlocutor. He gave serious consideration to terminating the push on Tichwin on account of the appalling state of the roads and would not hear of the scheme to crush the Oranienbaum bridgehead, feeling that the firepower available to its defenders (especially the heavy guns of the fortress of Kronstadt and the naval vessels based there) would turn such an operation into a Pyrrhic

---

[57] For a very detailed and well-sourced account of the fighting in and around Kalinin see Jack Radey and Charles Sharp, *The Defence of Moscow 1941: The Northern Flank* (Barnsley: Pen & Sword 2012).

[58] TB Leeb, pp 373, 374, 376, 380 (entries for 11, 13, 16 and 23 October 1941).

[59] Radey and Sharp, *Northern Flank*, pp 85–161

victory at best. He did, however, allow himself to be swayed by Leeb's arguments in favour of continuing the Tichwin operation.[60]

A day after his return, Leeb received a new set of orders effectively cancelling the operation against the Novgorod Front; he fired off a memo to OKH criticising the decision and drawing attention to the sacrifices made by 16. *Armee* in the process of tying down the forces of Novgorod Front.[61] In light of the fact that Brauchitsch had already indicated such a possibility to him only two days ago, Leeb's reaction would appear to be strange to say the least; it may well have reflected his frustration at realising that his last opportunity to play a more than subsidiary role in the imminent defeat of the Soviet armies west of Moscow had slipped away for good.

Barred from participating in the 'major leagues' where the war appeared to be weeks away from being decided, Leeb threw himself heart and soul into the next best thing: the progress of the campaign aimed at completely sealing off Leningrad from unoccupied Russia. On 29 October, he had pronounced the quality of the forces opposing XXXIX. *Korps'* advance to be very much 'a mixed bag' and expressed confidence in the operation's success;[62] the Luftwaffe withdrawing the bomber *Gruppe* it had detailed to support the operation appeared to be the only discordant note in the day's events.[63] The supporting offensive by I. *Armeekorps'* 11. and 21. *Infanteriedivisionen* advancing north on both sides of the Volkhov river was also making steady progress. Quite apart from the fact that seizing the town of Volkhov would present another opportunity to disrupt the flow of supplies from the interior, the advance along the river held out the promise of cutting off a large part of 54th Army, or failing that to at least widen the corridor that separated besieged Leningrad from the interior.

The offensive against Tichwin, however, soon slowed down to a crawl, and by 4 November, Leeb was already drawing up contingency plans with a view to abandoning the city after only a token period of occupation, long enough to wreck the railway crossing.[64] Three days later, with the German spearheads 8 km (5 miles) outside Tichwin, 16. *Armee* suggested to Leeb that he call off the operation; the army group commander did not record a verdict in his personal diary, but since both the corps and Franz Halder in faraway East Prussia

---

[60] A summary of the points discussed can be found in BA/MA, RH 19 III/771 'Aktennotiz über den Flug des Oberbefehlshabers der Heeresgruppe Nord zum O.K.H. am 26.10.1941 (29.10.1941)'.

[61] BA/MA, RH 2/1327 'Operationsabteilung IN Nr. 41 626/41 g.Kdos. an OKH Op Abt. (28.10.1941)'.

[62] TB Leeb, p 384 (entry for 29 October 1941).

[63] Bergström, *Air Battle*, p 94. I./*KG* 77 had suffered considerable losses as a result of having been ordered to support the advance with attacks delivered from very low altitudes.

[64] BA/MA, RH 19 III/771 'Heeresgruppenkommando Nord, Ia. Betr.: Beurteilung der Lage für die Abwehr im Winter (4.11.1941)'.

insisted on persevering in view of the tantalising proximity of the target, the advance continued.

On 9 November, Tichwin fell to XXXIX. *Armeekorps* and Leningrad lost its last lifeline with unoccupied Russia, leaving 16. *Armee* in possession of an oversized bulge it struggled to defend against almost daily counter-attacks. To achieve an even remotely tenable front line would have required I. *Armeekorps* to reach not just the town of Volkhov, but the mouth of the river of the same name by the shores of Lake Ladoga.[65] Leeb's most pressing priority on receiving the news of the fall of Tichwin hardly reflected such a realisation: on 11 November, he and members of his staff descended on the headquarters of 18. *Armee* outside Leningrad to impress upon the flabbergasted commander-in-chief, *Generaloberst* Georg von Küchler, that he needed to brace himself for an attack on the Oranienbaum bridgehead at the earliest opportunity. Both Küchler and the corps commander who was next on Leeb's list appear to have stated with remarkable candour that they felt a marked disinclination to prepare for an offensive that would see them abandon their recently finished winter quarters.[66] Leeb was having none of it. He reminded the hapless corps commander that the fighting around Tichwin provided plenty of proof that winter weather was no impediment to offensive action and that the idea of going into winter quarters was premature to say the least (*'Für Winterquartiere sei es noch zu früh'*),[67] an approach Halder and Brauchitsch would undoubtedly have approved of. This bullish attitude indicated that Leeb was actually one step ahead of the plans that Franz Halder put to the assembly of army and army group chiefs of staff at Orsha on 13 November.[68] The minutes that Leeb's chief of staff brought back from Orsha spelled out that OKH and OKW (displaying a rare consensus) expected *Heeresgruppe Nord* to link up with Finland's Karelian Army 'next year'.[69] A comparison with the relevant entry in *Heeresgruppe Mitte*'s war diary indicates that the intended time window was January, rather than June or July.[70] It appears that Leeb had, if anything, managed to successfully anticipate his superiors' wishes.

---

[65] A hypothetical scenario, which would still have had to factor in the need to garrison the southern shore of Lake Ladoga in wintertime, when that body of water froze over to a depth where it supported the weight of trucks.

[66] TB Leeb, p 389 (entry for 11 November), esp. fn 536, which gives Leeb's detailed itinerary for the day.

[67] Ibid.

[68] For a more detailed account of the Orsha talks, see below.

[69] BA/MA, RH 19 III/771 'Heeresgruppenkommando Nord, Kriegstagebuch Ia. Niederschrift über die Besprechung beim Chef des Heeres am 13.11.1941, Teil I (n.d.)', though apparently incomplete, complements other sources on Orsha in a useful way. It is used here for the first time.

[70] BA/MA, RH 19 II/387 'Heeresgruppenkommando Mitte, Kriegstagebuch Ia (entry for 15 November 1941)'.

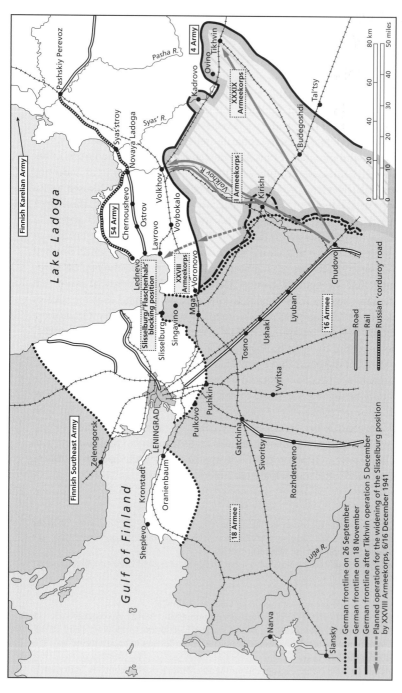

Map 7.2 The German attempt to isolate Leningrad, November–December 1941.

Over the next few days, the drive on the town of Volkhov reached a point a few kilometres from its southern suburbs. To finally dislodge the Soviet defenders, a drive into their flank by I. *Armeekorps* was laid on. Elements of four divisions were to sally forth from the eastern side of the 'corridor' and join hands with 11. *Infanteriedivison* as it made its way north on the western side of the Volkhov river. If successful, it would go a long way towards solidifying Leeb's position east of the Volkhov, thus putting him in a position to fulfil what Halder had demanded of *Heeresgruppe Nord* at the Orsha conference on the 13th: to reach the River Swir and create a solid link with the Finns. When the operation started on 16 November, the Russians managed to hold fast along most of the front line and effectively blunted the attack within a day; a report by 16. *Armee* put this unexpected reverse down to the fact that many of the units involved had been '*Ostkriegsungewohnt*' (that is, new to the conditions prevailing on the Russian Front).[71]

Over the next week it became increasingly obvious that Volkhov would not fall and that Tichwin would be increasingly difficult to hold onto; in light of these developments, it cannot have come as a surprise to Leeb that Hitler on the 18th decided to veto (once again) his pet project of destroying the Oranienbaum bridgehead.[72] On that same day, *Generaloberst* Ernst Busch of 16. *Armee* sent Leeb a report, which tried to put a brave face to things by expressing Busch's conviction that I. *Armeekorps* would still reach the shore of Lake Ladoga. At the same time, though, Busch drew attention to the fact that the size of the Tichwin bulge and the freezing over of many local lakes would require an extra four divisions if his command were to have a good chance of holding the line in the coming winter.[73] Leeb forwarded this paper to Brauchitsch and accompanied it with a covering letter where he put a forward a similar demand and even hinted at the obvious alternative – a retreat from Tichwin.[74] Only two days later, Soviet attacks on the bridgehead – as it had come to be called – meant that in the words of the army group's diarist, 'Tichwin is already more or less cut off,'[75] a development Leeb acknowledged to be a crisis point.[76] Halder and Hitler seem to have been more or less

---

[71] BA/MA, RH 19 III/766 'Armeeoberkommando 16, Ia Nr. 1127/41 g.Kdos an Heeresgruppe Nord (18.11.1941)'.

[72] BA/MA, RH 19 III/768 'Heeresgruppenkommando Nord, Kriegstagebuch Ia (entry for 18 November 1941)'.

[73] BA/MA, RH 19 III/766 'Armeeoberkommando 16, Ia Nr. 1127/41 g.Kdos an Heeresgruppe Nord (18.11.1941)'.

[74] BA/MA, RH 19 III/766 'Heeresgruppenkommando Nord Ia Nr. 2545/41 g.Kdos. an den Herrn Oberbefehlshaber des Heeres (20.11.1941)'.

[75] BA/MA, RH 19 III/768 'Heeresgruppenkommando Nord, Kriegstagebuch Ia (entry for 22 November 1941)'.

[76] TB Leeb, p 395 (entry for 22 November 1941).

oblivious of these developments, an omission attributable at least in part to the crisis developing around Rostov in the deep south.[77]

Over the next few days Soviet attempts to crush Tichwin decreased in intensity while the Volkhov sector saw some modest gains; by the 26th, Leeb was reassured enough to see the possibility of a 'sufficiently secured defensive front'.[78] By the end of the month, Tichwin was in fact gaining a perceived importance well ahead of Volkhov, a fact possibly brought about by the failure of another major 'push' against Volkhov by I. *Armeekorps* on 26 November,[79] and follow-up criticism from Hitler himself on the 30th.[80] By 1 December, the army group commander expressed reasonable confidence in holding Tichwin but all but gave up hoping for a breakthrough by I. *Armeekorps* into the flank of 54th Army to the north, settling for an expansion of the Slisselburg corridor instead. As for the long-term aim of the Tichwin operation – the link-up with the Finnish Karelian Army to the east – it was described as being 'out of the question'.[81]

As the continuation of Operation Taifun before Moscow lost all momentum, OKH warned Leeb to expect a major Soviet effort to relieve Leningrad.[82] This brought a commitment by Hitler to reinforce Leeb's two exhausted Panzer divisions with 100 new tanks, though this left Leeb rather nonplussed and even a little wary: he enquired of Halder whether such a gift might entail additional commitments, to which the army chief of staff responded that for the moment holding onto Tichwin would suffice, without however losing sight of the need to link up with the Finns.[83] Halder's diary suggests that this commitment was the result of a consensus arrived at between him and Hitler on the same day; though they were both resigned to abandoning the push on Moscow, they agreed that *Heeresgruppe Nord* needed to be reinforced in order to carry out an offensive along Lake Ladoga to completely seal off

---

[77] See 'Notizen von Generaloberst Halder für den Vortrag bei Hitler am 19. November 1941' and 'Notizen von Generaloberst Halder zu einer einleitenden Ansprache bei der Besprechung mit den Oberquartiermeistern der Armeen der Ostfront am 23. November 1941'; both in: KTB Halder III, pp 296–98, pp 305–7. The first of these two documents describes the prospects in the Tichwin/Ladoga theatre as 'promising'; the second one lists the link-up with the Finnish Karelian Army as one of the targets to be attained before the end of the year.

[78] TB Leeb, p 398 (entry for 26 November 1941).

[79] BA/MA, RH 19 III/771 'Der Chef d. Genst. der H.Gr. Nord. Besprechung beim A.O.K. 16 am 26.11.1941'.

[80] BA/MA, RH 19 III/768 Heeresgruppenkommando Nord, Kriegstagebuch Ia (entry for 30 November 1941).

[81] BA/MA, RH 19 III/769 'Heeresgruppenkommando Nord, Kriegstagebuch Ia (entry for 1 December 1941)'.

[82] BA/MA, RH 19 III/769 'Heeresgruppenkommando Nord, Kriegstagebuch Ia (entry for 3 December 1941)'.

[83] BA/MA, RH 19 III/769 'Heeressgruppenkommando Nord, Kriegstagebuch Ia (entry for 6 December 1941)'.

Leningrad and link up with the Finns. For this task, even the transfer of some units from the already seriously weakened VIII. *Fliegerkorps* outside Moscow was permissible.[84]

In the end, these deliberations would no longer affect the issue at Tichwin: by the afternoon of the 6th, the cumulative effect of the pressure exerted on all three sides of the salient by the Red Army led to a breakthrough, which in turn forced Leeb to abandon Tichwin within twenty-four hours;[85] Leningrad's life line was reopened.[86] This crisis resulted in a flurry of telephone calls between *Heeresgruppe Nord* on the one hand, and OKH and Keitel at OKW on the other. The latter's intervention in particular – he stressed he was just passing on Hitler's urgent wishes (*'seine persönliche Auffassung und seinen Wunsch'*) – is all the more striking in light of the fact that Hitler had been downright tepid in his commitment to the drive on Tichwin when he discussed it with Leeb on 26 October. As Keitel put it, Hitler was positively obsessed not just with the idea of securing a tight grip in Leningrad but also with retaining a sizeable bridgehead east of the Volkhov with a view to a later link-up with the Finns. In fact, Finland's Marshal Mannerheim himself, who had been dragging his feet over this issue for three months, was now said to be positively clamouring for such a move.[87] It goes without saying that this reaction needs to be seen against the backdrop of the cancellation of the drive on Moscow the day before. Having failed to secure one prize, Hitler must have found the prospect of finding himself barred from securing another one of similar political import-ance, if not now, than at least in the very near future, very hard to take. For the purposes of this study, however, a comment passed on by Keitel – an officer notorious throughout the German Army for being little more than 'his mas-ter's voice' – is much more revealing and carries much greater relevance. In expressing Hitler's 'personal opinion' over the telephone, he stressed that at

---

[84] 'Notizen aus der Führerbesprechung vom 6. Dezember 1941'; in: KTB Halder III, pp 329–31 (entry for 6 December 1941).

[85] On the planning and execution of the Soviet offensive, see David M. Glantz, *The Battle of Leningrad 1941–1944* (Lawrence: University Press of Kansas 2004), pp 104–11

[86] Since the fall of Tichwin, the Russians had been busy improvising a corduroy road through the local woodlands aimed at reaching Ladoga by a circuitous route, thus circumventing the German interdiction of the railway line. German intelligence only realised this after the Russian reconquest of Tichwin had made it redundant, see BA/MA, RH 19 III/769 'Heeresgruppenkommando Nord, Kriegstagebuch Ia (entry for 13 December 1941)'. For the story of this remarkable endeavour, see Bellamy, *Absolute War*, pp 366–71.

[87] Recent research does not support this contention. Mannerheim had repeatedly resisted German entreaties – the most recent one in late October – for an advance down the east or west shore of Lake Ladoga. Either of these moves could have rendered Leningrad's position untenable. For a comprehensive discussion of this problem, see Gerd Ueberschär, 'Kriegführung und Politik in Nordeuropa'; in: Horst Boog et al, *Der Angriff auf die Sowjetunion* (Stuttgart: DVA 1983) [= Das Deutsche Reich und der Zweite Weltkrieg, Bd. 4], pp 810–82, esp. pp 842–5. Henceforth quoted as DRZW.

this moment in time, 'Army Group North is the only critical flashpoint in the entire Eastern Front' (*'Die H.Gr. Nord ist z.Zt. der einzige kritische Punkt der Ostfront'*),[88] a truly remarkable statement if one takes into consideration that the Kalinin Front had started its counter-attack against *Heeresgruppe Mitte* on the 5th, and Western and Southwestern Fronts on 6 December.

In the meantime, the promises held out by a major lodgement east of the Volkhov took a long time to die. Hitler first insisted that XXXIX. *Armeekorps* pull back only to a position that would still allow intermittent shelling of Tichwin, a condition rescinded after half a day. On the 8th, the OKH's directive with regards to the *Ostheer*'s mission parameters during the winter insisted on the importance of 'bringing to a successful conclusion' the operations currently being conducted 'south of Ladoga Lake'.[89] Five days later, Leeb insisted that retaining a sizeable bridgehead on the east bank of the Volkhov was no longer realistic and risked the loss of several divisions; the military situation had deteriorated to a point where nothing less than a full retreat of all forces to the west bank would do. Eventually, Leeb and Küchler had to fly to the Wolfsschanze to plead their case in person, receiving permission to execute the retreat on the morning of 16 December.[90]

The story of the end of 16. *Armee*'s foray beyond the Volkhov in the second and third week of December is of particular interest because it coincided with the plans for another operation. This one was aimed at sealing the ring around Leningrad and had been sketched out in rough form by Halder and Hitler on the 6th. Even though it was essentially stillborn (it was not even given a code name), it reveals a lot about the frame of mind of Hitler and his key senior aides at a time when – according to conventional wisdom – OKW's and OKH's decision-making processes were already hamstrung by the crisis outside Moscow.

Even in the days before Tichwin was abandoned, Leeb, Halder and Hitler had been giving a lot of thought to extent that *Heeresgruppe Nord*'s tenuous grip on Leningrad could be stabilised. Holding on to Tichwin was the obvious first priority; however, after I. *Armeekorps*' march on Volkhov was defeated, Leeb was still left with an impossibly long salient to defend and the old problem of the *Flaschenhals* (bottleneck) which, while key to keeping Leningrad isolated, was also much too narrow to constitute a solid blocking position, especially if Leningrad's defenders and a relief force ever hit on the idea of crushing it with a coordinated

---

[88] BA/MA, RH 19 III/771 'Anruf Generalfeldmarschall Keitel an Chef des Genst H.Gru. (7.12.1941, 15.40 h)'.

[89] BA/MA, RH 2/1327 'Oberkommando des Heeres Gen.St.d.H./Op.Abt.(Ia) Nr. 1693/41 g.Kdos./Chefs. Weisung für die Aufgaben des Ostheeres im Winter 1941/42 (8.12.1941)'.

[90] BA/MA, RH 19 III/769 'Heeregruppenkommando Nord, Kriegstagebuch Ia (entries for 15 December, 17.35, and 16 December, 10.00)'.

offensive.[91] Accordingly, the idea of pushing back 54th Army with a view to widening the *Flaschenhals* began to take shape; though on the face of it less daring than 16. *Armee*'s double drive on Volkhov and Tichwin, it constituted a major challenge nonetheless, since it would constitute a frontal assault on the part of the front line where the Red Army was bound to have the greatest density of field units in the entire Leningrad sector. Halder rang Leeb's chief of staff in the small hours of 7 December and passed on the gist of the idea. He emphasised the need to hang onto Tichwin and promised reinforcements which, in light of the disaster narrowly averted to the west of Rostov six days earlier, was nothing short of breathtaking: a fresh Panzer regiment, 100 new tanks for 8. and 12. *Panzerdivision*, 22,300 men as reinforcements to flesh out the units that had suffered the worst attrition over the last few weeks as well as a new infantry division (81. *Infanteriedivision*).[92] With the exception of the infantry division, these assets were all to arrive by 23 December. Halder also insisted that a previous plan by the army group aimed at the same objective be cancelled because of the lack of assets available. Leeb's chief of staff, wholly unaccustomed by this stage of the war to such a cornucopia, unwittingly found himself pouring cold water on Halder's ideas by drawing his attention to the crisis brewing at Tichwin. Halder answered that evacuating Tichwin would be 'painful'; in particular, shrinking the lodgement east of the Volkhov in the proposed manner would reduce the scope for future cooperation with the Finns.[93]

Notwithstanding the tepid reception given to Halder's proposal, the scheme went ahead, with a formal order drafted hours later.[94] It specified a two-stage approach: a complete occupation of the area west of the River Volkhov and east of the *Flaschenhals* currently held by the Red Army, followed by an operation along the shores of Lake Ladoga to meet up with the Finnish Karelian Army. Rather remarkably, OKH described the latter notion as 'questionable' and suggested a more shallow advance that would merely increase the width of the *Flaschenhals* to ensure the isolation of Leningrad. A case was also made for a retreat of I. and XXXIX. *Armeekorps* from their lodgement east of the Volkhov, the idea being that Leeb simply lacked the forces to both undertake the imminent operation and defend the (albeit shrinking) perimeter east of

---

[91] A contingency which, rather remarkably, had yet to materialise by mid-December. See BA/MA, RH 19 III/771 'Aktennotiz über den Vortrag des O.B. beim Führer am 16.12.1941 (17.12.1941)'.

[92] BA/MA, RH 19 III/771 'Anruf Chef des Genst.d.H. an Chef des Genst.H.Gr.Nord (7.12.1941, 00.15 h)'.

[93] Ibid.

[94] BA/MA, RH 19 III/771 'Entwurf. Heeresgruppenbefehl Nr. 4 für die Fortführung der Operation (7.12.1941)'.

the river.[95] This in turn caused Hitler, who still seemed to think of the upcoming operation in terms of an advance all the way to the lower Volkhov and from there to a link-up with the Finns, to raise the question of whether such a move would not leave the right flank of the advancing force (XXVIII. *Armeekorps*) hanging in the air. Leeb saved the day by proposing an intermediate solution, and on the afternoon of 10 December 1941 the operation was confirmed.[96] For good measure, a strengthened SS battalion had in the meantime been added to the long list of reinforcements headed *Heeresgruppe Nord*'s way.[97]

The high expectations that Hitler invested in this enterprise can be gleaned from a non-military source. On the afternoon of 12 December, he hosted a meeting of the *Reichs- und Gauleiter* in his private quarters in the Reichskanzlei. This gathering has become notorious for being one of the few occasions when he spoke with candour about the subject of the recently initiated Holocaust. Of greater relevance for this chapter is the fact that he also dwelt at some length on his plans for the *Ostheer*'s winter campaign: in order to lessen the pressure on the army and facilitate the shifting of most mechanised units back to Germany where they would be reconstituted, *Heeresgruppe Mitte*'s front line would have to be pulled back in a number of places to make a purely defensive stance over the next few months practical. There would only be two exceptions to this general rule: operations planned for 'the next weeks' aimed at bringing about, first, the fall of Leningrad, to be followed quickly by that of Sevastopol.[98]

---

[95] BA/MA, RH 19 III/769 'Heeresgruppenkommando Nord, Ia Kriegstagebuch (entry for 9 December 1941, 02.50)'. It is noteworthy that Leeb proved rather reluctant to seize the towline Halder had thrown him, see BA/MA, RH 19 III/769 'Heeresgruppenkommando Ia, Kriegstagebuch (entry for 9 December 1941, 18.25)'.

[96] BA/MA, RH 19 III/769 'Heeregruppenkommando Nord, Kriegstagebuch Ia (entry for 10 December, 17.00)'.

[97] BA/MA, RH 19 III/769 'Heeresgruppenkommando Nord, Kriegstagebuch Ia (entry for 10 December 1941)'. Even though 1,100 men strong, it belonged to a formation that had been roughly handled in the Finnish theatre of war and was in need of retraining. Hence Leeb decided to deploy them in the 'quiet' sector of the Oranienbaum bridgehead.

[98] Elke Fröhlich (ed:), *Die Tagebücher von Joseph Goebbels: Teil II, Band 2 (Oktober–Dezember 1941)* (München: K. G. Saur 1996), p 495 (entry for 13 December 1941). If we allow for the fact that the operation against the south shore of Lake Ladoga was still a week or so in the future, the mere idea that it could have led to the collapse of Soviet resistance in and around Leningrad even before the success of the Sevastopol operation (hence by the turn of the year at the latest) seems preposterous at best. Rather than dismiss this notion outright, however, one must factor in the information Hitler was basing these calculations on, especially since he was in possession of intelligence on the desperate food situation in the city as early as 10 September. See 'Mittwoch, 10. September 1941'; in: Martin Vogt (ed.), *Herbst 1941 im 'Führerhauptquartier'. Berichte Werner Koeppens an seinen Minister Alfred Rosenberg.* (Koblenz 2002) [= Materialien aus dem Bundesarchiv, Heft 10], pp 16–18. On 7 December 1941, Halder commented to the chief

On 13 December 1941 preparations for the as yet unnamed offensive reached crisis point. In light of the battering that large parts of *Heeresgruppe Mitte* had been subjected to since 5 December, it would only have been natural for a sudden telegram, apprising Leeb of the redirection of his promised reinforcements, to have brought about the abrupt termination of the enterprise. Instead, the day started with Leeb admitting to Halder that he might have to order a wholesale retreat of all the troops east of the Volkhov, after all. Halder insisted that he at least put off such a move by a few days in order to tie down Soviet forces which would otherwise be turned around to face the impending offensive by 18. *Armee*'s XXVIII. *Armeekorps.*[99] *Generaloberst* Georg von Küchler, commander-in-chief of 18. *Armee*, then approached Leeb and confided in him that he had little faith in the offensive's prospects. He attributed this to the depth of the snow which had accumulated thus far. As he saw it, it was likely to greatly hinder the movements of both his infantry units and his tanks. In light of the fact that this particular problem was only likely to get worse over the next few days, he was reluctant to give the operation the go-ahead.[100]

The next event, however, could only be described as bizarre. In the evening, the war diarist of *Heeresgruppe Nord* recorded that OKH had copied Leeb into a telegram by Hitler to Brauchitsch, which in light of what had just happened at Rostov and would repeat itself a few days later outside Moscow, was nothing short of astonishing: the introductory sentence stated that Hitler had been apprised that *Heeresgruppe Nord*, while still willing enough to carry out his order for the upcoming offensive, no longer had 'faith and trust in the feasibility of this order'. This being the case, he asked Brauchitsch to assess whether the army group was capable of and willing to hold east of the Volkhov and, should this no longer be the case, whether the planned offensive along the south shore of Lake Ladoga should still be pursued.[101] The buck was duly passed onto 18. *Armee*, which sent one of its mechanised-warfare specialists to investigate. The findings he produced for Küchler were fast-tracked to Keitel, which provides a very strong indication that as late as the afternoon or evening of 15 December, Hitler had not yet given up on the idea of a big push south of Lake Ladoga at

of staff of *Heersgruppe Nord* that Hitler, 'based on the reports reaching him on the conditions in Leningrad, did not believe the city would be able to hold out for much longer'. See BA/MA, RH 19 III/769 'Heeresgruppenkommando Nord, Kriegstagebuch Ia (entry for 7 December 1941, 00.15)'.

[99] BA/MA, RH 19 III/769 'Heeresgruppenkommando Nord, Kriegstagebuch Ia (entry for 13 December 1941, 11.51)'.

[100] BA/MA, RH 19 III/769 'Heeresgruppenkommando Nord, Kriegstagebuch Ia (entry for 13 December, 18.45)'.

[101] BA/MA, RH 19 III/769 'Heeresgruppenkommando Nord, Kriegstagebuch Ia (entry for 13 December, 20.53)'.

some point in the next eight to ten days.[102] The report all but ruled out an advance along the planned axis, a verdict supported by the new commander of XXXIX. *Armeekorps, Generalleutnant* Hans-Jürgen von Arnim.[103]. When Leeb flew to see Hitler on the afternoon of the 16th to convince him of the need to pull back all the remaining elements of I. and XXXIX. *Armeekorps* still fighting east of the Volkhov, the attack aimed at widening the *Flaschenhals* was still discussed, though the proposed depth of the advance was considerably shrunk.[104] However, a war diary entry for the following day summarising an exchange with OKH about the operational priorities of the next weeks failed to mention this even in passing.[105]

Far more relevant than the eventual outcome of this debate is Hitler's reaction. Irrespective of the series of blows that were raining down on *Heeresgruppe Mitte* outside Moscow, between 7 and 12 December he thought nothing of directing quite substantial reinforcements to a theatre of war that in the grand scheme of things came dangerously close to being a sideshow. On the 10th, he appeared to waver briefly in his determination, though only because the commanders on the spot seemed to have found a way to fatally water down his original scheme. By the 13th, however, the news that Leeb or Küchler (or possibly both) appear to be unwilling to pull their full weight did not send him into a towering rage. Instead, we witness Hitler in the kind of mood that does not sit well with the popular image most people have of him: hesitant, confused even, anxious for advice rather than demanding slavish obedience.[106] Only a few days later, this brief moment would have passed and this same leader would be back to his old self, as seen during the Rostov crisis: issuing 'not one step back' orders, hectoring officers, sacking generals. The obvious explanation is that 13 December is the day on which the deteriorating situation in the main theatre of war (that is, outside Moscow) first starts to have an impact on his

---

[102] Further proof of this can be found in KTB Halder III, p 347 (entry for 15 December 1941).

[103] Arnim had taken over from Schmidt on 11 November. He is better known to readers in the English-speaking world as the last commander-in-chief of *Panzerarmee Afrika*, which he surrendered to the Allies in Tunisia in May 1943.

[104] BA/MA, RH 19 III/771 'Aktennotiz über den Vortrag des O.B. beim Führer am 16.12.1941 (17.12.1941)'.

[105] BA/MA, RH 19 III/769 'Heeresgruppenkommando Nord, Kriegstagebuch Ia (entry for 17 December 1941)'.

[106] This initial moment of insecurity finds confirmation in another set of sources. While at a meeting of the *Reichs- und Gauleiter* on 12 December, he spoke of the 'capitulation' of Leningrad by the turn of the year. In an interview with the Japanese ambassador twenty-four hours later, he would only commit himself to the 'continuation' of the siege of Russia's former capital. See TB Goebbels. Bd. II.2, p 495 (entry for 13 December 1941); 'Empfang des japanischen Botschafters General Oshima durch den Führer am 13.12.1941 von 13–14 Uhr in Anwesenheit des Reichsaußenministers' (n.d.); in: ADAP, Serie E, Bd. 1, pp 17–21.

perception of the developing crisis in the East. The Blitzkrieg may have run its course and his Panzer divisions may have been frozen in place for nearly ten days now, but the full implications of this are being driven home only now.

7.3.2   Crisis at Rostov: Heeresgruppe Süd, November–December 1941

By late October, the four armies of Gerd von Rundstedt's *Heeresgruppe Süd*,[107] after a rather slow start in June–July 1941, could look back on a string of impressive successes: the victory at Uman had been followed by their part in the pincer movement on the Soviet position around Kiev and the almost simultaneous piercing of what should have been an unassailable Soviet position on the Isthmus of Perekop, giving access to the Crimea by 11. *Armee* on 26 September. Another encirclement battle, rivalling that of Uman, came next by the Sea of Azov (7 October) and then the fall of Odessa to a Romanian–German force on 16 October. Finally, the important Ukrainian cities of Stalino and Kharkov fell to the 6. *Armee* on 21 and 24 October, respectively.[108] In the meantime, 11. *Armee* managed to break through the fallback position of the defenders of the Crimea, forcing them into a helter-skelter retreat into Sevastopol and the Kerch Peninsula in the east. The Red Army's evacuation of the eastern Ukraine also entailed the loss of the Donbass (or Donetsk) region with its coalfields and the iron ore mines of Krivoj Rojg on the Dnjepr. Evidence abounds that to the German dictator this event had far more wide-ranging implications than any other German success of 1941. In an exchange with senior officers in August, Hitler had described the region as the 'main foundation of the Russian economy', the loss of which 'would inexorably lead to an enemy collapse'.[109] Since at the time he was trying to make an argument for prioritising the Ukraine over Moscow, it cannot be ruled out that he may have been exaggerating for effect; even so, what at first glance appeared to be a sweeping statement made by an amateur economist reflected conventional wisdom at the time. A contemporary assessment by German military intelligence reached the conclusion that the loss of the Donbass would reduce

---

[107] From north to south: 6. *Armee* (*Generalfeldmarschall* Walter von Reichenau), 17. *Armee* (*Generaloberst* Hermann Hoth), 1. *Panzerarmee* (*Generaloberst* Ewald von Kleist) and 11. *Armee* (*General der Infanterie* Erich von Manstein).

[108] The pre-war population of Kharkov was in the region of 840,000, making it the Soviet Union's fourth-largest city. As a result of a large part of its inhabitants being called up to work in relocated factories or serve in the Red Army, it was down to 600,000 by December 1941. See BA/MA, RH 19 I/260 'Wi.Kdo. Kharkov Abt. La. Die Versorgung der Stadt Kharkov (10.12.1941)'.

[109] 'Besprechung gelegentlich Anwesenheit des Führers und Obersten Befehlshabers der Wehrmacht bei Heeresgruppe Mitte am 4. August 1941'; in: KTB OKW I, pp 1041–3. See also KTB Halder III, p 295 (entry for 19 November 1941).

Soviet steel production to 35 per cent of the pre-war output;[110] as for the consequences this was likely to have for the USSR's war-making capability, another analysis arrived at the following conclusion: 'This is likely to weaken the war economy of Russia to such an extent, that it will no longer be in a position to create the tools needed for a resumption of active operations west of the Urals in the summer of 1942'.[111] An entry in the Seekriegsleitung's war diary provides further confirmation of such an assessment. On 16 October, it recorded Hitler's decision to inform Mussolini of his intention to redeploy part of the Luftwaffe to the Mediterranean as soon as he was satisfied that operations had concluded in Russia for the year.[112] The letter in question was sent to Rome on 29 October – five days after the fall of Kharkov.

The successful evacuation of the substantial Odessa garrison to Sevastopol was the only thing Stavka was able to salvage from a six-week period of back-to-back fiascos. For the Germans, after such a fast-paced advance, the inevitable logistical problems reared their heads, and for the first time the idea of establishing a defensive line in order to settle down for the winter was discussed at the Heeresgruppe's headquarters. In the end, a decision was reached to continue the offensive by sending 1. Panzerarmee in the direction of Rostov, even though this meant reducing the advance of the three other army commands to a snail's pace.

Rostov – the historic gateway to the Caucasus – was an important enough objective, which the Red Army would no doubt defend with maximum effort. Resuming the offensive without the guarantee that 17. Armee to the north would be able to follow suit and hence protect the northern flank of 1st Panzer was not without risk. Hitler, for his part, stressed in those very days that while the advance of Heeresgruppe Süd should continue for a while to make the most of enemy disarray, the army group should then settle down for the winter on reaching the Don/Donec bend.[113] In the heady atmosphere created by the run of German successes of the last six weeks, this was, if anything, a remarkably

---

[110] BA/MA, RH D 7 11/4 'Oberkommando des Heeres, Gen.St.d.H. OQu IV – Abt. Fremde Heere Ost (II) Nr. 4700/41 geh. Die Kriegswehrmacht der Union der Sozialistischen Sowjetrepubliken (UdSSR). Teil I: Text', pp 129–31.

[111] BA/MA, RW 19/1251 '3. Abschrift, 2. Ausf., Wi Rü Amt Nr. 3208/41 gk Voraussichtliche Entwicklung der wehrwirtschaftlichen Lage Russlands mit Fortschreiten der Operationen nach Osten (early October 1941)'.

[112] Werner Rahn and Gerhard Schreiber (eds.), Kriegstagebuch der Seekriegsleitung, Teil A, Bd. 24 (Herford: Mittler & Sohn 1990) (entry for 16 October 1941). The term used ('mit dem diesjährigen Abschluss der Ostoperationen') hinted at the likelihood of further operations in 1942, but by implication was unambiguously clear that the initiative for this lay with the Ostheer alone.

[113] BA/MA, RH 24–34/42 'Höheres Kdo. XXXIV, Abt. Ia, Anlage zum KTB (27.10.1941)'. My thanks to Christian Hartmann (Potsdam) for drawing my attention to this source.

cautious aim. A senior visitor who arrived at Rundstedt's headquarters on the eve of the offensive had rather more ambitious ideas.

The *Oberbefehlshaber des Heeres*, Walther von Brauchitsch, though Franz Halder's superior, had thus far played an almost subsidiary role beside his proactive subordinate, a state of affairs that could be traced back, at least in part, to the important role attached to the position of chief of staff in modern German armies. It is significant that Halder was actually semi-immobilised as a result of a riding accident in Berlin when Brauchitsch called on Rundstedt in Poltava on 3 November.[114] After Rundstedt had explained to him in great detail the current logistical limitations of his army group, the army commander-in-chief sketched out his idea for the next phase of operations: Voronezh, Stalingrad and Maikop would all have to be seized 'as soon as possible'.[115] Since strong enemy resistance was 'not to be expected', the advance should be spearheaded by small detachments equipped with Panje ponies, rather than motor transport.[116] The relevant war diary entry is not quite clear about the extent to which Rundstedt continued to oppose such arrant nonsense. At some point, he seems to have ceded the stage to his chief quartermaster, who likewise does not appear to have made much of a dent in Brauchitsch's convictions. A memo sent to OKH the same day conceded that a drive by 1. *Panzerarmee* on Maikop by early January might just about be possible, but it would leave all its formations in such a state that come springtime they would be 'completely paralysed from an operational point of view'.[117]

Outward appearances might suggest that the army commander-in-chief had attempted to steal a march on his bedridden subordinate, but nothing could be further from the truth: Brauchitsch and Halder were actually in complete agreement. The latter's personal diary has several entries that testify to a boundless optimism with regards to the opportunities open to *Heeresgruppe Süd*. On 3 November, he expressed his view that the enemy seemed to be preparing for the evacuation of all territory to the west of the Volga in front of Rundstedt's army group, in order to concentrate their remaining assets for the defence of Moscow and the Caucasus.[118] The following day, Halder forced

---

[114] See Halder's own account of his convalescence in KTB Halder III, pp 277–8 (entries for 10 October–3 November 1941).

[115] At the time, the last two cities lay more than 480 km (300 miles) behind Soviet lines.

[116] BA/MA RH 19 I/87 'Heeresgruppenkommando Süd, Kriegstagebuch Ia (entry for 3 November 1941)'. Löffler's biography of Brauchitsch makes no reference to the stay of the *Oberbefehlshaber des Heeres* in Poltava or what transpired there. Jürgen Löffler, *Walther von Brauchitsch (1881–1948). Eine politische Biographie* (Frankfurt a.M.: Peter Lang 2001).

[117] BA/MA, RH 19 I/87 'Heeresgruppenkommando Süd, Kriegstagebuch Ia (entry for 3 November 1941)'.

[118] KTB Halder III, pp 278–9 (entry for 3 November 1941).

himself to be a little more conservative in his prognostications, but was still convinced that the enemy was ceding all the territory that lay between the Don ('and possibly beyond') and the spearheads of 6. *Armee*.[119] Only on 8 November did he finally concede that the intelligence suggesting a vast Soviet withdrawal had been overblown.[120] Together with the onset of winter (admittedly one marginally less brutal than in northern parts of the USSR) and the misgivings Rundstedt had expressed, this realisation should have been enough to cancel the informal instructions given to *Heeresgruppe Süd* to prepare for an operation against Maikop. This would involve 1. *Panzerarmee* moving beyond Rostov overland and 11. *Armee* crossing the Kerch Strait and staging a full-scale amphibious landing on the Taman Peninsula (Operation Wintersport). An interview Brauchitsch had with Hitler on 7 November about the strategic priorities of the next few months seemed to suggest that the Wehrmacht's commander-in-chief was in fact quite happy to postpone the conquest of the Caucasus oilfields until the next year; a move on Stalingrad was not even mentioned.[121] A mere two days later, in a remarkable about-face, the German leader confided to the *Reichs- und Gauleiter* of the NSDAP that the next few weeks would see a twin offensive aimed at encircling Moscow in the centre while *Heeresgruppe Süd* would strive to reach the Volga 'in several places' and cut off the Caucasus from the remainder of the USSR.[122]

A formal directive dated 11 November proves that this was more than just a flight of fancy; in it, Hitler consented to an 'extraordinary effort' to seize a number of key objectives before the onset of deep winter forced an immobilisation of all motorised units. Among the objectives listed were Vologda in the north and Maikop and Stalingrad in the south. Both the previous paper trail and the opening sentence of the document leave little room for doubt that this scheme had originated with Brauchitsch and Halder, and not Hitler.[123] Rundstedt's remonstrations were only factored in to the extent that 1. *Panzerarmee* would not be instructed to move on Maikop before early January. At the Orsha meeting of 13 November, which saw Franz Halder brief the chiefs of staff of the three army groups and most army commands on this last phase of Barbarossa, no minutes were taken; however, the informal notes taken by *Heeresgruppe Süd*'s chief of staff are extensive and give us a hint of Halder's priorities. According to this document, he vastly underrated the

---

[119] Ibid., p 280 (entry for 4 November 1941).

[120] Ibid., p 283 (entry for 8 November 1941).

[121] Ibid., p 283 (entry for 7 November 1941).

[122] TB Goebbels, Bd. II.2, pp 262–3 (entry for 10 November 1941).

[123] BA/MA, RW 4/578 'Oberkommando der Wehrmacht 1888/41 g.K. Chefs. WFSt/Abt. L (I Op.) an OKH, Op.Abt. (11.11.1941)'. In contrast to most orders from Hitler's command ('the Führer directs …'), this one merely stated that he 'agreed' with the idea to move on distant objectives like Maikop, if weather conditions allowed such a move.

importance of the Caucasus oilfields to the Soviet economy, but was nonetheless convinced that the Red Army would prioritise their defence to deny them to Germany.[124] A degree of ambiguity surrounded the capture of Stalingrad, which is listed among a number of other objectives and had been described as 'conceivable' in a preliminary OKH directive days before.[125] The capture of Maikop, on the other hand, is highlighted as the one objective he expected to be achieved by mid-January even if 11. *Armee* failed to stage a crossing of the Kerch Strait.[126] Rundstedt, realising that his opposition to Brauchitsch's plans during the latter's visit had not got him very far, produced a memo on 17 November, listing in painstaking detail the material assets needed if the operation against Maikop in particular was to have a fighting chance.[127] That same day, the drive by 1. *Panzerarmee* on Rostov, which had stalled due to a return of the *rasputitsa* (autumn rains), was resumed.

Objections to continuing the offensive into the northern Caucasus around the turn of the year were also voiced by *General der Infanterie* Erich von Manstein, the commander of 11. *Armee*. Only recently appointed to this command,[128] the general had the conquest of the Crimea as his first independent assignment. After defeating the Soviet defenders of the isthmus and bursting into the interior of the Crimea, he had attempted to cut off the enemy survivors before they could reach either the Kerch Peninsula in the east or Sevastopol in the south, but the lack of a motorised element in his command mostly prevented him from doing so. A sizeable body of Red Army soldiers either escaped to the mainland via Kerch or made it to the safety of Sevastopol, the main base of the Black Sea Fleet. There, together with the recently evacuated Odessa garrison, they manned an improvised outer defensive perimeter in sufficient strength to thwart any German attempt to seize the base off the line of march; thus, the scene was set for what would become one of the epic sieges of World War II.[129] Even when on 12 November OKH briefly formed the erroneous impression that the garrison seemed to be preparing for

---

[124] BA/MA, RH 19 I/281 'Vortragsnotiz über Chefbesprechung in Orscha am 13.11.41 (17.11.1941)'.

[125] BA/MA, RH 19 I/87 'Heeresgruppenkommando Süd, Kriegstagebuch Ia (entry for 7 November 1941)'.

[126] BA/MA, RH 19 I/281 'Besprechung Chef Gen.St.d.Heeres am 13.11. in Orscha, III. Teil (n.d.)'.

[127] BA/MA, RH 19 I/259 'Heeresgruppe Süd an O.K.H. – Gen.St.d.H./Op.Abt. (17.11.1941)'.

[128] Manstein had commanded LVI. *Panzerkorps* between June and September 1941. He succeeded *Generaloberst* Eugen Ritter von Schobert who had been killed in action on 12 September.

[129] Until quite recently, the Crimean theatre has been oddly neglected by Western scholars. This gap has been recently filled by the publication of Robert Forczyk, *'Where the Iron Crosses Grow': The Crimea 1941–44* (Oxford: Osprey 2014) and Mungo Melvin, *Sevastopol's Wars: Crimea from Potemkin to Putin* (Oxford: Osprey 2017), pp 441–581.

evacuation, it still insisted that any attempts to take the base only be made after thorough preparations.[130] Throwing caution to the winds, Manstein instead initiated a hasty attack that very day, even though half of his command was tied down driving the retreating Soviets out of the Kerch Peninsula. The operation enjoyed a measure of success in that it pushed back the southern half of the Soviet perimeter; *Luftflotte* 4's dive-bombers also managed to account for a light cruiser and a destroyer supporting the Soviet defenders. Even so, the line held and Manstein was forced to desist on 21 November.

After that, 11. *Armee* settled down to rest the troops and stock up on artillery ammunition in order to break into Sevastopol's defences in more methodical fashion.[131] The preliminary date for the next attack was 26 November, but the demands of the rest of the army group caused this to be pushed back time and again.[132] While engaged in these tasks, Manstein produced a rebuttal of his army's proposed part in Wintersport, which made Rundstedt's criticism appear tame by comparison. It went into the most minute detail regarding the assets needed for a successful crossing of the Kerch Strait, many of which were not yet even available in theatre. He pointed out that Soviet naval superiority and the presence of ice floes in the straits in winter constituted obstacles that could be countered only with difficulty or not at all. The report also stressed the need for a sequential approach: only after the fall of Sevastopol ('where the enemy can be relied upon to stage an all-out battle') could the focus be shifted to a crossing of the straits and the invasion of the Taman Peninsula.[133]

In the meantime, the sketchy ideas for Wintersport had finally been merged with a wider strategic scheme for the army group's continuation of operations into late autumn and early winter. According to this, 1. *Panzerarmee* and 11. *Armee* were instructed to head for Maikop, 17. *Armee* was allotted the task of driving on Stalingrad; 6. *Armee* drew the long straw insofar as its projected offensive against the Don was much shorter and was mainly tasked with closing the opening gap between Army Groups Centre and South.[134] Red Army forces capable of blocking the Wintersport offensive by 1.

---

[130] BA/MA, RH 19 I/87 'Heeresgruppenkommando Süd, Kriegstagebuch Ia (entry for 12 November 1941)'.

[131] Forczyk, *Crimea*, pp 80–4; Melvin, *Sevastopol's Wars*, pp 473–6. Manstein was remarkably successful in erasing this setback from the historical record. Neither his memoirs nor *Heeresgruppe Süd*'s war diary dwell on what was after all quite a substantial operation.

[132] BA/MA, RH 19 I/259 'Oberkommando der Heeresgruppe Süd. Der Chef des Generalstabes. Betr.: Lagebeurteilung (22.11.1941)'.

[133] BA/MA RH 19 I/250 'Armeeoberkommando 11 Abt. Ia Nr. 4326/41 geh.Kdos. an Oberkommando der Heeresgruppe Süd. Betr.: 'Wintersport' (22.11.1941)'.

[134] BA/MA, RH 19 I/259 'Oberkommando der Heeresgruppe Süd, Ia Nr. 2141/41 g.Kdos. Weisung Nr. 11 für die Weiterführung der Operationen im Winter 1941/42 (21.11.1941)'.

Panzerarmee and 11. *Armee* were assessed by the army group's intelligence officer as being in the region of fourteen infantry divisions in the North Caucasus and a further eight or nine in the Transcaucasus; it was assumed, however, that both their lower numerical strength and losses suffered thus far would have reduced their fighting power to the equivalent of seven and four full-strength infantry divisions, respectively.[135] The Wehrmacht's arithmetic aside, this was already quite a substantial increase over the estimate Franz Halder had recorded in his diary only twelve days before (five divisions),[136] and it was yet another worrying indicator of the Red Army's regenerative powers and *Fremde Heere Ost's* struggle to keep up with the latter. While OKW was busying itself with drawing up the paperwork that would be needed for the seizure of industrial facilities in Stalingrad,[137] the first cracks had already started to appear in the façade of Wintersport.

On 7 November, the head of the *Mineralölkommando Kaukasus* (the unit tasked with rehabilitating captured Soviet oilfields, attached to 1. *Panzerarmee*) reported to his superior officer that the *Panzerarmee's* chief of staff, *Oberst* Kurt Zeitzler, had told him that an advance on Maikop was quite out of the question. This was due to logistical issues, the losses suffered by his unit thus far, the likely demands of the spring campaign and the climatic conditions. Even in the improbable event of a Soviet evacuation of Rostov and the area to the east of it, 1. *Panzerarmee* was unlikely to take up the pursuit.[138]

Were the pessimistic forecasts of the kind made by Manstein and Zeitzler having any impact whatsoever at the level of the army group or that of OKH and OKW? The evidence available is somewhat contradictory. Rundstedt had proven thus far that he was, if anything, more cautious than many of his peers currently commanding armies or army groups, but there is plenty of evidence that even he had failed to understand that his units were running on empty and vulnerable to a major Soviet counterstrike. On 17 November, he agreed to detach two units, the 22. and the 62. *Infanteriedivisionen*, to take part in the so-called *Druschaktion* (harvest time) for the requisitioning of the harvest which was supposedly surplus to the requirements of the civilian population.[139] A few days later, the army group confirmed that Christmas holiday breaks for the

---

[135] BA/MA, RH 19 I/259 'Oberkommando der Heeresgruppe Süd, Abt. Ic. Feindlage (21.11.1941)'.

[136] KTB Halder III, p 284 (entry for 9 November 1941).

[137] BA/MA, RW 19/3211 'Oberkommando der Wehrmacht Az. 3i/34/33/ Wi Rü Amt/Wi (Via) Orientierung über die wehrwirtschaftliche Bedeutung der besetzten und im Bereich der Kampfhandlungen liegenden russischen Gebiete. Nr. 15. Industrie und Verkehrslage Stalingrads (24.11.1941)'.

[138] BA/MA, RW 19/1776 'Min. Kdo. K Ia. Br.Br.Nr. 5/41 gKdos. an Wi In Süd, z.Hd. des Chefs des Stabes Herrn Oberst Dietrich. Betr.: Vormarsch der 1. Panzerarmee in das Gebiet Maikop (7.11.1941)'.

[139] BA/MA, RH 19 I/87 'Heeresgruppenkommando Süd, Kriegstagebuch Ia (entries for 16 and 17 November 1941)'.

troops would be granted as planned, with the number of trains available being the only limiting factor.[140] The 22. *Infanteriedivision* had admittedly suffered considerable losses,[141] and it was slated to go to Germany in the near future to be restructured. Even so, it is undeniable that these measures give a sense of ordinary day-to-day life, rather than betraying a sense of urgency, much less crisis. At the same time, both Rundstedt and his chief of staff echoed 1. *Panzerarmee*'s demand for a full-strength mechanised corps if it was to continue operations into the winter season,[142] and they impressed on OKW that the notion of undertaking a major operation with the mechanised units available was 'mistaken'.[143] Such entreaties appear to have had some impact, since Halder's notes for a presentation to army quartermasters on 23 November listed Maikop as among the targets still to be taken in the near future, but admitted that reaching the Volga (that is, Stalingrad) before spring or summer was now out of the question.[144]

In the meantime, the campaign's most important preliminary target had fallen to German arms. On 20 November, 1. *Panzerarmee* took Rostov and even managed to seize one of the Don bridges intact. The taste of victory was somewhat soured by the fury of Soviet counter-attacks, which started the very next day and led Kleist to warn of the possible need to evacuate the city. These continued for the next three days and showed alarming signs of a well thought-out operational plan, aimed not just at pushing the Germans out of Rostov but at pinching off the bulk of the salient created by the advance of 1. *Panzerarmee*.[145] Kleist insisted that his command was not yet in the midst of a crisis, but at the same time hinted that barring major reinforcements coming his way, Operation Wintersport might already be fatally compromised[146] – a contradiction probably fostered by the unwelcome interest that Hitler himself was taking in the progress of the

---

[140] BA/MA, RH 19 I/259 'Der Oberbefehlshaber der Heeresgruppe Süd, Ia Nr. 3455/41 geh. An Befh.rückw.H.Geb.Süd und Befehlsstelle Süd/Gen.Qu. (23.11.1941)'.

[141] BA.MA, RH 19 I/259 'Stärkeaufstellung 11. Armee (n.d.)'. 22. *Infanteriedivision* had suffered 8.247 casualties thus far, while receiving only 3.848 replacements.

[142] BA/MA, RH 19 I/259 'Oberkommando Heeresgruppe Süd. Der Chef des Generalstabes. Betr.: Lagebeurteilung (22.11.1941)'. Especially in light of the priority accorded to operations outside Moscow, Rundstedt must have known that asking for a formation of the kind he described (two new Panzer divisions supported by two equally rested motorised divisions) was the equivalent of wishing for the moon.

[143] BA/MA, RH 19 I/87 'Heeresgruppenkommando Süd, Kriegstagebuch Ia (entry for 24 November 1941)'.

[144] KTB Halder III, pp 306–7 (entry for 23 November 1941).

[145] On the German assessment of Russian intentions with regards to the Rostov salient, see BA/MA, RH 19 I/87 'Heeresgruppenkommando Süd, Kriegstagebuch Ia (entries for 21, 22, 23 November 1941)'.

[146] BA/MA, RH 19 I/87 'Heeresgruppenkommando Süd, Kriegstagebuch Ia (entry for 22 November)'.

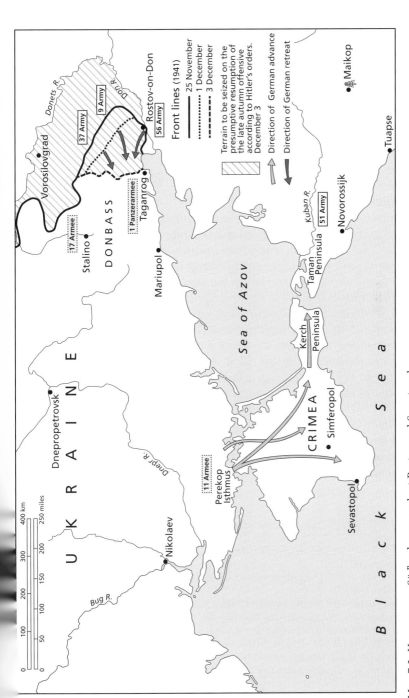

Map 7.3 *Heeresgruppe Süd's* advance ends at Rostov and Sevastopol.

battle.[147] After a three-day lull, the Red Army returned to the charge on 27 November. Rundstedt's only hope at this stage was to distract the enemy by prevailing upon 6. and 17. *Armee* to the north to engage in a maximum effort of their own. The former command proved particularly recalcitrant, leading to an angry exchange between Reichenau and Rundstedt at Poltava.[148] The compromise eventually arrived at – a diversionary attack by two of 6. *Armee*'s divisions – failed in its objective: Rostov was evacuated on the following day and Rundstedt used the opportunity to fire off a memo to OKH, which demanded the immediate cessation of any kind of offensive operations by his command until the coming of spring; any thoughts of at least reaching the line of the Don/Donec were dismissed out of hand.[149]

In view of the fact that as recently as 27 and 29 November, Hitler had expressed confidence in the prospects of a December drive into the northern Caucasus,[150] he accepted the retreat from Rostov without much demur, but a major quarrel arose between him and Rundstedt over the exact location for 1. *Panzerarmee* to turn around and face its pursuers. This may reflect the anxiety he and Halder felt over the need not to compromise the starting position of a renewed Wintersport; on the other hand, an interesting interpretation was put forward in 1983 to the effect that the catalyst for the ensuing quarrel may have been nothing more than a printing error on a situation map, leaving Hitler under the impression that Kleist was on the verge of giving up the important port of Taganrog, when in fact he fully intended to hold on to it.[151] The upshot of all of this was a message that arrived in the early hours of 1 December 1941, sacking Rundstedt and making Reichenau commander-in-chief of *Heeresgruppe Süd*; Reichenau would, however, continue to command 6. *Armee* for another month. For a day, the new army group commander tried to insist that 1. *Panzerarmee* carry out a staggered retreat, but he was eventually overwhelmed by events.[152]

---

[147] BA/MA, RH 19 I/87 'Heeresgruppenkommando Süd, Kriegstagebuch Ia (entry for 22 November)'.

[148] BA/MA, RH 19 I/87 'Heeresgruppenkommando Süd, Kriegstagebuch Ia (entry for 27 November 1941)'.

[149] BA/MA, RH 19 I/87 Heeresgruppenkommando Süd, Kriegstagebuch Ia (entry for 30 November 1941)

[150] In conversation with Finnish Foreign Minister Rolf Witting and Propaganda Minister Joseph Goebbels, respectively; see 'Empfang des finnischen Außenministers Witting durch den Führer in Anwesenheit des Reichsaußenministers am 27. November 1941 von 12–13 Uhr (28.11.1941)'; in: ADAP, Serie D, Bd. XIII.2, pp 694–9 as well as TB Goebbels, Bd. II.2, p 400 (entry for 30 November 1941).

[151] Ernst Klink, 'Heer und Kriegsmarine'; in: DRZW 4, pp 532–4.

[152] The exact sequence of events during those hectic days is chronicled in exhausting detail in the war diary of *Heeresgruppe Süd* and Franz Halder's personal notes.

On 2 December, Hitler himself arrived at the headquarters of 1. *Panzerarmee* in Mariupol, having travelled by air from Rastenburg. Such an unprecedented and quite risky move,[153] which ranks on a par with Churchill's flight to Egypt in August 1942, gives an indication of how exasperated he was by what had happened. Kleist was able to stand his ground by producing the paperwork proving that he had kept OKH abreast of the developing crisis at all times and by the support given to him by SS-*Obergruppenführer* 'Sepp' Dietrich, commander of the SS-*Leibstandarte* Regiment, who testified to the gravity of the crisis as it had unfolded between 29 November and 1 December. Hitler pronounced himself satisfied and even promised substantial reinforcements.[154] He left the following day, breaking his flight at *Heeresgruppe Süd*'s headquarters at Poltava on the way back. There, he stopped well short of apologising to Rundstedt, though he promised to reinstate him to a high command position in the near future.

The Rostov crisis has caught the eye of many historians of World War II because it appears to indicate a sea change in Hitler's command style: from this point onwards, he became less and less inclined to listen to dissenting opinions and as the war progressed abrupt sackings of senior officers would become more and more of a part of the routine at Führer's Headquarters. For the purposes of this study, a completely different aspect of Rostov is much more important: in the setting of the unfolding crisis of the *Ostheer* in autumn 1941, Rostov was a major red flag, arguably the last chance the German leader had to take stock of the situation with some calm before he would be overwhelmed by an avalanche of bad news. If he came back from the Ukraine with a sense of genuine crisis, this was likely to have major repercussions for German strategy at a global level. We are fortunate insofar as his thoughts on the subject, as he articulated them on the day in question, are recorded in two sources: in a report wired from Poltava to Oberkommando des Heeres at 16.00,[155] and

---

[153] At the time, Mariupol was a little more than 100 km (60 miles) from the new front line. For a contemporary assessment of the hazards involved in the trip, see BA/MA, RL 200/17 'Tagebuch Hoffmann von Waldau (entry for 3 December 1941)'. The post-war memoirs of Hitler's personal pilot echo Waldau's sentiments. Hans Baur, *Ich flog Mächtige der Erde* (Kempten: Albert Pröpster 1956), pp 211–13.

[154] BA/MA, RH 21-1/465a 'Panzerarmeeoberkommando 1, Kriegstagebuch Ia (entry for 3 December 1941)'. According to Kleist, Hitler had promised three battalions of paratroopers, 150 tanks, 50 self-propelled guns and an air lift as a stopgap measure, with 'several divisions' to follow. He delivered on the promised paratroopers, with *Fallschirmjägerregiment* 2 arriving between 6 and 19 December 1941, albeit mostly via rail and on foot. See Hans-Martin Stimpel, *Die deutsche Fallschirmtruppe 1942–1945. Einsätze auf Kriegsschauplätzen im Osten und Westen.* (Hamburg: Mittler 2001), pp 34–5.

[155] IWM, EDS, Group A 4/b AL 175 'Wehrmachtführungsstab Nr. 442058/41 g.K.Ch.Abt. L (I op). Abschrift (F.H.Qu., 3.12.1941)'. This document is the file copy produced for OKW's papers.

an entry into the war diary of *Heeresgruppe Süd*, which recorded his thoughts as he expressed them to a group of senior officers on the evening of 3 December 1941.[156]

In the first source, the dictator was still reflecting on the critical situation which *Panzerarmee* 1 had faced during the previous days; he reached the conclusion that Kleist's men had been spread too thinly over too wide a front to be able to mount an effective defence. He took solace in the fact that the enemy had managed to push them back by sheer weight of numbers alone. Hence he estimated the military potential of Russian soldiery to be 'essentially low' (*'an sich gering'*).[157] In the evening talk, he looked to the future: he insisted that the following weeks would in all likelihood afford the army group a window of opportunity, with ground that was frozen hard, on the one hand, and snow not yet thick enough to hinder the movement of mechanised units, on the other. Having promised reinforcements of up to six divisions from the army of occupation in France, he articulated his wish for Reichenau to resume operations against Rostov at some point in the next couple of weeks; once the advance reached the line of the lower Don and lower Donec, *Heeresgruppe Süd* should settle down for the winter and establish a base and launching point for the next spring campaign. The way the new army group commander-in-chief recorded Hitler's 'wishes' in the war diary suggests that outlandish targets like Stalingrad or Maikop were no longer on the list of operational priorities, but that Rostov, the Don/Donec line and Sevastopol definitely were.[158] Three days later, the German leader discussed the findings of his visit with Halder at the Wolfsschanze. He had come to the conclusion that the promise of reinforcements rashly entered into in Poltava had definitely been on the extravagant side; therefore, he expressly rejected the idea of shifting entire divisions out of France, having decided that 'combing out' rear areas would produce plenty of bodies for the task in hand. He also confirmed the need for a second offensive against Rostov during the winter, with a view to having a base for a drive on

---

[156] BA/MA, RH 19 I/88 'Heeresgruppenkommando Süd, Kriegstagebuch Ia (entry for 3 December 1941)'. Present were Hitler; the commander-in-chief of *Heeresgruppe Süd* and 6. *Armee*, *Generalfeldmarschall* Walter von Reichenau; his chief of staff, General Georg von Sodenstern; and *Oberst* Rudolf Schmundt, Hitler's adjutant for Wehrmacht matters.

[157] IWM, EDS Group A 4/b AL 175 'Wehrmachtführungsstab Nr. 442058/41 g.K.Ch.Abt. L (I op). Abschrift (F.H.Qu., 3.12.1941)'.

[158] BA/MA, RH 19 I/88 'Heeresgruppenkommando Süd, Kriegstagebuch Ia (entry for 3 December 1941)'. Even though Hitler chose to have his meals at the headquarters of 6. *Armee*, which was co-located at Poltava (undoubtedly because both Rundstedt and Reichenau were still using their respective previous HQs and mealtime conversations with the former would have been awkward at best), the war diary of that command does not add anything of substance. See BA/MA, RH 20–6/132 'Armeeoberkommando 6, Kriegstagebuch Ia (entries for 4 and 5 December)'.

Maikop the following spring.[159] Neither Stalingrad nor Maikop was mentioned as a possible target.

A reasonable case could be made that Hitler initially had shown a greater sense of realism about *Heeresgruppe Süd*'s remaining potential in early November 1941, until he allowed himself to be swept along by the misconceived enthusiasm of his senior military advisers, Halder and Brauchitsch. What is important is that neither at Rostov nor back at the Wolfsschanze three days later did he display the signs of a supreme leader who sensed that his master plan for the conquest of Soviet Russia had been fatally compromised. The scheme of operations previously agreed was adhered to; the key alterations made constituted nothing more than a return to the original scheme he had allowed Halder and Brauchitsch to tamper with.

In the meantime, Manstein found himself in the spotlight. On the one hand, he had penned an extensive memo to *Heeresgruppe Süd* on 2 December, spelling out in some detail why the force under his command was really too weak to guard the Crimea and take Sevastopol by storm at the same time.[160] On the other hand, the new army group commander-in-chief, Reichenau, let him know that that in light of the recent reverse at Rostov, a success at Sevastopol was highly desirable from a 'political point of view alone'.[161] By that time, Manstein's position outside Sevastopol bore a more than passing resemblance to that which Rommel had had to endure outside Tobruk for the last seven months: in both cases, the besieged force was able to fight from welldesigned fortifications and was being kept alive by a naval lifeline, which the aerial superiority of the Axis besiegers managed to interdict only on a few occasions. Also, while Rommel had to divide his forces between Tobruk and the Egyptian border, Manstein had to leave behind a substantial force on the Kerch Peninsula to guard against landings in his rear. In both cases, part of the command was made up of fellow Axis forces unlikely to withstand a major sally by the besieged or an offensive by a relieving force to lift the siege.[162]

---

[159] KTB Halder III, pp 328–33 (entries for 6 and 7 December 1941).

[160] BA/MA, RH 19 I/260 'Der Oberbefehlshaber der 11. Armee Ia Nr. 4445/41 an den Herrn Oberbefehlshaber der Heeresgruppe Süd (2.12.1941)'.

[161] BA/MA, RH 19 I/88 'Heeresgruppenkommando Süd, Kriegstagebuch Ia (entry for 3 December 1941)'. Hitler's confidence in the imminent fall of the naval base shines through in a conversation with the Romanian deputy prime minister days before. He refused to give a specific date for the fall of Leningrad or Moscow, but predicted the fall of Sevastopol in 'the next few days'. 'Aufzeichnung über die Unterredung zwischen dem Führer und dem rumänischen Vizeaußenminister Mihai Antonescu in Berlin am 28. November 1941 (3.12.1941)'; in: ADAP, Serie D, Bd. XIII.2, pp 726–29.

[162] Manstein's 11. *Armee* was made up of seven German divisions and three Romanian brigades. Manstein detailed them to guard parts of the coastline of the Kerch Peninsula, while noting: 'The Russians, should they please to do so, can land on Kerch anytime they want (the Romanians are not going to stop them)'. German generals were notorious for blaming their allies for assorted disasters after they had happened, but it is important to

Finally, in both cases the besiegers had to do without a working railway link, putting them at a logistical disadvantage over the force they were trying to dislodge.[163] When Manstein launched his assault on 17 December, the attrition suffered thus far by his infantry divisions forced him to limit his main effort to the northern half of the perimeter; he had also just been informed that a Stuka element to provide close air support promised by *Luftflotte* 4 would not be arriving for another twenty-four hours on account of other operational priorities and poor weather. Rather than postpone the operation yet again, Manstein decided to attack without the promised dive-bombers.[164] On 12 December, Hitler had held out the prospect of the fall of Leningrad and Sevastopol by the turn of the year in a confidential address to the *Gauleiter* in the Neue Reichskanzlei. When he met the Japanese ambassador the next day, he made the same claim with regards to Sevastopol and for good measure added a reference to a continuation of the drive in the general direction of the Caucasus – undoubtedly a hint at the planned occupation of Rostov and the Don/Donec bend. Only in the case of Leningrad did he choose his words more carefully than he had done the previous day.[165] The seriousness of the Sevastopol pledge in particular can be gleaned from the fact that *Heeresgruppe Süd*'s war diary recorded calls from Führer's Headquarters with the sole purpose of enquiring about the progress of operations at Sevastopol on 17, 18 and 21 December. Manstein soon realised that his forces – as he himself had hinted – were not up to the task and that the sole trump card which might have turned the tide, namely German air power, was prevented from intervening in sufficient strength by events elsewhere and, on more than a few occasions, the late autumn weather.[166]

Manstein kept banging on the gates of Sevastopol until nearly the end of the year when two major Soviet amphibious landings on the Kerch Peninsula forced him to cancel the operation. By that time, the defenders had been forced

---

realise that on this particular occasion the assessment preceded the setback. BA/MA, RH 19 I/260 'Der Oberbefehlshaber der 11. Armee Ia Nr. 4445/41 geh.Kdos. an den Herrn Oberbefehlshaber der Heeresgruppe Süd (2.12.1941)'.

[163] Railway communications with the main network in the Ukraine were only re-established in January 1942.

[164] BA/MA, RH 19 I/88 'Heeresgruppenkommando Süd, Kriegstagebuch Ia (entry for 17 December 1941)'. Manstein's rationale for doing so can only be explained in the light of Soviet reinforcements, the daily arrival of which took place under his very nose and the fact that the army group had only just taken away one of his divisions for another assignment. It is likely that he feared further inroads into his exiguous forces.

[165] 'Empfang des japanischen Botschafters General Oshima durch den Führer am 13.12.1941 von 13–14 Uhr in Anwesenheit des Reichsaußenministers (n.d.)'; in: ADAP, Serie E, Band I, pp 17–21.

[166] BA/MA, RH 19 I/88 'Heeresgruppenkommando Süd, Kriegstagebuch Ia (entry for 19 December 1941)'.

to give ground only in a few places.[167] In the meantime, the army group had settled down for the winter. The directive issued by Oberkommando des Heeres to all senior commands for the winding down of operations during the winter of 1941–2 had referred to the need to carry out 'during the winter, the overall situation permitting, the taking of Rostov and the Donec bend in order to create the prerequisite for the occupation of Maikop'.[168] There does not appear to be a record of Reichenau formally requesting this order to be rescinded; instead, other priorities (notably the assault on Sevastopol and continuing Soviet pressure on 1. *Panzerarmee*) appear to have gradually pushed it into the background. Even so, an element of ambivalence as to whether the 'wishes' expressed by Hitler on 3 December were still to be carried out appears for a while to have persisted. As late as 22 December, the chief of staff of *Luftflotte* 4 during a visit to Reichenau's headquarters felt compelled to clarify whether or not the army group was still planning for a push against Rostov. Only then was he unambiguously told that this notion had been written off and 'that everything was focused on a purely defensive stance'.[169]

7.3.3   Heeresgruppe Mitte: *the Continuation of Taifun*

For *Heeresgruppe Mitte*, the last week of October brought one last attempt to make good on a confident prediction rashly uttered by government spokes-man, Dr Otto Dietrich, at a press conference of 9 October, where on Hitler's instructions he had announced the imminent fall of the Soviet regime.[170] Seen against the backdrop of the events of the previous ten days, which had included the successful encirclement of sixty-four divisions and eleven tank brigades in two major pockets at Vyazma and Bryansk south of Moscow (Operation Taifun), this might have seemed like a reasonable forecast. The decisive moves of Taifun were concluded just before the onset of the dreaded autumn rains, and accordingly yielded a bag of prisoners and booty to rival that of the Kiev operation. The temporary resulting weakness of the Red Army to the west of Moscow allowed Bock one last success in that he managed to overrun all the fortified towns on which Stavka had hastily improvised the Mozhaisk defensive

---

[167] Forczyk, *Crimea*, pp 84–98.

[168] BA/MA, RH 2/1327 'Oberkommando des Heeres Gen.St.d.H./Op.Abt. (Ia) Nr. 1693/41 g.Kdos./Chefs. Weisung für die Aufgaben des Ostheeres im Winter 1941/42 (8.12.1941)'.

[169] BA/MA, RH 19 I/88 'Heeresgruppenkommando Süd, Kriegstagebuch Ia (entry for 22 December 1941)'.

[170] Dietrich already enjoyed a degree of notoriety with the Berlin press corps for his well-known tendency of playing fast and loose with the facts, but recent research indicates that on this occasion he was merely passing on a release that Hitler himself had dictated to him. See Stefan Krings, *Hitlers Pressechef Otto Dietrich (1897–1952). Eine Biografie* (Göttingen: Wallstein Verlag 2010), pp 413–20, esp. p 417. For a witness report of Hitler's exultant mood in mid-October, see BA/MA, ZA 3/264 'Zur amerikanischen Luftaufrüstung' (post-war deposition by Justus Koch and Fritz Siebel).

line. Kaluga had already fallen before the conclusion of Taifun (on 12 October). Mozhaisk and Maloiaroslavets followed on the 18th, and Volokolamsk fell on the 27th. However, the improvised forces detached for the defence of these places had put up an unexpectedly resolute fight, thus contributing to slowing down the German drive on the capital. The very same days also saw the virtual collapse of the logistics underpinning *Heeresgruppe Mitte*'s advance. This time, the weaknesses which had so far affected the German advance, such as receding railheads and the wear and tear of a multitude of truck types captured in the Blitzkrieg campaigns of 1939–40, mostly designed for hard-surfaced roads, were magnified many times over by roads which in many places had become bottomless quagmires.[171] Traffic first slowed down and in some areas came to a complete halt for several days.[172] The deterioration of the German situation in all likelihood contributed to Guderian's attempt to rush the defences of the city of Tula with a weak motorised force on 29–30 October. The failure of this *coup de main* left him in a situation that in due course would force him to resume his march on Moscow not with one, but two exposed flanks.

At the same time, Bock faced the fact that, as a result of his victorious advance and the nature of Russian geography, the frontage of his army group had increased from 500 to 800 km (310 to 500 miles) since the beginning of Barbarossa.[173] This in turn led to increasing demands by OKW and OKH that both operations still under way, as well as those belonging to the next phase of the advance, should be carried out along what were effectively divergent axes. The advance by Guderian's 2. *Panzerarmee* on Tula and beyond was at least geographically compatible with an operation aimed at an eventual encirclement of the Soviet capital from the west, southwest and south. The operation by that formation's XXXXVIII. *Panzerkorps* in the direction of Kursk (that is, away from Moscow) was already much more difficult to reconcile with this

---

[171] German commanders argued not just after, but also during the campaign in question that the autumn rains and the mud they brought were the key factor in allowing the Red Army to hold on to Moscow. See TB Bock, pp 295, 297, 299 (entries for 15, 19 and 21 October 1941) as well as TB Leeb, p 379 (entry for 22 October 1941). Also 'Letter by Oberst Hellmuth Stieff to his sister (17.10.1941)'; in: Mühleisen (ed.), *Briefe Stieff*, pp 130–1. For the impressions of a corps commander with 2. *Panzerarmee*, see 'Brief an die Frau (27.10.1941)', 'Bericht an die Familie (30.10.1941)' and 'Tagebuch (2.11.1941)'; all in: Johannes Hürter (ed.), *Notizen aus dem Vernichtungskrieg. Die Ostfront 1941/42 in den Aufzeichnungen des Generals Heinrici* (Darmstadt: WBG 2016), pp 82–6. For a well-argued case that conditions varied considerably between different sectors and that the Soviet defence and logistical inadequacies played a more important role in slowing the German advance, see Jack Radey and Charles Sharp, 'Was It the Mud?'; in: *Journal of Slavic Military Studies* Vol. 28 (Oct/Dec 2015), pp 646–76.

[172] For an excellent account of these conditions, see David Stahel, *Operation Typhoon: Hitler's March on Moscow, October 1941* (Cambridge: CUP 2013), pp 238–97.

[173] Stahel, *Typhoon*, pp 45, 191.

notion, especially when on 22 October OKH asked that it be extended beyond that city until it reached Voronezh.[174] Such a move would have meant an advance of nearly 300 km (190 miles) along a road which by that stage existed only in name. Though Kursk still fell on 4 November, the exiguous resources of the corps' sole Panzer division ruled out the implementation of such an idea.

In the meantime, a potentially far more serious distraction was emerging on the northern flank of *Heeresgruppe Mitte*. The under-resourced *Heeresgruppe Nord* had not kept pace with the advance of its neighbouring army group since 30 September, and Bock's command now found itself facing the Red Army not just to its east, but also along a northern shoulder. On 13 October, OKH had issued a directive for the continuation of operations after Taifun, which included the idea of having elements of 9. *Armee* (including its subordinate *Panzergruppe* 3) execute a 90-degree turn to the left and meet with *Heeresgruppe Nord's* 16. *Armee* halfway in order to cut off the bulk of the Soviet forces wedged in between the two German commands.[175]

The fall of the city of Kalinin with its Volga crossings to *Panzergruppe* 3 the next day provided what appeared to be an ideal jumping-off point for such an ambitious undertaking. However, by 28 October the focus of this operation had been shifted by about 90 degrees. Rather than meeting 16. *Armee*, both *Panzergruppe* 3 and 4 were now directed to attack in a northeasterly direction to seize first the towns of Yaroslavl and Rybinsk and then, after a brief pause, to carry on towards Vologda (approximately 400 km [250 miles] north of Moscow).[176] It is conceivable that the sudden shift may have been brought about by intelligence from the *Wehrwirtschaft- und Rüstungsamt*,[177] confirmed a few days later by the Washington embassy.[178] This pointed to the future importance of the railway hub, Vologda, in conveying to Moscow the first batch of Anglo–American supplies landed at the Arctic ports. A more likely explanation, however, involves German concerns over a different kind of Allied support. On 17 September, Hitler had had one of his monthly briefings with Kriegsmarine Commander-in-Chief Erich Raeder on the naval situation. One point involved the situation in the Barents Sea off northern Norway, where

---

[174] BA/MA, RH 19 II/124 'Heeresgruppe Mitte Ia Nr. 2134/41 g.Kdos. an A.O.K. 2 und Pz.A. O.K. 2 (24.10.1941, 15.10 h)'.

[175] BA/MA, RH 2/1327 'Oberkommando des Heeres Gen.St.d.H./Op.Abt. (I) Nr. 1584/41 g.Kdos.Chefs. Weisung für die Fortführung der Operationen der H.Gr. Mitte und Nord (13.10.1941)'.

[176] BA/MA, RH 19 II/124 'OKH, Gen.St.d.H./Op.Abt. (Ia) Nr. 319/14/41 g.Kdos. an Heereesgruppe Mitte (28.10.1941)'; RH 2/1327 Oberkommando des Heeres Gen.St.d.H. Op Abt (I) Nr. 1610/41 g.Kdos.Chefs. Weisung für die Fortführung der Operationen gegen die zwischen der Wolga und dem Ladogasee befindlichen Feindkräfte (30.10.1941)'.

[177] BA/MA, RM 7/94 'Wehrwirtschaft- und Rüstungsamt Abt. Wi Nr. 3409/41 gKdos. Beurteilung der Möglichkeiten einer materiellen Unterstützung Rußlands durch die angelsächsischen Mächte (22.10.1941)'.

[178] PA/AA, StS USA, Bd. 9, 'Thomsen an Auswärtiges Amt (26.10.1941)'.

General Dietl's advance on Murmansk had slowed to a crawl, though the fall of the city was still expected. British naval forays, however, had led to a situation where the resupply of his army was becoming more and more hazardous.[179] Moreover, both Raeder and Hitler were seriously concerned over the possibility of the British landing an expeditionary corps to support the Red Army. Such a move might jeopardise the German grip on the Petsamo nickel mines, which were located less than 100 km (60 miles) behind Dietl's front line. Towards the end of their exchange, Raeder insisted that not just Murmansk, but Archangelsk too, would have to be seized to thwart this threat. Hitler would not promise the latter, but gave the admiral the assurance that at the very least the railway line linking Archangelsk with Vologda and Moscow would be severed.[180]

The field commanders to whom these schemes were submitted were unimpressed. The normally optimistic Bock was highly critical of both schemes;[181] the commander of VIII. *Fliegerkorps*, on hearing of the impending Vologda operation, described it as unfeasible (*'nicht durchführbar'*) in his personal diary.[182] This pronouncement was all the more remarkable since it constituted a break with his habit of constantly blaming the army for its failure (alleged or real) to see promising operations through to a successful end. Quite apart from this, either advance would have brought the deployment of two formations, which thus far had been key to the success of the *Ostheer*, in missions where they could have rendered only marginal assistance to what should surely have been Halder's absolute priority, had he felt any genuine sense of urgency: the last chance to seize Moscow before the onset of winter.

A conversation between Brauchitsch and Hitler on 7 November was noteworthy above all because the German leader described the Mediterranean as taking 'priority' over any other theatre of war; with regards to Russia, he appeared happy to leave some unfinished work – especially the Caucasus – for the next spring.[183] Whether by coincidence or not, a missive from OKH bearing the same date arguably represents the very pinnacle of Halder's delusions of grandeur in those days. It was drawn up as a working paper for the benefit of the chiefs of staff of the armies and army groups of the *Ostheer*, whom he intended to meet in a few days' time. Setting out the Chief of Staff's ideas for the second phase of Taifun, it came with a map which illustrated Halder's ideas about maximum lines of advance that the Chief of Staff saw as desirable, feasible or

---

[179] In the small hours of 7 September, two transports ferrying troops of 6. *Gebirgsdivision* had narrowly avoided interception by two Royal Navy cruisers.

[180] 'OKM Skl B. Nr. 1 Skl Ib 1555/41 g.Kdos. Chefs. Vortrag des Ob.d.M. beim Führer am 17.9.1941 nachm. Wolfsschanze (n.d.)'; in: Gerhard Wagner (ed.), *Lagevorträge des Oberbefehlshabers der Kriegsmarine vor Hitler 1939–1945* (München: J.F. Lehmanns 1972), pp 286–9.

[181] TB Bock, pp 294, 304 (entries for 14 and 27 October 1941).

[182] BA/MA, N 671/8 'Tagebuch Wolfram von Richthofen (entry for 29 October 1941)'.

[183] KTB Halder III, p 283 (entry for 7 November 1941).

both. The 'minimum' line of advance would be anchored on the Swir river east of Lake Ladoga in the far north and the city of Rostov in the deep south; in the centre, it was supposed to reach a point 160 km (100 miles) east of Moscow. The 'maximum' line would have seen Heeresgruppe Nord in possession of Vologda and *Heeresgruppe Süd* establishing itself both in Stalingrad and Maikop; *Heeresgruppe Mitte* would have had to carry its advance beyond Moscow all the way to the industrial centre of Gorki, 400 km (250 miles) east of the Soviet capital.[184] Equally significant is the extent to which Halder was prepared to disperse his assets: *Panzergruppen* 3 and 4 were to bypass Moscow on their way to Vologda, 2. *Armee* would carry on with its advance on Voronezh and 2. *Panzerarmee* would drive on Gorki without making so much as a detour to Moscow. This left 4. *Armee* to seize the Soviet capital unassisted.

When Halder joined the gathering of chiefs of staff of all three army groups and seven of the ten army commands that made up the *Ostheer* at Orsha on 13 November,[185] he did so with a clear agenda: in order to hinder a Soviet recovery over the winter months, it was important that the tottering giant be dealt one final blow before deep winter set in.[186] According to the head of

---

[184] BA/MA, RH 21–2/879 'Der Chef des Generalstabes des Heeres an die Herren Chefs der Generalstäbe der Heeregruppen und Armee (7.11.1941)'.

[185] The absence of the chiefs of staff of 2. *Armee* (*Heeresgruppe Mitte*), 1. *Panzerarmee* and 11. *Armee* (both *Heeresgruppe Süd*) is a matter on which so far no historian of the campaign has dwelt. It should be remembered that in the case of 1. *Panzerarmee* and 2. *Armee*, the chief of staff, Kurt Zeitzler, and the commander-in-chief, Maximilian von Weichs, respectively, had been dismissive of the notion of late autumn campaigning pre-Orsha. Erich von Manstein, the commander-in-chief of 11. *Armee*, was equally critical in a memo he penned on 22 November and may have voiced such thoughts more informally sooner than that. Hence it appears likely that the sceptical attitude that prevailed in the HQs of these three commands had led to their exclusion from this important council of war. For Weichs' criticism, see BA/MA, RH 19 II/387 'Heeresgruppenkommando Mitte, Kriegstagebuch Ia (entries for 2 and 7 November 1941)'. *Panzergruppen* 3 and 4 did not send a representative because they were not yet, technically speaking, army commands.

[186] Even though no minutes were taken at Orsha, a number of the officers attending made notes which have survived to this day. The most extensive by far are those which can be found in the appended documents of the war diaries of *Heeresgruppe Nord* and *Süd*, see BA/MA, RH 19 III/771 'Niederschrift über die Besprechung beim Chef des Generalstabes des Heeres am 13.11.1941, Teil I (n.d.)', RH 19 I/281 'Vortragsnotiz über Chefbesprechung in Orscha am 13.11.41 (17.11.1941)' and RH 19 I/281 'Besprechung Chef Gen.St.d.Heeres am 13.11. in Orscha, Teil I-IV (n.d.)'. They should be complemented with a loose minute in the papers of 6. *Armee* and a detailed entry in the war diary of *Heeresgruppe Mitte*. See BA/MA, RH 20–6/142 'Besprechung in Orsha am 13.11.1941 (n.d.)' and BA/MA, RH 19 II/387, 'Heeresgruppenkommando Mitte, Kriegstagebuch Ia (entry for 15 November 1941)'. The points jotted down by Franz Halder in his diary are mainly useful for discerning how much time was devoted to the main subjects throughout the day: KTB Halder III, pp 288–9 (entry for 13 November 1941). See also the recollections of a staff officer present during part of the deliberations: Vincenz Müller, *Ich fand das wahre Vaterland* (Ost-Berlin: MV d. DDR 1962), p 382.

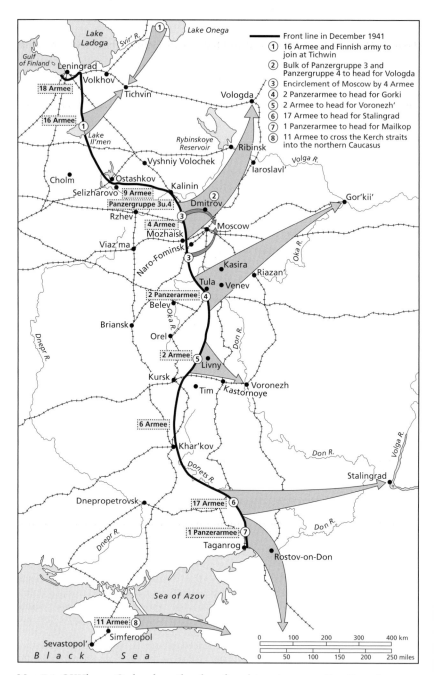

Map 7.4 OKH's pre-Orsha plans: the plans for a late autumn continuation of Barbarossa, which Franz Halder drew up in the days before the Orsha meeting, would mark him out as a decision maker who at the time was far more disconnected from military reality than Hitler.

Fremde Heere Ost, who travelled to Orsha with Halder, the USSR's residual strength remained considerable, with its output in artillery constituting a particular worry. By spring of the following year, it was likely the Red Army would have an order of battle of 150 divisions and 40 tank brigades. Even allowing for the fact that these Soviet formations would be under-strength,[187] much of the rank and file barely trained and their officers promoted beyond the usual proficiency levels, this was a worrying prospect. How would the Soviet leadership deploy this force to greatest effect? On 4 November, Halder had already elaborated on this theme during a telephone conversation with *Generalmajor* Hans von Greiffenberg, the chief of staff of *Heeresgruppe Mitte*; he had tried to impress on him that Moscow, for one, served as the equivalent of a bridgehead of 'Asian' Russia which would be used as a base from which new Soviet armies would sally forth in the near future to disrupt German attempts at exploiting the newly conquered territories.[188] Moreover, the losses suffered thus far by the *Ostheer* and the redirection of labour and raw materials towards the navy and air force would soon force Leeb, Bock and Rundstedt to fight a war with diminished forces, both in terms of quantity and quality. He also hinted at the possibility that 'the political leadership' might choose not to resume major campaigning in the East in 1942.[189]

Halder's sales pitch was tempered by his announcement that no reinforcements whatsoever could be expected from Germany and that the coming weeks would see the disbandment of eleven of the *Ostheer*'s divisions. The motorised divisions would have to part with 500 motor vehicles each and the infantry divisions undergo a process of de-motorisation in order to pool the surviving motor vehicles.[190] Accordingly, many of the officers attending remained unconvinced. Concerns about the weather and failing logistics featured prominently in most of their objections. Only one key player – Bock's chief of staff, *Generalmajor* Hans von Greiffenberg – was essentially on side as far as an advance on Moscow was concerned, while insisting that a complete encirclement of the capital, let alone an advance beyond it, was out of the question. The major bone of contention between him and Halder remained the *when*: the army's chief of staff, realising that the imminent winter weather made an early start of the operation imperative, rather disingenuously

---

[187] By May 1942, the Red Army's order of battle would in fact comprise a total of 172 tank brigades. It needs to be kept in mind, however, that at the time Halder gave his briefing, these formations had a paper strength of 67 tanks. Six months later, it had dropped to 46. See Walter Dunn Jr., *Hitler's Nemesis: The Red Army, 1930–1945* (London: Praeger 1994), pp 123–5.

[188] BA/MA, 19 II/387 'Heeresgruppenkommando Mitte, Kriegstagebuch Ia (entry for 4 November 1941)'.

[189] Ibid.

[190] BA/MA, RH 19 I/281 'Besprechung Chef Gen.St.d.Heeres am 13.11. in Orscha, Teil II (n. d.)'.

suggested that the army group spend another ten days replenishing prior to starting the offensive. Greiffenberg, keen to make the most of the disarray still prevailing amongst Soviet forces and with an eye on the effect that dropping temperatures would have on the availability of Luftwaffe close air support, insisted that a continuation of Taifun would only be viable if initiated within the next two to three days. Halder eventually relented, leaving a relieved Bock to record in his diary that 'the army group had been told to try and do its best'.[191] The rather tepid commitment to this plan of at least one of the key players involved (Günther von Kluge, commander-in-chief of 4. *Armee*) boded ill for the operation's success since his command was the biggest army-level formation in the army group.[192] It is difficult to discern the hand of Hitler – his reputation as an arch-meddler notwithstanding – in any of this. The theory that he was the driving force behind the continued drive on Moscow, with a view to encouraging Japan to initiate its war against the Western powers in Asia, does find some support in the odd contemporary source,[193] and it has been echoed by modern scholarship.[194] The overwhelming evidence, however, points towards a Hitler who during the weeks in question had shown an initial inclination to limit the depth of any further campaigning and had, moreover, temporarily given up on the idea of the Nipponese empire joining the Axis in the foreseeable future.[195] On the purely military side, the recollections of his army adjutant, Engel, for November convey the image of a leader who was either unable or unwilling to clearly express his wishes; he was unhappy with the priority accorded to the continuation of Taifun,[196] but equally failed to suggest a viable alternative. On two occasions Engel even recorded Halder and Brauchitsch leaving a long-winded briefing 'under the impression that the paucity of clear instructions really gave them leave to do as they pleased'.[197]

---

[191] TB Bock, p 317 (entry for 14 November 1941).

[192] See his communication to Bock two days after Orsha in BA/MA, RH 19 II/387 'Heeresgruppenkommando Mitte, Abteilung Ia, Anruf G.F.M. v. Kluge – O.B./H.Gr. Mitte (15 November 1941, 8.20 h)'.

[193] See BA/MA, RW 19/1282 'Besprechungsunterlagen für die Besprechung mit den Offizieren des Stabes am 26.1.1942 (n.d.)'. This minute summarises a briefing *Generalfeldmarschall* Keitel gave to the departmental heads of the *Wirtschaft- und Rüstungsamt* on the reasons for recent German setbacks in Russia and Libya. Accordingly, the document is riddled with ex post facto rationalisations that attempt to put a positive spin on a near-disaster. Keitel claimed that the offensives against Rostov, Tichwin and Moscow had all been executed to incentivise Japan to join the war and merely failed on account of the onset of Arctic temperatures.

[194] Most recently by Wolfram Pyta, *Hitler. Der Künstler als Politiker und Feldherr. Eine Herrschaftsanalyse* (München: Siedler 2015), pp 395–6.

[195] For a detailed discussion of this issue, see the chapter on German–Japanese relations.

[196] Kotze (ed.), *Aufzeichnungen Engel*, pp 114–15 (entries for 16 and 25 November and 8 December 1941).

[197] Kotze (ed.), *Aufzeichnungen Engel*, pp 114–15 (entries for 12 and 24 November 1941). The best analysis of the baleful consequences generated by this 'leadership crisis'

Crucially, the most detailed document to come out of the Orsha talks stresses that the 'political leadership' was primarily interested in linking up with the Finns and reaching Vologda in the north and seizing Maikop and Stalingrad in the south.[198] Moscow was not mentioned in this particular context.

Despite the fact that *Heeresgruppe Mitte*'s chief of staff, Greiffenberg, had enjoyed a measure of success at Orsha in dousing Halder's dangerous enthusiasm, it remains true that the continuation of Taifun was dangerously ill-conceived. While the Red Army had been in genuine disarray before Moscow in the fortnight after Vyazma-Bryansk, and Moscow had even witnessed a day or two of panic and civil disorder, measures to assert control were quickly taken. Stalin's trouble-shooter, General Georgii Zhukov, was given command of a newly created Western Army Group to defend the approaches to the capital on 10 October and a state of siege was declared nine days later. Substantial reinforcements had arrived by mid-November,[199] and a large part of the population had been put to dig anti-tank ditches outside the capital or drafted into militia units. The German side, on the other hand, witnessed a calamitous disconnect between means and ends, which in a way reflected the bigger problem of Barbarossa.

At the Orsha conference, all the attendees had agreed that the one thing consistently holding them back was erratic resupply by train. In the days immediately prior to resuming the drive on Moscow, Guderian signalled that he barely had enough fuel for one day of operations,[200] which was disconcerting to say the least since of all *Panzergruppen* his would face the longest advance by far. As for the number of trains arriving in the army group's railheads, Bock had aimed at a barely adequate thirty trains per day and OKH had committed itself to sending at least twenty-three,[201] but days like 16 November, when a mere twelve got through, were much more typical.[202] Together with a particularly effective spoiling attack by Soviet forces on Kluge's 4. *Armee*, this meant that the four army (2., 4., 9. and 2. *Panzerarmee*) and two *Panzergruppen* commands (3. and 4.) involved ended up attacking in a staggered fashion,[203] as and when

---

('*Führungskrise*') at the highest level of the Third Reich is to be found in Hürter, *Heerführer*, pp 302–50.

[198] BA/MA, RH 19 I/281 'Besprechung Chef Gen.St.d.Heeres am 13.11. in Orscha, Teil I and III (n.d.)'.

[199] Ten Siberian divisions arrived in the Moscow area between mid-October and mid-November alone. See Niklas Zetterling and Anders Frankson, *The Drive on Moscow 1941: Operation Taifun and Germany's First Great crisis in World War II* (Philadelphia: Casemate 2012), pp 266–9.

[200] BA/MA, RH 19 II/387 'Heeresgruppenkommando Mitte, Kriegstagebuch Ia (entry for 13 November 1941)'.

[201] In his personal diary, Bock described twenty-three trains as barely adequate to satisfy the daily needs of his units. TB Bock, p 313 (entry for 11 November 1941).

[202] David Stahel, *The Battle for Moscow* (Cambridge: CUP 2015), pp 128–30.

[203] A large part of 9. *Armee*'s infantry divisions were of course immobilised guarding the northern shoulder of the army group.

their supply situation allowed: one corps of 9. *Armee* on the 15th, *Panzergruppe* 3 on the 16th; the two corps that Guderian was able to spare from the siege of Tula and two corps of *Panzergruppe* 4 on the 18th; 2. *Armee*, two more corps of *Panzergruppe* 4 as well as one corps of 4. *Armee* on the 19th; and the remainder of 4. *Armee* on 1 December. The most important concession to operational realities on the ground lay in the fact that *Heeresgruppe Mitte* did not order its subordinate commands to fan out in a wide arc all over central Russia as originally envisaged by Halder pre-Orsha. Instead, and reflecting the impassability of much of the snowbound terrain and the completely inadequate logistics, Bock ordered frontal assaults delivered along the axis of the main roads leading to Moscow.

His original battle plan had envisaged a complete, albeit dangerously shallow encirclement of Moscow.[204] By 15 November, the failure of his logistical system and the pressure to get moving in a hurry forced the army group to adopt an approach that would have seen the advance ending at the Volga Canal to the north, and the Moskva river to the south of the city. Accordingly, only the western side of the capital would have found itself under close siege, with the remainder of the perimeter wide open to the Soviet hinterland. The prospects of using this precarious position as a jumping-off point for further operations were described by the army group's war diarist as desirable, but 'presently not foreseeable'.[205] Bock's mission thus boiled down to a very simple dilemma: he was tasked with neutralising the Soviet capital while at the same time lacking the logistics to bring about a complete encirclement; the only alternative – to force his way into the city and drive out the defenders in house-to-house fighting – had been adamantly ruled out by Hitler.[206]

It is certainly possible that Bock expected to run into a defence so weakened that the mere prospect of encirclement would lead to a hurried evacuation of the capital as had happened at Kharkov three weeks earlier. Failing such a lucky break, Bock's men were likely to spend the entire winter in open trenches besieging a city whose defenders had plenty of warm shelter – their campaign plan dictated as much. Nor was the Luftwaffe likely to tilt the balance in the *Ostheer*'s favour: it was if anything even worse affected than the army by the problems thrown up by deteriorating weather and poor logistics, and a shift to the Mediterranean first mooted by Hitler on 27 October would soon deprive *Luftflotte* 2 of more than half its squadrons.[207] The ramshackle nature of the

[204] TB Bock, p 314 (entry for 11 November 1941).
[205] BA/MA, RH 19 II/387 'Heeresgruppenkommando Mitte, Kriegstagebuch Ia (entry for 15 November 1941)'.
[206] BA/MA, RH 19 II/II 387 'Heeresgruppenkommando Mitte, Kriegstagebuch Ia (entry for 28 November 1941)'.
[207] BA/MA, RH 19 II/387 'Heeresgruppenkommando Mitte, Kriegstagebuch Ia (entry for 1 November 1941)'; RH 19 I/87 'Heeresgruppenkommando Süd, Kriegstagebuch Ia (entry for 29 November 1941)'; N 671/8 'Tagebuch Richthofen (entries for 15 November–4

continuation of Taifun alone is enough to cast serious doubt on the assumption that the drive on Moscow could have been part of a scheme to encourage Japan to initiate hostilities against the Western allies in the Pacific.

Even if we allow for the fact that Bock and Greiffenberg may have felt reasonably confident of their ability to find a way to bypass Hitler's ruling against entering Moscow, the historian is still struck by the cavalier attitude with which most of the generals of the army group launched into this adventure. Apart from the threadbare logistics, the simple fact remained that the falling temperatures made it more and more difficult to operate motor vehicles of all kinds.[208] An entry in the war diary of 2. *Panzerarmee* serves as a reminder that German mechanised forces had already experienced similar temperatures on one previous occasion. During the turn of the years 1939–40, preparations for a winter invasion of Western Europe had provided plenty of evidence that current Panzer makes could not be operated when the temperature dropped below –15°C.[209] In the week before the start of the offensive, temperatures had mostly hovered between 0° and –10° C, but worse lay in store, as shown during the night of 13 November which brought a drop to – 20°C. This was enough to immobilise the tanks of Guderian's *Panzerregiment* 6 and force the cancellation of a planned move south of Tula.[210] Needless to say, only a fraction of the troops had been issued with adequate winter garments,[211] and even winter camouflage for all vehicles had to be improvised with the help of lime.[212] A plausible case has been made that Brauchitsch, Halder and the army and army group commanders of the *Ostheer* all belonged to a generation seared by the trauma of the First Battle of the Marne; here, the Imperial Army had supposedly snatched defeat from the jaws of victory by heeding the voice of caution, rather than believing in the superiority of its training. The prospect of the Luftwaffe being soon grounded by the weather,[213] or shifted elsewhere,[214] as

December 1941)'. For a more detailed discussion of *Luftflotte* 2's temporary relocation to the Mediterranean theatre, see the chapter on the Luftwaffe.

[208] BA/MA, RH 19 II/387 'Heeresgruppenkommando Mitte, Kriegstagebuch Ia (entries for 13 and 14 November 1941)'.

[209] Stahel, *Battle for Moscow*, p 126.

[210] BA/MA, RH 21–2/v. 244 'Panzerarmeeoberkommando 2, Kriegstagebuch Ia (entry for 13 November 1941)'.

[211] BA/MA, RH 19 II/387 'Heeresgruppenkommando Mitte, Kriegstagebuch Ia (entry for 14 November 1941)' Also RH 21–2/v. 244 'Panzerarmeeoberkommando 2, Kriegstagebuch Ia (entry for 14 November 1941)'.

[212] Rolf Stoves, *1. Panzer-Division 1935–1945. Chronik einer der drei Stamm-Divisionen der deutschen Panzerwaffe* (Podzun: Bad Nauheim 1961), p 280.

[213] BA/MA, RH 19 II/387 'Heeresgruppenkommando Mitte, Kriegstagebuch Ia (entry for 15 November 1941)'.

[214] BA/MA, RH 19 II/387 'Heeresgruppenkommando Mitte, Kriegstagebuch Ia (entry for 10 November 1941)'.

well as a favourable weather forecast,[215] gave additional arguments to those who felt inclined to make the most of a window of opportunity that appeared to be closing fast.

The extent to which some of the generals gave at least an occasional thought to the hazards involved in the second phase of Taifun, and the possible penalties that might result, is very important because it gives us the frame of reference for their expectations. To begin with, it is crucial to realise the extent to which the stunning victories achieved in the first half of October had convinced not just Hitler and Otto Dietrich, but many German officers that a decisive corner had finally been turned in the war against Russia. A statement by General Alfred Jodl of the *Wehrmachtführungsstab* from 8 October nicely sums up the frame of mind of much of Hitler's military elite in those days. In it he declares to a group of dinner guests at the Wolfsschanze that the foreseeable outcomes of the current battles of Vyazma, Bryansk and the Sea of Azov mean that Germany has, 'without any exaggeration, won the war in irreversible fashion'.[216] In the Reichsluftfahrtministerium, *Generaloberst* Milch addressed a letter to fellow Luftwaffe production manager, Ernst Udet, drawing his attention to a stock of aerial ordnance well in excess of existing needs, seeing that 'the major campaign against Russia will be reaching its end in the very near future'.[217] The former naval attaché at the Moscow embassy, on being quizzed at the Seekriegsleitung about the Red Army's prospects for the winter, predicted a retreat beyond the Urals and a strategy prioritised at defending Siberia.[218] Many of *Heeresgruppe Mitte*'s senior officers like Bock, Greiffenberg, Richthofen, Guderian, Hoepner and Reinhardt, while rejecting the more outlandish schemes Halder proposed at Orsha, were all supportive of continuing the drive on Moscow.[219] Kluge, while not entirely convinced of the operation's viability, did not challenge it either.

As October turned into November, it became clear that the collapse of the USSR was not going to take place just yet, but the intoxicating effect of the unprecedented victories achieved by the *Ostheer* in the period between mid-

---

[215] TB Bock, p 322 (entry for 19 November 1941); BA/MA, RH 19 II/387 'Heeresgruppenkommando Mitte, Kriegstagebuch Ia (entry for 19 November 1941)'. Richthofen, for one, appears to have developed a marked scepticism towards the long-term weather forecasts pioneered by Professor Franz Baur. In his personal diary he poured scorn on his superior Kesselring's faith in them. See BA/MA, N 671/8 'Tagebuch Wolfram von Richthofen (entry for 11 November 1941)'.

[216] 'Mittwoch, 8. Oktober 1941'; in: Vogt (ed.), *Herbst 1941*, p 69.

[217] BA/MA, RL 3/50 'Der Staatssekretär der Luftwaffe und Generalinspekteur der Luftwaffe an den Herrn Generalquartiermeister (15.10.1941)'.

[218] KTB Seekriegsleitung, Teil A (entry for 26 October 1941).

[219] See Stahel, *Battle for Moscow*, pp 137–9. At *Heeresgruppe Nord*, the army group commander, Ritter von Leeb, as well as *Generaloberst* Ernst Busch, commander-in-chief of 16. *Armee*, and his chief of staff, were strongly supportive of resuming offensive operations. See Kotze (ed.), *Aufzeichnungen Engel*, p 113 (entry for 18 October 1941).

September and mid-October would take a long time to dissipate. The fact that in the following weeks, *Heeresgruppe Mitte*'s advance was slowed down as much by muddy roads as by Soviet resistance if anything reinforced this notion. In Franz Halder's case, his diary of November 1941 is replete with references to a particular corps or army being on its last legs and incapable of carrying on with a particular operation. The absence of any concern over that formation's vulnerability to sudden Soviet counterstrikes is conspicuous and seems to mark him out as the World War II equivalent of a Great War 'chateau general', but it has to be seen against the background just described. The personal diary of the commander-in-chief of *Heeresgruppe Mitte*, Fedor von Bock, is an exceptional source insofar as it allows us to share the thoughts of the man tasked with the hour-by-hour conduct of the battle for Moscow. Bock soon felt a degree of unease at the fact that the operation lacked depth,[220] but only after a fortnight of gruesome fighting did he express concern that it might turn into an attritional battle, where numbers would inevitably favour the Red Army; even at this point, his use of the simile of Verdun indicated fear of a bloody stalemate rather than an outright defeat.[221] By 1 December, he predicted that the offensive would in all likelihood run its course in a few days without having achieved its main objective and that some thought needed to be given to preparing a defence in depth, since at the moment the army group was incapable of checking a Russian counter-attack.[222] This was in many ways the most prescient assessment recorded at the time by a senior German officer involved in the second phase of Taifun, but finds no reflection in the orders issued by Bock's command over the following days.

At the other end of the spectrum were army and air force corps-level commanders, who were much closer to the front line, yet still retained a proximity to the highest command which gave them an idea of the bigger picture. Richthofen's meticulously kept diary only once expressed concern at the lack of depth that characterised the position of *Heeresgruppe Mitte* on the eve of the Soviet counterstrike.[223] All other entries up to and including 8 December 1941 either shrugged off the challenges and dangers inherent in the operation his airmen were currently supporting or reflected his anxiety about being left to rot in a backwater while the rest of his command was in the process of moving to the Mediterranean theatre.[224] The letters which *Panzergruppe* 4's commander-in-chief, Erich Hoepner, wrote home express exasperation with fellow senior officers and frustration at finding himself stopped at a time when Moscow seemed almost

[220] TB Bock, p 325 (entry for 21 November 1941).
[221] Ibid., p 332 (entry for 29 November 1941).
[222] Ibid., pp 334–5 (entry for 1 December 1941).
[223] BA/MA, N 671/8 'Tagebuch Richthofen (entry for 5 December 1941)'.
[224] BA/MA, N 671/8 'Tagebuch Richthofen (entries for 20 and 28 November and 8 December 1941)'.

within his grasp.[225] Hoepner's counterpart at *Panzergruppe* 3, Hans-Georg Reinhardt, in his surviving letters[226] and diary[227] expresses genuine empathy with his soldiers as well as exasperation at the lack of fuel. Even though his formation was one of the first to be targeted by Zhukov's offensive, it was not until 9 December that he expressed genuine appre-hension at the violence and success of the Soviet attack.[228] A memo penned on 27 November by the operations officer of LI. *Armeekorps*[229] dwelt at length on the options open to the leadership of the Red Army in the spring of 1942. In it, he blithely assumed that the German offensive would continue for at least a few more weeks and in all likelihood lead to the fall of Moscow and Maikop in the Caucasus as well as a link-up with the Finns to the east of Lake Ladoga. The possibility of the Red Army seizing the initiative in wintertime is not even mooted, possibly because the author estimated its residual strength at a mere sixty-five divisions.[230]

Last, but not least, we need to turn to the letters written to his family by General Gotthard Heinrici, commander of 2. *Panzerarmee*'s XXXXIII. *Armeekorps*. These documents are indicative of the thought process of a critical individual, who had learned to respect the challenges posed by the war of ideologies against the USSR, the resilience of its soldiers and the harshness of the local climate and terrain. It is thus highly noteworthy that when he and Heinz Guderian shared some thoughts on what the consequences of failing to inflict a war-winning defeat on the USSR by the end of the year might be, both guessed that the *Ostheer* might have to accept conditions of temporary stale-mate: incapable of achieving an outright victory, they saw themselves spending a period of 'hibernation' punctuated by occasional Soviet raids, with the coming of spring necessitating the chasing down of assorted armies as and when reconstituted by the Red Army in the previous months. The obvious comparison both officers agreed upon was the situation faced by the Japanese in China, where an outright victory appeared increasingly unlikely, but the superiority of the invading force certainly ruled out any serious setback.[231] On

[225] 'Brief vom 4. Dezember 1941'; in: Heinrich Bücheler (ed.), *Hoepner. Ein deutsches Soldatenschicksal des zwanzigsten Jahrhunderts* (Herford: Mittler 1980), p 160.

[226] BA/MA, N 245/2

[227] BA/MA, N 245/3

[228] BA/MA, N 245/2 'Private letter dated 9 December 1941'

[229] LI. *Armeekorps* at the time formed part of *Heeresgruppe Süd*'s northernmost army command (6. *Armee*).

[230] BA/MA, RM 7/1771 'Von Coelln, Major i.G., Ia 51. A.K. Wie kann und wird die Sowjetunion im Jahre 1942 den Krieg weiterführen? (27.11.1941)'. In the absence of a covering letter, one can only speculate as to the reasons which led to a document authored by a fairly junior army officer ending up in a Kriegsmarine file.

[231] 'Privattagebuch Gotthard Heinrici (entry for 29 October 1941)' as well as 'Gottthard Heinrici, Kriegsbericht an seine Familie (30 October 1941)'; both in: Hürter (ed.), *Aufzeichnungen Heinrici*, pp 83–4. The Heinrici papers are an excellent example of the

19 November, Heinrici had grown considerably more pessimistic about the army group's prospects, but still would not predict anything more daunting than a World War I-vintage *Stellungskrieg* along fixed lines for the winter.[232] Only on 11 December (the seventh day of the Soviet counteroffensive) did a letter to his family betray apprehension as to what the Red Army might do in the following days and weeks.[233]

We know of only one instance where a senior officer involved in the drive on Moscow recorded his dissent. Heinz Guderian, having supported the operation to begin with, told Bock on 20 November that 2. *Panzerarmee* simply lacked the resources to carry out its part in the drive on Moscow. Quite apart from the fact that this opinion was offered six days into the operation, Guderian then went on to deal a major blow to his credibility by twice changing his opinion on the topic over the following days. Bock was unimpressed and continued with the operation.[234]

As a contrast, we can use the assessments made by two opponents of the regime. In the case of *Oberstleutnant* Hellmuth Stieff, who had moved from OKH to the headquarters staff of 4. *Armee* in mid-September, the grounds for his scepticism were to a considerable extent due to non-military reasons. Over the course of the previous three years, he had turned into an opponent of the regime who by 1941 was referring to Hitler as a 'deranged proletarian' and a 'madman' in his private letters.[235] On the eve of the continuation of Taifun, he bemoaned the exhaustion of most units and made the forecast that in 1942 the *Ostheer* would find itself facing a resurgent Red Army at full strength.[236] However, he also conceded that the troops were willing to give their all for one more – albeit limited – push and for good measure added that 'the confrontation with Bolshevism had to come, and soon'.[237] Only eight days later, he reversed that judgement by announcing that he hoped for the onset of temperatures low enough to force the cancellation of the operation.[238] These inconsistencies would resolve themselves when he joined the Stauffenberg conspiracy against the regime, but in the context of 1941 they put him in the

---

sort of scholarly edition German historians are renowned for. A previous, shorter 2001 edition has recently become available in an English-language translation. Johannes Hürter (ed.), *A German General on the Eastern Front: The Letters and Diaries of Gotthard Heinrici 1941/42* (London: Pen & Sword 2014).

[232] 'Gotthard Heinrici, Brief an seine Frau (19 November 1941)'; in: ibid., pp 92–3.

[233] 'Gotthard Heinrici, Kriegsbericht an seine Familie (11 December 1941)'; in: ibid., pp 113–17, esp. p 115.

[234] The best account of Guderian's flip-flopping can be found in Stahel, *Battle for Moscow*, pp 164, 185–9.

[235] 'Brief Hellmuth Stieff an seine Frau (23.8.1941)' and 'Brief Hellmuth Stieff an seine Frau (5.11.1941)'; both in: Mühleisen (ed.), *Briefe Stieff*, pp 121–3, 131–3.

[236] 'Brief Hellmuth Stieff an seine Frau (11.11.1941)'; in: ibid., pp 133–4.

[237] Ibid.

[238] 'Brief Hellmuth Stieff an seine Frau (19.11.1941)'; in: ibid., pp 134–7.

same category as Guderian – somebody who, while conscious of the logistic inadequacies of his forces, is sorely tempted to take a risk because of the value of the prize at stake.

Gustav Hilger was a Russian-born German diplomat who had served on the staff of the Moscow embassy from 1923 to 1941; in that capacity he had conspired with Ambassador Schulenburg to deliver a thinly veiled warning to the Russians of the impending German aggression.[239] Upon his return to Berlin after June 1941, he ended up serving in an advisory role at the Auswärtiges Amt, where he warned of the folly of trying to subdue the communist giant by military means alone. Instead, he attempted to nudge German policy in the occupied territories of the USSR in a direction favourable to the rebirth of a sovereign, albeit truncated Russia. In this he found himself thwarted not just by Hitler and Ribbentrop, but also by Alfred Rosenberg, who favoured cooperation with a new Ukrainian state. Hilger's frustration and exasperation grew with every passing day. A memorandum that he finished in early December 1941 is of interest because it reflects, not any inside knowledge of the latest military developments to which he is unlikely to have been privy, but the views of a critic of German policies in Russia who was under no illusions about the residual economic potential of the USSR. Parts of the document, such as his assessment that the Soviet state had enough industrial redundancy to recover from the loss of the Donetsk provinces, echoed his earlier analyses.[240] He also dismissed the idea of an internal uprising or Soviet peace entreaties. At the same time, even a sceptic like Hilger had to concede that the staggering losses suffered by the Red Army would force it to adopt a purely defensive strategy in 1942. Any attempt at a counteroffensive would be strictly localised in scope and opportunistic in nature. A major offensive aimed at recovering large parts of the lost territories would not take place before 'a number of years' had passed.[241]

The continuation of Taifun was initiated by one corps of 9. *Armee* and *Panzergruppe* 3. They were tasked with extending the northern shoulder of the army group all the way to the Volga Reservoir and upon encountering the Volga Canal to follow its course in the direction of Moscow. To their south, *Panzergruppe* 4 headed more or less directly for the Soviet capital. The two *Panzergruppen* fielded a total of nine Panzer divisions and had only roughly 100 km (60 miles) to travel to their objective. It thus comes as little surprise that Zhukov regarded them as the principal threat to be countered. He was considerably aided in this task by the reluctance of Kluge's 4. *Armee* to get fully

---

[239] Jörn Happel, *Der Ost-Experte. Gustav Hilger – Diplomat im Zeitalter der Extreme* (Paderborn: Ferdinand Schöningh 2018), pp 252–5.

[240] 'Wie kann und wird die Sowjetunion den Krieg im Jahr 1942 weiterführen? (8.12.1941)'; partly reproduced in: ibid., pp 276–7.

[241] Ibid.

engaged in the operation. The Soviet spoiling attacks on two of his corps on the eve of the operation have been regarded by some historians as excellent examples of wasteful Soviet tactics at a time when Stavka had every reason in the world to carefully husband its resources.[242] However, it cannot be denied that they may have given a commander, who had shown a very tepid commitment to the operation to begin with, a perfect excuse to hang back for a while, rather than forcing his troops to abandon recently dug positions. As a result, 4. *Armee* committed only one of its corps on 19 November, putting Zhukov in a position to concentrate more forces against *Panzergruppen* 3 and 4. The latter formation was aided in its advance by quickly finding the seam between the defending 16th and 30th Armies, causing them to retreat in some disarray. On 23 November, *Panzergruppe* 3 was rewarded with the fall of Klin; its sister *Panzergruppe*, though numerically stronger, faced a tougher fight when it attempted to take its first intermediate objective, the city of Istra. The formation tasked with the mission, SS Division *Das Reich*, encountered 78th Division, a formation recently arrived from Siberia which was not only rested, but also nearly twice the size of the understrength divisions now making up the bulk of the Soviet field army. To make matters worse, the Soviet division held a position that could not be outflanked. Between 20 and 21 November, both formations engaged in a confrontation described by the German division as the worst its soldiers had encountered since the beginning of Barbarossa.[243] Even so, the SS troopers ended up taking Istra and 16th Army was forced to take up a new defensive line a mere 35 km (just over 20 miles) from Moscow. Hoepner's momentum, however, had been appreciably slowed. On the same day that the *Das Reich* took Istra, a reconnaissance element of *Panzergruppe* 3 managed to establish a lodgement on the eastern side of the Moskva–Volga Canal. Soviet counter-attacks, however, forced its abandonment on 29 November, thus arguably bearing out the prediction made by *Heeresgruppe Mitte*'s war diarist that moving beyond this body of water was likely to be unfeasible in the near future.

In view of Kluge's obvious reluctance to fully commit 4. *Armee* to the operation, the only possible support for Reinhardt and Hoepner had to come from Guderian's 2. *Panzerarmee* in the south. The first nine days of the continuation of Taifun had seen him fending off assorted Soviet attacks against his right and left flanks, with the latter emanating from the increasingly well-resourced Tula garrison. A few days into 2. *Panzerarmee*'s resumption of offensive operations, it became obvious that the need to somehow neutralise Tula was turning the drive on the Soviet capital into a secondary operation; by 29 November, Halder recorded his impression that Guderian had in all likelihood forfeited his chance of reaching Moscow's suburbs and would have to

[242] Kirchubel, *Barbarossa*, pp 339–40.
[243] Stahel, *Battle for Moscow*, p 151.

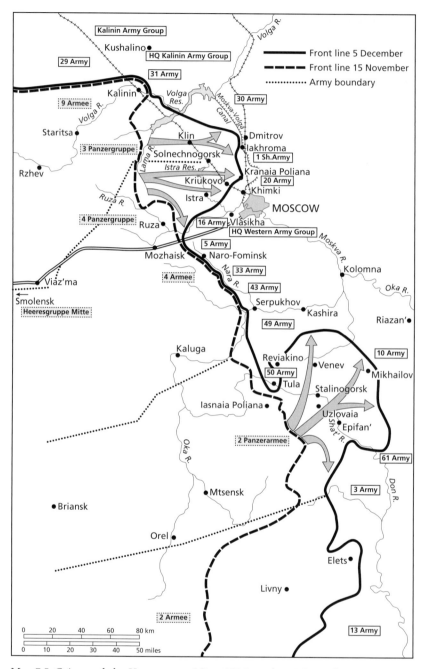

Map 7.5 Gains made by *Heeresgruppe Mitte*, 15 November–5 December 1941.

settle for establishing a defensive line for the winter, once the elimination of the pesky defenders of Tula had been accomplished.[244] A last-ditch attempt at a compromise saw an attempt to cut off Tula, with Heinrici's XXXXIII. *Armeekorps* providing the western pincer, while one motorised and one Panzer division were sent north to cut the railway line to Moscow. The latter operation had failed by 30 November, while the attempt to completely encircle Tula appeared to be near success on 4 December. This, however, had to be abandoned in the face of fierce Soviet resistance and plummeting temperatures the following morning.[245] It cannot be ruled out that *Heeresgruppe Mitte*'s southernmost army command, Schmidt's 2. *Armee*, might have been in a position to cover Guderian's right flank, thus allowing him to concentrate on Tula in a timely fashion. However, previous orders to send two of its divisions on an axis divergent from the rest of the army group to seize Yelez,[246] and the need to support these two formations, all but ruled this out.

In the meantime, Kluge had finally agreed to bring the remaining units of 4. *Armee* into the battle. They did so with some success on 1 December, but were recalled after only forty-eight hours, which meant that the ball was back in the Panzer leaders' court.[247] By that time, the catastrophic supply situation which Kluge had cited as the reason for the briefness of his foray had slowed Reinhardt's and Hoepner's rate of advance to a crawl, the proximity of the Soviet capital notwithstanding. Even though the operation had started in a staggered fashion, with the exception of 2. *Armee* all formations terminated offensive operations on 3 or 4 December 1941, a decision sanctioned by Bock on the 5th. The fact that temperatures had for the first time dropped below – 30° C the day before, while not causing this decision, certainly made it easier to justify.

Thus, Taifun concluded in a manner almost suggesting a natural death, with Army Group Centre pretty much frozen in place on the approaches to Moscow along a meandering front line hardly lending itself to defensive warfare. An entry in the *Heeresgruppe*'s war diary which served as Taifun's final epitaph hardly reflects Bock's brief moment of anxiety, which he had recorded in his personal diary only three days previously.[248] It gave the Red Army credit for

---

[244] KTB Halder III, p 316 (entry for 29 November 1941).

[245] 'Tagebuch, 4. Dezember 1941' and 'Tagebuch, 5. Dezember', both in: Hürter (ed.), *Aufzeichnungen Heinrici*, pp 97–111.

[246] For a succinct analysis of this little-known operation, which nearly resulted in the self-destruction of some of the units involved, see Hartmann, *Ostkrieg*, pp 367–75.

[247] See 'Brief Hellmuth Stief an seine Frau (7.12.1941)'; in: Mühleisen (ed.), *Briefe Stieff*, pp 138–41, where Kluge's operations officer blames himself for having urged 4. *Armee*'s commander-in-chief to finally commit his entire command: 'I have reproached myself in the most horrible way for having badgered Kluge to make this last attempt, despite his instinctive refusal to go along. He was right!'

[248] BA/MA, RH 19 II/122 'Heeresgruppenkommando Mitte, Kriegstagebuch Ia (entry for 4 December 1941)'.

good fieldwork in combination with profuse use of mines[249] and stressed the role played by new weapons' systems like heavy tanks and Katyusha rocket launchers. It also drew attention to the fact that Zhukov had had to resort to sudden lateral shifts of some units in order to resist the German pressure. Overall, the Soviet forces deployed in front of *Heeresgruppe Mitte* did not appear capable of launching a major counteroffensive in the short to mid-term.[250]

Hitler seemed to take the operation's failure in his stride. Rather than blaming the most obvious culprit (Kluge) for its collapse, he continued to hold the commander-in-chief of 4. *Armee* in high regard and would in fact promote him to the command of the entire army group two weeks later.[251] This is hardly surprising when we consider that the continuation of Taifun had only enjoyed the dictator's half-hearted support to begin with. Far more important to him was the attrition inflicted on the Soviet state thus far. As early as 25 October, he had given the Italian foreign minister, Count Ciano, a detailed breakdown of Soviet human losses, according to which the grand total of Red Army POWs (more than 3 million), dead (3 million) and those wounded so seriously that their return to combat in the near future could be safely ruled out (4 million) yielded a total return of 10 million.[252] This sort of grisly calculation could be easily dismissed as bragging calculated to shore up a flagging ally, but when the dictator received a confidential briefing on the situation in Russia by Halder on 6 December, the figures discussed were very similar. According to OKH's statistics, Red Army losses lay somewhere between 8 and 10 million men and 78,000 artillery pieces.[253] The fact that Hitler used similar figures in his Reichstag speech five days later has tended to devalue them in historians'

---

[249] For a number of good examples of how Soviet mine-laying slowed down the German advance in places, see Wolfgang Paul, *Brennpunkte. Die Geschichte der 6. Panzerdivision (1. Leichte) 1937–1945* (Osnabrück: Biblio 1977, rp 1984), pp 166–9 as well as Rolf Hinze, Hitze, *Frost und Pulverdampf. Der Schicksalsweg der 20. Panzerdivision* (Bochum: Heinrich Pöppinghaus 1981), pp 89–90, 94.

[250] BA/MA, RH 19 II/122 'Heeresgruppenkommando Mitte, Kriegstagebuch Ia (entry for 4 December 1941)'. For a similar assessment, see BA/MA, RH 2/2671 'Oberkommando des Heeres. Generalstab des Heeres. G.Qu.IV-Abt.Fr.H.Ost (II L) Nr. 4345 geh. Lagebericht Ost Nr. 170. Geheim ! (2.12.1941)'.

[251] When Keitel criticised Kluge in a discussion with the German leader in September 1942, Hitler defended him and even insisted 'that he had done a good job leading 4. *Armee*'. See Johannes Hürter and Matthias Uhl (eds.), 'Hitler in Vinnica. Ein neues Dokument zur Krise im September 1942'; in: *Vierteljahrshefte für Zeitgeschichte* Bd. 63 (2015), Nr. 4, pp 581–639, esp. p 632.

[252] 'Aufzeichnung der Unterredung zwischen dem Führer und dem Grafen Ciano im Hauptquartier am 25. Oktober 1941 (26.10.1941)'; in: ADAP, Serie D, Bd. XIII.2, pp 563–70, esp. p 565.

[253] 'Notizen aus der Führerbesprechung vom 6. Dezember 1941'; in: KTB Halder III, pp 329–31.

eyes: they are simply seen as outpourings of a delusional mind supported by a substandard military intelligence system.[254] Over and above the fact that the latest scholarship has tended to confirm these calculations,[255] what matters is that in the first week of December 1941, Hitler was convinced that the *Ostheer* had effectively wiped out the equivalent of the Red Army as it had existed on the eve of Barbarossa not once but twice over, with its third iteration currently manning the front line. Since there was good reason to assume that the Soviet forces before *Heeresgruppe Mitte* were near-crippled, the dictator had no problem with allowing partial withdrawals, provided a fallback position had been set up in the rear.[256] As far as the mid-term prospects for further fighting were concerned, his army adjutant noted a few days later that both OKH and Hitler had for once found themselves in agreement: winter outside Moscow would essentially amount to a twentieth-century equivalent of the 'encampment at Bunzelwitz'.[257]

No mention was made during the conversation of the attack that Konev's Kalinin Front had initiated against 9. *Armee* in the small hours of 5 December. In view of the fact that the area around Kalinin had been hotly contested since the Germans took the city on 14 October, yet another attack in the same area would not have set alarm bells ringing. The following day, three Soviet armies launched an attack against *Panzergruppe* 3 and a further one drove into Guderian's exposed eastern

---

[254] In the address of 11 December, he gave Soviet losses up to 1 December as the following: 3,806,865 POWs as well as 17,322 planes, 21,391 tanks and 32,541 artillery pieces captured or destroyed. It stands to reason that in the conversation with Halder the figure of 78,000 artillery pieces had also encompassed mortars upwards of a certain calibre. See Philipp Bouhler (ed.), *Der großdeutsche Freiheitskampf. Reden Adolf Hitlers*, III. Band (München: Franz Eher 1943).

[255] The figure for Soviet plane losses as quoted in the Reichstag speech was too low by at least 4,000. Artillery pieces (including medium mortars) lost totalled around 101,000, not 78,000. On the latest figures for Red Army human and material losses, see B. V. Sokolov, 'The Cost of War: Human Losses for the USSR and Germany, 1939–1945'; in: *Journal of Slavic Military Studies*, Vol. 9, No. 1 (March 1996), pp 152–93, esp. p 183; Christer Bergström and Andrey Mikhailov, *Black Cross, Red Star: Air War over the Eastern Front* (Pacifica, CA: Pacifica Military History 2000), pp 92, 252 and Lev Lopukhovsky and Boris Kavalerchik, *The Price of Victory: The Red Army's Casualties in the Great Patriotic War* (Barnsley: Pen & Sword 2017), pp 55, 67, 100, 133.

[256] 'Notizen aus der Führerbesprechung vom 6. Dezember 1941'; in: KTB Halder III, pp 329–31.

[257] Kotze (ed.), *Aufzeichnungen Engel*, pp 118–19 (entry for 18 December 1941). This exchange almost certainly took place in early, not mid-December. In August 1761 Frederick II of Prussia set up a fortified camp near the Silesian village of Bunzelwitz, where he was besieged by a superior Austro–Russian force for three weeks without, however, being attacked. See Christopher Duffy, *By Force of Arms: The Austrian Army in the Seven Years' War*, Vol. 2 (Chicago: The Emperor's Press 2008), pp 317–23.

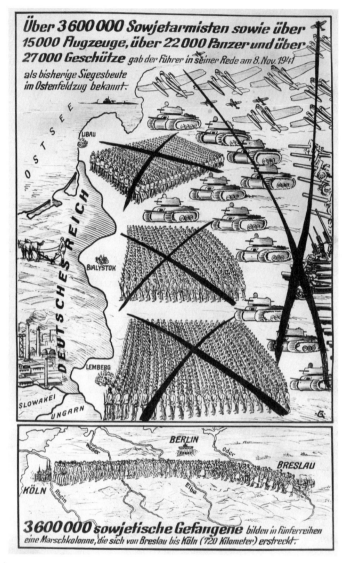

Figure 7.4 German propaganda poster, 1941: German intelligence on Red Army casualties in 1941 made for excellent propaganda material and also underpinned estimates of residual Soviet resistance to be expected in 1942. (ullstein bild/ullstein bild via Getty Images)

flank. Attacks by even small Soviet forces were greatly facilitated by the fact that at night many German units had taken to vacating the open ground between towns and villages because of the number of frostbite cases they had suffered over the last week;[258] even when an opportunity did present itself to engage the enemy, German soldiers where often horrified to discover that the cold had affected their artillery pieces and machine guns in such a way that they worked only intermittently or not at all.[259]

Contrary to what many publicists and scholars continue to imply to this day, the initial phase of the Red Army winter offensive was limited to localised counterstrikes. There is no evidence that either the scale or the impact of these early attacks warrants the use of adjectives like 'massive' or that they were enough to convey to Bock, never mind Halder and Brauchitsch, that they now had a major crisis on their hands.[260] When *Panzergruppe* 3 and 2. *Panzerarmee* initiated a retreat on the evening of 6 December, Hitler merely enquired if a local railway line could still be integrated into the new front line.[261] A fairly comprehensive retreat by *Panzergruppe* 4 a day later, mostly dictated by *Panzergruppe* 3's shift in position, was likewise sanctioned.[262] Halder registered these events in his diary, even though his overriding concern appears to have been about Hitler's recurring habit of communicating with the army

---

[258] Paul, *6. Panzerdivision*, p 169.

[259] Ibid., pp 169–73.

[260] For examples of this widespread misconception, see Janusz Piekalkiewicz, *Die Schlacht um Moskau. Die erfrorene Offensive* (Herrsching: Manfred Pawlak 1989 rp), p 227; Martin Gilbert, *Second World War* (London: Weidenfeld & Nicholson 1989), p 270; Alan Bullock, *Hitler and Stalin: Parallel Lives* (London: Harper Collins 1991), p 813; Klaus P. Fischer, *Nazi Germany: A New History* (London: Constable 1995), pp 472–3; Werner Haupt, *Army Group Centre: The Wehrmacht in Russia 1941–1945* (Schiffer: Atglen PA 1997), p 103; Heinz Magenheimer, *Hitler's War: German Military Strategy 1940–1945* (London: Arms & Armour 1998), p 114; Megargee, *Inside Hitler's High Command*, p 137; David Irving, *Hitler's War* (London: Focal 2002 rev. ed.), p 469; Ian Kershaw, *Hitler, 1936–1945. Hubris* (London: Allen Lane 2000), p 442; Ralf-Georg Reuth, *Hitler. Eine politische Biographie* (München: Piper 2003), p 550; Robert M. Citino, *The German Way of War: From the Thirty Years' War to the Third Reich* (Lawrence: Kansas UP 2005), p 300; Torsten Diedrich, *Paulus. Das Trauma von Stalingrad. Eine Biographie* (Paderborn: Ferdinand Schöningh, rev. ed. 2009), p 190; Gordon Corrigan, *The Second World War: A Military History* (London: Atlantic Books 2010), p 225; Alistair Horne, *Hubris: The Tragedy of War in the Twentieth Century* (London: Weidenfeld & Nicholson 2015), p 191; Peter Longerich, *Hitler. Biographie* (München: Siedler 2015), p 825; Gregory Liedtke, *Enduring the Whirlwind: The German Army and the Russo-German War 1941–1943* (Solihull: Helion 2016), p 162. The image conveyed by Michael Jones, *The Retreat: Hitler's First Defeat* (London: John Murray 2009), pp 145–6, that the mood at Führer's Headquarters already bordered on panic around 6–7 December appears to have as its only source a post-war account by Bock's chief of staff. It is not supported by contemporary sources. For the first challenge of this misconception, see Mawdsley, *December 1941*, pp 150–1.

[261] BA/MA, RH 19 II/122 'Heeresgruppenkommando Mitte, Kriegstagebuch Ia (entry for 7 December 1941)'.

[262] BA/MA, RH 19 II/127 'Fernschreiben von Kdo. der Panzergruppe 4 an H.Gr. Mitte, gleichlautend A.O.K. 4 (7.12.41, 18.40 h)'.

groups over OKH's head.[263] The fact that the army's commander-in-chief, *Generalfeldmarschall* Walther von Brauchitsch, offered Hitler his resignation on the 7th has occasionally been misinterpreted as a loss of nerve on his part in the face of the Red Army's winter offensive, but this is misleading.[264] He had been struggling with health issues for some time; in addition, the Rostov crisis and Hitler's on-off reluctance to go along with an offensive against Moscow had led to increasing friction between the two men.[265]

The first day to bring enough bad news to generate a feeling of crisis was arguably 8 December. *Panzergruppe* 3 had to deal with a breakthrough that came dangerously close to cutting the road through Klin, possession of which was a prerequisite for a more or less orderly withdrawal west,[266] forcing even Halder to admit to a 'very difficult situation'.[267] Deliberations between Bock and his army commanders about the likely possible need to continue the ongoing retreat of the two northern *Panzergruppen* produced the first admission that this was likely to result in the loss of a large amount of heavy equipment. Bock apprised his superior Halder of the fact that the army group no longer had the reserves to contain a major offensive; the two officers even struggled to establish a consensus on which crisis – the threat to Klin or the one to Kalinin – should be dealt with first, since doing both at the same time was clearly out of the question.[268] Finally, the official termination of offensive operations by 2. *Armee* on that same day in the south turned out to be something of a moot point because, within hours of the order going out, a drive by Soviet 13th Army crashed into the front of 2. *Armee*'s XXXIV. *Armeekorps*; by the 9th, it had become clear that attempts by two of its divisions to plug the gap were being nullified by the speed with which the attackers were streaming past, forcing 45. and 134. *Infanteriedivisionen* to grope their way back to German lines unassisted.[269]

A document that arrived with the army group on the morning of the 9th is remarkable insofar as it reflects the mindset prevailing at OKH until twelve hours earlier, which was only now being undermined on a daily basis.

[263] KTB Halder III, p 332 (entry for 7 December 1941)

[264] Löffler, *Brauchitsch*, p 255.

[265] BA/MA, MSg 2/12152 'handschriftl. Tagebuch von Gyldenfeldt (entries for 1 and 4 December)'.

[266] Reinhardt's own letters offer a vivid impression of the anxiety he experienced during those hours. See BA/MA, N 245/2 'Auszüge aus meinem vom November 1941 bis Januar 1942 nach Hause geschriebenen Briefen mit militärisch besonders bedeutenden Inhalt', especially letters dated 8, 9 and 10 December 1941.

[267] KTB Halder III, p 335 (entry for 8 December 1941).

[268] BA/MA, RH 19 II/122 'Heeresgruppenkommando Mitte, Kriegstagebuch Ia (entry for 8 December 1941)'.

[269] BA/MA, RH 19 II/127 'Fernschreiben von A.O.K. 2 Ia an H.Gr. Mitte (8.12.1941, 18.10 h)'; RH 19 II/122 'Heeresgruppenkommando Mitte, Kriegstagebuch Ia (entry for 9 December 1941)'.

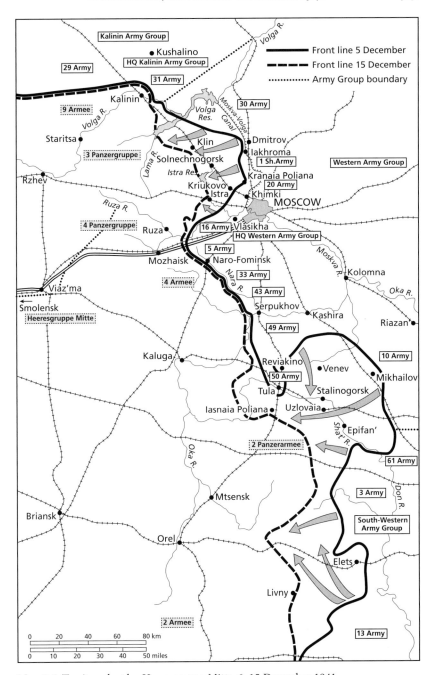

Map 7.6 Territory lost by *Heeresgruppe Mitte*, 6–15 December 1941.

The *Instructions for the Tasks of the Ostheer during the Winter of 1941/42*[270] only briefly touched on the fact that the Russians had yet to be 'finally beaten'. Instead it went into remarkable detail about how the *Ostheer* was to organise its winter positions, with a view to allowing the maximum number of troops to be pulled out of the front line to get some rest, particular stress being placed on the need to reconstitute the bulk of the mechanised forces in Germany. To that end, Guderian's 2. *Panzerarmee* was tasked with coordinating the move of 1., 3., 4., 5., 6. and 7. *Panzerdivision* back to Germany for a prolonged period of rest and refit.[271] Interestingly enough, the order reflected Hitler's thoughts as expressed to Halder on the 6th: rather than holding on to ground seized in the last days and weeks, the first priority would be to establish a front line that would lend itself to be defended with a minimum of troops. Only the retention of railway lines and important industrial facilities might justify a few bulges here and there. The sole specific reference to Russian offensive action was in the form of a warning about likely air raids on the accommodation the *Ostheer* would be reliant on to a greater degree than before, on account of the cold weather. Bock took his cue from the directive to issue orders to all his army commands to explore and prepare a fallback position following the line Kursk–Orel–Gshatsk–Rzhew.[272]

With the benefit of hindsight it is easy to see that the *Instructions* constituted nothing more than a house of cards about to be collapsed by the Red Army. It is important to understand, however, that the speed with which this process would be registered by the German leadership was by no means a foregone conclusion. The Red Army's historic penchant for mounting constant, often ill-conceived counter-attacks; local German defensive successes; the staggered, almost gradual nature of Zhukov's offensive; Hitler's interest in husbanding forces to facilitate operations expected to bring about the fall of Leningrad and Sevastopol in the next fortnight; to say nothing of the understandable reluctance of Halder and Brauchitsch to draw undue attention to the fact that an operation that had been very much their brainchild had left an entire army group at the end of its logistical tether, vulnerable to counter-attack and with no reserves or fallback positions to facilitate a safe retreat: all these factors would have a bearing on how fast Hitler came round to realising that the current Soviet offensive against *Heeresgruppe Mitte* constituted a threat far surpassing any previous counteroffensives by the Red Army.

The events of 9 December offer several examples of these dynamics at work. The previous day, Hitler had ruled out transferring entire divisions from other

---

[270] BA/MA, RH 2/1327 'Oberkommando des Heeres, Gen.St.d.H./Op.Abt.(Ia) Nr. 1693/41 g.Kdos.Chefs. Weisung für die Aufgaben des Ostheeres im Winter 1941/42 (8.12.1941)'.

[271] According to one post-war account, the staff of 6. *Panzerdivision* were still making preparations for this move as late as 12 December. Paul, *6. Panzerdivision*, p 186.

[272] BA/MA, RH 19 II/127 'Fernschreiben von Heeresgruppe Mitte an A.O.K. 2, Pz.A.O.K. 2, A.O.K.4 und A.O.K. 9 (9.12.1941, 22.30 h)'.

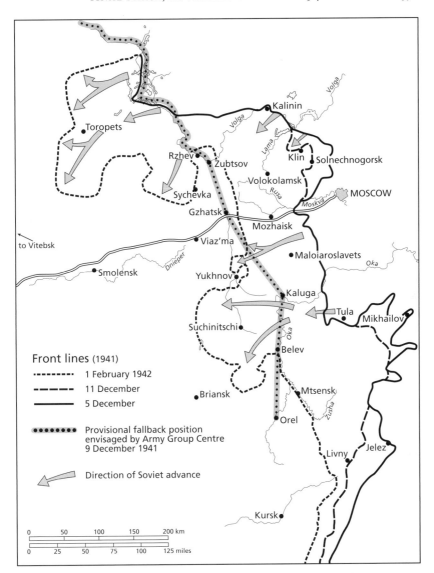

Map 7.7 Territory lost by *Heeresgruppe Mitte* to the Red Army, December 1941–January 1942.

fronts to Army Group Centre and some of the news pouring into Bock's HQ on the 9th now appeared to bear him out. Guderian was in the process of collapsing the bulge he had established to the east of Tula, but his retreat was still described as 'orderly'. To the north, Reinhhardt's *Panzergruppe* 3 had managed to defeat the Soviet breakthrough aimed at Klin through a timely counter-attack by 1. *Panzerdivision*;[273] *Panzergruppe* 4 fended off several Soviet attacks while continuing its retreat from the Klin bulge. Defending the army group's northern shoulder, 9. *Armee* expressed some confidence in stabilising its front by the 10th or 11th. Bock took a certain solace in the fact that thus far only three of his six armies (2. *Armee*, 2. *Panzerarmee*, 9. *Armee*) had been exposed to attacks lasting more than a couple of days, but nevertheless felt obliged to pass on some of his commanders' anxieties as to whether the extent of the crisis was being accurately reported to the highest leadership. In a telephone conversation he had with Halder on 9 December, the army chief of staff assured him that it was and finished the telephone conversation with a comment that indicated he was still drawing a lot of residual confidence from the intelligence estimates he had taken with him to Orsha just over three weeks before. He insisted that the recently terminated offensive on Moscow had spooked Zhukov into deploying a number of units he had originally intended to hold back for operations in 1942. Defeating them might take 'the last ounce of strength'. But the moment of respite was clearly in sight. After all, he went on, 'this level of activity will last until the middle or the end of the month and then ebb away'.[274]

One piece of good news arrived on 10 December (9. *Armee* reporting that the intensity of fighting appeared to be receding), along with news of some serious deterioration, including heavy fighting around the only road keeping the defenders of Klin supplied[275] and a widening of the gap torn by the Red Army in the front of 2. *Armee* in the south. At the same time, it provided an instructive insight into how far Bock and his subordinates still were from realising the true extent of the crisis they faced. Bock had drafted a telegram for Brauchitsch, the tone of which appeared to indicate he had finally reached a state of anxiety similar to what he had experienced during the peak of the Soviet Dushkovina and El'nia offensives in late August. In it, he predicted the direst consequences for his command if reinforcements did not arrive in the very near future. He all but ruled out a major withdrawal across the entire front since the partial withdrawals of the last few days had already shown that the freezing temperatures had created conditions in which such a shift resulted in large numbers of tanks, trucks and artillery pieces being left behind,[276] leaving the retreating troops even more defenceless when they reached a point where, in any case, no prepared positions awaited them.

---

[273] In a letter home, Reinhardt described the attack, which drove into the flank of the Soviet spearhead, as being 'a truly last minute affair'. See BA/MA, N 245/2 'Reinhardt, Auszüge, private letter dated 9 December 1941'.

[274] BA/MA, RH 19 II/122 'Heeresgruppenkommando Mitte, Kriegstagebuch Ia (entry for 9 December 1941, 11.15 h)'.

[275] For details of the fighting which allowed the Germans to keep open the road through Klin until 15 December, see Stoves, *1. Panzer-Division*, pp 296–317.

[276] For several examples of this, Paul, *6. Panzerdivision*, pp 180–4.

Figure 7.5 *Generalfeldmarschall* Fedor von Bock: in his capacity as commander-in-chief of *Heeresgruppe Mitte*, Bock played a crucial role in November–December 1941, assessing both the prospects of a continued drive on Moscow and the violence of the early phase of the Soviet winter offensive. (Heinrich Hoffmann/ullstein bild via Getty Images)

However, Bock desisted from sending this epistle because at noon a telephone call from OKH announced long-awaited good tidings: three divisions from occupied France had been given their marching orders to join *Heeresgruppe Mitte* and a fourth was being detached from *Heeresgruppe Süd* to join 2. *Armee*.[277] Quite apart from the fact that the new divisions would take nearly four weeks to arrive where they were needed in full strength, there was also the issue of scale to consider. Three (or four, depending on the count) divisions had been promised as reinforcement for the entire army group on exactly the same day that 2. *Armee*'s operations officer drew up an estimate of the number of troops he deemed necessary to re-establish a coherent front line in his comparatively small sector and protect the vitally important railway link between Kursk and Orel: whether by coincidence or not, he too arrived at a

---

[277] BA/MA, RH 19 II//122 'Heeresgruppenkommando Mitte, Kriegstagebuch Ia (entry for 10 December 1941)'.

total of four divisions.[278] This morsel of information would have made for a powerful argument in Bock's daily exchanges with Halder, but if he made use of it, it is not reflected in the army group's telephone log. Nor does it appear in his personal diary.

The 11th brought more bad news from 2. *Armee*: the Soviet progress continued unchecked.[279] Most of 2. *Panzerarmee* established a preliminary defensive line which was, however, rendered less than perfect by a gaping hole between it and its XXXXIII. *Armeekorps* to the west; for the first time, 4. *Armee* was subjected to a violent attack on one of its corps. On a positive note, *Panzergruppe* 3's 1. *Panzerdivision* scored a major success when it defeated yet another Soviet attempt to interdict the road leading out of Klin[280] and 9. *Armee* expressed confidence that it would be able to hold on to Kalinin. Back at OKH, Halder recorded his opinion that by the evening the situation in Russia appeared to be 'by and large, devoid of tension'.[281]

On 12 December, Guderian returned to a theme he had been sounding for some time. Implying that somewhere along the line his reports were being edited prior to being presented to Hitler, he insisted that the time had come to report to him directly.[282] As it happened, that same evening Hitler, bypassing Halder, did indeed make a direct enquiry through his army adjutant, Major Engel. It concerned the situation at 2. *Armee*, but instead of enquiring about the prospects of holding the supply centre of Liwny or the Kursk–Orel railway line, he asked whether anything had been learned about the fate of the two divisions trying to make their way back to German lines in the wake of the Soviet advance. The motive may have been genuine interest or, more likely, the hope that fragments of these units might reappear in time to be turned around to help plug the two holes comprom-ising the front at 2. *Armee* and 2. *Panzerarmee*.[283] It is difficult to read into this a major concern for the long-term capacity of the army group to stand up to further Soviet offensives.

Someone else, however, was nurturing serious concerns about the matter. On the face of it the day had not been markedly worse than those before (only a motorised division that held the joint between 9. *Armee* and *Panzergruppe* 4

---

[278] BA/MA, RH 19 II/127 'Armee-Oberkommando 2 Ia Nr. 672/41 g.Kdos. Beurteilung der Lage vom 10.12.1941 (10.12.1941)'.

[279] According to *Heeresgruppe Mitte*'s war diarist the corps command in question 'appeared to have lost the reins'. BA/MA, RH 19 II/122 'Heeresgruppenkommando Mitte, Kriegstagebuch Ia (entry for 11 December 1941)'.

[280] Stoves, *1. Panzer-Division*, pp 305–7.

[281] KTB Halder III, p 339 (entry for 11 December 1941).

[282] BA/MA, RH 19 II/122 'Heeresgruppenkommando Mitte, Kriegstagebuch Ia (entry for 12 December, 10.00 h)'.

[283] BA/MA, RH 19 II/122 'Heereesgruppenkommando Mitte, Kriegstagebuch Ia (entry for 12 December 1941, 21.40 h)'.

struggled to hold its place in the line).[284] Nonetheless, the accumulated stress
and strain of nearly four weeks of fighting, together with the need to decide on
the feasibility of executing in the next few days the first phase of the planned
withdrawal (to the line Rusa–Wolokolamsk–Sztaritza) over clogged and icy
roads, produced a situation that was described by Halder in a telephone
conversation with Bock as the 'most critical of both wars'.[285] This exchange
may or may not have contributed to Bock's decision on this very day finally to
cancel all leave for his troops; overdue or not, it certainly reflected the fact that
it had taken the *Ostheer*'s key decision maker between seven and eight days to
fully realise the potential threat of Zhukov's winter offensive.[286] Halder, on the
other hand, managed to finish the day on a mildly positive note. While
realising that further retreats by 2. *Armee* and 2. *Panzerarmee* were certainly
imperative, he took comfort in the fact that *Panzergruppen* 3 and 4 appeared to
be fending off the latest Soviet attacks and, most importantly, that 4. *Armee*
had enjoyed yet another 'quiet day'.[287] Ever since the beginning of the Soviet
offensive, Kluge's command had become the bedrock of the army group;
Soviet attacks might tear holes into the bulges presented by units at the flanks,
but the centre at least remained virtually unscathed.

   On the 13th, two new threats developed: first, a Soviet attack managed to
find the seam between *Panzergruppe* 3 and *Panzergruppe* 4; second, to the
south, a continuation of the thrusts against 4. *Armee*'s VII. *Armeekorps* threatened to pry that formation apart from *Panzergruppe* 4. If these breaches were
to be exploited, they would leave both of *Panzergruppe* 4's flanks exposed.[288]
Since 4. *Armee*'s centre still remained untouched, Guderian made the suggestion that Kluge turn over one or two divisions to him, a suggestion the field
marshal failed to take him up on.[289] Indeed Kluge stressed to Bock that the
fallback line which the current retreat was aimed at occupying (Rusa–
Wolokolamsk–Sztaritza) could only serve as a position in which to gather
strength for another shift to the rear. This was the situation when the commander-in-chief of the army, Walther von Brauchitsch, and Hitler's OKW
adjutant, *Oberst* Rudolf Schmundt, arrived in Bock's headquarters at
Smolensk. To Brauchitsch, Bock described the situation facing him as one

[284] BA/MA, RH 19 II/122 'Heeresgruppenkommando Mitte, Kriegstagebuch Ia (entry for 12
December 1941)'.
[285] BA/MA, RH 19 II/122 'Heeresgruppenkommando Mitte, Kriegstagebuch Ia (entry for 12
December 1941)'.
[286] BA/MA, RH 19 II/127 'Heeresgruppenkommando Mitte, Aktenvermerk (12.12.1941)'.
[287] KTB Halder III, p 341–2 (entry for 12 December 1941).
[288] By the evening of 13 December, even the notoriously unflappable Richthofen was
expressing serious concern at the advance rate achieved by the Red Army against the
flanks of *Panzergruppe* 4, see BA/MA, N 671/8 'Tagebuch Richthofen (entry for 13
December 1941)'.
[289] BA/MA, RH 19 II/122 'Heeresgruppenkommando Mitte, Kriegstagebuch Ia (entry for 13
December 1941, 10.45 h)'.

transcending purely military decision making. Both holding the line and ordering a major retreat risked the destruction of the army group. Crucially, he had also undergone a major change of heart on the subject of the reinforcements en route from occupied France. While on the 10th, the promise of these units arriving in four weeks' time had been enough to make him desist from sending the equivalent of a formal complaint to Brauchitsch, he now felt that the reserves promised by OKH would in any case arrive too late to make a difference. As he saw it, he was no longer in a position to recommend anything.[290] One of the staff officers accompanying Brauchitsch recorded in his personal diary that the conversations he had at Smolensk featured allusions to both Napoleon's disastrous 1812 campaign and the need for a negotiated peace in order to facilitate 'an exit with honour'.[291]

Faced with such a situation, Hitler could do little more than demand from East Prussia that Bock discuss with Brauchitsch the location of the fallback position he deemed himself capable of hanging onto for the remainder of the winter. The mere fact that Hitler had to ask for this information raises the question of to what extent he had been kept abreast by Halder or Brauchitsch about the events of the last forty-eight hours. An exchange that took place in the late evening certainly supports the notion that while Oberkommando des Heeres may not have been engaged in an outright conspiracy of silence, it was being parsimonious with the unvarnished truth. In Bock's command, 2. *Armee* had undoubtedly been the higher formation most seriously hit in the last six days and since it formed the hinge between Army Groups Centre and South, the headquarters of the latter grew increasingly concerned. When *Heeresgruppe Süd*'s operations officer enquired of OKH's *Chef der Operationsabteilung* about 2. *Armee*'s status, he was told that since the day had passed without further enemy attacks on 2. *Armee*'s southern flank, the situation had 'improved somewhat'. As for the embattled army's situation in general, he described it as 'a tactical unpleasantness' (*'eine taktische Unannehmlichkeit'*) which in all likelihood would soon be rectified.[292]

On 14 December Bock's attempts at keeping his army group together finally threatened to come unstuck. Thus far, he had enjoyed a measure of success in doing so for two reasons. First of all, Soviet blows had always been delivered in a staggered fashion, meaning that with – arguably – the exception of 2. *Armee* and 2. *Panzerarmee*, all other major formations had always enjoyed at least two or three days if not of outright calm, then certainly of only desultory fighting

---

[290] BA/MA, RH 19 II/122 'Heeresgruppenkommando Mitte, Kriegstagebuch Ia (entry for 13 December 1941, 15.00 h)'. The war diary does not record whether Schmundt was present during this particular exchange or not.

[291] BA/MA, MSg 2/12152 'handschriftl. Tagebuch von Gyldenfeldt (entry for 13 December 1941)'.

[292] BA/MA, RH 19 I/88 'Heeresgruppenkommando Süd, Kriegstagebuch Ia (entry for 13 December 1941)'.

between major crises. Secondly, by virtue of the brevity of its active participation in the operation and the comparatively little attention devoted to it by Zhukov, Kluge's 4. *Armee* had become the anchor which more or less held Bock's command in place. This was about to change, with the Soviet Western Front exploiting the previous day's gains into *Panzergruppe* 4's southern flank, forcing Hoepner to warn Bock he would have to pull back further and faster than agreed, while – in all likelihood – abandoning most of his artillery in the process.[293] Together with a similar crisis at *Panzergruppe* 3, this would inevitably lead to exposing the right flank of 9. *Armee*. In the meantime, further south, the Red Army had found and exploited the gap between Guderian's XXXXIII. *Armeekorps* and 4. *Armee* to the north. By 14.15, Bock and Kluge's chief of staff agreed that the long-term prospects of keeping 4. *Armee* in place were becoming questionable. Shortly afterwards, Brauchitsch and Bock in another telephone conference with Hitler received instructions to collapse the front of the two northern *Panzergruppen* and 9. *Armee* by abandoning the area around Klin and Kalinin; Hitler also gave permission for 2. *Armee* and 2. *Panzerarmee* to continue their respective retreats. He did however specify that beyond this, no further retreats should take place until at least a makeshift position had been prepared to receive the troops arriving in the rear.[294]

It seems that no one impressed on the German leader that these orders would soon be rendered impractical by virtue of the northern and southern ends of 4. *Armee* being turned and the inconvenient fact that no fallback position (makeshift or otherwise) had been prepared in the rear area. Even so, 14 December still appears to be have been the day on which the true gravity of *Heeresgruppe Mitte*'s deteriorating position finally registered with Hitler. The sudden onset of Soviet media coverage of the offensive the previous day appeared to indicate a new confidence among the Red Army's leadership in exploiting the success of the previous week.[295] However, while this may have contributed to sensitising the politician Hitler, the impressions that Schmundt had gathered at Smolensk and Roslavl[296] and then passed on to his Führer over the telephone were as likely as not the true catalyst for the first of several radical steps he took over the next forty-eight hours. Around midnight, he had a

---

[293] BA/MA, RH 19 II/122 'Heeresgruppenkommando Mitte, Kriegstagebuch Ia (entry for 14 December 1941)'.

[294] BA/MA, RH 19 II/122 'Heeresgruppenkommando Mitte, Kriegstagebuch Ia (entry for 14 December 1941)'.

[295] TB Goebbels, Bd. II.2, p 503 (entry for 14 December 1941). For a Soviet perspective on the media management of the campaign, see Rodric Braithwaite, *Moscow 1941: A City and Its People at War* (London: Profile 2006), p 309.

[296] On the 14th, Schmundt and Brauchitsch travelled from Smolensk to 2. *Panzerarmee*'s field headquarters at Roslavl, where they conferred with Kluge and Guderian. See BA/MA, RH 19 II/122 'Heeresgruppenkommando Mitte, Kriegstagebuch Ia (entry for 14 December 1941)'.

meeting with *Generaloberst* Friedrich Fromm, head of the *Ersatzheer* (Replacement Army) and, as such, the overlord of all recruiting and training establishments of the German Army.[297] Hitler demanded that he make ready at short notice four infantry divisions made up of half-trained draftees for use in the sector of *Heeresgruppe Mitte*. Lack of proficiency would have to be compensated for by equipping them for mobile warfare in snowbound terrain.[298] The German Army rightly prided itself on the high standards of its training system and such interference constituted an obvious infringement of the rigorous rules which had made these possible. The embattled 2. *Armee*, in making a demand for deployment of units from the *Ersatzheer* to shore up *Heeresgruppe Mitte*'s front, had admitted that such a move was likely to result in a drop in fighting power[299] and predicted dire consequences for the 'war as a whole'.[300]

By the evening of 14 December, even Halder was making liberal use in his diary of terminology ('weakened', 'dire', 'serious') he had thus far used only sparingly. Kluge's army, which only in the morning had been the bulwark of the defence was now poised to join the retreat of its sister formations; the likely ditching of heavy kit during this move caused Halder considerable concern.[301] In conversation with Brauchitsch and Schmundt, Bock admitted that a fallback position that could be used by the retreating troops with a view to establishing a new front line did not as yet exist.[302] Lastly, Klin was finally abandoned and orders went out to give up Kalinin as well. While the former by this time merely symbolised the high-water mark of German success, Kalinin was the second major Soviet city (after Rostov) from which the Germans were retreating in only a fortnight. Something was clearly wrong.

On 15 December, *Führerweisung* No. 39a was issued, addressing itself to the same topic that Hitler and Fromm had broached in their midnight talk. As a stopgap measure, the four under-strength German divisions garrisoning Serbia and northern Croatia were to be immediately pulled out and shifted

---

[297] Fromm has recently become the subject of what is by quite a margin the most comprehensive scholarly biography of any senior military leader of World War II. See Bernhard Kroener, *'Der starke Mann im Heimatkriegsgebiet'. Generaloberst Friedrich Fromm. Eine Biographie* (Paderborn et al: Schöningh 2005).

[298] BA/MA, RW 4/578 'Abteilung Landesverteidigung (L b V) Aktenvermerk über Besprechung Führer – Generaloberst Fromm in der Nacht 14./15.12.1941 (15.12.1941)'.

[299] As was amply borne out by the experience of these formations upon arrival in Russia. See Günther Rathke, '"Walküre"-Divisionen 1941/42. Letzte Aushilfe in der Winterkrise'; in: *Militärgeschichte* 1996, Nr. 4, pp 47–54.

[300] BA/MA, RH 19 II/127 'Armee-Oberkommando 2 Ia Nr. 672/41 g.Kdos. An den Oberbefehlshaber der Heeresgruppe Mitte, Herrn Generalfeldmarschall v. Bock (15.12.1941)'.

[301] KTB Halder III, p 345 (entry for 14 December 1941).

[302] BA/MA, RH 19 II/122 'Heeresgruppenkommando Mitte, Kriegstagebuch Ia (entry for 14 December 1941)'.

to Russia, with their place to be taken by Italian and Bulgarian units.[303] At Bock's HQ, the same day was bookended by two orders giving details for the retreat to be carried out to the line Kursk–Orel–Kaluga–Gshatsk–Rzhew by 20 December: the first order gave the lines that would separate the commands once they held the new line;[304] the second confirmed Hitler's permission for 9. *Armee* and the two northern *Panzergruppen* to collapse the northeastern corner of the army group's front, which had been under such consistent Soviet attacks over the last ten days. The orders for the other three commands to do likewise would follow in short order.[305] On the face of it, this appeared to vindicate the pleas of all the senior officers of the army group who over the previous days had repeatedly insisted that the retreat from Moscow be accelerated. Between these two sets of instructions going out, however, a number of events occurred that would call into question the feasibility of the move.

Panzergruppe 3 was momentarily under less pressure and thus in a position to retreat in good order.[306] Furthermore, 9. *Armee*, on abandoning Kalinin, managed to blow the crucially important road bridge spanning the Volga, which only a day before had looked likely to fall intact into Soviet hands,[307] thus slowing the rate of the expected pursuit by the Red Army. On the other hand, *Panzergruppe* 4 felt the need to pick up the speed of its withdrawal and, in the south, Heinrici's XXXXIII. *Armeekorps* gave way before another Soviet push, thus widening the gap between 4. *Armee*'s southern flank and Guderian's 2. *Panzerarmee*. By 19.00 Kluge was talking to Bock of the imminent danger of his army being 'unhinged' and forced to abandon its position prematurely. In the evening, Schmundt and Brauchitsch left Bock's HQ for the *Führerhauptquartier*. Before doing so, Bock gave Schmundt the opportunity to speak to all army commanders (he had already met and spoken to Guderian and Kluge at Roslavl) over the telephone.[308] If somebody had indeed been 'editing' reports presented to Hitler from the Eastern Front, this move was likely to throw a monkey wrench into the machinery of that process.

---

[303] Concern over leaving a number of important mines in the care of the Italian Army eventually led to the cancellation of the move. See Klaus Schmider, *Partisanenkrieg in Jugoslawien* (Hamburg: Koehler & Mittler 2002), pp 97–8.

[304] BA/MA, RH 19 II/127 'Heeresgruppe Mitte Ia Nr. 3101/41 g.Kdos. an A.O.K. 2, Pz.A.O. K. 2, A.O.K. 4, A.O.K. 9, Panzergruppe 3, Panzergruppe 4 und Bef.r.H.Geb.Mitte (15.12.1941, 01.15 h)'.

[305] BA/MA, RH 19 II/127 'Heeresgruppe Mitte, Ia Nr. 3111/41 geh.Kdos.Chefs. an A.O.K. 2, Pz.A.O.K. 2, A.O.K. 4, Pz.Gr. 4, A.O.K. 9, Bef. rückw.H.Geb.Mitte und VIII. Fl.Korps (15.12.1941, 22.00 h)'.

[306] BA/MA, N 245/3 'Tagebuch Reinhardt (entry for 15 December 1941)': 'The worst threats appear to be receding'.

[307] 9. *Armee* had reported the day before that lack of explosives threatened to make the demolition 'problematic'. BA/MA, RH 19 II/122 'Heeresgruppenkommando Mitte, Kriegstagebuch Ia (entry for 14 December 1941)'.

[308] TB Bock, p 351 (entry for 15 December 1941)

On 16 December the crisis came to a head.[309] While previous days had seen occasional references to units having to abandon some of their tanks, trucks, prime movers and artillery pieces due to slippery roads, snow drifts or lack of fuel, the war diary of *Heeresgruppe Mitte* for the 16th has no fewer than six such entries, all of them referring to specific cases. Hoepner, whose warnings about his *Panzergruppe* being stuck in an untenable position had been belittled by Kluge only the day before, was now echoed and supported by the latter quite emphatically. At noon, a preliminary order arrived from Führer's Headquarters which no doubt reflected the tidings which Schmundt had brought with him on his return from Russia. While it confirmed the permission granted to 9. *Armee*, *Panzergruppe* 3 and *Panzergruppe* 4 to continue their retreat it added that they were to do so 'only if no other option presented itself'. All other commands were admonished to stand fast and 2. *Armee* and 2. *Panzerarmee* specifically instructed to plug the gaping holes in their front lines around Liwny and Tula, respectively.[310] This message caused Bock to wire back that he no longer had any reserves with which to carry out these orders and that he had said as much to Brauchitsch during the latter's visit to Smolensk on the 13th. A lengthy telephone conversation followed with Schmundt, who in the meantime had been made point man for all communications with *Heeresgruppe Mitte*, so that Brauchitsch was now essentially removed from the command loop. Hitler's adjutant expressed his opinion that Brauchitsch had given Hitler a watered-down version of what he had seen and heard in Russia and that, crucially, he had not passed on Bock's comments about the army group's cupboard being completely bare as far as reserves were concerned.[311] The commander of *Heeresgruppe Mitte* insisted that a decision still had to be made about whether to execute the retreat that was already under way in some units. Hitler called in the early hours of 17 December and decided that for the time being, everybody was to hold the existing front line,[312] a decision some commanding officers in *Heeresgruppe Mitte* actually greeted with relief,[313] despite post-war protestations to the contrary. Germany's supreme leader now undoubtedly realised that he had a major crisis on his hands. Even so, a conversation with Goebbels on the

---

[309] While the war diary of *Heeresgruppe Mitte* is the best source to follow the day's events, it should be complemented with the entries from Halder's and Bock's personal diaries.

[310] BA/MA, RH 19 II/122 'Heeresgruppenkommando Mitte, Kriegstagebuch Ia (entry for 16 December 1941, 12.10 h)'.

[311] Ibid.

[312] For an almost verbatim transcript of Bock's telephone conversations with Schmundt and Hitler, see BA/MA, RH 19 II/122 'Heeresgruppenkommando Mitte, Kriegstagebuch Ia (entry for 16 December 1941)', esp. pp 130–3.

[313] Reinhardt's comment can be taken as an example: BA/MA, N 245/3 'Tagebuch Reinhardt (entry for 17 December 1941)': 'Finally, clarity through a Führer's order!' A candour not normally reflected in post-war accounts. For a rare exception see Hinze, *20. Panzerdivision*, p 97.

afternoon of the 17th, in which he expressed the hope of soon withdrawing all armoured and motorised divisions to Germany for an urgently needed refit, seems to indicate that its full extent had not yet sunk in.[314] This may well have happened soon after, when the Red Army on the 18th for the first time attacked *Heeresgruppe Mitte* across its entire frontage. After a heated exchange the following day, Hitler decided that rather than retain Brauchitsch as a cipher, the *Generalfeldmarschall* would have to go, the considerable public relations fallout from this move notwithstanding.[315]

7.3.4   Conclusion: Operation Barbarossa

Historians have tended to look at the defeat of Operation Barbarossa in December 1941 through the prism of the Wehrmacht's hubris or the shift in power at the top of the Third Reich, which saw Hitler emerge as head of the army. It is the author's contention that the exact sequence with which the German disaster unfolded is of far greater importance, since the perception of the *Ostheer*'s situation could not but have the most enormous implications for the decision to declare war on the USA. While it was clear that the USSR was not yet defeated, the question to be answered was whether it had been sufficiently crippled to make a gradual shift of the Third Reich's strategic focus to the west a safe proposition. A USSR on its last legs, metaphorically speaking, might still be able to land a few painful blows, but would otherwise still be an easy prey once the onset of spring in 1942 allowed the Germans to recover their full mobility and mop up the remainder of the Red Army. Conversely, a Soviet state only just getting its second wind would conceivably place Germany between two juggernauts in 1942 and thus in a horrible dilemma.

Most of the available evidence points to a Hitler who had resigned himself as far back as August to a continuation of Barbarossa into 1942 and saw this as perfectly feasible provided the USSR was first deprived of its Donbass industrial heartland. In the meantime, he still needed to turn to his military advisers to accurately assess the residual powers of resistance of the Red Army on a day-to-day basis. There is plenty of evidence that in October and November 1941, Brauchitsch's and Halder's optimism in particular far outdid his own. What of the field commanders? It is important to remember that prior to 10–11 December, few if any of them expressed genuine concern even in the privacy

---

[314] TB Goebbels, Bd. II.2, p 537 (entry for 18 December 1941). Of the nineteen Panzer divisions deployed in Russia in mid-December, only three (6th, 7th and 10th) would eventually be shifted west in May 1942 for a complete refit. All others remained in place and were reequipped while holding a position in or near the front line. See www.lexikon-der-wehrmacht.de/Gliederungen/Panzerdivisionen (accessed 2 May 2017).

[315] See David Stahel, *Retreat from Moscow: A New History of Germany's Winter Campaign, 1941–1942* (New York: Farrar, Straus & Giroux 2019), pp 115–31.

of their diaries or letters home. Bock and Richthofen had genuine flashes of insight but managed to suppress these within a day. When the question of continuing the autumn campaign came up, Leeb and Bock had shown themselves to be more than willing to roll the dice one more time by going for a risky late autumn campaign; Rundstedt was the only army group commander to oppose such a course of action. While it is true that the commitment shown by some of the army and *Panzergruppen* commanders was either lukewarm (Kluge) or veered from one extreme to the other (Guderian), only one of them (Weichs) went on record right from the start as consistently opposing the idea of campaigning into December. Even so, it is important to stress that both Rundstedt and Weichs were urging caution because they feared the consequences of having their troops caught in the open by the onset of winter and at the end of their logistical tether; neither appears to have lived in fear of the power of a resurgent Red Army. Even observers like Heinrici and Hilger, who had concluded that the USSR had the military and economic resources to go on fighting for a long time yet, were confident in ruling out Soviet offensive action for the foreseeable future.

It could, of course, be argued that since the offensives on Rostov, Moscow and Tichwin had all failed before Hitler drove to the Reichstag on 11 December 1941 to read out his declaration of war, he found himself in the first ten days of December in his own personal 'last chance saloon'. Did the evidence before him justify a last-minute diplomatic about-turn which would have ruined, possibly permanently, the chances of a Japanese alliance?

In the case of Rostov, the evidence available at the time strongly suggested that this reverse had much more to do with a failure of communications on the German side than with the power of a resurgent Red Army. Rather than tracing a defensive line, Reichenau was ordered to proceed with planning for the storming of Sevastopol and another attempt to seize Rostov and the Don/Donec bend before the end of the year. These demands indicated that Hitler was engaged in a process of scaling back the expectations that had been fostered by Halder's original outlandish ideas, but in a gradual way. *Heeresgruppe Nord* was forced to abandon Tichwin (7 December), but this setback was soon pushed aside by renewed planning for another offensive which, while less ambitious in scope, was still expected once and for all to render Leningrad's position untenable. In the case of Moscow, the situation was different insofar as the largest of three army groups had been left stranded in the approaches to Moscow while bereft of reserves or logistics that might have put it in a position to defend its meandering front line. While no written record exists of the briefings that Brauchitsch gave Hitler on the situation of *Heeresgruppe Mitte*, it is certainly significant that as late as 9 December Halder still seemed convinced that Bock was up against a hodgepodge army equally composed of neophytes and a smattering of fresh units brought in from the Far East. Bock was in a much better position to judge these matters, but on 10

December he was still ready to muzzle his protest after he was fobbed off with the promise of four divisions, still weeks away from arriving. A day later, Halder's diary recorded a fairly stable situation in the sector of *Heeresgruppe Mitte*. Only on the 13th did Bock finally confront Brauchitsch with intelligence which suggested that collapse was more than just a remote possibility; even then, circumstantial evidence suggests that Brauchitsch on his return failed to pass on an unvarnished report of this to Hitler. There may have been a crisis, but it is difficult to see how news of it could have reached the Wolfsschanze before 11 December.

Without a doubt, the agonising slowness of this process can be explained at least in part by the fact that the Germans felt that the Red Army's way of war by now held few surprises for them. Since the first week of Barbarossa, the hallmark of Soviet warfare had been constantly counter-attacking the enemy, whether in piecemeal manner or in strength. Many, if not most, of these attacks had been conducted in an ill-coordinated and disjointed manner and had actually brought little but loss to the Soviet side. All the same, they were a fact of life. There was a certain rationale to them insofar as the Red Army of that period found it hard to keep up with the Wehrmacht when it was manoeuvring. Hence a German spearhead slowing down or even coming to a complete halt, as happened at El'nia, Dnepropetrovsk or Rostov, offered the Red Army a chance to engage a target that for once was stationary. It is only logical that the first four or five days of the Soviet winter offensive should barely have registered as something out of the ordinary in the German generals' minds. The violence or impact of the attacks experienced during that period was still a long way from matching that of the Red Army counter-strikes at Staraya Russa and Smolensk in August 1941; furthermore, permission was quickly granted to collapse the most vulnerable bulges created by the advance at the northern and southern ends of *Heeresgruppe Mitte*'s front line, thus ruling out a repeat of the situations that arose at El'nia and Dnepropetrovsk (month-long attrition to no clear purpose) or Rostov (a brief, though real danger of seeing a mechanised spearhead cut off).

The available evidence indicates that it was only on 14 December, with the trusted Schmundt relaying the bad news straight from Smolensk, that Hitler began to understand that several factors had come together to create a crisis which surpassed anything witnessed thus far on the Eastern Front. It is important to realise that even then he did not avail himself of the most obvious option, namely to immediately cancel the planned offensives against Leningrad and Sevastopol and redirect some or all of the assets tied up in these endeavours to support Bock's beleaguered command. Earlier in the campaign, the shift from outlandish targets, such as Maikop, Stalingrad and a link-up with the Finns east of Ladoga, to 'manageable' ones, such as Rostov, Sevastopol and a broadening of 18. *Armee*'s blocking position east of Leningrad, had been the result of a gradual process that had taken between three days and three weeks; it was only logical that the realisation that an entire army group was not just increasingly hard-pressed, but facing an unprecedented existential crisis, should take a similar period of time.

7.4   The German Assessment of Lend-Lease Aid

The impact which Lend-Lease deliveries had on the fighting in Russia is usually associated with the vast amount of materiel (especially motor vehicles) delivered to the Red Army post-1942 and which greatly facilitated its twin drives on Berlin and Budapest. In 2006 and 2009, Alexander Hill was the first scholar to put forward the theory that even the first batch of Lend-Lease tanks (in this case, British Matildas and Valentines) may have played an important, if not quite decisive, role in the battle for Moscow in December 1941.[316] Irrespective of their small number (an approximate total of ninety, not all of which may have seen combat[317]) their disproportionate impact can be explained by Red Army losses of the previous months and the fact that Soviet industry's production of its much superior T-34 had bottomed out at 185 units in October 1941; an adequate tank was preferable to no tank at all.[318] For the purposes of this book, the limited impact that a few British tanks and American planes were having on the battlefields of the autumn of 1941 is less important than the manner in which the German leadership in general and Adolf Hitler in particular would have perceived them.

The proclamation of the First Protocol at the end of the Moscow Conference (1 October 1941) might still have been dismissed as a public relations stunt aimed at supporting the tottering Soviet regime, but a surprise encounter of I. *Gruppe* of JG 77 with a group of Hurricanes near Murmansk on 12 September had provided the first evidence that Allied support was a reality. On 13 October, II./JG 51, supporting *Heeresgruppe Mitte*'s advance on Moscow, encountered a squadron of Curtiss P-40s which had likewise arrived with the first Arctic convoy; as if to drive the point home, American radio actually broadcast a major feature on the role played by American-produced planes in

---

[316] For this discussion, see David Glantz, *Colossus Reborn: The Red Army at War, 1941–1943* (Kansas: Kansas UP 2005), pp 249–50, 659, and in greater detail, Alexander Hill, 'British "Lend-Lease" Tanks and the Battle for Moscow, November–December 1941 – a Research Note'; in *Journal of Slavic Military Studies* 2006, Nr. 19, pp 289–94 and Alexander Hill, 'British "Lend-Lease" Tanks and the Battle for Moscow, November–December 1941 – Revisited'; in: *Journal of Slavic Military Studies* 2009, No. 22, pp 574–87.

[317] The bulk of the British and American tanks delivered in 1941 (a total of 646) arrived too late to take part in the battle for Moscow. See Glantz, *Colossus*, p 659.

[318] Both British designs suffered from similar inadequacies as German Panzers when exposed to the Russian winter and were handicapped by the small calibre of their main armament; on a positive note, the thickness of their armour rendered them virtually invulnerable to the 37 mm Pak anti-tank gun, which at the time was still the most widely used German anti-tank asset.

the fight for Russia a fortnight later.[319] Voices in English picked up by German listening stations in the sector of *Heeresgruppe Mitte* undoubtedly belonged to the instructors whom the USAAF had thoughtfully provided to introduce Soviet pilots to their new mounts.[320] The first German document to address itself – albeit briefly – to the desirability of blocking routes of access for Allied aid was penned by *Generalleutnant* Walter Warlimont of the OKW's *Wehrmachtführungsstab* on 6 August. In a ten-page memorandum discussing the likely consequences of a continuation of the war against the USSR into 1942, he skipped any discussion of the routes through Archangelsk and Murmansk, but drew his readers' attention to the fact that an extension of the campaign made a contribution by Japan desirable, since this would put the Tripartite powers in a position to block the arrival of 'Allied support through the Far East'.[321]

On 22 October, *Generalmajor* Georg Thomas of the OKW's *Wehrwirtschafts- und Rüstungsamt* presented a comprehensive report into the conceivable impact that American arms shipments might have in prolonging Soviet resistance.[322] Unlike his comrade in arms, Boetticher in Washington, he did not yield to the temptation of blithely assuming that American industry would be stretched to breaking point by the burden of supplying both a host of 'vassal states' and its own armed forces; instead, he limited himself to examining whether Allied shipping on the one hand, and the Soviet transportation system on the other, were in a position to deliver goods he knew to be available. Existing choke-points notwithstanding (the limited capacity of the roads and railway lines linking the ports in the Persian Gulf to the interior of the USSR), he came to the conclusion that, especially if Vladivostok remained accessible, nothing stood in the way of importing up to 12 million tonnes of goods a year. He correctly identified the Soviet need for a number of raw materials (especially bauxite, the base material for aluminium), but estimated that in light of the disruption of most of the Soviet pre-war economy, the Russians' need for

---

[319] Bergström, *Air Battle*, pp 79, 105. Also: Valeriy Romanenko, 'The P-40 in Soviet Aviation'; in: *Journal of Slavic Military Studies*, Nr. 22 (2009), pp 97–124 and Vladimir Kotelnikov, *Lend-Lease and Soviet Aviation in the Second World War* (Solihull: Helion 2017), pp 165–90. The radio feature is highlighted in PA/AA, StS USA, Bd. 9, 'Thomsen & Boetticher an Auswärtiges Amt (31.10.1941)'.

[320] See TB Bock, p 317 (entry for 14 November 1941), which specifically refers to the presence of British or American airmen in front of *Heeresgruppe Mitte*. The voices intercepted were likely as not those of Lieutenants John Alison and Hubert Zemke (the latter a future famous ace) who were serving as instructors to VVS airmen making the transition to the P-40. Romanenko, *P-40 in Soviet Aviation*, p 99.

[321] BA/MA, RM 7/258 'Abt. Landesverteidigung-Chef. Nr. 441339/41 Kurzer strategischer Überblick über die Fortführung des Krieges nach dem Ostfeldzug (6.8.1941)'.

[322] BA/MA, RM 7/94 'Wehrwirtschafts- und Rüstungsamt Abt.Wi Nr. 3409/41 gKdos. Beurteilung der Möglichkeiten einer materiellen Unterstützung Rußlands durch die angelsächsischen Mächte – Abschrift (22.10.1941)'.

Figure 7.6 Overturned Matilda tanks outside Moscow, winter 1941–2: they serve as an apt image of Hitler's fatal underestimation of Lend-Lease deliveries. (Alexander Ustinov/Slava Katamidze Collection/Hulton Archive via Getty Images)

tanks, planes and ammunition would probably take precedence in the short to mid-term.[323] These Roosevelt was in a position to deliver in important quantities; the main limiting factor was the extent to which he was prepared to send weapons earmarked for domestic or British use to the Red Army instead. In fact, a redirection of the entire export quota of the US armaments industry to this new ally was likely to make good the crippling damage inflicted on the Russian war economy by the loss of much of the western USSR.[324] Thomas briefly touched on developments that might affect American will (the recent Soviet defeat at Vyazma-Bryansk) or capability (a Japanese blockade of Vladivostok) to carry out Lend-Lease, but did not allow these musings to affect his devastating conclusion: as long as the main

---

[323] Thomas was broadly correct in that the first Soviet lists handed over to the US government in July prioritised planes and anti-aircraft artillery, as well as high-octane gasoline for the former. Tanks were not singled out. When Stalin met US envoy Harry Hopkins in the Kremlin on 28 July, the Soviet dictator by and large re-emphasised this order of priorities, while adding aluminium. See Robert Huhn Jones, *The Roads to Russia: United States Lend-Lease to the Soviet Union* (Norman: Oklahoma UP 1969), pp 37, 48–9.

[324] BA/MA, RM 7/94 'Wehrwirtschafts- und Rüstungsamt Abt. Wi Nr. 3409/ gKdos. Beurteilung der Möglichkeiten einer materiellen Unterstützung Rußlands durch die angelsächsischen Mächte – Abschrift (22.10.1941)', pp 6–7.

ports and the railway lines serving them remained open, Lend-Lease was likely to turn into a major challenge to German prospects of victory in Russia.

In the week after Thomas filed his report, the Washington embassy reported on the American perspective of the same issue: even in 1941 Washington, the routing of Lend-Lease shipments was a rather unlikely topic for public debate, but had turned into exactly that because of concerns that the route to Vladivostok might conceivably lead to a hardening of the Japanese stance at the ongoing talks over the future of the Far East. In the face of the well-known inadequacies of the Iranian route, the government all but publicly pledged to ship most goods for the foreseeable future through Archangelsk or Murmansk.[325] Within a few days of each other, two sources close to the German leadership had thus singled out the importance of both the Arctic ports and the railway hub at Vologda which served as their key link to Moscow and beyond. The idea of a move against Vologda in 1941 had first been articulated in an exchange between Raeder and Hitler in mid-September, during which the dictator expressed his concern over recent British naval activity in these waters and saw this as a harbinger of a possible British lodgement via Archangelsk or Murmansk. Blocking this route promised to be difficult, since the former port in particular was likely to remain out of reach for some time; instead, Hitler had promised the admiral to cut off its communications with central Russia by severing the railway line that ran to Moscow via Vologda.[326] The next few weeks witnessed further spectacular victories by the *Ostheer*; by late October, an emboldened Halder was, as we have already seen, drafting plans for a late autumn campaign that would have seen *Heeresgruppe Nord* link up with the Finns, *Heeresgruppe Mitte* reach Moscow and Vologda and possibly even Gorki and *Heeresgruppe Süd* execute an operation along diverging lines against Maikop and Stalingrad. Though these ideas were considerably scaled down in the days after the Orsha conference, Hitler – who had shown, if anything, a rather tepid commitment to Halder's wilder schemes – commented to the army chief of staff on 19 November that he would still like the operation against Moscow to include Vologda if at all possible.[327]

This as likely as not reflected his previous interest in blocking a British lodgement in the far north. One way of ascertaining without doubt what lay behind the dictator's interest in Vologda is by examining the abundant notes taken at the Orsha talks. *Heeresgruppe Nord*'s summary of the conference alleges that OKW's (and hence it is fair to surmise, Hitler's) interest in the

---

[325] PA/AA, StS USA, Bd. 9, 'Thomsen an Auswärtiges Amt (26.10.1941)'.

[326] 'Oberkommando der Kriegsmarine. Seekriegsleitung B.Nr.1.Skl. Ib 1555/41 g.Kdos. Chefs. Vortrag des Ob.d.M. beim Führer am 17.9.1941 nach. Wolfsschanze (n.d.)'; in: Wagner (ed.), *Lagevorträge*, pp 286–9.

[327] KTB Halder III, p 295 (entry for 19 November 1941).

railway junction reflects the perceived need to 'interdict the flow of Anglo–American war materiel'.[328] The two sets of notes produced by the delegation from *Heeresgruppe Süd* are contradictory: the first report, while assuming that Anglo–American deliveries might to some extent make up for the tank and aircraft losses suffered by the Red Army in 1941, mentions Vologda only in the context of 'preventing a joint Anglo–Russian move out of the Far North'.[329] One part of a second, more exhaustive report (a compilation of four separately themed sections) likewise stresses the need to block any British attempts to establish a lodgement in the far north and makes no mention of Lend-Lease.[330] A different section, however, has Halder claiming that both Vologda and Stalingrad have been included because 'the political leadership' has decided to prioritise objectives likely to facilitate the processing of Allied shipments.[331] This could of course be an accurate rendition of his latest briefing by Brauchitsch, but it might also reflect an attempt on his part to deflect some of the criticism that a few of his brother officers – astonished at the scope of the late autumn campaign forced on them – directed at him at Orsha.

Until such time as a source appears that allows us to make sense of this welter of contradictions, we cannot ascertain with any certainty which strategic threat aroused Hitler's interest in Vologda in mid-November:[332] the possibility of a British expeditionary corps joining hands with the Red Army or the gradually increasing flow of Lend-Lease from the Arctic ports.

In due course, orders to pass on intelligence indicating the presence of Western weapons and/or advisers were issued by OKH: over the following days and weeks, and belying the fact that the impact of Anglo–American weapons on the field of battle was as yet minimal, *Fremde Heere Ost* and the commands making up *Heeresgruppe Mitte*, in particular, carefully recorded every morsel of intelligence pointing to the increasing presence of Western planes (and as of late November, tanks) over or near the

---

[328] BA/MA, RH 19 III/771 'Niederschrift über die Besprechung beim Chef des Heeres am 13.11.41, Teil I (n.d.)'.

[329] BA/MA, RH 19 I/281 'Vortragsnotiz über Chefbesprechung in Orscha am 13.11.41 (17.11.1941)'.

[330] BA/MA, RH 19 I/281 'Niederschrift über die Besprechung beim Chef des Heeres am 13.11.41, Teil III (n.d.)'.

[331] BA/MA, RH 19 I/281 'Besprechung Chef Gen.St.d.Heeres am 13.11. in Orscha, I. Teil (n.d.).' In TB Goebbels, Bd. II.3 (entry for 20 March 1942), pp 510–11, Hitler complained to Goebbels how Brauchitsch had 'ruined' his idea of driving on the Volga in order to 'cut off the Caucasus and hit the Soviet system at its most vulnerable spot' by instead driving on Moscow. However, Goebbels failed to record why Hitler believed this to be such an Achilles heel.

[332] The source which might provide final proof (the diary of Franz Halder) is of no help in this case, on account of its author's convalescence after a riding accident. He only resumed his diary notes on 4 November.

front.[333] Some of these reports were only based on hearsay, others were downright fanciful,[334] lending credence to the theory that the mere knowledge of impending Allied arms supplies on any scale depressed the Germans to the same extent that it gave heart to the Russians.[335]

The evidence thus far would seem to indicate a slowly growing appreciation on the part of the German leadership of the potential of Lend-Lease deliveries to breathe new life into a Red Army crippled by material loss on a truly staggering scale. However, other parts of the strategic picture do not offer equally conclusive pointers.

On 26 September 1941 the attaché in Washington relayed the gist of a recent article in a journal directed at the US business community. The piece argued that the industry available to the USSR the east of the Urals was unlikely to be an even remotely adequate substitute for the mines and facilities being lost to the Germans, because of the degree of interdependence that had existed between both general areas on the outbreak of war.[336] The article went into quite specific detail, no doubt a reflection of the knowledge that had accumulated in the USA through the role played by American contractors in the crash industrialisation of the Soviet Union between the wars. Not even US help, Boetticher added for good measure, would be able to make good the shortfall thus created.[337]

As far as finding an access point for any aid was concerned, the outlook seemed similarly bleak. In two reports from Washington, the German attaché went into considerable detail explaining the inadequacies of the Iranian route. All the evidence pointed towards the available berthing facilities, roads, railway lines and rolling stock being either in poor repair or unavailable.[338] Some of the solutions proposed as stopgap measures clearly smacked of desperation,

---

[333] BA/MA RH 19 II/124 'Panzergruppe 3. Betr.: Gefangenenvernehmung (22.10.1941)'; RH 2/2670 'Fremde Heere Ost, Lagebericht vom 4.11.1941'; RH 2/2670 'Fremde Heere Ost, Lagebericht vom 13.11.1941'; RH 2/2670 'Fremde Heere Ost, Lagebericht vom 24.11.1941', KTB Halder III, p 326 (entry for 4 December 1941); TB Bock, p 317 (entry for 14 November 1941).

[334] As in the case of the SS-*Leibstandarte Adolf Hitler*, fighting with *Heeresgruppe Süd*'s 1. *Panzerarmee*, which reported sighting American tanks in its sector. At the time, only a handful of American tanks had even arrived in the USSR, and none saw combat before the year was out. See BA/MA, RH 19 I/88 'Heeresgruppenkommando Süd, Kriegstagebuch Ia (entry for 7 December 1941)'.

[335] For this interpretation, Stahel, *Battle for Moscow*, pp 172–80.

[336] PA/AA, Handakten Etzdorf, 'Politische Berichte Washington. Meldung Mil.Att. Washington vom 26.9.1941 (29.9.1941)'.

[337] Ibid.

[338] PA/AA, Handakten Etzdorf. 'Politische Berichte Washington. Meldung Mil.Att. Washington vom 6.10.1941 (9.10.1941)'. Only one (single-track) railway line linked an underdeveloped port in the Persian Gulf with the Iranian northwest, without connecting with the Soviet railway network. Accordingly, the first year witnessed a laborious system of relays whereby aid to the USSR was shipped north via barges on the Tigris, the Iraqi

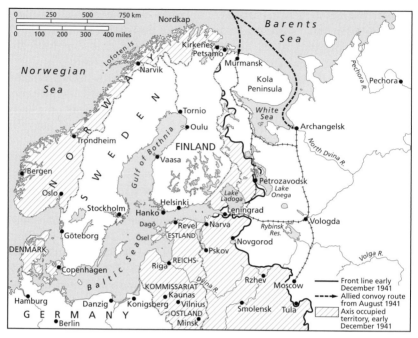

Map 7.8 The approaches to Murmansk and Archangelsk: in 1941–2, initial uncertainty over Japan's stance and the inadequacies of the Iranian transport infrastructure forced the Allies to prioritise delivery of Lend-Lease goods to the USSR via the Arctic ports, the proximity of German bases notwithstanding.

the general gleefully reported.[339] In contrast to Basrah and Bander Shapur, the USSR's Arctic ports of Archangelsk and Murmansk had a functioning rail link with the Russian interior and were thus the most obvious point of entry for Lend-Lease shipments in 1941. The branch line from Murmansk into the interior was left highly vulnerable by Finland's entry into the war on Germany's side, but a combination of a thoroughly disjointed Axis strategy together with timely US diplomatic pressure on the Finns put the Red Army in a position to parry these thrusts.[340] This left the Kriegsmarine and Luftwaffe as

---

railway network and truck convoys. Ashley Jackson, *Persian Gulf Command: A History of the Second World War in Iran and Iraq* (New Haven: Yale UP 2018), pp 294–309.

[339] See PA/AA, Handakten Etzdorf. 'Politische Berichte Washington. Meldung Mil.Att. Washington vom 3.11.1941 (7.11.1941)', which makes reference to a proposed relay system that would involve the use of, first, flying boats and, then, trucks to reach the Caspian Sea, giving Boetticher reason to muse about 'the confusion' reigning in Washington.

[340] A major monograph on the war in this theatre is still very much a desideratum. Chris Mann and Christer Jorgensen, *Hitler's Arctic War: The German Campaign in Norway,*

the two services that were in a position to interdict Allied convoys making for one of the two ports. As such, they should really have featured quite prominently in the agenda of the briefings on naval affairs held between Raeder and Hitler. As it was, the talks held on 17 September mentioned the Arctic mainly in the context of securing a naval supply route for Eduard Dietl's embattled *Gebirgskorps* outside Murmansk in the face of Allied naval superiority; Hitler also brought up the subject of the Kriegsmarine's capital ships, which he wanted moved to a place like Norway, where they would both be safe from air attack and could help with securing the Third Reich's northern flank;[341] a Führer's Directive from 22 September, ordering the cessation of offensive operations against Murmansk and a thrust to commence forthwith against the railway that constituted the port's lifeline, made quite detailed reference to the role to be played in this plan by aircraft and light naval forces. Careful reading of the document, however, makes it quite clear that these assets were to be deployed solely with the mission of either protecting Dietl's supply route or interdicting that of his Soviet opponents,[342] an interpretation also supported by an entry into the war diary of the Seekriegsleitung.[343]

In a briefing on 7 October Kurt Fricke attempted to convince the dictator that a feared British amphibious descent in the rear of Dietl's front line was all but ruled out by the lack of natural light in this latitude in wintertime.[344] Hitler, however, would not be dissuaded. The way he saw it, any kind of British reinforcements for the Soviet defenders around Murmansk was likely to be a mere harbinger of worse things. A British bomber force based in the area would be in a position to raid with ease the Petsamo mines, which were an asset of 'crucial importance' to the German war economy. He also expressed hope that a last-ditch attempt to reach and cut the railway line, which was the Arctic ports' main lifeline, might still be successful, but only in the context of

Finland and the USSR 1940–1945 (London: Ian Allan 2002), pp 62–185, is a good introduction to the subject. The events of 1941 in the Murmansk sector are well covered in Alf R. Jacobsen, *Miracle at the Litza: Hitler's First Defeat on the Eastern Front* (Philadelphia and Oxford: Casemate 2017).

[341] 'Vortrag des Ob.d.M. beim Führer am 17.9.1941 nachm. Wolfsschanze'; in: Wagner (ed.), *Lagevorträge*, pp 286–9.

[342] 'Der Führer und Oberste Befehlshaber der Wehrmacht Nr. 441 578/41 g.K. Chefs. WFSt/ L (I Op.) Weisung Nr. 36 (22.9.1941)'; in: Walther Hubatsch (ed.), *Hitler's Weisungen für die Kriegführung 1939–1945. Dokumente des Oberkommandos der Wehrmacht* (Koblenz: Bernard & Graefe 1983), pp 154–7

[343] KTB Seekriegsleitung, Teil A (entry for 23 September 1941). The Seekriegsleitung actually decided to put its own gloss on Hitler's instructions by using a planned stopover of the new *Tirpitz* in Trondheim for 'brief forays' against the Allied traffic to Archangelsk, something not discussed in the talks of the 17th or the directive of 22 September.

[344] KTB Seekriegsleitung, Teil A (entry for 7 October 1941). This diary entry is the only existing source for this exchange, which is omitted from the Wagner edition.

pre-empting a British lodgement or rendering it less of a threat. The potential of Murmansk as a gateway for Allied supplies was not mentioned even in passing.[345]

This is also reflected in the next directive concerning itself with the Arctic sideshow, which followed three days later. *Führerweisung* No. 37 ordered all German troops to stand down until the end of winter, when offensive warfare would be resumed. In the meantime, protection of the vitally important nickel mines of Petsamo would become the first priority of Dietl's *Gebirgskorps*. Almost an entire page of the directive discusses the role of air and sea power in supporting this scheme. While Murmansk is actually mentioned by name, it is merely in the context of its role as a base for possible Soviet offensive operations that might one day threaten Petsamo.[346] Hitler's next meeting with his naval leadership took place on 27 October and had the strategic shift to the Mediterranean as its only topic;[347] finally, on 13 November, both the ongoing operations of a handful of U-boats in Arctic waters and the possible shift of most of the Kriegsmarine's remaining heavy units to northern Norway were discussed at considerable length. However, it is clear from the minutes that the former had been ordered to fight Soviet coastal convoys, while the idea of deploying the latter to Norway had developed out of Hitler's growing anxiety to finally move the ships to a base where they would not be exposed to a major RAF air raid once or twice a month.[348] The meeting on 12 December was overshadowed by the entry of Japan into the war and appears to have skipped the issue of the war in the Arctic altogether.[349]

Only on 29 December, and as likely as not as the result of a major British raid on the port of Vagsoo two days before, did Hitler show himself positively anxious about the security of the German position in Norway and order the navy to move its remaining heavy units (three capital ships and three heavy cruisers) to the far north. The minutes do imply that intercepting an Allied invasion force would in all likelihood take precedence over interdicting British convoys to Archangelsk (a successful landing in the Narvik area was described as a turning point in the war), but a clear order of priority was not established

---

[345] Ibid.

[346] 'Der Führer und Oberste Befehlshaber der Wehrmacht OKW/WFSt/Abt. L (I Op.) Nr. 441696/41 g.K. Chefs. (10.10.1941)'; in: Hubatsch (ed.), *Weisungen*, 161–6.

[347] 'Niederschrift der Besprechung des Führers mit dem Chef des Stabes der Seekriegsleitung, Vizeadmiral Fricke, über Einsatz deutscher Marine-Streitkräfte im Mittelmeer (27.10.1941)'; in: Wagner (ed.), *Lagevorträge*, pp 301–4. On this occasion, the Seekriegsleitung's chief of staff, *Vizeadmiral* Kurt Fricke, had to stand in for Raeder.

[348] 'Vortrag Ob.d.M. beim Führer am 13. November 1941, nachmittags in Wolfsschanze'; in: Wagner (ed.), *Lagevorträge*, pp 304–10.

[349] 'Vortrag des Ob.d.M. beim Führer in Berlin am 12.12.1941 (15.12.1941)'; in: ibid., pp 325–7.

and, in fact, never would be.[350] A second set of minutes from the same meeting, however, clearly indicates that the events of the last fortnight had caused the dictator to fundamentally rethink his previous assessment that Lend-Lease goods could not possibly pull the embattled USSR back from the brink. When Raeder questioned the wisdom of including the relatively slow heavy cruisers of the *Deutschland* class in the wholesale shift to Norway, Hitler retorted that, if given a choice, he would prefer to forego the sinking of 100,000 GRT in the South Atlantic in exchange for a mere four merchantmen bringing tanks to the Eastern Front.[351]

In his report of 22 October, *Generalmajor* Thomas had stressed the potential of Vladivostok in serving as the most important port of entry for Lend-Lease shipments, provided the Japanese did not blockade it. Even though the idea of a Japanese intervention in support of Barbarossa was encouraged intermittently by the German side between late June and mid-November 1941,[352] the evidence is rather patchy that concerns over the Pacific port's possible role as a back door for American supplies may have been the main driving force behind this. The first time Vladivostok was mentioned in the run-up to Barbarossa appears to have been on 20 April 1941, when Hitler and Raeder were discussing the results achieved during the recent visit by Japanese Foreign Minister Matsuoka. According to the dictator, even though the Soviet–Japanese Neutrality Pact signed by their visitor on his return journey had come as something of a surprise, it was a development he thoroughly approved of. The way he saw it, it was likely to keep the Japanese from 'making a move against Vladivostok and instead encourage them to attack Singapore'.[353] On 8 June, *Staatssekretär* Ernst von Weizsäcker summarised in a private letter the gist of recent conversations with Ambassador Oshima on the idea of Japan finally throwing in its lot with its ally Germany by initiating hostilities against one of the major Allied powers. Oshima seems to have confided in Weizsäcker that he would attempt to steer Japanese strategy in the general direction of the Soviet Pacific port, a prospect the *Staatssekretär* appears to have met with complete indifference.[354]

On 28 June, and then again on 1 July, in the full flush of initial victory, Ribbentrop did instruct his ambassador in Tokyo to urge the Japanese to join the war immediately. Here was a chance which, if seized in a timely manner,

---

[350] 'Vortrag des Ob.d.M. beim Führer am 29.12.1941 abends in Wolfsschanze'; in: ibid., pp 334–7.

[351] BA/MA, RM 7/133 'Besprechungsniederschrift vom 29. Dez. 1941. Anwesend: Der Führer, Grossadmiral Raeder, Generalfeldmarschall Keitel, Vizeadmiral Fricke, Kapitän zur See von Puttkamer (1.1.1942)'.

[352] More on this topic in the chapter on Japanese–German relations.

[353] 'Seekriegsleitung B.Nr. I op 515/41 gKdos.Chefs Vortrag Ob.d.M. beim Führer am 20. April 1941 (n.d.)'; in: Wagner (ed.), *Lagevorträge*, pp 217–21, esp. 220 (quote).

[354] 'Note by Weizsäcker (8.6.1941)'; in: Hill (ed.), *Weizsäcker-Papiere*, p 258.

meant that German and Japanese spearheads might still make contact in Siberia before the onset of winter.[355] This probably reflected Hitler's stance at least up to a point; on 8 July the dictator told his propaganda minister that he was 'utterly convinced' of Japanese intervention. Japan might still prevaricate a little, he went on, but it would still join Berlin faster than the USSR had done after Germany's invasion of Poland in 1939.[356] This might explain another wire which Ribbentrop sent to the embassy in Tokyo two days later, in which he re-emphasised his earlier argument and urged Ott to make haste.[357] However, none of these telegrams or statements betray any anxiety over the possibility that Allied supplies conveyed through Vladivostok might extend or even reverse the Soviet Union's terminal crisis. This hardly constitutes a surprise if we keep in mind that the German initiative was, in fact, driven by a hidden agenda to wreck a diplomatic rapprochement between Tokyo and Washington. It would appear that the first warning about Vladivostok's potential to affect the course of the Russo–German war was put forward not by a German, but by a Japanese official. In mid-July, Vice Admiral Naokuni Nomura expressed concern to *Konteradmiral* Otto Groos of the Seekriegsleitung that in the aftermath of the collapse of Soviet military power to the west of the Urals, a residual state might hold on in most of Siberia if supported by Anglo–American deliveries from the Pacific. Groos' answer is highly revealing: such worries were groundless, since the losses already suffered by the USSR were 'impossible to replace in the foreseeable future'.[358]

In the meantime, the Japanese leadership continued sending mixed messages about joining the war, but called up several reservist classes and reinforced the army in Manchuria, thus keeping the issue on the boil.[359] On 6 August 1941 Groos and Nomura met again for another discussion of Japan's strategic options. The German officer took extensive notes which he then had typed up and submitted to the Seekriegsleitung's chief of staff, *Vizeadmiral* Kurt Fricke.[360] Fricke liberally peppered the document with marginal comments, most of them sarcastic barbs directed at Nomura's transparent attempts

---

[355] PA/AA, Handakten Ritter Japan 18 'Ribbentrop an Ott (1.7.1941)'.

[356] TB Goebbels, Bd. II.1, p 34 (entry for 9 July 1941). Since this implied a Japanese declaration of war on the very date Goebbels and Hitler were having this conversation (a clear impossibility), it is likely the propaganda minister made a slight error here.

[357] PA/AA, Handakten Ritter Japan 18 'Ribbentrop an Ott (10.7.1941)'.

[358] BA/MA, RM 12 II/249 'Kriegstagebuch Marineattache Tokio, Eingang Telegr.Matt 3791 gK (entry for 3 September 1941)'. This summary of the conversation with Nomura was wired to the attaché in Tokyo on 3 September. It appears to be the only surviving record of this exchange.

[359] In PA/AA, StS Japan, Bd. 4, 609 'Ott an Auswärtiges Amt (25.7.1941)', the German ambassador in Tokyo stressed that the ongoing call-up of reservists had reached a point where it was 'impossible to cover up'.

[360] BA/MA, RM 7/94 'Abschrift zu B.Nr. 1. Abt. Skl 17934/41 g.Kdos. Abschrift. Unterredung mit Vizeadmiral Nomura am 6.8.1941 (n.d.)'

to avoid any kind of commitment. The most remarkable thing about the document, however, is dissent between Groos and Fricke. While the former repeatedly tried to sell his Japanese interlocutor on the idea of an attack against the USSR in general and Vladivostok (which he described as a 'link' between the USA and the USSR) in particular, three of Fricke's marginal notes argue against this most emphatically.[361] With the Seekriegsleitung's chief of staff not just more senior, but also closer to the centres of power, this constitutes proof that anxiety over Vladivostok's potential was not a driver of German strategy in August 1941.

On 18 August, Goebbels and Hitler had one of their periodic private meetings in which, apart from reminiscing about the days of 'the struggle', they would also discuss issues of both a military and domestic nature. On this occasion, the Führer briefly turned to the subject of Japan. He expressed 'his conviction that Japan would attack the Soviet Union. This did not hinge on whether the German advance had reached Moscow or not, but on the rainy period coming to an end, something to be expected in the near future'.[362] In the same exchange, Hitler dwelt at length on the fact that the sheer numbers of tanks and planes deployed by the Red Army in the last few weeks had come as something of a shock,[363] but the subject of large-scale Allied aid was not brought up. The reference to Soviet numerical strength is no doubt a reflection of the ferocity of Soviet resistance in the Smolensk area, where despite inflicting staggering losses on the defenders, *Heeresgruppe Mitte* found itself slowed down to a point where the odds of it reaching Moscow before the *rasputitsa* period began to appear doubtful for the first time. This, in turn, may have compelled Ribbentrop to hold Ott's feet to the fire yet again. On 22 August, the latter had reported on the adamant refusal of virtually all Japanese officials to be drawn on the subject of blocking access to Vladivostok, much less on outright war. According to Ott, while the navy tended to favour a move south, some (but by no means all) army leaders were willing to consider a move against the USSR; both the looming threat of US intervention and the number of units tied up in China meant that any of the two courses would be fraught with considerable risk even in a best-case scenario.[364] Under a system not known for smooth and effective decision making at the best of times, a

---

[361] Where Groos takes note of Nomura's complaint at Germany's sudden demand that Japan now turn against the USSR, Fricke noted: 'Most definitely not something we should ask for'; where Groos' records his own plea that Japan should invade Siberia to re-establish rail communications with Europe, Fricke just commented that 'this would weaken their main effort in the south', further elaborating a little later by adding that the sheer distances involved would mitigate against the success of such an endeavour: 'neither we nor the Japanese will get far enough'. See ibid.

[362] TB Goebbels, Bd. II.1, p 263 (entry for 19 August 1941).

[363] Ibid., p 260.

[364] PA/AA, Handakten Ritter Japan, Bd. 18, 'Nr. 7633 Ott an Auswärtiges Amt (22.8.1941)'.

consensus was impossible to establish under these conditions. What is important is that Ott, in trying to make a case for intervention against the USSR with
one or several navy representatives, had argued that 'in view of the changed
situation'[365] (an obvious allusion to Barbarossa) a confrontation with the
USSR had to take priority.

Ribbentrop's answer mainly dwelt on an argument made by Boetticher and
Thomsen many times over, namely that American policy was so much bluff and
provided Japan acted speedily and did not touch US sovereign territory on its
march of conquest, it could do pretty much as it pleased. Accordingly, the German
foreign minister went on, the empire should seize the moment, 'finish off Russia
quickly' and, with its back free, turn south to fulfil its Greater Asian mission.[366]
More relevant to this chapter than this Ribbentropian flight of fancy is the
argument he developed over the last three pages of the telegram. No doubt
realising that the problem of the first American tankers making landfall at
Vladivostok in a couple of weeks' time was unlikely to be solved by Japan having
conveniently gone to war against the USSR by then, he explored in elaborate detail
for Ott's benefit why such a contingency must not come about. Along the way, he
even made a couple of quite ingenious suggestions that would allow the Japanese
to block access to the Soviet Pacific port without having to go to war over this
issue.[367] He stressed time and again that this was a problem which it was really in
Japan's own interest to solve (the Americans must not be allowed to set a
precedent, Japan's prestige was at stake, increased Soviet military potential in the
Far East would one day be turned against it). While this approach fits seamlessly
with the aim of German diplomacy to instigate a Russo–Japanese clash in order to
wreck the talks between Washington and Tokyo, the beseeching words he used
could suggest that this was the first instance where a German policymaker had
realised the potential of Vladivostok as a conduit for Allied help.[368]

Any attempt to assess the extent to which this plea also reflected Hitler's
thinking at the time must remain tentative. Ribbentrop was hardly known for
conducting foreign policy against Hitler's wishes and the crisis facing
Heeresgruppe Mitte outside Smolensk could, of course, have encouraged as
yet underdeveloped ideas about the value of Japanese belligerence. If the

---

[365] Ibid. Ott's interlocutors are not identified by name.
[366] PA/AA, Handakten Ritter Japan, Bd. 18, Nr. 7633 'Ribbentrop an die Botschaft in Tokio
(25.8.1941)'.
[367] See ibid. With the geography of the region already favouring a Japanese blockade of
Vladivostok, Ribbentrop suggested the proclamation of a Japanese variant of the Pan-
American Neutrality Zone of 1939, which would formally bar access to all foreign
merchantmen carrying military hardware. Alternatively (or complementing such a
scheme), merchant vessels attempting to run the blockade should be intercepted, and
rather than sunk, be escorted to a Japanese port where their cargo would be impounded
and the vessel then released.
[368] Ibid.: 'I must warn Japan earnestly to follow this fateful course of action'; 'Should Japan
allow a single transport to pass, she would have lost the game.'

German leader reached such a conclusion, it dissipated quickly. Two documents from early September suggest quite strongly that Hitler's attitude
towards involving the Japanese was tepid at best. In a loose minute by
Ambassador Hasso von Etzdorf dated 8 September 1941, he is described as
being opposed to the idea of exerting serious pressure on the Japanese, because
this might be interpreted as a sign of weakness in Tokyo.[369] Confirmation of
this can be found in a diary entry recorded by the army chief of staff, Franz
Halder, two days later.[370]

As far as the potential of US deliveries to reverse Russian military fortunes
was concerned, the dictator was still sanguine. In the second week of
September, he is on record as explaining to his entourage that even a four-
year output by the US armaments industry would not suffice to make good the
losses suffered thus far by the USSR.[371] A few days later, Joseph Goebbels met
his Führer at the Wolfsschanze for another exchange of ideas. In contrast to
their last meeting a month before, the military situation in Russia had changed
out of all recognition: Leningrad had been cut off on 8 September, and on 15
September spearheads of Army Groups Centre and South had met to the east
of Kiev, encircling the bulk of five Soviet armies. Now the 'cauldron' was being
collapsed from all sides and every few hours new data came pouring in of the
number of prisoners taken and booty secured. Where Smolensk had appeared
to be a harbinger of stalemate, Kiev had all the makings of a war-winning
victory. Rather unsurprisingly, Hitler allowed himself to explore the options
still open to the Soviet government, especially if – as he correctly predicted –
the Donetsk with its coal and iron ore deposits were to be lost next. A sudden
collapse, retreat beyond the Urals or asking for terms of surrender, all appeared
to be definite possibilities.[372] Even so, he was not yet prepared to rule out the
possibility of Stalin continuing the struggle with Allied help and he even briefly
reflected on the possible routes this might take. The imminent German
advance into the Caucasus would soon enough block the Iranian route;
using Vladivostok was 'easier said than done', with deliveries then having to
undergo a time-consuming railway journey of several thousand kilometres.
The phrase 'easier said than done' may well have been a reference to expected
Japanese opposition to the use of that route and, by implication, an admission
that geographical remoteness by itself was not enough of a factor to stop it
from becoming an important asset to the enemy. In any case, in light of further

---

[369] 'Auszug aus den Notizen des Vertreters des Auswärtigen Amts beim OKH (n.d.)'; in:
ADAP, Serie D, Bd. XIII.1, p 381.

[370] KTB Halder III, p 219 (entry for 10 September 1941).

[371] '8. und 9.9.1941 nachts und 10.9.1941 mittags, abends und nachts (Wolfsschanze)'; in:
Henry Picker (ed.), Hitler's Tischgespräche im Führerhauptquartier (München:
Propyläen 2003), pp 93–8. Provided his frame of reference was US industrial output as
of late summer 1941, the estimate would in fact have been quite accurate.

[372] TB Goebbels, Bd. II.1, pp 481–7, esp. p 482 (entry for 24 September 1941).

deterioration of the Soviet position, Japan might still decide to finally cast its lot once and for all with the Axis.[373]

The Kriegsmarine had always been of two minds where the desirability of Japan joining the war against the USSR was concerned; to many of the admirals at the Seekriegsleitung, Japan's strategy should be aimed first and foremost at the Western powers and Singapore, with war against Russia only being a means towards this end or something to be avoided altogether.[374] In the three weeks that followed Goebbels's interview with Hitler, the Russian position deteriorated even further, with the Red Army losing around a million men at the battles of Vyazma, Bryansk and the Sea of Azov. Coming within a mere fortnight of the Kiev disaster, these events convinced most of the German leadership that the collapse of the USSR was, if not mere days away, then certainly something that would occur in the very near future, a development that could not but have a major impact on how the issue of Vladivostok was perceived.

In a conversation with Admiral Nomura in mid-October, *Vizeadmiral* Kurt Fricke, the Seekriegsleitung's chief of staff, did his utmost to actually dissuade his Japanese interlocutor from going to war against the USSR. Such a move might tie down the remainder of its army for years and, on account of the distances involved, might not even succeed in reopening the Trans-Siberian Railway within a reasonable time frame.[375] Worst of all, it would not even help Germany, since the Anglo–American shipments which thus far had made it to Vladivostok were 'completely irrelevant' and those following in their wake would arrive too late to make a difference.[376] Such a statement actually flew in the face of what officially was still accepted government policy and by rights should have earned Fricke a reprimand or worse. As it turned out, his estimate was fast becoming accepted consensus. Hitler himself had described the Red Army's situation as hopeless in conversation with the Italian foreign minister, Galeazzo Ciano, on the 25th and in a letter to Mussolini on the 29th. In light of the critical logistical situation facing the Axis forces in North Africa, he may well have exaggerated for effect. However, he had already expressed himself along very similar lines on the 24th to members of his entourage. In view of the disastrous Soviet situation he doubted that the Americans would be inclined to ship any goods at all, since this would be tantamount to supporting a lost cause; only if the Russians managed to put a new army in the field during the winter might they feel compelled to do so, and the distances involved in getting

---

[373] Ibid., p 484.

[374] For examples, see as well BA/MA, RM 12 II/250 'Kriegstagebuch Marineattache Tokio (entry for 24 October 1941)'.

[375] BA/MA, RM 7/253a 'Der Chef des Stabes der Seekriegsleitung. Vertraulich ! (15.10.1941)', esp. p 9.

[376] Ibid., pp 8–10.

goods from Vladivostok to where they were needed meant a long enough delay (he mentioned three months) to diminish or even negate the effect they might have.[377]

Further confirmation of this view can be found in the exchange he had with the Seekriegsleitung's chief of staff on 27 October. Fricke, who was standing in for his boss Raeder, had come to Führer's Headquarters for the monthly discussion of naval affairs. The German leader agreed with the admiral's assessment that a 'Japanese advance on Vladivostok by itself would not constitute a relief for German strategy; Japan's main strategy must be accomplished through [an] advance into the South'.[378] It appears that this rather momentous change of strategy had not been communicated to Ott in Tokyo, when on 18 November 1941 he cabled Ribbentrop to inform him of the first Japanese proposals that Germany join Tokyo in an upcoming war with the United States. On his own initiative, he strongly recommended that any such move should be tied to the issue of the often promised, but as yet unrealised Japanese blockade of Vladivostok.[379] He also raised this issue of his own volition with one of his Japanese interlocutors on 23 November.[380] Ribbentrop himself raised the option with Oshima on 3 December, when the ambassador came to see him to ask for an interview with Hitler. Even if the foreign minister was taking his cue from Ott in Tokyo on this occasion, this does not mean that he did so out of any concern over the situation outside Moscow. He had already made the same suggestion to Oshima on 28 November, but only as a last-minute resort after the poorly briefed Japanese ambassador had shown himself completely clueless as to the war plans being hatched in Tokyo. No doubt fearing that this might reflect another last-minute U-turn on the part of the Japanese government, Ribbentrop had then fallen back on the policy of torpedoing a US–Japanese détente by pushing Tokyo and Moscow into a confrontation.

His conversation with Oshima on 3 December took place against a backdrop of heightened tension in the Pacific and was a clear pointer towards a looming US–Japanese confrontation. However, since over the previous two or three days Ribbentrop had issued instructions regarding future propaganda work in

---

[377] 'Sonntag, 25. Oktober 1941. Militärische Lage, 24.10'; in: Vogt (ed.), *Herbst 1941*, pp 103–7, esp. p 105. The phrase used by Hitler to describe the current Soviet predicament was *'augenblicklichen Sauhaufen'* ('the current mess').

[378] KTB Seekriegsleitung, Teil A (entry for 28 October 1941). This assessment may or may not have been influenced by reports that the Trans-Siberian Railway had collapsed under the weight of traffic being run through it. See ibid., p 458 (entry for 27 October 1941).

[379] PA/AA, StS Japan, Bd. 5, '615 'Ott an Reichsaußenminister (18.11.1941)'.

[380] PA/AA, StS Japan, Bd. 5, '615 Ott an Auswärtiges Amt. Für Herrn Reichsaußenminister (23.11.1941)'.

the USA, this clearly indicated that war with the USA was not yet regarded as a certainty.[381] Thus, it stands to reason that by mentioning the possibility of an exclusion zone for the second time in five days, he was simply hedging his bets. Three days later, after Hitler had committed to joining the Japanese in war against the USA, Japanese Foreign Minister Togo rejected the idea of an exclusion zone. Ribbentrop promptly dropped the request.[382]

The last high-level assessment of the USSR's residual military potential predating Pearl Harbor is a comprehensive report by *Fremde Heere Ost* which bears the date 1 December 1941. It runs to 139 pages and offers an exhaustive review of the human and material resources still available to Stalin after the loss of much of the western Soviet Union.[383] Though a reference in the text to the recent outbreak of the Pacific War[384] indicates that it was, in fact, backdated and hence in all likelihood not available before Pearl Harbor, it still gives a valuable insight into how OKH's military intelligence section perceived Soviet war-making potential in the late autumn of 1941. Lend-Lease is mentioned several times in the text, even to the extent of giving the seal of approval to the *Wehrwirtschafts- und Rüstungsamt's* rather ominous prediction of 22 October that US imports could conceivably make up for the devastating loss and disruption suffered by the Soviet economy so far. With regards to the importance of Vladivostok, the report is downright contradictory, one sub-chapter pronouncing the port to be 'blockaded' on account of the outbreak of hostilities,[385] with other references to it making no such assumption. A common thread that does run through the *Kriegswehrmacht der UdSSR*, however, is the – reasonably accurate – estimate that Anglo–American help would not have an appreciable impact before May 1942, when the three German army groups would awake from their hibernation and resume

---

[381] PA/AA, StS USA, Bd. 10 'Covering note signed by Dieckhoff (2.12.1941)'

[382] No trace exists of this exchange in German records. For a reconstruction from Japanese sources, see Gerhard Krebs, 'Deutschland und Pearl Harbor', in: *Historische Zeitschrift*, Bd. 253 (1991), pp 313–69, esp. pp 351, 355.

[383] BA/MA, RH D 7 11/4 'Oberkommando des Heeres. Gen.St.d.H. OQu IV – Abt. Fremde Heere Ost (II) Nr. 4700/41 geh. Die Kriegswehrmacht der Union der Sozialistischen Sowjetrepubliken (UdSSR). (Stand Dezember 1941). Teil I: Text (1.12.1941)'.

[384] Ibid., p 104.

[385] Ibid., p 104. An identical reference to such a blockade in an OKW assessment analysing the impact of Japan's entry into the war appears to indicate that this misconception was widely held in German military circles during the first week of the Pacific war. See BA/ MA, RM 7/258 'WFSt/Abt.L (I K Op) Nr. 44 2173/41 g.K. Chefs. Überblick über die Bedeutung des Kriegseintritts der U.S.A. und Japans (14.12.1941)'. The Seekriegsleitung' s war diary first referred to a Japanese intention to blockade the Soviet port 'if possible', followed by another entry two days later which confirmed such a move, see KTB Seekriegsleitung, Teil A (entries for 10 and 12 December 1941). A military briefing for Joseph Goebbels around that time also reflected this erroneous assessment: TB Goebbels, Bd. II.2, p 479 (entry for 12 December 1941).

large-scale campaigning.[386] According to the German intelligence report, the reasons for this were manifold, but all tied to the geography of the region. Archangelsk (the bigger of the Arctic ports) was known to be icebound until May, thus severely limiting the flow of goods that could be conveyed by that route. The Persian Gulf route was limited in its impact by the lack of a line linking the Iranian and Soviet railway networks. Only by laboriously shifting goods onto river barges and trucks could either a Soviet railhead or a Caspian port be reached. The latter option permitted much better economies of scale, but was ruled out for the time being by the fact that ports and river estuaries on the north shore of the Caspian Sea were themselves icebound until April.[387] Finally, the authors addressed the extent to which the Soviet railway network would be able to cope with the colossal task of ferrying troops, shifting back dismantled factories and supplying industrial facilities which had just lost their Donetsk coal source with alternative supplies brought in over ridiculous distances from Siberia, all on a network with far less built-in redundancy than that which had been available in the western regions of the USSR. A major influx of Western goods would only further tax an infrastructure already on the brink of collapse. When the report expressed the considered opinion that the time needed to stabilise the rail network would no doubt be 'considerable', the implication was clear:[388] it would come too late to save the USSR from defeat in the spring and summer of 1942.

Within a fortnight of Hitler's speech to the Reichstag, the German high command was forced to reassess its estimates regarding Lend-Lease and its future impact on Soviet fighting power. The second half of December and most of January saw *Heeresgruppe Mitte* desperately fending off a whole series of ferocious Soviet attacks.[389] First to give up large swathes of territory were 2. *Panzerarmee* and 2. *Armee*, when they collapsed the large bulges to the east and south of Tula, and by Christmas Eve found themselves struggling to hold a line that followed the course of the River Oka. This state of affairs made it possible for a substantial Soviet raiding force to slip past them and threaten the highway bearing much of the army group's supply. In the meantime, 4. *Armee*, which had been the bulwark of Bock's defence in the days after 5 December, found its position compromised when its southern flank was turned by an attack by 49th Army between 17th and 19th of December. On the 24th, two Soviet armies

---

[386] BA/MA, RH D 7 11/4 'Oberkommando des Heeres, Gen.St.d.H., OQu 4 – Abt. Fremde Heere Ost (II) Nr. 4700/41 geh. Die Kriegswehrmacht der Union der Sozialistischen Sowjetrepubliken (UdSSR). (Stand Dezember 1941). Teil I: Text (1.12.1941)', p 107.

[387] Ibid., pp 112, 132.

[388] Ibid., p 121

[389] This campaign has recently become the subject of a major revisionist work. See David Stahel, *Retreat from Moscow: A New History of Germany's Winter Campaign, 1941–1942* (New York: Farrar, Straus & Giroux 2019).

penetrated the seam between Panzergruppe 4 and 4. Armee, threatening to render the latter's position wholly untenable. Guarding the army group's northern shoulder was 9. *Armee*, which had one of its corps ground down between 29 and 31 December. The overly ambitious Soviet plan governing these moves, which entailed an encirclement of the entire army group, appeared to be feasible for a few days. Apart from a number of Soviet operational blunders,[390] what saved the Germans in these desperate days, was the meagreness of the resources available to the Red Army (the number of tanks in particular was wholly inadequate to the vastness of the task in hand[391]) and the fact that Stalin decided to go over to the offensive in other parts of the front as well. In a manner reminiscent of Manstein's prediction, a double amphibious descent on the Kerch Peninsula (25 and 29 December) forced the Germans to immediately terminate operations against Sevastopol and face this new threat. Kerch was lost, and with a third Soviet landing on the west coast of the Crimea (5 January 1942), an evacuation of the entire peninsula appeared to be on the cards for a couple of days. In the north, two Soviet groupings began operations with a view to relieving Leningrad and disrupting German communications along the seam of Army Groups Centre and North on 7 and 9 January, respectively. Finally, on 18 January 1942 in the Ukraine, one of 17. *Armee*'s corps failed to prevent 57th Army from carving out a major bulge in the front line and capturing the army's supply depot. The situation eventually stabilised in the second half of January, after Hitler rescinded his order forbidding any retreat. By that time, the conflicts that had arisen between the dictator and his field commanders over the extent to which his directive was to be applied to the letter or not, led to one army group commander suffering a stroke (Reichenau) as well two army group commanders (Bock and Leeb) and one army commander (Strauß) being sent away on extended sick leave. Four army commanders (Falkenhorst, Guderian, Hoepner and Kübler), together with a number of corps commanders, received straight sackings. When set against OKW's and OKH's expectations of slightly over a month ago, the scene was one of utter devastation.

Even though Allied equipment and weapons' systems did not as yet feature in a major way in any of the attacks raining down on the *Ostheer*, these events inevitably brought in their train a revision of the rose-tinted estimates of Soviet residual strength from autumn 1941. This process first manifested itself in a rather improbable fashion, namely an exchange of diplomatic notes between the new allies, Germany and Japan. On 13 December, the Japanese expressed the wish to complement the alliance treaty of 11 December with a document

---

[390] For a few examples, see Reinhardt, *Wende*, pp 235 (fn 275), 241–5.

[391] In mid-December 1941, the Red Army units engaged in combat operations had at their disposal 1,958 tanks (roughly 10 per cent of what had been available on the eve of the German invasion). This figure included part of the British tanks that had arrived in the country by then (361). See Lopukhovsky and Kavalerchik, *Price of Victory*, pp 100–1.

that would spell out the specifics of Axis military cooperation in the field. When set against the backdrop of the lacklustre manner in which the German leadership had addressed the issue of Vladivostok in previous months, these documents show a remarkable zeal on the part of German decision makers to broaden their strategic horizons. Hitler was first past the post, when he suggested to Japanese Ambassador Oshima on 14 December that the Japanese find a way of blocking American access to Vladivostok. It is significant that this should have happened on the very day when he finally realised that *Heeresgruppe Mitte* was facing a serious crisis outside Moscow.[392] Oshima's answer as given in the German minutes appears to suggest that he had either failed to understand the question or preferred to prevaricate.[393] On 23 December, OKH expressed an interest in having the Japanese interdict Allied supply routes in the Arabian Sea which fed the Iranian route for Lend-Lease goods.[394] A day later, the same command elaborated on this point by expressing the expectation that Germany would 'demand' of Japan that it maintain current force levels in Manchuria to tie down the Far Eastern Army and block access to Vladivostok forthwith. Finally, the hope was expressed that Japan would enter the war against the USSR after its 'southern operation' was finished.[395] This agenda jarred with Ribbentrop's concern that any conditions put to Japan might cause ill will, possibly even to the point of making its government reconsider its political options, a notion not too far-fetched in light of the territories already seized.[396]

In the end the matter was put before Hitler and a compromise reached. The German side would not insist on any conditions or changes to the draft treaty, but OKW's representative at the signing ceremony would be given an opportunity to bring up these issues with the Japanese representatives in an informal manner. A first draft of the note listing these points

[392] 'Empfang des japanischen Botschafters General Oshima durch den Führer am 14.12.1941 von 13–14 Uhr in Anwesenheit des Reichsaußenministers (n.d.)'; in: ADAP, Serie E, Bd. I, pp 17–21.

[393] Ibid. Oshima attempted to reassure the German dictator by reminding him that all the straits giving access to the Sea of Japan were so narrow that they could be covered by land-based artillery, a rather disingenuous answer which completely missed the wider point.

[394] PA/AA, Handakten Ritter Japan 17, 'Nr. 7632, Der Chef des Sonderstabes HWK im Oberkommando der Wehrmacht und Leiter der militärischen Kommission des Dreimächtepaktes an den Herrn Reichsaußenminister. z.Hd. Herrn Botschafter Dr. Ritter (23.12.1941)'.

[395] PA/AA, Handakten Ritter Japan 17, 'Nr. 7632, Der Chef des Sonderstabes HWK im Oberkommando der Wehrmacht und Leiter der militärischen Kommission des Dreimächtepaktes an den Herrn Reichsaussenminister, z.Hd. Herrn Botschafter Dr. Ritter (24.12.1941)'.

[396] See the loose minute on this subject prepared by Ribbentrop for Hitler's attention: PA/AA, Handakten Ritter Japan 17, 'Nr. 7631, Für den Vortrag beim Führer über die militärische Vereinbarung mit Japan (30.12.1941)'.

had been couched in a language that would have been unthinkable only two weeks before. In it, the issue of Japanese assistance in interdicting Allied access to ports capable of processing Lend-Lease goods in bulk (Vladivostok was singled out) was described as being 'a matter of urgency' (*'dringend'*).[397] A revised version of the same document a few days later dispensed with the implied urgency and in fact even recognised that the Americans did not appear to be making much use of Vladivostok at the moment. It went on to say, however, that a possibility existed that Lend-Lease deliveries would start arriving in the Far Eastern port at some point in the future; in this case, the German side expressed the wish that the Japanese Navy would interdict any such traffic.[398]

On 2 January, it was Ribbentrop's turn again. In a meeting with Ambassador Oshima, he expressed German 'interest' that Japan should continue to tie down as many Red Army units in the Far East as possible, and for good measure initiate hostilities in May. Oshima, however, did not budge and this time produced a completely new argument. He insisted that in light of the absence of the bulk of the Imperial Japanese Navy on operations in the South Pacific, the 100 submarines available to the Red Navy at Vladivostok constituted too much of a threat against Japan's domestic sea lanes.[399] Ribbentrop's riposte that surely it should be possible to pre-empt such a threat by a Pearl Harbor-style air strike may have reflected his zeal to get the Japanese moving in the direction of the Soviet Pacific base, sheer incredulity in light of his own familiarity with the very limited impact the Soviet submarine arm had thus far had in the Baltic and Black seas, or both. Even so, Oshima held his ground and limited himself to a promise not to allow US goods on Soviet merchantmen passage through one of the four straits giving access to the Sea of Japan.[400] Oshima's stonewalling on the subject of Vladivistok was in all likelihood the reason why Hitler did not bring it up when the Japanese ambassador

---

[397] PA/AA, Handakten Ritter 17, 'Nr. 7631, Entwurf eines Schreibens von Generalfeldmarschall Keitel (n.d.; 30.12.1941)'. The date on this document coincides with the lowest point of German military fortunes in Russia.

[398] PA/AA, Handakten Ritter 17, 'Nr. 7631, 'Stichworte für eine Unterredung des Generalfeldmarschalls Keitel mit Nomura (und Banzai) nach der Unterzeichnung, am besten bei dem Frühstück (n.d.)'.

[399] 'Aufzeichnung über die Besprechung des Herrn Reichsaußenministers mit dem japanischen Botschafter Oshima am 2. Januar 1942 in Steinort (2.1.1942)'; in ADAP, Serie E, Bd. I, pp 148–55, esp. p 150. Submarines available to the Soviet Pacific Fleet at the time numbered around 90 in total. See Jürgen Rohwer, *Chronology of the War at Sea, 1939–1945: The Naval History of World War Two* (Annapolis: USNIP 2005), p 80.

[400] 'Aufzeichnung über die Besprechung des Herrn Reichsaußenministers mit dem japanischen Botschafter Oshima am 2. Januar 1942 in Steinort (2.1.1942)'; in: ADAP, Serie E, Bd. I, p 150.

met him for a two-hour interview the next day.[401] When Ribbentrop, who was also present, at one point interjected that Japan might be able to invade the Soviet Pacific provinces by May, it was Hitler who was ready to concede the point that Japan had to concentrate its assets against the targets that would loom once it reached the Malay Barrier, namely India and Australia.[402]

In the three weeks after Hitler's declaration of war on the USA, the German leadership – though to varying degrees in individual cases – came round to a major reassessment of the potential of Lend-Lease and Vladivostok's role in it, even though the facts as such were not novel: they had been spelled out with remarkable prescience in Thomas' memorandum of 22 October. The events of those days brought about the implied admission that the USSR was almost certain to go on fighting at a terrific pace and largely unassisted throughout the winter and well into spring. The fact that Lend-Lease was never likely to make a major impact of its own before mid-1942 had always underpinned German calculations; both the comparatively small volume of deliveries Roosevelt had pledged himself to, as well as the shortfall in what was actually delivered, would go a long way towards bearing them out.[403] Before mid-December, however, these estimates had been predicated on a USSR in terminal decline, the rate of which would only be increased by any attempt on the part of the Soviet leadership to go over to the offensive. It had become obvious by the turn of the year that this cornerstone of German strategy had just collapsed.

---

[401] In those months, a residual Soviet concern over Japanese reactions meant that most of the goods shipped on Soviet vessels from the US west coast to Vladivostok were of a non-military nature (especially foodstuffs and petroleum products). No evidence has as yet surfaced that Hitler could have known of this. The history of the Pacific Lend-Lease route is as yet inadequately covered in the existing literature. A few glimpses of its workings can be found in Jones, *Roads to Russia*, pp 112–13, 123, 209–10, as well as in Joan Beaumont, *Comrades in Arms: British Aid to Russia 1941–1945* (London: Davis-Poynter 1980), pp 82–3, 105, 167.

[402] 'Aufzeichnung über das Gespräch des Führers mit Botschafter Oshima am 3. Januar 1942 im Beisein des Reichsaußenministers in der Wolfschanze von 16.15–18.00 Uhr' (n. d.); in: ADAP, Serie E, Bd. I, pp 157–64.

[403] With regards to the tanks (2,250 pledged, 2,249 delivered) and Jeeps (5,000 pledged, 6,823 delivered) promised to the Soviet government under the First Protocol (October 1941 to June 1942), the US administration did remarkably well. As far as planes (1,800 pledged, 1,285 delivered) and armoured scout cars (624 pledged, 400 delivered) were concerned, the shortfall was important. In the case of trucks (85,000 pledged, 36,865 delivered), 37 mm anti-tank guns (756 pledged, 63 delivered) and 90 mm anti-aircraft guns (152 pledged, 4 delivered), it was nothing short of disastrous. The Germans were conscious of the fact that some of the slack would be picked up by British deliveries, but since this in turn implied creating a greater need for more Lend-Lease deliveries on their part, they were not unduly worried. Wolfgang Schlauch, *Rüstungshilfe der USA an die Verbündeten im Zweiten Weltkrieg* (Darmstadt: Wehr und Wissen 1967), p 152.

7.4.1   Conclusion: Lend-Lease

There are not many statements on record from Hitler on the subject of Lend-Lease in 1941 and some of these are rather inconclusive. When seen against the backdrop of military events, it appears that with regards to the military situation in Russia he was by and large inclined to dismiss its potential, because he felt any goods delivered would be too small in number and, in any case, come too late to make a meaningful contribution to the Red Army's struggle. Only the second half of August appears to strike a dissonant note, with some genuine anxiety on Hitler's part over the logjam outside Smolensk; Ribbentrop's telegram of 25 August, which warned the Japanese against allowing US shipments into Vladivostok, could conceivably have been a reflection of this anxiety; on the other hand, it would have been perfectly consistent with his strategy to alienate Japan from the USA by goading them into war with the USSR. The contradictory evidence on Hitler's interest in mid-November (as articulated by Halder) in a drive for Vologda poses a similar problem: it may well have reflected the dictator's interest in blocking Allied weapons shipments, but this interpretation is rather contradicted by the fact that the crucial role of the Arctic ports in the processing of Lend-Lease shipments is completely absent from the discussions he had with the naval leadership throughout this period. Thus, we have to assume that his very emphatic agreement with Fricke on the subject of Vladivostok's limited potential (27 October) remained broadly unchanged throughout the following weeks, or at least was not subjected to the kind of reassessment that might have caused him to include it in the negotiations with Tokyo, which both preceded and followed Pearl Harbor. He did, however, broach the subject of the Soviet Pacific base in the talks with Oshima on 14 December, thus indicating at least a partial reconsideration; the meeting with the naval leadership on 29 December provides hard evidence of a truly radical reassessment of the impact of Lend-Lease on his part. It is obvious that this process took place in close synchronicity with the crisis facing *Heeresgruppe Mitte*, a crisis that on 11 December had still appeared to be of manageable proportions.

The available evidence thus suggests very strongly that Hitler was willing to disregard the impact Lend-Lease might have on Barbarossa for the very simple reason that by late October and early November he was convinced the Red Army was, if not quite a broken reed, certainly past the point where Allied help would be able to pull it back from the brink.

8

The Battle of the Atlantic

8.1   Introduction

As far as waging the Battle of the Atlantic was concerned, the 1940–1 period saw Adolf Hitler in a position frequently at odds with the image we have of him today. While in continental Europe the flimsiest pretext was good enough to escalate the conflict and invade yet another country, Kriegsmarine operations on the high seas were, if not crippled, than certainly somewhat hamstrung by the increasingly muscular deployment of units of the US Navy's Atlantic Fleet. By the early summer of 1941, this had led to a state of affairs where Germany's dictator was issuing orders calling for his U-boats to refrain from engaging unidentified escorts lest they turn out to be US vessels. In doing so, he showed an astonishing willingness to go to what seemed like self-defeating lengths to prevent the cold war with the USA from turning hot. At the same time, the kill rate achieved by German submersibles remained well below the threshold deemed necessary to effectively interdict Britain's lifelines through the second half of 1941.

The afternoon of 11 December would witness the termination of this bizarre state of affairs. Forty-eight hours after ordering Kriegsmarine commander-in-chief, Erich Raeder, to rescind all orders that had been given for the sparing of US vessels, the German dictator stepped up to the lectern prepared for him at the Kroll Opera to read out the speech justifying his declaration of war on the USA. While it also featured the inevitable verbiage about 'international Jewdom', another topic took up rather more space. In harking back to the days of 1939–40, he listed a litany of cases where German merchant vessels making for Germany had been trailed, boarded or delivered into British hands by the US Navy.[1] On top of that, by allowing British warships the use of US shipyards under Lend-Lease legislation, occupying Iceland and issuing the shoot-on-sight order of 11 September, the American President had put

---

[1] 'Rede vor dem Großdeutschen Reichstag 11. Dezember 1941'; in: Philipp Bouhler (ed.), *Der großdeutsche Freiheitskampf. Reden Adolf Hitlers, III. Band (16. März 1941 bis 15. März 1942)* (München: Franz Eher 1943).

Germany in a position where it faced a stark choice: to declare war or allow its submarine campaign to be 'rendered worthless', just like its predecessor had been in 1915–16.[2] The fact that he bothered to go into so much detail over this issue appears to lend credence to General Walther Warlimont's post-war interpretation that the dictator had had to suppress 'his mounting anger' over many months of US transgressions and that the declaration of war was tantamount to releasing this fury 'with a blast'.[3]

The problem with this train of thought is that it is not really borne out by statements the dictator made pre-Pearl Harbor: only in the days and weeks after he received news of the Japanese strike against the Pacific Fleet did he stress this point, almost as if seeking to reassure himself of the rationale behind the momentous decision he had just made.[4] While the undeclared US–German naval war of 1941 features prominently in every history of World War II, thus far it has only been analysed within the framework of its operational impact.[5] This chapter will endeavour to find an answer to the question of whether the information put before Hitler at any point in the summer and autumn of 1941 would have led him to conclude that the US Navy's intervention in the Battle of the Atlantic had been instrumental in stalling the Kriegsmarine's war effort against Britain's Atlantic lifeline.

[2] Ibid.

[3] 'Interview with General der Artillerie Walter Warlimont by Major Kenneth W. Hechler (28.7.1945)'; in: Donald S. Detwiler (ed.), *World War II German Military Studies: A Collection of 213 Special Reports on the Second World War Prepared by Former Officers of the Wehrmacht for the United States Army*, Vol. 2, Part II (New York and London: Garland Publishing 1979), p 12. My thanks to my colleague Simon Trew for drawing my attention to this source.

[4] Elke Fröhlich (ed.), *Die Tagebücher von Joseph Goebbels. Teil II.* Bd. 2 (München et al: K.G. Saur 1996), pp 464, 494 (entries for 10 and 13 December 1941); 'Empfang des japanischen Botschafters General Oshima durch den Führer am 14.12.1941 von 13 bis 14 Uhr in Anwesenheit des Reichsaußenministers'; in: *Akten zur deutschen auswärtigen Politik (ADAP)*, Serie E, Bd. I (Göttingen: Vandenhoeck & Rupprecht 1969) pp 17–21; Hans Frank, *Im Angesicht des Galgens* (Neuhaus bei Schliersee: Eigenverlag 1955), p 397; '23.3.1942 Montag abends (Wolfsschanze)'; in: Henry Picker (ed.), *Hitlers Tischgespräche im Führerhauptquartier* (München: Propyläen 2003), pp 186–7. Also Henrik Eberle and Mathias Uhl (eds.), *Das Buch Hitler. Geheimdossier des NKWD für Josef W. Stalin, zusammengestellt aufgrund der Verhörprotokolle des Persönlichen Adjutanten Hitlers, Otto Günsche und des Kammerdieners Heinz Linge, Moskau 1948/49* (Bergisch Gladbach: Lübbe 2005), p 157.

[5] H. P. Willmott, *The Great Crusade* (London: Michael Joseph 1989), p 184; W. J. R. Gardner, *Decoding History: The Battle of the Atlantic and Ultra* (Annapolis: USNIP 1999), pp 148, 176–7; Adam Tooze, *The Wages of Destruction* (London: Allen Lane 2006), pp 399–400; Antony Beevor, *The Second World War* (London: Weidenfeld & Nicholson 2012), p 279; Phillips Payson O'Brien, *How the War Was Won* (Cambridge: CUP 2015), pp 182–3, have all made a case for the Atlantic Fleet's contribution in 1941 having been important. David Kaiser, *No End Save Victory: How FDR Led the Nation into War* (New York: Basic Books 2014), p 278, sees the American role as 'marginal'.

8.2   The Kriegsmarine's War on British Commerce until July 1941

Admiral Erich Raeder, the Reichsmarine (as of May 1935: Kriegsmarine) commander-in-chief, had watched Hitler's accession to power with some trepidation. This was down to the latter having repeatedly expressed scathing criticism of Imperial Germany's bungled naval arms race with Britain, criticism which he then extended to the modest naval rearmament undertaken by the late Weimar Republic in the early 1930s. In due course, however, the two men found common ground. Hitler assured the admiral that a war against Britain was something he could safely rule out for the foreseeable future.[6] Raeder was greatly relieved by this and delighted to discover that Germany's new ruler had after all discovered a place in his heart for capital ships. By 1935 Hitler was even making changes to existing blueprints in order to give the next generation of battleships more displacement and heavier guns.[7] Along the way, he had acquired a knowledge of naval hardware that was quite detailed and impressed many a visitor. His grasp of matters of naval strategy, however, was far shakier and usually limited to the sphere of force projection or the interdiction of the same.[8] An initial fascination with capital ships could be traced back to the power of their symbolism as the embodiment of the modern state's power.[9]

By the spring of 1938 Hitler's pledge to keep Britain neutral in any future conflict was starting to look increasingly brittle, and by October that year it had collapsed altogether. Raeder sought a way out of this dilemma by suggesting to the dictator that all building work on battleships be stopped for the time being and shipyard space and workers allocated to building additional *Panzerschiffe* instead. By virtue of its 280 mm (11-inch) armament, this type might still have passed muster as a battleship in 1914, but by the late 1930s was closer to most heavy cruisers. Its diesel engine plant gave it superior range and proven reliability, thus making it ideal for overseas commerce warfare. However, the dictator rejected this suggestion and insisted on continuing with the projected battleship designs. He even briefly reallocated resources to the navy which led to the Z-Plan of January 1939. Its stated aim was that in addition to 2 battleships still in the process of being built and the 2 battlecruisers, 3 *Panzerschiffe*, 3 heavy cruisers, 6 light cruisers, 22 destroyers and 20 torpedo boats currently in service or being fitted out, the following units would

---

[6] On the early relationship between the two men, see Keith Bird, *Erich Raeder. Admiral of the Third Reich* (Annapolis: USNIP 2006), pp 91–102.

[7] Ibid., p 124.

[8] For a pithy analysis of Hitler's grasp of naval warfare, the reader is referred to the memoirs of his naval adjutant: Karl Jesko von Puttkamer, *Die unheimliche See. Hitler und die Kriegsmarine* (Wien and München: Karl Kühne 1952), pp 11–12.

[9] Otto Dietrich, *12 Jahre mit Hitler* (Köln: Atlas 1955), p 115; Nicolaus von Below, *Als Hitlers Adjutant* (Selent: Pour le Merite 1999 rp), p 150.

be joining the fleet by 1947–8: 4 aircraft carriers, 6 battleships, 5 heavy cruisers, 15 *Panzerschiffe*, 44 light cruisers, 68 destroyers, 90 torpedo boats and 249 U-boats.

Raeder, realising he might soon find himself in a strategic situation even more daunting than that faced by his counterparts in 1914, attempted to find a role for a fleet that on paper was structured to challenge the British (and possibly the Americans) by the mid-1940s, but would struggle to do more than commerce raiding in 1939–40. Taking his cue from his own research into commerce warfare in World War I,[10] he tentatively developed a concept that called for the formation of task forces made up of two capital ships, possibly supported by an aircraft carrier, which would then operate in the Atlantic for months on end.[11] Pressure thus exercised would force the enemy to withdraw naval assets from other theatres, though to exactly what strategic end was never made clear. Another loose end – Britain's commanding position at both exits from the North Sea – was reflected in the demand increasingly mooted by naval leaders in 1938–9 for bases in Scandinavia and/or Western Europe.

The outbreak of World War II found the Kriegsmarine in a weak position in a variety of ways. To begin with, Erich Raeder soon revealed himself to be less than adept as a political operator. In the Third Reich, time spent with (or just near) Hitler translated into power. The admiral developed a routine of travelling to Führer's Headquarters and briefing Hitler there about once every three to four weeks. In contrast to his successor Dönitz, who would usually make a point of arriving on the eve of the briefing and then staying for another day, thus allowing himself a maximum amount of time to interface with other power brokers of the Third Reich, Raeder would always clear off as fast as he decently could. On the other hand, he would not hesitate to demand the dictator's attention on matters wholly unconnected to the war effort but concerning the 'honour' of the navy. In this manner, the marriage of one of his officers to a lady of supposedly ill repute could be important enough to warrant an unscheduled meeting. A bizarre topic such as this could easily end up taking an hour or two of the dictator's time, leaving him mystified and exasperated in equal measure.[12]

As far as the navy's combat assets were concerned, the surface element available in September 1939 (two battlecruisers, two *Panzerschiffe*, one heavy

---

[10] Bird, *Raeder*, pp 51–6.

[11] Ibid., pp 116–31, for an interesting analysis of the viability of this concept. The prospect of such a task force operating against convoys on the North Atlantic route had caused the Royal Navy some concern before the war. On this, see Marcus Faulkner, '"A Most Disagreeable Problem": Admiralty Perceptions of the Kriegsmarine's Aircraft Carrier Capability'; in: Christopher Bell and Marcus Faulkner (eds.), *Decision in the Atlantic: The Allies and the Longest Campaign of the Second World War* (Lexington: Kentucky UP 2019), pp 169–94.

[12] For an example, see Below, *Adjutant*, p 170–1.

Figure 8.1 Erich Raeder with Admiral Adolf von Trotha: sometimes a picture really is worth a thousand words. Here, an adjutant presents Trotha with the scale model of a capital ship while Erich Raeder looks on wistfully. (Keystone-France/Gamma-Keystone via Getty Images)

cruiser, six light cruisers) made it the weakest of the great power navies by a wide margin, its good quality notwithstanding. The subsurface element amounted to a mere fifty-seven combat-ready submarines, only twenty-seven of them ocean-going types capable of operating west of the British Isles. These submarines were basically improved versions of the diesel-electric U-boats of 1918. With the exception of improved surface range and a few enhancements aimed at increasing their military potential, they shared all the features of their predecessors:[13] very basic creature comforts, extremely low underwater speed and range, surface speed adequate for stalking a convoy but not most modern warships.[14] What set them apart from their World War I predecessors was the

---

[13] Apart from improved periscopes they also incorporated two innovations not available in 1918: discharging a torpedo no longer left a large telltale air bubble pinpointing the submarine's position; and surface attacks could be carried out with the help of the UZO (*Überwasserzieloptik*) apparatus, whereas in World War I it had mainly been a matter of guesswork.

[14] In point of fact, the two main U-boat types of World War II were based on designs from World War I . The *U-81* to *U-86* subseries built at the Germaniawerft in Kiel was the rough blueprint for the transoceanic Type IX, while the medium Type VII's DNA could be traced back to the UB III design of 1915–16, which had spawned nearly 100 U-boats

wealth of experience acquired during 1914–18 and a centralised command structure under the *Befehlshaber der U-Boote* (BdU), Karl Dönitz,[15] which was a vast improvement over the cumbersome arrangements prevailing during World War I.[16] Dönitz had also worked out a strategy for undertaking a renewed war against Allied shipping, specifically designed to overcome the tactic of convoying which had checkmated the U-boats in 1917–18. A group of several U-boats would search the shipping lanes in a rake-like formation with several kilometres between them, the idea being that although individual ships might manage to slip through the net, a major convoy would not. When one of the U-boats established contact with the pack's prey, it would call the others to the scene, making use of improved radio technology which had not been available in 1918. The coordination of the group was to lie in the hands of a flotilla commander travelling for that purpose on one of the U-boats. Attacks were preferably to be carried out at night and on the surface, thus negating the advantage conferred on the Royal Navy by its possession of sonar – an active underwater search device using high frequency sound waves which every British destroyer carried.[17]

Thus it was that Germany went to war with a hybrid fleet. Plans to expand the U-boat fleet many times over were drawn up within a month of the war's outbreak.[18] This 'expanded U-boat building programme' called for a monthly production of thirty submersibles, which (allowing for losses) would have given Raeder an underwater armada of 368 by the end of 1941. The scheme was soon compromised by two factors. The preparation of the two other services for the invasion of Western Europe took absolute precedence and

put to operational use in the second half of the Great War. See Bodo Herzog, *Deutsche U-Boote 1906–1966* (München: J.F. Lehmanns 1968, rp 1990) p. 50, 58, 195.

[15] Title adopted on 17 October 1939 with his promotion to *Konteradmiral* (rear admiral).

[16] In 1914–18 German submarines had come under four different operational commands: the flotillas based in the North Sea were part of the High Seas Fleet; those based in occupied Belgium took their orders from *Marinekorps Flandern*; while those (starting in May 1915) sent to the Mediterranean Command were subordinated to the admiralty. Even the few boats detached to the Baltic were part of the local command's order of battle. See Joachim Schröder, *Die U-Boote des Kaisers. Die Geschichte des deutschen U-Bootkrieges gegen Großbritannien im Ersten Weltkrieg* (Bonn: Bernard & Graefe 2003) pp 44–5.

[17] Naval units dedicated to anti-submarine warfare (ASW) in World War I had been limited to sound-detecting hydrophones (= passive sonar) in locating their prey. This device gave only a very general indication as to a submerged submarine's bearing, speed and depth. Sonar was first trialled in 1919, too late obviously to be of use in World War I. By 1939, it was still limited in its range (generally 1,500 m on either beam), but gave accurate readings for bearing and speed. Calculating the depth took an experienced operator until the summer of 1944, when improved sets were introduced.

[18] 'Vortrag des Oberbefehlshabers der Kriegsmarine beim Führer am 10. Oktober 1939, 17.00 Uhr'; in: Gerhard Wagner (ed.), *Lagevorträge des Oberbefehlshabers der Kriegsmarine vor Hitler 1939–1945* (München: J.F. Lehmanns Verlag 1972), pp 26–9.

soon led to a reduced quota of twenty-one U-boats per month,[19] and even that would not be met until June 1942.[20] In addition, the crucially important allocation of labour and shipyard space continued to reflect Raeder's zeal for finding a role for his surface units well into 1942. The fact that the Z-Plan was shelved did not by itself amount to much, since work had not even started on the majority of the ships it provided for. Only the immediate cancellation of some or all of the major naval units, which had recently been launched, but were still in the process of being fitted out (battleships *Bismarck* and *Tirpitz*, heavy cruisers *Prinz Eugen*, *Blücher* and *Seydlitz*, aircraft carrier *Graf Zeppelin*) and tying up thousands of workers, could have brought a radical shift in favour of the U-boat arm.[21] Hitler is on record as making a rather half-hearted suggestion to that end, but Raeder was adamant that such a move would bring only little gain and hence not justify the upset this would cause to his building programme.[22] The dictator never raised the topic again, but before the end of the year another issue arose which provided the first glimpse of the different priorities the two men attached to commerce warfare with surface units. When the pocket battleship *Graf Spee* took refuge in Montevideo and scuttled itself off the Uruguayan port in December after being damaged in a fight with three British cruisers, a critical observer might have drawn attention to the fact that losing a third of the Kriegsmarine's pocket battleship force in exchange for eleven merchantmen hardly constituted a ringing endorsement of Raeder's strategy of commerce warfare.[23] Instead, Hitler expressed exasperation over the fact that *Graf Spee* had scuttled herself without first finishing off her most grievously stricken opponent, the cruiser HMS *Exeter* (a point most naval historians would probably agree with).[24] To him, the loss

---

[19] 'Aktennotiz Chef Wi.Rü.Amt Betr.: Vortrag bei Generaloberst Keitel am 8.2.1940 (8.2.1940)'; in: Hans-Adolf Jacobsen (ed.), *Kriegstagebuch des Oberkommandos der Wehrmacht*, Bd. I (Frankfurt a.M.: Bernard & Graefe 1965), p 962 (Document No. 14).

[20] Guntram Schulze-Wegener, *Die deutsche Kriegsmarine-Rüstung* (Hamburg et al: Mittler 1997), p 49

[21] Such an admittedly radical move would have had history on its side. Even after the *Flottenchef* Reinhard Scheer had reported to the emperor after the Battle of Jutland that further fleet actions of this kind would have to be avoided and strategic focus shifted to the U-boats, construction on a number of capital ships continued for months. The number of man-hours wasted in this fashion left the U-boat arm short by at least twenty oceanic submersibles in the first half of 1917, when Allied shipping was at its most vulnerable. See Schröder, *U-Boote des Kaisers*, pp 241–2, 365.

[22] Hitler's suggestion was in any case limited to halting construction of the carrier *Graf Zeppelin*. See 'Vortrag des Oberbefehlshabers der Kriegsmarine beim Führer am 10. Oktober 1939, 17.00 h'; in: Wagner (ed.), *Lagevorträge*, pp 26–8.

[23] A fact recognised by Hans Langsdorff, the *Graf Spee*'s captain, in conversation with an Argentine naval officer. Eric Grove, *The Price of Disobedience: The Battle of the River Plate Reconsidered* (Stroud: Sutton 2000), p 170.

[24] 'Vortrag des Ob.d.M. beim Führer am 30.XII.39'; in: Wagner (ed.), *Lagevorträge*, pp 65–7. See also Puttkamer, *Unheimliche See*, pp 27–8.

of a capital ship was closely tied to questions of wider national prestige – it could only be stomached if comparable damage was inflicted on the enemy in the same action. This divergence of views would come back to haunt the relationship between dictator and admiral in 1941.

In the meantime, the meagre U-boat force available to Dönitz was at first held in check. This was because Adolf Hitler, mindful of the role played by unrestricted submarine warfare in bringing about the US declaration of war in 1917, issued a whole series of restrictions regarding the sinking of civilian shipping. These concerned the type of ship, its nationality, the way it was being handled (zigzagging, blackout at night) and the need to board in order to inspect the vessel's papers in accordance with the London Submarine Protocol of 1936. These regulations were gradually dismantled over the next year or so. In the meantime, the naval leadership showed little inclination to engage in the sort of political power play with which their predecessors of World War I had blackmailed the government of that day into unleashing unrestricted commerce warfare well before the submarine arm was ready for it.[25] This undoubtedly played a role in limiting the potential of the U-boat arm, but to not nearly the same extent as the technical issues that beset German torpedoes in 1939–40. They ran too deep, exploded well before the target or not at all. What at first appeared to be an inconvenience turned into a full-blown crisis when U-boats deployed to counter the Allied landings at Narvik and Namsos in April 1940 found a cornucopia of targets, only to be frustrated time and again by their unreliable weapons. A thorough investigation discovered flaws in both the contact as well as the magnetic exploder. That the former problem should be solved by copying the design of a recently captured British torpedo is probably a good indicator of the mixture of desperation and exasperation afflicting U-boat command by that time.[26] German U-boats finally went to sea with improved detonators after June 1940, but the reason behind the erratic depth-keeping was in fact not discovered until January 1942.

A major break came with the fall of Norway and France in June 1940. Bases in both countries enabled the Kriegsmarine to shift its U-boats to bases which outflanked the British blockade; as a first reaction, the British government, as of July 1940, found itself forced to reroute all its merchant traffic (a large part of which had been convoyed since October 1939) to the northwestern approaches. This in turn created a bottleneck that would make the U-boats' task of tracking their victims that much easier. To make matters worse, the Royal Navy's destroyer force had suffered serious losses during the Norwegian

---

[25] Schröder, *U-Boote des Kaisers*, pp 184–7.
[26] For an account of the 'torpedo crisis' as it came to be called, see Oliver Krauß, *Rüstung und Rüstungserprobung in der deutschen Marinegeschichte – Die Torpedoversuchsanstalt* (Bonn: Bernard & Graefe 2010) [= Wehrtechnik und wissenschaftliche Waffenkunde, Bd. 17], pp 190–216.

operation and the Dunkirk evacuation, with much of the remainder of the force being tied down in the Mediterranean and in home waters in expectation of the German invasion of the United Kingdom. On 24 May 1940 Dönitz was finally given a clearly defined 'operational zone' around the British Isles where any form of shipping was fair game.[27] Once it was expanded to 20 degrees of longitude west in mid-August, it greatly facilitated his task of interdicting Britain's lifelines with the outside world. The only thing standing in the way of wholesale slaughter on the scale of spring 1917 was the number of U-boats. By 1 June 1940, losses suffered in the previous nine months and a woefully inadequate replacement rate meant that the number of ocean-going submarines had actually decreased by three to a grand total of twenty-four.[28] Since the basic plan for expansion of the U-boat fleet was to stand, however, this meant that as of September 1940 a disproportionate number of the U-boats available were tied up as training boats for crews, who needed to be available in enough numbers as soon as the yards finally began commissioning enough boats.[29] As a result, the ratio of operational boats to those used for training or still engaged in 'working up' (being put through their paces by their new crews), which had stood at 1:1 in August 1940, rose to 1:2. Between January and June 1941, it was never less than 1:3 and occasionally got close to 1:4.[30] An impassioned plea by Raeder in late December 1940 that Hitler should finally make good on his pledge to release the steel, copper and skilled labour to turn a U-boat fleet of 300-plus into reality translated into a promise to Dönitz of an extra 192 U-boats by December 1941.[31] This was already a substantial decrease from the numbers that had appeared possible for a brief time in October 1939, but it would still allow the BdU to cast a wide enough net if the increase of anti-submarine warfare (ASW) forces operating in or close to the northwestern approaches forced Dönitz to shift his search patterns farther to the west. Rather ominously, Hitler had stressed to Raeder that in case of a confrontation with the USSR this cheque might bounce again.

For the time being, these were future problems. Despite a ridiculously small number of boats, the force under Dönitz's command achieved its best-ever efficiency ratio from August to October 1940, with sinkings totalling just under

---

[27] Clay Blair, *Hitler's U-Boat War: The Hunters, 1939–1942* (London: Weidenfeld & Nicholson 1997), pp 161, 179.

[28] Blair, *The Hunters*, p 167.

[29] The idea of temporarily neglecting the training process in order to make the most of the short-term British weakness was rejected by Raeder, Dönitz and Hitler alike. See 'Vortrag Ob.d.M. beim Führer am 21.5.40 mittags'; in: Wagner (ed.), *Lagevorträge*, pp 103–4. Also Puttkamer, *Unheimliche See*, pp 57–8.

[30] See the tables provided in V. E. Tarrant, *The U-boat Offensive, 1914–1945* (London: Arms & Armour Press 1989), pp 96, 103.

[31] Werner Rahn and Gerhard Schreiber (eds.), *Kriegstagebuch der Seekriegsleitung, Teil A, Band 17.* (Herford: Mittler & Sohn 1990) (entry for 6 January 1941). Henceforth quoted as KTB Seekriegsleitung, Teil A.

Figure 8.2 U-boat launch: no other factor limited U-boat sinking rates in 1941 so much as the numbers of boats available, kept down by competing priorities for skilled labour. Only by November–December 1941 was a corner finally turned. (Hanns Hubmann/ ullstein bild via Getty Images)

or (in the case of October) well over 300,000 GRT each month. Operating against convoys whose escorts were inexperienced, few in number or even forced to turn around after reaching a drop-off point well short of mid-Atlantic, they savaged several of them to an unprecedented degree.

Small numbers, defective torpedoes, the gradual escalation of the campaign and Raeder's failure to redirect at least some of the German shipyard work-force away from capital ships had thus robbed the initial phase of the German assault on shipping of some of the impact it might otherwise have had. As yet, this relative failure was wholly unconnected to events in the USA.

US President Franklin Delano Roosevelt, who had been an increasingly vocal critic of the Axis powers throughout the 1930s, found himself faced with an increasingly isolationist mood in his country on the outbreak of war. Thus, on 5 September 1939, he felt obliged to proclaim a war zone around the British Isles and the approaches to Gibraltar, which American vessels were forbidden from entering. US citizens travelling on board for-eign ships would do so at their own risk. This move was complemented by the creation of the Panamerican Neutrality Zone in conjunction with the

Latin American republics. This provided for a neutral buffer zone, which the warring powers were expected to respect. For obvious reasons, it excluded Canada. The line drawn on a map roughly followed the outline of the North and South American continents south of Newfoundland, with the distance to the nearest coastline in the Western Hemisphere averaging between 500 and 700 nautical miles (926 and 1296 km). In due course, the Roosevelt administration would find all sorts of ways to make this arrangement work to the advantage of the Allied powers, and it is these steps that have tended to attract the interest of historians. Even so, it is important to realise that at least for the next two years, this state of affairs would work to the advantage of Germany in one key area: in contrast to the days of World War I, when the Wilson administration had always insisted on the concept of the 'freedom of the seas' and the safety of its seafaring citizens irrespective of ongoing wars, in 1939 the US government had all but voluntarily surrendered this position and retreated into its hemisphere the moment the first shot was fired. For the time being at least, the Atlantic would be seen as a moat rather than highway. Retrenchment, rather than intervention, appeared to be the guiding principle of US strategy.

In due course, however, US policy would give Raeder and Dönitz cause for concern. The amendment of 11 November 1939 to the 1935 Neutrality Law, which allowed the Allies to buy arms and munitions in the USA provided they paid in cash and transported them in their own ships (Cash-and-Carry), hardly came as a surprise, but the manner in which the Panamerican Neutrality Zone was policed did. Not only were Allied vessels given virtual freedom of movement, but the Americans made no attempt to enforce their neutrality whenever the British or French navies intercepted Axis merchantmen which had been holed up in Latin American ports and were now trying to make a break for Germany. On a few occasions, German blockade runners even made the disconcerting discovery that their position was broadcast in the clear by US Navy vessels trailing them, which then proceeded to just stand by when they were intercepted and boarded by British warships – all of this well within the zone and on at least one occasion even within US territorial waters.[32] The Kriegsmarine, on the other hand, was expressly forbidden by Hitler even from stationing two U-boats off the Canadian port of Halifax, which, while adjacent to the Panamerican Zone, was not part of it. As Hitler put it to the admiral, such action, operationally promising as it was, was ruled out by the likely

---

[32] As US–German relations deteriorated, Admiral Raeder twice compiled a list of these transgressions for Hitler in the hope of convincing him of the need to adopt a more aggressive stance towards American policy. See 'Besprechung des Ob.d.M. beim Führer am 14.11.40, 13 Uhr. Anlage 2: Verletzungen der Panamazone'; also 'Vortrag Ob.d. M. beim Führer am 20. April 1941. Anlage 1: Britische Verletzungen der Panama-Zone'. Both in Wagner (ed.), *Lagevorträge*, p. 158, 223–4.

'psychological impact' it would have in the USA.[33] However, such restraint was not echoed by the US President. On 17 June 1940, only three days after Congress had passed a bill that put the seal on a massive naval expansion, he upped the ante by proposing to legislators a doubling of the already considerable increase. The aim, as he put it, was to build a Two-Ocean Navy capable of simultaneously seeing off challenges coming from the German and the Japanese fleets.[34] An armada of such a size would relegate even the Kriegsmarine of the Z-Plan to the status of a perpetual runner-up.

Over the winter, Dönitz's U-boat campaign proceeded in a lacklustre fashion, hampered as much by the low number of boats as by the winter weather. The one ray of hope was the effective cooperation of other elements of the Wehrmacht with the U-boat arm. The first *Gruppe* of Kampfgeschwader 40 had only just arrived at Bordeaux–Merignac airport. The Condor bombers they fielded (converted airliners of the Focke-Wulf 200 type) were enjoying rich pickings against stragglers or even ships travelling in convoy, as yet poorly armed against an aerial threat.[35] They should also have been suited to the role of maritime reconnaissance, but were limited in this by their crew's notoriously poor navigational skills. Between 9 and 12 February, for the first time in the war, one U-boat cooperated directly with five FW-200s in an attack on a convoy (HG-53) and for good measure also brought the heavy cruiser *Admiral Hipper* to the scene. *Hipper* ended up tearing into an altogether different convoy which was supposed to join up with HG-53, but even so the tally was impressive: sixteen ships sunk over a period of just four days. A number of factors had to be in place to create such a perfect storm, and in fact it remained a unique event, never to be repeated.

Overall, the balance sheet for March and April was a mixed one. In mid-March, the Seekriegsleitung had a major breakthrough when the *Marinenachrichtendienst* broke the British Naval Merchant Code,[36] giving Dönitz unique insights into sailing dates and routes. Hard on the heels of this, Hitler, looking for a way to retaliate against the proclamation of US Lend-Lease, finally gave way on the issue of the war zone around the British Isles and, effective from 23 March, agreed to expand it to the west and northwest, bringing into it the waters around British-occupied Iceland.[37] Partly as a result of this, U-boat operations brought a richer yield in March and April,

---

[33] 'Vortrag des Ob.d.M. beim Führer am 23.2.40, 10.30 h'; in: Wagner (ed.), *Lagevorträge*, pp 80–4.

[34] In the same speech, the President would go on to make the demand for an output of 50,000 military aircraft per year, a demand utterly beyond the capabilities of the US aircraft industry at the time.

[35] On the exploits of this unit, see Sönke Neitzel, *Die deutsche Luftwaffe im Einsatz über dem Nordatlantik und der Nordsee 1939–1945* (Bonn: Bernard & Graefe 1995), pp 49–120.

[36] KTB Seekriegsleitung, Teil A (entry for 17 March 1941).

[37] KTB Seekriegsleitung, Teil A (entries for 20, 24, 25 and 27 March 1941).

with figures rising to a total tonnage just shy of 250,000 GRT. However, Dönitz's plan to intercept convoys farther out to sea with much greater regularity than had been possible so far was getting nowhere on account of the numbers available.[38] A U-boat crew would on average need six months' training before it was handed its own boat. This was then followed by three to four months of shakedown cruises and live-fire exercises with a training flotilla in the Baltic. Minor flaws discovered in the course of this process would usually necessitate a return to the shipyard for at least a month or two, to be capped by the final equipping of the U-boat with every item needed to initiate a month-long cruise. In late 1940 and early 1941 a number of factors came together to drastically cut down the numbers which had been promised to Dönitz at the turn of the year. Apart from the well-known shortages in steel, copper and other metals, labour allocation was turning into the biggest obstacle that stood in the way of a truly exponential growth of the U-boat arm. What with the other two services preparing for the invasion of the Soviet Union, it was obvious that the navy would have to stand in line and await its turn. In March, the Luftwaffe managed to have 22,000 men exempted from military service and returned to the factories, but no such privilege was accorded to the Kriegsmarine.[39]

This meant that the advent of good spring weather would find Dönitz in a position where promising opportunities would go begging, because the number of boats actually deployed with front-line flotillas had increased only marginally beyond what had been available in September 1939. Thus, the number of U-boats commissioned was not an accurate reflection of the numbers actually joining the front-line flotillas in France and Norway. As just explained, some new boats would be assigned to training flotillas, while others, having been taken on the shakedown cruise by their first crew, would then spend months clogging up the Baltic shipyards while the inevitable final repairs (the so-called *Restarbeiten*) were finished. A comparison between the numbers promised to Dönitz by the Seekriegsleitung on 6 January 1941, with the numbers ordered and those actually reporting for duty in French or Norwegian bases, respectively, is instructive. In January 1941 twelve boats due to be commissioned on paper translated into eight new deliveries from the shipyards and only two new additions to the front; February 1941 came close to a reasonable match with eight boats planned for, eight delivered and six reporting for duty; in March 1941, the quota foresaw fourteen new boats; thirteen were actually delivered, but only five reached the front-line flotillas; in

---

[38] KTB Seekriegsleitung, Teil A (entry for 15 April 1941). On 1 April, the number of available ocean-going boats (most of the coastal types having been relegated to training) stood at forty-one. In nineteen months of war, the submarine arm had thus increased by a grand total of fourteen boats.

[39] 'Vortrag des Ob.d.M. beim Führer am 18.3., 16.00 Uhr', especially 'Anlage 5'; in: Wagner (ed.), *Lagevorträge*, p 216.

April 1941 a reasonable match was again achieved between boats as laid out according to plan (sixteen) and those actually delivered (fourteen); however, only three arrived to increase the order of battle of Dönitz's command. Only towards the end of the year did new arrivals in Lorient or Brest finally begin to bear a reasonable resemblance to the number of new boats commissioned as laid out by the Seekriegsleitung's planning. The commissioning of nineteen new boats had been pencilled in for December 1941 and fifteen actually joined the ranks of the front-line flotillas.[40]

Despite stagnating U-boat strength, however, a combination of factors saw the losses of the Allied merchant navies increase. For starters, between February and March, four of the heavy units of the Kriegsmarine (*Gneisenau* and *Scharnhorst* as a task force, *Admiral Hipper* and *Admiral Scheer* on their own) were at large in the Atlantic and for several weeks wrought havoc on a considerable scale.[41] The *Scharnhorst–Gneisenau* sortie in particular (Operation Berlin) briefly appeared to suggest that Raeder's pre-war concept of using capital ships in twos and threes as commerce raiders might be viable after all, especially since it would force the British Admiralty to deploy an increasing number of capital ships to act as escorts for particularly valuable convoys.

In April, losses suffered to mines, U-boats, surface raiders, the prowling Condors and German air attacks on the merchantmen tasked with supporting the British expeditionary force deployed in Greece would combine to make that month the worst of the war so far for the British (687,901 GRT lost to all causes, including 249,375 of them to submarines).[42] However, events such as the Greek campaign were not a regular feature of commerce warfare and the share of the Condors in actual sinkings was already dropping by April.[43] Only the U-boats could be relied upon to inflict attrition in a consistent and predictable way. This they continued to do in late spring, with May and June 1941 the only months that year when sinkings by U-boat alone would exceed the magical marker of 300,000 GRT. Two convoys were savaged in a manner almost reminiscent of the October battles of 1940.

As far as Hitler is concerned, a clear preference for one form of commerce warfare over the other can be inferred, if not proven beyond any doubt. It is

---

[40] Blair, *The Hunters*, pp 703–5.

[41] Tearing into several convoys, the four vessels managed to sink or capture just shy of 300,000 GRT of Allied shipping. Jürgen Rohwer, *Chronology of the War at Sea, 1939–1945: The Naval History of World War Two* (Annapolis: USNIP 2005), pp 57–64.

[42] Losses suffered by Greek and British merchant shipping during the transfer of the BEF to Greece in March (Operation Lustre) came to approximately 100,000 GRT; supplying the Empire forces during their brief campaign and then evacuating them in April (Operation Demon) cost another 145,000 GRT. For a more detailed breakdown of these figures, see Rohwer, *Chronology*, pp 62, 67, 69–70

[43] Neitzel, *Luftwaffe*, pp 77, 82, 85, 135. From summer 1941, successful attacks by FW-200s on convoys were becoming a rare occurrence.

certainly significant that the expansion of the U-boat fleet was a topic he got into the habit of bringing up in conversation more and more frequently, even when his interlocutor only had the most tenuous link to naval affairs.[44] As far as capital ships were concerned, victory over France had led him to approve in principle the resumption of battleship construction halted with the shelving of the Z-Plan,[45] even though this was soon rescinded. Eight months later, he pointed out to a gathering of senior officers that the best yardstick by which to gauge the progress of American rearmament was the progress made by the US Navy in commissioning a new class of super-battleship;[46] he also stressed that upon the victorious conclusion of the Russian campaign, German war production would have to focus on a major building programme for the Kriegsmarine which would feature a number of capital ships. On 9 April, Erich Raeder in a meeting at the Seekriegsleitung made it clear that this priority transcended the current conflict. A major building programme of capital ships should, according to the dictator's wishes, be initiated 'immediately upon the conclusion of hostilities'.[47] At the same time, Hitler had started to show some concern at the vulnerability of these behemoths to modern air power.[48] What is significant is that while the dictator had made a point of bragging to a number of people about the devastation his growing armada of submarines would inflict on Allied merchantmen, there is no record of him gleefully anticipating the next sortie by his capital ships to the same end. It would appear that – in contrast to Erich Raeder – using these expensive behemoths for commerce warfare was not something he readily contemplated.

Upon the introduction of Lend-Lease for the United Kingdom on 11 March, the German dictator for once departed from his line of caution. Effective 1 April, he expanded the operations zone as far out as 38 degrees west, thus

---

[44] Klaus Gerbet (ed.), *Generalfeldmarschall Fedor von Bock. Zwischen Pflicht und Verweigerung. Das Kriegstagebuch* (München: Herbig 1995), pp 170, 194 (entries for 3 December 1940 and 14 June 1941); TB Goebbels, Bd. I.9, pp 120–1, 351 (entries for 1 February 1941 and 4 June 1941); Bd. II.1, p 483 (entry for 24 September 1941) and Bd. II.2, p 51 (entry for 4 October 1941). Also 'Aufzeichnung über die Unterredung zwischen dem Führer und dem Duce in Anwesenheit des RAM und des Grafen Ciano auf dem Brenner am 2. Juni 1941 (3.6.1941)'; in: ADAP, Serie D, Bd. XII.2, pp 785, 788.

[45] 'Vortrag des Ob.d.M. beim Führer am 11. Juli 1940 (Obersalzberg)'; in: Wagner (ed.), *Lagevorträge*, p 108–10.

[46] 'Besprechung durch Führer am 30.3.1941 in Reichskanzlei' (n.d.); in: Susanne Heim et al (eds.), *Sowjetunion mit annektierten Gebieten I. Besetzte sowjetische Gebiete unter deutscher Militärverwaltung, Baltikum und Transnistrien* (München: Oldenbourg Verlag 2011) [= Die Verfolgung der europäischen Juden durch das nationalsozialistische Deutschland 1933–1945, Bd. 7], pp 117–19.

[47] KTB Seekriegsleitung, Teil A (entry for 9 April 1941).

[48] This change of heart on his part is normally associated with the impact made by the Fleet Air Arm's spectacular raid on Taranto in November. 'Vortrag des Ob.d.M. beim Führer am 11. Juli 1940 (Obersalzberg)'; in: Wagner (ed.), *Lagevorträge*, p 110, would seem to indicate a more gradual process.

including the waters around Iceland.[49] Less well known, but arguably much more significant, is the fact that he also briefly pondered the possibility of allowing Raeder to expand commerce warfare across the entire North Atlantic without any regard for the US Neutrality Zone. Under this scheme, only US territorial waters would have been safe from attack.[50]

On 9 April, the orphaned Danish colony of Greenland was placed under US protection, thus bearing out an earlier statement by White House spokesmen that it and the waters surrounding it were seen as part of the Western Hemisphere.[51] Three days later, Hitler expressed considerable scepticism at Raeder's claim that the attempt to engage in submarine warfare against all neutral (even US) shipping outside the German war zone could, if waged according to Prize Regulations, bring about a sizeable increase in sinkings.[52] This point was basically rendered moot when the Americans announced a much more militant stance on 18 April. The former Neutrality Zone proclaimed at Panama in 1939 changed names to become a Security Zone while being expanded into the eastern half of the North Atlantic. This new patrol area's eastern limit had been settled as the 26th meridian a week before,[53] though the delimitation was never formally announced. The Chief of Naval Operations, Admiral Harold Stark, emphasised that the vessels of the US Navy's Neutrality Patrol tasked with policing the new zone would from now on range as far as 4830 km (3,000 miles) from the American continent 'in places',[54] though he corrected this to 3220 km (2,000 miles) on 29 April. The *New York Times* hazarded the guess that US vessels would now be covering the North Atlantic as far out as the 30th meridian west.[55] By either of the two measurements the new Security Zone overlapped with the operations zone proclaimed by the Kriegsmarine on 26 March 1941. The scene was now set for an inadvertent clash. To begin with, the President was adamant in refusing to give a delimitation that might have helped Raeder in keeping a safe distance, and on 29 April Roosevelt even stressed that the German operations zone would be disregarded 'if and when necessary', since the Atlantic Fleet's only priority lay in 'protecting the hemisphere'.[56] When seen against the backdrop of the US Navy's policy of reporting in the clear the position of Axis vessels and

---

[49] KTB Seekriegsleitung, Teil A (entry for 27 March 1941).

[50] 'Seekriegsleitung B.Nr. I op 355/41 g.K. Vortrag des Ob.d.M. beim Führer am 18.3., 16.00 Uhr (n.d.)'; in: Wagner (ed.), *Lagevorträge*, p 202.

[51] KTB Seekriegsleitung, Teil A (entry for 27 March 1941).

[52] PA/AA, StS USA, Bd. 5, 'Fernschreiben an Ministerbüro Berlin für Botschafter Ritter (12.4.1941)'.

[53] Waldo Heinrichs, *Threshold of War: Franklin D. Roosevelt and American Entry into World War II* (Oxford: OUP 1988), pp 46–7.

[54] Ibid. p 33.

[55] Ibid.

[56] Ibid. Also: 'Confidential. Press Conference #738, Executive Office of the White House, April 25, 1941, 10.45 AM'; 'Confidential. Press Conference # 739, Executive Office of the

submarines encountered in 'their' zone, and the fact that the Kriegsmarine did not limit its war on shipping to the operations zone (it just tended to be more discriminating about target selection when outside it), this new state of affairs essentially preordained the outbreak of a shooting war.[57] Shifting the Security Zone this far east constituted a deliberate challenge which, taken together with the deliberately obfuscating language used by the President in announcing this measure, virtually guaranteed that it would happen sooner rather than later.[58] Even though Roosevelt within a week followed up his proclamation with a renewed pledge that the vessels of the steadily growing Atlantic Fleet would only 'patrol' these waters without providing convoys with close escort, the Seekriegsleitung's concerns were not assuaged.[59] To them, this latest development was something that was bound to have the most serious impact on the effectiveness of German commerce warfare even if the British prime minister had not provided them with a running commentary on how the US Navy's presence in mid-Atlantic was easing the task of the British escorts.[60] From now on, isolationist senators and German admirals alike would closely monitor the slightest changes in the US Navy's rules of engagement in the knowledge that they were the most reliable gauge by which to judge Roosevelt's willingness to inch ever further in the direction of war. In the meantime, the Seekriegsleitung, basing its decision on the obfuscating statements from US government sources and its own intelligence, issued instructions to its vessels to consider the 38th meridian west as the outer limit of the new US Security Zone.[61]

President, April 29, 1941, 4.10 PM'. Both in: www.fdrlibrary.marist.edu/_resources/images/pc/pc0116.pdf (accessed 9 October 2019).

[57] So far, most of the surface raiders had operated well outside the war zone proclaimed around Britain. Small groups of U-boats had operated off the approaches to the West African port of Freetown in November and December 1940 and March 1941. Blair, *The Hunters*, pp 208–9, 255.

[58] A speech by the President on 27 May 1941 confirmed that the area being patrolled by the Atlantic Fleet had just been extended, but again failed to give a specific demarcation line. See Douglas M. Norton, 'The Open Secret: The US Navy in the Battle of the Atlantic, April–December 1941'; in: *Naval War College Review* 26 (1974), No. 4, pp 63–83, esp. p 79. For a German appreciation of this shift in US policy, KTB Seekriegsleitung, Teil A (entries for 30 April 1941 and 27 May 1941).

[59] Between April and October 1941 what had been an appendage to the main fleet in the Pacific would grow from 159 ships to 355. See Patrick Abbazia, *Mr. Roosevelt's Navy: The Private War of the U.S. Atlantic Fleet, 1939-1942* (Annapolis: USNIP 1975), p 173.

[60] KTB Seekriegsleitung, Teil A (entry for 27 April 1941). In a public speech, the British prime minister had stressed that the patrols by the Atlantic Fleet had allowed the Royal Navy to concentrate its assets in the general area of the eastern Atlantic and the western approaches.

[61] BA/MA, RM 7/1700 'Oberkommando der Kriegsmarine an Flotte, Gruppe West und Gruppe Nord (10.5.1941)'.

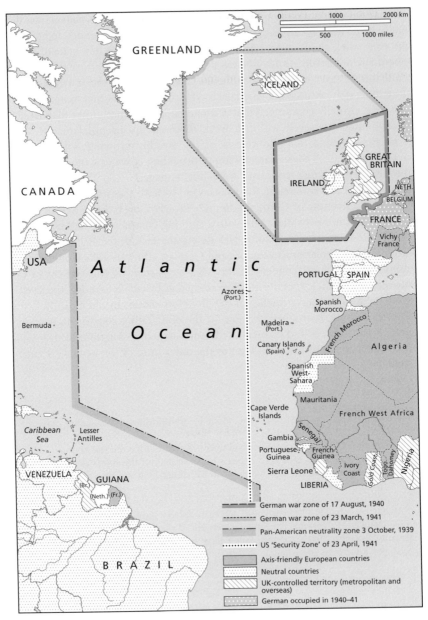

Map 8.1 Operational areas in the North Atlantic, April 1941.

For Dönitz, these events were to cast a pall over the otherwise good sinking results achieved in May. When a dearth of sightings in the northwestern approaches led him to plan a probe by a wolf pack south of Greenland just outside the operational zone, he and Raeder soon found themselves in a three-way debate with the Auswärtiges Amt and Hitler about the rules of engagement to adapt in this contingency. On 16 May one of the U-boats concerned (*U-74*) came across the battleship USS *New York* and her destroyer escort near 34 degrees west. This led to serious consideration being given to pulling back the entire wolf pack into the operations zone in order to rule out any possible clashes with US forces.[62] Even though it did not come to that, U-boat commanders were issued a set of orders, which had the potential to cramp their style. Prior to the sally outside the zone in May, they had already been impressed with the need to discriminate between US and British escorts when attacking a convoy. The former were not to be attacked at all unless they had initiated hostilities. The Seekriegsleitung's diarist had wistfully added that such a contingency seemed not likely to arise since as yet no intelligence had been received that joint convoying was actually being undertaken by the US and British navies.[63] After *U-74*'s sighting report, further instructions followed on 17 May: outside the zone, warships travelling on their own were to be attacked only after they had been positively identified as British; since night-time all but ruled out such an identification, blacked-out warships were not to be attacked at all. In night-time attacks on convoys, warships were to be attacked 'if the situation demanded it'. US merchantmen were to be spared within and outside the war zone.[64] Preposterous as these instructions were from a tactical point of view, the intelligence reaching Hitler from the USA in these weeks made it understandable that he should have opted to put the U-boat arm on a short leash. All the indications were that Roosevelt was actively courting war but taking great care that Germany should be seen to have fired the first shot.[65] Since the last two wars fought by the USA (against Spain in 1898, against the Central Powers in 1917–18) had both been preceded by 'controversial' sinkings with heavy loss of American lives, it did not take a leap of the imagination to foresee a scenario where a similar incident might give the Roosevelt administration the pretext for a declaration of war.

Even so it must have been obvious to all concerned that the limitations of the elaborate rules of engagement drawn up by the Seekriegsleitung would soon be revealed by the harsh realities of naval warfare in the North Atlantic. The sinking of the American merchantman *Robin Moor* on 21 May off the West African coast by *U-69* was carried out without loss of life and in any case could

---

[62] KTB Seekriegsleitung, Teil A (entry for 16 May 1941).
[63] KTB Seekriegsleitung Teil A (entry for 13 May 1941).
[64] KTB Seekriegsleitung Teil A (entry for 17 May 1941).
[65] Fears which were probably stoked by an article published in the *New York Post* on 12 May 1941. It alleged that Roosevelt would resist the temptation to start convoying and wait for the Germans to strike first instead. See KTB Seekriegsleitung, Teil A (entry for 14 May 1941).

be blamed on a misunderstanding – the former British vessel having only recently been acquired by a US company.

Raeder was fully aware that his next attempt to prove the validity of using capital ships as commerce raiders had the potential to produce many more misunderstandings of this kind. Accordingly, he gave a great deal of thought to how the task force made up of the battleship *Bismarck* and the heavy cruiser *Prinz Eugen* should engage American vessels during their cruise (Operation Rheinübung). His chief concern undoubtedly lay in having his surface raiders or their support ships tailed by US Navy units which would then broadcast their position to the British; the need to spare US merchantmen outside the German war zone was another major source of irritation.[66] The fact that his U-boats were largely immune to this form of harassment appears to have been cold comfort to him.[67] When these problems had first been put to him, Hitler had just received news of the introduction of Lend-Lease and was accordingly more inclined to consider possible methods of reprisal. Accordingly, he had even toyed with the idea of turning the Rheinübung task force loose within the US Neutrality Zone.[68] No doubt encouraged by this, Raeder on 20 April suggested that all Kriegsmarine units or, failing that, *Bismarck* and *Prinz Eugen* be given permission to sink US merchantmen according to Prize Regulations. This would put them in a position to make use of their armament if a hailed merchantman used its wireless, declined to stop or decided to make a run for it. Raeder admitted that this would in all likelihood only produce a temporary hike in sinkings, but it would serve notice on the Americans that their ever-growing inventiveness in rewriting the rights of neutrals was no longer being tolerated. By that point, however, the dictator's initial exasperation over Lend-Lease had mostly evaporated. Thus, on 20 April he insisted to Raeder that recent German victories in Libya and the Balkans had created a climate of opinion in the United States which made increased intervention on Britain's side less likely than only a few weeks before.[69] Accordingly, the Rheinübung task force sailed with instructions that both US merchantmen and the old Neutrality Zone had to be respected; moreover, even US Navy vessels trailing *Bismarck* and *Prinz Eugen* from a distance while broadcasting their

[66] 'Anlage zu OKM I op 515/41 Handelskrieg gegen USA-Schiffahrt nach Prisenordnung'; also: 'Seekriegsleitung B.Nr. 1 Skl I Op. 721/41 g.Kdos.Chefs Anlage 1: Das gegenwärtige Problem der Seekriegsführung im Atlantik im Hinblick auf die Haltung der USA (Mai 1941)'; both in: Wagner (ed.), *Lagevorträge*, pp 224–6, 231–6.

[67] In ibid., p 233, he admitted that U-boat operations would 'not face an insoluble problem'; surface units, on the other hand, would be 'most severely affected'. See also KTB Seekriegsleitung, Teil A (entry for 16 May 1941).

[68] 'Skl B.Nr. I op 355/41 g.K. Vortrag des Ob.d.M. beim Führer am 18.3., 16.00 Uhr (n.d.)'; in: Wagner (ed.), *Lagevorträge*, pp 201–6. See also KTB Seekriegsleitung, Teil A (entry for 20 March 1941).

[69] KTB Seekriegsleitung, Teil A (entry for 21 April 1941).

position in the clear (as had happened to many German blockade runners) must on no account be engaged; instead, the resulting encumbrance to operations 'would have to be accepted'.[70]

The Seekriegsleitung promised the task force commander, *Vizeadmiral* Günther Lütjens, that it would attempt to have these restrictive rules of engagement amended even after the task force sailed. Thus, on 22 May, Raeder raised the subject with the dictator. In light of the recent encounter of *U-74* with USS *New York*, his timing could not have been worse. Hitler was adamant in his rejection. He pointed out to the admiral that unless Japan's entry into the war could be guaranteed at the same time, he was unwilling to risk war with the USA 'for the sake of sinking a few extra 100,000 GRTs'.[71] Even though there is no specific reference to a particular agency of naval warfare, there can be no doubt that the 'temporary hike in sinkings' discussed in the previous month is the clue to Hitler's remark about 'sinking a few extra 100,000 GRTs'. Shackled by such restrictive rules of engagement, the task force's potential was bound to be considerably circumscribed. Under these circumstances, Hitler's last-minute suggestion that they cancel the operation, while somewhat belated, made perfect sense. Raeder, however, stood his ground and pointed to the time-consuming preparations that had been necessary to get this far.[72] Under these auspices, Rheinübung continued.

The task force's foray resulted in what is without a doubt the best-known naval engagement of World War II in Europe. *Bismarck* and *Prinz Eugen* found the exit into the Atlantic at the Denmark Strait blocked by a British force of two capital ships and two cruisers, which though superior had to retreat after losing the battlecruiser *Hood* to the *Bismarck*'s accurate shooting. Over the following days, a dramatic chase ensued which would have resulted in the *Bismarck*'s escape had she not had her steering crippled in a strike by British carrier planes. While *Prinz Eugen* reached a French port, *Bismarck* was cornered and sunk by elements of the Home Fleet on 27 May.

Though Rheinübung was defeated without the Atlantic Fleet playing any role, the aftermath ensured that the spectre of US interference remained uppermost in Erich Raeder's mind: eight of Rheinübung's supply ships, which had been pre-positioned in various parts of the North Atlantic, were intercepted and sunk throughout June by the Royal Navy. To Raeder, this confirmed his growing premonitions about the vulnerability of the Kriegsmarine's surface element in general and that of the supply ships

---

[70] BA/MA, RM 7/1700 'Oberkommando der Kriegsmarine an Flotte, Gruppe West und Gruppe Nord (10.5.1941)'.

[71] Institut für Zeitgeschichte (IfZ), ED 100–78 'Tagebuch Walther Hewel (entry for 22 May 1941)'.

[72] Puttkamer, *Unheimliche See*, pp 47–8 for the impressions of Hitler's naval adjutant who witnessed the exchange.

Figure 8.3 *Bismarck* sets sail for Rheinübung. The rules of engagement issued to *Bismarck* and her consort *Prinz Eugen* for their May 1941 foray threatened to make a nonsense of the operation. (ullstein bild/ullstein bild via Getty Images)

underpinning raider operations in particular. Ignorant of the fact that Bletchley Park had led the British to the floating service stations intended for the Rheinübung task force, he and the Seekriegsleitung soon jumped to the obvious conclusion: at least some of them must have been spotted by the increasingly omnipresent patrols of the Atlantic Fleet which were constantly in touch with the British Home Fleet to report the movements of unidentified vessels.[73]

Every history of World War II which discusses the demise of Rheinübung goes on to stress that this setback meant the end of Raeder's attempts to deploy his capital ships against the United Kingdom's Atlantic sea lanes. This conclusion, while true, is also misleading. In a briefing he gave for Hitler on 6 June, the admiral laid out his reasons for continuing with the campaign throughout the summer and possibly beyond. More than anything, he hoped to keep up the disruptive impact which had been achieved during Operation Berlin; he would only concede that the timing of the *Bismarck*'s sailing had been

---

[73] BA/MA, RM 7/120 'OKM, Seekriegsleitung I op 1313/41 Lagebetrachtung über die ausserheimische Kriegführung (1.7.1941)'.

misjudged.[74] Even though this episode marked the beginning of the process of estrangement between the two men, which would eventually culminate with the admiral's resignation eighteen months later, this was not apparent at first sight. Hitler, apart from voicing his exasperation over the squadron commander's failure to finish off HMS *Hood*'s damaged consort, urged Raeder not to invite another similar setback for the next six weeks since this would give the British heart to the extent that it might even cushion the psychological impact of the USSR's impending fall.[75] Raeder, who in any case did not have a cruiser or battleship ready to sail within this time frame, concurred. His insistence on prioritising sorties by heavy units, if not in word, then certainly in deed, became obvious a fortnight later. When Dönitz asked for the war zone in which the U-boats could wage unrestricted commerce warfare to be extended to the south, he as likely as not expected Raeder to reject this out of hand out of concern for American reactions. Even though he was turned down, the reason for this was an entirely different one, as recorded by the Seekriegsleitung's war diary: such a move 'would spread disquiet in an area which thus far has been of use to us for the deployment of tankers which are absolutely crucial for later fleet operations'.[76] This order of priorities found further confirmation in a series of memoranda produced within the Seekriegsleitung over the following weeks. These conceded that tactics would have to be adjusted to the fact that the British were becoming more and more vigilant, but remained adamant that commerce warfare with capital ships was still regarded as a key component in the Kriegsmarine's armoury.[77]

On the same day that the secondary importance of the U-boat war was driven home to Dönitz, an encounter between a US and a German warship took place, which could quite easily have made the issue of a declaration of war a moot point. On 20 June, the battleship USS *Texas* was on patrol well beyond the admittedly ill-defined boundary of the new US Security Zone. When spotted by *U-203* she had just entered the German zone of operations at 32 degrees west. The U-boat commander recognised a vessel of American design but, since the limitations issued on 17 May only pertained to action outside the

---

[74] 'B. Nr. 1. Skl (Ib) 885/41 op Chefs. Anlage 2. Betrachtungen zur Weiterführung des Atlantikhandelskrieges mit Überwasserstreitkräften'; in: Wagner (ed.), *Lagevorträge*, pp 252–7.

[75] 'B. Nr.1. Skl. (Ib) 885/41 op Chefs. Vortrag Ob.d.M. beim Führer am 6.6.1941 auf dem Berghof'; in: Wagner (ed.), *Lagevorträge*, pp 239, 257.

[76] KTB Seekriegsleitung, Teil A (entry for 20 June 1941).

[77] BA/MA, RM 7/120 'Oberkommando der Kriegsmarine, Seekriegsleitung Iop 1313/41. Lagebetrachtung über die ausserheimische Kriegführung (1.7.1941)'; RM 7/1058 'Durchbruch von Überwasserstreitkräften zum Atlantik' (n.d.); RM 7/1058 'Anlage zu OKM op 1240/41 Geheime Kommandosache ! Einige Überlegungen zu Operationen von Überwasserstreitkräften (n.d.; summer 1941)' strikes a slightly dissonant note. Its unknown author makes a case for deploying capital ships but argues for shorter raids from Brest against the convoys on the Gibraltar route.

German war zone, he took up pursuit. He tried for hours to get into a firing position, being thwarted in this only by the battleship's superior speed and constant zigzagging. When he radioed a contact report, there was an almighty flap at the Tirpitzufer and the Reichskanzlei, the upshot of which was an order that prohibited attacks on any warship encountered either outside or within the German war zone unless it was a capital ship that had been positively identified as British. This essentially meant that the U-boat's mortal enemies – the destroyers and assorted escorts of the British and Canadian navies – were out of bounds for the time being.[78]

Unbeknownst to Dönitz, fuming at the orders to detail submarines to support Rheinübung, one of his U-boat commanders had, in fact, allowed the unthinkable to happen: on 10 May, *U-110* was depth-charged and forced to the surface by Royal Navy destroyers escorting convoy Outbound-318. No one thought to jettison the boat's electromechanical Enigma encoding machine, an error compounded by the failure to properly rig *U-110* for scuttling. As a result, a boarding party from HMS *Bulldog* was able to retrieve the machine and an abundance of paperwork regarding encoding procedures.[79] The Government Code and Cypher School at Bletchley Park had been reading the Luftwaffe general Enigma code with regularity since 22 May 1940, thus providing British military leaders with high-grade (Ultra) intelligence on a number of developing threats, like the *Afrikakorps*' arrival in Libya or the German plans for the airborne invasion of Crete.[80] In the naval sphere, however, they had so far been defeated by the greater professionalism shown by the Kriegsmarine's Enigma operators. The yield secured by HMS *Bulldog*, together with those recovered from a German trawler (4 March) and the two weather ships *München* and *Lauenburg* (7 May and 28 June),[81] produced a torrent of readily actionable intelligence. Previously, the time spent between reading and breaking an encoded Kriegsmarine transmission had ranged from eighteen days (best case) to a month; most of the time, it was altogether impossible.[82] In June and July 1941, the time lag was reduced to one hour. For the rest of 1941, it was usually thirty-six hours or less, though on a number

---

[78] KTB Seekriegsleitung Teil A (entries for 20 and 21 June, 1941).

[79] The dramatic story of the boarding of *U-110* has been told and retold in many publications. Blair, *The Hunters*, pp 277–85, offers a good summary of the key points.

[80] Ralph Erskine, 'Breaking Air Force and Army Enigma'; in: Michael Smith and Ralph Erskine (eds.), *Action This Day: Bletchley Park from the Breaking of the Enigma Code to the Birth of the Modern Computer* (London: Bantam Press 2001), pp 47–76, esp. pp 55–7.

[81] The former was the result of a chance encounter during the Lofoten raid carried out that day; the weather ships, however, were deliberately targeted because it was believed their remote positions would force their crew to carry encryption material not just for weeks, but the months ahead. Hugh Sebag-Montefiore, *Enigma: The Battle for the Code* (London: Weidenfeld & Nicholson 2000), pp 145–53.

[82] Sebag-Montefiore, *Enigma*, pp 73–6, 118–19.

Figure 8.4 A Kriegsmarine Enigma operator: the compromise of the Enigma-based U-boat code by mid-1941 led to numerous reroutings of Atlantic convoys. As a result, clashes between the Kriegsmarine and the US Navy were less frequent than might otherwise have been the case. (Pen and Sword Books/Universal Images Group via Getty Images)

of days it could stretch up to seventy-five.[83] In this fashion, in the last week of June 1941, convoy HX-133 became the first convoy to benefit from the intelligence windfall when its escort was reinforced just in time to blunt the full force of an impending wolf pack attack.

It was in 1941 that the British learned through trial and error how to make use of the Ultra intelligence without compromising it. In the course of this process, they would occasionally tend towards extremes. For instance, they were cautious almost to the point of being self-defeating when they very nearly decided against the capture of the weather ship *Lauenburg*.[84] In the new few weeks, however, the British Admiralty if anything, veered towards the other extreme: from 3 to 23 June, it used Ultra intelligence to intercept and sink

---

[83] Francis Harry Hinsley et al., *British Intelligence in the Second World War: Its Influence on Strategy and Operations*, Vol. 2 (London: HMSO 1981), p 163; Ralph Erskine, 'Breaking German Naval Enigma on Both Sides of the Atlantic'; in: Smith and Erskine (eds.), *Action this Day*, pp 179–80.

[84] Sebag-Montefiore, *Enigma*, pp 145–6.

a total of nine raider supply ships and one blockade runner, the first six going down in a period of just four days. The geographical area covered during this operation ranged from the southern tip of Greenland to the waters off Natal (Brazil). It was believed that the current German overestimation of the capabilities of British radar would be enough of a smokescreen to hide the real source of information.[85] Three months later, the Admiralty decided to top this by sending the submarine HMS *Clyde* to ambush a meeting of three U-boats in remote Tarafal Bay in the Cape Verde Islands on the evening of 27 September 1941; the trap was sprung, but all three Kriegsmarine vessels escaped, duly carrying the news of this unexpected encounter back to the Seekriegsleitung. In light of the unique experience gathered by the Royal Navy in the art of hunting U-boats with other submersibles,[86] this was easily one of the most gratuitous blunders ever perpetrated by the Allied side in World War II and constituted an act of criminal folly that should by rights have blown the lid off the Ultra secret.[87] Dönitz insisted that naval intelligence investigate the matter but was assured that breaks into Enigma could only happen occasionally. Even in a worst-case scenario, the daily change of settings would black out an enemy codebreaker who had been enjoying a streak of good luck.

As the German armies crashed into the Soviet Union in the last week of June, Dönitz would have been encouraged both by a slight rise in the number of operational U-boats (that month had seen an all-time high of thirteen joining the front-line flotillas) and the amount of GRT sunk. Much of the latter, however, was the result of a group of long-range Type IX U-boats exploiting British weaknesses off Freetown and the Gulf of Guinea. In the crucial North Atlantic theatre two successful convoy battles had been fought in May (Outbound-318, Halifax-126), but only one in June (Halifax-133); more to the point, the price exacted by the escorts in the case of the latter (six merchantmen sunk in exchange for two U-boats lost and another heavily damaged) was not at all in keeping with the exchange rate Dönitz had in mind. Until now, U-boat losses in 1940–1 had been fairly light. The loss of two or three boats in a pitched convoy battle seemed to confirm the forebodings

---

[85] A belief fostered by reports from *Bismarck* on the persistence of her shadowers both before and after the Denmark Strait action. These messages were decrypted by Bletchley Park. Blair, *The Hunters*, p 298.

[86] British submarines had accounted for eighteen German U-boats over the course of World War I as well as nine Axis (three German and six Italian) submersibles thus far in the currently ongoing conflict. These encounters, together with the far more numerous instances where the quarry was narrowly missed, should have indicated that the odds against disposing of three U-boats in one encounter were insurmountable, quite apart from the fact that some survivors would inevitably have reached the nearby shore. On this niche subject in general, see Harald Bendert, *U-Boote im Duell* (Berlin et al: Mittler 1996).

[87] Neither the Cape Verdes nor the waters around them had so far been used as a clandestine meeting point by Axis submarines or surface raiders.

Raeder had voiced to Hitler as far back as November 1940 about the increased numbers and proficiency of the escorts. Basing escort groups in Iceland, in particular, made it possible to provide more and more convoys with an anti-submarine escort for the entire voyage, HX-129 being the first to enjoy such protection in early June.[88] The greater number of escorts and the greater proficiency of their crews in turn made it practical to hound U-boats to destruction; previously, this would have meant leaving a convoy without any escort at all. Should an exchange rate of 1:3 become the norm, the BdU would need a much greater influx to his front-line flotillas than the thirteen he received in June.

8.3   Between a Rock and a Hard Place: the Decline in Sinkings, July–December 1941

For the Seekriegsleitung, July was ushered in with a bombshell. A few days after an isolationist senator in Washington had already given the game away,[89] a brigade of US Marines and supporting units proceeded to occupy Iceland and relieve part of the British force garrisoning it. It was obvious they would soon be followed by air and naval units. To the Kriegsmarine leadership, the consequences of this action were unambiguous. During a meeting with Hitler on 9 July, Raeder asked whether he was to consider this move a formal act of war.[90] Though he was quietly determined to dislodge the Americans from the island in the long run,[91] Hitler demurred for the moment, pointing out that the soon-to-be-expected collapse of the USSR would go a long way towards checking American expansionism.[92] He also made allow-ances for increased US traffic to and from Iceland by issuing orders on the following day which stressed the need to spare unidentified escorts and US merchantmen traversing the German war zone. He did, however, add: 'This should not be read as a duty to identify the nationality of a merchantman, since the Führer is well aware of the challenges of U-boat warfare. A case of mistaken identity in the war zone will not lead to recriminations being levelled against a U-boat commander.'[93] Only time would tell to what extent such

---

[88] Rohwer, *Chronology*, p 76.
[89] KTB Seekriegsleitung, Teil A (entry for 3 July 1941).
[90] An assessment shared by Admiral Stark, the US Navy's Chief of Naval Operations. Norton, 'Open Secret', p 71.
[91] 'Geheime Reichssache Füh 42/41. Aufzeichnung über die Unterredung des Führers mit Graf Oshima in Anwesenheit des Reichsaußenministers im Führerhauptquartier am 14. Juli 1941, von 17 bis 19 Uhr (15.7.1941)'; in ADAP, Serie D, Bd. XIII.2, pp 829–34.
[92] 'Besprechung des Ob.d.M. beim Führer im Hauptquartier Wolfsschanze am 9.VII.1941 nachmittags (10.7.1941)'; in: Wagner (ed.), *Lagevorträge*, pp 264–6.
[93] BA/MA, RM 7/845 'B. Nr. 1 Abt. Ic 15300/41 gKdos. Fernschreiben an B.d.U. Op. Abschrift (10.7.1941)'.

contradictory orders would end up shaping the reality of naval warfare in the North Atlantic.

It stands to reason that Raeder in particular would have been a lot more upset had he been privy to the secret instructions which the US Atlantic Fleet had been receiving in the context of the occupation of Iceland. With a view to protect the troop convoy making its way to Iceland, Admiral Ernest King, the commander-in-chief of the Atlantic Fleet, had ordered the commanders of his vessels to engage any Axis warship 'within sight or sound contact' of American shipping. On 7 July, in a message to Congress, the President emphasised that the US Navy had received orders to 'insure the safety of communications in the approaches between Iceland and the United States and all other strategic outposts'; the following day, he deflected a journalist's question about the ever-shifting limits between the two hemispheres with a joke: 'That is, I say, depending on the geographer I had seen the previous night.'[94]

Permanently resupplying a US garrison located within a German war zone would of course require rather more specific rules of engagement. Drafting them would be a somewhat delicate task, since the Secretary of the Navy and the Chief of Naval Operations were due to testify before the Naval Affairs Committee on 11 July. This session had been called to examine rumours that had been making the rounds about the extent to which the US Navy's far-ranging Neutrality Patrol was in the process of being turned into escort for British convoys in all but name. Thus, it was only a few hours after Knox and Stark had managed to satisfy the senators' curiosity that Hemisphere Defence Plan No. 4 was issued, becoming effective on 26 July. It provided for close escort of all US and Iceland-flagged ships travelling to and from Iceland. Encounters with German surface or subsurface raiders near these routes were 'to be viewed as actuated by a possibly unfriendly intent', thus strongly hinting at a shoot-first order.[95] For the Atlantic Fleet, Admiral King took this to mean that any U-boat which came within 160 km (100 miles) of an American convoy making its way to or from Iceland was fair game.[96] Crucially, in a manner similar to the expansion of the Atlantic Fleet's patrol area in April, both Roosevelt and Knox refused to give a geographical marker (like a longitude meridian) beyond which US vessels would not operate, thus increasing the likelihood of inadvertent clashes.

---

[94] 'Confidential. Press Conference # 753, Executive Office of the President, July 8, 1941 – 4.10 P.M., EST'; in: www.fdrlibrary.marist.edu/_resources/images/pc/pc0120.pdf (accessed 2 July 2020).

[95] B. Mitchell Simpson III, *Admiral Harold R. Stark: Architect of Victory, 1939–1945* (University of South Carolina Press 1989), pp 88–9.

[96] 'Operation Order No. 6–41 (19.7.1941)' as quoted in David Gannon, *Operation Drumbeat: The Dramatic True Story of Germany's First U-boat Attacks along the American Coast in World War II* (New York: Harper & Row 1990), pp 87–8.

Raeder's concerns that the US Navy's habit of shadowing any Axis vessel and reporting its current position in the clear might soon render the operations of the slower surface units and their supply ships impractical came one step closer to realisation on 1 August,[97] when the Atlantic Fleet deployed Task Force 1 (battleships *Arkansas*, *New York* and *Texas* plus numerous escorts) with exactly such a task in mind. To be rotated between Newfoundland and an improvised base in Hvalfjördhur (Iceland), these capital ships bordered on individual obsolescence, but their combined armour and armament posed a major challenge to an attempt by any surface unit of the Kriegsmarine to break out into the open Atlantic via one of the two obvious avenues to the east and west of Iceland. Moreover, King would have been secure in the knowledge – confirmed by the tactics followed by *Scharnhorst* and *Gneisenau* in Operation Berlin – that German capital ships would try to avoid a head-on confrontation with Allied vessels of their class, rather than allow themselves to be crippled by relatively minor combat damage far from their home bases. The mere presence of Task Force 1 would therefore serve as a major obstacle to any attempt by the Seekriegsleitung to repeat an operation along the lines of Berlin or Rheinübung.

However, finding a way to somehow reconcile the presence of such a powerful force with Washington politics and international law took several weeks. The Newfoundland summit (9–12 August 1941) between Churchill and Roosevelt gave the Chief of Naval Operations the necessary leverage, as it constituted a major break with much of the ambiguity that so far had been characteristic of Roosevelt's developing policy on this matter. During the course of the talks, the US Navy's commitment to escorting convoys (as opposed to patrolling), promised in March, was confirmed in principle, and some practical specifics were even addressed. A near-defeat in Congress then made the President hesitate again, causing much disappointment in London. On 25 August, the American government finally agreed to extend the remit of the growing naval force by now concentrated along the rim of the northwestern Atlantic. Effective from that date, US Navy forces were allowed to engage Axis surface units 'which attacked shipping along the sea lanes between North America and Iceland or which approached these lanes sufficiently closely to threaten such shipping'.[98] The latter definition in particular was of course loose enough to give naval commanders a great deal of flexibility. When a large part of the Atlantic Fleet joined the British in a fruitless hunt for a reported German heavy cruiser on the loose from 27 to 31 August they covered waters from northern Brazil to the

---

[97] 'Besprechung auf dem Berghof Ob.d.M. beim Führer am 22. Mai 1941. Anlage 1: Das gegenwärtige Problem der Seekriegführung im Atlantik im Hinblick auf die Haltung der USA (Mai 1941)'; in: Wagner (ed.), *Lagevorträge*, pp 227–36, esp. 233.

[98] Norton, 'Open Secret', p 73.

Denmark Strait.[99] It is unclear whether the commanders of the five task groups involved still operated under the instructions inherited from the Neutrality Patrol of old or whether they were carefully weighing the implications of the new set of instructions, since the sinking of a German vessel off Bermuda would have been difficult to justify with a view to protecting the Iceland–Newfoundland route. On 1 September, an order from the commander-in-chief of the Atlantic Fleet brought clarity on this point: it confirmed that all Axis raiders, whether of the surface or submarine variety, that appeared to be threatening shipping anywhere along the Iceland–North America shipping routes were to be engaged and destroyed. The same rules of engagement were also extended to the entirety of the old Neutrality Zone.[100]

For Dönitz, who was blissfully ignorant of the problems Knox and Roosevelt were encountering in their efforts to get the US Navy involved in the Atlantic, July and August would constitute all-time lows in the war against British shipping. New additions to his force were in keeping with the trend set in June: fourteen and sixteen boats. Mysteriously, however, convoy sightings were far more difficult to come by than in the days when his force had been substantially smaller. Both the compromise of naval Enigma and (to a lesser extent) the decision taken in mid-June to include merchantmen capable of steaming between 13 and 15 knots in the convoy system had temporarily swept the seas clean of merchantmen.[101] Only once in July was a meaningful concentration of U-boats achieved against a convoy; British losses to Axis submarines in this month totalled a miserly 94,000 GRT. Even so, wasted patrols did not yet make Dönitz suspicious: on 11 July he described the dearth of targets as 'temporary',[102] and on the 15th he consoled himself that an influx of additional boats would go a long way towards solving the problem.[103] Days later, he redeployed the bulk of his force to the north, from where it had been temporarily shifted in an effort to appease the Americans. However, results achieved in these waters were not much better. On the two occasions that a wolf pack was successfully concentrated against a convoy in August, the

---

[99] Rohwer, *Chronology*, p 94.

[100] Reproduced in: Robert C. Stern, *The US Navy and the War in Europe* (London: Seaforth 2012), pp 48–9.

[101] Gardner, *Decoding History*, p 154. How much Allied tonnage was 'saved' in this fashion by the Bletchley Park codebreakers in 1941 has been the subject of some controversy. Figures given by various authors range from 0.5 million to nearly 2 million GRT. See Sönke Neitzel, 'The Deployment of the U-boats'; in: Stephen Howarth and Derek Law (eds.), *The Battle of the Atlantic 1939–1945* (London: Greenhill Books 1994), pp 276–301, for a high, Gardner, *Decoding History*, pp 171–7, for a more conservative estimate.

[102] KTB Seekriegsleitung, Teil A (entry for 11 July 1941).

[103] BA/MA, RM 87/14 'Kriegstagebuch Befehlshaber der Unterseeboote (BdU), entry for 15 July 1941'. Henceforth quoted as 'KTB BdU'.

results were mixed. By then, Dönitz's command benefitted from an important change to their rules of engagement. As of 9 August, permission was granted to engage any kind of warship, unless it was positively identified as American, within the original war zone. In the extended war zone, permission was restricted to engage those enemy vessels (not just capital ships) that had been positively identified as belonging to the Royal Navy. The instructions to spare US merchantmen caught traversing the extended German war zone on their way to and from Iceland remained in place.[104] It would appear that the change came about as the direct result of reports from Dönitz that his U-boats had engaged and sunk at least two escorts in previous convoy battles. Rather remarkably, the Seekriegsleitung did not even attempt to allege self-defence on the part of the commanders involved, thus essentially owning up to the violation of a Führer's directive.[105]

The question before the historian is whether Raeder and Dönitz established a causal link between the U-boat arm's lack of success and an increased American presence. The evidence before us is ambiguous. On 1 July, an assessment by the Seekriegsleitung had voiced the suspicion that US Navy vessels had been involved in at least some of the losses incurred by German supply ships in early June.[106] On 9 July, at an emergency meeting called to discuss the US occupation of Iceland, Raeder had stressed the problems that a US Navy presence in the waters around the island was likely to create for both surface and subsurface raiders.[107] In a lengthy memo, dated 17 July, he went out of his way to stress that the US naval presence would allow the Royal Navy to concentrate its assets in the eastern Atlantic, thus facilitating its task; more specifically, the threat to the supply tankers which were key to surface raider operations had led to a marked 'worsening' of operating conditions. Irrespective of this, Raeder insisted, surface units would continue to be deployed for reasons 'of grand strategy and to support the U-boat war'.[108] When on 25 July, both Raeder and Dönitz came to the Wolfsschanze to brief the dictator on a number of points, it must have become clear to an attentive listener that the two admirals were starting to diverge in their assessment of the

[104] KTB Seekriegsleitung, Teil A (entry for 9 August 1941).

[105] KTB Seekriegsleitung, Teil A (entries for 6 and 9 August 1941). No such sinkings did in fact occur; what is remarkable is the candour displayed by all levels of command involved.

[106] BA/MA, RM 7/120 'OKM, Seekriegsleitung Iop 1313/41 Lagebetrachtung über die ausserheimische Kriegführung (1.7.1941)'.

[107] 'Der Oberbefehlshaber der Kriegsmarine B. Nr. I b 1266/41 op Chefs. Besprechung beim Führer im Hauptquartier Wolfsschanze am 9.VII. 1941 nachmittags (10.7.1941)'; in: Wagner (ed.), Lagevorträge, pp 264–71.

[108] BA/MA, RM 7/1058 'Der Oberbefehlshaber der Kriegsmarine und Chef der Seekriegsleitung B.Nr.1. Skl.Ia 1263/41 g.Kdos Chefs. an Gruppe West, Gruppe Nord, Befehlshaber der Schlachtschiffe, Befehlshaber der Kreuzer, B.d.U., F.d.Z. Betr.: Weiterer Einsatz der Überwasserstreitkräfte (17.7.1941)'.

situation. Though Raeder appears to have done most of the talking, Dönitz was given the opportunity to speak about the situation in the North Atlantic. The Kriegsmarine commander-in-chief stressed that the occupation of Iceland had made operations for all service branches involved in the Battle of the Atlantic more hazardous. He also implied that the recent drop in sinkings was down in equal measure to American and British actions.[109] Dönitz, for his part, listed a number of points he felt were behind the poor pickings: the insufficient number of available U-boats, the lack of experience of some crews, the recent loss of resupply tankers in the central Atlantic and poor weather. As far as he was concerned, the first point was the most important by far.[110] If he so much as mentioned American intervention even in passing, the minutes do not reflect it. And if Hitler picked up on the subtle discrepancy between the two briefings, he did not bring it out into the open.

Since Dönitz found himself in the peculiar position of giving a briefing for the supreme warlord of the Third Reich while in the presence of his own commander-in-chief, the possibility that he followed instructions to leave certain subjects to Raeder while speaking in front of Hitler cannot be ruled out. Fortunately, we also have a record of a visit the BdU paid to the Seekriegsleitung just a fortnight earlier in order to discuss at length any concerns he had about the state of play of the U-boat war. There he noted the recent drop in convoy sightings, the growing proficiency of British escorts as well as the desirability of occupying the Azores and commissioning the first U-boat tankers. He was also full of praise for the types of attack boat his command was equipped with. At no point did he address the issue of American interference.[111]

Raeder's admission that by now the surface units were supporting the U-boat war rather than the other way around was not reflected in the only area where it really mattered: the allocation of skilled German labour. More and more indicators suggested that the window of opportunity to inflict mortal damage on Britain's Atlantic lifeline was closing fast and that the maintenance alone of the battleships and cruisers made calls on the workforce, which was not really reflected in the sinkings achieved by these units.[112] Even so, it does not appear to have occurred to the admiral to cancel the two remaining capital ships (heavy cruiser *Seydlitz* and aircraft carrier *Graf Zeppelin*), which were

[109] 'Der Oberbefehlshaber der Kriegsmarine B. Nr. Skl. Ib 1321/41 g.Kdos Chefs. Vortrag des Ob.d.M. beim Führer am 25. Juli nachm. in Wolfsschanze (n.d.)'; in: Wagner (ed.), *Lagevorträge*, pp 271–7.

[110] Ibid., p 275.

[111] 'Vortrag BdU (Vizeadmiral Dönitz) über Stand U-Bootkrieg'; in: KTB Seekriegsleitung, Teil A (entry for 11 July 1941).

[112] BA/MA, RM 7/845 'B.Nr. Skl.-U II 2495/41 g.Kdos. Rückgang des U-Bootneubaus und seine Auswirkungen auf den weiteren Aufbau der Unterseebootwaffe, n.d. (August 1941)'.

still a year or more from their commissioning date. When Hitler gave his tentative approval to carry on with fitting out both ships, Raeder seized it with both hands and included the two vessels in a long shopping list, which he mailed to a horrified armaments minister.[113]

Dönitz was now well past believing that this dearth of targets was just 'temporary'. What with having had an all-time high daily average of thirty-six U-boats on the lookout for convoys in August and even before the incident in Tarafal Bay, he ordered a full-blown investigation by the Marinenachrichtendienst into the security of the U-boat's encoded communications.[114] It was produced on 20 October and by and large tended to give Enigma a clean bill of health. British successes in pinpointing the location of gathering wolf packs were put down to the assumed range and effectiveness of British radar and high-frequency direction finding (HF/DF) sets. When on one occasion no record was found of radio communications by a group of U-boats that HF/DF could have homed in on, the report just assumed that this had happened nonetheless against instructions.[115]

Dönitz did not wait for the submission of the report before carrying out a number of preliminary security measures. Most of these were for nought since they assumed an internal security leak of a human nature. He did, however, also insist that in future communications giving the position of a U-boat be double-enciphered. In the time it took Bletchley Park to detect this ruse and find a remedy to it, the period for decoding a signal was never less than fifty hours.[116] This, together with the breaking of Admiralty Naval Cypher No. 3 by the B-Dienst in the first week of September,[117] meant that for the next four weeks Dönitz had a fighting chance of assembling a strong enough wolf pack before the British Admiralty could reroute the prey he was stalking. Partly as a result of this, he was able to concentrate eleven U-boats against SC-42 between 9 and 16 September. They lost two of their number but accounted for nineteen merchantmen (75,574 GRT) sunk, a balance sheet no

---

[113] BA/MA, RM 7/845 'Der Oberbefehlshaber der Kriegsmarine B.Nr.Skl.-UI II 2495/41 g.Kdos. an den Chef des Oberkommandos der Wehrmacht und den Reichsminister für Bewaffnung und Munition Herrn Dr. Ing. Todt (31.7.1941)'. See also BA/MA, RM 7/94 'Seekriegsleitung B.Nr. 1.Skl. IIIa 16703/41 gKdos an SKL Qu A I, SKL Qu A II und M Wa (A Wa). Betrifft: Führerweisung vom 14.7.1941 (24.7.1941)', which clearly prioritises the fitting out of *Seydlitz* and *Graf Zeppelin*.

[114] This had been triggered by a B-Dienst intercept of a message from the British Admiralty dated 6 September giving the current positions of the U-boats of a wolf pack to within a few kilometres. KTB Seekriegsleitung, Teil A (entry for 19 September 1941).

[115] See the discussion in R. A. Ratcliff, 'Searching for Security: the German Investigations into Enigma's Security'; in: *Intelligence and National Security*, Vol. 14, No. 1 (1999), pp 146–67, esp. pp 151–2.

[116] Hinsley et al, *British Intelligence*, Vol. 2, pp 173–4 (+ appendix 9).

[117] KTB Seekriegsleitung Teil A (entry for 23 September 1941). The B-Dienst would continue to read this code until the end of the year.

doubt made possible by the inexperience of the Canadian escort group.[118] The arrival of timely reinforcements from Iceland increased the number of escorts from six to fifteen and in all likelihood prevented a massacre. Total sinkings for the month were finally beginning to bear a relation to the number of U-boats on station: 202,820 GRT.

In the meantime, Hitler's attempts to de-escalate the situation in the North Atlantic by issuing restrictive rules of engagement had suffered another major setback. On 4 September, the US destroyer *Greer* cooperated with an Iceland-based Lockheed Hudson in pinpointing the position of the submerged *U-652* and locking the U-boat in her sonar beam; incapable of outrunning the American vessel, the commander of *U-652* fired a torpedo, which missed and was in turn subjected to a depth-charge attack, which likewise failed to find its target. To the US President, who a only a few weeks earlier had had his Secretary of the Navy and the Chief of Naval Operations grilled by the Senate Naval Affairs Committee on the extent to which the US Navy was allowing itself to be dragged into a shooting war, the *Greer* incident was a major break. In a speech broadcast to the nation on 11 September, he omitted to mention the role played by the bomber and instead reminded his listeners that the vessel had not been involved in convoying (the politically hot potato amongst critics of his policy), but had just been engaged on a peaceful mission of 'carrying the American mail to Iceland', when she suddenly found herself under attack. As a result of this action, the President vowed that from now on US 'naval vessels and planes will protect all merchant ships – not only American ships but ships of any flag – engaged in commerce in our defensive waters'. He likewise placed great emphasis on the need to protect 'the freedom of the seas'.[119] Secretary Knox was only marginally more specific when he announced the introduction of convoying in all but name on 15 September. Merchantmen bearing Lend-Lease goods from 'the United States to countries neighbouring Iceland', he said, would be given all possible protection.[120] For the US Navy, this meant that orders first issued in great secrecy in early July had finally and irrevocably been committed to by the administration. Convoying by US Navy escorts began the following day, when five destroyers joined the UK-bound HX-150. Over the following weeks, they would generally shepherd Allied ships across the central part of the North Atlantic limited by the two MOMP (Mid-Ocean

---

[118] The Royal Canadian Navy was afflicted with growing pains like no other belligerent navy involved in World War II, the result of a twenty-fold increase in its strength in 1939. See Roger Sarty et al., *No Higher Purpose: The Official Operational History of the Royal Canadian Navy in the Second World War, 1939–1943*. Volume II, Part 1 (Ontario: Vanvbell Publishing 2002).

[119] For the full text of the speech, see Samuel I. Rosenman (ed.), *The Public Papers and Addresses of Franklin D. Roosevelt, 1941: The Call to Battle Stations* (New York: Harper & Brothers 1950), pp 384–92.

[120] KTB Seekriegsleitung, Teil A (entry for 16 September 1941).

Meeting Point) drop-off points. This meant a penetration of the eastern half of the North Atlantic as far as 22 degrees west, thus broadly staying within the geographical limit set by the inclusion of Iceland in the US Navy's operational area. In actual fact, American participation in the close escort of transatlantic convoys (as opposed to those headed for outposts like Iceland) marked a major step up the escalatory ladder.

For the Germans, this meant that the phase of American retrenchment was now well and truly over. The American refusal to unambiguously spell out even the approximate limits of terms such as 'defensive waters' and 'the neighbourhood of Iceland', thus taking the by now customary obfuscation to a new level, only added insult to injury.[121] Raeder likened the President's announcement to 'a locally limited declaration of war' and asked Hitler on 17 September for a relaxation of the rules of engagement still limiting the U-boat commanders' freedom of action. Specifically, he suggested reducing the old US Neutrality Zone to 32 km (20 miles) and insisted that the part of the August directive which forbade attacks on US vessels, if they had been identified as such prior to an attack, should be rescinded if they were caught in the act of escorting an enemy convoy. The dictator again demurred and asked Raeder for four more weeks, by which time he believed the Russian campaign would have entered its final phase. Rules of engagement as decreed on 9 August essentially remained in place.[122]

Dönitz, who was present at the same meeting, supported his commander-in-chief in asking for the existing rules of engagement to be scrubbed. Over and above this, he stressed that one current problem far outweighed all others: the British success in evading his patrol lines time and again, something that could only be rectified by increasing the number of submersibles on patrol at any given time. The fact that the US Navy was starting to provide escorts for these convoys was immaterial if his U-boats failed to get to grips with them more than occasionally.[123]

The Seekriegsleitung chief of staff, Kurt Fricke, on the other hand, could not bring himself to shrug off quite so easily the irritation posed by American interventionism. In a conversation with Ambassador Karl Ritter, he was adamant that 'the extreme consideration shown to the USA was having major military disadvantages'.[124]

In October 1941, the work of the Bletchley Park codebreakers made it possible to successfully reroute fifteen convoys. Luckily for the British, Dönitz did not take this as his cue to question Enigma's security again. As it

---

[121] KTB Seekriegsleitung, Teil A (entries for 13, 14, 16 and 20 September 1941).
[122] 'Vortrag des Ob.d.M. beim Führer am 17.9.1941 nachm. Wolfsschanze'; in: Wagner (ed.), *Lagevorträge*, pp 286–304, esp. pp 286, 295–6, 300–1.
[123] Ibid., p 288.
[124] KTB Seekriegsleitung, Teil A (entry for 1 October 1941).

happened, he was able to attribute a poor rate of intercepted convoys to a number of other factors. First, the disruption of training schedules in the Baltic due to the invasion of the USSR in June meant that in October his front-line flotillas only received a total of four new U-boats. Secondly – and much more seriously – the previous weeks had seen him fight and lose a battle over U-boat deployment. By the beginning of October seven boats had been deployed to the Arctic and a total of six to the Mediterranean. A number of others had to take time off their sorties to escort blockade runners or report on weather patterns near the Arctic Circle. The Mediterranean and Arctic boats were shifted to these theatres to support the army by interdicting traffic engaged in resupplying the besieged British outposts of Malta and Tobruk as well as the Soviet forces defending Murmansk. However, the vessels involved in the Tobruk run in particular were few in number, small in tonnage and generally of a shallow draft, which made them poor targets. The Mediterranean U-boats did at least account – in an almost incidental way – for a number of major warships before the end of the year,[125] but their comrades in the Arctic did not successfully engage even one of the British PQ convoys being run to Archangelsk or Murmansk before March 1942, when PQ-13 lost two merchantmen.[126] Finding himself thus short-changed by at least twenty-three U-boats, Dönitz had to be content with a total monthly tonnage sunk of 156.554 GRT. To make matters worse, he then learned that Raeder and Fricke had accepted a demand of Hitler's to more than quadruple the number of U-boats in the Mediterranean in order to support Rommel's position in Libya.[127] As a result of this idiosyncratic decision, over the course of the next seven weeks, Dönitz had to part with twenty-six more U-boats, which would never return to the Atlantic theatre. Three of them were lost in action within days of entering the Mediterranean; three more were lost and six heavily damaged in attempting to force their way past the British defences of the Strait of Gibraltar.[128]

Set against this, however, was a development of a more positive sort for the U-boat arm. Whether by coincidence or not, the relaxation of the rules of engagement governing encounters with warships had seen an immediate rise

---

[125] Carrier HMS *Ark Royal* (13 November), battleship HMS *Barham* (25 November) and light cruiser HMS *Galatea* (14 December). See David Brown, *Warship Losses of World War Two* (London: Arms & Armour, rev. ed. 1996), pp 52–4.

[126] This despite the fact that the Seekriegsleitung had been aware of the running of these convoys since the first week of October 1941. See KTB Seekriegsleitung, Teil A (entry for 7 October 1941) and 'Lagebetrachtung der Seekriegsleitung zur weiteren Kampfführung gegen England (Stand 20.10.1941)'; in: Michael Salewski (ed.), *Die deutsche Seekriegsleitung 1935–1945. Band III: Denkschriften und Lagebetrachtungen 1938–1944* (Frankfurt am Main: Bernard & Graefe 1973), pp 215–34, esp. p 228.

[127] KTB Seekriegsleitung, Teil A (entry for 28 October 1941).

[128] Blair, *The Hunters*, p 403.

in Allied escorts sunk. Within hours of Dönitz stressing to his U-boat commanders engaged in the battle for convoy HG-70 that escorts were fair game again, *U-568* engaged and sank the British corvette HMS *Picotee* off Iceland on 12 August. One escort destroyer and two more corvettes followed over the course of the two next months.[129] Then came the battle for SC-48 (15–18 October 1941). When it became obvious the convoy was being stalked, Allied commanders in Newfoundland and Iceland rushed in reinforcements, including a group of five US Navy destroyers. The US Navy had escorted its first convoy to a MOMP in mid-September and had in fact very nearly found itself in the position of having to fight off a wolf pack on its first escort detail. Now, seniority meant that the American commander assumed tactical control on 16 October over a force comprising British, Canadian, US and Free French vessels. The ensuing problems of command and control no doubt assisted the Germans during the continuation of the attack. When they called it off, they had accounted for nine merchantmen and two escorts. *U-568* also hit and very nearly sank the USS *Kearny*, which just about made it back to Iceland with eleven of her crew dead. That Hitler's original order on sparing escorts bore no relation whatsoever to the reality of naval war in the North Atlantic can be gleaned from the fact that the commander of *U-562* – who made no attempt to hide that he had deliberately targeted a destroyer – was in no way penalised or reprimanded. Still, a threshold had been crossed. The belligerent status of the USA had been underwritten with blood.[130]

To a generation brought up on stories of the outrage caused in the USA by the sinking of the *Lusitania*, the consequences of this incident were rather unexpected. It just so happened that over the previous weeks the omissions in the President's account of the *Greer* incident had come to light in the course of a hearing before the Senate Naval Affairs Committee which the Chief of Naval Operations was obliged to testify to.[131] This may have contributed to muffling cries for vengeance when the news of the *Kearny*'s torpedoing was received. On the other hand, the incident does not appear to have significantly boosted the cause of isolationism in the United States. When the Atlantic Fleet prepared for the challenges inherent in the ABC-1941 US–British staff talks in Washington, Roosevelt had refused to give King draftees with which to man his ships.[132] As result of this the sailors killed on the USS *Kearny* were widely considered to have become victims of their profession. Roosevelt waited for nearly two weeks to make a statement on the incident, and when he did, his speech on Navy Day (27 October),

---

[129] For details of these sinkings, see Brown, *Warship Losses*, pp 49–51.

[130] The most detailed account of the *Kearny*'s torpedoing is provided by Abbazia, *Roosevelt's Navy*, pp 265–80.

[131] Norton, 'Open Secret', p 75.

[132] A decision soon rendered untenable by manpower shortages and finally rescinded on 25 November 1941, Abbazia, *Roosevelt's Navy*, p 338.

while tinged with emotion,[133] did little more than reinforce the points already made in his previous exposition on 11 September. Even at this late stage in the game, the fact that the USS *Kearny* had been engaged in escorting a convoy was kept from the public. Only time would tell how long this state of undeclared war could persist without precipitating a deliberate escalation.

The next incident was inconclusive because of its timing and the fact that no lives were lost: only two days after the President's address, the US Navy tanker *Salinas* was attacked and severely damaged by *U-106* while travelling as part of westbound ONS-28. She survived two torpedo hits and reached St John's on Newfoundland under her own steam on 3 November. In the meantime, before either the navy or the American public had had a chance to take stock of this latest incident, another clash had occurred which effectively pushed the attack on the *Salinas* to the sidelines and – arguably – into historical oblivion altogether. In the small hours of 31 October 1941, *U-552* torpedoed and sank the destroyer USS *Reuben James* with heavy loss of life. In many ways, the destruction of the *Reuben James* was an accident waiting to happen. Even though the attack occurred at night, it probably would not have made much of a difference if *U-552* had engaged her in daytime, since the vessel shared the characteristic four-stack silhouette with the fifty US-built destroyers which had been delivered to the Royal Navy as part of the destroyers-for-bases deal of September 1940. Furthermore, the USS *Reuben James* had been in the process of escorting eastbound convoy HX-156 and found herself in the area in which the new Security Zone claimed by the USA overlapped with the operational area declared by the Germans in March of that year.[134] Even though this incident had a markedly different quality from the previous ones – a sizeable US vessel had actually been sunk – the political reaction in Washington remained fairly restrained.[135] Apart from the fact that again no draftees had been involved, the gradual escalation which had been the hallmark of the clashes in the Atlantic so far (the *Greer* incident, where no blood was drawn; two torpedoings, only one of which involved loss of life; finally, an outright sinking) may well have inured the American public to the existence of a shooting war, which involved one of their armed services but as yet did not affect them at a personal level.[136]

---

[133] Norton, 'Open Secret', p 76, describes the speech as 'histrionic'.

[134] For a more detailed account of this action, the reader is again referred to Abbazia, *Roosevelt's Navy*, pp 293–308.

[135] The war diarist of the Seekriegsleitung stressed the fact that both Roosevelt and Hull had exercised considerable restraint in their public statements ('*während Roosevelt und Hull sich auf der Pressekonferenz sehr zurückhalten . . .* '). KTB Seekriegsleitung, Teil A (entry for 4 November 1941).

[136] On the American public mood in those days, see Norton, 'Open Secret', p 77; Abbazia, *Roosevelt's Navy*, 305–6.

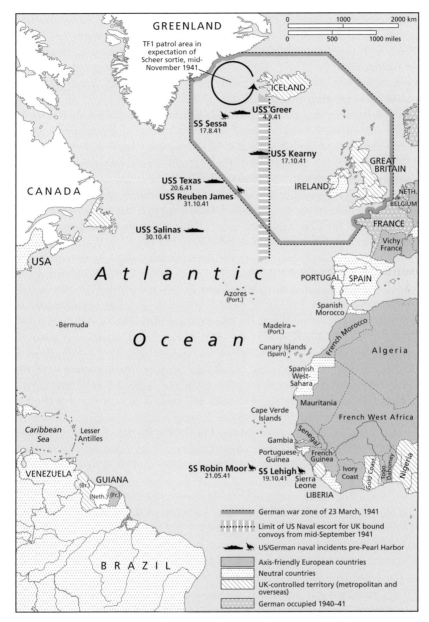

Map 8.2 Operational areas in the North Atlantic and location of US–German naval encounters, May–December 1941.

Among Washington legislators, the incident encouraged many who had previously been sceptical to rally round the flag and acquiesce in the President's further dismantling of laws and regulations standing in the way of further military mobilisation: after the Coast Guard was put under the operational command of the Atlantic Fleet (2 November), Lend-Lease was extended to the embattled Soviet state (7 November). As a next step, the last obstacle standing in the way of direct US assistance to Britain – the Neutrality Legislation of 1939 – was rendered virtually toothless by amendments which were passed first by the Senate (7 November) and then the House (13 November). As a result, from the moment the President signed the Bill into law (17 November), US merchantmen could be armed to fend off U-boats and – crucially – would be allowed to enter the harbours of belligerents.

While all this was happening and unbeknownst to Hitler or Raeder, the stage was being set for a confrontation which, had it been played out, would have made open war inevitable. Although history has taught us that the doomed sortie of the *Bismarck* was the last by a German capital ship into the Atlantic, at the time the Seekriegsleitung had other plans. *Prinz Eugen*, *Scharnhorst* and *Gneisenau* had spent months marooned in Brest, with the last two vessels suffering important damage in persistent British air raids – *Gneisenau* on 6 April, *Scharnhorst* on 24 July.[137] These setbacks left Hitler seriously exasperated and by 17 September led him for the first time to question in Raeder's presence the viability of Brest as a base and suggest relocating the squadron to Norway instead.[138] The admiral insisted that further Atlantic forays were 'the only right way' and pleaded for more time. He suggested early 1942 as the moment when the three ships should be turned loose on the Atlantic sea lanes;[139] a lengthy entry in the Seekriegsleitung's diary a few days later likewise made a detailed case for a two-pronged foray into the North Atlantic by both the Brest group and the *Tirpitz* with at least one heavy cruiser. The two task forces were to annihilate at least one convoy and then retreat back to Norwegian bases together.[140]

Admiral Rolf Carls, commander of *Marinegruppenkommando Nord*, one of the commands which would inevitably be involved in the deployment of the *Tirpitz*, once she and her crew concluded the last shakedown cruise, concurred, but advised a postponement: the way the war appeared to be going for Germany, by the end of the year pro-Axis neutrals would be flocking to the

---

[137] The Bristol Beaufort piloted by Flying Officer Kenneth Campbell scored a torpedo hit which wrecked *Gneisenau*'s starboard screw and propeller shaft, confining her to port for six months. Rohwer, *Chronology*, p 67, 88.

[138] 'OKM. Seekriegsleitung B. Nr. 1. Skl I b 1555/41 g.Kdos Chefs. Vortrag des Ob.d.M. beim Führer am 17.9.1941 nachm. Wolfsschanze.(n.d.)'; in: Wagner (ed.), *Lagevorträge*, pp 286–9.

[139] Ibid.

[140] KTB Seekriegsleitung, Teil A (entry for 23 September 1941).

German cause. This would probably allow the Seekriegsleitung to base the *Tirpitz* and any consort at Casablanca or the Spanish navy base of El Ferrol, thus making possible repeated sorties without having to undergo the perilous journey past Iceland several times while at the same time avoiding the attentions of the RAF.[141] The emphasis on commerce warfare with capital ships, however, remained unchanged.

A mere three weeks later, the forecasts made by Carls had to be toned down substantially: in light of continued Soviet resistance, a collapse of the USSR and the redirection of key Wehrmacht assets in the general direction of Morocco and northern Spain were no longer on the cards, thus confining the main units to their current bases. In an address to senior Wehrmacht officers on 8 November Raeder was even willing to concede that the U-boats were now the main agents of German commerce warfare.[142] His ire over this state of affairs, however, was not directed at the Royal Navy's command of the seas or the recuperative powers of the Red Army, but the interfering US Atlantic Fleet. What is most revealing is that the *Grossadmiral* should single out not the destroyers now routinely acting as escorts for British convoys, but the cruisers and battleships of the Neutrality Patrol. In and of itself a leftover from 1939, it had turned into a major pebble in Raeder's shoe because in his perception its cruises had reached a point where by their very presence they compromised forays by Kriegsmarine surface raiders to a degree where their resumption was called into question. Camouflaged raiders making their way to the South Atlantic or Indian Ocean might still elude shadowers by means of subterfuge, but a repeat by the battleships of the Berlin operation against Britain's North Atlantic lifeline – Raeder's perpetual pet project – was looking increasingly improbable. Moreover, the tankers they depended on were liable to be picked off one by one as had happened in June 1941.[143] The Royal Navy on its own might not have been in a position to provide enough prying eyes to scour the surface of the sea for the Kriegsmarine's floating service stations, but the US Navy – with little else to keep it occupied at present – could.

During his presentation Raeder glossed over a point which, if anything, was even more crucial to capital ship operations than the presence of the US Atlantic Fleet: fuel availability. The *Ostheer*'s failure to defeat the Red Army had the unexpected effect of keeping army and Luftwaffe fuel consumption in the Russian theatre of operations at a level which according to pre-Barbarossa calculations should have begun to decrease

---

[141] BA/MA RM 7/1058 'Oberbefehlshaber Marinegruppenkommando Nord op 1913/41 an den Oberbefehlshaber der Kriegsmarine Herrn Großadmiral Dr.h.c. Raeder (15.10.1941)'.

[142] BA/MA, RM 7/1771 'Probleme und Aufgaben der deutschen Seekriegführung. Stand Anfang November 1941. Vortrag bei der Tagung der Befehlshaber und Kommandierenden Generale am 8.XI.1941'.

[143] Ibid., pp 68–71 (post-war pagination).

from mid-September onwards.[144] The simultaneous failure to reach even the northernmost of the Caucasus oil wells meant that Germany had to demand that her ally Romania increase domestic production. The timing for this could not have been less propitious, since relations between the two Axis powers were strained by a number of economic issues. Romania had pledged itself to supply Germany with grain and oil and pay for the needs of German servicemen based on its national territory, a definition that the Germans had taken to include all units passing through Romanian territory on their way to and from the Eastern Front. Private purchases by German soldiers had also led to rampant inflation. A struggling oil industry, the output of which had been stagnating for five years,[145] as likely as not contributed in some measure to the escalating war of words between diplomats from both countries, until the Romanians terminated any further deliveries to Germany and Italy in mid-November. A resumption was made contingent upon payment of the gold equivalent of 20 million Reichsmark.[146]

As these issues were being ironed out, Raeder had to own up to the dictator that fuel availability, British superiority in the air and the growing US naval presence ruled out a major sortie by the *Tirpitz* for the time being. He did insist, however, that the Brest group should still be left in place to execute shorter forays against convoys plying the UK–Gibraltar route.[147] Four days later, in a paper summarising the gist of his talks at the Wolfsschanze for his senior subordinates, he admitted that a sortie along the lines of the Berlin operation would put at risk not just two or three capital ships but also fuel reserves that would have to be pre-positioned at a number of meeting points for the marauding task force. In light of the 'the current fuel situation' such cargo had to be seen as 'irreplaceable' and hence too valuable to be risked.[148] A fortnight later fuel allocation for the Kriegsmarine as a whole (only the U-boat service was excepted) was slashed by 50 per cent.

Despite this unpromising backdrop, Raeder clung to the notion of seeing through one long-range operation involving a surface raider: plans were ready

[144] Wilhelm Meier-Dörnberg, *Die Ölversorgung der Kriegsmarine 1935 bis 1945* (Freiburg: Rombach 1973) [= Einzelschriften zur militärischen Geschichte des Zweiten Weltkrieges, Bd. 11], pp 57–63.

[145] Romanian oil production had peaked at over 8 million tons in 1936, but had dropped to 6.24 million tons in 1939 and 5.81 million tons in 1940. Sebastian Balta, *Rumänien und die Großmächte in der Ära Antonescu, 1940–1944* (Stuttgart: Franz Steiner 2005) [= Quellen und Studien zur Geschichte des östlichen Europa, Bd. 69], p 223.

[146] 'B.Nr.1. Skl. Ib 2133/41 op g.Kdos. Chefs. Vortrag des Ob.d.M. beim Führer in Berlin am 12.12.41 (15.12.1941)', esp. Anlage 4; in: Wagner (ed.), *Lagevorträge*, pp 325–38.

[147] 'Der Oberbefehlshaber der Kriegsmarine und Chef der Seekriegsleitung B. Nr. 1 Skl. Ib 1951/41 op g.Kdos. Chefs. Vortrag Ob.d.M. beim Führer am 13. November 1941, nachmittags in Wolfsschanze'; in: Wagner (ed.), *Lagevorträge*, pp 304–10.

[148] BA/MA, RM 7/1058 'Seekriegsleitung B.Nr.1 Skl Ia 1905/41 g.Kdos. Chefs. Betr.: Einsatz der Schlachtschiffe und Kreuzer (17.11.1941)'.

for the pocket battleship *Admiral Scheer* to exit through the Denmark Strait and engage in commerce warfare as far as the Indian Ocean. On 13 November, Raeder had put the matter to Hitler, who eventually declined to give the go-ahead, since he openly admitted fearing the blow to German prestige should the vessel be lost. The paperwork linked to the mission offers interesting insights into the evolution of the undeclared war between Germany and the USA. Even though it is not quite clear whether the admiral was aware of the presence of Task Force 1 in the waters around Iceland, he had had the foresight to prepare an elaborate set of rules of engagement that covered any encounters with US ships by Kriegsmarine surface vessels in general and the *Scheer* in particular. To some extent, they still reflected Hitler's concerns to avoid further escalation in the Atlantic and stressed the need to avoid contact whenever possible. At the same time, instructions for dealing with shadowers could not have been more different from the ones issued to the Rheinübung task force in May – in such a situation, the commanding officer was admonished not to dither and once fire had been opened, to 'make sure of the annihilation of the enemy'.[149] The dictator's hand in this becomes evident in a marginal note by a staff officer explaining another step up the escalatory ladder: the Führer, who until now had always reined in the navy's natural tendency to engage American units, now insisted that camouflaged raiders challenged by US vessels should feign willingness to submit to a search, then torpedo the American warship as the boarding party came aboard.[150]

Unbeknownst to Raeder, Bletchley Park had been decoding much of the traffic which accompanied the preparations for the *Scheer*'s sortie, and as a result the Admiralty in London was preparing an ambush in the waters around Iceland. The new battleship *King George V* was assigned the area to the east of the Arctic island, while the vessels of Task Force 1 (battleships *Idaho* and *Mississippi*, cruisers *Wichita* and *Tuscaloosa*) were to lie in wait in the Denmark Strait. They operated under the rules of engagement given to the US Atlantic Fleet on 25 August for the engagement of Axis surface raiders in the waters around Iceland, though it is unclear to what extent these orders would have covered their subordination under British tactical command. The pocket battleship's advantage in speed might have been enough to outrun the old US battleships,[151] but the same did not apply to the supporting cruisers or, for that matter, *King George V*. Had *Scheer* been lost – as she very well might have been – to a force partly made up of US ships, it is difficult to see how this could

---

[149] 'Vortrag Ob.d.M. beim Führer am 13. November 1941, nachmittags in Wolfsschanze. Anlage 2: Richtlinien für das Verhalten beim Zusammentreffen mit amerikanischen Streitkräften'; in: Wagner (ed.), *Lagevorträge*, pp 312–3.

[150] Ibid.

[151] Even though *Idaho* and *Mississippi* were modernised in the early 1930s, this resulted in only a marginal speed increase to 21.5 knots. Top speed for the *Deutschland*-class pocket battleships is given by various sources as ranging from 26 to 28 knots.

have been hushed up for more than a couple of days, especially since the British would have had a major stake in leaking the information to the world's media. Once the dictator's concerns led to *Scheer*'s sortie being scrubbed, the last four weeks prior to the German declaration of war turned into something of an anticlimax. Historian Patrick Abbazia has put this down to both sides finding themselves in a situation where they could neither afford to back down nor (as yet) declare war.[152] While essentially true in a wider sense, this assessment does not quite tally with the operational situation that Dönitz faced in those days. The eight U-boats he had been forced to detach to support the *Scheer* sortie were now free to resume commerce warfare, albeit with half-empty fuel tanks. However, to the admiral this was cold comfort in view of other assignments he found himself lumbered with. Apart from the six or seven boats now permanently detached to the Arctic, there was also the new Mediterranean assignment. The latter, he had been told on 29 October, would have to be increased from the originally intended six to a total of twenty-four U-boats 'as soon as possible'.[153] The expected protest was cut off with a truly astonishing statement: it was 'out of the question' to question this directive since 'the Führer is even willing to cease submarine warfare in the Atlantic until the Mediterranean situation has been led to a satisfactory conclusion'.[154] What with deliveries of new boats to the front-line flotillas hitting an all-time low of five in October, Dönitz predicted the end of commerce warfare in the Atlantic by mid-November.[155] As it turned out, he was out by only one week, when a small pack operating off Newfoundland was shifted to Gibraltar to ward off a feared British–Gaullist operation against French North Africa. For want of U-boats actually engaged in operations on the North Atlantic run, the possibility of further US–German naval clashes had for the time being become a moot point.

8.4   A Time for Reflection? The Late Autumn Impasse

On 28 September 1941, the Seekriegsleitung's Third Department, which concerned itself with the tonnage available to the Allies, put together a detailed estimate of the progress made so far in the war against Allied merchant shipping. They estimated the average monthly loss to have been in the region of 450,000 GRT, which was an overestimate of at least 20 per cent, even when losses to other agencies (aircraft, surface raiders, accidents) are included. The estimated replacement rate of 900,000 GRT built in British and Empire yards in 1941 alone, on the other hand, was quite close to the truth. The report

---

[152] Abbazia, *Roosevelt's Navy*, p 280.
[153] KTB Seekriegsleitung, Teil A (entry for 29 October 1941).
[154] Ibid.
[155] KTB Seekriegsleitung, Teil A (entry for 3 November 1941).

factors in the growing US contribution (800,000 GRT in 1941, an estimated 4,000,000 GRT in 1942), but makes no mention of the numerous Norwegian, Dutch and Greek merchantmen, which joined the Allied side once their countries had been overrun by the Wehrmacht. Crucially, the conclusions drawn from this evidence were not far removed from contemporary British estimates: in view of the booming trade being done by Allied shipyards by mid-1942, new production would only just keep up with the rate of attrition; at some point after that, it would fall behind it. Hence, the report went on, a truly 'lethal' rate of attrition would have to lie somewhere between 800,000 and 1,000,000 GRT per month[156]. In view of the sinkings achieved in the second half of 1941, such an aim would appear to be overambitious to say the least. Given that the contribution made by other parts of the Wehrmacht (long-range bombers or surface raiders) had been steadily declining throughout this period, with a major comeback by the latter increasingly unlikely, the prospect for such a sinking rate appears downright utopian.

At this point, the key question to be asked is how Hitler, Raeder and Dönitz perceived the situation in the autumn 1941. The Führer was perfectly aware of the fact that sinkings from June onwards had been inadequate. He knew that U-boat numbers were still a long way away from what had been promised to the Kriegsmarine, but took solace in the number of submersibles now under construction in Germany's shipyards. The drop in sinkings he was willing to put down at least in part to the long summer days, which made wolf pack attacks (invariably a night-time activity) more difficult. The increased interference by the US Atlantic Fleet does not appear to have unduly concerned him.[157] As for Raeder, he had repeatedly put it to Hitler that a state of undeclared war already existed between Germany and the USA, and the Kriegsmarine was experiencing all the drawbacks and none of the benefits of such a state of affairs. At the same time, Raeder lacked Dönitz's single-minded commitment to submarine warfare: though the Seekriegsleitung's war diary freely admitted that successes against major warships in the Mediterranean would – impressive 'firsts' notwithstanding – as likely as not turn out to be one-offs,[158] he acquiesced in paralysing the war against Allied commerce by sending nearly a third of the U-boat force into the Mediterranean. He also clung to the strategy of using capital ships for commerce raiding long after the

---

[156] KTB Seekriegsleitung, Teil A (entry for 28 September 1941). An estimate already arrived at by *Korvettenkapitän* Heinz Aβman of the Seekriegsleitung in a major memorandum which was circulated among all the other service chiefs in July 1941. 'Denkschrift zum gegenwärtigen Stand der Seekriegführung gegen England Juli 1941 (Draft copy, 21.7.1941)'; in: Salewski (ed.), *Seekriegsleitung* III, pp 189–217, esp. 207.

[157] TB Goebbels, Bd. II.1, p 483 (entry for 24 September 1941) as well as Bd. II.2, p 51 (entry for 4 October 1941).

[158] KTB Seekriegsleitung, Teil A (entry for 15 November 1941). Two days previously, *U-81* had accounted for the fleet carrier HMS *Ark Royal* east of Gibraltar.

aerial and naval presence established by the British and American navies in the North Atlantic should have made it abundantly clear that such sorties had moved from being calculated risks to outright gambles.

What of his subordinate Dönitz? We are fortunate in that the *Befehlshaber der Unterseeboote* used the period of enforced leisure which the lull in commerce warfare had given him to take stock of the situation as he saw it. The end result was a lengthy letter to Raeder, dated 26 November, in which he exposed the challenges and opportunities which the next months would bring.[159] The omissions in this letter are every bit as interesting as the points he dwells on at length. For openers, there is not a single mention of the US Navy's presence (whether in the form of patrols or as escorts for British convoys) actually cramping his submariners' style. Nor does he advocate taking the U-boat war into the Western Hemisphere. If nothing else, this clearly reflects the fact that by November American intervention was not seen as big a problem as it may have appeared in May and June when a stream of orders emanating from the Seekriegsleitung at first glance appeared to place a ridiculous burden on the battle against convoys. In actual fact, stagnating U-boat numbers and the failure to find more than a few convoys played such an overwhelming role in blunting the edge of the German offensive in summer and autumn 1941 that any possible inhibitions about engaging the Americans cannot have affected the issue in any but the most marginal way. By late October, as is borne out by the minutes of a meeting of the *Führungsstab* at the Seekriegsleitung, the prospect of encountering US Navy vessels in a particular operational area no longer played even a minimal role in determining the allocation of U-boat wolf packs,[160] despite British hopes to the contrary.[161] Moreover, as we have seen, by this point rules of engagement governing encounters between German submersibles and Allied escorts had been sufficiently relaxed to make this problem more apparent than real.[162] Since even the sinking of the USS *Reuben*

---

[159] 'B.d.U. an den Ob.d.M. (26.11.1941)'; in: Wagner (ed.), *Lagevorträge*, pp 320–5. The original copy with barbed marginal comments by Raeder and his operations officer Gerhard Wagner can be found in BA/MA, RM 7/845.

[160] BA/MA, RM 7/170 'Besprechungspunkte mit Ia op Führungsstab (31.10.1941)'. The otherwise excellent O'Brien, *How the War Was Won*, p 183, is in error here.

[161] TNA, CAB 65/24 'W.M. (41) 112th Conclusions, Minute 1. Confidential Annex (12.11.1941)'.

[162] Between 9 August (when the rules on sparing escorts were relaxed) and 9 December 1941 (when all restrictions on engaging US vessels were removed), U-boats operating in the North Atlantic accounted for a total of eight Allied escort vessels: corvette HMS *Picotee* (12 August), escort destroyer HMS *Bath* (19 August), corvette HMS *Zinnia* (23 August), corvette HMCS *Lewis* (20 September), corvette HMS *Gladiolus* (16 October), escort destroyer HMS *Broadwater* (18 October), destroyer HMS *Cossack* (23 October) and destroyer USS *Reuben James* (31 October). This list does not include unsuccessful attacks or losses suffered by Allied navies in the Mediterranean. For further details, see Brown, *Warship Losses*, pp 47–53.

James had provoked neither a general war nor a rocket from Führer's Headquarters, it is easy to see why Dönitz might now be inclined to turn to other, more pressing worries.

Another notable omission is cypher security. While it is possible that the investigation into this matter carried out by the *Marinenachrichtendienst* satisfied him up to a point, it is equally important to consider that the dearth of convoy interceptions in October and November had a much more obvious explanation: the poor ratio of patrolling U-boats to square kilometres of North Atlantic at any given time. This problem (as Dönitz saw it) was caused by the more random routing and increased speed of Allied convoys, and then compounded many times over by the constant siphoning off of German units to other tasks or other theatres of war.

This problem was Dönitz's cue to turn to his main demand. Rather than ask – as he would from mid-1942 on – for add-on technology to increase the military potential of his boats or even a completely new type of submersible capable of higher underwater performance,[163] he insisted that the basic Type VII diesel-electric represented very much state of the art technology and was crewed by men who knew their trade inside out. Allied escorts had become more numerous and more skilled, but had only occasionally been able to inflict an outright defeat on an attacking wolf pack. The problems faced by his force at this point, both as regards finding convoys and overwhelming their escorts, could easily be solved by bringing more U-boats to the front line faster than before. He went on to touch on the perpetual bugbear of U-boat production – lack of skilled German labour – but then offered a solution to this problem that he must have known would displease Raeder massively: looking back on the sorry outcome of the planned *Scheer* sortie and the deleterious impact it had had on his operations, he bluntly stated that the capital ships of the German Navy (he included destroyers for good measure) had essentially outlived their strategic usefulness. In view of the calls they made on his U-boats whenever a sortie was even considered, they actually had the effect of saving the Allies lost tonnage. At best, such an operation might just about balance the books, but without any net gain. Barring a major operation like an amphibious descent on the Azores or the Cape Verdes, the admiral went on to argue, they should lose their priority call on skilled labour in favour of his U-boats. As far as the presence of the US Navy in general and its dreaded Neutrality Patrol in particular were concerned, Dönitz could not resist giving his report a note of bravado. He practically shrugged off the loss of the tanker network and

---

[163] 'Schreiben des Befehlshabers der U-Boote, Admiral Karl Dönitz, an Oberbefehlshaber der Kriegsmarine (24.6.1942)' as well as 'Schreiben Befehlshaber der U-Boote, Admiral Karl Dönitz, an Oberkommando der Kriegsmarine (1.9.1942)'; both in: Werner Rahn, 'Einsatzbereitschaft und Kampfkraft deutscher U-Boote 1942'; in: *Militärgeschichtliche Mitteilungen* Nr. 1/1990, pp 73–132, esp. pp 107–12.

stressed that 'to the U-boat, an increased presence of enemy capital ships in the operational area is to be equated with a highly welcome multitude of targets, not an increased danger'. In light of what Raeder had had to say on the same topic nine days previously, it is difficult to see how the admiral cannot have felt this as a deeply personal insult bordering on open insubordination.[164]

Blissfully unaware of the compromise of his codes and with little evidence as yet that the old diesel-electric subs were dangerously close to being turned into blunt weapons by a whole array of new Allied weapons, Dönitz was essentially echoing the assessment made by the Seekriegsleitung on 28 September: Germany had to make the most of the opportunity 1942 would afford it. That he did not raise the issue of penetrating American waters may seem strange to a generation of students of naval history brought up on tales of the massacre the U-boats would inflict off the US eastern seaboard that year, but this needs to be seen in the context of the time. In fact, his letter of 26 November is downright dismissive of the opportunities that operations off US harbours were likely to bring for more than a couple of weeks. Dönitz likely as not was allowing himself to be guided by the first U-boat campaign in these waters (March–October 1918) which had been something of a flop. The first submarine sent over to cruise off the US east coast enjoyed rich pickings, but the five that followed were thwarted by the quick implementation of convoying. Accordingly, the five U-boats that were sent out in December 1941 were very nearly recalled on 22 January 1942 on Raeder's orders and only kept on station for a little longer at the insistence of Hitler.[165]

Hence, it is important to realise that Karl Dönitz envisaged a campaign for 1942 which involved the same strategy his force had followed throughout 1941: stay out of reach of land-based air power whenever possible, seek out convoys in the eastern and central portions of the North Atlantic, overwhelm the escorts by sheer weight of numbers without making any fundamental changes to the tried and tested formula of wolf pack attack. American involvement was of relevance only insofar as the assistance of their shipyards to the British cause meant there was a real danger of the U-boat's successes being negated by Allied production. At no point does the danger of a major setback appear to have entered the admiral's mind; in view of the relatively low losses suffered throughout the fifteen months since Germany declared unrestricted submarine warfare in August 1940, this does not appear too surprising. At its heart, the Dönitz letter is best described as an assessment that is equally dismissive of the opportunities to be found in US coastal waters as it is of the US Navy's threat potential.[166]

---

[164] The distribution list at the head of Raeder's memo indicates that it was copied to Dönitz' command.

[165] KTB Seekriegsleitung, Teil A (entries for 22 and 23 January 1942).

[166] Only post-war did the admiral change his stance to one where US intervention before Pearl Harbor is described as an obstacle to the operations of his command. See BA/MA, RM 6/374 'Die deutsche Seekriegführung, n.d.' (summer 1945), pp 23–4, which he

The last assessment by the Seekriegsleitung on the US role in the Battle of the Atlantic prior to Pearl Harbor came on 2 December and provided further proof of the increasingly divergent assessments of BdU and Seekriegsleitung. It called for a series of measures in response to the gutting of the US Neutrality Law, which have to be seen against the backdrop that nobody in the Kriegsmarine would as yet have had any certainty on the topic of Japanese belligerency. The report was prefaced by an introduction, which stated that under the current set of orders prioritising (if only on paper) the avoiding of incidents on the high seas, 'commerce warfare likely to lead to success is no longer possible'.[167] The points listed ranged from demands almost guaranteed to bring about a US declaration of war (an extension of commerce warfare into US territorial waters as well as an inclusion of neutral and US shipping taking raw materials to the USA[168]) to those that had been rendered irrelevant by operational developments (requesting permission to engage US escorts or merchantmen travelling as part of UK-bound convoys). Moreover, though operations with capital ships were not mentioned in so many words, the demands singled out by the author strongly point to such an agenda, undoubtedly fired by the hope that permission for a sortie by the *Admiral Scheer* might still be granted after all.[169] World events would soon render the document's judgement questionable, but it gives an important insight into how Raeder and his staff could not bring themselves to finally let go of the idea of commerce warfare with capital ships.

Dönitz's plea for the radical reallocation of skilled labour would remain essentially unanswered for another seventeen months.[170] But even without this radical move the plans he presented to Raeder on 26 November were

compiled while awaiting trial. By the 1970s he was even claiming that German restraint had forced his U-boats to 'abandon attacks on convoys' on various occasions, see Karl Dönitz, *Zehn Jahre und zwanzig Tage* (München: Bernard & Graefe 1975), p 186. None of this is supported by any of the admiral's contemporary statements. It appears likely that he decided to rewrite the historical record in collusion with his son-in-law *Korvettenkapitän* Günter Hessler who was engaged by the Royal Navy in 1945–6 to write up the operational record of the U-boat arm. In it, he claimed that the orders aimed at sparing US vessels had 'greatly increased the U-boat's difficulties' in convoy battles. See Ministry of Defence, Navy (ed.), *The U-Boat War in the Atlantic 1939–1945* (London HMSO 1989 rp), p 87.

[167] BA/MA, RM 7/256 'Oberkommando der Kriegsmarine B.Nr. 1 Skl Ia 24608/41 gKdos. an OKW/WFSt, OKW/WFSt./L, OKW Ausland und Ausw. Amt z.Hdn. von Botschafter Ritter. Abschrift (2.12.1941)'.

[168] On the grounds that these were likely to be turned into weapons for Britain and its allies in US factories.

[169] Ibid.

[170] On the events of April and May 1943 that led to Hitler signing off on the *Flottenbauprogramm 1943*, which effectively put U-boat production on an equal footing with tank output, see the excellent account in Schulze-Wegener, *Kriegsmarine-Rüstung*, pp 111–29.

supported by an impressive number of submarine hulls being turned into viable weapons systems on the slipways of the Baltic. After the disappointing numbers delivered in October, nine U-boats arrived in French bases in November, fifteen would do so in December 1941. However, these numbers would barely be enough to make good the depletion of the previous weeks and many of them would in any case go on their first sortie under the command of rookie skippers; to deliver on what Dönitz appears to have had in mind, a regular monthly delivery in accordance with the latest production plan (twenty-five boats) was definitely called for. Raeder promised as much to Hitler on 12 December 1941,[171] and it stands to reason that the Führer factored in this increase in numbers when he weighed his options before declaring war on the USA.

This still begs the question as to whether the Atlantic Fleet's transgressions had by themselves been enough of a reason to play a major part in the German declaration of war. Raeder's briefings could certainly have had such an effect, since they continuously implied that German commerce warfare was being fatally compromised by the US Navy's patrols and convoy escorts. It is unclear to what extent the dictator realised that Raeder's view was completely skewed insofar as he mostly had operations by his beloved capital ships in mind. Since Hitler had fallen out of love with the idea of deploying these after the Rheinübung disaster, it does not seem likely that keeping them in port for any other reason would have caused him too many sleepless nights. What of the submarine arm? Here the evidence is more contradictory. While it is true that the deployment of US escorts for convoy duty had allowed the Royal Navy to free up some assets, thus far the clashes between the US Navy and Dönitz's U-boats had been depressingly one-sided. Neither the Seekriegsleitung nor the BdU at the time regarded forays by the submarine force into the waters of the Western Hemisphere as a major missed opportunity. Any allegations that the Seekriegsleitung's orders to spare US merchantmen and vessels had cramped the U-boat commander's style in a major way tends to rest on post-war statements, the first weeks in June–July possibly excepted. It can be safely ruled out that Dönitz had made such a case to his commander-in-chief, because that would have been grist to Raeder's own arguments and would almost certainly have been discussed at length at one of the briefings on naval affairs at Führer's Headquarters. Also, and more importantly, the tepid US reaction to each and every one of the clashes that had occurred appeared to indicate that there was little danger of continued sinkings of US Navy escorts leading to a rupture in diplomatic relations, much less a declaration of war. Finally, it needs to be kept in mind that even a hint on

---

[171] 'Vortrag des Ob.d.M. beim Führer in Berlin am 12.12.41 (15.12.1941)'; in: Wagner (ed.), *Lagevorträge*, p 326.

the part of Hitler that he was beginning to see American naval transgressions as a major obstacle to successful commerce warfare would have been immediately rushed to Raeder and carefully recorded in the Seekriegsleitung's war diary. On the contrary, Hitler's willingness in late October 1941 to temporarily cease submarine warfare in the North Atlantic because of his overblown concerns over the strategic security of the Axis position in Norway or Libya clearly indicates that he did not feel that the war was being won or lost in the campaign for Britain's supply lines to the New World.

As a dwindling U-boat presence all but shut down the Battle of the Atlantic, an intelligence report was making its way to Germany, which provided additional detail on the growing importance of American help to the British in the battle. The extant file copy is a sixty-page manuscript bearing the straightforward title *The British Home Fleet*. Even though lacking a date, it is possible to narrow down the time window in which it must have been finished to 14–25 November 1941.[172] It is significant that it came not from a *Marinenachrichtendienst* source but went directly to Hitler's headquarters, from where it was forwarded in late December 1941 to the Seekriegsleitung.[173] The accompanying paper trail, such as covering letters, appears to have been lost, making it difficult to assess the possible identity of the author or, more importantly, the exact date on which it was presented to the dictator. What can be ascertained, however, is that an entry in the Seekriegsleitung's war diary indicates that report's contents had been judged to be genuine.[174] The document gives a comprehensive appraisal of the Home Fleet's strengths and weaknesses in the autumn of 1941 and touches on such subjects as design flaws in specific weapons systems, operational losses, damage suffered by shipyards during the Blitz, cooperation with the USA and morale. A theme that recurs throughout the report is the strain the Royal Navy has been under over the last two years and its increasing reliance on US help of both a direct kind (convoy escort by US vessels) and an indirect one (supply of all kinds of

---

[172] BA/MA, RM 7/132 'Die britische Home-Fleet. Abschrift (n.d.)'. The report makes reference to the recent passing of the amendments to the US Neutrality Laws by the House of Representatives (which occurred on 13 November), and refers to the imminent sailing of a convoy in 'the last week of November'.

[173] See the entry in KTB Seekriegsleitung, Teil A (entry for 24 January 1942): 'A report on the Home Fleet compiled approximately around mid-November 1941 by a special English source was forwarded to the Seekriegsleitung from the Führerhauptquartier in late December.'

[174] KTB Seekriegsleitung, Teil A (entry for 24 January 1942): '... contains extremely valuable intelligence and constitutes a brilliant vindication of our own strategy in the first two years of this war' ('... *enthält eine Fülle wertvoller Nachrichten und bildet eine glänzende Bestätigung für die Richtigkeit unserer eigenen Kriegführung in den ersten beiden Kriegsjahren*').

hardware,[175] overhauling of British vessels in American shipyards). Without this assistance, so the anonymous informant notes, Britain would not be able to maintain its navy (*'Aus eigener Kraft kann die Insel die navy nicht mehr erhalten'*).

The key reason given for the wear and tear of the Home Fleet's main units is the need to provide the most important convoys with an escort of at least one capital ship, in view of the Kriegsmarine's residual capability to mount a sortie against the convoy traffic in the North Atlantic with one or more of its major surface units. In the author's judgement this trump card might soon be rendered void by recent developments: the dismantling of the Neutrality Laws by both Houses of Congress would allow US merchantmen to ferry their cargo straight to British ports. The manner in which this was likely to happen had just been demonstrated at the beginning of the month: on 6 November, a convoy of unprecedented size (an alleged ninety-seven ships) reached the North Channel after an uneventful crossing from the Western Hemisphere. It had done so under close escort by one, at times two, British capital ships and two American cruisers, who then turned around at 40 degrees west. A convoy of even greater size (between 102 and 107 ships) was already slated to leave towards the end of the month, with the imminent extension of US Navy capital ship escort all the way into British ports seen as the obvious next step. Taken in conjunction with the US bases currently under construction in Ulster and Scotland, this appeared to presage a future where even a successful sortie by the three capital ships based in Brest, or by the brand-new *Tirpitz* from Germany staging through Norway (potentially a worst-case scenario for the Royal Navy), might be rendered meaningless by the presence of heavy units of a powerful neutral interposing themselves as a shield between the Kriegsmarine and any convoy worthy of such a major operation.[176]

What is important is that the daily OKW situation report produced for a circle of senior officers and civilians on 6 December carried a brief, but unambiguous reference to a morsel of intelligence contained in *Die britische Home Fleet*.[177] Thus, it is possible to ascertain that this intelligence scoop was

---

[175] BA/MA, RM 7/132 'Die Home-Fleet': 'the American help is of key importance, the first thousand tons of armour plating which arrived in June were regarded as a crucial last-minute relief.'

[176] A fortnight earlier, the sailing instructions for the *Admiral Scheer* had in fact specified that the presence of US Navy vessels was reason enough to terminate the attack on a convoy, no matter how promising the tactical situation appeared to be. See in: 'Vorlage Ob.d.M. beim Führer am 13. November 1941, nachmittags in Wolfsschanze, Anlage 2'; in: Wagner (ed.), *Lagevorträge*, p 313.

[177] Each of the entries in Goebbels' diaries is prefaced by the military situation report of the previous day. On 7 December, the paragraph on naval affairs makes reference to a report 'from an obscure source' giving figures on recent British submarine losses and highlighting the fact that the Royal Navy had ten US submarines on order to make good these

in all likelihood put before Adolf Hitler at some point in the preceding days and possibly in time to influence his final decision on 4 December to stand by Japan should it decide to unilaterally initiate hostilities with the USA. While the presence of US capital ships is unlikely to have exercised him as much as Admiral Raeder, the fact remains that the report, when seen against the backdrop of the US presence on Iceland, convoying by the US Navy, the abolition of US Neutrality Laws and intelligence on bases being built in Ireland and Scotland for the future use of the US Navy, must have confirmed in his mind that the very idea of avoiding further clashes on the high seas was unrealistic.

To a German of his generation, the idea of regular traffic of convoyed American merchantmen into British ports could not but lead to a *Lusitania* analogy. Such an incident would leave a substantial number of dead American civilians in its wake and raise the question whether the American public and its legislators would react as calmly as they had when professional servicemen had perished on the USS *Kearny* and the USS *Reuben James*. The marginal, but critical support which the sinkings of SS *Sessa* and SS *Steel Seafarer* in September and of the SS *Lehigh* in November had generated for the US government's drive to legitimise the shoot-on-sight order and the gutting of the Neutrality Law appeared to make this questionable.[178]

The question of the political impact of major incidents at sea became a moot point when Germany and the USA found themselves at war on 11 December. As far as the operational side of the matter is concerned, the U-boat arm had reached a point where enough submarines to saturate the North Atlantic sea lanes were finally becoming available. In contrast to the September 1939–June 1941 period, when due to the requirements of an expanded training programme the number of operational submarines (*Frontboote*) had stagnated at around thirty, things were definitely beginning to look up by mid-November with a total of eighty-four *Frontboote* available. Even though twenty-four of these had either moved to the Mediterranean or had received orders to do so in the next days and weeks, this net loss would be amply compensated for over the following weeks and months by the seventy-nine submarines still engaged in shakedown cruises and final repairs.[179] We will never know how this armada would have fared against Anglo–American sea power in the first half of 1942, because fate decreed against the deployment. Starting in late December, only days after Raeder had promised Hitler a major increase in the number of

---

losses. TB Goebbels, Bd. II.2, p 442 (entry for 7 December 1941). This tallies exactly with the information found in BA/MA, RM 7/132 'Die britische Home Fleet', p 13.

[178] For Hitler's thoughts on this matter as expressed to some of his closest collaborators a day or two before 11 December, see Frank, *Galgens*, p 397.

[179] 'Anlage zu O.K.M. op 1951/41 Stand der U-Bootsverteilung, 10.11.1941'; in: Wagner (ed.), *Lagevorträge*, pp 313–4.

U-boats to be delivered in winter and spring,[180] and the dictator had boasted of that prospect to Japanese Ambassador Oshima,[181] Europe was hit by a winter second only in harshness and duration to the already legendary one of 1939–40. Soon ports and river estuaries in the Baltic began to freeze over; fluvial traffic came to a complete halt on 15 January 1942.[182] The thickness of the ice was such that even the movement of capital ships was occasionally called into question.[183] A number of U-boats and crews engaged in the last phases of training or tied up with final repairs were still shifted to North Sea bases in time,[184] but by mid-February the training and fitting out process had more or less ground to a halt. In mid-December, Dönitz had already complained that the lack of skilled labour was extending final repairs to up to two months.[185] This problem was now compounded many times over by the weather, with the seventy-eight U-boats commissioned between November 1941 and February 1942 taking up to seven to eight months to work their way through the system after being handed to their crews.[186] Deliveries to the front-line flotillas plummeted as a result: fifteen in January, thirteen in both February and March, eight in April, six in May. In a briefing for Hitler in mid-May, Dönitz admitted that the disruptive effect of this had been considerable: at present, the U-boat force had to make do with 124 operational submarines, instead of the 173 that would otherwise have been available.[187] As the *Eisstau* (in reference to the bottleneck created by ice

[180] 'Vortrag des Ob.d.M. beim Führer in Berlin am 12.12.1941 (15.12.1941)'; in: Wagner (ed.), *Lagevorträge*, p 326.

[181] 'Empfang des japanischen Botschafters General Oshima durch den Führer am 14.12.1941 von 13–14 Uhr in Anwesenheit des Reichsaußenministers (n.d.)'; in: ADAP, Serie E, Bd. I, pp 17–21

[182] KTB Seekriegsleitung, Teil A (entry for 26 February 1942). On the history of how the Wehrmacht's meteorologists were caught flat-footed by what were admittedly freak climatic conditions (the two previous winters had already been notably harsh, the one in 1939–40 outstandingly so), see Andreas Frey, 'Kalt erwischt. Der Meteorologe Franz Baur stellte Hitler's Wehrmacht im Winter vor 70 Jahren eine folgenschwere Wetterprognose. Eine Erinnerung zum 125. Geburtstag'; in: *Frankfurter Allgemeine Sonntagszeitung*, 12 February 2012, 'Wissenschaft' supplement.

[183] KTB Seekriegsleitung, Teil A (entries for 27 January, 5 February and 3 March 1942)

[184] KTB Seekriegsleitung, Teil A (entries for 26 January, 4 and 10 February 1942).

[185] BA/MA, RM 87/19 'KTB BdU (entry for 16 December 1941)'.

[186] For these figures see Blair, *The Hunters*, p 486. For an assessment by Dönitz on the impact the weather was having on training schedules, BA/MA, RM 87/21 'Kriegstagebuch BdU (entry for 6 February 1942)'. At this time, the admiral was still pinning his hopes on an improvement in weather conditions in the foreseeable future, pessimistic forecasts from previous days notwithstanding. For the latter, see BA/MA, RM 7/2164 'OKM Skl HW N V an B.d.U – Abschrift (25.1.1942)' as well as RM 7/2164 'Amtsgruppe Nautik an 1. Skl (3.2.1942)'.

[187] 'Vortrag des B.d.U. beim Führer am 14.5.1942 in Gegenwart des Oberbefehlshabers der Kriegsmarine Anlage zu OKM 1375/52 (n.d.)'; in: Wagner (ed.), *Lagevorträge*, pp 393–6, esp. p 393.

conditions) was gradually reduced, June finally brought a slight improvement with fifteen boats delivered, but not until July (twenty-two), August (thirty-one) and September (thirty-four) was the backlog worked off. By that time, the worst period of Allied vulnerability both in terms of dysfunctional US defence arrangements in the Western Hemisphere and tonnage availability had passed. Since the period between February 1942 and March 1943 also saw the U-boats operating under the cloak provided by a new secure Enigma machine, with sinkings rarely dropping to less than 400,000 GRT per month, the importance of the unexpected impact of the winter of 1941–2 is hard to overstate.[188] According to calculations made by historian Axel Niestle, the delays imposed on the training regime by the winter weather added up to a total of 4,977 operational days lost to the U-boat arm. Extrapolating from the success rates their brethren were achieving at the time, even the most conservative estimate of Allied tonnage saved in this fashion between February and September 1942 comes to a figure of 850,000 GRT.[189]

8.5   Conclusion

On 23 March 1942 the German dictator, while in the company of a few acolytes at the Wolfsschanze, reflected on the American actions that had led him to declare a state of war between the two countries. The way he saw it, Roosevelt would have been well advised to remain neutral and stay on his side of the ocean for the remainder of the war.[190] Had he done so, Lend-Lease goods from the USA could have been trans-shipped from American to British bottoms waiting in Iceland; in this manner, the weapons and munitions being delivered in this fashion would have been immune from German attack for two-thirds of their crossing of the Atlantic.[191] Taken together with what he said to Goebbels on 9 December, in the address he gave to the *Gauleiter* on 12 December and in his interview with Oshima two days after that, this appears to confirm that the increasingly assertive role played by the US Navy in the Battle of the Atlantic still exercised him months later. Did it also play a role in determining his decision to go to war?

---

[188] The manner in which this crucial event is completely overlooked by otherwise comprehensive histories of the Battle of the Atlantic or wartime events in the Baltic is nothing short of startling. John Terraine, *Business in Great Waters: The U-boat Wars, 1916–1945* (London: Leo Cooper 1989), Jonathan Dimbleby, *The Battle of the Atlantic* (London: Penguin 2015) and Poul Grooss, *The Naval War in the Baltic, 1939–1945* (London: Seaforth 2017) are all cases in point.

[189] Figures communicated by Axel Niestle (Berlin) to the author in email from 4 July 2018.

[190] '23.3.1942, Montag abends (Wolfsschanze)'; in: Henry Picker (ed.), *Hitlers Tischgespräche im Führerhauptquartier* (München: Propyläen 2003), pp 185–7.

[191] Ibid. The process sketched out by the German dictator, while attractive on paper, would have been impossible to realise for a number of practical reasons, the lack of sufficient docking facilities in Iceland among them.

It is important to remember that throughout 1940–1, Hitler's commitment to commerce warfare in any shape or form had always been conditional: so as not to upset the US government, no U-boats were allowed to operate in the approaches to Halifax and the Rheinübung task force was ordered to operate under rules of engagement so restrictive they called into question the very rationale behind the operation. Orders sparing enemy escorts were issued in late June with a view to soothing American nerves while Barbarossa was still raging; overblown concerns over a British descent on northern Norway led to the detachment of half a dozen U-boats to the Barents Sea; Rommel's critical position in Libya led to nearly thirty U-boats being denied to Dönitz by the end of the year. These moves all came about, not as a result of a specific political or strategic crisis, but of concern over the mere possibility of one arising. In each case, the prospects of commerce warfare were deliberately and consciously compromised. The American entry into the war did not change this: in April 1942 the dictator showed a revitalised interest in sinking enemy tonnage, but only with the view to limiting the enemy's potential for future amphibious operations.[192]

Hence, it does not come as a surprise that prior to Pearl Harbor, the only statements decrying the supposedly crippling effect of American interference on the Kriegsmarine's war against Britain's lifelines came from Raeder and his chief of staff, Fricke, and were very much focused on the effect the patrols of the Atlantic Fleet had on the feasibility of ever resuming commerce warfare with capital ships. No comparable statements are on record from Karl Dönitz, the claims he made in his post-war writings notwithstanding. The dictator himself, who in any case had become increasingly disillusioned with the idea of using capital ships for commerce warfare, only began fuming about American interference with German naval operations in the days and weeks after he had declared war on the United States. The often alleged notion that both the dictator and his admirals hankered to unleash the U-boats on the Western Hemisphere meets with exactly the same problem:[193] Dönitz was downright

---

[192] 'Skl. B Nr. 1. Skl. Ib 785/42 gKdos. Chefs. Vortrag Ob.d.M. beim Führer in Wolfsschanze am 13.4.42 abends (16.4.1942)'; in: Wagner (ed.), *Lagevorträge*, pp 372–87. 'Führer agrees with estimate by the Oberbefehlshaber der Marine that the annihilation of as much merchant tonnage on the Anglo-Saxon side is of decisive importance to the outcome of the war, since all offensive operations by the enemy are liable to be hampered or even rendered impossible in this fashion.'

[193] Norman Rich, *Hitler's War Aims: Ideology, the Nazi state and the Course of Expansion* (London: Andre Deutsch 1973), p 246; Gerhard Weinberg, 'Germany's Declaration of War on the US: A New Look'; in: Hans L. Trefousse (ed.), *Germany and America: Essays on Problems of International Relations and Immigration* (New York: Columbia UP 1980) [= Brooklyn College Studies on society in change, Vol. 21], pp 54–70; Rainer Zitelmann, *Adolf Hitler. Eine politische Biographie* (Göttingen: Musterschmidt 1990), p 156; Williamson Murray and Alan Millett, *A War to Be Won: Fighting the Second World War* (New Haven: Yale UP 2000), pp 135–6; Ian Kershaw, *Fateful Choices: Ten Decisions*

dismissive of the idea, Raeder only willing to deploy a small wolf pack for less than a month; Hitler did go on record as insisting to Raeder that operations in US coastal waters had to be persevered with for longer than that in order to at least test the viability of the idea, but this too occurred well after he had declared war on the USA.

Instead, the exchange between Raeder and Hitler on 13 November is a clear pointer to the area that most gravely concerned the dictator: the western approaches to Great Britain. As the intelligence report on US support for the Royal Navy from early December would confirm in greater detail, this was the area where a US–German clash would almost certainly originate. After the gutting of the Neutrality Law, US merchantmen and passenger liners would start crossing the Atlantic in ever-increasing numbers. As the dearth of sinkings in the past months indicated, a large part might escape the wolf packs lurking in mid-Atlantic, but they would still end up converging on the approaches to British ports and there the Luftwaffe and Kriegsmarine, short of receiving orders to stand down, would eventually sink enough of them (and kill American civilians in the process) to generate a *Lusitania* effect. After briefly toying with the idea of escalating commerce warfare in the immediate aftermath of the proclamation of Lend-Lease, the dictator spent the rest of the year engaged in keeping his U-boats on a tight leash. At various points in May, June, July and September, he insisted that the U-boats exercise restraint lest they trigger a US declaration of war that might prevent Germany from reaping the full political benefit from the impending fall of the USSR. In mid-November, this logic was if anything even more compelling since *Heeresgruppe Mitte* was in the process of unleashing its final offensive on Moscow. This time, however, no orders went out asking the Seekriegsleitung for 'four more weeks'. This shift in attitude is undoubtedly linked to the vote in the Senate which dismantled the key articles of the Neutrality Law; when the dictator met Raeder on 13 November, the vote in the lower house was still a few hours away, but now Hitler was resigned to meeting the Atlantic Fleet's interference with force of his own. If nothing else, the numbers of U-boats joining the submarine arm would have told him that the means to do so with some confidence were finally becoming available. Six weeks later, the freak weather conditions of the incoming winter dealt these expectations a devastating blow.

that Changed the World, 1940–1941 (London: Allen Lane 2007), pp 382–430; P. M. H. Bell, *Twelve Turning Points of the Second World War* (New Haven: Yale UP 2011), pp 77–8; Beevor, *Second World War*, p 279 and Volker Ullrich, *Adolf Hitler. Die Jahre des Untergangs, 1939–1945. Biografie* (Frankfurt a.M.: Fischer 2018), pp 254–5.

The Luftwaffe on the Eve of Global War

9.1 Introduction

On 14 November 1940, Kriegsmarine Commander-in-Chief Erich Raeder arrived at the Neue Reichskanzlei to brief Adolf Hitler on the naval situation. These meetings took place at least once a month and usually addressed a wide range of issues. The two men discussed mine warfare, recent successes by the Kriegsmarine's U-boats in the Atlantic and the desirability of a closer coordination between the navy and Luftwaffe in the war against Britain's merchant fleet. On this occasion, the discussion turned to the strategic second-order effects of Operation Felix – the codename for the imminent entry of German forces into Spain with a view to eliminating the British base at Gibraltar.[1] Both men quickly agreed that before such an operation could be given the green light, steps would have to be taken to reinforce the Spanish position in the Canary Islands in case the British retaliated by staging an attack on the Atlantic archipelago.

Dictator and admiral struggled, however, to reach a final agreement on the subject. Raeder wanted the German invasion of the Iberian peninsula to be limited to Spain, excluding Portugal and, by extension, the Azores and Cape Verdes, in the hope that the latter territories would not end up being targeted by the British. The Führer, on the other hand, predicted a British descent on the Azores 'immediately upon our [Germany's] entry in Spain'; it was not a prospect he faced with equanimity. As he explained to Raeder, were the Germans, rather than the British, to take possession of the Azores, it would give the Wehrmacht 'the only facility for attacking America, if she should enter the war, with a modern plane of the Messerschmidt [sic] type which has a range of 12,600 km [7,830 miles]. Thereby America would be forced to build her own anti-aircraft defence, which is still completely lacking, instead of assisting Britain.'[2]

---

[1] 'Seekriegsleitung Iop 2486/40 Besprechung des Ob.d.M. beim Führer am 14.11.40. 13.00 Uhr'; in: Gerhard Wagner (ed.), *Lagevortäge des Oberbefehlshabers der Kriegsmarine vor Hitler 1939–1945* (München: J.F. Lehmanns 1972), pp 151–5.

[2] Ibid., p 154.

While this source features prominently in analyses of the stillborn operation against Gibraltar, its implications for the dictator's understanding of air power are far more momentous.[3] Beyond the fact that a US–German war had not so far broken out, the bomber the dictator was alluding to still only existed in the form of a blueprint. The Messerschmitt company had not yet been formally tasked with the production of the prototype – this would only happen in January 1941. Even if design and production of the new aircraft were to be given the highest priority and proceeded without a glitch, the first fully worked-up *Gruppe* (36–40 planes) was unlikely to be ready for operational deployment before the turn of the years 1943–4, at the earliest.[4]

The dictator's grasp of technical matters relating to land warfare can only be described as very good and those relating to the war at sea as adequate. This exchange seems to suggest that his understanding of aeronautical technology was limited in the extreme and thus tends to confirm the post-war judgement of one of his collaborators that the German leader lacked even the most basic concept of aeronautical matters.[5] This chapter will look at Hitler's understanding of the strategy and technology that underpinned air warfare in the 1940s, exploring the extent to which any inadequacies in this area could have skewed his view of the strategic realities in autumn 1941 and contributed to his decision to declare war on the USA.

9.2   The Early Luftwaffe: Perception and Reality

During the years 1939 to 1941, Hermann Göring enjoyed Hitler's complete trust in all matters concerning air power. In addition, although technically subordinate to the Oberkommando der Wehrmacht (OKW), the unique position he held in the power structure of the Third Reich (heir apparent to Hitler, head of the Four Year Plan, cabinet minister and Luftwaffe commander-in-chief) meant that the dictator's instructions to him effectively bypassed the normal command chain. There are several reasons for Hitler's high regard for Göring. The important role he had played in the NSDAP's rise to power was one factor, as was the Luftwaffe commander-in-chief's widespread popularity – unlike most of the rest of the party's upper echelons – among Germans from all

---

[3] Most recently the excellent monograph by Norman Goda. Goda, *Tomorrow the World: Hitler, Northwest Africa and the Path toward America* (College Station: Texas A & M UP 1998), pp 120–1.

[4] The development of the Junkers 88 medium bomber, which saw the cutting of many corners, is a case in point. It was rushed into front-line service after a development of thirty-four months (December 1936–October 1939), leaving a number of flaws unnoticed. This necessitated important design changes and the retraining of crews. See William A. Medcalf and Eddie Creek, *Junkers Ju-88: From Schnellbomber to Multi-Mission Warplane*, Vol. 1 (Manchester: Crecy 2013), esp. pp 23–82.

[5] Otto Dietrich, *12 Jahre mit Hitler* (Köln: Atlas 1955), pp 117–18, 121–2.

walks of life.[6] Another reason was the crucial role the Luftwaffe's close air support of the army had played in facilitating the victories of the Blitzkrieg years (1939 to mid-1942). This seemed to confirm that Göring, his boastful nature notwithstanding, was delivering on his promises.

Göring's advantageous position, which enabled him to circumvent OKW, meant that the air force had a bureaucratic head start over the other services. Yet this was squandered by the dysfunctional nature of its top layer of command: Göring in theory oversaw a power structure in which, since mid-1937, the Luftwaffe general staff and the ministry for air (Reichsluftfahrtministerium, RLM) coexisted side by side as separate, yet equal entities.[7] The problem was that the new commander-in-chief had a poor grasp of many key technological issues and harboured a pathological distrust of his senior subordinates. He was also overindulgent and lethargic to a point where he would think nothing of summoning senior aides to his hunting lodge at Rominten for a high-level conference, then interrupt the meeting for one and a half hours to go on a sleigh-ride.[8] *Generaloberst* Hans Jeschonnek, the chief of the air staff responsible for operations between February 1939 and August 1943, while hard-working, was consumed with a zeal for the new regime that led to many a questionable decision. *Generaloberst* Ernst Udet (who was *Generalluftzeugmeister* between February 1939 and November 1941) and *Generalfeldmarschall* Erhard Milch (state secretary at the air ministry) oversaw aircraft design and production, respectively, at the RLM. Milch was a capable enough administrator, but Udet, who was very much a pilot's pilot, found himself increasingly out of his depth as a manager. The fact that the relationship between these four men was often fraught with personality clashes was not the problem. Nor did it mark out the Luftwaffe as substantially different from the top command structure of any other armed service of the period, be it Allied or Axis. What rendered it problematic was Göring's habit of discharging his duties as overall coordinator very erratically, while at the same time stoking the flames of his subordinates' rivalry.[9]

The reason for this lay undoubtedly in a personal insecurity rooted in his poor grasp of many of the technological issues which dominated discussions about the next generation of aircraft and the place they should take in the air

---

[6] See BA/MA, ZA 3/336 'Hermann Göring, der Oberbefehlshaber der deutschen Luftwaffe. Ein Versuch'. In this post-war biographical précis, a former Luftwaffe officer relates witness testimony from the autumn of 1944, according to which Hitler rejected the idea of sacking Göring with these words: 'The party would not understand me.'

[7] David Irving, *The Rise and Fall of the Luftwaffe: The Life of Field Marshal Erhard Milch* (Focal Point electronic rp 2002), pp 62–3.

[8] BA/MA, RL 3/60 'Besprechung in Rominten, den 21.3.1942 (21.3.1942)'.

[9] On these issues, Nicolaus von Below, *Als Hitlers Adjutant 1937–1945* (Selent: Pour le Merite 1999 rp), pp 53, 106–7.

force's inventory. Yet Göring's weak understanding of the technical dimension did not stop him from acquiescing to demands from Hitler that were completely unfeasible. The most notorious instance of this occurred well before the outbreak of the war. In October 1938 the dictator demanded that air strength be boosted, which resulted in the so-called *Konzentriertes Flugzeugmusterprogramm*, an initiative which would increase the number of the Luftwaffe's front-line flying units fivefold. Had it been completed, the German Air Force of early 1942 would have boasted an establishment of fifty-eight bomber, twenty-eight day fighter[10] and twelve dive-bomber wings.[11] To put this into perspective, it was only through the most strenuous wartime exertions that by early 1943 the Luftwaffe would eventually field seventeen bomber, fifteen day fighter and four dive-bomber wings. Apart from the fact that the October 1938 programme relied on large numbers of two aircraft types which had not yet reached the prototype stage, the quantities of fuel and aluminium alone required for such an expansion would have made considerable inroads into the supplies needed for the civilian economy and the other services. One senior official had the courage to point out the obstacles facing the scheme, but despite his objections, the *Konzentriertes Flugzeugmusterprogramm* was accepted with only minor amendments.[12] As late as June 1941, long after the original scheme should have been revealed as grotesquely overambitious, Erhard Milch unveiled a marginally scaled-down version of the *Flugzeugmusterprogramm*, known as the *Göring-Programm*. This version was predicated on a quick collapse of the USSR and a simultaneous freeing-up of army resources (especially skilled labour) for Luftwaffe production. It involved a fourfold, rather than fivefold increase of flying units.[13] If those in positions of top command agreed to implement schemes such as this, no matter how overambitious and unrealistic in scope, it comes as no surprise that their Führer believed the German aircraft industry to possess human and material resources in significant quantities which it simply did not.

Göring encouraged unrealistic expectations in his lord and master in more ways than one. An air show laid on for the dictator's benefit at Rechlin on 3 July 1939 featured a number of new aircraft types and weapons. A few were just mock-ups, but even the airworthiness of a prototype (like the Heinkel 280 jet fighter) would belie the fact that a design was still years away from being

---

[10] Divided between sixteen single-engined and twelve twin-engined (Zerstörer) wings.

[11] Lutz Budrass, *Flugzeugindustrie und Luftrüstung in Deutschland 1918–1945* (Düsseldorf: Droste 1998) [= Schriften des Bundesarchivs, Bd. 50], p 558.

[12] Budrass, *Luftrüstung*, pp 559–61.

[13] 'Chef des Stabes, Nr. 134/41 g.Kdos. Chefsache. Besprechung Staatssekretär Milch am 26.6.1941 (26.6.1941)'; in: Hans-Adolf Jacobsen (ed.), *Kriegstagebuch des Oberkommandos der Wehrmacht*. Band I (Frankfurt a.M.: Bernard & Graefe 1965), pp 1016–18.

ready for front-line service. As Hitler and Göring made their way from one display to the next, the latter's shaky grasp of some of the technological detail and his wish to impress the Führer made for a fateful mix. Hitler's Luftwaffe adjutant would claim after the war that a number of serious misconceptions arose out of the Rechlin air show, although the exact degree to which Göring fed Hitler false information is impossible to determine.[14] Nonetheless, the way in which in September 1942 Göring attempted to shift the blame for the Rechlin presentation to representatives of the aircraft industry does suggest that he had been embarrassingly reminded by Hitler of some of the promises rashly made in July 1939, which had still not been delivered on three years later.[15]

Despite this, Göring enjoyed a period of grace until early 1942. Not only did his boasts about yet-to-be-built aircraft types and air fleets go unchallenged, but instances of the dictator meddling in the operational conduct of the air war remained few and far between.[16] After the war, a number of key witnesses as well as Göring himself described the period from 1939 to 1941 as the one in which he enjoyed the dictator's complete trust in general and in matters concerning air power in particular.[17] Finally, in 1940–1, the Führer's main

---

[14] Hitler's Luftwaffe adjutant wrote after the war that 'Hitler had little understanding of aircraft, but was drawn towards technical gimmicks and the potential of weapons. Following that reasoning, Göring and Udet had tasked the Testing Site with laying on the exhibition', see Below, *Adjutant*, pp 172–4. Also Edward L. Homze, *Arming the Luftwaffe: The Reich Air Ministry and the German Aircraft Industry, 1919–1939* (Lincoln: Nebraska UP 1976), pp 248–9.

[15] BA/MA, RL 3/60 'Stenographischer Bericht über die Besprechung des Reichsmarschalls Göring mit Vertretern der Luftfahrtindustrie über Entwicklungsfragen am Sonntag, dem 13. September 1942, vorm. 11 Uhr im Reichsluftministerium (n.d.)'. This baseless accusation appears to have rankled, since it produced a rare rebuttal by the spokesman of the German aeronautical industry: BA/MA, RL 3/51 'Der Präsident des Reichsverbandes der deutschen Luftfahrtindustrie an den Staatssekretär und Generalinspekteur der Luftwaffe (1.11.1942)'.

[16] Such as shifting the focus of Luftwaffe bombing raids from Fighter Command's sector stations to London (September 1940), a couple of instances where he meddled with close air support operations in Russia (summer 1941) and the termination of intruder operations by the Luftwaffe's night fighter arm over Britain (October 1941). It is important to stress that in the first case (by far the most serious), he had the support of one of the two *Luftflotten* commanders involved. See Kenneth Macksey, *Kesselring: The Making of the Luftwaffe* (New York: David McKay 1978), pp 76–8, and Horst Boog, *Die deutsche Luftwaffenführung 1935–1945. Führungsprobleme, Spitzengliederung, Generalstabsausbildung* (Stuttgart: DVA 1982), pp 523–36.

[17] *Der Prozeß gegen die Hauptkriegsverbrecher vor dem Internationalen Militärgerichtshof, 14. November 1945–1. Oktober 1946*, Bd. IX (Nürnberg: Verlag der Friedrich Kornschen Buchhandlung 1947), p 490–1; KTB OKW I, p 232 E (deposition by Oberstleutnant Friedrich Greffrath); 'Befragung von Alfred Jodl, 17.6.1945'; in: Matthias Uhl et al (eds.), *Verhört. Die Befragungen deutscher Generale und Offiziere durch die sowjetischen Geheimdienste 1945–1952* (Oldenbourg: deGruyter 2015), p 124; Ulrich Schlie (ed.),

focus with regards to air warfare increasingly shifted to a new challenge that even the enormous aerial armada envisaged in the *Konzentriertes Flugzeugmusterprogramm* could not have met.

9.3 Home Defence

In mid-October 1941, General Hoffmann von Waldau, the Luftwaffe's chief of operations, declared himself to be supremely unconcerned about the bombing offensive which the RAF's Bomber Command had been waging against German urban areas since May 1940. As he put it, 'The night attacks of the English [sic] have had no impact on the war economy, despite having suffered relatively high losses in the process.'[18] Few historians would disagree with this assessment. Every history of the bombing war draws attention to the problems experienced by a campaign that played itself out almost entirely at night on account of German interceptor action against the British bombers, which had been massacred during a few early daylight raids in 1939.[19] Severely handicapped in finding their targets by a lack of adequate navigation aids, the bombers struggled to inflict serious damage on the rare occasions when they did reach them. The early phase of Bomber Command's war on German urban centres, culminating in the notorious *Butt Report* which highlighted these failings in painful fashion, is often depicted as a textbook example of an exercise in futility.[20] It is, however, important not to fall into the trap of adopting an ahistorical perspective by using as sole yardstick the firestorms which devastated so many German towns and cities from July 1943 onwards.

A number of individuals and institutions of the time would most likely have emphatically disagreed with General Waldau's cold marshalling of the facts. Both the disruption of sleep patterns caused by air-raid sirens and the growing number of instances where bomb damage went beyond the superficial left more and more civilians shaken. Even those living in areas untouched by

---

Albert Speer. Die Kransberg-Protokolle 1945 (München: Herbig 2003), p 126; Dietrich, *12 Jahre*, pp 117–21.

[18] BA/MA, RL 200/17 'Tagebuch Hoffmann von Waldau (entry for 16 October 1941)'. A statement backed up by the very detailed monthly assessments produced by the *Wirtschafts- und Rüstungsamt*. The reports for 1941 are filed away under BA/MA, RW 19/99. The period of May 1940 to November 1941 saw the loss of 1,024 British bombers in night-time raids. Around 10 per cent of these losses would have occurred in attacks on non-German targets (i.e., in occupied countries and Italy). Martin Middlebrook and Chris Everitt, *The Bomber Command War Diaries: An Operational Reference Book, 1939–1945* (New York: Viking Penguin 1985), p 219.

[19] Daytime raids were effectively terminated by the RAF after a sortie by twenty-four Vickers Wellingtons against shipping targets in the German Bight suffered the loss of half the force in December 1939.

[20] Available in full on the world wide web: https://etherwave.wordpress.com/2014/01/03/document-the-butt-report-1941 (accessed 12 June 2020) .

British bombing registered anxiously the spread of the campaign and air-raid precautions taken by their local authorities.[21] The German admiralty soon found itself echoing these sentiments because many of its bases on the North Sea coast were within easy flying range for Bomber Command; moreover, their proximity to water made targeting comparatively easy whenever moonlight coincided with a clear sky. When in April 1941 Kiel suffered what were by the standards of the period a number of fairly damaging raids, concern about the future reached such levels that in talks between the Seekriegsleitung and civilian authorities the evacuation of the city by all Kriegsmarine facilities was even briefly considered (if ultimately rejected).[22]

Nor was the civilian leadership of Nazi Germany unconcerned about the impact of the early British bombing raids. The German dictator took the air threat very seriously indeed and, as early as 1938, had taken to task the RLM over its 'antiquated views' on air-raid shelter design; his preference for anti-aircraft guns over fighter aircraft as the mainstay of modern air defence also appears to have predated the outbreak of the war.[23] This is reflected in Göring's canny decision to integrate the Flak arm into the Luftwaffe.

That Flak was clearly a key pillar of home defence is further confirmed by a source from June 1940 in which one of Hitler's generals reveals the emphasis the dictator placed on anti-aircraft warfare. In an impromptu gathering at Hitler's field headquarters in France, held at a time when the French surrender was imminent, General Jodl briefed General Thomas of the *Rüstungsamt* on the dictator's thoughts regarding production priorities: 'the Führer sees the solution in a strong Flak defence. Flak assets will have to be increased.'[24] Hitler's determination to invest in Flak assets for home defence seems vastly disproportionate to what the situation called for: Germany had already been steadily increasing its Flak arm since the outbreak of the war,[25] and it was on the cusp of achieving an unprecedented victory over France. The dictator's continued concern over protecting and consolidating the home front with

[21] Many contemporary letters and diaries reflect this feeling. For a good example, see Marianne Feuersenger, *Im Vorzimmer der Macht. Aufzeichnungen aus dem Wehrmachtführungsstab und Führerhauptquartier 1940–1945* (München: Herbig 2001), pp 31–5, 38, 65, 68, 73–5 (letters dated 29 and 31 August, 9 and 17 September, 16 October, 15 November 1940 and 29 March, 13 and 18 April, 9 May, 26 July, 8 and 15 August 1941).

[22] Werner Rahn and Gerhard Schreiber (eds.), *Kriegstagebuch der Seekriegsleitung 1939–1945, Teil A*, Bd. 20 (Herford: Mittler & Sohn 1990) (entries for 10 and 14 April 1941).

[23] Below, *Adjutant*, pp 41, 115, 131–2.

[24] IWM, Speer Coll., FD 5447/45 'Aktennotiz. Besprechung am 18.6.40 im Führerhauptquartier bei General Jodl (21.6.1940)'.

[25] Heavy guns increased from 2,628 to 3,095, light guns from 6,700 to 9,817. See Edward B. Westermann, *Flak: German Anti-Aircraft Defences, 1914–1945* (Lawrence: Kansas UP 2001), pp 97–8.

boosted Flak raises interesting questions as to whether he ever truly believed Britain would succumb to diplomatic blandishments or military threats.

In the following months, further orders were issued to ensure the continued expansion of the Flak arm. Even the industrial areas of the German east, which until then had been left untouched by the bombing war, were to come under the umbrella of a *Flakschutz Ost*. The proximity of Soviet-occupied territory appeared to warrant this move, as did the supposed need to 'demonstrate' to British fliers that Silesian industry enjoyed the same protection as that of other provinces.[26] The extension of the Flak arm would mean an increase in ammunition production. This was not only because of the increase in the number of Flak batteries but also because the batteries needed to use copious amounts of shellfire to make up for the difficulty in accurately targeting and bringing down enemy planes at night. Regardless of the large amounts of copper (a scarce non-ferrous metal) this would demand, the dictator ordered the production of 88 mm shells to be increased to 1 million per month.[27]

Autumn saw the introduction of two major schemes which clearly indicate that the political leadership was now prioritising home defence. The *Erweiterte Kinderlandverschickung* encouraged parents dwelling in large cities to allow the NSDAP to move their children into camps organised in rural areas. At the same time, the *Führer-Sofortprogramm* addressed the issue of air-raid shelter construction on a truly massive scale: by October 1941, sixty-one cities within range of the RAF were to be provided with enough concrete bunkers to offer shelter for most of their inhabitants.[28] Destined to fall well short of expectations, it nevertheless amounted to a massive investment, with the concrete poured into it surpassing that used in the Westwall fortifications as early as mid-1941.[29] The most visible legacies of this and other related schemes betray the dictator's close personal interest in it: three enormous Flak towers which doubled as shelters for civilians in Berlin, Vienna and Hamburg followed a rough design put forward by him before the war; in occupied France, he played a key role in prioritising bunker construction for U-boat berths long before the idea of targeting them had occurred to anyone at RAF Bomber Command.[30]

---

[26] 'OKW, WFSt/Abt. L (IL) Nr. 00643/40 gKdos. FHQu, den 18.9.1940'; in: KTB OKW, Bd. I, p 968. Also IWM, AL 1571 'Betr. Vortrag des Amtschefs beim Gen.F.M. Keitel am 21.9.40 (n.d.)'.

[27] IWM, EDS, AL 1571 'Betr.: Vortrag des Amtschefs beim Gen.F.M. Keitel am 21.9.40'.

[28] Ralf Blank, 'Kriegsalltag und Luftkrieg an der "Heimatfront"'; in: Jörg Echternkamp (ed.), *Die deutsche Kriegsgesellschaft 1939–1945. Politisierung, Vernichtung, Überleben* (München: DVA 2004) [=Das Deutsche Reich und der Zweite Weltkrieg, Bd. 9/1}, pp 357–464, esp. pp 396–7.

[29] IfZ, ED 100–18–40 'Der Staatssekretär der Luftfahrt und Generalinspekteur der Luftwaffe an den Herrn Reichsmarschall. Betr.: Reisebericht über Besichtigungen des Luftschutzes (5.4.1941)'.

[30] KTB OKW, Bd. I, p 158 (entry for 7 November 1940).

The last case is a clear indication of Hitler's prioritisation of military over civilian matters. Even so, this beehive of activity around developing anti-air raid plans and building air-raid shelters, well before Bomber Command was in a position to inflict more than the occasional pinprick of a damaging raid, can only be understood if it is seen in context of the dictator's concern for civilian morale. The first British raids on German urban areas and Berlin in particular left him sufficiently rattled to make a public commitment on 4 September to reprisal raids on British cities. The Luftwaffe's shift from targeting RAF Fighter Command bases to raids on London (and hence, it could be argued, German defeat in the Battle of Britain) was the consequence.[31] At a meeting with Milch on 15 October 1940, Hitler concerned himself with the most minute detail of civil protection, which had just been added to the general's tasks. He enquired about what kind of light would be best for use in a blacked-out urban area (blue), flagged the need for air-raid shelters to be provided with heating and a duty physician and went into considerable detail about the way in which Berliners had been alerted to the latest British air raid. Apparently, coordination between the Luftwaffe and civil defence had been less than perfect, as a result of which two alarms had been sounded, rousing people twice from their beds. This would never do, Hitler chided his subordinate: 'One had to be very careful with sounding the all clear, since for the sick in particular two alarms constitute an extraordinary burden.'[32]

These concerns may appear vastly overblown in light of the actual threat facing German cities at the time, but they are indicative of the mindset of many in the Nazi elite. *Reichsleiter* Alfred Rosenberg showed himself seriously concerned when faced with the actually very scant damage Bomber Command managed to inflict on central Berlin in September and October 1940 and decided to seek refuge in the countryside for a while.[33] The air raids also had the undivided attention of Heinrich Himmler, overlord of the SS empire. As early as the summer of 1940, he was recording in his personal diary every *Luftalarm* in the Berlin area down to the exact timings; by mid-September he was even making separate entries on those occasions when the night had passed without an alert.[34] To an even greater extent than

---

[31] For other factors that may also have had a bearing on this decision, see the excellent discussion in Richard Overy, *The Bombing War: Europe, 1939–1945* (London: Allen Lane 2013), pp 82–6.

[32] BA/MA, RL 3/54 'Der Staatssekretär der Luftfahrt und Generalinspekteur der Luftwaffe an den Herrn Reichsmarschall (15.10.1940)'.

[33] Jürgen Matthäus and Frank Bajohr (eds.), *Alfred Rosenberg. Die Tagebücher von 1934 bis 1944* (Frankfurt a.M.: S. Fischer 2015) pp 343, 348 and 352 (entries for 11 and 13 September and 12 October 1940).

[34] Markus Moors and Moritz Pfeiffer (eds.), *Heinrich Himmlers Taschenkalender 1940. Kommentierte Edition* (Paderborn: Ferdinand Schöningh 2013), pp 337–41, 345 (entries for 14, 16, 17, 18, 19 and 26 September 1940).

Himmler, *Reichspropagandaminister* and Berlin *Gauleiter* Joseph Goebbels turned himself into a faithful chronicler of the bombing war; he adopted the habit of beginning every entry in his personal diary by summarising the nightly tit-for-tat in the Anglo–German bombing war, thus providing the historian with a unique insight into the perception of this campaign by one of Hitler's top collaborators. He failed to draw much solace from the fact that, right up until July 1941,[35] the exchange of blows between Germany and Britain, both in terms of sorties flown and bombers actually finding their targets, undoubtedly favoured the Germans. Goebbels professed himself to be ecstatic whenever London or Liverpool was dealt a damaging blow by the Luftwaffe, but was just as quickly downcast whenever Bomber Command dealt out a fraction of the damage on a German city: in his diary, the human losses and material damage inflicted by the British in a series of raids on Berlin, Bremen and Wilhelmshaven were routinely described as 'heavy', 'considerable' and 'devastating' even though the number of fatalities was usually between twenty and forty, and sometimes fewer than that.[36]

Both Hitler and Goebbels were in agreement that the British raids would significantly increase over the following months.[37] This was all the more reason for concern because the dictator had reached the conclusion that bombing raids carried out under the cover of darkness, as he had put it to Goebbels, 'were impossible to counter'. Such a conclusion appeared to be validated by both the consistently low losses thus far suffered by the Luftwaffe in its night-time Blitz against the British Isles as well as the problems encountered in designing a radar set small enough to fit into a heavy fighter.[38] In the meantime, German interceptors operating at night remained dependent either on a full moon or support from searchlights; unsurprisingly, pickings tended to be small on most nights.

It is important to keep in mind Hitler's perception of Britain's bomber arm as a serious threat when looking at the address he gave on 9 January to his military leadership and the foreign minister, Ribbentrop. The talk was aimed at

---

[35] For a convincing argument that the Blitz did last beyond the widely accepted end date (10 May), see Stephen Moore, 'Reconsidering the Historical Evidence for the End Date of the Blitz against the United Kingdom in 1941' (forthcoming article in *Global War Studies*).

[36] Elke Föhlich (ed.), *Die Tagebücher von Joseph Goebbels, Teil I*, Bd. 9 (Dezember 1940-Juli 1941) (München: K.G. Saur 1998), pp 67, 78, 87, 98 and 186 (entries for 24 December 1940 and 3, 10 and 18 January and 14 March 1941). The only British raid of the 1940–1 period that matched the level of devastation routinely visited on British cities by the Luftwaffe occurred on 8–9 May 1941, when 185 people were killed in Hamburg. Middlebrook and Everitt, *War Diaries*, pp 152–3.

[37] TB Goebbels, Bd. I.9, p 90 (entry for 11 January 1941).

[38] Ibid., p 34 (entry for 4 December 1940). For a summary of the early history of German airborne radar, see Gebhard Adders, *Geschichte der deutschen Nachtjagd 1917–1945* (Stuttgart: Motorbuch 1978), pp 64–9.

convincing the Wehrmacht's top brass of the need for a war of aggression against the USSR. A victory over the communist state, the dictator emphasised, would then have to be followed by building 'a comprehensive Flak screen and the shift of the most important industry into areas removed from the reach of enemy air power. Germany would then be unassailable.'[39]

This forecast is both ridiculously pessimistic in the short to mid-term and astonishingly prescient at the same time: Germany was in a strong, even unassailable position when this address was made, but it quite accurately lays out the challenges the German home defence would be facing from mid-1943 onwards. Further utterances were in keeping with this sombre appreciation. On 16 March 1941 Hitler gave a public speech in which for the first time he dwelled on the hardships the civilian population had had to put with as a result of the British bombing war.[40] Two weeks later a conversation with Goebbels indicated that he really appeared to be at his wits' end. On hearing of the latter's impressions of a visit he had just made to bomb-damaged Wilhelmshaven, he ended up clutching at straws in a fashion almost suggestive of the crisis situations he would be faced with in the last months of the war. At least the cities of northern Germany, which had received more than their share of raids because of their proximity to the United Kingdom, were, as he put it, 'made up of the best racial stock. They are the most likely to keep it together in a crisis.'[41] In the context of early 1941, such statements reflected the dictator's genuine resignation before the apparent invulnerability of the strategic bomber operating at night. Goebbels, for his part, continued to put his faith in increased construction of air-raid shelters for as many Berliners as possible.[42]

The dictator's somewhat gloomy view of Germany's prospects was not destined to last, however. After bemoaning the situation to Goebbels, the leader of the Third Reich made no more demands for the wholesale shift of entire industries to Silesia or East Prussia, nor did he continue to pin his hopes on the supposed 'racial hardiness' of north Germans. Instead, the dictator slowly began to show a degree of optimism about the prospects of German home defence. Addressing the top tier of the Wehrmacht on 30 March, he stuck to his earlier insistence that the Flak arm be enhanced, but added that from now on the anti-aircraft crews on the ground would get support from 'a new apparatus for night firing'.[43]

---

[39] KTB OKW, Bd. I, p 258 (entry for 9 January 1941).

[40] Max Domarus (ed.), Hitler. Reden und Proklamationen 1932–1945, Bd. II.2 (Wiesbaden: R. Löwitt 1973), pp 1673–5.

[41] TB Goebbels, Bd. I.9, p 217 (entry for 1 April 1941).

[42] Ibid., pp 90, 192 and 252–3 (entries for 11 January, 18 March and 17 April 1941).

[43] 'Aufzeichnung von Hermann Hoth über Hitlers Ansprache vor Generälen der Wehrmacht am 30.3.1941 in der Reichskanzlei'; in: Susanne Heim et al (eds.), Sowjetunion mit annektierten Gebieten I. Besetzte sowjetische Gebiete unter deutscher Militärverwaltung. Baltikum und Transnistrien (München: Oldenbourg Verlag 2011) [=

The device the dictator was referring to was the Telefunken company's *Funkmessgerät* (FuMG) 39 T Würzburg. This radar set operated on a different wavelength from previous early-warning radars such as the Freya. The Würzburg had a far inferior range but boasted an accuracy that permitted its use as gun-laying radar in the war against the night-time intruders of Bomber Command. A British raid on Berlin in November 1940 had found a number Würzburg prototypes ready and waiting: the results fully justified the priority its production had already been given. Needless to say, demand far outstripped production and would in fact do so until the end of the war. Nonetheless, by March 1942 a third of all Flak batteries in Germany were supported by a Würzburg set.[44] German anti-aircraft defences thus acquired a lethality far ahead of anything Allied airmen would ever encounter in the skies of other Axis countries.[45]

This development was all the more important because a prototype Lichtenstein airborne radar which would finally free the night fighter force from the shackles of searchlight support was not trialled until August 1941 and not issued in appreciable numbers until the following spring.[46] Hitler had in any case, as we have already seen, a strong preference for the Flak arm as the main tool of home defence and was unfazed by this. Reflecting on the Würzburg's growing success rate he said to Goebbels on 18 August 1941: 'This is a clear manifestation of the cycles governing air warfare. Every weapon will give rise to a weapon designed to counter it. This may take a little while; but there is no precedent in military history for the invention of one weapon conferring on one side a permanent superiority over the other. That's precisely what we are currently witnessing in the air war.'[47]

There can be little doubt that this development played at least a contributory role in the regime's decision to allow the gradual return of some of the Berlin children sent to live in rural areas, a decision which had ended up generating some serious discontent among the parents affected.[48] In the meantime, the dictator had made sure that Flak artillery retained the highest production priority.[49] The events of autumn 1941 certainly appeared to indicate that the

Die Verfolgung und Ermordung der europäischen Juden durch das nationalsozialistische Deutschland 1933–1945], pp 117–19.

[44] On the early history of the Würzburg, see Westermann, *Flak*, pp 95–108.

[45] See Daniel T. Schwabe, *Burning Japan: Air Force Bombing Strategic Change* (Nebraska UP: Potomac Books 2015), pp 25–7, 161, on the deficiencies of the Japanese anti-aircraft arm, which allowed the US strategic bombing campaign to be switched from high-altitude daytime raids to low-altitude night-time incursions in early 1945.

[46] Aders, *Nachtjagd*, pp 66–7.

[47] TB Goebbels, Bd. II.1, p 264 (entry for 19 August 1941).

[48] Ibid., p 474 (entry for 23 September 1941).

[49] BA/MA, RW 19/822 'Der Reichsminister für Bewaffnung und Munition Nr. M 5467/41 (19.9.1941)'; ibid., 'Der Chef des Oberkommandos der Wehrmacht an Chef Wi Rü Amt. Geheime Kommandosache (19.9.1941)'.

balance in the bombing war was now tilting more and more in Germany's favour, notwithstanding the absence of radar-equipped fighters. The events of 17 November provided powerful evidence to that end. That night saw a maximum effort by Bomber Command against Berlin and other targets. The British suffered an unprecedented loss rate (14 per cent) for a mission of such size: 37 out of 169 aircraft failed to return. For the remainder of 1941, raids on German urban areas were limited to coastal towns and a few cities in the Ruhr, thus not requiring a lengthy exposure to enemy defences. Even so, a further 141 planes were lost by the end of the year, an overall loss rate that would play a key role in the removal of Air Vice Marshal Sir Richard Peirse, Bomber Command's commander-in-chief.[50]

To anyone today it seems baffling that Hermann Göring was able so easily to dispel the dictator's concerns at the appearance around this time of a small, but slowly growing number of four-engined bombers with Bomber Command (the Short Stirling was soon followed by the Handley Page Halifax and the Boeing B-17), but this has to be seen against the backdrop of the RAF's losses in the late summer and autumn of 1941.[51] These are likely to have coloured Hitler's assessments of the air war to a far greater extent than the limited impact made by the three types of heavy bomber deployed in very small numbers in 1941.

When Hitler addressed the *Gauleiter* in the Neue Reichskanzlei on 12 December 1941 he gave them an overview of the military situation. Unbeknownst to him, his assessment of the situation on the Eastern Front was just forty-eight hours away from collapsing like a house of cards. His assessment of the air war, on the other hand, was an accurate reflection of military reality in the short to mid-term. Once again, Joseph Goebbels left a pithy summary of these thoughts for posterity: 'As far as the air attacks were concerned, the Führer felt that their impact would diminish more and more with the passage of time. Our defensive weapons against the air threat have yielded such a rate of successes that it is not too far-fetched to view the future of the air war with some scepticism. In the long term, every weapon will find its match in a weapon

---

[50] Westermann, *Flak*, pp 134–5.

[51] 'Freitag, 24. Oktober 1941'; in: Martin Vogt (ed.), *Herbst 1941 im 'Führerhauptquartier'. Berichte Werner Koeppens an seinen Minister Alfred Rosenberg* (Koblenz 2002) [= Materialen aus dem Bundesarchiv, Heft 10], pp 98–9. According to Joachim von Ribbentrop, Göring had insisted to Hitler in 1941 or early 1942 that the American B-17 was vulnerable and 'easy to shoot down'. See Joachim von Ribbentrop, *Zwischen London und Moskau. Erinnerungen und letzte Aufzeichnungen.* (Druffel-Verlag: Leoni am Starnberger. See 1961), pp 270–1. With regards to the early 'C' version of the B-17 trialled by the RAF's No. 90 Squadron between July and September 1941, this statement actually had a core of truth: the aircraft was rejected by the British for a number of technical reasons. See Donald Caldwell and Richard Muller, *The Luftwaffe over Germany: Defence of the Reich* (London: Greenhill Books 2007), p 45.

Figure 9.1 A Boeing B-17 C at a flypast laid on for Winston Churchill. The inadequacies of the early versions of the B-17 and the kill rate of the Würzburg gun-laying radar contributed to allaying Hitler's early fears about the potential of the RAF's strategic bombing campaign. (Bettmann via Getty Images)

designed to counter it.'[52] This estimate was undoubtedly correct so far as the growth of the Flak arm,[53] the introduction of Würzburg and rising British losses were concerned. Confirmation that the December address to the *Gauleiter* was an accurate reflection of the dictator's estimates can be found in a comment he made three weeks later to a small group of visitors at the Wolfsschanze. To them, he confessed that he had, if anything, been guilty of overrating the British air

---

[52] TB Goebbels, Bd. II.2, p 497 (entry for 13 December 1941).
[53] The Flak arm had more than doubled its already impressive size since the beginning of the war: from 9,828 (1 October 1939) to 22,090 (1 January 1942). See Rolf-Dieter Müller, 'Die Mobilisierung der deutschen Wirtschaft für Hitlers Kriegsführung'; in: DRZW Bd. 5/1, p 638.

threat in 1941. This in turn had led him to issue directives which resulted in the production of anti-aircraft shells considerably in excess of the needs of the moment.[54] Serious doubt, however, would soon be cast on the other pillar of Germany's 'defensive weapons'. On 28 January 1942 Milch announced to Hitler that the German building industry could simply no longer cope with the demands set by the *Führer-Sofortprogramm*. He recommended a significant reduction in the building of bunkers and the redirection of resources to the strengthening of basements instead. In light of the original aims of the *Führer-Sofortprogramm*, this was clearly an unsatisfactory solution. Even so, the dictator agreed.[55]

9.4   The Shift to the South

As with any other senior party official of the NSDAP, Hermann Göring's guiding principle throughout his time as Hitler's lieutenant was 'to work towards the Führer', irrespective of the number of empty promises he ended up making to that end. By that yardstick, the letter he dictated on 20 October has to be seen as one of the more unusual documents to emerge out of the history of the Third Reich. For weeks now, the growing losses suffered by Axis convoys supplying Rommel's forces in Libya had led to serious concerns about the viability of maintaining an active theatre of war in the Western Desert. Both the Italian and German high commands were blissfully unaware that the compromise of assorted Axis codes was greatly facilitating this attrition, but they did know where the majority of the planes, submarines and surface vessels inflicting the damage were based: the island of Malta which conveniently straddled the convoy routes leading from southern Italy to Tripoli and Benghazi. The Kriegsmarine had already been ordered to detach six submarines to the Mediterranean in September, with a view to interdict the traffic which kept both the island and the besieged fortress of Tobruk resupplied. In many ways, relocating elements of the Luftwaffe to Sicilian bases seemed to be the more obvious solution, since from January to mid-May X. *Fliegerkorps* had already waged a highly successful campaign from these against Malta, managing in the process to cripple a British fleet carrier and sink a heavy cruiser. Elements of the force were then shifted to eastern Europe for the invasion of the USSR, while a rump moved to bases in southern Greece. From here the latter waged a strategic air campaign against logistics facilities in the Nile Delta, while occasionally detaching a few squadrons to reinforce its sub-command *Fliegerführer Afrika* fighting in the desert in direct support of Rommel.[56]

---

[54] 'Wolfsschanze, 5.1.1942 mittags. Gäste Reichsminister Dr. Todt, Sepp Dietrich, General Gause, Oberst Zeitzler. H/Fu.'; in: Werner Jochmann (ed.), *Adolf Hitler. Monologe im Führerhauptquartier 1941–1944* (München: Orbis 2000), pp 178–9.

[55] Blank, 'Kriegsalltag und Luftkrieg', pp 396–7.

[56] Karl Gundelach, *Die deutsche Luftwaffe im Mittelmeer, 1940–1945* (Frankfurt a.M.: Peter Lang 1981), pp 92–146, 224–34, 267–78.

This successful precedent notwithstanding, Göring tried his best to have a repeat of the move cancelled or at least postponed. He argued that the units would still be needed in the upcoming offensive by *Heeresgruppe Süd* on the Eastern Front, aimed at seizing the Maikop oilfields before winter closed in. In addition, he stressed that refit, rest and recuperation would mean a delay of at least fifty-four days before the first squadrons materialised in Sicily and insisted that the improved defences of Malta would now require a far stronger force than the one which had temporarily suppressed the base in winter. For good measure, he demanded the subordination of all Italian air force units engaged in the same mission. There may have been a variety of motives for this unusual attempt at obstruction.[57] What is certain is that at this very time moves were afoot for a wholesale shift of Luftwaffe units away from Russia which, even allowing for the near-catastrophic losses inflicted on the Red Army at Kiev and Vyazma-Bryansk, were nothing short of staggering. While the latter battle was still raging, *Luftflotte 2* in the central sector alone had fielded fourteen bomber, ten fighter and nine Stuka *Gruppen*. In a briefing for Halder on 8 October, Luftwaffe operations chief, Hoffmann von Waldau, explained that by the end of the year, Luftwaffe presence along the entire Eastern Front would be reduced to a grand total of eight bomber, ten and a half fighter and one single Stuka *Gruppe*.[58] The commander of VIII. *Fliegerkorps*, Wolfram von Richthofen, far from sharing Göring's caution in the matter, in a private letter written on 26 October, appeared to welcome the idea of this move, because it would facilitate the long overdue rest and refit of some of the units concerned. The document conveys no sense of urgency or even a hint that these units might be sorely missed by *Heeresgruppe Mitte* upon its resumption of operations.[59]

A mere eight days after Göring penned his futile attempt to ward off the unwanted relocation to the Mediterranean, the war diary of the Seekriegsleitung gave specific figures for the future employment of some of these units. From the current strength of the remainder of X. *Fliegerkorps* – three *Gruppen* of bombers, one *Gruppe* of Stukas and one *Gruppe* of heavy fighters[60] – Luftwaffe strength in the Mediterranean was to be boosted to a total of twelve *Gruppen* of bombers, nine *Gruppen* of

[57] Gundelach, *Luftwaffe*, pp 331–3. Gundelach makes an argument that Göring in his capacity as plenipotentiary for the Four Year Plan was becoming concerned about Germany's fuel situation and hence more inclined to prioritise the capture of Maikop. Confirmation of this can be found in BA/MA, RW 19/2334 'Chef Wi Rü Amt. Aktennotiz über Vortrag beim Reichsmarschall am 4.9.41 im Reichsjägerheim Rominten (5.9.1941)'.

[58] Hans-Adolf Jacobsen (ed.), *Generaloberst Halder. Kriegstagebuch. Tägliche Aufzeichnungen des Chefs des Generalstabes des Heeres 1939–1942*, Bd. III (Stuttgart: Kohlhammer 1964), pp 272–3(entry for 8 October 1941).

[59] BA/MA, N 671/8 'General der Flieger von Richthofen an Oberst Meister (26.10.1941)'.

[60] Gundelach, *Luftwaffe*, p 304.

Stukas and nine *Gruppen* of fighters (six *Gruppen* of bombers, six *Gruppen* of Stukas and six *Gruppen* of fighters on Sicily and Sardinia and six bomber, three Stuka and three fighter *Gruppen* in the Aegean).[61] Since the units already deployed on North African soil were not even included in this count, the Luftwaffe's order of battle for early spring 1942 would have seen the bulk of its Stukas, together with half its bombers and a third of its fighter force, deployed in the Mediterranean. Thus far, Luftwaffe strength in the region had never sufficed to combine close air support for Rommel with convoy escort and regular air raids on both Malta and the Nile Delta, a focus on just two of these remits invariably leading to the neglect of the other two. With a force of the kind now envisaged, these dilemmas would be a thing of the past.

In a letter which by his standards was a masterpiece of tact and diplomacy, the German dictator gave a strategic tour d'horizon to Mussolini on 29 October. He did so in a manner that helped render the main reason for his communication – Italian acquiescence in a large-scale Luftwaffe deployment in southern Italy – somewhat more palatable, allowing his Italian counterpart to grant the necessary permission without construing the move as a slight to Italian honour or sovereignty.[62] First, he gave a lengthy summary of the events which had led to the recent near-catastrophic Soviet defeats at Kiev, the Sea of Azov and Vyazma-Bryansk, taking care to stress the honourable role played in the first of these three battles by the Italian corps fighting in the ranks of *Heersgruppe Süd*. In light of the fact that '70–90 per cent' of Soviet 'mines and industrial sites' were now in German hands or just days away from falling into them, he concluded the first part of the letter by stating that the 'Bolshevik empire is beaten'. He then shifted his attention to the British, running through a number of strategic options still open to them, including highly implausible ones like a major landing in Western Europe. Only towards the end of the letter did he turn to the far more pressing problem of shoring up Rommel's position and suppressing Malta. Despite the Regia Aeronautica's failure since May to do just that, he assured Mussolini that he felt 'that this main task could only be solved by the Italian air force'. He was, however, willing to offer a few specialist Luftwaffe units, like long-range night fighters for intruder work.[63] Thus mollified and reassured, Mussolini on 6 November graciously agreed to receive an entire air corps in Sicily.[64] Once this exchange had allowed a consensus to be reached, the destruction

---

[61] KTB Seekriegsleitung, Teil A (entry for 28 October 1941).
[62] 'Der Führer an den Duce (29.10.1941)'; in: ADAP, Serie D, Bd. XIII.2, pp 580–5.
[63] Ibid.
[64] 'Der Duce an den Führer. Geheime Reichssache (6.11.1941)'; in: ADAP, Serie D, Bd. XIII.2, pp 613–18.

Figure 9.2 An Italian air raid on Malta: by November 1941, the limited impact of the Regia Aeronautica's forays against Malta forced Hitler to redeploy important parts of the Luftwaffe fighting in Russia to the Mediterranean. (ullstein bild/ullstein bild via Getty Images)

of yet another southbound convoy by a Malta-based task force in the small hours of 9 November worked wonders to concentrate the minds of all concerned and led to orders from Hitler to prioritise the move south from the USSR forthwith.[65]

November saw the withdrawal from Russia gather pace with, by the end of the month, General Wolfram von Richthofen put in charge of the entire central sector as a kind of caretaker *Luftflotte* commander. He was decidedly unhappy at this development, confiding in his diary that he feared being 'left to rot' in what appeared to be a sideshow where the weather alone would leave him and his men with little to do.[66] By 5 December 1941 the order of battle of his command showed a strength of seven bomber, three Stuka and six fighter *Gruppen* – a decrease of more than 50 per cent.[67] *Heeresgruppe Mitte* was not best pleased with this development and even before the Soviet counteroffensive before Moscow turned into a major crisis asked Halder that further relocations

---

[65] Gundelach, *Luftwaffe*, p 297.
[66] BA/MA, N 671/8 'Tagebuch Richthofen (entries for 11 November and 3 December 1941)'.
[67] BA/MA, RL 8/280 'VIII. Fliegerkorps order of battle (5.12.1941)'.

to Germany be halted for the time being.[68] The continuing deterioration in the days after 13 December meant that on 17–18 December 1941 four bomber *Gruppen* had to be rushed back to the Eastern Front.[69] When the crisis reached existential levels around the turn of the year, more reinforcements followed in haste, notwithstanding the limitations imposed on daily operations by the brutal winter weather.[70] By early January 1942, Richthofen would have a total fifteen bomber, three Stuka and six fighter *Gruppen* under his command.[71] In contrast to the pace of operations in November, when a low cloud ceiling had sufficed to stand the entire force down, wing commanders were now being admonished to fly sorties in any kind of weather and in doing so 'accept any kind of risk'.[72]

Not only had *Heeregruppe Mitte* been left dangerously short of air support for a brief, though critical moment in time, the consequences for the new Mediterranean strategy soon made themselves felt as well. At its peak in March and April 1942, II. *Fliegerkorps* in Sicily would have a strength of five bomber and six fighter *Gruppen* together with a miniscule Stuka element. This constituted but a temporary high, since in the first days of May, two *Gruppen* each of bombers and fighters had to be returned to Russia.[73] While this already constituted a considerable diminution of what had been originally planned in October, it was as to nothing compared with what happened to the second pillar of the new *Schwerpunkt* of Luftwaffe strategy. Not only did X. *Fliegerkorps* in the Aegean receive no reinforcements whatsoever, on several occasions it had to share its slender resources either with the newcomers on Sicily or *Fliegerführer Afrika* in Libya. In the end, only half of the reinforcements envisaged in October 1941 had actually made it to the Mediterranean by March 1942, and would only remain there for a brief moment in time. In contrast to the 1939–41 period, when it had always been possible to deploy the bulk of the Luftwaffe's bomber and Stuka force in one theatre at a time, the German leadership was now being confronted with the dilemmas of a two-front war.

---

[68] BA/MA, RH 19 II/127 'Fernschreiben von Heeresgruppe Mitte an OKH Gen.St.d.H./Op. Abt. (9.12.1941)'.

[69] BA/MA, RL 8/280 'Gefechtsbericht über den Verlauf der Operationen und Einsatz des VIII. Fliegerkorps, 2. Teil (30.11.41–5.1.42)'.

[70] BA/MA, RL 200/17 Tagebuch Hoffmann von Waldau (entry for 2 December 1941): 'There is a shortage of ground crew and heating apparatus rather than aircraft.'

[71] BA/MA, RL 8/280 'Generalkommando VIII. Fliegerkorps Ia Br.B.Nr. 2950/41 g.Kdos. – Abschrift. Befehl über Gliederung und Befehlsführung innerhalb des VIII. Fliegerkorps ab 6.1.1942 (30.12.1941)'.

[72] BA/MA, RL 8/280 'Fernschreiben an KG 76, 15./KG 53, II./KG 3, III./KG 53, II./KG 53, Gef.Verb. Rettberg, III.St.G. 2. (F)/11, 4. (F)/11, III./JG 51, Quartiermeister f. unterst. Verbände, Lufttransportführer, Nakafü 2 (nachr.), AOK 9 (nachr.) (4.1.1942)'.

[73] Gundelach, *Luftwaffe*, pp 340–6, 362.

9.5 New Aircraft Designs

Generaloberst Wolfram von Richthofen was cursed with a notoriously short fuse. This trait, though undoubtedly exasperating to his headquarters staff, is reflected in the colourful language used in his personal diaries, making them an unusually entertaining primary source. In April 1941, while his VIII. *Fliegerkorps* was supporting the German invasion of Yugoslavia and Greece, he once again had reason to vent his anger as he reflected on the day's events. Even though victorious in all sectors, the German operation was not without the occasional glitch. In this instance, serviceability rates of the Junkers 88 medium bomber had failed to meet his expectations. Since the aircraft had first joined front-line squadrons more than a year ago, this was not a state of affairs he deemed acceptable. The Ju-88, he fumed in his diary on 20 April 1941, was *'ein kriegsunbrauchbarer Mistschlitten'* (loosely translated as 'a good-for-nothing crate').[74]

Although most aviation historians of World War II would probably see this judgement as unduly harsh and as much indicative of the general's temper as any shortcomings of the aircraft in question, it is an important indication of the wider constraints German aircraft designers were labouring under by the late 1930s. From 1936 onwards, the RLM did its utmost to force firms to concertina the process between building the first mock-up and the start of factory production so that prototype testing, the production of a preliminary series and the freezing of the design overlapped each other, rather than being executed sequentially.[75] In the case of the Ju-88, this caused a number of issues compounded by the RLM's insistence that a design initially developed to prioritise speed be given a dive-bombing capability as well. This meant that the new bomber had a rocky start in life, its operational premiere marred by all sorts of teething problems.[76] Most of these were eventually overcome, and the *'Mistschlitten'*, Richthofen's harsh judgement notwithstanding, would go on to become one of the Luftwaffe's more successful designs.

By late 1941, a whole family of highly advanced aircraft that were slated to replace or complement much of the German Air Force's existing inventory were nearing operational deployment: the FW-190 single-engined fighter, the Me-210 fast bomber/heavy fighter and the He-177 heavy bomber were all either in the process of joining their first front-line squadrons or just a couple of months away from doing so. The Me-264 long-range bomber would take somewhat longer, but it is included in this line-up both because of its potential as a weapons system theoretically capable of reaching the USA

---

[74] BA/MA, N 671/6 'Tagebuch Wolfram von Richthofen (entry for 20 April 1941)'.

[75] For a discussion of this process, see Ralf Schabel, *Die Illusion der Wunderwaffen. Die Rolle der Düsenflugzeuge und Flugabwehrraketen in der Rüstungspolitik des Dritten Reiches* (München: Oldenbourg Verlag 1994), pp 115–23.

[76] Budrass, *Luftrüstung*, pp 622–36.

and because Hitler – as we have seen – appears to have been under the impression that its operational deployment was more or less imminent too. In the case of the Ju-88, the basic soundness of the design eventually carried the day, but the production practices that had nearly compromised the new bomber meant that the margin of error had dwindled to almost nothing.

In all likelihood, the Me-264 project first lodged in the mind of Adolf Hitler during a visit to the Messerschmitt works on 22 November 1937. According to the post-war testimony of Nicolaus von Below, Professor Willy Messerschmitt, at the time still chief designer and CEO of the Messerschmitt company, hijacked the choreography of the event by dramatically unveiling before the dictator a mock-up of an oversized four-engined bomber. In front of an aghast Milch, he went on to make all sorts of extravagant claims about the range and speed of the as yet unrealised plane. Hitler expressed a certain interest but no preliminary decision seems to have been reached on the spot.[77] Indeed, a few weeks later Jeschonnek assured Below that there were no plans to include the Me-264 in the current production plan.[78] Hitler believing otherwise may explain his comment to Raeder in November 1940 about deploying the bomber from the Azores.[79] That the admiral relayed this to his staff is the most plausible explanation for a Seekriegsleitung memo from mid-April 1941, which makes a passing reference to the imminent deployment of the first two Me-264s for combat operations.[80] A rough production plan drawn up at the Messerschmitt company a few days later made it clear that nothing could be further from the truth. It estimated that if all the skilled labour and the necessary raw materials were to be made available the two prototypes would be available by November 1941.[81] The company planned a production run of fifty aircraft. This figure may seem small, but it is also realistic when considering the new type's intended mission. Contrary to what has been alleged by some

---

[77] IfZ, ZS 7/1 'Notes taken during interview with Oberst i.G. a.D. Nicolaus von Below at his home in Bochum from 4 pm-10.30 pm, 19th Nov. 1969'. Also Below, *Adjutant,* pp 52–3. Messerschmitt gained a certain notoriety for the way in which he would make untenable promises in order to gain a commercial advantage. A test pilot from the period later went on record as follows: 'He had a gift to insinuate himself into the drift of a major conference. Nor was he averse, in order to achieve his aim, to throw around figures which were impossible to fulfil.' See DM, NL 271/2 'Private letter by Erich Warsitz to Dieter Köhler (16.11.1979)'.

[78] Below, *Adjutant,* pp 54–5.

[79] Göring would claim in 1946 that he had originally put the idea of seizing the Azores to Hitler in October 1940, without, however, tying it to the idea of staging raids on the USA through air bases there. Werner Bross, *Gespäche mit Hermann Göring während des Nürnberger Prozesses* (Flensburg and Hamburg: Christian Wolff 1950), pp 78–9.

[80] BA/MA, RM 7/1058 'Seekriegsleitung B.Nr. 1Skl. Iop 429/41 Gdos. Chefs. Betr.: Durchbruchmöglichkeiten von und nach dem Atlantik (13.4.1941)'.

[81] BA/MA, RL 3/552 'Messerschmitt AG Augsburg, Planung Me 264 (24.4.1941)'.

historians, who have seen the plane as a tool for world domination,[82] the Me-264's intended mission in 1940–1 was of a political more than a military nature. Or as Claudius Dornier reminded his fellow aircraft designer Willy Messerschmitt in a 1942 communication: 'the original intention driving this design was to develop a long-range plane capable of dropping propaganda leaflets over America in order to show the Americans that they would have to create a civilian and military home defence command with a view to a possible war'.[83]

The Messerschmitt company's plan to have two airworthy prototypes by November was most likely run past the dictator in some form, since in another conversation with Raeder on 22 May he modified his earlier estimate and suggested that missions flown from the Azores would be possible by autumn.[84] On the face of it, this was still wildly optimistic, the German aircraft industry having little experience in the design of heavier-than-air aircraft of this size. If the priority, however, was to get a mere two to three prototypes ready to make a small number of incursions into US airspace for the purposes of deterrence, it would appear to be a realistic idea.

In the next twenty-four hours it became clear that the Me-264 was unlikely to be ready to take to the skies in any shape or form by the end of 1941. In a four-paged, tightly spaced letter the Messerschmitt company informed Milch and Udet that due to the lack of aluminium the programme would be cut back to thirty planes. In fact, even producing this quantity would be difficult unless the company was quickly supplied with additional skilled labour and various types of machinery.[85] If the dictator was made aware of this development he managed to hide it during his next summit with Benito Mussolini. Meeting on the Brenner on 2 June, the German treated his fellow dictator to a forecast of the Axis' strategic fortunes in which all was well. He virtually apologised to his ally for the fact that a new type of bomber with an enormous range would only enter series production by 'the end of the year'.[86]

On 30 July 1941 another communication from Messerschmitt finally put paid to that hope. Citing a lack of available materials, the company announced that production of the Me-264 had temporarily been reduced to three

[82] See Jochen Thies, *Hitler's Plans for Global Domination: Nazi Architecture and Ultimate War Aims* (New York and Oxford: Berghahn Books 2012), pp 139–50.

[83] IWM, FD 4355/45, Vol. 3 'Claudius Dornier an Willy Messerschmitt (23.12.1942)'.

[84] 'Seekriegsleitung B.Nr. 1 Skl I Op. 721/41 g.Kdos. Chefs. Besprechung auf dem Berghof Ob.d.M. beim Führer am 22. Mai 1941 (n.d.)'; in: Wagner (ed.), *Lagevorträge*, pp 227–31, esp. p 229.

[85] BA/MA, RL 3/1103 'Messerschmitt AG an das Reichsluftfahrtministerium LC 2 (23.5.1941)'.

[86] 'Aufzeichnung über die Unterredung zwischen dem Führer und dem Duce in Anwesenheit des RAM und des Grafen Ciano auf dem Brenner am 2. Juni 1941, Füh. 34g, Rs (3.6.1941)'; in: ADAP, Serie D, Bd. XII.2, pp 783–92.

prototypes, leaving the factory floor sequentially in January, February and March 1942. Provided the dearth of materials was ameliorated by then, the balance of the production run might follow from September 1942[87].

Long before that point was reached, the entire project reached a crisis point, and in the last week of 1941 it was nearly terminated by Erhard Milch. He was then in the process of taking over the office of Ernst Udet, who had taken his own life in despair in mid-November. In doing so, Milch discovered an alarming lack of oversight, transparency and accountability: aircraft designers had been given far too much leeway in pursuing projects not key to the war effort and allowed to hoard materials well in excess of their needs. Milch, in attempting to cut down on waste and duplication of effort, took a hard look at a number of delayed projects. In the case of the Me-264, a preliminary inspection revealed that the bomber was unlikely to have the range needed for a return trip to the US east coast while carrying a useful payload. Messerschmitt, citing the work already invested and the lack of any viable rival designs, insisted that he be permitted to submit all the evidence to a senior Luftwaffe engineer. This was done in late April 1942. The report stated that in its present configuration the aircraft would reach the US east coast 'only just' and placed primary importance on the aircraft's uses as a long-range reconnaissance plane in the ongoing Battle of the Atlantic.[88] The project was allowed to continue.

Soon after the prototype's much delayed maiden flight (24 December 1942), the Messerschmitt company's main focus on fighter production pushed the project further and further into the background. An attempt to farm it out to the Dornier company failed;[89] it was only briefly brought back into the limelight when Hitler expressed a renewed interest during a meeting with several aircraft designers at his Berghof residence on June 27.[90] It is important to stress that this comeback was no longer tied to his earlier hopes of using the aircraft for a small number of raids against

[87] BA/MA, RL 3/552 'Messerschmitt AG an das Reichsluftfahrtministerium Abteilung LC 2 I A z.Hd. d.H. Ing. Belter (30.7.1941)'.

[88] 'Kommando der Erprobungsstellen der Luftwaffe, Obstlt. u. Kommandeur Petersen, betr. Überprüfung der Arbeiten am Flugzeugmuster Me-264 an Verteiler v. 7.5.1942, Nr. 15200/42 geh. Kdos'., reproduced in full in: Hans J. Ebert et al, *Willy Messerschmitt – Pionier der Luftfahrt und des Leichtbaus. Eine Biographie* (Bonn: Bernhard & Graefe 1992), p 214.

[89] IWM, FD 4355/45, Vol. 3 'Unsigned note addressed to Firma Dornier GmbH, Friedrichshafen (11.1.1943)'; BA/MA, RL 3/1103 GL/C-B 2/II (A) 'Aktenvermerk. Betr.: Me-264 (16.3.1943)'.

[90] Ernst Heinkel, *Stürmisches Leben* (Stuttgart: Mundus 1953), pp 459–62 and DM, FA 001/0212 'Letter to Karin Engel (29.6.1943)'; BA/MA, ZA 3/191 'Aus GL-Besprechung am 8.7.1943'. Older accounts that give a date in April or May for this meeting are in error.

Figure 9.3 Yesterday's deterrent: the Me-264 prototype in flight, Christmas Eve, 1942. (PF-(sdasm3) / Alamy Stock Photo)

cities on the eastern seaboard in order to force the US government into adopting a more defensive posture. He admitted to Admiral Dönitz ten days after the Berghof conference 'that he had dropped the idea of a bombing campaign against the USA, since the few aircraft likely to reach their targets would not make a difference, but might galvanise the civilian population into a greater commitment to the war'.[91] The dictator's interest resulted in a brief flurry of activity, but it soon became clear that an aircraft industry forced by round-the-clock Allied air raids to turn out an increasing number of fighters lacked the means to resuscitate a project that harked back to a time when Germany had briefly been in a position to contemplate waging air campaigns spanning oceans.[92]

While the Me-264 owed its very existence to an idiosyncratic intervention by Germany's dictator, the Messerschmitt 210 was a different matter altogether. As a twin-engined heavy fighter/fast bomber, it was designed to become the

---

[91] Skl.B.Nr. 1 Skl Ib 2164/43 'g.K. Chefs. Niederschrift über die Besprechung des Ob.d. M. beim Führer am 8.7.1943 um 16.30 h im Hauptquartier 'Wolfsschanze' (31.7.1943)'; in: Wagner (ed.), *Lagevorträge*, pp 517–22, esp. p 518.

[92] BA/MA, RL 3/61' Stenografische Mitschrift der Besprechung des Reichsmarschalls mit GL und Industrierat am Donnerstag, den 14. Oktober 1943, 12 Uhr in der Neuen Reichskanzlei, Berchtesgaden (n.d.)'.

successor to the much better known Me-110 heavy fighter.[93] The latter's maiden flight in June 1936 had been just a few months in the past when the RLM approached the Messerschmitt company with an offer to begin design work on a successor. Although the Me-110 had started life as a pure fighter, the RLM was now in the process of reconsidering its operational priorities. The new plane it was asking for, while still able to operate as a heavy fighter, would also need to be able to carry a ton of bombs; moreover, the ministry insisted on enhanced defensive armament.[94] This in-built ambiguity would never be satisfactorily resolved and materially contributed to the design's failure.

In the meantime, however, the Me-210 became a key component in the Luftwaffe's future order of battle. The *Flugzeugmusterprogramm* of October 1938 relied on the new plane to equip eight new *Zerstörer* (heavy fighter) wings and eventually the majority of twelve dive-bomber wings.[95] In contrast to the Me-264, originally designed with just one very specific contingency in mind, the Me-210 was seen as absolutely crucial to the Luftwaffe of 1942–3, irrespective of the type of campaign the German armed forces' youngest service might be called upon to undertake next.

After a maiden flight that coincided with the outbreak of World War II, Messerschmitt and his test pilots set about fine-tuning the design of the Me-210. A swathe of problems soon emerged, the process of solving them rendered more problematic by simultaneous demands from the RLM for a number of last-minute design changes. The situation was further compounded when the Luftwaffe, with a view to equipping at least two wings by the spring of 1942, insisted on initiating series production before testing was finished.[96] The aircraft's wing loading turned out to be on the high side and gave it a poor climbing rate, a direct consequence of the attempt to combine the design of a fighter with the tasking of a bomber. Both the fuselage and the undercarriage were shown to be too weak. In addition, stability was an issue, with the aircraft showing an alarming habit of stalling in a banking manoeuvre. Rather than lengthening the fuselage, as he appears to have been advised by at least one test pilot, Messerschmitt tackled the problem by installing leading edge slats.[97] Udet was increasingly driven to distraction by the delays to the project and in

---

[93] This plane is often referred to as the Bf-110, thus reflecting the Messerschmitt company's original name (Bayerische Flugzeugwerke) in 1936. For the sake of simplicity and consistency, the acronym 'Me' will be used for this aircraft throughout the text.

[94] On the early design history of the type, see Ebert, *Pionier*, pp 164–9; Heinz Mankau and Peter Petrick, *Messerschmitt Bf 110-Me 210-Me 410. Die Messerschmitt-Zerstörer und ihre Konkurrenten* (Oberhaching: Aviatic 2001), pp 89–90, 247–54 as well as Peter Petrick and Werner Stocker, *Messerschmitt Me 210/Me 410 Hornisse/Hornet: An Illustrated Production History* (London: Ian Allan 2007), pp 8–14.

[95] Petrick and Stocker, *Hornet*, p 11.

[96] Ibid., *Hornet*, pp 16–17.

[97] Ebert et al, *Messerschmitt*, pp 170–1.

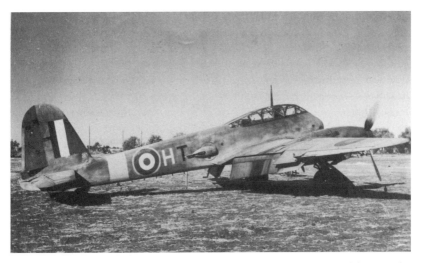

Figure 9.4 Me-210 in RAF colours: Willy Messerschmitt's problems in delivering the Me-210 in 1942 turned into the biggest weapons procurement scandal of the Third Reich. The pictured specimen was displayed by the RAF after the war. (Bettmann via Getty Images)

late July 1941 took Messerschmitt to task. He complained of the plethora of changes that had been made to the original design (while conveniently omitting the Luftwaffe's own role in insisting on some of these) and reminded Messerschmitt that he had been given a task that carried with it an enormous responsibility. As he put it, the care invested in the project had to reflect the fact that the Me-210 was nothing less than 'a type likely to decide the outcome of the war'.[98]

In the meantime, the supposedly imminent introduction, from May 1941 onwards, of the Me-210 led to a gradual decrease in production of the earlier Me-110, with a view to ending it altogether in September that year.[99] Producing both types side by side would not only have been regarded as wasteful, but near-impossible, since they both used the same in-line engine. As a result, in view of the delays besetting the new Messerschmitt design, it was decided in early July to continue production of the Me-110, though on a comparatively small scale. Over the following months, the exact number of planes on order was increased or decreased virtually every month, giving

---

[98] 'Brief des Generalluftzeugmeisters an Prof. Messerschmitt (25.7.1941)'; reproduced in full in: Mankau and Petrick, *Messerschmitt-Zerstörer*, p 94.

[99] BA/MA, RL 3/1104 'GL/C-B 2 No. 492/42 g.K. (I) Aktenvermerk. Betr.: Programm-Entwicklung Me-110 bzw. Me-210 (5.2.1942)'.

a good idea of the confusion that reigned in Udet's office.[100] These shifts would have had a major disruptive effect even under the most favourable circumstances. But circumstances were far from favourable: it was discovered that the Daimler-Benz 601 F engine used for the version of the Me-110 chosen for continued production – the Me-110 F – suffered from problems with oil pressure. As a result, 60 per cent of the aircraft of this production batch had to be withheld from front-line service.[101] By late 1941, the *Zerstörer* arm of the Luftwaffe thus faced a crisis, likely to have the direst ramifications in light of the Me-110's versatility: whether as convoy escort off Norway and in the Mediterranean, as close air-support and reconnaissance aircraft in Russia and North Africa or as a night-time interceptor, the Me-110 had become a veritable jack of all trades and one of the Luftwaffe's key assets. Prioritising the allocation of the rapidly dwindling number of heavy fighters became such a contentious issue that in early November 1941 Hitler himself broke his customary habit of leaving Luftwaffe affairs to Göring and took matters into his own hands.[102]

It is against this backdrop that the visit to the Messerschmitt factory in Augsburg by a delegation of three experienced pilots and engineers on 12 December 1941 has to be seen. Udet had taken his life three weeks before and now his successor Milch was in the process of assessing which aircraft projects were likely to pass muster and which ones would have to be terminated. The three men reported back that matters appeared to be in hand and that the Me-210 was now in the final stages of becoming a viable combat aircraft.[103] Predictably enough, however, there was one last-minute alteration desired by the RLM (dive-bombing capability was now de-emphasised in favour of low-level attacks). Apart from this, things were heading in the right direction.[104]

Elation soon turned to horror and disbelief when the first substantial number of aircraft were put in the hands of rookie pilots in advanced training units. In the second half of January, a total of eight aircraft crashed. After a brief hiatus, ten more crashes followed between 3 and 9 March 1942.[105] As late as 25 January 1942 Milch had announced in a report to Jeschonnek that they would soon be in a position to finally and permanently phase out the Me-

[100] See ibid. For a slightly different chronology of events, see Mankau and Petrick, *Messerschmitt-Zerstörer*, pp 203–4. The disruption caused by these changing priorities is reflected in BA/MA, RL 3/552 'Messerschmitt AG Augsburg an das Reichsluftfahrtministerium zu Hd. von Herrn Oberst i.G. Vorwald (18.10.1941)'.

[101] BA/MA, RL 3/1104 'GL/C-E 2 III Aktenvermerk. Betr.: Bf-110 Anlauf der Baureihe F (5.2.1942)'.

[102] BA/MA, RM 7/170 'Ergebnis der Besprechung 1.Skl./I L bei Robinson am 3.11.1941 (n. d.)'. Also KTB Skl, Teil A (entry for 1 January 1942).

[103] Petrick and Stocker, *Hornet*, p 17

[104] Mankau and Petrick, *Messerschmitt-Zerstörer*, p 95.

[105] Ibid., pp 96–7.

110.[106] By early March 1942, the Luftwaffe leadership thus found itself confronted with the very real prospect of campaigning for the remainder of 1942 with a completely inadequate number of heavy fighters.

At a conference held at Göring's country residence on 6 March, Milch, Jeschonnek and Göring decided to immediately summon Messerschmitt and some of his key collaborators. They openly discussed the possible cancellation of the Me-210 that day, but if Göring was particularly agitated by any of this, the minutes do not reflect it; either the passing reference to a possible substitute aircraft (the inferior Arado 240[107]) led him to believe that he still had an ace up his sleeve or the Me-210's long history of producing a multitude of bugs that were all ultimately addressed encouraged him in the hope that the next round of talks with Messerschmitt would reveal that the latest issues were rectifiable as well.

When the two men, Göring and Messerschmitt, finally met three days later on the former's special train, any such hopes had apparently been dashed, since the *Reichsmarschall* was a changed man. He described the failure of the Me-210 as 'the worst blow to hit him since the creation of the Luftwaffe and claimed that he 'envied *Generaloberst* Udet' because he was no longer around to witness such a failure.[108] In the ensuing exchange, the Luftwaffe commander-in-chief did make one valid criticism that went to the heart of the matter: as far as he was concerned, the failure to fully diagnose the seriousness of the stability problems during the twenty-eight months that had elapsed between the first flight and the Me-210 being issued to trainee pilots constituted a mystery, which could only be explained either by the test pilots' extraordinary proficiency or by their total lack of guts.[109]

Further to this criticism, the exchange made clear the truly breathtaking lack of oversight by either Udet or Göring in handling this matter. Their ineptitude soon came to the fore when the Luftwaffe commander-in-chief claimed that both Messerschmitt and Udet had repeatedly assured him that the Me-210 would easily pass all tests, because the design was at heart little more than an improved version of the Me-110, rather than a completely new design of

---

[106] IWM, Speer Collection FD 5514/45 'Der Staatssekretär der Luftfahrt und Generalinspekteur der Luftwaffe an den Herrn Chef des Generalstabes (25.1.1942)'.

[107] BA/MA, RL 3/60 'Besprechungsnotiz Nr. 46/42 g.Kdos. Carinhall, 6.3.1942, 11.20 h-14.10 h und 15.20 h-19.05 Uhr (n.d.)'. A handwritten marginal note in pencil (probably from the hand of an anonymous staff officer) clarified that the Arado 240 would in any case only be ready in 1943.

[108] IWM, Speer Coll., FD 5514/45 'Bericht über die Besprechung betr. Me 210 im Sonderzug des Herrn Reichsmarschall am 9.3.1942 (10.3.1942)'.

[109] Ibid. The comparative ease with which a seasoned pilot was able to compensate for the aircraft's faults can be gleaned from the impressions of Johannes Kaufmann of ZG 1, who flew it between November 1941 and March 1942. See Peter Schmoll, *Nest of Eagles: Messerschmitt Production and Flight Testing at Regensburg, 1936–1945* (Hersham, Surr.: Ian Allan 2010), pp 38–9.

considerable complexity.[110] While this accusation may indeed have been true, it is more revealing in that it shows the extent of Göring's ignorance: only a complete lack of interest in the new fighter could have left him under the impression that the latest addition to the Luftwaffe's order of battle was nothing more than an improvement on an existing design. The *Reichsmarschall* must have sensed that his position was fast becoming indefensible, and accordingly showed himself increasingly thin-skinned: when some of those present in the train challenged him on a matter of minor importance that had only a tangential bearing on the issue being discussed (whether civilian engineers had had sufficient access to front-line units to gather the views of air crew), Göring got so agitated that his interlocutors quickly decided to change the subject ('the attempt to clarify the matter of trips to the front was dropped in light of the irritation of the *Reichsmarschall*').[111]

Production of the Me-210 was stopped four days later and the entire project cancelled a month after that.[112] Even so, the saga of 'trying to make this truly malevolent flying machine behave itself' (in the immortal words of aviation journalist, Bill Gunston) was not yet over.[113] In a move that undoubtedly reflects the amount of investment already poured into the project, a resurrection of sorts was eventually facilitated in September 1942.[114] This was done by lengthening the fuselage by 950 mm (37.4 in), choosing a marginally more powerful engine and giving the type a new denomination (Me-410). In this guise, the aircraft gave adequate service as a fast bomber and daytime interceptor from September 1943 on. Even though this solution might suggest a happy ending of sorts, it has to be seen against the backdrop of the events of early 1942: that a model well past the testing phase and deemed absolutely crucial to the Luftwaffe had had to be cancelled at such an advanced stage was without precedent. The disruption the cancellation caused at the Messerschmitt plant was bad enough,[115] but far worse was the need to run down Me-110 production to make room for that of the Me-210, which was

---

[110] IWM, Speer Coll., FD 5514/45 'Bericht über die Besprechung betr. Me-210 im Sonderzug des Herrn Reichsmarschall am 9.3.1942 (10.3.1942)'.

[111] Ibid. This report is also reproduced in Mankau and Petrick, *Messerschmitt-Zerstörer*, pp 98–100.

[112] IWM, Speer Coll., FD 5514/45 'Aktenvermerk über Besprechung betr. Auswirkungen des Befehls des Herrn Reichsmarschalls über Weiterlauf Me-210 (12.3.1942)'.

[113] Bill Gunston, *Classic World War II Aircraft Cutaways* (London: Bounty Books 2013 rp), p 78.

[114] Or as Milch put it a year later: 'I would never have produced the Me-410 were it not for the fact that the Me-210 had created certain facts of life.' 'Generalluftzeugmeisterbesprechung (29.10.1943)', reproduced in: Mankau and Petrick, *Messerschmitt-Zerstörer*, pp 131–3.

[115] For some graphic examples of this, see the witness statements in Schmoll, *Nest of Eagles*, pp 42–3.

only just beginning. An investigation by the RLM highlighted that without the burden of shifting production to the flawed Me-210 the two companies licensed to build the new fighter together with Messerschmitt (Luther-Werke Braunschweig and Gothaer Waggonfabrik) would have been able to produce an additional 1,000 Me-110s.[116] Since the RLM report was filed at a time when Milch was looking for any shred of evidence that might help him take Messerschmitt down a peg or two, a degree of exaggeration is more than likely.[117] However, in view of the Luftwaffe's lack of heavy fighters, even half that figure would still have constituted a highly welcome reinforcement for the embattled *Zerstörer* arm.

The story of a third plane is similar to that of the Me-210. The Heinkel 177 *Greif* heavy bomber was also a second-generation design, the rough specifications of which were initially submitted in 1936. It received an important boost when the belated conclusion that Great Britain was likely to confront Germany over her next attempted land-grab led to it being included in the *Flugzeugmusterprogramm* of October 1938 in considerable strength.[118] Göring intended to use this model to intercept British merchant shipping to the west of the British Isles, a task the Ju-88 would not be able to carry out from German bases. Unlike the Me-264, which could be described as a boutique product for the needs of a niche market, the He-177 – together with the Ju-88 – was intended to become one of the two mainstays of the Luftwaffe's bomber arm by early 1942. The *Göring-Programm* of June 1941 accordingly aimed at the production of 120 aircraft of this type per month.[119]

The new Heinkel's maiden flight took place in November 1939. The next two years witnessed attempts to iron out assorted design flaws with a conspicuous lack of success. Nonetheless, by early 1942 the Luftwaffe was considering the new bomber not just for maritime interdiction, but for a number of other missions as well; those in command anticipated the readiness of this type as eagerly as that of the Me-210.

In many ways the key design flaw that would ultimately doom the aircraft was far more obvious than in the case of the Me-210. Ernst Udet insisted that

---

[116] IWM, Speer Coll. FD 5514/45 'Untersuchungen bei der Gothaer Waggonfabrik; Untersuchungen bei den Luther-Werken Braunschweig (15.4.1942)'.

[117] The Messerschmitt board of directors yielded to the pressure by releasing a statement on 30 April which explained that Willy Messerschmitt would henceforth 'focus on his task as chief designer'. He was succeeded as chairman by Theo Croneiß. Ebert, *Messerschmitt*, p 174.

[118] Budrass, *Luftrüstung*, p 558. The original version of the programme had called for ten wings of He-177s; for once the irrepressible optimist Jeschonnek had to yield to common sense and agree to plan for four instead.

[119] BA/MA, RL 3/51 'Ansprache des Staatssekretärs der Luftfahrt und Generalinspekteurs der Luftwaffe, Generalfeldmarschall Milch an den Industrierat und die Führer der neu gebildeten Industrieringe (Ringführer) am 18.9.1941 im Reichsluftfahrtministerium (n.d.)'

the Heinkel company give the heavy bomber a dive-bombing capability. This made sense in light of the expected anti-shipping assignment the model would have to undertake, since at the time the Luftwaffe did not yet have torpedoes or guided bombs.[120] Based on previous experience with the Ju-88, it was feared that a four-engined heavy bomber might be aerodynamically unstable in a dive. Therefore, Heinkel produced a design which featured one engine nacelle in each wing, each nacelle housing two engines driving one propeller. According to Nicolaus von Below's memoirs, Hitler himself, on being shown a scale model or blueprint of the new bomber in November 1938, expressed doubts as to the practicality of the twin-engine arrangement.[121] Around this time, and possibly prompted by the dictator's remark, Ernst Heinkel allegedly suggested producing a couple of prototypes with four engine nacelles, but this idea was rejected by Udet.[122]

Heinkel does not appear to have raised the point again. In all likelihood this was because for about a year his company faced the prospect of seeing its orders dry up. By the spring of 1940, Messerschmitt had cornered the market for fighters and Junkers for bombers and transport aircraft; even an excellent new single-engined fighter design by Focke-Wulf for a time appeared unlikely to find a toehold in the market. Apart from the as yet barely tested He-177, Heinkel was stuck with the He-111 medium bomber which the Luftwaffe intended to phase out by early 1942 and a prototype jet fighter (the He-280) unlikely to see service in this war. Admiral Lahs, the spokesman (despite his naval rank) of the German aircraft industry, thus suggested that the company give some serious thought to license-building other companies' models. Heinkel would have regarded such a thought as an insult at best, a thinly veiled threat at worst, and it cannot have been much of an incentive to question the rationale behind his principle remaining project, technologically dubious though it may have been.[123]

In the following months, two He-177 prototypes crashed with the loss of their entire crews and a third had to belly-land. Yet far from raising the alarm, this was regarded as par for the course. As a result of the first crash, changes were made to the tail unit which made the aircraft more stable in a dive. The remaining stability issues were described as 'bearable' at an October 1940

---

[120] The two guided weapons which would see operational service with the Luftwaffe, the SD 1400 (Fritz X) and the Henschel 293, were first tested in June and September 1940, respectively. J. Richard Smith and Eddie J. Creek, *Heinkel He-177 Greif: Heinkel's Strategic Bomber* (Hersham, Surr.: Ian Allan 2008), pp 69–71.

[121] Below, *Adjutant*, pp 137–8.

[122] Heinkel, *Leben*, pp 220, 459. The post-war memoirs of Heinkel appear to be the only source for this proposal.

[123] DM, FA 001/0255 'Aktennotiz über Besprechung mit Admiral Lahs am 2.6.1940 betr. Entwicklungsaufgaben (3.6.1940)'.

conference.[124] When in February 1941 two pilots of *KG* 40, which at the time was still using converted airliners of the FW-200 type for its maritime interdiction missions, came calling, conversation quickly turned to relatively minor changes the design might still need. The engineer who had been hosting the two officers stressed the enthusiasm they had shown for the new aircraft and that the company should feel encouraged to do more to promote 'the importance of the He-177 for the war effort'.[125]

As it turned out, any concern that the He-177 project might languish because of a lack of interest was wholly unfounded. On 11 July, Ernst Udet stressed to Heinkel the need to get the new bomber ready for combat as soon as possible with a view not just to support the U-boats, but also to carry out a mission which no other bomber could fulfil: to stage regular raids with useful payloads on Iceland. Even though British and Canadian forces had occupied the island since May 1940, this was the first time such a mission was mentioned in the paperwork connected with the He-177. There can be little doubt that it was linked to the arrival of a US occupation force on Iceland five days earlier, a matter known to have exasperated the German dictator to a considerable degree.[126] This new development, paired with the original brief to interdict shipping west of the British Isles, caused Udet to stress that the new type was now 'in highest demand' and that its delivery had 'the highest priority'.[127]

The following weeks saw further tinkering on the coupled engines, which continued to cause trouble: the need to cram a large number of pipes into a very small space turned them into a potential fire hazard, and even when they did work smoothly they were difficult to service. Nonetheless, the project continued to make headway and Heinkel indicated to the Luftwaffe and Kriegsmarine that factory production would be initiated in spring 1942, with two squadrons ready for duty in early summer of that year.[128] By October, there was even talk of initiating series production slightly earlier than

---

[124] DM, FA 001/0255 'Aktennotiz. Betr.: He-177. Besprechung am 1.10.1940 im RLM (2.10.1940)'.

[125] DM, FA 001/0860 'Besprechungsniederschrift von Konstruktionsleitung. Besuch der Herren: Major Petersen (KG 14 – sic), Hauptmann Düsing (Generalstab) am 20. Februar 1941 in Marienehe (21.2.1941)'.

[126] 'Geheime Reichssache Füh42/41. Aufzeichnung über die Unterredung des Führers mit Graf Oshima in Anwesenheit des Reichsaußenministers im Führerhauptquartier am 14. Juli 1941, von 17 bis 19 Uhr (15.7.1941)'; in: ADAP, Serie D, Bd. XIII.2, pp 829–34.

[127] DM, FA 001/0259 'Aktennotiz ! Betr.: Frühzeitiger Serienauslauf He 111 H 6 (11.7.1941)'.

[128] BA/MA, RM 7/258 'Oberkommando der Wehrmacht W.F.St./L Nr. 441465/41 g.K.Ch. Die strategische Lage im Spätsommer 1941 als Grundlage für die weiteren politischen und militärischen Absichten' (27.8.1941)'. See also BA/MA, RL 3/1833 'Luftrüstungsvergleich Deutschland + Italien und Grossbritannien + USA 1939–1943. Stand: 1. Juli 1941. Erster Teil', which Udet forwarded to Göring, Milch and Jeschonnek on 30 August 1941.

anticipated and of exceeding the agreed production quota of 120 aircraft per month.[129] Such projections appear to have encouraged the Luftwaffe to prepare for the first full *Gruppe* (three squadrons) of He-177s to join *Fliegerführer Atlantik* as early as March.[130] Hitler himself, in a long letter to Mussolini on 29 October, dwelt at some length on the progress the new design was currently making, extolling its range, payload and speed.[131] Hitler repeatedly made a point of shoring up weaker allies by references to superior German weapons technology, but only rarely where air power was concerned. This shows that he had been closely following the progress made by the new Heinkel bomber.

In a manner eerily reminiscent of the events surrounding the final testing phase of the Me-210, the He-177 project entered a major crisis in January and February 1942. This was most likely caused by the urgency of the situation: testing of the new type would need to be pushed to new limits if it was to be ready by early spring for handover to the first front-line squadrons. January saw two prototypes crash, one of which was caused by Daimler-Benz using the wrong type of rivet in the crankshaft. Events in February proved that the design suffered from far more serious flaws than simple human error. Not counting a number of non-fatal accidents (such as an engine catching fire while the aircraft was still in the process of taxiing), a total of six aircraft crashed with the loss of most of their crews. Five of the six crashes involved engine fires. All further flights were immediately stopped until further notice.[132] An extensive memo penned in mid-February by Major Petersen of *KG* 40 on the operational vistas which the introduction of the He-177 would soon open up for maritime air warfare was destined to remain a pipe dream.[133]

In May Hermann Göring visited the Rechlin testing centre. His criticism of the coupled-engine design echoed his clash with Messerschmitt over the Me-210 two months before ('I believe I am right in saying that you cannot even take out the spark plugs without pulling the whole engine apart'). But while his criticism of the design was essentially accurate, his claim that this was the first time that this feature had come to his notice was a different matter.[134] Even the

[129] DM, FA 001/0860 'Aktennotiz. Betr.: Göring-Programm. Bau der He-177 in Marienehe, Verlegung der Ju 88-Flächen aus Oranienburg (15.10.1941)'; BA/MA, RL 3/1104 'Entwurf – Aktenvermerk über die Programmbesprechung bei Herrn Generalfeldmarschall Milch vom 21. Oktober 1941 (22.10.1941)'.

[130] BA/MA, RM 7/170 'Ergebnis der Besprechung 1. Skl./I L bei Robinson am 3.11.1941 (n.d.)'.

[131] 'Brief Hitlers an Mussolini (29.10.1941)'; in: ADAP, Serie D, Bd. XIII.2, pp 580–5.

[132] DM, FA 001/0862 'Heinkel Berlin an Heinkel Rostock. Betr.: He-177 – Triebwerksbrände/Sperrung (25.2.1942)'.

[133] DM, FA 001/0862 'Gedanken über den Einsatz der He-177 im Atlantik ab Sommer 1942 (12.2.1942)'.

[134] BA/MA, RL 3/60 'Stenographischer Bericht über die Besprechung des Reichsmarschalls Göring mit Vertretern der Luftfahrtindustrie über Entwicklungsfragen am Sonntag, dem 13. September 1942, vorm. 11 Uhr im Reichsluftfahrtministerium (n.d.)'.

most cursory glance at a scale model or drawing would have revealed the fundamental problem with the design: to an even greater degree than had been the case with the Me-210, the He-177's entire design history was linked to one particular and quite unique design requirement (the alleged need for the coupled-engine arrangement) and all the concomitant problems and limitations arising therefrom. Göring's claim that he had somehow spent two and a half years since the type's maiden flight in ignorance of this basic fact beggars belief. It signals to a far greater degree than any other incident in his career as Luftwaffe commander-in-chief that he was unfit for a senior command position of any kind.

In due course, test flights were resumed, but at a price. On 19 June, the crash of another He-177 was witnessed by two regime VIP's. Erhard Milch and Albert Speer happened to be present at Peenemünde for the test launch of the V-2 ballistic missile when a fully bombed up He-177 plummeted to the earth before their very eyes, thus virtually guaranteeing that the unfolding disaster would be the talk at Führer's Headquarters for weeks to come.[135] However, even before this embarrassing incident, a note by Heinkel to one of his engineers stated that the readying of the He-177 for front-line service, was 'earnestly desired by the highest authority' – a clear and ominous allusion to the highest decision maker in the Third Reich.[136] In the meantime, thought was finally given to producing a version with four separate engine nacelles, without, however, terminating the original version.[137] Göring also acquiesced in foregoing the need for a dive-bombing capability.[138] Even so, the process of turning the He-177 into a dependable 'workhorse' (as Milch had demanded in July) continued to be marked by a strange ambiguity. Not only did work on the original (clearly flawed) design continue, but at a November conference at the Heinkel works persistent problems with stability were clearly prioritised over the more fundamental problem with the engines.[139]

In a further comprehensive report by Major Edgar Petersen of *KG* 40 in August, he listed all of the existing flaws in considerable detail, but expressed the hope that a 'promising' deployment of the new Heinkel with *Fliegerführer Atlantik* might still be possible by March 1943'.[140] Those at the

---

[135] Smith and Creek, *He 177*, p 46.

[136] DM, FA 001/0863 'Herrn Schwärzler – Notizen für den Brief an Herrn Nallinger (17.6.1942)'.

[137] BA/MA, RL 3/60 'Besprechungsnotiz Nr. 109/42 g.Kdos. Reichsjägerhof, den 29.6.1942, 18.45–21.15 Uhr (n.d.)'.

[138] 'GL-Besprechung (15.9.1942)'; reproduced in: Georg Hentschel (ed.), *Die geheimen Konferenzen des Generalluftzeugmeisters. Ausgewählte und kommentierte Dokumente zur Geschichte der deutschen Luftrüstung und des Luftkrieges 1942–1944* (Koblenz: Bernard & Graefe 1989), p 110–11.

[139] DM, NL 271/1 'Aktennotiz über die Besprechung bei Generalfeldmarschall Milch am 14.11.42 (n.d.)'.

[140] IWM, Speer Coll., FD 5514/45 'Oberstleutnant Petersen an R.d.L. u. Ob.d.L. (13.8.1942)'.

Figure 9.5 Heinkel He-274 prototype: problem solved? By mid-1944 the
He-274 prototype (pictured in French Air Force service after the war) proved
that with four engine nacelles, the *Greif* could have been a viable combat
aircraft. The type came too late to see combat in World War II. (-/AFP via Getty
Images)

very top of the chain of command, however, were unwilling to wait that
long. On 28 October 1942 Hans Jeschonnek wrote to Erhard Milch with the
news that 'the Führer in the last few days has repeatedly expressed his
interest in seeing this type deployed on the Eastern Front even in
a primitive form'. By this he meant 'night attacks in horizontal flight on
targets which on account of their distance from our front cannot be reached
with other aircraft types'.[141] The support for the U-boat war, while clearly
still important, was to be relegated to a secondary priority for the time
being; the spell cast over the project by the perceived need of the dive-
bombing configuration appeared to have been finally broken.

[141] BA/MA, RL 3/50 'Der Chef des Generalstabes der Luftwaffe Nr. 03720/42 g.Kdos. an
Herrn Generalfeldmarschall Milch, RLM (28.10.1942)'.

Needless to say, the time lost could no longer be made good as became clear a mere eleven days later, when a third contingency unexpectedly materialised. The Allies had landed in French North Africa and while the Luftwaffe was just about able to reach the beachheads in Algeria, the lodgements in Morocco were well out of flying range, considerably easing the Allies' task. In a conversation overheard by his army adjutant, Hitler expressed his utmost exasperation at the aircraft industry's failure to provide him with a long-range bomber that was viable, rather than a design burdened by the idea that it should be of 'universal use'. He pledged to summon the key aircraft designers to his residence and 'take them by the hand, just as he had already done with those working for the army'.[142]

No such meeting occurred until seven months later, thus negating any good that might conceivably have come of it.[143] In the meantime, a small detachment of improved He-177s was sent to southern Russia to help with the airlift set up to support the beleaguered 6. *Armee* in and around Stalingrad. During the course of a deployment which lasted just over a fortnight, a total of seven of the new Heinkels were destroyed and three damaged in quick succession. Of the aircraft lost, only one fell due to enemy action, with engine fires claiming five and structural failure one.[144] It was obvious that the He-177 was still a far cry from becoming the 'workhorse' Milch had demanded in July.

After the Stalingrad disaster Hitler expressed open doubts that the continued tinkering with the design could ever produce 'something usable'.[145] Nonetheless, in a similar fashion to the Me-210, a number of improved He-177s would eventually make their much delayed appearance at the front and even score the occasional success against Allied shipping. But that lay in the future. In early 1942, the Luftwaffe leadership's plans for the introduction of a whole family of second-generation aircraft lay in ruins. Only the FW-190 had turned into a success story, but in the eyes of a political leadership still fixated on offensive warfare and thus inevitably inclined to prioritise bombers, this only served to throw the failure of the other types into even starker relief.

At a conference with designers and Luftwaffe senior officers held at his country residence in mid-March 1943, Göring expressed his disappointment at what had come to pass. He spoke of his 'utmost bitterness' about the 'failure' of the German aeronautical industry in a number of areas, singling out for special attention three types. In the case of the Me-264, he highlighted the fact that Messerschmitt had failed to deliver on his promises regarding the type's

---

[142] Hildegard von Kotze (ed.), *Heeresadjutant bei Hitler 1938–1943. Aufzeichnungen des Majors Engel* (Stuttgart: DVA 1974), p 134(entry for 8 November 1942).

[143] Heinkel, *Leben*, pp 459–62; Conradis, *Kurt Tank*, pp 245–48.

[144] Smith and Creek, *Heinkel 177*, pp 51–4.

[145] 'Oberbefehlshaber der Kriegsmarine B.Nr. 1 Skl Ib 680/43 gKdos. Chefs. Niederschrift über den Vortrag des Ob.d.M. beim Führer im Führerhauptquartier Winniza am 26. II.1943 (5.3.1943)'; in: Wagner (ed.), *Lagevorträge*, pp 470–1.

range and payload. He then moved on to the 'wonder plane Me-210', which he described as 'one of the biggest disappointments' he had ever experienced and highlighted the disruptive effect it had had on production planning in general.[146] He saved his greatest ire for the new Heinkel. The failure to get the He-177 ready for front-line service (as Stalingrad had just made clear) 'was the worst blow' of all. He added – rather presciently, as it turned out – that even in the unlikely event of 'that bitch' finally becoming an airworthy plane in another year or so, it would by then probably be obsolete. In frustration, he urged the designers present simply to copy the design of one of the Allied four-engined bombers then criss-crossing Germany's skies in ever-increasing numbers.[147]

Hitler's assessment of the same situation appears to have been briefer and more to the point. Even before the fiasco of the He-177's brief deployment to Stalingrad, he identified 'overblown expectations on the part of Luftwaffe development' as the core problem. In a conversation with Albert Speer, he pointed out that the 'He-177 was simultaneously designed as a four-engined long-range bomber and a dive bomber. Only one of these mission briefs could be fulfilled and as a consequence development had stretched out for years. Exactly the same went for the Me-210.'[148]

9.6   Conclusion

On 29 March 1942 only two months after Milch had owned up to the fact that the building of bunkers for the civilian population would not keep up with demand, the German dictator received a far more shattering indication that all was not well on the air front. Thus far, the growing successes of radar-guided Flak and Bomber Command's spectacular defeat over Berlin on 17 November 1941 appeared to indicate that the concerns he had voiced in early 1941 had been misplaced. The British bombing offensive, if not quite defeated, had certainly been successfully checked.

This assumption was brutally shaken when Bomber Command resumed its war against German urban areas under a new commander-in-chief, Arthur Harris, in March 1942. It was aided in this by increased numbers and a newly introduced system of navigational beams (Gee), similar to those used by the Luftwaffe during the Blitz. On 28 March, a record number of 234 bombers raided the port city of Lübeck. What the attack lacked in precision (it lay just outside the range of Gee) when compared to some Luftwaffe raids of 1940–1, it

---

[146] BA/MA, RL 3/60 'Stenographische Niederschrift über die Besprechung beim Reichsmarschall am 18. März 1943 in Karinhall. Beginn: 11 Uhr vormittags (n.d.)'.

[147] Ibid.

[148] IWM, Speer Coll., FD 5514/45 'Ministeramt. Auszug aus der Führerbesprechung am 3./4./5.1.43 (11.1.1943)'. Speer had these impressions typed up and forwarded to his political ally Milch.

more than made up for in the level of devastation caused. The centre of town was heavily damaged and casualties among the population considerably higher than during any previous raid by Bomber Command on a German target. In conversation with his acolytes, the dictator made a telling observation. Attacks on such a scale, he said, could no longer be defeated by Flak alone – a clear recognition that Würzburg would not be enough to inflict unsustainable casualties on a growing bomber force, as had appeared possible in the summer and autumn of 1941.[149]

The common denominator between these developments and the disaster that unfolded in the German aeronautical industry is timing. At the time of Pearl Harbor, German defences appeared to be in the process of significantly checking British night-time raids. While it seemed unlikely that the British incursions would be banished altogether (like daytime raids were from December 1939 onwards), the prospects that they would be reduced to an important nuisance appeared to be good and the current rate of air-raid shelter building would offer plenty of protection from those raiders who still got through. At the same time, where the offensive dimension of air warfare was concerned, the Luftwaffe appeared to be just a few months away from unhinging the Allied position in the Mediterranean, while also taking delivery of a long-range bomber of trans-Atlantic range, a heavy strategic bomber and a heavy fighter, which could also double as a powerful close air-support aircraft. Only three months later, one of these had fallen well short of its promised performance, another had just suffered a rash of crashes which seemed likely to delay the project for more than a year and the third had been cancelled altogether. Previous studies have engaged in a great deal of analysis to apportion the blame for this disaster among Luftwaffe bureaucrats and aircraft designers; in doing so, they have uncovered a system which at times bordered on the dysfunctional. By comparison the German dictator is almost treated as a bystander. His one key decision (to prioritise Flak over fighters in Home Defence) actually turned out to be beneficial when the British shift to night attacks temporarily put Luftwaffe interceptors at a disadvantage. With regards to aircraft design, the unease he expressed over the He-177's coupled engines can be set alongside the fact that he appears to have realised as early as November 1940 that bombing raids on US targets by the Me-264 with a useful bomb load would require bases on the Azores. Both suggest that, while a dilettante in air power questions, Hitler at least had an eye for technical details that seem to have escaped Udet's or Göring's notice.

What ultimately matters to this narrative is that around the time of Pearl Harbor, Adolf Hitler had no reason to assume that within the next three to four months a series of events would call into question the viability of existing home

---

[149] '29.3.1942 (Wolfsschanze)'; in: Henry Picker (ed.), *Hitlers Tischgespräche im Führerhauptquartier* (München: Propyläen 2003) pp 217–18.

defence arrangements, the future deployment of the bomber and Stuka arm and future aircraft designs. On the eve of Germany's declaration of war on the USA, RAF Bomber Command's losses to radar-directed Flak were on the rise, air-raid shelter construction was making good progress and military successes in Russia offered the opportunity for a major strategic shift to the Mediterranean; in addition, the He-177 and Me-210 were just a few months away from joining front-line squadrons in strength. In the three months that lay between the turn of the year and late March, all these developments were called into question: air-raid shelter construction was subject to unexpected compromises, parts of the Russian Front came close to collapsing before a Red Army counter-attack, the new aircraft types were revealed to be costly failures and Bomber Command returned to the fray with numbers and tools that put it in a position to swamp the defenders and deal out crippling damage. This process would turn out to be irreversible: the Luftwaffe's capability to support the other services and defend Germany's cities deteriorated with every month, and played a crucial role in Germany's ultimate defeat.

10

The Holocaust

10.1 Introduction

On 12 December Adolf Hitler addressed the *Reichs- und Gauleiter* in his private rooms in the Reichskanzlei. The majority would already have been in attendance the previous day in the Reichstag when he read out his declaration of war on the United States. Such gatherings of the NSDAP's elite had become a common feature of the regime's way of doing business, though an appearance by Hitler was by no means axiomatic. Sometimes a major political event would be the main point of business, while in other instances it would be a more routine affair.[1] The gathering on 12 December definitely fell into the former category. Since no minutes were kept, the gist of the dictator's address has been handed down to us by Joseph Goebbels and Hans Frank; the former took notes that day,[2] while the latter reflected on the event in his memoirs.[3] The entry in Goebbels' diary is by a wide margin the most detailed source. Apart from briefing his audience on the situation on the fronts in Russia and Libya, the dictator justified the declaration of war on military grounds and also discussed the 'Jewish question'. Reminding his audience of his so-called prophecy of 30 January 1939, when he had threatened the Jews with 'extinction' should they once again conspire to bring about a Great War in Europe, he now concluded that since 'the World War is now a fact, the annihilation of Jewry must be the necessary consequence'.[4]

It is the timing of this statement, rather than its content, which is of some importance to our analysis. The main debate among the second generation of

---

[1] The importance of these gatherings went unrecognised by historians for a surprisingly long time. See now Martin Moll, 'Steuerungsinstrument im Ämterchaos? Die Tagungen der Reichs- und Gauleiter der NSDAP'; in: *Vierteljahrshefte für Zeitgeschichte* 2001, Nr. 2 (April), pp 215–73.

[2] Elke Föhlich (ed.), *Die Tagebücher von Joseph Goebbels*. Teil II, Bd. 2 (München et al: K. G. Saur 1996), pp 494–500, esp. pp 498–9 (entry for 13 December 1941).

[3] Hans Frank, *Im Angesicht des Galgens. Deutung Hitlers und seiner Zeit auf Grund eigener Erlebnisse und Erkenntnisse* (Neuhaus bei Schliersee: Eigenverlag 1955), p 397.

[4] TB Goebbels, Bd. II.2, pp 498–9 (entry for 13 December 1941).

Holocaust historians has been about Hitler's key role in issuing the orders which led to the Shoa. The 'functionalists' like Martin Broszat and Hans Mommsen maintained that input from a number of senior-level subordinates was at times as important as that of the dictator, with David Irving taking this view to the implausible extreme of seeing the dictator essentially reduced to a bit player. The 'intentionalists' (Eberhard Jäckel, Helmut Krausnick, Klaus Hildebrand, Philippe Burrin, Gerald Fleming) insisted that input from the dictator was central every step of the way. In recent years, some scholars have attempted to find a compromise between the two approaches by stressing that a broad (and possibly vaguely worded) directive was in all likelihood delayed in its implementation by interest clashes between various agencies of the German state and lack of resources.[5]

This study, while broadly siding with the 'intentionalist' school of thought, has a different focus. Rather than look at the role of individuals or institutions, it will endeavour to examine the questions of timing and strategic context and the extent to which military strategy was influenced by an agenda for genocide or the other way around. The address of 12 December would appear to suggest a strong causal link between Hitler's obsessive anti-Semitism and the declaration of war on the USA. A case has been made for the former being, in fact, the reason behind the latter.[6] At least three historians have argued that the decision to move from localised ethnic cleansing to continental-scale genocide reflected the actions of a man who realised his plans for victory had been irredeemably compromised by continued Soviet resistance and the imminence of US intervention; he thus decided to prioritise the genocide of the European Jews over the conduct of military operations.[7] On the other hand, numerous preparatory measures for the mass murder of the Jews of central and eastern Europe suggest an earlier date, very probably tied to the high-water mark of success achieved by the *Ostheer* in its war against the USSR. In such a scenario, the Holocaust would have to be seen as a decision taken from a position of perceived strength, not despair; concerns over US intervention would accordingly have to be reassessed as well.

---

[5] For a good example of this, see Götz Aly, *'Endlösung'. Völkerverschiebung und der Mord an den europäischen Juden* (Frankfurt am Main: S. Fischer 1995). For an excellent overview of Holocaust historiography, see Ian Kershaw, 'Hitler's Role in the "Final Solution"'; in: *Yad Vashem Studies* 34 (2006), pp 7–43.

[6] Victor Rothwell, *War Aims in the Second World War* (Edinburgh: Edinburgh UP 2005), pp 82–3; A. N. Wilson, *Hitler: A Short Biography* (London: Harper Press 2012), p 147.

[7] Sebastian Haffner, *Anmerkungen zu Hitler* (Fischer: Frankfurt a.M. 1981), pp 140–1; Arno J. Mayer, *Why Did the Heavens Not Darken? The 'Final Solution' in History* (New York: Pantheon Books 1988); Tobias Jersak, 'Die Interaktion von Kriegsverlauf und Judenvernichtung. Ein Blick auf Hitler's Strategie im Spätsommer 1941'; in: *Historische Zeitschrift* Bd. 268 (1999), pp 311–74. While Jersak saw the critical juncture as mid-August, Mayer argued for early December 1941. Jersak's case is weakened by a number of serious factual errors made in assessing military events of those months.

10.2 Early Attempts at Demographic Engineering, 1939–1940

In the first months of the war, the collapse of the Polish republic led to a situation where a regime already notorious for its anti-Semitic policies found itself controlling the most populous part of inter-war Poland, more than 2 million Jewish subjects included. The situation thus created would soon be exacerbated by an influx over the following months of ethnic Germans from abroad. Originally hailing from Romania, Italy and the USSR as well as the three Baltic republics, their 'return to the Reich' had been agreed between their host countries where they had dwelt for generations and the new German regime. In Berlin's logic, geographic remoteness meant that many of these people would have been lost to Germany if they had been left in their forlorn outposts; back in the fatherland, they could serve a useful purpose by providing some demographic muscle to the expansion of Germany's border areas.[8] This mammoth task of demographic engineering fell to Heinrich Himmler who had been granted a roving commission as *Reichskommissar für die Festigung des deutschen Volkstums*. Accordingly, the Polish western regions annexed to Germany proper in the form of two *Gaue* under Arthur Greiser and Albert Forster would soon be vacated of their Polish inhabitants, their place to be taken wholly or in part by the newly arrived settlers.[9] The expellees would be forced across the border into Hans Frank's *Generalgouvernement*, which encompassed the bulk of what might be called the historic core of Poland. Ethnic Germans living in Frank's empire were likewise uprooted and shifted into Greiser's or Forster's *Gaue*.

Needless to say such a process would not have been smooth at the best of times. The sheer disruption caused was something a country at war could easily have done without, and protests were soon raised. Furthermore, for people who had been uprooted from an urban environment and were now expected to settle down in the countryside, or vice versa, it was often difficult to find dwellings or job opportunities. Very soon, the whole process seized up, with many of the returnees constrained to wait on events in makeshift camps under deteriorating conditions. Even though Jews soon emerged as the minority who could expect the least consideration in what was – at best – a rough-and-ready enterprise, it is important to stress that at this time very little

---

[8] On this topic, see Aly, *Völkerverschiebung*.

[9] Both the *Reichsgau Wartheland* under Arthur Greiser and *Danzig-Westpreussen* under Albert Forster included the lands Germany had lost to the new Polish state in 1919, but also incorporated a substantial share of territory that lay beyond the old border. Before the onset of deportations into the *Generalgouvernement*, the German population was outnumbered almost 10:1 by the local Poles. Detailed figures are provided by Maria Rutowska, 'Nationalsozialistische Verfolgungsmassnahmen gegenüber der polnischen Zivilbevölkerung in den eingegliederten polnischen Gebieten'; in: Jacek Andrzej Mlynarczyk (ed.), *Polen unter deutscher und sowjetischer Besatzung 1939–1945* (Osnabrück: fibre 2009), pp 197–216.

pointed towards mass murder, much less genocide, as an option under consideration. Himmler himself was far more interested in getting Germans resettled than having Jews murdered,[10] and in a confidential communication of January 1940 he even described the 'Bolshevik method of physical extermination' as something 'un-German and impossible'.[11]

Instead, large-scale resettlement was the preferred option in 1939–40. An attempt in October 1939 to shift German and Czech Jews into an area west of Lublin in the *Generalgouvernement* (often referred to as the 'Nizko experiment') was more or less stillborn because its progenitor *SS-Obersturmbannführer* Adolf Eichmann went off half-cock without having the backing of a number of key officials.[12] Even a much smaller scale endeavour to deport just a few hundred Jewish Germans from Stettin into the *Generalgouvernment* in February 1940 foundered on the twin rocks of Frank's opposition and the attention this brought in its wake, especially among US journalists.[13] In the summer of 1940, in the heady months following the Blitzkrieg campaigns against northern and western Europe, the possibility of a compromise peace with Britain brought the so-called Madagascar plan to the fore. It was suggested by a senior official of the Auswärtiges Amt and envisaged the shifting of the entire Jewish population of continental Europe to the tropical island. Neither the death toll to be expected in such a move, nor the fact that such a protectorate would have been extremely difficult to police effectively, even in a world where both France and Britain had acknowledged the hegemony of the Third Reich, appears to have deterred the planners. Only the continuation of British resistance caused this bizarre scheme to be shelved in autumn.[14]

In the meantime, Himmler had not given up on his resettlement schemes. With a large part of the *Generalgouvernement*'s Jewish population now isolated in ghettoes, further major demographic exchanges between the new *Reichsgaue* in eastern Germany and the *Generalgouvernement* were being prepared for early 1941. It took a last-minute alliance between Hans Frank and Oberkommando des Heeres to stop this move in its tracks. The army's intervention was key, since the argument it put forward trumped all others: it had to have first call on all the resources of the *Generalgouvernement*, because within weeks, millions of German servicemen would begin pouring into the

---

[10] Christopher Browning, *The Origins of the Final Solution: The Evolution of Nazi Jewish Policy, 1939–1942. With a Contribution by Jürgen Matthäus* (London: Arrow Books pb 2005), pp 65, 67.

[11] Ibid., p 107.

[12] Ibid., pp 36–43. Eichmann's position as the *Judenreferent* in Amt IV of the Reichssicherheitshauptamt meant that he was involved – if only in the margins – in a number of key decisions that led to the Holocaust.

[13] Ibid., p 65.

[14] Ibid., pp 81–9.

region. Central Poland had been designated as the main launch pad for the German invasion of the USSR.[15]

10.3   The Evolution of Genocide: the War in Russia, June–September 1941

In the immediate run-up to Operation Barbarossa, talk about 'Germanising' former Polish territory by one means or another subsided in favour of an even more grotesquely ambitious endeavour: rather than shifting 'racial undesirables' to ever more confined parts of the old Polish state or islands in the Indian Ocean, the same task could be undertaken on a much wider scale on the territory of the soon-to-be-invaded (and, presumably, vanquished) USSR. By March 1941, Hitler himself seemed to be hinting at such a scheme: he promised Frank that the entirety of the *Generalgouvernement* would have to be Germanised in the manner of Greiser's and Forster's *Gaue*.[16] In light of the fact that the apparently straightforward process of making room in West Prussia and the Warthegau by deporting Jews and the majority of 'undesirable' gentile Poles across the border had just failed spectacularly, this indicated that the regime, far from being daunted by such setbacks, was envisaging a much vaster task of demographic engineering for the near future.

These ideas ushered in a campaign of mass murder that would seamlessly move over into genocide in late 1941. It was spearheaded by four battalion-sized task forces (*Einsatzgruppen*), who were given orders for the apprehension and assassination of functionaries of the Communist Party of the Soviet Union (CPSU) or anybody else suspected of abetting the Stalinist regime by word or deed.[17] The wording of the orders these units received, however, was highly ambiguous insofar as they also reflected the obsession inherent in Nazi ideology that communism and the Jewish community were essentially two sides of the same coin. Hence, *Einsatzgruppen* officers were admonished to prioritise the apprehension or murder of members of the CPSU who were also Jewish, as these were deemed to constitute a particular threat to the occupying power. Great stress was also placed on the need for showing initiative when faced with contingencies not covered by the original brief. The ambiguity thus created would be seen as an opportunity by Himmler and his subordinate Reinhard Heydrich, since their plans for the SS to take over the administration of the conquered western Soviet Union wholesale had just been stymied when Alfred Rosenberg was made *Reichsminister* for the occupied Eastern Territories. Their

---

[15] Ibid., pp 98–101.

[16] Ibid., pp 104–5.

[17] For the first major work of scholarship on the *Einsatzgruppen*, see Helmut Krausnick and Hans-Heinrich Wilhelm, *Die Truppe des Weltanschauungskrieges: die Einsatzgruppen der Sicherheitspolizei und des SD, 1938–1942* (Stuttgart: DVA 1981). While still valuable, it has now been superseded in parts by Browning and Matthäus, *Final Solution*, pp 213–308.

control over the actions of the *Einsatzgruppen* and assorted police formations supporting them remained for the moment their main instrument to mould the shape of the future *Lebensraum* in the East.[18] The available evidence, however, does not support the testimony of the majority of surviving *Einsatzgruppen* officers after 1945 that Heydrich issued an unambiguous (albeit oral) order to murder all Soviet Jews on the eve of the invasion.[19] Mass murder of Jews could only take the form of pogroms by local gentiles; inciting these events was desirable, but must not result in a visible association between them and the occupying power.

In the early days of Barbarossa, the leaders of the four *Einsatzgruppen* and their subordinate *Einsatzkommandos* interpreted the orders given to them rather differently: while *Einsatzgruppe A*, following *Heeresgruppe Nord* through the former Baltic republics, lost no time in engaging in a campaign of mass murder, *Einsatzgruppe B* (bringing up the rear of *Heeresgruppe Mitte*) proceeded with greater caution. Over the next few weeks, however, this reluctance was cast aside, leading to a campaign that evolved from a scheme originally aimed at ferreting out individuals most likely to support a future insurgency to mass murder on a growing scale. The latter was increasingly aimed at Jewish civilians, irrespective of any affiliation to the CPSU they may or may not have had. This dynamic might have come about in any case, but it is certainly striking that a major step up the escalatory ladder was more often than not preceded by a 'visit from head office', when units that appeared to show any reluctance in this regard could expect a telling-off.[20] Throughout the entire period, there is only one recorded instance of an officer in the field being admonished by Himmler for showing too much murderous zeal; this event constituted a highly significant break from the usual pattern and will be discussed in greater detail later in the chapter.

With body counts soon running into the tens of thousands, the only thing separating the assassination squads from all-out genocide was the murder of women and children. This became commonplace by mid-August, with the arrival of three SS brigades over the previous three weeks who provided the numbers needed to execute such an extended brief.[21] Two plausible explanations have been put forward to explain the development. Jürgen Matthäus and Martin Cüppers see it as the result of the German dictator issuing a verbal order to that effect in mid-July, when the destruction of much of the first

---

[18] Robert Gerwarth, *Reinhard Heydrich. Biographie* (München: Siedler 2011), pp 240–1.
[19] For a discussion of this point, see Browning and Matthäus, *Final Solution*, pp 214, 226–7.
[20] Peter Longerich, *Heinrich Himmler. Biographie* (München: Siedler 2008), p 544.
[21] Martin Cüppers, 'Auf dem Weg in den Holocaust. Die Brigaden des Kommandostabes Reichsführers-SS im Sommer 1941'; in: Jan Erik Schulte et al (eds.), *Die Waffen-SS. Neue Forschungen* (Paderborn: Ferdinand Schöningh 2014), pp 286–301. The three brigades totalled 19,000 men, thus dwarfing the aggregate strength of the four *Einsatzgruppen* many times over.

echelon of the Red Army deployed near the border suggested an imminent victory over the USSR.[22] According to Alex Kay, the move to all-out genocide can be explained by the momentary crisis experienced by *Heeresgruppe Mitte* in the weeks between late July and the first days of September. Logistical strain was compounded many times over by a series of furious Soviet counter-attacks east of Smolensk; Red Army stragglers and the first partisans began to strike at German supply convoys. Against this backdrop, any residual inclination of German army commanders to put a brake on Himmler's genocidal agenda vanished and help extended by the comrades of the SS in any shape or form was gratefully accepted.[23] The fact that the majority of Soviet Jews dwelt in towns and cities meant that most of them lived near a road or rail line that was of some importance or even absolutely crucial to the German campaign; this fact alone appeared to give credence to the theory that their very presence constituted a potential menace to German operations. When this notion that the Jews were a menace to security actually appeared to be confirmed by events on the ground, it twice led to massacres with a death toll of more than 30,000 lives.[24]

Within less than three months a campaign which started out with an agenda that, while murderous, was at least still geared to the political realities on the ground had escalated into out-and-out genocide. The extent to which the perpetrators had deliberately opted for an approach of gradual escalation, in order to avoid a possible head-on confrontation with other agencies such as the Wehrmacht or the contingents of Axis allies, is still a subject for future research.[25] The key lesson is that by early autumn a point had been reached where the leadership of the Third Reich could conclude that genocide was a practical proposition. The fact that the victims had belonged to the group of the much pilloried '*Ostjuden*' and that their murder had occurred in an area which was effectively still a war zone had certainly made the perpetrators' task

---

[22] Browning and Matthäus, *Final Solution*, pp 313.

[23] See the argument put forward in Alex Kay, 'Transition to Genocide, July 1941: Einsatzkommando 9 and the Annihilation of Soviet Jewry'; in: *Holocaust and Genocide Studies* 27, No. 3 (Winter 2013), pp 411–42.

[24] This occurred when timed explosive charges planted by the retreating Red Army in Kiev and Odessa led to heavy loss of life among the newly established German and Romanian occupiers. Browning and Matthäus, *Final Solution*, pp 291–3.

[25] The willingness of Germany's Axis partners to support or even join in the genocidal designs of the SS varied considerably, with the Romanians being the keenest, the Finns the most reluctant. For an introduction to this topic, see Wendy Lower, 'Axis Collaboration: Operation Barbarossa and the Holocaust in Ukraine'; in: Alex Kay et al (eds.), *Nazi Policy on the Eastern Front, 1941: Total War, Genocide and Radicalization* (New York: Rochester UP 2012), pp 186–219, and Bastian Matteo Scianna, *The Italian War on the Eastern Front, 1941–1943: Operations, Myths and Memories* (London et al: Palgrave Macmillan 2019), pp 238–61.

much easier. Would it be possible to extend the geographical scope of this mass crime if one or both of these factors no longer applied?

10.4   Sketching Out Plans for Genocide, September–December 1941

On 18 August 1941 another lengthy meeting took place between Hitler and his *Reichspropagandaminister* Joseph Goebbels.[26] The dictator, worn out by a bout of illness, quarrels with the army leadership and mounting intelligence on the Red Army's formidable order of battle, was happy to indulge in a walk down memory lane to take his mind off the day-to-day business of running Operation Barbarossa. Goebbels took advantage of this and, wearing his hat as *Gauleiter* of Berlin, chose this moment to bring up the topic of the Jews who still lived in the German capital. He once again made a case for their deportation and suggested passing legislation that would force them to wear a sign on their clothing that would mark them out as not belonging to the Aryan *Volksgemeinschaft*.[27] Hitler conceded the latter but – yet again – balked at the former. He did, however, promise Goebbels that he would permit deportation of the Jewish Berliners 'to the East' as soon as operations in Russia had reached a conclusion.[28] Only then would such an endeavour become logistically feasible;[29] this clear sense of priorities on his part is something that needs to be kept in mind whenever the evolution of the Holocaust in 1941 is discussed.

Mid-September, however, brought a turnaround. Either on 17 or 18 September, Hitler acquiesced into the wholesale deportation of German and Czech Jews to the East. A combination of factors is said to have played a role in finally forcing his hand. The first in chronological order would have been the speech by President Franklin Delano Roosevelt, in which he announced rules of engagement for the US Atlantic Fleet that effectively turned Washington into a belligerent. Next came the Soviet deportation of the Volga Germans into the interior of the USSR.[30] Alfred Rosenberg took this as his cue to suggest the deportation of Germany's Jews as a measure of retaliation. On 16 September, the *Gauleiter* of Hamburg, Karl Kaufmann, whose city just had suffered damage in a British bombing raid, renewed the case for deportation in order to find dwellings for those made homeless the previous night.[31] Rather remarkably, most Holocaust historians tend to ignore

---

[26] TB Goebbels. Bd. II.1, pp 259–72 (entry for 19 August 1941).
[27] Ibid., p 265.
[28] Ibid., p 278 (entry for 20 August 1941).
[29] Ibid., p 266 (entry for 19 August 1941).
[30] The Presidium of the Supreme Soviet had announced this decision as far back as 28 August. It appears that the Germans did not expect Stalin to act on this straightaway and were caught flat-footed when the deportations actually began on 13 September.
[31] Browning and Matthäus, *Final Solution*, p 324–5, 387.

the impact another development would have had on Hitler's frame of mind: on 14 September, the pincers of the armoured elements of army groups *Mitte* and *Süd* linked up near the town of Lokhvitsa, in doing so sealing the encirclement of forty-three Soviet divisions and making the fall of most of the Ukraine a foregone conclusion.[32] Even though a few thousand Soviet servicemen would escape the net over the next two weeks, it still amounted to the most catastrophic defeat so far suffered by the Red Army in its disaster-littered initial confrontation with the *Ostheer*. It also meant a triumphant vindication of Hitler's idiosyncratic stand against the majority of his generals, who throughout the month of August had insisted on deploying the bulk of the available strength on the Moscow axis.[33] It was thus while his spirits were boosted by news of military success in the field that he took the first concrete step towards deportation, though mass murder does not appear to have been on the cards just yet. As Himmler explained it in a letter to Arthur Greiser on 18 September, it was 'the removal to the East' of Jewish Germans, concentrating on the urban areas of western Germany first, that was to have priority.[34] It is certainly possible – though by no means certain – that a cataclysmic event such as the Kiev battle could have rekindled hopes of an imminent Soviet collapse, thus giving the original schemes of shifting all surviving European Jews to the wastes of northern Russia a new lease of life.

The following weeks saw a flurry of meetings and exchanges between assorted agencies of the Third Reich to turn this 'wish' of the Führer into gruesome reality. On 15 October, the first deportation train headed for Lodz left Vienna, to be followed by twenty-four more over the next fortnight.[35] The closing off of the last possibilities of emigration from German-occupied territory on 23 October also appeared to clearly indicate a commitment by Berlin towards mass extermination, which was as unambiguous as it was closely coordinated.

In other areas, escalation appeared to be driven more by the initiative of local Nazi chieftains than by any directives emanating from the centre. Occupied Serbia was a case in point. The satellite state witnessed the murder of more than 5,000 Jews, who were shot between September and November in reprisals for fatalities suffered by the Wehrmacht while quelling a local insurgency. Some of them were not even Serb nationals, thus making a nonsense of the rationale that usually underlay hostage shootings even in Nazi Germany.[36]

---

[32] David Stahel, *Kiev 1941: Hitler's Battle for Supremacy in the East* (Cambridge: CUP 2012), pp 225–9.

[33] Ibid., p 230.

[34] Browning and Matthäus, *Final Solution*, pp 325–6.

[35] For a detailed compilation of all trains that left in the first deportation waves, see ibid., pp 375–7.

[36] Walter Manoschek, *'Serbien ist judenfrei.' Militärische Besatzungspolitik und Judenvernichtung in Serbien 1941/42* (München: Oldenbourg 1993), pp 91–6.

It could be argued that this event was dependent on external factors, but other developments which took place at the same time came with an agenda that was much more clear-cut in its genocidal intent. In the *Generalgouvernement* district of Lublin, the SS and Police leader, *SS-Brigadeführer* Odilo Globocnik, who at the time was still prioritising the settlement of Germans from abroad in Poland, was experimenting with a stationary gassing facility on his own initiative. Strong circumstantial evidence indicates that in a meeting with Himmler on 13 October, he was given the order to turn this trial project into something more permanent;[37] building work on the death camp at Belzec began on 1 November. This would mark the beginning of the organised mass murder of Jewish Poles.[38] In another district of Frank's empire, the former Soviet province of Eastern Galicia had witnessed sporadic violence against adult male Jews before and after it was attached to the *Generalgouvernment* on 1 August. However, a major spike in killings from mid-October to the end of the year brought several large-scale massacres that also included women and children. By the end of the year, it left 30,000 people dead. The fact that it appeared to be driven by a local agenda (reducing the numbers of the Jewish population so as to make concentration in a few ghettos practical) has led some historians to question the extent to which it was part of a genocidal scheme that encompassed all of former Poland, much less the entirety of Europe.[39]

Only in Arthur Greiser's *Warthegau* can a direct causal link be established between the decision to deport German and Czech Jews and the local beginnings of the Holocaust. The ghetto in Lodz (or Litzmanstadt) was chosen by Himmler as an intermediate stop on the way east, but Greiser pointed to the crowded conditions there and obliged the *Reichsführer-SS* to agree to a compromise: instead of the 60,000 deportees he had been told to expect, the two men settled on 25,000.[40] Though the paper trail is incomplete, there is evidence to suggest that Greiser then asked for (and received) permission to

---

[37] Peter Witte et al (eds.), *Der Dienstkalender Heinrich Himmlers 1941/42* (Hamburg: Hans Christians 1999), pp 233–4 (entry for 13 October 1941). The team behind this remarkable edition decided to combine Himmler's appointment book and his telephone log into one. Though many of the entries are rather cryptic, this is more than made up for by the contextual background provided by the stupendous research work into a multitude of other related sources and which is presented in nearly 2,000 footnotes.

[38] Whether Belzec was already designed with the genocide of all Polish Jews in mind, or initially just those of Lublin, is a matter as yet unresolved. See Robert Seidel, *Deutsche Besatzungspolitik in Polen. Der Distrikt Radom 1939–1945* (Paderborn et al: Ferdinand Schöningh 2006), pp 282–5, and Jan Erik Schulte, 'Initiative der Peripherie. Globocniks Siedlungsstützpunkte und die Entscheidung zum Bau des Vernichtungslagers Belzec'; in: Jan Erik Schulte (ed.), *Die SS, Himmler und die Wewelsburg* (Paderborn et al: Ferdinand Schöningh 2009), pp 118–37.

[39] For a summary, see Browning and Matthäus, *Final Solution*, pp 347–52.

[40] Michael Alberti, *Die Verfolgung und Vernichtung der Juden im Reichsgau Wartheland 1939–1945* (Wiesbaden: Harrassowit 2006), pp 385–95.

murder up to 100,000 *Warthegau* Jews no longer deemed 'fit for work' as a quid pro quo. Throughout the autumn, several thousand of these unfortunates fell victim to mass shootings, while the remainder were gassed at the Chelmno extermination camp which began operating on 8 December 1941[41].

It has been alleged that the evidence for an all-out commitment to genocide is tenuous at best as late as early November, by which time the Soviet Union's survival into 1942 appeared more and more likely, hence ruling out the deportation of millions into the Russian interior. The only two death camps nearing completion within the foreseeable future did not have the capacity to even begin a Europe-wide campaign of mass murder, although the construction of two more at Riga and Mogilev (Belorussia) appears to have been under way. An often-quoted letter from 25 October sent by an official in the Ostministerium to Hinrich Lohse, the newly appointed *Reichskommissar Ostland*, provides unambiguous evidence that not just Polish, but also German Jews would now be murdered by gas; what is often overlooked is that he referred to 'those unfit for work', rather than Jewish Germans in their totality.[42] This makes sense if one keeps in mind that the sources from this particular period routinely refer to the mass murder of 'those incapable of work'. In light of the way in which the term was used at the Wannseekonferenz, it is all too easy to dismiss this as a cynic's code for genocide pure and simple.[43] In terms of what would still transpire, however, it will soon become obvious that the regime was still hesitating to issue unambiguous orders for the murder forthwith of all Jews.

Leaving aside the lack of available death factories and continuing Soviet resistance, the most obvious reason for holding back on initiating the Holocaust undoubtedly lay in the possible reactions of others. As far back as 1934, Hitler had allegedly described Jewish Germans as hostages, possession of whom would allow him to influence American policy to a certain extent.[44] In mid-September 1941, Hitler had expressed the hope that it might be possible to influence American foreign policy by treating the Jews of Germany as hostages, who would suffer the consequences if their *Rassegenossen* (racial kin) in America did not prevail on the Roosevelt administration to desist from further

---

[41] Ibid., p 400–7, for a detailed discussion of this move.

[42] Gerald Fleming, *Hitler and the Final Solution* (London: Hamish Hamilton 1984), p 92. Also: Peter Klein, 'Die Wannsee-Konferenz als Echo auf die gefallene Entscheidung zur Ermordung der europäischen Juden'; in: Norbert Kampe and Peter Klein (eds.), *Die Wannsee-Konferenz am 20. Januar 1942. Dokumente. Forschungsstand. Kontroversen* (Köln: Böhlau 2013), pp 182–201, esp. p 193. For another source that corroborates this piece of evidence, see Browning and Matthäus, *Final Solution*, p 369.

[43] For a recent interpretation that this rationale may still have applied throughout much of 1942, see Christian Gerlach, *The Extermination of the European Jews* (Cambridge: CUP 2016), pp 86–8.

[44] Ernst Hanfstaengl, *Zwischen Weissen und Braunem Haus* (München: Piper 1970), pp 304–5.

moves against Germany.[45] Could this hope have been extinguished at some point, thus leading the dictator to give the Holocaust the final go-ahead? On 7 November, news of not just one, but two events important enough to warrant such an interpretation reached Berlin. One was the announcement from the White House that the USA had included the USSR in the list of Lend-Lease recipients.[46] The other was the vote by the Senate which gutted the existing Neutrality Law by rescinding its Articles 2, 3 and 6, thus allowing the resupply of Britain by US merchantmen. Irrespective of their negligible short-term strategic impact, both measures would have would have gone a long way towards confirming Hitler's deep-seated obsessions about the Jews and their supposed ability to corrupt and control societies as fundamentally different and even antagonistic as the USA and USSR. When Hitler and Himmler met extensively over the next two days to attend the memorial celebrations for the dead of the 1923 coup attempt in Munich, it seems far-fetched to assume that the subject did not come up.[47]

According to a deposition given by Friedrich Jeckeln, Higher SS- and Police leader *Ostland*,[48] immediately after the war, Himmler instructed him on 10 or 11 November that 'all the Jews to be found in the *Ostland* would have to be annihilated down to the last man'.[49] It is to be noted that his instruction was bereft of the sort of qualifications (as per age, gender, nationality, fitness for work) that had until now dominated the genocidal agenda of the early Holocaust. Such an order would certainly tally with a sudden change in the perpetrators' modus operandi. Thus far, it was Lithuanian, Belorussian or Polish Jews who had been murdered to make room in their ghettos for newly arrived German deportees. The 20,000 German Jews who arrived in Lodz between 15 October and 4 November, that is, just before Himmler's order of 10 or 11 November, were subjected to atrocious living conditions, but not murdered and not even included in the first transports to Chelmno in early 1942. In the case of the seven trains that brought 7,000 deportees to Minsk

---

[45] 'Sonntag, 21. September 1941'; in: Martin Vogt (ed.), *Herbst 1941 im 'Führerhauptquartier'. Berichte Werner Koeppens an seine Minister Alfred Rosenberg* (Koblenz 2002) [= Materialien aus dem Bundesarchiv, Heft 10], pp 34–5.

[46] Wolfgang Schlauch, *Rüstungshilfe der USA an die Verbündeten im Zweiten Weltkrieg* (Darmstadt: Wehr & Wissen 1967), pp 112–14.

[47] For Hitler's movements on those days, see Witte et al (eds.), *Dienstkalender*, pp 257–8 (entries for 8 and 9 November 1941).

[48] In November 1941 the *Reichskommissariat Ostland* was made up of those parts of the western USSR (Belorussia, Lithuania and Latvia) that had passed to civilian control once the advance of *Heeresgruppe Nord* and *Heeresgruppe Mitte* had made this practical. Estonia would follow on 1 December. See DRZW, Bd. 4, Beiheft, map 27.

[49] 'Ausforschungsprotokoll des Verhafteten Friedrich Jeckeln, Riga, 14. Dezember 1945'; in: Wassili Christoforow, Wladiimir Makarow, Matthias Uhl (eds.), *Verhört. Die Befragungen deutscher Generale und Offiziere durch die sowjetischen Geheimdienste 1945-1952* (Oldenbourg: de Gruyter 2015), pp 347–55.

Figure 10.1 NSDAP ceremony at the Feldherrnhalle, Munich: the 1941 memorial for the fallen of the botched 1923 coup in all likelihood served as the backdrop for a verbal order to extend the Holocaust to German and Austrian Jews.(Imagno/Hulton Archive via Getty Images)

between 11 and 25 November, the same restraint appears to have been exercised at first, though protests by the local *Generalkommissar*, Wilhelm Kube, at the inclusion of 'half-Jews' and veterans of World War I in the deportation transports, in all likelihood played a role there.

Events in the Baltic states, however, appear to indicate that without such special circumstances, indiscriminate murder was by now the order of the day. In Kaunas (Lithuania) a total of 4,934 Jewish Germans arrived in two batches on 25 and 29 November. They were murdered in their entirety by *Einsatzkommando* 3 without any attempt having been made to discriminate between those still 'capable of work' and those who were not. The same happened to the 1,000 occupants of the first train to arrive in Riga on the evening of 29 November, bringing the total to nearly 6,000. This appears to confirm the nature of the orders Jeckeln claimed to have received from Himmler on 10 or 11 November and is also supported by the reflections on the topic by two of Hitler's senior henchmen in the intervening period. While Alfred Rosenberg, with breathtaking candour, announced the need for the upcoming 'biological extermination of Jewdom in Europe' to an audience of tame journalists in Berlin,[50] the *Reichsführer-SS* was more discrete, yet in his own way as chillingly devoid of any ambiguity. All matters pertaining to Jews, he recorded in his diary on 24 November, from now on 'belong to me'.[51] Finally, 28 November saw the passing of legislation which officially despoiled the deportees of any remaining physical possessions the moment the train carrying them left German soil. A minor point in the grand scheme of things, but a clear indication that the perpetrators now had put in place the cogs and wheels of a process encompassing all conceivable aspects of a long-term project.[52]

Then, in the afternoon of 30 November, an event occurred which appeared to call into question the existence of an unambiguous extermination order for all Jews, German ones included. Himmler's telephone log recorded a conversation with Heydrich in Prague at 13.30. Whatever passed between the two men can be surmised up to a point by the note Himmler recorded in his log: 'Transport of Jews from Berlin. No liquidation' (*'Judentransport aus Berlin. Keine Liquidierung'*).[53] A British radio intercept of the time confirms that the two SS chieftains had indeed agreed to spare the transport of Jewish Berliners which had just arrived in Riga the previous night. Since they had all been murdered that very morning, the intervention came too late by a few hours. Himmler appeared genuinely infuriated when he found this out and let Jeckeln know the following day that he 'fully intended to punish unilateral acts and violations' in the future.[54] Even if one allows for the possibility that an unambiguous order to initiate the Holocaust had not yet been issued, this still begs the question why Himmler had chosen this moment to vent his spleen on Jeckeln, when the previous five days had already witnessed the murder of 5,000 Jewish Germans in Riga. Moreover, while there are quite a few recorded instances of SS or police officers involved in the early phase of the Holocaust in 1941 receiving a major telling-off for not showing enough murderous zeal, this is the only one we know of where the opposite happened. The very fact that Himmler and Heydrich had spent several minutes on the phone discussing this issue, and that the former thought it worthwhile to make a note of the agreement reached, strongly points to one conclusion: the wholesale murder

[50] 'Rede von Reichsminister Rosenberg anläßlich des Presseempfangs am Dienstag, 18. Nov. 1941, 15.30 h im Sitzungssaal des Reichsministeriums für die besetzten Ostgebiete'; in: Jürgen Matthäus and Frank Bajohr (eds.), *Alfred Rosenberg. Die Tagebücher von 1934 bis 1944* (Frankfurt a.M.: S. Fischer 2015), pp 574–8.

[51] Witte et al (eds.), *Dienstkalender*, pp 273–74 (entry for 24 November 1941).

[52] Cornelia Essner, *Die 'Nürnberger Gesetze' oder die Verwaltung des Rassenwahns, 1939–1945* (Paderborn et al: Schöningh 2002), pp 292–4.

[53] Witte et al (eds.), *Dienstkalender*, pp 277–8 (entry for 30 November 1941).

[54] Richard Breitman, *Official Secrets: What the Nazis Planned, What the British and Americans Knew* (London: Allen Lane 1999), pp 82–3.

of the Berlin deportees – short of an immediate order countermanding it – was to be expected in due course and that would not have been possible without an existing order or directive to that effect.

Historians have put forward several theories to explain away the inconsistency of Himmler's behaviour on this occasion.[55] The majority have settled for the protests raised from several quarters about the inclusion of so-called half-Jews and war veterans in some of the early transports from Germany.[56] It is doubtful, however, that Himmler would have been sufficiently rattled by this to make him threaten Jeckeln in the manner he did, especially as it is extremely unlikely that he would already have been in receipt of the only protest with some major political weight behind it – that put forward by Kube in Minsk.[57] Protests by the army at the use of its railway lines in Russia for this task at a time when they were logistically stretched to the limit have also been mentioned in this context. Such a protest did indeed occur and did bring deportations to Minsk (though not the Baltic states) to a temporary halt, but is hard to see in what way army logistics could have been affected by the murder of deportees who had already been moved. A personality clash between Jeckeln and the local *Kommandeur der Sicherheitspolizei* in Riga, *SS-Sturmbannführer* Rudolf Lange, which appears to have reached a new level over the manner in which the murder of the Jewish Berliners was carried out, has also been put forward as a possible reason for the controversy surrounding the shootings.[58]

---

[55] Klein, 'Wannsee-Konferenz als Echo'; in: Kampe and Klein (eds.), *20. Januar 1942*, pp 182–201, offers the most detailed account of events on the ground, without, however, unambiguously committing himself as to the reasons that could have caused them.

[56] See Christian Gerlach, 'The Wannsee Conference: The Fate of German Jews and Hitler's Decision in Principle to Exterminate All European Jews'; in: *The Journal of Modern History*, Vol. 70, No. 4 (December 1998), pp 759–812, esp. 766–71; Richard Breitman, 'Friedrich Jeckeln – 'Spezialist' für die Endlösung im Osten'; in: Ronald Smelser and Enrico Syring (eds.), *Die SS. Elite unter dem Totenkopf. 30 Lebensläufe* (Paderborn et al: Schöningh 2000), pp 267–75; Mark Roseman, *The Villa, the Lake, the Meeting: Wannsee and the Final Solution* (London: Allen lane 2002), pp 53–4. Both Christopher Browning and Jürgen Matthäus (with a nuanced difference) tend towards this theory, but stress a high factor of uncertainty. Browning and Matthäus, *Final Solution*, pp 305, 394. Fleming, *Hitler and the Final Solution*, pp 76–7, while not ruling out the possibility of 'momentary hesitations before America's entry into the war', tends to see the inclusion of elderly World War I veterans as the main reason for the exchange, a point also stressed in Gerlach, *Extermination*, p 79.

[57] See the detailed argument in Hans Safrian, *Eichmann's Men* (Cambridge: CUP 2010), p 260 (fn 68), that it was unlikely that Himmler could already have been in receipt of Kube's protest before his telephone conversation with Heydrich.

[58] Peter Klein, 'Die Erlaubnis zum grenzenlosen Massenmord – das Schicksal der Berliner Juden und die Rolle der Einsatzgruppen bei dem Versuch, Juden als Partisanen "auszurotten"'; in: Rolf-Dieter Müller and Hans-Erich Volkmann (eds.), *Die Wehrmacht. Mythos und Realität* (München: Oldenbourg 1999), pp 923–47. For a supporting assessment, see David Cesarani, *Final Solution: The Fate of the Jews, 1933–1949* (London: Macmillan 2016), pp 426–7.

A violation of an existing order by Hitler to spare central European Jews as long as they could serve as hostages while dealing with the US government has also been suggested, even though this begs the question of Himmler's previous orders to Jeckeln and the fact that more than 5,000 Jewish Germans had already been murdered prior to the controversial shootings at Riga.[59]

The sequence of events strongly points to a scenario where either Hitler or Himmler had made a preliminary decision on the subject and was then forced to reverse it, albeit it only temporarily. What could have caused such an embarrassing climb-down? As the previous chapters have shown, over the course of 1941, Germany's willingness to confront the USA was tied not just to the progress of operations in Russia, but also increasingly to Japan's willingness to rise to the challenge posed by US power in the Pacific. The ability of the Auswärtiges Amt to accurately gauge this willingness was repeatedly called into question by the countless vacuous promises made by various Japanese officials with regards to their government's inclination to invade Siberia or seize parts of Southeast Asia in the foreseeable future. Even when they were not hedged by absurd preconditions like a successful German invasion of Britain, they would invariably be revealed as the mirages they were after a couple of weeks at the most.

The German foreign minister's interview with Ambassador Oshima on 28 November has to be seen against this unique backdrop.[60] By this time, Ribbentrop's expectations would have been framed by a stream of reports from the Tokyo embassy indicating that over the previous fortnight several senior Japanese officers of both services had beaten a path to the doors of German representatives in Tokyo, and with unprecedented consistency had virtually beseeched their Tripartite partner for its support in an upcoming war between Japan and all Western powers with possessions in the Pacific or Far East. In his interview with Ribbentrop, Oshima, not known for being a shrinking violet in matters of war and peace, suddenly suggested a campaign plan that must have left Ribbentrop thoroughly bewildered, because it was so completely at odds with what he had learned over the previous days: far from Japan girding itself to do battle with five Western powers, the ambassador felt that Japan should initiate hostilities against The Netherlands alone, in the expectation that both Britain and the USA would then shy away from intervening in a Far Eastern war.[61] Oshima had in the past made occasional references to his German hosts

[59] Peter Longerich, *Der ungeschriebene Befehl. Hitler und der Weg zur Endlösung* (München: Piper 2001), p 133.

[60] 'Geheime Reichssache, RAM 58. Aufzeichnung über den Empfang des japanischen Botschafters Oshima durch den Herrn RAM am 28.11.1941 abends' (n.d.); in: *Akten zur deutschen auswärtigen Politik* (ADAP), Serie D, Bd. XIII.2 (Göttingen: Vandenhoeck & Ruprecht 1970), pp 708–10.

[61] Ibid.

that Tokyo was keeping him out of the loop,[62] and it is certainly possible that Ribbentrop may have rationalised away such a colossal inconsistency by putting it down to poor communications on the Japanese side. The evidence provided by the first fourteen months of the Tripartite Alliance, however, is likely to have been far more compelling. Thus far, every single Japanese promise or pledge to confront, never mind initiate hostilities against, Britain or the USSR, even when delivered in a very detailed or specific form, had come to nothing; the dysfunctional Japanese system of government had never managed to achieve the elaborate consensus between the armed services and the various civilian power centres required for such a decision. It is more than likely, then, that at least for the next four days (at the end of which Oshima presented himself in Ribbentrop's office, virtually demanding to see Hitler so that specifics of a new wartime alliance could be set in stone forthwith), the German foreign minister would have felt he was being treated to yet another episode of the by now well-known internal squabbling in Tokyo. He would have assumed that one (or even several) factions within the Japanese armed services were making another doomed attempt to force an agenda for war through the political system and would undoubtedly fail to get their way when blocked by other power brokers.

Ribbentrop undoubtedly shared these impressions with Hitler, quite possibly when they boarded the same train from Berlin to the Wolfsschanze on the evening of 29 November. The man who in turn would have been in the best position to relay the developments to Himmler was his chief adjutant and the head of his personal staff, Karl Wolff. He was usually in attendance wherever Hitler happened to have his headquarters, with the brief to relay to Himmler any morsel of intelligence that seemed in any way relevant to the *Reichsführer-SS*. Having just played a critical role in defusing a major clash between the SS and Auswärtiges Amt four months previously, he was left in place as the perfect and unchallenged conduit for the passage of information between both institutions.[63] He would most certainly have been present at either the Neue Reichskanzlei on the 29th or the Wolfsschanze on the 30th and may even have travelled between the two places on the same train as Hitler and Ribbentrop. Since Himmler did not phone Heydrich until 13.30, it is likely that Wolff learned of this new development at some point after the train's arrival at the Wolfsschanze at 09.00.[64] Japan hesitating – yet again – to rise to the American challenge would certainly have indicated to all concerned that

---

[62] PA/AA, StS Japan, Bd. 5, 615 'Fernschreiben an den Herrn Reichsaußenminister über Büro RAM (17.11.1941)'.

[63] Brendan Simms, 'Karl Wolff – Der Schlichter'; in: Syring and Smelser (eds.), *Elite*, pp 441–56.

[64] On Hitler's and Ribbentrop's movements during these two days, see Harald Sandner, *Hitler. Das Itinerar. Aufenthaltsorte und Reisen von 1889 bis 1945. Band IV, 1940–1945* (Berlin: Berlin Story 2016), p 1972 .

the current state of cold war between Germany and the USA would continue for some time yet, and would have put a different gloss on any utterances by Hitler with regards to the Jews' supposedly diminishing value as 'hostages'.

It thus seems likely that when Hitler and Himmler attended the celebrations to commemorate the dead of the botched 1923 coup on 9 November, the twin subject of recent American actions and the supposed Jewish role in them came up.[65] The dictator either gave a verbal order for mass murder that would encompass even German Jews or gave Himmler something along the lines of 'an approving nod' (Mark Roseman),[66] which was eagerly seized by the *Reichsführer-SS*, who in turn relayed it to Jeckeln two days later. When Ribbentrop's interview with Oshima appeared to indicate that the cheque signed by the Imperial Japanese armed forces was likely to bounce again, Hitler either qualified his earlier statement or (more likely) Himmler realised that he may have acted rashly in interpreting whatever casual gesture or remark the dictator may have made in Munich in the manner that he did. Only in this way does the bizarre inconsistency which ensued in the aftermath of the Riga and Kaunas massacres make any kind of sense. It is likely that this would have been the last instance when Hitler found himself again – albeit briefly – in the improbable role of a 'moderate' which he had already played on previous occasions: while party radicals invariably pressed for an escalation of anti-Semitic measures, he would occasionally make a point of withholding approval if domestic or foreign policy priorities made it advisable to do so.[67] Within a fortnight, he was able to drop the pretence: twenty-four hours after his declaration of war on the USA, the dictator made it clear to the *Reichs- und Gauleiter* that genocide had now become one of Germany's war aims. Earlier statements had still carried some ambiguity, with deportation into the east blurring into mass murder, subject to changes imposed by local circumstance and – more importantly – foreign policy. From now on, mass murder could only be overridden by military priorities.

Proof of this can be found in the fact that by the time the subject of Jewish Germans deported to the Baltic states came up again in January 1942, Himmler is on record as hesitating, but only about the method of execution to be used: gassing facilities had been planned, but were not yet installed, while mass shootings were still a viable option.[68] In the meantime, two unexpected developments would impose a temporary hiatus on the Holocaust: the near-collapse of the railway logistics on which the *Ostheer* depended reduced the

---

[65] Sandner, *Itinerar*, p 1967; Witte et al (eds.), *Dienstkalender*, pp 257–8 (entries for 8 and 9 November 1941).

[66] Roseman, *Wannsee*, p 54

[67] Examples of this abound, with the abrupt termination of the 1933 boycott of Jewish retailers and the overall toning down of anti-Semitic rhetoric on the eve of the 1936 Olympic Games being the most obvious ones.

[68] Browning and Matthäus, *Final Solution*, p 397.

flow of transports from Germany to a trickle,[69] while the depth to which the unexpectedly harsh winter had frozen the ground made disposal of the victims' bodies virtually impossible. The period of December 1941 to March 1942 thus saw a pause in the execution of the Shoah, but nothing indicates that it was caused by any further hesitations on the part of the perpetrators.[70]

10.5   Conclusion

The available evidence thus suggests three conclusions: Hitler as likely as not considered the Jews of central Europe as hostages whose treatment could, to some extent, influence US foreign policy. The small-scale deportation of just a few hundred Jewish Germans from Stettin in early 1940 provided plenty of evidence for this. At the same time, there is no evidence for the assumption that the German dictator at any point in 1941 allowed his anti-Semitic views to influence his grand strategy in general, much less determine his thinking on bringing the USA into the war.

Two examples should be enough disabuse anybody of this idea. As David Cesarani has recently stressed, the resources allocated to putting the genocide into practice by late 1941 still bordered on the inadequate. The manpower devoted to the *Einsatzgruppen* was downright minute, and the extermination facilities available by late 1941 or early 1942 were wholly inadequate to the task they were about to undertake.[71] The events of 30 November, moreover, show the workings of a regime where even the key proponent and facilitator of the genocidal programme has a clear understanding of the priorities: military strategy and foreign policy have to come first, ethnic cleansing second.

Finally, if one allows for the fact that the Holocaust was probably not the result of one, but several directives – that, in short, it needed between one and three months to evolve from a programme originally aimed at deportation and gradual decimation to one that unambiguously strove for mass murder – the overwhelming evidence points towards the key steps being taken between

---

[69] Even though a number of factors played a role in bringing about this crisis, one stands out: the extreme drop in temperatures led to poorly winterised German locomotives suffering serious damage to their piping, a problem compounded by the lack of heated repair sheds; as a result, serviceability rates hovered around 20–40 per cent for weeks. For an exhaustive analysis, see Klaus-Friedrich Schüler, *Logistik im Rußlandfeldzug. Die Rolle der Eisenbahn bei Planung, Vorbereitung und Durchführung des deutschen Angriffs auf die Sowjetunion bis zur Krise im Winter 1941/42* (Frankfurt a.M.: Peter Lang 1987), pp 518–636, esp. pp 556, 572.

[70] The near-collapse of the railway network in Poland and the western USSR during the winter of 1941–2 is a factor rarely considered by Holocaust historians attempting to rationalise the drop in deportations and killings during that period. For a rare exception, see Florent Bayard, 'To What Extent Was the "Final Solution" Planned?'; in: *Yad Vashem Studies* 36 (2008), pp 73–109, esp. pp 92–3, 96, 98.

[71] Cesarani, *Final Solution*, pp 458–9.

mid-September and mid-December. As the previous chapters have made clear, nothing that happened during this period would have suggested to the German dictator that he was in any danger of losing the war. While there may have been an element of hesitation in targeting German Jews in the same manner as Polish and Russian ones, this was simply born out of a residual reluctance to add to the many factors contributing to the deterioration of US–German relations while Japan's position was still unclear.

Whatever else it may have indicated, the Holocaust cannot be seen as evidence of the despair which overcame the German leadership upon realising that their cause was lost.

~~~

Conclusion

On 3 January 1942 Ambassador Oshima paid his second house call on the German dictator in fewer than three weeks. Hitler's fondness for the Japanese envoy notwithstanding, such a minimal gap between two visits was unheard of and could only be justified by the need to brief the new Far Eastern ally on some unforeseen event. As was to be expected, much of the time the two men spent in conference was an attempt by the dictator to cover up the near-collapse of the German frontline outside Moscow. Hitler may have held the Japanese diplomat in high regard, but he still resorted to bare-faced lying to counter any rumours about the *Ostheer*'s crisis that may have reached the Japanese embassy. Oshima was treated to a version of events where only the sudden onset of Arctic temperatures had averted the fall of Moscow, and the number of German soldiers who had suffered frostbite which had necessitated the amputation of limbs numbered fewer than 100. Inevitably, the new belligerent Berlin and Tokyo had just dragged into the war also featured in the exchange. Here, Hitler made a rather remarkable admission to his guest: 'He professed to have no knowledge of how to defeat the US.'[1] An error on the part of an overworked stenographer can safely be ruled out, since on 15 January Hitler made an assertion that was if anything even more astonishing. Speaking to a group of hangers-on, he claimed that 'should this war turn out to be winnable at all, it will only be won by America'.[2]

Supporters of the Hillgruber school of thought have invariably pointed to these statements to back their claim that declaring war on the USA was either a propaganda 'gesture' or a nihilistic move calculated to escalate the war in a way that would somehow be conducive to facilitating the Holocaust and bringing ruin down on Germany. It is the contention of this historian that the contradiction is more apparent than real. A close analysis of the military situation of Germany's armed forces and the branches of the economy

---

[1] 'Aufzeichnung über das Gespräch des Führers mit Botschafter Oshima am 3. Januar 1942 im Beisein des Reichsaußenministers in der Wolfsschanze von 16.15–18.00 Uhr (n.d.) Füh. 2/42 g. Rs.' (n.d.); in: *Akten zur deutschen auswärtigen Politik*, Serie E, Bd. I (Göttingen: Vandenhoeck & Rupprecht 1969), pp 156–64.

[2] 'Wolfsschanze 15.1.1942, abends H./Fu.'; in: Werner Jochmann (ed.), *Adolf Hitler, Monologe im Führerhauptquartier 1941–1944* (München: Orbis 2000), p 199.

supporting them as late as the eve of the declaration of war on the USA would have given the country's supreme warlord a balance sheet that was still broadly reassuring.

While the war against Britain's sea lanes had been yielding disappointing results since June, the perceived bugbear – insufficient U-boat numbers – was finally on the path to being rectified. American interference in the Battle of the Atlantic may occasionally have been exasperating to Admiral Raeder, but no evidence has come to light to suggest that the German leader linked the U-boats' relative lack of success to the US Navy's growing presence. As for the opportunities that beckoned in the waters of the Americas for the 'grey wolves', neither he nor Erich Raeder nor Karl Dönitz is on record as having regarded these as a major missed opportunity. The Luftwaffe had managed to check RAF Bomber Command's war against Germany's cities and was just a few months away from taking delivery of three new aircraft types of which great things were expected. Factory output of many weapon and ammunition types was stalling, but the dictator felt that here too the reasons for this had been identified and were rectifiable. The manner in which the ammunition crisis of early 1940 had been tackled offered an obvious pointer. As regards Russia, it is of crucial importance to realise that, as far back as August, the dictator had foreseen a continuation of the war against the USSR into 1942. Hence, *Heeresgruppe Mitte*'s failure to neutralise the Soviet capital by early December (an operation which in any case had only enjoyed Hitler's tepid support) was unlikely to be interpreted by him as a major setback. The recent defeats suffered by the Red Army in the battles of Kiev, Vyazma-Bryansk and the Sea of Azov, on the other hand, had inflicted human and material losses on the Soviet Union that seemed to make recovery to a level capable of supporting a more than mainly defensive war effort questionable, especially when seen against the backdrop of the loss of the Donetsk industrial area. The USSR was now in a far worse situation than in August, and the prospect of continuing Barbarossa into 1942 was much less daunting than had been the case three months before. The relief the German dictator must have felt at this becomes obvious in his orders to shift the bulk of *Luftflotte* 2 to the Mediterranean and the way in which he belittled Anglo–American attempts to ship Lend-Lease goods to the USSR via Archangelsk and Vladivostok.

It goes without saying that a favourable assessment of Germany's strategic situation was not by itself enough to trigger a declaration of war. As far as the assessment of enemy threat potential was concerned, it is safe to say that Hitler never underestimated the United States. Throughout the 1920s and 1930s, his judgements on *die amerikanische Union* consistently dwelt on the raw industrial power and penchant for technical innovation that were at the heart of the 'the American way of life'. This was a theme he returned to with remarkable consistency in private conversation and public speeches as well as published and unpublished writings, which even the impact of the Great Depression on the American economy could not dent. Only the consistently non-committal attitude of the American President to the transgressions of the early Third Reich briefly led Hitler to disregard that country as a great power in 1937–8. A greater willingness by the US government to openly take sides progressively changed this from March 1939. Even so, there is no evidence that the dictator at any point before mid-March 1941 seriously entertained the notion of going to war with the USA or contemplated any such prospect with equanimity. In a process that culminated with the signing of Führer's Directive No. 24 on cooperation with Japan (March 1941), Hitler and Ribbentrop consistently sought to keep Washington out of the war, whether by insisting to their Japanese ally that war in the South Pacific be limited to European possessions or by issuing restrictive rules of engagement to U-boat skippers to minimise the likelihood of an unwanted naval clash. Neither the plans for a German blue-water navy as sketched out in early 1939 and again briefly in July 1940, nor the Me-264 project, are valid counterarguments to this. The planned fleet, while large, would still have struggled to do more than secure the Atlantic approaches to continental Europe against either an Anglo–American combination or (assuming a British neutralisation of some kind by 1945–6) the USA's newly created two-ocean navy. The same goes for the Me-264 transatlantic bomber; the available paper trail points quite strongly to a project never intended to be used as a viable weapons system in large numbers; instead, a handful of prototypes were supposed to be available in time to show the flag in the skies over Boston and New York in order to deter, rather than provoke, American belligerency.

March 1941 witnessed an event which, while less visible than the delivery of fifty destroyers to the Royal Navy the previous September, would have far more momentous consequences. In contrast to most of his senior aides, the dictator immediately grasped the long-term implications of Lend-Lease. The extent to which this unsettled him can be inferred from three separate events. First, 18 March has the dictator on the record as considering the extension of Kriegsmarine operations into the US Neutrality Zone. On 30 March he makes an unambiguous reference to Washington as the main rival of the new Germany in an address given to 100 senior officers in the Neue Reichskanzlei. Finally, there is the offer to Matsuoka on 4 April to join him in war against Washington should a Japanese move on Singapore be met by an American armed intervention. It is important to stress that this commitment did not cover a Japanese attack on the USA – it assumed a hypothetical American move against a Japanese invasion of Southeast Asia that had initially spared US possessions. At the same time, it still constituted an important clarification of Germany's duties towards Japan under the Tripartite Pact. It goes without saying that both statements practically disregarded the possibility of the invasion of the USSR stretching into 1942, never mind beyond.

While the seemingly spontaneous offer to Matsuoka appears to indicate that at some point after the passing of Lend-Lease the German leader had already made up his mind with regards to a war with the USA, this is not supported by other statements on the subject. A comment he made to Raeder on 30 March about the design of Germany's next generation of capital ships clearly indicated that he preferred to finish both the current war against Great Britain and the imminent conflict with the USSR before any possible war with the USA. This explains the orders given to the Rheinübung task force on the subject of encounters with US Navy vessels, which came close to being self-defeating. Another comment he made, in May, at a military briefing at the Berghof indicated that he still very much preferred to keep the Americans out of the conflict, since doing so might allow him to finish the war by the end of the year. However, he was willing to concede that Japan's posture had to be considered as 'key'. Hence, the mere preservation of Japan as an ally in waiting became a crucial task for German diplomacy from March to November 1941. When an assessment of the German ambassador in Tokyo all but ruled out a Japanese move on Singapore or Batavia on account of Japanese reluctance to provoke American hostility, but suggested that an attack on the USSR was just about possible, Hitler and Ribbentrop, rather than repeating and clarifying the offer made to Matsuoka in Berlin, simply switched targets. From now on, German foreign policy would be directed at encouraging Japan to move against the USSR. That the embassy staff in Washington continued to sell their Japanese counterparts the old idea of moving on Singapore may appear bizarre to a present-day observer. However, this thoroughly opportunistic scattergun approach to coalition politics as likely as not came about because the Germans had realised that the tribal nature of Tokyo politics not only made this desirable, but possibly more promising. Whatever the outcome, Japan would end up irrevocably committed to the cause of the Axis and permanently alienated from the United States.

In early July, the US occupation of Iceland brought in its train an increased likelihood of a US–German confrontation in the mid to long term. To Oshima, the German dictator was unambiguous in stating his intention of having the Americans removed from the island. The Heinkel company was instructed to hurry along the He-177 project because it would soon be needed for raids on the Arctic island, a mission profile which thus far had not been part of the design history of the new bomber. Around the same time, the dictator's perception of Japan's role also underwent a shift. A conference with Oshima in mid-July had seen Hitler upbeat and optimistic about how things were going in Russia and almost indifferent to how exactly a Japanese intervention might one day be brought about. August, however, saw him manifesting an interest in an active Japanese participation in the war against the USSR with a consistency that seemed to belie the purely political agenda of sabotaging a possible US–Japanese détente. It is impossible to separate this from the stalemate *Heeresgruppe Mitte* found itself in outside Smolensk. Goebbels' personal diary gives us a dictator who for the first time in the war appears genuinely concerned about retaining the strategic initiative and accordingly inclined to bring Japan into the war against the USSR as quickly as possible.

That crisis over, the months of September and October witnessed a remarkable waning of Hitler's interest in attracting Japan into the Axis camp. He repeatedly went on record as rejecting outright the idea of Japan's participation in the Russian campaign and at times even expressed a tepid interest in, at best, mobilising Japan against British possessions in the Far East. Quite apart from his genuine belief that a corner in the war against the USSR had finally been turned, this may stem from the accumulated weariness of three years spent trying to get any kind of coherent strategic commitment out of Tokyo. Although General Ichiro Banzai's notorious visit to OKH on 4 August constituted the high-water mark of this process, it has to be seen against a multi-facetted backdrop. Starting with Konoe's series of bungled attempts at ending the Sino–Japanese war in one form or another, this extended to the apparent impossibility of convincing Tokyo of the imminence of Barbarossa and Matsuoka's penchant for blowing hot and cold (very nearly sabotaging the Tripartite Pact on the eve of its signing, ignoring Hitler's offer to discuss the possibility of war against the USA during the Berlin summit, rashly committing his country to the Russo–German war while reneging on this later), to say nothing of the ongoing 'John Doe talks' and the concerns over the Kwantung Army's willingness to follow any kind of script. Finally, there were the perennial Japanese demands that Germany prepare the ground for a Japanese intervention by first defeating the United Kingdom. All of this had meant that managing the putative Far Eastern ally had been a taxing and exhausting job at the best of times.

Crucially, interest in confronting the USA in any form decreased virtually in step with the declining likelihood of a Japanese alliance. By late October, the dictator appeared willing enough to put up with further American provocations and leave the ultimate confrontation with the USA to 'the next generation'. Even as the ultimate tripwire against US interference was activated with the gutting of the Neutrality Law on 13 November, Ribbentrop was redoubling his efforts to steer Japan into a conflict with Great Britain and The Netherlands, while making sure it would spare the USA as it did so. Six days later, Franz Halder found himself being sounded out by Germany's supreme warlord on the implausible notion of a compromise peace with the British Empire and its budding ally, the USA. This clearly indicated that irrespective of the permission Hitler had just given to the Kriegsmarine's surface units to engage US Navy vessels in certain tactical situations, he was essentially clueless as to his next move. One day later, the offer from Tokyo appeared to offer a way out of the impasse: what with the imminent arrival in European waters of a growing number of US merchant vessels, conflict with the USA in 1942 was a near-certainty, but now Germany would be able to wage it with a powerful new ally by its side. More importantly, the German dictator had known for nearly a year that Tokyo's first strategic priority lay in the seizure of Southeast Asia. As a result of this, those US factories that had just been laboriously retooled to produce tanks, trucks and military aircraft were soon likely to find themselves short of a key commodity – rubber – substitutes for which were not yet available in meaningful quantities in the USA. To preclude such a massive shift in the economic balance of power between the two blocs, Roosevelt would have no choice but to shift the bulk of the navy and all combat-ready units of the army to Southeast Asia in short order.

The timing of events proves conclusively that it took the gutting of the Neutrality Law by Congress for the German dictator to depart from a policy he had rigorously adhered to for the last fourteen months: war with the USA was something to be either avoided or entered into only if Washington had taken the crucial first step (like intervening against a Japanese move against Southeast Asia). If there was an ideological streak in this line of reasoning, it was contempt for the democratically constituted state: only in this manner can we account for the estimate – maintained even in the days after Pearl Harbor – that the US government would seriously contemplate handing over large parts of Southeast Asia to Tokyo as a 'reward' for future good behaviour. Tojo may have been unaware of this, but this assumption gave him a diplomatic leverage which in turn compelled his German allies to commit to the idea of a military alliance with a truly bizarre display of haste. Strangely enough, the racist Hitler refused to contemplate the notion that the racist dispositions of the US elite of the time would have been enough to kill at birth the idea of a large-scale Far Eastern Munich-style deal over Japanese expansion into Southeast Asia.

The rather remarkable statement of 15 January 1942 about the odds now favouring a US victory were not an expression of undiluted Hitlerian nihilism, but simply a reflection of the events of the last month. In the six days since the declaration of war on the USA, the previously localised attacks on *Heeresgruppe Mitte* had escalated into an offensive against the entire breadth of Bock's command. These attacks rivalled those of August 1941 for sheer ferocity, but were now raining down on German formations that were far more exhausted. Days later, the onset of an unexpectedly harsh winter all but crippled the U-boat training programme, thus calling into question Raeder's recent promises about the long-overdue expansion of the submarine service. Crucially, on 10 January Hitler had had to give in to the concerted pressure of Todt, Thomas and Fromm to redirect the resources of the war industry away from the planned expansion of the navy, air force and Panzer arm, and towards the rebuilding of the field army fighting in Russia. The odds of fulfilling even one of these tasks were not good, since most of the factory workers and miners originally slated for release from the army in Russia – some of them as late as 11 December – would now have to stay there. The grand strategy that had guided the German war effort on the day of the declaration of war lay in tatters, a fact that would be compounded many times over in the weeks and months that followed: 1942 would witness both the compromise of key projects associated with German air defence and aircraft production as well as the beginnings of an entire industry in the USA dedicated to the production of synthetic rubber.

While such an avalanche of disasters would have been hard for anyone to foresee, the fact remains that declaring war on the USA while the United Kingdom stood by to serve as an enormous aircraft carrier and naval base was a momentous decision to say the least. It only becomes intelligible when we accept three facts amply borne out by contemporary sources. The dictator, OKH and indeed many of the senior field commanders of the *Ostheer* agreed that the USSR appeared to be essentially crippled and unlikely to be capable of waging more than a defensive campaign for the remainder of the war. Based on past form, the Japanese offer of an alliance might well turn out to be nothing more than a Fata Morgana; at best, it was probably nothing more than the manifestation of a short-lived consensus among various factions in Tokyo likely to dissipate as suddenly as it had appeared. If it was to be turned into something tangible, it would have to be seized with alacrity. Finally, these two developments coincided with the gutting of the last remaining article of the US Neutrality Law, which the dictator himself had named in 1939 as the critical indicator of American willingness to enter hostilities. A war with the USA now appeared to be only a few months away at the most. The coincidence of these three events produced a window of opportunity, which events in Russia and elsewhere would soon reveal for the illusion that it was; however, it remained intact just long enough to incite the German leader to gamble on a move, which may have appeared an excellent bet at the time, but would doom the Third Reich. As far as we know, Hitler did not ask for anybody's advice before going ahead with this decision. That Fritz Todt was the only key player of the Third Reich (and a NSDAP veteran at that) known to have confronted the dictator with evidence that Germany lacked the means to further escalate the war speaks volumes for the extent to which the traditional elites had been either cowed or intoxicated by the recent run of spectacular victories in France and Russia.[3] As for Hitler, he seems to have realised by the turn of the years 1941–2 that he had just made the strategic miscalculation of the century. Paradoxically, and in contrast to the equally fateful decision to invade the USSR, this one really appears to have been determined solely by military estimates, rather than ideological paradigms.

---

[3] Even though Goebbels' personal diary makes clear that he was deeply concerned about war with the USA, it is not clear whether he ever shared these thoughts with Hitler. *Generaloberst* Fromm had voiced the same concerns as Todt, but only in a memo addressed to Keitel; he could not have known for certain that the latter would show it to Hitler.

BIBLIOGRAPHY

Archival sources

Bundesarchiv-Lichterfelde (Berlin)

NS 5/VI 37204 (Deutsche Arbeitsfront)
R 55/792 (Ministerium für Volksaufklärung und Propaganda)
R 3112 /99 (Reichsamt für den Wirtschaftsausbau)

Bundesarchiv-Koblenz (Koblenz)

N 1348/4, 5 (Aufzeichnungen Morell)
Bestand Film B/123530/1

Bundesarchiv/Militärarchiv (Freiburg)

MSg 2/11357 (Beauftragter der Führers für die militärische Geschichtsschreibung)
MSg 2/12152 (Tagebuch von Gyldenfeldt)
N 245/2, 3 (Nachlass Reinhardt)
N 671/6, 8 (Tagebuch Wolfram von Richthofen)
N 745/4 (Nachlass Below)
RH 2/1327, 1521, 1825, 2671, 2670, 2942 (Oberkommando des Heeres)
RH 14–4 (Chef der Heeresrüstung und Befehlshaber des Ersatzheeres)
RH 19 I/87, 88, 250, 259, 260, 281 (Heereesgruppe Süd)
RH 19 II/122, 124, 127, 387 (Heeresgruppe Mitte)
RH 19 III/766, 768, 769, 771 (Heeresgruppe Nord)
RH 20–6/132 (6. Armee)
RH 21–2/v. 244, 879 (Panzergruppe 2/2.Panzerarmee))
RH 24–34/42 (Höheres Kommando XXXIV)
RH 67/49, 50, 53 (Militärattaches/Attachegruppen im Generalstab des Heeres)
RH D 7–11/4 (Amtsdrucksachen)
RL 3/50, 51, 54, 60, 61, 552, 1103, 1104, 1833 (Reichsluftfahrtministerium)
RL 8/280 (VIII. Fliegerkorps)

RL 200/17 (Tagebuch Hoffmann von Waldau)
RM 6/374 (Oberkommando der Kriegsmarine)
RM 7/94, 120, 132, 133, 166, 170, 253, 253 a, 256, 258, 845, 1058, 1700, 1771, 2164, 3381 (Seekriegsleitung)
RM 11/68, 77, 83 (Marineattachegruppen der Kaiserlichen Marine, Reichsmarine und Kriegsmarine)
RM 12 II/249, 250 (Marineattache Tokio)
RM 87/14, 19, 21 (Befehlshaber der Unterseeboote)
RW 4/578 (Oberkommando der Wehrmacht)
RW 19/99, 165, 166, 177, 199, 259, 559, 654, 822, 1251, 1467, 1568, 1776, 1914, 1970, 1971, 2071, 2334, 3211 (OKW, Wehrwirtschafts- und Rüstungsamt)
ZA 3/191, 264, 336

Deutsches Museum (München)

FA 001/0255, 0259, 0860, 0862, 0863 (Heinkel Flugzeugwerke)
NL 271/1, 2 (Nachlaβ Köhler)

Imperial War Museum

FD 386/46
FD 3049/49
FD 4479 (Speer Coll.)
FD 5514/45 (Speer Coll.)
FD 5447/45 (Speer Coll.)
FD 5450/45 (Speer Coll.)
FD 5450/50 (Speer Coll.)
FD 4355/45, Vol. 3
EDS, Mi 14/433 (II)
EDS Mi 14/463 (III)
EDS Group A4/b AL 175

Institut für Zeitgeschichte (München)

ED 100–78 (Tagebuch Walther Hewel)
ED 100–18-40 (Milch Papers)
ZS 7/1 (Below interview 1969)
ZS 285/1–4 (Puttkamer interview)
ZS/A 32, Bd. 8 (Nachlass Ott)

John Rylands Library (Manchester)

Auchinleck papers, AUC 392

Politisches Archiv des Auswärtigen Amtes (Berlin)

Handelspolitische Akten Wiehl, Bd. 2
Staatssekretär Japan, Bd. 3, 4, 5
Handakten Ritter Japan 17, 18
Staatssekretär USA, Bd. 5, 6, 7, 8, 9, 10
Handakten Etzdorf. Politische Berichte Washington
Handakten Luther. Schriftverkehr N-Sch.
Inland II g 337, 338, 339, 340, 440, 477 a, 477 b, 477 c
R 27487 'Betr.: Botschafter Hewel. Vorlagen beim Führer vom Januar 1940 bis
    April 1942'

The National Archives (TNA)

CAB 65/24 W.M. (41)
CAB SO/96 C.O.S. (45) 490 (o)

Published primary sources

*Der Prozeß gegen die Hauptkriegsverbrecher vor dem internationalen
    Militärgerichtshof, 14. November 1945–1. Oktober 1946*, Bd. IX (Nürnberg:
    Verlag der Friedrich Kornschen Buchhandlung 1947)
Various editors: *Hitler. Reden. Schriften. Anordnungen*, Bd. I-VI (München: KG
    Saur 1992–7)
Akten zur deutschen auswärtigen Politik (ADAP), Serie D (1937–1941), Bd. I –
    XIII.2 (various publishers 1950–70)
Akten zur deutschen auswärtigen Politik (ADAP), Serie E (1941–1945), Bd. I
    (Göttingen: Vandenhoeck & Rupprecht 1969)
Bavendamm, Dirk and Heß, Wolf-Rüdiger (eds.): *Rudolf Heß. Briefe 1908–1933*
    (München: Langen Müller 1987)
Bouhler, Philipp (ed.): *Der großdeutsche Freiheitskampf. Reden Adolf Hitlers*, Bd.
    III (München: Franz Eher 1943)
Bridge, Carl (ed.): *A Delicate Mission: The Washington Diaries of Richard G. Casey
    1940–1942* (Canberra: National Library of Australia 2008)
Bücheler, Heinrich (ed.): *Hoepner. Ein deutsches Soldatenschicksal des zwanzigsten
    Jahrhunderts* (Herford: Mittler 1980)
Detwiler, Donald S. (ed.): *World War II German Military Studies: A Collection of
    213 Special Reports on the Second World War Prepared by Former Officers of
    the Wehrmacht for the United States Army*. Vol. 2, Part II (New York and
    London: Garland Publishing 1979)
Domarus, Max (ed.): *Hitler. Reden und Proklamationen, 1932–1945*, Bd. I & II
    (Wiesbaden: R. Löwitt 1973)
Eberle, Henrik and Uhl, Matthias (eds.): *Das Buch Hitler. Geheimdossier des
    NKWD für Josef W. Stalin, zusammengestellt aufgrund der Verhörprotokolle*

des Persönlichen Adjutanten Hitlers, Otto Günsche, und des Kammerdieners Heinz Linge, Moskau 1948/49 (Bergisch Gladbach: Gustav Lübbe 2005)

Feuersenger, Marianne: *Im Vorzimmer der Macht. Aufzeichnungen aus dem Wehrmachtführungsstab und Führerhauptquartier* (München: Herbig 1999)

Foreign Relations of the United States (FRUS), 1940: General and Europe, Vol. II (Washington 1957)

Fröhlich, Elke (ed.): *Die Tagebücher von Joseph Goebbels,* Teil I, Bd. 3/II, 4, 8 & 9 (München : KG Saur 1998–2006)

(ed.): *Die Tagebücher von Joseph Goebbels,* Teil II, Bd. 1, 2, 3, 4 & 15 (München: KG Saur 1993–6)

Fröhlich, Paul and Kranz, Alexander (eds.): *Tagebuch des Chefs des Stabes beim Chef der Heeresrüstung und Befehlshaber des Ersatzheeres 1938 bis 1943* (forthcoming)

Gerbet, Klaus (ed.): *Generalfeldmarschall Fedor von Bock. Zwischen Pflicht und Verweigerung. Das Kriegstagebuch* (München: Herbig 1995)

Hartmann, Christian et al (eds.): *Hitler. Mein Kampf. Eine kritische Edition* (München: Institut für Zeitgeschichte 2016)

Heilmann, H. D. (ed.): 'Aus dem Kriegstagebuch des Diplomaten Otto Bräutigam'; in: Götz Aly et al (eds.): *Biedermann und Schreibtischtäter. Materialien zur deutschen Täter-Biographie* (Berlin: Rotbuch Verlag 1987), pp 123–87

Heim, Susanne et al (eds.): *Sowjetunion mit annektierten Gebieten I. Besetzte sowjetische Gebiete unter deutscher Militärverwaltung, Baltikum und Transnistrien* (München: Oldenbourg 2011) [= Die Verfolgung der europäischen Juden durch das nationalsozialistische Deutschland 1933–1945, Bd. 7]

Hentschel, Georg (ed.): *Die geheimen Konferenzen des Generalluftzeugmeisters. Ausgewählte und kommentierte Dokumente zur Geschichte der deutschen Luftrüstung und des Luftkrieges 1942–1944* (Koblenz: Bernard & Graefe 1989)

Hill, Leonidas (ed.): *Die Weizsäcker-Papiere 1933–1950* (Frankfurt a.M.: Propyläen 1974)

Hillgruber, Andreas (ed.): *Japan und der 'Fall Barbarossa'. Japanische Dokumente zu den Gesprächen Hitlers und Ribbentrops mit Botschafter Oshima von Februar bis Juni 1941*; in: Wehrwissenschaftliche Rundschau, Bd. 18 (1968), pp 326–9

Hubatsch, Walther (ed.): *Hitlers Weisungen für die Kriegführung 1939–1945. Dokumente des Oberkommandos der Wehrmacht* (Koblenz: Bernard & Graefe 1983)

Hürter, Johannes and Uhl, Matthias (eds.): *Hitler in Vinnica. Ein neues Dokument zur Krise im September 1942*; in: *Vierteljahrhefte für Zeitgeschichte* Bd. 63 (2015), Nr. 4, pp 581–639

Notizen aus dem Vernichtungskrieg. Die Ostfront 1941/42 in den Aufzeichnungen des Generals Heinrici (Darmstadt: WBG 2016)

Ike, Nobutaka (ed.): *Japan's Decision for War: Records of the 1941 Policy Conferences* (Stanford: Stanford UP 1967)

Istituto Poligrafico dello Stato (ed.): *I documenti diplomatici italiani (DDI)*. Ottavia serie. Vol. XIII: 1935–1939 (Rome: Libreria dello Stato 1953)

Jäckel, Eberhard and Kuhn, Axel (eds.): *Hitler. Sämtliche Aufzeichnungen 1905–1924* (Stuttgart: DVA 1980)

Jacobsen, Hans-Adolf (ed.): *Dokumente zur Vorgeschichte des Westfeldzuges 1939–1940* (Göttingen: Musterschmidt 1956)

(ed.): *Generaloberst Halder. Kriegstagebuch. Band III. Der Rußlandfeldzug bis zum Marsch auf Stalingrad, 22. 6.1941–24.9.1942* (Stuttgart: Kohlhammer 1964)

(ed.): *Kriegstagebuch des Oberkommandos der Wehrmacht, Bd. I: 1. 8.1940–31.12.1941* (Frankfurt a.m. 1965)

(ed.): *Karl Haushofer. Leben und Werk, Bd. I. Lebensweg 1869–1946 und ausgewählte Texte zur Geopolitik* (Boppard a.Rh.: Harald Boldt 1979) [= Schriften des Bundesarchivs, Bd. 24/I]

(ed.): *Karl Haushofer. Leben und Werk, Bd. II. Ausgewählter Schriftwechsel 1917–1946* (Boppard a.Rh.: Harald Boldt 1979) [= Schriften des Bundesarchivs, Bd. 24/II]

Joachimsthaler, Anton (ed.): *Christa Schroeder. Er war mein Chef. Aus dem Nachlaß der Sekretärin von Adolf Hitler* (Coburg: Nation Europa 1985)

Jochmann, Werner (ed.): *Adolf Hitler. Monologe im Führerhauptquartier* (München: Orbis 2000)

Kido, Koichi: *The Diary of Marquis Kido, 1931–1945* (Fredrick: Maryland: University Publications of America 1984)

Kotze, Hildegard von (ed.): *Heeresadjutant bei Hitler 1938–1943. Aufzeichnungen des Majors Engel* (Stuttgart: DVA 1974)

Krausnick, Helmut and Deutsch, Harold C. (eds.): *Helmuth Groscurth. Tagebücher eines Abwehroffiziers 1938–1940* (Stuttgart: DVA 1970)

Matthäus, Jürgen and Bajohr, Frank (eds.): *Alfred Rosenberg. Die Tagebücher von 1934 bis 1944* (Frankfurt a.M.: S. Fischer 2015)

Mayer, Georg (ed.): *Generalfeldmarschall Wilhelm Ritter von Leeb. Tagebuchaufzeichnungen und Lagebeurteilungen aus den zwei Weltkriegen* (Stuttgart: DVA 1976)

Minuth, Karl-Heinz (ed.): *Akten der Reichskanzlei 1933–1938. Die Regierung Hitler. Teil I: 1933/34, Bd. 1 (30. Januar bis 31. August 1933)* (Boppard am Rhein: Harald Boldt 1983)

Moll, Martin (ed.): *Führer-Erlasse 1939–1945* (Stuttgart: Franz Steiner 1997)

Moors, Markus and Pfeiffer, Moritz (eds.): *Heinrich Himmlers Taschenkalender. Kommentierte Edition* (Paderborn: Ferdinand Schöningh 2016)

Mühleisen, Horst (ed.): *Hellmuth Stieff. Briefe* (Berlin: Siedler 1991)

Overy, Richard (ed.): *Interrogations: The Nazi Elite in Allied Hands* (London: Allen Lane 2001)

Picker, Henry (ed.): *Hitlers Tischgespräche im Führerhauptquartier* (München: Propyläen 2003)

Rahn, Werner (ed.): *Einsatzbereitschaft und Kampfkraft deutscher U-Boote 1942*; in: Militärgeschichtliche Mitteilungen Nr. 1/1990, pp 73–132

Rahn, Werner and Schreiber, Gerhard (eds.): *Kriegstagebuch der Seekriegsleitung 1939–1945. Teil A*, Bd. 17–32 (Herford and Bonn: Mittler & Sohn 1990)

Rosenman, Samuel I. (ed.): *The Public Papers and Addresses of Franklin D. Roosevelt, 1941: The Call to Battle Stations* (New York: Harper & Brothers 1950)

Salewski, Michael (ed.): *Die deutsche Seekriegsleitung 1935–1945. Band III: Denkschriften und Lagebetrachtungen 1938–1944* (Frankfurt a.M.: Bernard & Graefe 1973)

Schlie, Ulrich (ed.): *Albert Speer. Die Kransberg-Protokolle 1945* (München: Herbig 2003)

(ed.): *Ulrich von Hassel. Römische Tagebücher 1932–1938* (München: Herbig 2004)

Semmler, Rudolf : *Goebbels: The Man Next to Hitler* (London: Westhouse 1947)

The 'Magic' Background of Pearl Harbor (MBPH), Vols. I-V with appended documents (United States, Department of Defense 1977) also available on: https://archive.org/details/MagicBackgroundOfPearlHarbor.

Treue, Wilhelm et al (eds.): *Deutsche Marinerüstung 1919–1942. Die Gefahren der Tirpitztradition* (Herford: Mittler & Sohn 1992)

Trial of the Major War Criminals (TMWC), Vols. II, X (Nürnberg 1947)

Turner, Henry Ashby (ed.): *Hitler aus nächster Nähe. Aufzeichnungen eines Vertrauten 1929–1933* (Frankfurt a.M.: Ullstein 1978)

Uhl, Matthias et al (eds.): *Verhört. Die Befragungen deutscher Generale und Offiziere durch die sowjetischen Geheimdienste 1945–1952* (Oldenbourg: de Gruyter 2015)

Vogt, Martin (ed.): *Herbst 1941 im 'Führerhauptquartier'. Berichte Werner Koeppens an seinen Minister Alfred Rosenberg* (Koblenz 2002) [= Materialien aus dem Bundesarchiv, Heft 10]

Vormann, Nikolaus von: *So begann der Zweite Weltkrieg. Zeitzeuge der Entscheidungen – als Offizier bei Hitler, 22. 8.1939–1.10.1939* (Leoni: Druffel-Verlag 1988)

Wagner, Gerhard (ed.): *Lagevorträge des Oberbefehlshabers der Kriegsmarine vor Hitler 1939–1945* (München: J.F. Lehmanns 1972)

Witte, Peter et al (eds.): *Der Dienstkalender Heinrich Himmlers 1941/42* (Hamburg: Hans Christians 1999)

Secondary sources

Abbazia, Patrick: *Mr. Roosevelt's Navy: The Private War of the US Atlantic Fleet, 1939–1942* (Annapolis: USNIP 1975)

Aders, Gebhard: *Geschichte der deutschen Nachtjagd 1917–1945* (Stuttgart: Motorbuch 1978)

Alberti, Michael: *Die Verfolgung und Vernichtung der Juden im Reichsgau Wartheland 1939–1945* (Wiesbaden: Harrasowitz 2006)

Allard, Dean C.: 'Naval Rearmament, 1930–1941: An American Perspective'; in: Jürgen Rohwer (ed.), *Rüstungswettlauf zur See, 1930–1941* (Bonn: Bernard & Graefe 1991), pp 45–54

Aly, Götz: 'Endlösung'. Völkerverschiebung und der Mord an den europäischen Juden (Frankfurt a.m.: S. Fischer 1995)

Anderson, Irvine H.: 'The 1941 De Facto Oil Embargo of Japan: A Bureaucratic Reflex'; in: Pacific Historical Review, Vol. 44, No. 2 (1975), pp 201–31

Asada, Sadao: From Mahan to Pearl Harbor: The Imperial Japanese Navy and the United States (Annapolis: USNIP 2006)

Baer, George W: One Hundred Years of Sea Power: The US Navy, 1890–1990 (Stanford: Stanford UP 1994)

Balta, Sebastian: Rumänien und die Großmächte in der Ära Antonescu, 1940–1944 (Stuttgart: Franz Steiner 2005) [= Quellen und Studien zur Geschichte des östlichen Europa, Bd. 69]

Barnhart, Michael A.: Japan Prepares for Total War: The Search for Economic Security, 1919–1941 (Ithaca and London: Cornell UP 1987)

Barrett, John Q. (ed.): 'That Man': An Insider's Portrait of Franklin D. Roosevelt (Oxford: OUP 2003)

Bauer, Kurt: 'Hitler und der Juliputsch 1934 in Österreich. Eine Fallstudie zur nationalsozialistischen Aussenpolitik in der Frühphase des Regimes'; in: Vierteljahreshefte für Zeitgeschichte, No. 2 (2011), pp 193–227

Bauer, P. T.: The Rubber Industry: A Study in Competition and Monopoly (London: Longmans 1948)

Baumunk, Bodo-Michael: Colin Ross: ein deutscher Revolutionär und Reisender 1885–1945 (unpublished MA thesis, Universität Tübingen 1991)

Baur, Hans: Ich flog Mächtige der Erde (Kempten: Albert Pröpster 1956)

Bayard, Florent: 'To what extent was the "Final Solution" planned?'; in: Yad Vashem Studies 36 (2008), pp 73–109

Beaumont, Joan: Comrades in Arms: British Aid to Russia, 1941–1945 (London: Davis-Poynter 1980)

Beck, Alfred M.: Hitler's Ambivalent Attaché: Lt. Gen. Friedrich von Boetticher in America, 1933–1941 (Washington DC: Potomiac Books 2005)

Beevor, Antony: The Second World War (London: Weidenfeld & Nicholson 2012)

Bell, Christopher: Churchill and Sea Power (Oxford: OUP 2013)

Bell, P. M. H.: Twelve Turning Points of the Second World War (New Haven: Yale UP 2011)

Bellamy, Chris: Absolute War: Soviet Russia in the Second World War (London: Macmillan 2007)

Below, Nicolaus von: Als Hitlers Adjutant 1937–1945 (Selent: Pour le Merite 1999 rp)

Bendert, Harald: U-Boote im Duell (Berlin et al: Mittler 1996)

Bercuson, David J. and Herwig, Hoger : One Christmas in Washington: Churchill and Roosevelt Forge the Grand Alliance (London: Weidenfeld & Nicholson 2005)

Bergamini, David: Japan's Imperial Conspiracy (London: Heinemann 1971)

Berger, Gordon M.: 'Politics and Mobilization in Japan'; in: Peter Duus (ed.), *The Cambridge History of Japan, Vol. 6. The 20th Century* (Cambridge: CUP 1998), pp 97–153

Bergström, Christer and Mikhailov, Andrey: *Black Cross, Red Star: Air War over the Eastern Front* (Pacifica, CA: Pacifica Military History 2000)

Barbarossa: The Air Battle, July-December 1941 (London: Ian Allan 2007)

Bird, Keith: *Erich Raeder: Admiral of the Third Reich* (Annapolis: USNIP 2006)

Blair, Clay: *Hitler's U-boat War: The Hunters, 1939–1942* (London: Weidenfeld & Nicholson 1997)

Blake, John: *Northern Ireland in the Second World War* (Belfast: Blackstaff Press 2000 rp)

Blank, Ralf: 'Kriegsalltag und Luftkrieg an der "Heimatfront"'; in: Jörg Echternkamp (ed.), *Die deutsche Kriegsgesellschaft 1939-1945. Politisierung, Vernichtung, Überleben* (München: DVA 2004) [= Das Deutsche Reich und der Zweite Weltkrieg, Bd. 9/1], pp 357–464

Bloch, Michael: *Ribbentrop* (London: Bantam Press 1992)

Bloβ, Hartmut: 'Die Zweigleisigkeit der deutschen Fernostpolitik und Hitlers Option für Japan 1938'; in: *Militärgeschichtliche Mitteilungen*, 1/1980, pp 55–92

Boehm-Tettelbach, Karl: *Als Flieger in der Hexenküche* (Mainz: Hase & Koehler 1981)

Boelcke, Willi A.: *Die deutsche Wirtschaft 1930-1945. Interna des Reichswirtschaftsministeriums* (Düsseldorf: Droste 1983)

Boog, Horst: *Die deutsche Luftwaffenführung 1935-1945. Führungsprobleme, Spitzengliederung, Generalstabsausbildung* (Stuttgart: DVA 1982)

Brailey, Nigel: 'Thailand, Japanese Pan-Asianism and the Greater East Asia Co-Prosperity Sphere'; in: Saki Dockrill (ed.): *From Pearl Harbor to Hiroshima: The Second World War in Asia and the Pacific, 1941–1945* (London MacMillan Press 1994), pp 119–33

Braithwaite, Rodric: *Moscow 1941: A City and Its People at War* (London: Profile 2006)

Braunmühl, Anton von: 'War Hitler krank?'; in: Stimmen der Zeit 79 (1954), pp 94–102

Breitman, Richard: 'Friedrich Jeckeln – "Spezialist" für die Endlösung im Osten'; in: Ronald Smelser and Enrico Syring (eds.): *Die SS. Elite unter dem Totenkopf. 30 Lebensläufe* (Paderborn et al: Schöningh 2000), 267–75

Official Secrets: What the Nazis Planned, What the British and Americans Knew (London: Allen Lane 2002)

Brett, Peter: *The USA and the World, 1917-1945* (London: Hodder & Stoughton 1997)

Bross, Werner: *Gespräche mit Hermann Göring während des Nürnberger Prozesses* (Flensburg and Hamburg: Christian Wolff 1950)

Brown, David: *Warship Losses of World War Two* (London: Arms & Armour 1995 rev. ed.)

Browning, Christopher: *The Origins of the Final Solution: The Evolution of Nazi Jewish Policy, 1939–1942. With a contribution by Jürgen Matthäus* (London: Arrow Books pb 2005)

Budrass, Lutz: *Flugzeugindustrie und Luftrüstung in Deutschland 1918–1945* (Düsseldorf: Droste 1998) [= Schriften des Bundesarchivs, Bd. 50]

Budrass, Lutz: *Adler und Kranich. Die Lufthansa und Ihre Geschichte 1926–1955* (München: Karl Blessing 2016)

Budrass, Lutz et al: 'Demystifying the German 'Armament Miracle' during World War II. New insights from the annual audits of German aircraft producers' [= Economic Growth Centre, Yale University, Centre Discussion Paper No. 905, January 2005], pp 1–40

Bullock, Alan: *Hitler and Stalin: Parallel Lives* (London: Harper & Collins 1991)

Burr, Lawrence: *US Fast Battleships, 1936–1947* (Oxford: Osprey 2010)

Butow, Robert J.: *The John Doe Associates: Backdoor Diplomacy for Peace, 1941* (Stanford: Stanford UP 1974)

Caldwell, Donald and Muller, Richard: *The Luftwaffe over Germany: Defense of the Reich* (London: Greenhill Books 2007)

Canosa, Romano: *Mussolini e Franco. Amici, alleati, rivali; vite parallele di due dittatori* (Milano: Mondadori 2008)

Casey, Steven: *Cautious Crusade: Franklin D. Roosevelt, American Public Opinion and the War against Nazi Germany* (New York: OUP 2001)

Cesarani, David: *Final Solution: The Fate of the Jews, 1933–1949* (London: MacMillan 2016)

Cescotti, Roderich: *Fernflug. Erinnerungen 1919–2012* (Moosburg: NeunundzwanzigSechs 2012)

Charmley, John: *Churchill – The End of Glory: A Political Biography* (London: Hodder & Stoughton 1993)

Citino, Robert M.: *The German Way of War: From the Thirty Years' War to the Third Reich* (Lawrence, KS : Kansas UP 2005)

Clifford, J. Garry and Wilson, Theodore A.: 'Blundering on the Brink, 1941: FDR and the 203–202 Vote Reconsidered'; in: J. Garry Clifford and Theodore A. Wilson (eds.): *Presidents, Diplomats and Other Mortals* (Columbia: Missouri UP 2007), pp 99–115

Coates, Austin : *The Commerce in Rubber: The First 250 Years* (Oxford: OUP 1987)

Coffman, Edward M.: *The Regulars: The American Army, 1898–1941* (Cambridge and London: Harvard UP 2004)

Conradi, Peter: *Hitler's Piano Player: The Rise and Fall of Ernst Hanfstaengl, Confidant of Hitler, Ally of FDR* (London: Duckworth 2005)

Conradis, Heinz: *Nerven, Herz und Rechenschieber. Kurt Tank: Flieger, Forscher, Konstrukteur* (Göttingen: Musterschmidt 1955)

Cook, James F.: *Carl Vinson: Patriarch of the Armed Forces* (Macon, GA: Mercer UP 2004)

Coox, Alvin D.: 'Japanese Foreknowledge of the Soviet-German War, 1941'; in: *Soviet Studies* 23, No. 4 (April 1972), pp 554–72

Nomonhan: Japan against Russia (Stanford, CA: Stanford UP 1985)

'Japanese Net Assessment in the Era before Pearl Harbor'; in: Williamson Murray and Allan R. Millett (eds.): *Calculations: Net Assessment and the Coming of World War II* (New York: The Free Press 1992)

Corrigan, Gordon: *The Second World War: A Military History* (London: Atlantic Books 2010)

Cüppers, Martin: 'Auf dem Weg in den Holocaust. Die Brigaden des Kommandostabs Reichsführer-SS im Sommer 1941'; in: Jan-Erik Schulte et al (eds.): *Die Waffen SS. Neue Forschungen* (Paderborn: Ferdinand Schöningh 2014), pp 286–301

Diedrich, Torsten: *Paulus. Das Trauma von Stalingrad. Eine Biographie* (Paderborn: Ferdinand Schöningh, rev. ed. 2009)

Dietrich, Otto: *12 Jahre mit Hitler* (Köln: Atlas 1955)

Dimbleby, Jonathan : *The Battle of the Atlantic* (London: Penguin 2015)

Dönitz, Karl: *Zehn Jahre und zwanzig Tage* (München: Bernard & Graefe 1975)

Downing, David: *The Moscow Option: An Alternative Second World War* (London: Greenhill Books 2001)

Drea, Edward J.: *Japan's Imperial Army: Its Rise and Fall, 1853–1945* (Lawrence: Kansas UP 2009)

Drea, Edward J. and van de Ven, Hans: 'An Overview of the Major Military Campaigns during the Sino-Japanese War, 1937–1945'; in: Mark Peattie, Edward Drea and Hans van de Ven (eds.), *The Battle for China: Essays on the Military History of the Sino-Japanese War of 1937–1945* (Stanford: Stanford UP 2011), pp 27–47

Dreifort, John E.: *Myopic Grandeur: The Ambivalence of French Foreign Policy towards the Far East, 1919–1945* (London: Kent State UP 1991)

Duffy, Christopher: *By Force of Arms: The Austrian Army in the Seven Years' War*, Vol. 1 (Chicago: The Emperor's Press 2008)

Dunn, Susan: *A Blueprint for War: FDR and the Hundred Days That Mobilized America* (New Haven and London: Yale UP 2018)

Dunn, Walter: *Hitler's Nemesis: The Red Army, 1930–1945* (London: Praeger 1994)

Eberle, Henrik and Neumann, Hans-Joachim : *War Hitler krank? Ein abschliessender Befund* (Bergisch Gladbach: Gustav Lübbe 2009)

Hitlers Weltkriege (Hamburg: Hoffmann & Campe 2014)

Ebert, Hans J.: *Willy Messerschmitt – Pionier der Luftfahrt und des Leichtbaus. Eine Biographie* (Bonn: Bernard & Graefe 1992)

Ehrengardt, Christian J. and Shores, Christopher: *L'aviation de Vichy au combat, tome II. La campagne de Syrie, 8 juin-14 juillet 1941* (Paris: Lavauzelle 1987)

Erker, Paul: *Vom nationalen zum globalen Wettbewerb. Die deutsche und die amerikanische Reifenindustrie im 19. und 20. Jahrhundert* (Paderborn: Ferdinand Schöningh 2005)

Erskine, Ralph: 'Breaking Air Force and Army Enigma'; in: Michael Smith and Ralph Erskine (eds.): *Action This Day: Bletchley Park from the Breaking of the Enigma Code to the Birth of the Modern Computer* (London: Bantam Press 2001), pp 47–76

'Breaking German Naval Enigma on Both Sides of the Atlantic'; in: Michael Smith and Ralph Erskine (eds.): *Action This Day: Bletchley Park from the Breaking of the Enigma Code to the Birth of the Modern Computer* (London: Bantam Press 2001), pp 174–96

Esser, Cornelia: *Die 'Nürnberger Gesetze' oder die Verwaltung ds Rassenwahns 1939–1945* (Paderborn et al: Schöningh 2002)

Evans, Richard J.: *The Third Reich at War* (London: Allen Lane 2008)

Faulkner, Marcus: '"A Most Disagreeable Problem": Admiralty Perceptions of the Kriegsmarine's Aircraft Carrier Capability'; in: Christopher Bell and Marcus Faulkner (eds.): *Decision in the Atlantic: The Allies and the Longest Campaign of the Second World War* (Lexington: Kentucky UP 2019), pp 169–94

Fest, Joachim: *Hitler Eine Biographie* (Frankfurt: Propyläen 1973)

Speer. Eine Biographie (Berlin: Alexander Fest Verlag 1999)

Field, Andrew: *Royal Navy Strategy in the Far East 1939–1945* (London and New York: Frank Cass 2004)

Finlay, Mark F.: *Growing American Rubber: Strategic Plans and the Politics of National Security* (New Brunswick, NJ: Rutgers UP 2009)

Fischer, Klaus P.: *Hitler and America* (Philadelphia: Pennsylvania UP 2011)

Fleischmann, Peter: *Hitler als Häftling in Landsberg am Lech* (Neustadt a.d. Aich: P. H. C. W. Schmitt 2015)

Fleming, Gerald: *Hitler and the Final Solution* (London: Hamish Hamilton 1984)

Fleming, Thomas: *The War within World War II: Franklin Delano Roosevelt and the Struggle for Supremacy* (London: Perseus Press 2011)

Forczyk, Robert: *Panzerjäger vs KV-1* (Oxford: Osprey 2012)

'Where the Iron Crosses grow': *The Crimea, 1941–1944* (Oxford: Osprey 2014)

Tank Warfare on the Eastern front, 1941–1942 (London: Pen & Sword 2015)

Förster, Jürgen: 'Das Unternehmen Barbarossa – eine historische Ortsbestimmung'; in: Horst Boog et al (eds.): *Der Angriff auf die Sowjetunion* (Stuttgart: DVA 1983) [= Das Deutsche Reich und der Zweite Weltkrieg, Bd. 4], pp 1086–8

Frank, Hans: *Im Angesicht des Galgens* (Neuhaus bei Schliersee: Eigenverlag 1955)

Frey, Andreas: 'Kalt erwischt. Der Meteorologe Franz Baur stellte Hitlers Wehrmacht im Winter vor 70 Jahren eine folgenschwere Wetterprognose. Eine Erinnerung zum 125. Geburtstag'; in: Frankfurter Allgemeine Sonntagszeitung (12.2.2012), 'Wissenschaft' supplement

Frieser, Karl-Heinz: *Blitzkrieglegende. Der Westfeldzug 1940* (München: Oldenbourg 1996)

Fritz, Stephen G.: *The First Soldier: Hitler as Military Leader* (New Haven and London: Yale UP 2018)

Fröhlich, Paul: *'Meine Reise ergab in dieser Beziehungen sehr gute Aufklärung für unsere Belange'. Die militärische Zusammenarbeit der Reichswehr mit der US Army 1918–1933* (unpublished MA thesis, Universität Potsdam 2009)

'Der unterirdische Kampf'. Das Wehrwirtschafts- und Rüstungsamt 1924–1943 (Paderborn: Ferdinand Schöningh 2018)

Gannon, David: *Operation Drumbeat: The Dramatic True Story of Germany's First U-boat Attacks along the American Coast in World War II* (New York: Harper & Row 1990)

Gardner, W. J. R.: *Decoding History: The Battle of the Atlantic and Ultra* (Annapolis: USNIP 1999)

Gerlach, Christian: 'The Wannsee Conference, the Fate of German Jews and Hitler's Decision in Principle to Exterminate All European Jews'; in: *The Journal of Modern History*, Vol. 70, No. 4 (December 1998), pp 759–812

The Extermination of the European Jews (Cambridge: CUP 2016)

Gerwarth, Robert: *Reinhard Heydrich. Biographie* (MüSnchen: Siedler 2011)

Gibbels, Ellen: 'Hitler's Parkinson-Syndrom. Eine postume Motilitätsanalyse in Filmaufnahmen der Deutschen Wochenschau 1940–1945'; in: *Der Nervenarzt*, 59 (1988), pp 521–8

'Hitlers Nervenleiden. Differentialdiagnose des Parkinson-Syndroms'; in: *Fortschritte der Neurologie, Psychiatrie*, Bd. 57, Nr. 12 (Dezember 1989), pp 505–17

Hitler's Parkinson-Krankheit. Zur Frage eines hirnorganischen Psychosyndroms (Berlin: Springer 1990)

'Hitler's Nervenkrankheit'; in: *Vierteljahrshefte für Zeitgeschichte*, Bd. 42, Nr. 2 (1994), pp 155–210

Gilbert, Martin: *Second World War* (London: Weidenfeld & Nicholson 1989)

Glang, Nele Friederike: 'Germany and Chongqing: Secret Communication during World War II'; in: *Intelligence and National Security*, Vol. 30, Nr. 6 (2015), pp 871–89

Glantz, David M.: *The Battle of Leningrad, 1941–1944* (Lawrence: Kansas UP 2004)

Colossus Reborn: The Red Army at War, 1941–1943 (Kansas: Kansas UP 2005)

Barbarossa Derailed: The Battle for Smolensk, 10 July–10 September 1941, Vol. 1 (Solihull: Helion 2010)

Barbarossa Derailed: The Battle for Smolensk, 10 July–10 September 1941, Vol. 2 (Solihull: Helion 2012)

'The Impact of Intelligence Provided to the Soviet Union by Richard Sorge on Soviet Deployments from the Far East to the West in 1941 and 1942'; in: *Journal of Slavic Military Studies*, Vol. 30, Nr. 3 (2017), pp 453–81

Goda, Norman J. W.: *Tomorrow the World: Hitler, Northwest Africa and the Path toward America* (College Station: Texas A & M UP 1998)

Gole, Henry G.: *Exposing the Third Reich: Colonel Truman Smith in Hitler's Germany* (Lexington: Kentucky UP 2013)

Goodwin, Doris Kearns: *No Ordinary Time – Franklin and Eleanor Roosevelt: The Home Front in World War II* (New York: Simon & Schuster 1995)

Gorodetsky, Gabriel: *Grand Delusion: Stalin and the German Invasion of Russia* (New Haven and London: Yale UP 1999)

Görtemaker, Heike B.: *Hitlers Hofstaat. Der innere Kreis im Dritten Reich und danach* (München: C. H. Beck 2019)

Grampp, Hermann: 'Großonkel Leitwolf'; in: *Frankfurter Allgemeine Zeitung* (25.7.2018) – 'Geisteswissenschaften' supplement

Grandin, Greg : *Fordlandia: The Rise and Fall of Henry Ford's Forgotten Jungle City* (London: Icon Books 2010)

Groos, Poul: *The Naval War in the Baltic, 1939–1945* (London: Seaforth 2017)

Grove, Eric: *The Price of Disobedience: The Battle of the River Plate Reconsidered* (Stroud: Sutton 2000)

Gundelach, Karl: *Die deutsche Luftwaffe im Mittelmeer 1940–1945* (Frankfurt a.M.: Peter Lang 1981)

Gunston, Bill: *Classic World War II Aircraft Cutaways* (London: Bounty Books 2013 rp)

Guttmann, Henry: *Die Rohstoffe unserer Erde. Das materielle und geistige Potential der Welt* (Berlin: Safari 1952)

Haffner, Sebastian: *Anmerkungen zu Hitler* (München: Kindler 1978; Fischer pb 2003)

Hanfstaengl, Ernst: *Zwischen Weißem und Braunem Haus* (München: Piper 1970) *Hitler: The Missing Years* (New York: Arcade 1994 rp)

Happel, Jörn : *Der Ost-Experte. Gustav Hilger – Diplomat im Zeitalter der Extreme* (Paderborn: Ferdinand Schöningh 2018)

Hardesty, Von and Grinberg, Ilya: *Red Phoenix Rising: The Soviet Air Force in World War II* (Lawrence: Kansas UP 2012)

Harrington, Dale: *Mystery Man: William Rhodes Davis, Nazi Agent of Influence* (Dulles, VA.: Brassey's 1999)

Harris, John and Wilbourn, Richard: *Rudolf Hess: A New Technical Analysis of the Hess Flight, May 1941* (Stroud: Spellmount 2014)

Harrison, Richard W.: 'Soviet Planning for War, 1936–1941: the "Preventive Attack" Thesis in Historical Context'; in: *Journal of Military History*, 83 (July 2019), pp 769–94

Hart, B. H. Liddell: *History of the Second World War* (New York: G. P. Putnam's Sons 1970)

Hastings, Max: *Finest Years: Churchill as Warlord, 1940–1945* (London: Harper Press 2009)
All Hell Let Loose: The World at War, 1939–1945 (London: Harper Press 2011)

Haupt, Werner: *Army Group Centre: The Wehrmacht in Russia, 1941–1945* (Atglen, PA.: Schiffer : 1997)

Haushofer, Karl: *Japan und die Japaner. Eine Landeskunde* (Leipzig: B.G. Teubner 1923)

Hearden, Patrick: *Roosevelt Confronts Hitler: America's Entry into World War Two* (Dekalb: Northern Illinois UP 1987)

Heinkel, Ernst: *Stürmisches Leben* (Stuttgart: Mundus 1953)

Heinrichs, Waldo: *Threshold of War: Franklin D. Roosevelt and American Entry into World War II* (Oxford: OUP 1988)
'The Russian Factor in Japanese-American Relations, 1941'; in: Hilary Conroy and Harry Wray (eds.): *Pearl Harbor Re-examined: Prologue to the Pacific War* (Honolulu: University of Hawaii Press 1990), pp 163–78
Hemming, Henry: *Our Man in New York: The British Plot to Bring America into the Second World War* (London: Quercus 2019)
Herbst, Ludolf: 'Walther Funk – Vom Journalisten zum Reichswirtschaftsminister'; in: Ronald Smelser et al (eds.): *Die braune Elite II. 21 weitere biographische Skizzen* (Darmstadt: WBG 1993), pp 91–102
Herde, Peter: Italien, *Deutschland und der Weg in den Krieg im Pazifik* (Wiesbaden: Franz Steiner 1983) [= Sitzungsberichte der Wissenschaftlichen Gesellschaft an der Johann Wolfgang Goethe-Universität Frankfurt am Main, Bd. XX, Nr. 1]
Herwig, Holger: 'Geopolitik: Haushofer, Hitler and Lebensraum'; in: *Journal of Strategic Studies*, Vol. 22, Nos. 2 & 3 (June/September 1999), pp 218–41
The Demon of Geopolitics: How Karl Haushofer 'Educated' Hitler and Hess (New York and London: Rowman & Littlefield 2016)
Herzog, Bodo: *Deutsche U-Boote 1906–1966* (München: J. F. Lehmanns 1968, rp 1990)
Heston, Leonard L. and Heston, Renate: *The Medical Casebook of Adolf Hitler* (London: William Kimber 1979)
Hett, Benjamin Carter: *The Death of Democracy: The Rise of Hitler* (London: Heinemann 2018)
Hill, Alexander: 'British "Lend-Lease" Tanks and the Battle for Moscow, November–December 1941 – A Research Note'; in: *Journal of Slavic Military Studies*, No. 19 (2006), pp 289–94
'British "Lend-Lease" Tanks and the Battle for Moscow, November–December 1941 – Revisited'; in: *Journal of Slavic Military Studies*, No. 22 (2009), pp 574–87
The Red Army and the Second World War (Cambridge: CUP 2017)
Hillgruber, Andreas: *Hitlers Strategie. Politik und Kriegführung 1940–1941* (Frankfurt a.M.: Bernard & Graefe 1965)
Deutsche Großmacht- und Weltpolitik im 19. und 20. Jahrhundert (Düsseldorf: Droste Verlag 1978)
'Hitler und die USA 1933–1945'; in: Otmar Franz (ed.): *Europas Mitte* (Göttingen: Musterschmidt 1987), pp 125–44
Hiltzik, Michael: *The New Deal: A Modern History* (New York: Free Press 2011)
Hinsley, Francis Harry et al: *British Intelligence in the Second World War: Its influence on Strategy and Operations*, Vol. 2 (London: HMSO 1981)
Hinze, Rolf: *Hitze, Frost und Pulverdampf. Der Schicksalsweg der 20. Panzerdivision* (Bochum: Heinrich Pöppinghaus 1981)
Holwitt, Joel Ira: *'Execute Against Japan': The US Decision to Conduct Unrestricted Submarine Warfare* (College Station: Texas A & M UP 2009)

Hone, Thomas C.: 'The Evolution of the U.S. Fleet, 1933–1941: How the President Mattered'; in: Edward J. Marolda (ed.): *FDR and the US Navy* (New York: St. Martin's Press 1998), pp 65–114

Horne, Alistair: *Hubris: The Tragedy of War in the Twentieth Century* (London: Weidenfeld & Nicholson 2015)

Hotta, Eri: *Japan 1941: Countdown to Infamy* (New York: Alfred Knopf 2013)
    'Japanese Policy, Thinking and Actions'; paper delivered at the 'Five Days in December' conference of the Centre on Geopolitics, Peterhouse, Cambridge (28.9.2019)

Howard, Frank A.: *Buna Rubber: The Birth of an Industry* (New York: D. van Nostrand 1947)

Hübner, Stefan: 'National Socialist Foreign Policy and Press Instructions, 1933–1938: Aims and Ways of Coverage Manipulation Based on the Example of East Asia'; in: *International History Review*, Vol. 34, No. 2 (June 2012), pp 271–91

Hürter, Johannes: *Hitlers Heerführer. Die deutschen Oberbefehlshaber im Krieg gegen die Sowjetunion 1941/42* (München: R. Oldenbourg 2011)

Iriye, Akira: *The Origins of the Second World War in Asia and the Pacific* (London: Longman 1987)

Irving, David: *Wie krank war Hitler wirklich? Der Diktator und seine Ärzte* (München: Heyne 1980)
    Hitler's War 1942–1945 (London: Papermac 1983)
    Hitler's War (London: Focal 2002 rev. ed.)
    The Rise and Fall of the Luftwaffe: The Life of Field Marshal Erhard Milch (Focal Point electronic rp 2002)

Isaev, Aleksei: *Dubno 1941: The Greatest Tank Battle of the Second World War* (Solihull: Helion 2017)

Jäckel, Eberhard: 'Die deutsche Kriegserklärung an die Vereinigten Staaten von 1941'; in: Fredrich J. Kroneck and Thomas Oppermann (eds.): *Im Dienste Deutschlands und des Rechts. Festschrift für Wilhelm G. Grewe zum 70. Geburtstag am 16. Oktober 1981* (Baden-Baden: Nomos-Verlagsgesselschaft 1981), pp 117–37
    'Neue Erkenntnisse zur Fälschung von Hitler-Dokumenten'; in: *Vierteljahrshefte für Zeitgeschichte*, Bd. 32 (1984), Nr. 1, pp 163–9
    Hitler in History (London: New England UP 1984)

Jackson, Ashley: *Persian Gulf Command: A History of the Second World War in Iran and Iraq* (New Haven: Yale UP 2018)

Jacobsen, Alf R.: *Miracle at the Litza: Hitler's First Defeat on the Eastern Front* (Philadelphia and Oxford: Casemate 2017)

Jeffreys, Diarmuid: *Hell's Cartel: IG Farben and the Making of Hitler's War Machine* (London: Bloomsbury 2008)

Jennings, Eric T.: *Free French Africa in World War II: The African Resistance* (Cambridge: CUP 2015)

Jersak, Tobias: 'Die Interaktion von Kriegsverlauf und Judenvernichtung. Ein Blick auf Hitlers Strategie im Spätsommer 1941'; in: *Historische Zeitschrift*, Bd. 268 (1999), pp 311–74

Johnsen, William T.: *The Origins of the Grand Alliance: Anglo-American Military Collaboration from the Panay Incident to Pearl Harbor* (Lexington: Kentucky UP 2016)

Johnson, David E.: *Fast Tanks and Heavy Bombers: Innovation in the US Army, 1917–1945* (Ithaca and London: Cornell UP 1998)

Jones, Robert Huhn: *The Roads to Russia: United States Lend-Lease to the Soviet Union* (Norman: Oklahoma UP 1969)

Jones, Michael: *The Retreat: Hitler's First Defeat* (London: John Murray 2009)

Jordan, Jonathan: *American Warlords: How Roosevelt's High Command Led America to Victory in World War II* (New York: Penguin 2015)

Jordan, Rudolf: *Erlebt und erlitten. Weg eines Gauleiters von München bis Moskau* (Leoni: self-published 1971)

Jun, Tsunoda: 'On the So-called Hull-Nomura Negotiations'; in: Hilary Conroy and Harry Wray (eds.): *Pearl Harbor Re-examined: Prologue to the Pacific War* (Honolulu: University of Hawaii Press 1990), pp 89–95

Junker, Detlef (ed.): *Kampf um die Weltmacht. Die USA und das Dritte Reich 1933–1945* (Düsseldorf: Schwann 1988)

Jünger, Wolfgang: *Kampf um Kautschuk* (Leipzig: Goldmann 1940)

Kaiser, David: *No End Save Victory: How FDR Led the Nation into War* (New York: Basic Books 2014)

Kaufmann, J. E. and Kaufmann, H. W.: *The Sleeping Giant: American Armed Forces between the Wars* (Westport, CT: Praeger 1996)

Kay, Alex: 'Transition to Genocide, July 1941: *Einsatzkommando* 9 and the Annihilation of Soviet Jewry'; in: *Holocaust and Genocide Studies* 27, No. 3 (winter 2013), pp 411–42

Keitel, Wilhelm: *Mein Leben. Pflichterfüllung bis zum Untergang* (Berlin: edition q 1998 rp)

Kershaw, Ian: *Hitler: A Profile in Power* (London: Longman 1991)
Hitler, 1936–1945: Nemesis (London: Allen Lane 2000)
'Hitler's Role in the Final Solution'; in: *Yad Vashem Studies*, 34 (2006), pp 7–34
Fateful Choices: Ten Decisions that Changed the World (London: Allen Lane 2007)
The Nazi Dictatorship: Problems and Perspectives of Interpretation (London and New York: Bloomsbury 1985, rev. ed. 2015)

Kiesel, Hellmuth: 'War Adolf Hitler ein guter Schriftsteller?'; in: *Frankfurter Allgemeine Zeitung* (4.8.2014) – 'Feuilleton' supplement

Kimball, Warren F.: *Forged in War: Roosevelt, Churchill and the Second World War* (New York: William Morrow 1997)

King, David : *The Trial of Adolf Hitler* (London: MacMillan 2017)

Kirchubel, Robert: *Operation Barbarossa: The German Invasion of Soviet Russia* (Oxford: Osprey 2013)

Kissenkoetter, Udo: *Gregor Straßer und die NSDAP* (Stuttgart: DVA 1978)

Kitchen, Martin: *Rommel's Desert War* (Cambridge: CUP 2009)

Klein, Maury: *A Call to Arms: Mobilizing America for World War II* (New York: Bloomsbury Press 2015 pb)

Klein, Peter: 'Die Erlaubnis zum grenzenlosen Massenmord – das Schicksal der Berliner Juden und die Rolle der Einsatzgruppen be idem Versuch, Juden als Partisanen "auszurotten"'; in: Rolf-Dieter Müller and Hans-Erich Volkmann (eds.): *Die Wehrmacht. Mythos und Realität* (München: Oldenbourg 1999), pp 923–47

'Die Wannsee-Konferenz als Echo auf die gefallene Entscheidung zur Ermordung der europäischen Juden'; in: Norbert Kampe and Peter Klein (eds.): *Die Wannsee-Konferenz am 20. Januar 1942. Dokumente, Forschungsstand, Kontroversen* (Köln: Böhlau 2013), pp 182–201

Knox, MacGregor: *Mussolini Unleashed 1939–1941: Politics and Strategy in Fascist Italy's Last War* (Cambridge: CUP 1982)

Koch, Sigrid: 'Buna wird zum Symbol eines Triumphs der Chemie'; in: Ulrich Giersch and Ulrich Kubisch (eds.): *Gummi. Die elastische Faszination* (Ratingen: Dr. Gupta 1995), pp 116–25

Komatsu, Keiichiro: *Origins of the Pacific War and the Importance of 'Magic'* (Richmond: Curzon 1999)

Kopper, Christopher: *Hjalmar Schacht. Aufstieg und Fall von Hitlers mächtigstem Bankier* (München: Hanser 2006)

Kordt, Erich: *Nicht aus den Akten* (Stuttgart: Union Deutsche Verlagsgesellschaft 1950)

Kotani, Ken: *Japanese Intelligence in World War II* (Oxford: Osprey 2009)

Kotelnikov, Vladimir : *Lend-Lease and Soviet Aviation in the Second World War* (Solihull: Helion 2017)

Krauß, Oliver: *Rüstung und Rüstungserprobung in der deutschen Marinegeschichte – Die Torpedoversuchsanstalt* (Bonn: Bernard & Graefe 2010) [= Wehrtechnik und wissenschaftliche Waffenkunde, Bd. 17]

Krebs, Gerhard: *Japans Deutschlandpolitik 1935–1941. Eine Studie zur Vorgeschichte des Pazifischen Krieges* (Hamburg 1984) [= MOAG- Mitteilungen der Gesellschaft für Natur- und Völkerkunde Ostasiens e.V., Bd. 91]

'Deutschland und Pearl Harbor'; in: *Historische Zeitschrift*, Bd. 253 (1991), pp 313–69

'Die etwas andere Kriegsgefangenschaft'; in: Overmanns, Rüdiger (ed.): *In der Hand des Feindes. Kriegsgefangenschaft von der Antike bis zum Zweiten Weltkrieg* (Köln: Böhlau 1999), pp 323–37

Japan im Pazifischen Krieg. Herrschaftssystem, politische Willensbildung und Friedenssuche (München: IUDICUM 2010) [= Monographien aus dem Deutschen Institut für Japanstudien, Bd. 46]

Krings, Stefan: *Hitler Pressechef Otto Dietrich (1897–1952). Eine Biografie* (Göttingen: Wallstein Verlag 2010)

Kroener, Bernhard: 'Der "erfrorene Blitzkrieg". Strategische Planungen der deutschen Führung gegen die Sowjetunion und die Ursachen Ihres Scheiterns'; in: Bernd Wegner (ed.): *Zwei Wege nach Moskau. Vom Hitler-Stalin Pakt zum Unternehmen Barbarossa* (München: Piper 1991), pp 133–48

'Zwischen Blitzsieg und Verhandlungsfrieden. Der Chef der Heeresrüstung und Befehlshaber des Ersatzheeres fordert im Herbst 1941 die Beendigung des Krieges'; in: Wolfgang Elz and Sönke Neitzel (eds.): *Internationale Beziehungen im 19. und 20. Jahrhundert. Festschrift für Winfried Baumgart zum 65. Geburtstag* (Paderborn et al: Ferdinand Schöningh 2003), pp 341–60

'*Der starke Mann im Heimatkriegsgebiet'. Generaloberst Friedrich Fromm. Eine Biographie* (Paderborn: Ferdinand Schöningh 2005)

Kube, Alfred: *Pour le Merite und Hakenkreuz. Hermann Göring im Dritten Reich* (München: Oldenbourg 1987)

Kümmel, Gerhard: *Transnationale Wirtschaftskooperation und der Nationalstaat. Deutsch-amerikanische Unternehmensbeziehungen in den dreißiger Jahren* (Stuttgart: Franz Steiner 1995)

Lacey, James: 'World War II's Real "Victory Program"'; in: *Journal of Military History*, Vol. 75 (July 2011), pp 811–34

Langford, Michael: 'South American Leaf Blight of Hevea Rubber Trees'; in: US Department of Agriculture, Washington DC, Technical Bulletin No. 882 (January 1945), pp 1–31

Leighton, Richard M. and Coakley, Robert W.: *The War Department: Global Logistics and Strategy, 1940–1943* (Washington D.C.: Office of the Chief of Military History, Department of the Army 1955)

Liebermann, Abraham: 'Adolf Hitler Had Post-encephalitic Parkinsonism'; in: *Parkinsonism and Related Disorders*, Vol. 2, No. 2 (1996), pp 95–103

'Hitler's Parkinson's Disease Began in 1933'; in: *Movement Disorders*, Vol. 12, No. 2 (1997), pp 239–40

Liedtke, Gregory: *Enduring the Whirlwind: The German Army and the Russo-German War, 1941–1943* (Solihull: Helion 2016)

Lindner, Roland: 'Schneesturm und Seelenfinsternis'; in: *Frankfurter Allgemeine Zeitung* (30.4.2019), p 3

Loadman, John: 'Der Baum, der weint. Vom Blutgummi zum Plantagenkautschuk'; in: Ulrich Giersch and Ulrich Kubisch (eds.): *Gummi. Die elastische Faszination* (Ratingen: Dr. Gupta 1995), pp 32–47

Longerich, Peter: *Der ungeschriebene Befehl. Hitler und der Weg zur Endlösung* (München: Piper 2001)

Heinrich Himmler. Biographie (München: Siedler 2008)

Hitler. Biographie (München: Siedler 2015)

Lopukhovsky, Lev and Kavalerchik, Boris: *The Price of Victory: The Red Army's Casualties in the Great Patriotic War* (Barnsley: Pen & Sword 2017)

Love, Robert: *History of the US Navy, 1775–1941* (Harrisburg: Stackpole 1992)

Lowenthal, Mark: 'Roosevelt and the Coming of War: The Search for United States Policy, 1937–1942'; in: *Journal of Contemporary History*, Vol. 16 (1981), pp 413–40

Lower, Wendy: 'Axis Collaboration, Operation Barbarossa and the Holocaust and the Holocaust in Ukraine'; in: Alex Kay et al (eds.): *Nazi Policy on the Eastern*

Front, 1941: Total War, Genocide and Radicalization (New York: Rochester UP 2012), pp 186–219

Löffler, Jürgen: Walther von Brauchitsch (1881–1948). Eine politische Biographie (Frankfurt a.M.: Peter Lang 2001)

Lüdicke, Lars: Griff nach der Weltherrschaft. Die Aussenpolitik des Dritten Reiches 1933–1945 (Berlin: be.bra 2009)

  Hitlers Weltanschauung. Von 'Mein Kampf' bis zum 'Nero-Befehl' (Paderborn: Ferdinand Schöningh 2016)

Lukacs, John: The Hitler of History (New York: Alfred Knopf 1997)

Macksey, Kenneth: Kesselring: The Making of the Luftwaffe (New York: David McKay 1978)

Magenheimer, Heinz: Hitler's War: German Military Strategy, 1940–1945 (London: Arms & Armour 1998)

Mann, Chris and Jorgensen, Christer: Hitler's Arctic War: The German Campaigns in Norway, Finland and the USSR, 1940–1945 (London: Ian Allan 2002)

Manoschek, Walter: 'Serbien ist judenfrei'. Militärische Besatzungspolitik und Vernichtungspolitik in Serbien 1941/42 (München: Oldenbourg 1993)

Marshall, Jonathan: To Have and Have Not: Southeast Asian Raw Materials and the Origins of the Pacific War (Berkely et al: California UP 1995)

Martin, Allan: Robert Menzies: A Life, Volume 1, 1894–1943 (Melbourne: Melbourne UP 1993)

Martin, Bernd: Japan and Germany in the Modern World (Oxford: Berghahn 1995)

Marvell, David G.: 'Ernst Hanfstaengl – des 'Führers' Klavierspieler'; in: Ronal Smelser et al (eds.): Die braune Elite II. 21 weitere biographische Skizzen (Darmstadt: WBG 1993), pp 137–149

Maslov, Mikhail: Polikarpov I-15, I-16 and I-153 aces (Oxford: Osprey 2010)

Matthews, Owen: An Impeccable Spy: Richard Sorge, Stalin's Master Agent (London: Bloomsbury 2019)

Mauch, Peter: 'A Bolt from the Blue? New Evidence on the Japanese Navy and the Draft Understanding between Japan and the United States, April 1941'; in: Pacific Historical Review, Vol. 78, No. 1 (2009), pp 55–79

Mawdsley, Evan: '"Crossing the Rubicon": Soviet Plans for Offensive War, 1940–1941'; in: International History Review, Vol. 24, No. 4 (2003), pp 818–65

  Thunder in the East: The Nazi–Soviet War, 1941–1945 (London: Hodder Arnold 2005)

  World War II: A New History (Cambridge: Cambridge UP 2009)

  December 1941: Twelve Days that Began a World War (New Haven: Yale UP 2011)

Mayer, Arno: Why Did the Heavens Not Darken? The 'Final Solution' in History (New York: Pantheon Books 1988)

Mayers, David: FDR's Ambassadors and the Diplomacy of Crisis: From the Rise of Hitler to the End of World War II (Cambridge: CUP 2013)

McComb, Dave: US Destroyers 1934–45: Pre-war classes (Oxford: Osprey 2010)

McNab, Chris: MG 34 and MG 42 Machine Guns (Oxford: Osprey 2012)

Medcalf, William A. and Creek, Eddie: *Junkers Ju-88: From Schnellbomber to Multi-Mission Warplane*, Vol. 1 (Manchester: Crecy 2013)

Medvedev, Zhores and Medvedev, Roy: 'Stalin's Personal Archive: Hidden or Destroyed?'; in: Medvedev, Zhores and Medvedev, Roy (eds.), *The Unknown Stalin* (London: I. B. Tauris 2003), pp 57–94

Megargee, Geoffrey: *Inside Hitler's High Command* (Kansas: Kansas UP 2000)

Meier-Dörnberg, Wilhelm: *Die Ölversorgung der Kriegsmarine 1935 bis 1945* (Freiburg: Rombach 1973) [= Einzelschriften zur militärischen Geschichte des Zweiten Weltkriegs, Bd. 11]

Melvin, Mungo: *Sevastopol's Wars: Crimea from Potemkin to Putin* (Oxford: Osprey 2017)

Merrick, Ken: *Handley Page Halifax: From Hell to Victory and Beyond* (London: Ian Alan 2009)

Michalka, Wolfgang: 'Joachim von Ribbentrop – vom Spirituosenhändler zum Außenminister'; in: Ronald Smelser and Rainer Zitelmann (eds.): *Die braune Elite. 22 biographische Skizzen* (Darmstadt: WBG 1989), pp 201–11.

Middlebrook, Martin and Everitt, Chris: *The Bomber Command War Diaries: An Operational Reference Book, 1939–1945* (New York: Viking Penguin 1985)

Miller, Edward M. : *Bankrupting the Enemy: The US Financial Siege of Japan before Pearl Harbor* (Annapolis: USNIP 2007)

Ministry of Defence, Navy (ed.): *The U-Boat War in the Atlantic, 1939–1945* (London: HMSO 1989 rp)

Misch, Rochus: *Der letzte Zeuge. Ich war Hitlers Telefonist, Kurier und Leibwächter* (München: Piper 2008, 2013 pb)

Mitani, Taichiro: 'The Establishment of Party Cabinets, 1898–1932'; in: Peter Duus (ed.), *The Cambridge History of Japan, Vol. 6, The 20th century* (Cambridge: CUP 1998), pp 55–96

Mitter, Rana: *China's War with Japan, 1937–1945: The Struggle for Survival* (London: Allen Lane 2013)

Molesworth, Carl: *Curtiss P-40: Long-nosed Tomahawks* (Oxford: Osprey 2013)

Moll, Martin: 'Steuerungsinstrument im 'Ämterchaos'? Die Tagungen der Reichs- und Gauleiter der NSDAP'; in: *Vierteljahrshefte für Zeitgeschichte* 2001, No. 2 (April), pp 215–273

Montefiore, Hugh Sebag: *Enigma: The Battle for the Code* (London: Weidenfeld & Nicholson 2000)

Moore, Stephen: 'Reconsidering the Historical Evidence for the End Date of the Blitz against the United Kingdom in 1941'; in: *Global War Studies*, forthcoming

Morley, James William (ed.): *The Final Confrontation: Japan's Negotiations with the United States, 1941* (New York: Columbia UP 1994) [= Japan's road to the Pacific War, Vol. 6]

Morris, Peter J. T.: *The American Synthetic Rubber Research Program* (Philadelphia: Pennsylvania UP 1989)

Müller, Rolf-Dieter: 'Die Mobilisierung der deutschen Wirtschaft für Hitler Kriegführung'; in: Bernhard Kroener, Rolf Dieter Müller and Hans Umbreit : *Organisation und Mobilisierung des deutschen Machtbereichs* (Stuttgart: DVA 1988) [= Das Deutsche Reich und der Zweite Weltkrieg, Bd. 5/1], pp 346–689

'Albert Speer und die Rüstungspolitik im totalen Krieg'; in: Bernhard Kroener et al (eds.): *Organisation und Mobilisierung des deutschen Machtbereichs. Kriegsverwaltung, Wirtschaft und personnelle Resourcen 1942–1944/45* (Stuttgart: DVA 1999) [= Das Deutsche Reich und der Zweite Weltkrieg, Bd. 5/2], pp 275–773

'"Für Hitler war Uran nur ein Metall". Wie aus einem Geschoß für den Notfall dennoch eine Waffe für den Masseneinsatz wurde'; in: *Frankfurter Allgemeine Zeitung*, 'Die Gegenwart' supplement (21.2.2001)

Müller, Vincenz: *Ich fand das wahre Vaterland* (Ost-Berlin: MV der DDR 1962)

Murray, Williamson and Millett, Alan : *A War to Be Won: Fighting the Second World War* (New Haven: Yale UP 2000)

Nasaw, David: *The Chief: The Life of William Randolph Hearst* (Boston and New York: Houghton & Mifflin 2001)

Nedialkov, Dimitar : *In the Skies of Nomonhan: Japan versus Russia, May-September 1939* (Manchester: Crecy Publishing 2011)

Neitzel, Sönke: 'The Deployment of the U-boats'; in: Stephen Howarth and Derek Law (eds.): *The Battle of the Atlantic 1939–1945* (London: Greenhill Books 1994), pp 276–301

Die deutsche Luftwaffe im Einsatz über dem Nordatlantik und der Nordsee 1939–1945 (Bonn: Bernard and Graefe 1995)

Neitzel, Sönke and Welzer, Harald : *Soldaten, Protokolle vom Töten, Kämpfen und Sterben* (Frankfurt a.M.: S. Fischer 2011)

Newpower, Anthony: *Iron Men and Tin Fish: The Race to Build a Better Torpedo during World War II* (Westport and London: Praeger 2006)

Norton, Douglas M.: 'The Open Secret: The US Navy in the Battle of the Atlantic, April-December 1941'; in: *Naval War College Review* 26, No. 4 (1974), pp 63–83

O'Brien, Phillips Payson: *How the War Was Won: Air-Sea Power and Allied Victory in World War II* (Cambridge: CUP 2015)

Ohler, Norman : *Der totale Rausch. Drogen im Dritten Reich* (Köln: Kiepenheuer & Witsch 2015)

Overy, Richard: *War and Economy in the Third Reich* (Oxford: Clarendon Press 1995 pb)

The Bombing War: Europe 1939–1945 (London: Allen Lane 2013)

Paul, Wolfgang: *Brennpunkte. Die Geschichte der 6. Panzerdivision (1. Leichte) 1937–1945* (Osnabrück: Biblio 1984 rp)

Petrick, Peter and Mankau, Heinz: *Messerschmitt Bf 110-Me 210-Me 410, Die Messerschmitt-Zerstörer und Ihre Konkurenten* (Oberhaching: Aviatic 2001)

Petrick, Peter, Mankau, Heinz and Stocker, Werner: *Messerschmitt 210/Me 410 Hornisse/Hornet: An Illustrated Production History* (London: Ian Alan 2007)

Perret, Geoffrey: *There's a War to Be Won: The United States Army in World War II* (New York: Random House 1991)

Winged Victory: The Army Air Forces in World War II (New York: Random House 1993)

Piekalkiewicz: *Die Schlacht um Moskau. Die erfrorene Offensive* (Herrsching: Manfred Pawlak 1989)

Pike, Francis: *Hirohito's War: The Pacific War, 1941–1945* (London: Bloomsbury 2015)

Plöckinger, Othmar: *Geschichte eines Buches. Adolf Hitlers Mein Kampf 1922–1945* (München: Oldenbourg 2006)

Plumpe, Gottfried: 'Industrie, technischer Fortschritt und Staat. Die Kautschuksynthese in Deutschland 1906–1944/45'; in: *Geschichte und Gesellschaft* 9 (1983), pp 564–97

Pogue, Forrest C.: *George C. Marshall: Ordeal and Hope, 1939–1942* (New York: Viking Press 1966)

Pommerin, Reiner: *Das Dritte Reich und Lateinamerika. Die deutsche Politik gegenüber Süd- und Mittelamerika 1939–1942* (Düsseldorf: Droste 1977)

Ponting, Clive : *Churchill* (London: Sinclair-Stevenson 1994)

Prange, Gordon W.: *Target Tokyo: The Story of the Sorge Spy Ring* (New York: McGraw Hill 1984)

Puttkamer, Karl-Jesko von: *Die unheimliche See. Hitler und die Kriegsmarine* (Wien and München: Karl Kühne 1952)

Pyta, Wolfram: 'Weltanschauliche und strategische Schicksalsgemeinschaft: die Bedeutung Japans für das weltpolitische Kalkül Hitlers'; in: Martin Cüppers et al (eds.): *Naziverbrechen. Täter, Taten, Bewältigungsversuche* (Darmstadt: WBG 2013)

Hitler. Der Künstler als Politiker und Feldherr. Eine Herrschaftsanalyse (München: Siedler 2015)

Radey, Jack and Sharp, Charles: *The Defence of Moscow 1941: The Northern Flank* (Barnsley: Pen & Sword 2012)

'Was It the Mud?'; in: *Journal of Slavic Military Studies*, Vol. 28 (Oct./Dec. 2015), pp 646–76

Ratcliff, R. A.: 'Searching for Security: The German Investigations into Enigma's Security'; in: *Intelligence and National Security*, Vol. 14, No. 1 (1999), pp 146–67

Rathke, Günther: '"Walküre"-Divisionen 1941/42. Letzte Aushilfe in der Winterkrise'; in: *Militärgeschichte*, No. 4 (1996), pp 47–54

Reinhardt, Klaus: *Die Wende vor Moskau. Das Scheitern der Strategie Hitlers im Winter 1941/42* (Stuttgart: DVA 1972)

Recktenwald, Johann: *Woran hat Adolf Hitler gelitten? Eine neuropsychiatrische Deutung* (München and Basel: Reinhardt 1963)

Redlich, Fritz: *Hitler: Diagnosis of a Destructive Prophet* (Oxford: OUP 1998)

Reuth, Ralf-Georg : *Hitler. Eine politische Biographie* (München: Piper 2003)
Kurze Geschichte des Zweiten Weltkriegs (Berlin: Rowohlt 2018)

Reynolds, David: 'The "Atlantic Flop": British Foreign Policy and the Churchill-Roosevelt Meeting of August 1941'; in: Douglas Brinkley and David R. Facey-Crowther (eds.): *The Atlantic Charter* (New York: St Martin's Press 1994), pp 129–50
America: Empire of Liberty (London: Allen Lane 2009)

Rhys-Jones, Graham: *The Loss of the* Bismarck*: An Avoidable Disaster* (London: Cassell 1999)

Ribbentrop, Joachim von: *Zwischen London und Moskau. Erinnerungen und letzte Aufzeichnungen* (Leoni: Druffel-Verlag 1961)

Rich, Norman: *Hitler's War Aims: Ideology, the Nazi State and the Course of Expansion* (London: Andre Deutsch 1973)

Roberts, Andrew: *The Storm of War: A New History of the Second World War* (London: Allen Lane 2009)

Rohland, Walter: *Bewegte Zeiten. Erinnerungen eines Eisenhüttenmannes* (Stuttgart: Seewald 1978)

Rohwer, Jürgen: *Chronology of the War at Sea, 1939–1945: The Naval History of World War Two* (Annapolis: USNIP 2005)

Romanenko, Valeriy: 'The P-40 in Soviet Aviation'; in: *Journal of Slavic Military Studies*, No. 22 (2009), pp 97–124

Roseman, Mark: *The Villa, The Lake, The Meeting: Wannsee and the Final Solution* (London: Allen Lane 2002)

Rosen, Erwin: *Amerikaner* (Leipzig: Dürr & Weber 1920)

Ross, Davis R. B.: 'Patents and Bureaucrats: US Synthetic Rubber Development before Pearl Harbor'; in: Joseph R. Frese and Jacob Judd (eds.); *Business and Government: Essays in 20th Century Cooperation and Confrontation* (New York: Sleepy Hollow Press 1985), pp 119–56

Rothwell, Victor: *War Aims in the Second World War* (Edinburgh: Edinburgh UP 2005)

Rutowska, Maria: 'Nationalsozialistische Verfolgungsmassnahmen gegenüber der polnischen Zivilbevölkerung in den eingegliederten polnischen Gebieten'; in: Jaceck Andrzej Mlynarczyk (ed.): *Polen unter deutscher und sowjetischer Besatzung 1939–1945* (Osnabrück: fibre 2009), pp 197–216

Ryback, Timothy: *Hitlers Bücher. Seine Bibliothek. Sein Denken* (Köln: Fackelträger 2010)

Safrian, Hans: *Eichmann's men* (Cambridge: CUP 2010)

Salewski, Michael: *Die deutsche Seekriegsleitung 1939–1945*, Bd. 1 (Frankfurt a.M.: Bernard & Graefe 1970)

Sander-Nagashima, Berthold: *Die deutsch-japanischen Marinebeziehungen 1919–1942* (unpublished Ph.D, Hamburg University 1998)

Sandner, Harald: *Hitler. Das Itinerar. Aufenthaltsorte und Reisen von 1889 bis 1945*, Bd. IV, *1940–1945* (Berlin: Berlin Story 2016)

Schabel, Ralf: *Die Illusion der Wunderwaffen. Die Rolle der Düsenflugzeuge und Flugabwehrraketen in der Rüstungspolitik des Dritten Reiches* (München: Oldenbourg Verlag 1994)

Schäfer, Kirstin: *Werner von Blomberg – Hitlers erster Feldmarschall. Eine Biographie* (Paderborn: Ferdinand Schöningh 2006)

Scheil, Stefan: *Ribbentrop. Oder: die Verlockung des nationalen Aufbruchs* (Berlin: Duncker & Humblot 2013)

Schenck, Ernst Günther: *Patient Hitler. Eine medizinische Biographie* (Düsseldorf: Droste 1989)

Schlauch, Wolfgang: *Rüstungshilfe der USA an die Verbündeten im Zweiten Weltkrieg* (Darmstadt: Wehr und Wissen 1967)

Schlie, Ulrich: *Kein Friede mit Deutschland. Die geheimen Gespräche im Zweiten Weltkrieg, 1939–1941* (München and Berlin: Langen Müller 1994)

Schmider, Klaus: 'The Mediterranean in 1940/41: Crossroads of Lost Opportunities?'; in: *War and Society*, Vol. 15, No. 2 (1997), pp 19–41

Partisanenkrieg in Jugoslawien (Hamburg: Koehler & Mittler 2002)

Schmidt, Jürgen W.: 'Eugen Ott – Freund und Quelle von Richard Sorge'; in: Heiner Timmermann et al (eds.): *Spionage, Ideologie, Mythos – der Fall Richard Sorge* (Münster: LIT 2005) [= Dokumente und Schriften der Europäischen Akademie Otzenhausen, Bd. 113], pp 88–104

Schmidt, Paul: *Statist auf diplomatischer Bühne. Erlebnisse des Chefdolmetschers im Auswärtigen Amt mit den Staatsmännern Europas* (Bonn: Athenäum Verlag 1950)

Schmidt, Rainer F.: *Der Zweite Weltkrieg. Die Zerstörung Europas* (Berlin: Be.bra 2008)

Schmidt, Udo: *Hitlers Englandbild und seine strategischen Entscheidungen im Zweiten Weltkrieg* (München: GRIN Verlag 1998)

Schmied, Jürgen-Peter: 'Hitlers Amerikabild vor der 'Machtergreifung''; in: *Geschichte in Wissenschaft und Unterricht*, No. 12 (2002), pp 714–26

Schmoll, Peter: *Nest of Eagles: Messerschmitt Production and Flight Testing at Regensburg 1936–1945* (Hersham: Ian Allan 2010)

Schölgen, Gregor: *Jenseits von Hitler. Die Deutschen in der Weltpolitik von Bismarck bis heute* (Berlin: Propyläen 2005)

Schröder, Joachim: *Die U-Boote des Kaisers. Die Geschichte des deutschen U-Bootkrieges gegen Großbritannien* (Koblenz: Bernard & Graefe 2003)

Schulte, Jan-Erik: 'Initiative der Peripherie. Globocniks Siedlungsstützpunkte und die Entscheidung zum Bau des Vernichtungslagers Belzec'; in: Jan Erik Schulte (ed.): *Die SS, Himmler und die Wevelsburg* (Paderborn et al: Ferdinand Schöningh 2009), pp 118–37

Schulze-Wegener, Guntram: *Die deutsche Kriegsmarine-Rüstung* (Hamburg et al: Mittler 1997)

Schüler, Klaus-Friedrich: *Logistik im Rußlandfeldzug. Die Rolle der Eisenbahn bei Planung, Vorbereitung und Durchführung des deutschen Angriffs auf die Sowjetunion bis zur Krise im Winter 1941/42* (Frankfurt a.M.: Peter Lang 1987)

Schwabe, Daniel T.: *Burning Japan: Air Force Bombing Strategic Change* (Lincoln, NE: Potomac Books 2015)

Schwarz, Birgit: *Geniewahn: Hitler und die Kunst* (Wien: Böhlau Verlag 2009)

Scianna, Bastian Matteo: *The Italian War on the Eastern Front, 1941–1943: Operations, Myths and Memories* (London et al: Palgrave Macmillan 2019)

Seidel, Robert: *Deutsche Besatzungspolitik in Polen. Der Distrikt Radom 1939–1945* (Paderborn et al: Ferdinand Schöningh 2006)

Seidler, Franz W.: *Fritz Todt. Baumeister des Dritten Reiches* (München: Herbig 1986)

Seki, Eiji: *Mrs Ferguson's Tea Set – Japan and the Second World War: The Global Consequences Following Germany's Sinking of the SS* Automedon *in 1940* (Folkestone: Global Oriental 2007)

Seligmann, Rafael: *Hitler. Die Deutschen und ihr Führer* (München: Ullstein 2004)

Shores, Christopher, Massimello, Giovanni and Guest, Russell: *A History of the Mediterranean Air War, 1940–1945 – Vol. 1: North Africa, June 1940–January 1942* (London: Grub Street 2012)

Short, Neil: *The Stalin and Molotov Lines: Soviet Western Defences, 1928–1941* (Oxford: Osprey 2008)

Shrader, Charles Reginald (ed.): *Reference Guide to United States Military History, 1919–1945* (New York: Facts on File 1994)

Simms, Brendan: 'Karl Wolff. "Der Schlichter"'; in: Ronald Smelser and Enrico Syring (eds.): *Die SS. Elite unter dem Totenkopf. 30 Lebensläufe* (Paderborn et al: Schöningh 2000), pp 441–56

'"Against a World of Enemies": The Impact of the First World War on the Development of Hitler's Ideology'; in: *International Affairs* 90:2 (2014), pp 317–36

Hitler: Only the World Was Enough (London: Allen Lane 2019)

Simons, Peter: *German Air Attaché: The Thrilling Story of the German Ace Pilot and Wartime Diplomat Peter Riedel* (London: AirLife 1997)

Simpson, B. Mitchell: *Admiral Harold R. Stark: Architect of Victory, 1939–1945* (Columbia: South Carolina UP 1989)

Sirois, Herbert: *Zwischen Illusion und Krieg. Deutschland und die USA, 1933–1941* (Paderborn: Schöningh 2000)

Smith, Richard J. and Creek, Eddie J.: *Heinkel He-177 Greif. Heinkel's Strategic Bomber* (Hersham: Ian Allan 2008)

Smith, William G. Clarence: 'Rubber Cultivation in Indonesia and the Congo from the 1910s to the 1950s: Divergent Paths'; in: Ewout Frankema and Frans Buelens (eds.): *Colonial Exploitation and Economic Development: The Belgian Congo and The Netherlands Indies Compared* (London: Routledge 2013), pp 193–210

Sokolov, B. V.: 'The Cost of War: Human Losses for the USSR and Germany, 1939–1945'; in: *Journal of Slavic Military Studies*, Vol. 9, No. 1 (March 1996), pp 152–93

Sommer, Theo: *Deutschland und Japan zwischen den Mächten 1935–1940. Vom Antikominternpakt zum Dreimächtepakt* (Tübingen: Paul Siebeck 1962)

Spang, Christian W.: 'Wer waren Hitlers Ostasien-Experten?' Teil I & II; in: *OAG-Notizen* (4/2003), pp 10–16 and *OAG-Notizen* (5/2003), pp 12–24

Karl Haushofer und Japan. Die Rezeption seiner geopolitischen Theorien in der deutschen und japanischen Politik (München: IUDICUM 2013) [= Monographien aus dem Deutschen Institut für Japanstudien, Bd. 52]

Stahel, David: *Operation Barbarossa and Germany's Defeat in the East* (Cambridge: CUP 2009)

Kiev: Hitler's Battle for Supremacy in the East (Cambridge: CUP 2012)

Operation Typhoon: Hitler's March on Moscow, October 1941 (Cambridge: CUP 2013)

The Battle for Moscow (Cambridge: CUP 2015)

Retreat from Moscow: A New History of Germany's Winter Campaign, 1941–1942 (New York: Farrar, Straus & Giroux 2019)

Steffahn, Harald: 'Hitler als Soldat und militärischer Führer'; in: Christian Zentner and Friedemann Bedürftig (eds.): *Das große Lexikon des Zweiten Weltkriegs* (München: Südwest Verlag 1993), pp 254–57

Steinert, Marlis: *Hitler* (München: C. H. Beck 1994)

Stern, Robert C.: *The US Navy and the War in Europe* (London: Seaforth 2012)

Stimpel, Hans-Martin: *Die deutsche Fallschirmtruppe 1942–1945. Einsätze auf Kriegsschauplätzen im Osten und Westen* (Hamburg: Mittler 2001)

Stockings, Craig and Hancock, Eleanor: *Swastika over the Acropolis: Reinterpreting the Nazi Invasion of Greece in World War II* (Leiden and Boston: Brill 2013)

Stoler, Mark A.: *Allies and Adversaries: The Joint Chiefs of Staff, the Grand Alliance and US Strategy in World War II* (Chapel Hill and London: North Carolina UP 2000)

Stone, Norman: *A Short History of World War Two* (London: Penguin 2014 pb)

Stoves, Rolf: *1. Panzer-Division 1935–1945. Chronik einer der drei Stamm-Divisionen der deutschen Panzerwaffe* (Podzun: Bad Nauheim 1961)

Streb, Jochen: 'Technologiepolitik im Zweiten Weltkrieg. Die staatliche Förderung der Synthesekautschukproduktion im deutsch-amerikanischen Vergleich'; in: *Vierteljahrshefte für Zeitgeschichte* Bd. 50 (Juli 2002), pp 367–98

Syring, Enrico: 'Hitlers Kriegserklärung an Amerika vom 11. Dezember 1941'; in: Wolfgang Michalka (ed.): *Der Zweite Weltkrieg. Analysen, Grundzüge, Forschungsbilanz* (München: Piper 1989 pb), pp 683–96

'Walther Hewel – Ribbentrop's Mann beim "Führer"'; in: Ronald Smelser et al (eds.): *Die braune Elite. 21 weitere biographische Skizzen* (Darmstadt: WBG 1993), pp 150–165

Hitler. Seine politische Utopie (Berlin: Propyläen 1994)

Taliaferro, Jeffrey: 'Strategy of Innocence or Provocation? The Roosevelt Administration's Road to World War II'; in: Jeffrey Taliaferro et al (eds.): *The Challenge of Grand Strategy* (Cambridge: CUP 2012), pp 193–223

Tarleton, Robert: 'What Really Happened to the Stalin Line? Part 1'; in: *Journal of Soviet Military Studies*, Vol. 5 (June 1992), No. 2, pp 187–219

'What Really Happened to the Stalin Line? Part 2'; in: *Journal of Slavic Military Studies*, Vol. 6, No. 1 (March 1993), pp 21–61

Tarrant, V. E.: *The U-Boat Offensive, 1914–1945* (London: Arms & Armour Press 1989)

Taschka, Sylvia: *Diplomat ohne Eigenschaften? Die Karriere des Hans Heinrich Dieckhoff (1884–1952)* (Stuttgart: Franz Steiner 2006 [= Transatlantische Historische Studien, Bd. 25]

Terraine, John: *Business in Great Waters: The U-Boat Wars 1916–1945* (London: Leo Cooper 1989)

Thies, Jochen: *Hitler's Plans for Global Domination: Nazi Architecture and Ultimate War Aims* (New York and Oxford: Berghahn Books 2012)

Thompson, Leroy: *The M 1 Garand* (Oxford: Osprey 2012)

Todman, Daniel: *Britain's War: Into Battle, 1937–1941* (London: Allen Lane 2016)

Toland, John: *Adolf Hitler* (New York: Doubleday 1976)

Tooze, Adam: 'No Room for Miracles: German Industrial Output in World War II Reassessed'; in: *Geschichte und Gesellschaft*, Bd. 31 (2005), pp 439–64

The Wages of Destruction (London: Allen Lane 2006)

Toughill, Thomas: *A World to Gain: The Battle for Global Dominance and Why America Entered WW II* (Forest Row: Clairview 2003)

Treher, Wolfgang: *Hitler-Steiner-Schreiber. Ein Beitrag zur Phänomenologie des kranken Geistes* (Emmendingen 1966)

Treue, Wilhelm: *Gummi in Deutschland. Die deutsche Kautschukversorgung und Gummi-Industrie im Rahmen wirtschaftlicher Entwicklungen* (F. Bruckmann: München 1955)

Turner, Henry Ashby: 'Otto Wagener. Der vergessene Vertraute Hitlers'; in: Ronald Smelser et al (eds.): *Die braune Elite II. 21 weitere biographische Skizzen* (Darmstadt: WBG 1993), pp 243–53

Tuttle, William M.: 'The Birth of an Industry: The Synthetic "Rubber Mess" in World War II'; in: *Technology and Culture*, Vol. 22 (1981), Pt.1, pp 35–67

Ullrich, Volker: *Adolf Hitler. Die Jahre des Untergangs, 1939–1945. Biografie* (Berlin: Fischer 2018)

Volkmann, Hans-Erich: 'Die NS-Wirtschaft in Vorbereitung des Krieges'; in: Wilhelm Deist et al (eds.): *Ursachen und Voraussetzungen des Zweiten Weltkriegs* (rev. ed.,Frankfurt a.M.: Fischer TB 1989) [= Das Deutsche Reich und der Zweite Weltkrieg, Bd. 1], pp 211–435

Wallace, G. L.: 'Economic and Social Aspects of the Industry'; in: P. Schirdrowitz and T. R. Dawson (eds.): *History of the Rubber Industry* (Cambridge: Heffer & Sons 1952), pp 320–36

'Statistical and Economic Outline'; in: P. Schidrowitz and T.R. Dawson (eds.): *History of the Rubber Industry* (Cambridge: Heffer & Sons 1952), pp 337–45

Walter, John: *The Kaiser's Pirates: German Surface Raiders in World War One* (London: Arms & Armour Press 1994)

Warlimont, Walter: *Im Hauptquartier der deutschen Wehrmacht 1939–1945. Grundlagen, Formen, Gestalten* (Frankfurt a.M.: Athenäum 1964)

Weber, Thomas: *Hitler's First War* (Oxford: OUP 2010)

Wegner, Bernd: 'Hitlers Strategie zwischen Pearl Harbor und Stalingrad'; in: Horst Boog et al (eds.): *Der Globale Krieg. Die Ausweitung zum Weltkrieg und der Wechsel der Initiative 1941–1943* (Stuttgart: DVA 1990) [= Das Deutsche Reich und der Zweite Weltkrieg, Bd. 6], pp 97–217

'Von Stalingrad nach Kursk'; in: Karl-Heinz Frieser (ed.): *Die Ostfront 1943/44. Der Krieg im Osten und an den Nebenfronten* (München: DVA 2007) [= Das Deutsche Reich und der Zweite Weltkrieg, Bd. 8], pp 17–39

'Warum verlor Deutschland den Zweiten Weltkrieg? Eine strategiegeschichtliche Interpretation'; in: Christian Müller and Matthias Rogg (eds.): *Das ist Militärgeschichte ! Festschrift für Bernhard Kroener* (Paderborn: Ferdinand Schöningh 2013), pp 103–21

Weinberg, Gerhard L.: 'Germany's Declaration of War on the US: A New Look'; in: Hans L. Trefousse (ed.): *Germany and America: Essays on Problems of International Relations and Immigration* (New York: Columbia UP 1980) [= Brooklyn College Studies on society in change, Vol. 21], pp 54–70

A World at Arms: A Global History of World War II (Cambridge: CUP 1994)

Werr, Sebastian: *Heroische Weltsicht. Hitler und die Musik* (Köln: Böhlau Verlag 2014)

Westermann, Edward: *Flak: German Anti-Aircraft Defences, 1914–1945* (Lawrence: Kansas UP 2001)

Wettstein, Adrian: *Die Wehrmacht im Stadtkampf 1939–1942* (Paderborn: Ferdinand Schöningh 2014)

Whitman, James Q.: *Hitler's American Model: The United States and the Making of Nazi Racial Law* (Princeton and Oxford: Princeton UP 2017)

Whymant, Robert: *Stalin's Spy: Richard Sorge and the Tokyo Espionage Ring* (London and New York: I. B. Tauris 1997)

Wiedemann, Fritz: *Der Mann, der Feldherr werden wollte* (Velbert: Blick + Bild 1964)

Willmott, H. P.: *Battleship* (London: Cassell 2002)

Wilson, A. N.: *Hitler: A Short Biography* (London: Harper Press 2012)

Wilt, Alan F.: *War from the Top: German and British Military Decisionmaking during World War II* (London and New York: I. B. Tauris & Co. 1990)

Winterhagen, Johannes: 'Rund erneuert. Der Reifen der Zukunft muss vor allem energieeffizient sein'; in: *Frankfurter Allgemeine Zeitung* – 'Technik und Motor' supplement (6.11.2012)

Wolf, Howard and Howard, Ralph: *Rubber: A Story of Glory and Greed* (New York: Covici Friede 1936)

Wortman, Marc: *1941: Fighting the Shadow War* (New York: Atlantic Monthly 2016)

Wüstenbecker, Katja: *Deutsch-Amerikaner im Ersten Weltkrieg. US-Politik und nationale Identitäten im Mittleren Westen* (Stuttgart: Franz Steiner 2007)

Yergin, Daniel: *The Prize: The Epic Quest for Oil, Money and Power* (New York: Simon & Schuster 1991)

Yu, Maochun: *The Dragon's War: Allied Operations and the Fate of China, 1937–1945* (Annapolis: USNIP 2006)

Zabecki, David: *The German 1918 Offensive: A Case Study in the Operational Level of War* (London: Routledge 2006)

Zehnpfenning, Barbara: *Adolf Hitler: Mein Kampf. Studienkommentar* (München: Wilhelm Fink 2011)

Zelle, Karl-Günther: *Hitlers zweifelnde Elite. Goebbels-Göring-Himmler-Speer* (Paderborn: Ferdinand Schöningh 2010)

   Mit Hitler im Gespräch. Blenden-überzeugen-wüten (Paderborn: Ferdinand Schöningh 2017)

Zetterling, Niklas and Frankson, Anders: *The Drive on Moscow 1941: Operation Taifun and Germany's First Great Crisis in World War II* (Philadelphia: Casemate 2012)

Zitelmann, Rainer: *Adolf Hitler. Eine politische Biographie* (Göttingen: Musterschmidt 1990)

Internet sources

https://etherwave.wordpress.com/2014/01/03/document-the-butt-report–1941
www.bibliotecapleyades.net/sociopolitica/sociopol_igfarben02.htm
www.nizkor.org/trials-of-german-major-war-criminals
www.lexikon-der-wehrmacht.de/Gliederungen/Panzerdivisionen/Gliederung .htm
www.fdrlibrary.marist.edu/_resources/images/pc/pc0120.pdf

INDEX